WITHDRAWN
UTSA Libraries

HANDBOOK OF
DEMENTIA

HANDBOOK OF

DEMENTIA

Psychological, Neurological, and Psychiatric Perspectives

Edited by

PETER A. LICHTENBERG, DANIEL L. MURMAN,
and ALAN M. MELLOW

WILEY

John Wiley & Sons, Inc.

Copyright © 2003 by John Wiley & Sons. All rights reserved.

Published by John Wiley & Sons, Inc., Hoboken, New Jersey.
Published simultaneously in Canada.

Library of Congress Cataloging-in-Publication Data:

Handbook of dementia : psychological, neurological, and psychiatric perspectives / edited
  by Peter A. Lichtenberg, Daniel L. Murman, and Alan M. Mellow.
    p.   cm.
  Includes bibliographical references and index.
  ISBN-0-471-41982-6 (alk. paper)
    1. Dementia—Handbooks, manuals, etc.   2. Dementia—Psychological
aspects—Handbooks, manuals, etc.   I. Lichtenberg, Peter A.   II. Murman, Daniel L.   III.
Mellow, Alan M.
  [DNLM: 1. Dementia. 2. Alzheimer Disease. WM 220 H2368 2003]
  RC521.H364 2003
  616.8′3—dc21

                                                                      2002044607

Printed in the United States of America.

10   9   8   7   6   5   4   3   2   1

Contents

Contributors

Cameron J. Camp, PhD
Myers Research Institute
Mcnorah Park Center for Senior
    Living
Beachwood, Ohio

Mary E. Haines, PhD
Medical College of Ohio
Toledo, Ohio

Judith L. Heidebrink, MD, MS
Department of Neurology
University of Michigan
    Health System
Neurology Service
Ann Arbor VA Medical Center
Ann Arbor, Michigan

M. Saleem Ismail, MD
Department of Psychiatry
University of Rochester Medical
    Center
Rochester, New York

Helen C. Kales, MD
Division of Geriatric Psychiatry
University of Michigan
Geriatric Psychiatry Clinic
Health Services Research and
    Development
VA Ann Arbor Healthcare System
Ann Arbor, Michigan

Peter A. Lichtenberg, PhD, ABPP
Institute of Gerontology
Wayne State University
Detroit, Michigan

Susan E. MacNeill, PhD, ABPP
Henry Ford Health System
Detroit, Michigan

Benjamin T. Mast, PhD
University of Louisville
Louisville, Kentucky

Donna Masterman, MD
Neurology Department
University of California
Los Angeles, California

Alan M. Mellow, MD, PhD
Division of Geriatric Psychiatry
Department of Psychiatry
University of Michigan
Psychiatry Service
VA Ann Arbor Healthcare System
VISN 11 Mental Health Service Line
Department of Veterans Affairs
Ann Arbor, Michigan

Daniel L. Murman, MD, MS
Department of Neurology
Michigan State University
East Lansing, Michigan

Elizabeth H. Nasser, MA
Myers Research Institute
Menorah Park Center for Senior Living
Beachwood, Ohio

Margaret P. Norris, PhD
Private Practice
College Station, Texas

Gregory H. Pelton, MD
Department of Psychiatry
New York State Psychiatric Institute
Columbia University College of
    Physicians and Surgeons
New York, New York

Anton P. Porsteinsson, MD
Department of Psychiatry
University of Rochester Medical
    Center
Rochester, New York

**Gustavo C. Román, MD, FACP,
    FRSM**
University of Texas HSC
Audie L. Murphy Memorial Veterans
    Hospital Geriatric Education and
    Clinical Center
San Antonio, Texas

J. Michael Ryan, MD
Department of Psychiatry
University of Rochester Medical
    Center
Rochester, New York

Mary Sano, PhD
Research and Development
VA Medical Center
Department of Psychiatry
Mount Sinai School of Medicine
Bronx, New York

Margaret Swanberg, DO
Department of Neurology
University of California-Los Angeles
Los Angeles, California

Pierre N. Tariot, MD
Department of Psychiatry
University of Rochester Medical
    Center
Rochester, New York

R. Scott Turner, MD, PhD
Department of Neurology
Institute of Gerontology
Neuroscience Program
University of Michigan Health System
Veterans Affairs Medical Center
Geriatric Research Clinical and
    Education Center
Ann Arbor, Michigan

Christine Weber, PhD
Taub Institute for Alzheimer's
    Disease Research
Department of Neurology
College of Physicians and Surgeons
Columbia University
New York, New York

Introduction

Peter A. Lichtenberg, Daniel L. Murman, and Alan M. Mellow

BASIC PRINCIPLES: PSYCHOLOGICAL PERSPECTIVES

Using psychological techniques in the assessment of and intervention with persons having dementia is optimized when three principles are integrated into the work. These principles are briefly highlighted and then explained. Psychological perspectives are unique in dementia evaluation and treatment because they incorporate parts of both the medical and psychosocial model.

Principle 1: Accurate Assessment of Both Cognitive Abilities and Noncognitive Behaviors Is Based on Thorough Knowledge of the Tools Utilized

The assessment of cognition and, in particular, memory loss, has been found to be one of the most sensitive measures of early cognitive decline and dementia. Psychological techniques include the valid interpretation of thorough psychometric testing. Whereas it is common in physician offices to use very brief mental status measures (e.g., Mini-Mental State Exam) to document cognitive decline, psychological techniques more thoroughly assess cognitive functioning and, in particular, domains of cognitive functioning. As a result, neuropsychological assessment measures are typically more sensitive, specific, and provide better positive and negative predictive power than do screening exams alone (Becker, Boller, Lopez, Saxton, & McGonigle, 1994). While these instruments can be quite powerful, there are many caveats to their proper usage and interpretation. All cognitive assessment is based on a deficit model in which one individual's score is typically compared to a range of "normative" values. All too often, practitioners look for single cutoff scores that can be used across populations. This practice, although common, is fraught with difficulty, as those with less education, older age, and those from minority groups are often deemed "impaired," when in fact they are not (Lichtenberg, 1998). Tests of memory and of other cognitive functions are impacted by sociodemographic information such as age, education, and literacy. Practitioners need to use appropriate normative data when interpreting cognitive test scores.

Practitioners need to know the strengths and weaknesses of scales used in the assessment of noncognitive behaviors as well. In particular, the value of the input (self-report) from the person with dementia or suspected dementia must be balanced with the ratings of family or professional caregivers. In the assessment of depression, for example, obtaining some aspects of self-report from the person with dementia (e.g., mood, withdrawal) can provide unique and useful information that adds to the report of the caregiver. Similarly, the person with dementia's own report of suspicions, delusions, or hallucinations can be useful and can add unique information to that provided by the caregiver.

Principle 2: Comorbidity Is Common in Dementia

In discussing interdisciplinary teams and how models of functioning can lead to conflicts, Lichtenberg (1994) reported that whereas the medical model emphasizes a "ruling out" of influences until a diagnostic entity is determined, the psychosocial model emphasizes a "ruling in" of influences on behaviors. In applying the psychosocial model to dementia, psychological practitioners need to be aware of the relatively common occurrence of comorbidities. Depression often accompanies dementia. Delirium occurs more frequently among those with dementia. Environmental stresses, such as caregiver burden, relocation, boredom, or overstimulation, can heighten behavioral disturbances among those with dementia. Caregiver functioning impacts the care recipient's cognitive and noncognitive behaviors. Further, as the disease progresses, so do comorbidities. Thus, memory decline is associated with functional decline, risk of delirium episodes, and loss of independence in self-care abilities. These losses, in turn, are related to increased caregiver burden, caregiver depression, and nursing home placement. Thus, the psychosocial model helps to understand behavior by assessing the characteristics of the person with dementia, the caregiver's characteristics, and the interaction of the psychosocial and physical environment in which care is given.

Principle 3: Treatment Interventions Should Be Based on Conceptual Frameworks and Tested Empirically to Determine Efficacy and Effectiveness

Behavioral and psychosocial interventions with persons with dementia and with family and professional caregivers are based on the conviction that persons with dementia, similar to those with any chronic disease, can have an improved quality of life. Because dementia attacks both cognitive and noncognitive aspects of functioning, interventions are geared to both. Learning theory and cognitive-behavioral theory are the underpinnings of many successful interventions with persons with dementia. Learning theory has been applied to cases of dementia, demonstrating how best to maximize cognitive abilities, use whatever cognitive strengths remain, and integrate all of this into daily life. Behavioral theory has been applied to the understanding of mood and depressive disorders in those with dementia demonstrating clinical effectiveness in reducing depressive symptoms. Each of these interventions has as its aim to affect the patient's behavior and to improve the psychosocial and physical environment for both the person with dementia and the caregiver(s).

The psychological perspectives on dementia offered in this book highlight these three principles over and over. Assessment instruments are created, extensively validated, and carefully (validly) applied to appropriate groups of persons with dementia or suspected dementia. Broad-based assessments that incorporate the person with dementia and the family or professional caregiver attempt to "rule in" all those important elements that contribute to cognitive and noncognitive symptom exacerbation. Finally, treatments aimed at improving quality of life are based on conceptual frameworks and evaluated empirically.

BASIC PRINCIPLES: NEUROLOGICAL PERSPECTIVE

The neurologic chapters in this handbook stress three general principles of neurology as applied to dementia. These principles are not unique to neurology, but are routinely used by neuroscientists and clinical neurologists. These chapters and approaches emphasize the biomedical model of disease causation and treatment and demonstrate that their application can result in more accurate diagnosis and more appropriate and effective treatments.

Principle 1: Biomedical Research Can Lead to a Better Understanding of the Pathophysiology of Dementing Diseases and the Development of Disease-Modifying Treatments

Each of the neurology chapters summarizes scientific advances in our understanding of the pathophysiology of the most common causes of dementia and progress in the development of safe and effective disease-altering treatments. An example from Alzheimer's disease (AD) biomedical research demonstrates the multidisciplinary nature of this type of research and shows how discoveries can move from patients to the laboratory and back to patients again. For example, genetic researchers identified families with early-onset autosomal dominant AD. Blood samples taken from these families were used to identify specific genetic mutations in three genes that can produce this type of AD. Transgenic animal models of AD were developed using these genes. These animal models have been used to develop drugs and treatments that are effective in delaying or stopping the development of AD pathology. Promising drugs are then moved into clinical trials for testing in patients with AD. Additionally, the development of genetic tests for specific mutations that cause early-onset, autosomal dominant AD allows their clinical use for at-risk patients who desire presymptomatic genetic testing. Similar multidisciplinary research is occurring that focuses on the other major causes of dementia also, with the ultimate goal of developing safe and effective disease-altering treatments for each of the major causes of dementia. The successes achieved so far toward this goal are outlined in each of the neurology chapters.

Principle 2: A Careful History and Neurologic Examination, Supplemented by Knowledge of Dementing Diseases and Selected Ancillary Tests, Can Result in an Accurate Diagnosis for Patients Suffering from Dementia

Traditionally, neurology has emphasized the importance of an accurate diagnosis in the care of patients with neurologic disease. The specialty of neurology uses a systematic approach to the evaluation of patients with neurologic complaints described by some as neurologic problem solving. The principles of neurologic problem solving are at the foundation of diagnostic evaluations of patients with dementia. In neurologic problem solving, the clinician uses the history to gain information about the time course of the disease (e.g., acute, subacute, chronic) and to understand other coexisting factors that may be causing or influencing the patient's symptoms and signs. The neurologic examination is used to identify signs of neurologic dysfunction. This information is used along with knowledge of neuroanatomy and brain-behavior relationships to localize the area in the nervous system where there are signs of dysfunction. Information about the time course of disease and location within the nervous system is combined with knowledge of diseases of the nervous system to generate a differential diagnosis. This differential diagnosis helps dictate which diagnostic tests are ordered. The results of the diagnostic tests are used to refine or confirm the diagnosis or diagnoses.

In the evaluation of dementia, each of these aspects of neurologic problem solving is important. For example, a detailed understanding of the time course of a dementing illness is important for differentiating potential causes (e.g., AD vs. vascular dementia). The history may also provide clues as to other factors (e.g., medications, comorbid diseases, depression) that may be contributing to the patient's symptoms of cognitive impairment. The neurologic examination then tests cognitive functioning in multiple cognitive domains to determine what brain regions are involved. The pattern of brain involvement helps distinguish the major causes of dementia, especially early in their course. The neurologic examination also provides information about whether there are signs of parkinsonism, cerebrovascular disease, mass lesions, or hydrocephalus. Clinicians then use their knowledge of the typical presentation and natural history of the major causes of dementia to generate differential diagnoses and to help decide what additional testing is needed. Useful ancillary tests include neuropsychological testing, laboratory tests, and brain imaging. Finally, information from the history, the exam, and the ancillary testing are combined to reach a conclusion as to the cause or causes of a patient's dementia. The neurology chapters in this handbook provide summaries of the common presentations, natural histories, and current approaches to the diagnosis of the major causes of dementia.

Principle 3: A Correct Diagnosis Is Essential for Providing Accurate Information about Prognosis and Initiating an Appropriate Treatment Plan

The major causes of dementia in the elderly (e.g., Alzheimer's disease, vascular dementia, dementia with Lewy bodies, frontotemporal dementia) have unique causes, clinical features, and natural histories. Despite individual patient differences, there are important similarities in presentation, disease course, and response to treatment in those patients with the same cause of dementia. By making a specific dementia diagnosis, a clinician can better predict a patient's prognosis and expected disease course, better identify atypical variations in the expected disease course that may signify a new problem (e.g., depression or delirium), and better determine which treatments may provide benefit to a patient based on clinical research conducted on patients with a similar, specific dementia diagnosis. In addition, based on Principle 1, it is anticipated that in the future, disease-specific treatments will be effective in those with the disease and ineffective in those without the disease (e.g., inhibitor of or secretases for treating AD). If such treatments become available, it will be increasingly more important to make an accurate diagnosis, especially if the treatments have negative side effects or are costly. While some new therapies may work for several causes of dementia (e.g., neuroprotective agent that reduces oxidative stress or excitotoxicity), it will still be important to be able to determine who is at risk for developing dementia in the future and to determine who is developing initial symptoms of dementing disease. Each of the neurologic chapters reviews current treatment options and discusses potential future treatment approaches.

MANAGEMENT OF DEMENTIA—PSYCHIATRIC PRINCIPLES

As is evident throughout this volume, the management of patients with dementia is a challenge that spans time as well as an interdisciplinary approach. Psychiatric management requires simultaneous attention to psychiatric syndromes, both clear-cut and mixed; comorbid medical illnesses; social supports; family dynamics; and both pharmacologic and nonpharmacologic interventions. The following principles are useful anchors to the effective diagnosis and management of those psychiatric syndromes that complicate dementia illnesses.

Principle 1: Psychiatric Complications of Dementia Are Often the Major Contributor to Disability, Patient and Family Distress, and Costs of Care

Although the core cognitive impairment associated with dementia of all types certainly represents personal and family tragedy, the complications of depression, agitation, and psychosis often represent perhaps the greatest challenge to patients, caregivers, and healthcare providers. Psychiatric symptoms often increase caregiver burden, create crises for patient management and safety, and lead to need for more specialized care and institutionalization.

Principle 2: Differential Diagnosis Should Always Include Underlying Medical Illnesses, Both Minor and Serious, Which Might Be Contributing to Behavior Change

Elderly patients are susceptible to delirium, and patients with dementia have an even greater risk of developing delirium with consequent behavioral disturbance, as a result of even minor medical illnesses, such as a urinary tract infection or viral syndrome. In addition, more serious, potentially life-threatening symptoms could have behavioral concomitants in susceptible patients with dementia. For this reason, it is imperative, in the evaluation of such patients, to thoroughly evaluate for comorbid states. Assuming that acute behavioral changes in a dementia patient are only part of the dementia can often delay diagnosis of comorbid states and can lead to unnecessary interventions for behavior.

Principle 3: Effective Treatments for Psychiatric Complications Are Available and Should Be Vigorously Pursued, Even in Patients with Advanced Cognitive Impairment

Relief of symptoms of depression, anxiety, agitation, and psychosis can be effected with both pharmacologic and nonpharmacologic interventions. Such interventions often greatly improve the quality of patients' and caregivers' lives, even if underlying dementia progression or core cognitive impairment is unaffected. Particularly for the pharmacologic interventions, as with other such treatment in the elderly, one often must "start low and go slow," but "don't quit."

Principle 4: Psychiatric Symptoms, and Hence the Indicated Treatment, May Change over the Course of the Patient's Illness

Dementia patients, over the course of their illness, may experience various combinations of psychiatric syndromes, so diagnostic approaches and treatment strategies must be flexible to meet patients' needs over time. For example, patients may develop depression early in their illness, with good response to an antidepressant, but later may require antipsychotic or mood stabilizer treatment. Alternatively, patients may develop anxiety and agitation early on, becoming more withdrawn and depressed in later stages.

REFERENCES

Becker, J. T., Boller, F., Lopez, O., Saxton, J., & McGonigle, K. L. (1994). The natural history of Alzheimer's disease. *Archives of Neurology, 51,* 585–594.

Lichtenberg, P. A. (1994). *A guide to psychological practice in geriatric long term care.* Binghamton, NY: Haworth Press.

Lichtenberg, P. A. (1998). *Mental health practice in geriatric health care settings.* Binghamton, NY: Haworth Press.

CHAPTER 1

Neurologic Aspects of Alzheimer's Disease

R. Scott Turner

> *... they grew melancholy and dejected ...*
>
> *At fourscore ... they ... have no remembrance of anything but what they learned in their youth, and even that is very imperfect.*
>
> *At ninety, they forget the ... names ... of ... their nearest friends and relations ...*
>
> *They are ... the most mortifying sight I ever beheld, and the women more horrible than the men.*
>
> *My keen appetite for perpetuity of life was much abated.*
>
> Quoted from *Gulliver's Travels* by Jonathan Swift, 1726,
> on learning that although the Struldbruggs (immortals)
> live forever, they were not "a living treasury of knowledge
> and wisdom ... [and] oracle of the nation" but became
> progressively demented with age. As for much of human
> history, average life expectancy was 20 to 30 but by 1801
> reached 35.9 years in England and Wales.

> *"The answer ... is ... Forty-two," said Deep Thought ...*
>
> Quoted from *The Hitchhiker's Guide to the Galaxy* by
> Douglas Adams, 1980—before recent knowledge led
> to the amyloid hypothesis of Alzheimer's disease.

HISTORICAL ASPECTS

Although age-related progressive cognitive decline has been known since antiquity, a case report by Alois Alzheimer described the neuropathology

---

This work was supported by the Department of Veterans Affairs Geriatrics Research Education and Clinical Center, grants from the Alzheimer's Association and NIA/NIH (P50 AG08671), and a Beeson Faculty Scholar in Aging Research Award from the American Federation for Aging Research. The author thanks Dr. M. L. Steinhilb for artwork in Figure 1.1.

associated with a "peculiar" dementing syndrome (Alzheimer, 1907). Dr. Alzheimer, a psychiatrist in Munich, reported the five-year clinical course of a 51-year-old woman with progressive dementia and autopsy findings of neuronal loss, neurofibrillary tangles, and miliary amyloid plaques found under light microscopic examination of Bielshowsky silver-stained brain sections. Thus, he was the first to suggest a link, perhaps causal, between this dementing disease and the abnormal proteinaceous aggregates in the brain. Or were they merely "tombstone" epiphenomena? The debate continues. However, in recognition of Dr. Alzheimer's seminal observations, the disorder became known as Alzheimer's disease (AD). AD was initially considered extremely rare and limited to the presenium (age of onset less than 60 or 65)—both false notions overturned many decades later.

EPIDEMIOLOGY

AD now affects approximately 2% to 3% of individuals at age 65, with an approximate doubling of incidence for every five years of age afterward. Thus, the prevalence of AD in one study (Evans, Funkenstein, Albert, Scherr, Cook, et al., 1989) approaches 50% of those over age 85. AD is not inevitable with aging, however, and "escapees" warrant further study. In 1990, there were an estimated 4 million people in the United States with AD. Because of an expanding population and increasing life expectancy in affluent societies, the number of affected individuals will increase to 14 million in 2050. Most patients who live and die with AD are women because of a higher risk and a longer life expectancy than men. In 1998, the annual direct and indirect costs for care of a patient with AD was approximately $40,000, in part because AD has two victims—patient and caregiver. The high prevalence of AD results in an enormous economic impact. As the elderly population also increases in less affluent countries, large numbers of patients with AD will emerge and face intense competition from the younger populace for scarce health care resources. The slow progression of the disease (average of 7 years, range 2 to 18) engenders many years of health care costs. As dementia becomes severe and patients become progressively more dependent on caregivers for basic activities of daily living, expenditures increase. A major cost for many patients in the latter stages of AD is assisted living and nursing home care.

   The major risk factor for AD is aging. Even subjects with Down's syndrome or those carrying gene mutations and polymorphisms linked to familial AD require a degree of aging before signs and symptoms commence. It remains unknown, however, what specific factors associated with aging increase risk of AD. Genetic and environmental risk factors appear to accelerate certain age-dependent processes leading to AD. Having a first-degree relative with AD increases a person's risk of developing AD approximately two- to fourfold, and this risk grows higher with increasing numbers of affected first-degree relatives. These familial risks clearly implicate genetic factors in AD pathogenesis.

Much has been learned about the molecular basis of AD by the study of rare families with early-onset AD. Other than a pedigree analysis showing an early-onset (presenile) highly penetrant autosomal dominant pattern of inheritance, these familial forms of AD are strikingly similar, clinically and pathologically, to the overwhelming majority (> 95%) of patients with sporadic (senile) AD. Thus, proposed pathogenic mechanisms of familial AD may be extrapolated to sporadic AD. The first gene mutation linked to AD was a missense mutation in the amyloid precursor protein (APP) gene on chromosome 21. Subsequently, other APP missense mutations were found in other pedigrees of AD. However, most familial AD has no APP mutation, implicating other affected genes. By study of these pedigrees, mutations were identified in presenilin-1 (for *presenile*) or the homologous gene presenilin-2. Of the rare familial forms of AD, the most commonly found mutation is a missense mutation in presenilin-1. Polymorphisms in Apolipoprotein E (ApoE), α2-macroglobulin (α2-M), low-density lipoprotein-related receptor protein (LRP), loci on chromosomes 9 and 10, and other unconfirmed loci increase the risk of sporadic late-onset AD. The high prevalence of progressive dementia in subjects with Down's syndrome (trisomy 21) led to autopsy observations of typical AD pathology, including neurofibrillary tangles and amyloid plaques, in aging brains. However, the onset of dementia occurs in the third to fifth decade of life and neuropathology is found even earlier. A hypothesis for the cause of AD must also include this category of high-risk patient.

In addition to genetic factors, several environmental factors increase the risk of AD. For example, severe head trauma with loss of consciousness and a low level of education increase risk. Conversely, advanced education may be protective. For unclear reasons, female gender also increases risk of AD (Turner, 2001), hypothesized to be due to a lack of postmenopausal estrogen. Recently, a resurgence of studies in risk factors for stroke, such as hypertension, diabetes mellitus, smoking, hypercholesterolemia, and possibly

FAMILIAL SPORADIC

ENVIRONMENTAL

hyperhomocysteinemia, may also increase risk of AD. Whether these factors act directly on AD pathogenic mechanisms, indirectly by vascular compromise, or both remains unclear. Proposed environmental risks now discarded include exposure to aluminum.

GENETICS

Down's syndrome, including translocation Down's (21q), is clearly linked to AD (Evenhuis, 1990). The mechanism may be a gene dosage phenomenon because APP is encoded on the long arm of chromosome 21. Cells of Down's syndrome patients express about 1.5 times the normal amount of APP and secrete a higher level of Aß peptides. Aß peptides derived from APP are the major component of amyloid plaques in AD brains. Not coincidentally, the missense mutations in APP found in familial AD pedigrees cluster near the two proteolytic cleavage sites that release Aß from APP; the originally unidentified proteases were termed ß-secretase and γ-secretase (see Figure 1.1). The location of these APP mutations immediately suggested a pathologic mechanism favoring amyloidogenic over nonamyloidogenic APP catabolism (a toxic gain of function). This hypothesis was

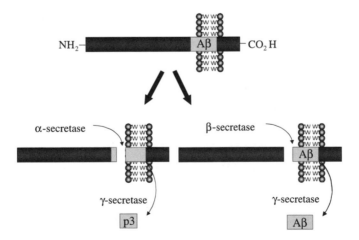

Figure 1.1 Amyloid precursor protein (APP) processing. APP is a transmembrane protein that may be cleaved either by α- and γ-secretases to release p3 and a large amino-terminal ectodomain (the nonamyloidogenic pathway) or by ß- and γ-secretases to release 4 kD Aß peptides including Aß40 and Aß42 and a large amino-terminal ectodomain. Aß is the major component of amyloid plaques in AD brain.

confirmed by study of the effects of the mutations in cell culture, samples taken from affected patients, and in transgenic mouse models of AD. A transgenic organism carries a gene from another species—in this case, a mutant human APP gene is expressed in a mouse brain (specifically, in neurons). These transgenic mice exhibit age-dependent behavioral decline in learning and memory tasks and progressive amyloid deposition in the brain (Games, Adams, Alessandrini, Barbour, Berthelette, et al., 1995; Hsiao, Chapman, Nilsen, Eckman, Harigaya, et al., 1996). However, they develop neither neurofibrillary tangles nor neuronal loss. Thus, they are at best a partial AD-like model of human disease.

A double missense mutation in APP (K670N/M671L, in the 770 isoform numbering system) near the ß-secretase cleavage site increases both Aß40 and Aß42 generation. In contrast, any one of several single missense mutations in APP (T714I, V715M, I716V, V717I, G, F, or L, and L723P) near the γ-secretase site increases Aß42 secretion specifically. In vitro studies of these peptides reveal that Aß42 is more spontaneously amyloidogenic than Aß40, again suggesting a disease mechanism. In fact, immunohistochemical stains reveal that early Aß deposits in aging brains are primarily Aß42. These preamyloid deposits (diffuse plaques) may evolve into mature neuritic plaques and thus have been likened to fatty streaks that develop into atherosclerotic plaques in blood vessels. Diffuse plaques, unlike neuritic plaques, are thought to be benign because they are not linked with clinical dementia or surrounded by dystrophic neurites (swollen and deformed axonal and dendritic neuronal processes) and reactive gliosis (microglial and astrocytic).

Missense mutations in APP are also known within the Aß sequence at positions 692, 693, and 694 and thus near the α-secretase cleavage site (see Figure 1.1). These mutations result in vascular and parenchymal amyloid deposition in the brain—thus producing a mixed clinical presentation of dementia and lobar hemorrhagic or microvascular ischemic strokes. The APP E693Q mutation found in hereditary cerebral hemorrhage with amyloidosis of the Dutch type (HCHWA-D) results in an increased propensity of Aß to form amyloid and a clinical presentation of lobar hemorrhages. The APP A692G mutation leads to microvascular amyloidopathy and AD pathology and presents with dementia and occasional cerebral hemorrhages; this mutation promotes Aß production from APP. Cerebral congophilic amyloid angiopathies with dementia are not limited to Aß, however, but to other amyloidogenic proteins such as cystatin C and transthyretin. Taken together, the data on the effects of APP mutations linked to AD led to the amyloid hypothesis—that amyloid deposition in the brain is the *causal* or initiating event in AD pathogenesis (Selkoe, 2001).

Another major advance in the genetics of AD was the discovery of the link between Apolipoprotein E (ApoE) polymorphisms on chromosome 19 and sporadic late-onset AD (Strittmatter, Saunders, Schmechel, Pericak-Vance, Enghild, et al., 1993). ApoE is synthesized in the liver and plays a role in lipid and cholesterol transport in lipoprotein particles in blood. In the brain, ApoE is secreted by glia with receptors on neurons. The function of ApoE in the brain is unclear, but it may be involved in central lipid and cholesterol metabolism. Three ApoE polymorphisms—2, 3, and 4—result in six possible genotypes. These polymorphisms differ by only one or two amino acids at positions 112 and 158 (of 299). The gene frequency in the population is 3 > 4 > 2. Having either one or two apoE4 alleles increases the risk of developing late-onset AD and lowers the average age of onset with a gene dosage effect. In other words, the hierarchy of individual risk is ApoE4/4 > ApoE4/x > ApoEx/x. The ApoE2 allele is slightly protective, and ApoE3 is intermediate in risk. The mechanism whereby ApoE polymorphisms affect AD risk is unknown. ApoE does not influence APP metabolism; rather, in vivo and in vitro evidence suggests that ApoE4 promotes the formation of insoluble fibrillar amyloid from soluble Aß peptides. For example, double transgenic mice have been developed expressing mutant human APP and either human ApoE3 or ApoE4; similar to humans, mice expressing human ApoE4 develop a greater amyloid burden in the brain. ApoE knockout mice expressing human mutant APP develop no amyloid plaques, again suggesting a role for ApoE in amyloidogenesis. However, additional mechanisms whereby ApoE4 increases risk of AD have not been completely excluded.

Most pedigrees of familial AD have no APP mutation but linkage to other genes on other chromosomes. Thus, mutations were identified in novel genes named presenilin-1 on chromosome 14 and presenilin-2 on chromosome 1. The identification of these gene mutations provided a test for the amyloid hypothesis. Would they alter APP metabolism and Aß generation? Again, studies of cells in culture, samples taken from affected patients, and transgenic mice reveal that presenilin mutations increase Aß42 generation from APP (a toxic gain of function). Double transgenic mice expressing both human mutant APP and human mutant presenilin-1 exhibit markedly accelerated amyloid deposition in the brain compared to single human mutant APP transgenic mice. Thus, in common to all known familial AD mutations is an increased production of Aß42 from APP. However, presenilin mutations are speculated to have other detrimental effects promoting AD, for example, by increasing neuronal apoptosis.

Other than ApoE, genetic linkages to sporadic AD remain controversial. Several candidate genes are being investigated. For example, risk of sporadic AD is linked with polymorphisms in α2-macroglobulin (α2-M) and the low-density lipoprotein-related receptor protein (LRP), both on chromosome 12, and genes on chromosome 9 (possibly X11α that modulates Aß production) and on chromosome 10 (possibly insulin-degrading enzyme that also degrades Aß). Perhaps not coincidentally, α2-M and ApoE, both ligands for Aß and the LRP, may play a role in Aß clearance or deposition in the brain. Genetic risks may be additive, for example, in ApoE4-positive individuals with APP mutations, but the ApoE allele has no impact on the most aggressive, earliest onset form of AD found in individuals with presenilin-1 mutations.

PATHOPHYSIOLOGY

In the late 1970s, a profound cholinergic deficit was discovered in human AD cerebral cortex. The source of this deficit is loss of cholinergic neurons in the basal forebrain (nucleus basalis of Meynert) that project widely to the hippocampus and neocortex (Davies & Maloney, 1976). Anatomic lesion studies of animals and pharmacologic studies of animals and humans demonstrated the requirement of these cholinergic systems for learning and memory. These observations led to the hypothesis that supplementation of central cholinergic systems may be an effective treatment strategy for AD. This approach proved remarkably successful in a different neurodegenerative disease with a (far more discrete) central neurotransmitter deficit—dopaminergic supplementation such as *levo*-dopa for the treatment of Parkinson's disease. However, because of limited efficacies and peripheral side effects, use of the first aceylcholinesterase inhibitor (tacrine, Cognex) for the treatment of AD patients was not approved by the U.S. Food and Drug Administration until 1993. Compared to drugs for Parkinson's disease, efficacy of AD medications is limited by more global damage to multiple neurotransmitter systems. Approval of other acetylcholinesterase inhibitors soon followed, but other central cholinergic supplementation strategies (cholinergic precursors, muscarinic cholinergic receptor agonists, etc.) failed to prove efficacy.

The discovery of gene mutations in the late 1980s and 1990s linked to familial AD and a study of their effects led to the amyloid cascade hypothesis of AD. This hypothesis moves Aß generation and amyloid deposition upstream from the other pathologies found in AD. This hypothesis, in fact, states that Aß generation and amyloid deposition *cause* AD. In favor of this hypothesis is the evidence that Down's syndrome, APP and presenilin mutations, and ApoE polymorphisms linked to AD either promote Aß generation, especially Aß42, or its deposition in the brain as amyloid (see Figure 1.2). Evidence against the amyloid hypothesis is the poor correlation of neuritic plaque burden, compared to neurofibrillary tangle density or synaptic loss, to clinical dementia and weak evidence for linkage to other putative downstream pathologies. For example, Aß peptides are thought to be neurotoxic, but in vivo evidence is suggestive, and mechanisms, perhaps involving elevated intracellular calcium levels, are unclear. In addition, there is poor linkage of amyloid to the development of the other defining neuropathology of AD—neurofibrillary tangles. Proponents of the amyloid hypothesis are quick to point out that amyloid may be necessary but is not sufficient to

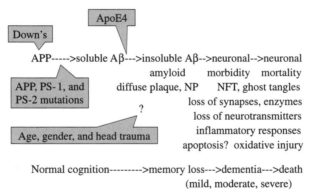

Figure 1.2   The amyloid cascade hypothesis of Alzheimer's disease (AD). Aß, derived from APP, forms insoluble neuritic plaques (NP) in brain, leading to neuronal morbidity, neurofibrillary tangles (NFT), and neuronal mortality. A ghost tangle remains when a neuron containing a NFT dies. In this model, risk factors for AD (Down's syndrome, mutations in APP, presenilin-1 [PS-1], or presenilin-2 [PS-2], and the apolipoprotein E4 [ApoE4] polymorphism) are located proximally, implying their *causal* roles in AD pathogenesis. The mechanisms whereby age, female gender, and head trauma increase risk are obscure. In parallel with these pathologic events in brain, cognitively normal elderly individuals become progressively amnestic and demented until death.

cause AD; neurofibrillary tangle formation and neuronal and synaptic loss, albeit downstream of amyloid deposition, are equally important pathogenic events. Despite its drawbacks, the amyloid cascade hypothesis of AD is providing new targets for screening strategies and rational drug design and driving novel therapeutic approaches for prevention and treatment. Although AD affects only the brain, a similar age-dependent disease process in skeletal muscle may result in the progressive and fatal myopathy inclusion body myositis (Askanas & Engel, 2001).

DIAGNOSIS

The clinical diagnosis of AD remains rooted in a thorough history and physical examination. The history must be obtained from both the patient and a reliable family member or historian and should include a review of centrally active medications and inquiries as to stroke, head trauma, alcoholism, educational and occupational attainment, and family history of neurologic or psychiatric disease. Cognitive decline, functional decline, behavioral changes, and impact on daily life should all be assessed. The onset of AD is insidious and difficult to pinpoint. Most patients recognize no or only minimal and insignificant cognitive deficits (anosagnosia), and this history often contrasts sharply with reports from family members. AD usually begins with difficulties with memory and orientation, with subsequent gradual and progressive decline in visuospatial skills, language and calculation, praxis (learned motor skills), gnosis (perception), and frontal and executive functions, such as reasoning, judgment, foresight, and insight. More complex activities of daily living such as handling finances and driving and shopping become increasingly difficult. Although old memories remain relatively intact, formation of new memories is progressively impaired. Patients may ask questions repeatedly, exhibit frequent word-finding pauses in conversation, and forget conversations, appointments, and medications. The history and examination should exclude depression and delirium and note the presence of asymmetry, focal signs, or parkinsonism. Routine serum laboratory tests, including a hematologic panel and chemistry battery (glucose, electrolytes, renal and liver function tests), should also rule out vitamin B_{12} deficiency and hypothyroidism as well as syphilis if suspected (Knopman, DeKosky, Cummings, Chui, Corey-Bloom, et al., 2001). The routine use of the Mini-Mental State Examination (MMSE) in suspect

patients (Tangalos, Smith, Ivnik, Petersen, Kokmen, et al., 1996) and referral for neuropsychologic batteries if dementia is questionable or uncertain
are useful in clinical diagnosis (Costa, Williams, Albert, Butters, Folstein,
et al., 1996).

A small fraction of patients develop myoclonus, seizures, or spastic
paraparesis, and many develop weight loss and extrapyramidal signs. Patients may become lost in their own homes and fail to recognize family
members. In latter stages of the disease, basic activities of daily living such
as dressing, grooming, bathing, mobility and transfers, toileting, and eating are progressively affected. After years of cognitive and functional decline, patients become vegetative, mute, unresponsive, incontinent, and
bed-bound before death ensues—often from pneumonia and overwhelming
infection. Issues of tube feeding, hydration, antibiotic use, and cardiopul-
monary resuscitation become ethical debates for family members and may
have devastating consequences when opinions differ. Thus, decisions as to
advance directives for medical, financial, and legal affairs should be made
with the patient and family in early stages of AD while the patient is com-
petent to participate. Hospice care offers an alternative to patients in the
terminal stage of AD.

As part of the initial clinical evaluation of dementia, patients should
undergo a structural (anatomic) neuroimaging study—either cerebral
computed tomography (CT) or magnetic resonance (MR) imaging, typically noncontrast, to rule out other causes of cognitive decline such as
intracranial mass lesions (tumor, subdural hematoma), strokes, and perhaps normal pressure hydrocephalus (Knopman et al., 2001). The neuroimaging findings associated with AD, particularly in early stages, are
nonspecific—cerebral atrophy, including medial temporal lobe atrophy,
periventricular white matter changes (leukoaureosis), and enlarged ventricles (hydrocephalus *ex vacuo*). There are no structural imaging abnormalities specific to AD.

Although not routinely recommended, the classic findings of AD on
functional neuroimaging studies, whether single photon emission computed tomography (SPECT), [^{18}F] fluorodeoxy-glucose positron emission
tomography ([^{18}F]FDG-PET), or functional MR, are hypoperfusion and
hypometabolism in temporoparietal association and posterior cingulate
cortices bilaterally; prefrontal cortices are also progressively affected in
latter stages. In contrast, primary sensory cortices (auditory, visual, and

somatosensory) and primary motor cortex are spared, explaining the selective decline in higher cortical functions. This pattern of abnormalities is also found (in milder degrees) in asymptomatic genetically at-risk (ApoE4 positive) elderly individuals, suggesting its potential use as a predictor or biomarker of AD in preclinical stages. Although PET is more sensitive than SPECT imaging, PET is currently limited to research applications. SPECT imaging may be useful in differentiating frontotemporal dementias from AD, but sensitivity, especially in early stages, is limited. Functional MR imaging is becoming widely available and has the advantage of no radioactive exposure, but it requires further study.

To date, there is no established biomarker of AD, despite decades of intense investigation. Measurements of Aß peptides in blood or Aß40, Aß42, and tau levels in cerebrospinal fluid appear promising with post hoc analysis, but prospective studies are lacking. A widely marketed test for AD— elevated urine or cerebrospinal fluid neural thread protein (NTP, AD7C)—has not adequately proven clinical utility. ApoE4 genotyping is commercially available, but its application should be limited to research studies because this test adds very little to the predictive value of clinical diagnosis, adds cost, and requires genetic counseling for the patient and family members. Individuals with ApoE4 may not necessarily develop AD, and many patients with AD do not carry the ApoE4 allele.

The *Diagnostic and Statistical Manual of Mental Disorders,* 4th edition (*DSM-IV;* American Psychiatric Association [APA], 1994) or the National Institute of Neurologic, Communicative Disorders and Stroke-AD and Related Disorders Association (NINCDS-ADRDA) criteria (McKhann, Drachman, Folstein, Katzman, Price, et al., 1984) are used for the clinical diagnosis of AD. These criteria are similar and require a gradually progressive dementia severe enough to impair social or occupational functioning with other etiologies of dementia excluded. By definition, dementia requires a decline in memory and at least one other cognitive domain—visuospatial skills, language and calculation, praxis, gnosis, or frontal and executive function. Dementia cannot be diagnosed in the presence of significant depression or delirium. Depression is a harbinger of dementia in some patients, and demented individuals are at high risk for delirium (often induced by infection, dehydration, or centrally-active medications). A diagnosis of definite AD requires light microscopic examination of brain tissue sections (by autopsy, or rarely by brain biopsy). Thus, only possible and probable AD are diagnosed clinically. Possible AD is diagnosed when uncertainty arises from an additional secondary etiology of dementia or the dementia has an atypical onset, course, or presentation. Diagnostic accuracy, compared to autopsy, for possible and probable AD by NINCDS-ADRDA criteria is approximately 50% to 60% and 80% to 90%, respectively, in specialized centers.

The Khachaturian (1985) pathologic criteria for AD require that the density of amyloid plaques and neurofibrillary tangles in brain sections exceed a given threshold that increases with age. In contrast, the Consortium to Establish a Registry for Alzheimer's Disease (CERAD) criteria focus exclusively on the density of amyloid plaques (the sine qua non marker of AD) in brain sections compared to given high-power microscopic fields. In part because neurofibrillary tangles are not specific to AD, they were not considered essential to the diagnosis (Mirra, Heyman, McKeel, Sumi, Crain, et al., 1991). The recent "Reagan criteria" for AD, however, require both amyloid plaques and neurofibrillary tangles in multiple brain regions and declare all such pathology abnormal. These criteria incorporate the CERAD plaque density scale as well as Braak and Braak (1991) staging of the density and distribution of pathologic abnormalities found in AD brain (National Institute on Aging and Reagan Institute Working Group on Diagnostic Criteria for the Neuropathologic Assessment of Alzheimer's Disease, 1997). Despite numerous other profound neuropathologic changes in the brain (neuronal and synaptic loss, gliosis, inflammation, cholinergic deficits, microvascular amyloid angiopathy, oxidative damage, etc.), the mainstay of pathologic diagnosis remains silver staining of brain sections and light microscopic examination of the density and distribution of amyloid plaques and neurofibrillary tangles—in other words, methods used by Dr. Alzheimer in 1907. As documented by Braak and Braak (1991), the neuropathology of AD is not random but affects entorhinal cortex and hippocampus followed by other limbic structures and neocortex. However, rare focal variants of AD, including posterior cortical atrophy (occipitoparietal) or frontal lobe variants, present a diagnostic challenge. As is true for all neurodegenerative diseases, the etiology of the selective vulnerability of different brain regions to AD pathologies remains obscure. Like all amyloidopathies, the ß-pleated sheet conformation of Aß in amyloid plaques and blood vessels results in their fluorescence with thioflavin-S staining as well as apple-green birefringence in Congo red-stained sections visualized with polarized light.

TREATMENT

To prove both statistically and clinically significant benefits, clinical trials of drugs for AD include cognitive and functional outcome measures. This is a mandate for drug approval from the U.S. Food and Drug Administration. Thus, scales routinely used in clinical trials with AD patients include the MMSE, Alzheimer's Disease Assessment Scale, Cognitive Subscale (ADAS-Cog), the Clinical Global Impression of Change Scale, and the Clinician Interview-Based Impression of Change Scale (CIBIC; Mayeux & Sano, 1999). To date, the only drugs with proven efficacy in the treatment of patients with AD are acetylcholinesterase inhibitors (Doody, Stevens, Beck, Dubinsky, Kaye, et al., 2001; see Figure 1.3). The first of these medications was tacrine (Cognex, approved in 1993; Knapp, Knopman, Solomon, Pendlebury, Davis, et al., 1994). However, this drug is limited by its q.i.d. dosing and titration, side effects (especially nausea, vomiting, diarrhea, and hepatotoxicity), and requirement for serum alanine aminotransferase (ALT) monitoring. Thus, newer acetylcholinesterase inhibitors without hepatotoxicity—donepezil (Aricept, approved in 1996; Rogers & Friedhoff, 1996), rivastigmine (Exelon, approved in 2000), and galantamine (Reminyl, approved in 2001)—have eclipsed tacrine (Cognex). There are no direct comparison trials, but efficacy in improving or maintaining outcome measures over time appears comparable. Therefore, clinical usage is determined by their dose frequency, titration schedule, and frequency of side effects. Donepezil has the advantages of having once-daily (q.d.) dosing, only one titration step, and infrequent or often temporary side effects such as nausea,

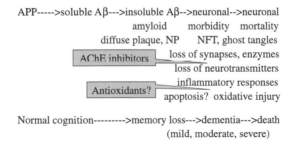

APP----->soluble Aβ--->insoluble Aβ-->neuronal-->neuronal
                                amyloid   morbidity mortality
                  diffuse plaque, NP   NFT, ghost tangles

AChE inhibitors   loss of synapses, enzymes
                            loss of neurotransmitters
                               inflammatory responses
Antioxidants?   apoptosis? oxidative injury

Normal cognition--------->memory loss--->dementia--->death
                                (mild, moderate, severe)

Figure 1.3   The amyloid cascade hypothesis of AD. Current drug treatments for AD such as acetylcholinesterase (AChE) inhibitors and perhaps antioxidants (vitamin E) act on putative distal targets, allowing only modest, symptomatic, and temporary clinical benefits.

vomiting, and diarrhea. Despite modest and temporary benefits, cost-benefit analyses favor drug usage because of reduced requirements for other medical resources, including delayed nursing home placement. Interestingly, caregiver education and support such as respite care may also delay nursing home placement of AD patients. When to withdraw medication is unclear because most studies enroll only patients with mild to moderate dementia.

Other medications have questionable efficacy for the treatment of AD. Clinical trials of *Ginkgo biloba* extract in patients with mixed dementias are inconclusive, and rare side effects include bleeding. The antioxidants α-tocopherol (vitamin E) and selegiline (Deprenyl) delay functional decline and death in AD patients (Sano, Ernesto, Thomas, Klauber, Schafer, et al., 1997), perhaps due to peripheral effects. No cognitive benefits were found, but these were secondary endpoint measures. There was no additive effect of the two compounds, but either was superior to placebo. Despite flaws in this study, vitamin E (1,000 I.U. b.i.d.) is routinely recommended to patients with AD. Vitamin E is inexpensive, available without a prescription, and virtually without side effects but should not be used in patients with a coagulopathy (e.g., those taking warfarin [Coumadin]) because of an increased bleeding risk. Only one dosage of vitamin E was used in this study—it remains unknown if a lower dose is efficacious.

Although epidemiologic and pilot data are promising, treatment trials with estrogens have shown no beneficial cognitive effect in postmenopausal women with AD. Likewise, despite a considerable inflammatory response to amyloid in the brain and promising pilot studies of older nonsteroidal antiinflammatory inhibitors (NSAIDs), drugs inhibiting cyclooxygenase-2 specifically (COX-2 inhibitors) have also proven disappointing in AD patients. Prednisone treatment is also without cognitive benefit in AD patients. Because retrospective epidemiologic studies appear promising, *statins* that lower serum cholesterol levels are being explored for potential benefit in prevention or treatment of AD. Some clinical trials are focusing on more proximate events with the hypothesis that treatment of AD patients may be "too little, too late." Thus, trials in progress are enrolling individuals with mild cognitive impairment (MCI), a predementia syndrome with high risk of conversion to dementia (Petersen, Stevens, Ganguli, Tangalos, Cummings, et al., 2001). For example, treatment with estrogen in postmenopausal women, donepezil (Aricept), or vitamin E is being studied in patients with MCI for potential efficacy in delaying or preventing the onset of dementia and AD. The exact neuropsychometric boundaries among normal aging, MCI, and dementia, however, are controversial.

In addition to cognitive and functional outcomes, many clinical trials of AD patients focus on behavioral outcome measures. Abnormal behaviors eventually affect the majority of patients with AD and include depression, apathy, anxiety, agitation, wandering, pacing, aggression, hostility, delusions, paranoia, hallucinations, disinhibition, catastrophic reactions, and sleep-wake cycle disturbances. With some patients, the presenting complaints of the family or caregiver are not cognitive and functional decline but intolerable behaviors. Such patients may more likely present to a geriatric psychiatrist than a neurologist. In addition to onset of bowel and bladder incontinence and loss of a caregiver, disruptive behaviors are a major precipitant of nursing home placement. Thus, treatment of behavioral problems is a very important aspect of AD management. Unfortunately, well-designed clinical trials of behavioral management are few, leading to empiric treatment trials. Examples of behavioral outcome measures employed in clinical trials are the Neuropsychiatric Inventory, Geriatric Depression Scale, and the Cohen-Mansfield Agitation Inventory. Treatment with neuroleptics (especially newer atypical neuroleptics), anticonvulsants, anxiolytics, and antidepressants (especially selective serotonin reuptake inhibitors [SSRIs]) may be indicated based on the problem behaviors (Sutor, Rummans, & Smith, 2001). Interestingly, acetylcholinesterase inhibitors also improve behavioral outcome measures in patients with AD, although there are anecdotal reports of their worsening behavior. Nonpharmacologic strategies for behavioral management such as the use of scheduled music and exercise should be exhausted before resorting to drug treatment and should be used concurrently. Further, education of caregiving staff minimizes the use of neuroleptics for agitation (Doody et al., 2001).

To date, all treatments for AD are thought to be symptomatic only with no beneficial effect on underlying progressive disease processes. In support of this hypothesis, cessation of donepezil (Aricept) results in acute loss of clinical benefits. Recent experimental strategies, however, such as inhibitors of ß- or γ-secretases, metal chelation, or immunization with Aß (more later) may retard underlying pathologic processes. The development of these therapies will be a test of the amyloid hypothesis of AD.

ISSUES IN DIAGNOSIS AND TREATMENT

Although AD is the most frequent cause of dementia in affluent societies, vascular dementia and Lewy body dementia are also common in the elderly. Thus, many patients with AD have these comorbid diagnoses. In fact, although Lewy body dementia may occur in pure form, most patients also qualify clinically and neuropathologically for AD. The McKeith criteria for the diagnosis of Lewy body dementia include progressive dementia with coincident parkinsonism, neuroleptic sensitivity, fluctuations in cognition, and spontaneous (not drug-induced) visual hallucinations (McKeith, Galasko, Kosaka, Perry, Dickson, et al., 1996; McKeith, Perry, & Perry, 1999). If indicated, patients may be given a combined diagnosis of AD and Lewy body dementia. This combination is also termed the Lewy body variant of AD.

The Hachinski Ischemic Score (HIS; Hachinski, Lassen, & Marshall, 1974) as modified by Rosen, Terry, Fuld, Katzman, and Peck (1980) is an autopsy-validated index for the diagnosis of vascular dementia. This scale includes a history of sudden onset, stepwise progression, stroke risk factors, stroke or transient ischemic attack, asymmetry or focal signs on examination, and so on. Again, patients may have a combined diagnosis of AD and vascular dementia. Finally, other potentially confounding diagnoses are the frontotemporal dementias linked to neurofibrillary tangles (the tauopathies). Phosphorylated tau is the major component of neurofibrillary tangles, and some familial frontotemporal dementias are linked to mutations and polymorphisms in the tau gene on chromosome 17. Frontotemporal dementia may be distinguishable from AD by consensus criteria (Neary, Snowden, Gustafson, Passant, Stuss, et al., 1998) such as early loss of personal and social awareness, hyperorality, stereotyped perseverative behavior, and impaired word fluency and executive functions. These criteria, however, are unvalidated. Patients with frontotemporal dementia may present with marked personality changes such as impulsivity, distractibility, perseveration, and disinhibition. The tauopathies include frontotemporal dementia plus parkinsonism, corticobasal degeneration, progressive supranuclear palsy, and Pick's disease spectrum including primary progressive aphasia. Although these disorders present very differently in early clinical stages, they may be difficult to distinguish from AD in late and vegetative stages.

For unclear reasons, the risk of developing AD is higher in Black and Hispanic compared to White populations. Although the influence of the ApoE4 polymorphism on increased AD risk is apparent in Blacks, it appears to be less potent compared to Whites. Interestingly, although Black populations in Africa and the United States have similar ApoeE4 allele frequencies, the risk of AD is much higher in the age-matched U.S. Black population. This suggests that unknown environmental factors such as diet or resultant comorbidities may be important culprits. Until recently, vascular dementia was the leading cause of dementia in Japan, but this is shifting to AD, despite a low ApoE4 allele frequency, as life expectancy increases and stroke risk factors such as hypertension are better managed.

NEW DIRECTIONS

Presenilin-1 testing is commercially available and may be diagnostic for AD in the rare patient with early-onset dementia (usually age 30 to 55) and a pedigree showing an autosomal-dominant pattern of inheritance. Because more than 60 different mutations in presenilin-1 are known (almost all single missense mutations), the entire presenilin-1 gene is sequenced, and this sometimes uncovers novel mutations. As is true for all genetic markers, presenilin-1 testing should not be obtained in minors; and with consenting symptomatic adults (or their legal guardian), testing must be obtained only if genetic counseling is available. Prenatal screening and testing of asymptomatic adults in affected pedigrees raise ethical questions. Due to their rarity, genetic testing for APP, presenilin 2, and tau mutations are not commercially available. New genetic linkages for increased risk of AD will no doubt be found in the future, and this effort will be aided by bioinformatics—analysis of massive databases of the human genome sequence with single nucleotide polymorphisms (SNPs) and studies of large populations (such as the Icelandic study). This information will shed further light on the pathogenesis of AD, and every genetic linkage identified will be a test of the amyloid hypothesis.

The diagnosis of AD remains based in the history and physical examination. Potential biomarkers for AD under investigation include ApoE and other gene polymorphisms, Aß40 and Aß42 levels in blood, Aß40, Aß42, and tau levels in cerebrospinal fluid, neural thread protein (AD7C, NTP) levels in cerebrospinal fluid or urine, APP processing in platelets, neuropsychologic measures, and structural or functional neuroimaging markers. One neuropsychometric measure that may predict risk of AD decades later is linguistic ability as a young adult (Snowdon, Kemper, Mortimer, Greiner, Wekstein, et al., 1996). For some proposed biomarkers, repeated measures over time may be required, such as medial temporal lobe thickness measured by MR imaging. To date, there is no imaging modality able to detect amyloid plaques and neurofibrillary tangles in humans in vivo. Many proposed biomarkers have been discounted such as the pupillary response to topical muscarinic cholinergic receptor agonists. Surrogate markers of AD will be useful in diagnosis and in determination of efficacy of therapeutic strategies for disease prevention or arrest but must first meet accepted threshold criteria (The Ronald and Nancy Reagan Research Institute of the Alzheimer's Association and the National Institute on Aging Working Group, 1998).

Construction of the amyloid cascade hypothesis and recent identification of the ß- and γ-secretases responsible for the release of Aß from APP have sparked an intense search for inhibitors of these proteases as potential treatments for AD (see Figure 1.4). For example, γ-secretase inhibitors are now being studied in clinical trials. There is strong evidence to suggest that presenilins either are γ-secretases or an important component of the γ-secretase complex (Selkoe, 2001). Unfortunately, these proteases are not

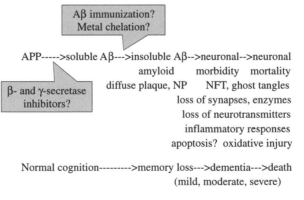

Figure 1.4   The amyloid hypothesis of AD. Novel potentially disease-modifying treatments may prevent or treat AD by targeting more proximate causal events. These approaches include developing ß- or γ-secretase inhibitors to retard Aß formation, metal chelation to prevent Aß/amyloid deposition, and immunization to promote Aß/amyloid clearance.

specific to APP and have other important normal functions. For example, γ-secretase cleaves both APP and Notch, a protein essential to normal mammalian development and adult processes such as hematopoesis. Underscoring its importance in normal development, presenilin-1 knock-out mice are lethal in utero and resemble Notch knock-out mice. A γ-secretase inhibitor may, therefore, have dose-limiting toxic side effects. Another promising approach is inhibition of ß-secretase, because mice with this gene (BACE-1) knocked out are viable and appear normal. Inhibitors of ß-secretase are in the preclinical phases of investigation.

Despite their shortcomings, the availability of transgenic mouse models of AD that develop age-dependent progressive amyloid deposition in brain and cognitive decline has greatly facilitated development of putative AD therapeutics. Whether any of these therapies will be useful for humans, however, remains to be seen. Because of inflammatory responses to amyloid in AD brain tissue, it was hypothesized that immunization of human APP transgenic mice with Aß may exacerbate disease. In stark contrast, immunized mice develop little or no amyloid deposition, indicating a novel therapeutic strategy (Schenk, Barbour, Dunn, Gordon, Grajeda, et al., 1999). The mechanism of action remains to be determined, but immunization may promote Aß and amyloid clearance by anti-Aß immunoglobulin (IgG) complexes and phagocytic cells (microglia) in the brain; peripheral immune-mediated Aß clearance (a "sink"?) has not been excluded. Immunization not only prevents but also removes established amyloid plaques in transgenic mouse brain. In support of the amyloid hypothesis, immunization prevents both plaque deposition in transgenic mouse brain and behavioral decline in learning and memory tasks. However, a Phase II clinical trial of Aß42 vaccination of patients with AD was halted due to encephalitic complications in about 5%.

An alternate strategy with orally administered Clioquinol, a metal chelator, has also demonstrated success in prevention of amyloid plaque deposition in aging transgenic APP mouse brain (Cherny, Atwood, Xilina, Gray, Jones, et al., 2001). Aß peptides bind selectively to Cu^{2+} and Zn^{2+} and chelators of Cu^{2+} and Zn^{2+} solubilize Aß amyloid deposits in the AD brain. Interestingly, in this study soluble Aß levels in transgenic mouse brain were increased with drug treatment. Effects of treatment on mouse behavior are unknown. Phase I clinical trials of Clioquinol (with vitamin B_{12}) have demonstrated safety and a Phase II trial is in progress.

Gene therapy for AD and other neurologic diseases faces enormous barriers, such as access to the central nervous system, limited duration and extent of gene expression, and detrimental host responses to the vector or gene product. Nevertheless, a small Phase I clinical trial of transfected fibroblasts expressing nerve growth factor (NGF) injected into the brain of AD patients is underway. NGF promotes survival of neurons, including cholinergic neurons in the basal forebrain. Other gene therapy approaches with genes that modulate APP expression or catabolism, or provide trophic support to neurons, remain speculative. Replacement of defective gene products by somatic cell gene therapy is now having limited clinical success in other diseases, and heritable repair of a defective mutant gene by germ-line gene therapy may also be technically feasible. Conversely, a gene targeting strategy has generated "humanized" human APP transgenic mice in part by replacing the mouse Aß sequence with the human sequence (Reaume, Howland, Trusko, Savage, Lang, et al., 1996).

A major ethical debate for the new millennium is inheritable genetic modification of man, which is now and for the near future rightfully banned (Frankel & Chapman, 2001). Neither do we understand AD pathogenesis enough to warrant this approach. Interestingly, longer lived mammals that share the human amyloidogenic Aß sequence, such as canine, *ursus* (bear), and nonhuman primate species, also share the risk of developing AD-like pathologies with aging. In contrast, the three amino acid differences in the mouse and rat Aß sequence render this peptide relatively nonamyloidogenic. Inheritable modification of the Aß sequence in human APP may become feasible with modern molecular techniques as shown by our ability to manipulate and transmit genes in a variety of animal and plant species (including genetically modified foods). Nonamyloidogenic Aß may be generated by introducing a single nucleotide polymorphism, perhaps found naturally in another species, within the Aß sequence of the human APP gene. More than 1.6 million SNPs are already known in the human genome, although most are in noncoding (intronic) sequences. This strategy may interfere the least with the normal functions of APP, which remain unclear. Small steps toward creating "designer humans" with enhanced beauty or intellectual, artistic, or athletic ability have already been taken, for example, in fertility clinics. However, if inheritable genetic modification of man is ever exploited in the distant future, a far more justifiable application will be disease eradication (Stock & Campbell, 2000).

As we approach the 100-year anniversary of Dr. Alzheimer's case report, his words are more prescient than ever—"It is evident we are dealing with a peculiar little-known disease process. In recent years, these particular disease-processes have been detected in great numbers. This fact should stimulate us to further study and analysis of this particular disease" (Alzheimer, 1907). After decades of persistent anosagnosia writ large and therapeutic nihilism, the fruits of modern biochemical pathology and molecular biology and genetics have quickly brought us to the threshold of safe and effective *disease-modifying* therapies for the prevention and treatment of AD. These may be pharmacologic, immunologic, and, perhaps, ultimately genetic. Further study and analysis are now essential to maintain quality of life.

REFERENCES

Alzheimer, A. (1907). Über eine eigenartige Erkrankung der Hirnrinde (Translation: A characteristic disease of the cerebral cortex). *Allgemeine Zeitschrift fur Psychiatrie und Psychisch-gerichtliche Medizin, 64,* 146–148.

American Psychiatric Association. (1994). *Diagnostic and statistical manual of mental disorders* (4th ed.). Washington, DC: Author.

Askanas, V., & Engel, W. K. (2001). Inclusion-body myositis: Newest concepts of pathogenesis and relation to aging and Alzheimer's disease. *Journal of Neuropathology and Experimental Neurology, 60,* 1–14.

Braak, H., & Braak, E. (1991). Neuropathologic staging of Alzheimer related changes. *Acta Neuropathologica, 82,* 239–259.

Cherny, R. A., Atwood, C. S., Xilinas, M. E., Gray, D. N., Jones, W. D., McLean, C. A., et al. (2001). Treatment with a copper-zinc chelator markedly and rapidly inhibits ß-amyloid accumulation in Alzheimer's disease transgenic mice. *Neuron, 30,* 665–676.

Costa, P. T., Williams, T. F., Albert, M. S., Butters, N. M., Folstein, M. F., Gilman, S., et al. (1996). *Recognition and initial assessment of Alzheimer's disease and related dementias* (Clinical Practice Guideline No. 19; AHCPR Publication No. 97–0702). Rockville, MD: U.S. Department of Health and Human Services, Public Health Service, Agency for Health Care Policy and Research.

Davies, P., & Maloney, A. J. F. (1976). Selective loss of central cholinergic neurons in Alzheimer's disease. *Lancet, 2,* 1403.

Doody, R. S., Stevens, J. C., Beck, C., Dubinsky, R. M., Kaye, J. A., Gwyther, L., et al. (2001). Practice parameter: Management of dementia (an evidence-based review). *Neurology, 56,* 1154–1166.

Evans, D. A., Funkenstein, H. H., Albert, M. S., Scherr, P. A., Cook, N. R., Chown, M. J., et al. (1989). Prevalence of Alzheimer's disease in a community population of older persons. Higher than previously reported. *Journal of the American Medical Association, 262,* 2551–2556.

Evenhuis, H. M. (1990). The natural history of dementia in Down's syndrome. *Archives of Neurology, 47,* 263–267.

Frankel, M. S., & Chapman, A. R. (2001). Facing inheritable genetic modifications. *Science, 292,* 1303.

Games, D., Adams, D., Alessandrini, R., Barbour, R., Berthelette, P., Blackwell, C., et al. (1995). Alzheimer-type neuropathology in transgenic mice expressing V717F ß-amyloid precursor protein. *Nature, 373,* 523–527.

Hachinski, V. C., Lassen, N. A., & Marshall, J. (1974). Multiinfarct dementia: A cause of mental deterioration in the elderly. *Lancet, 2,* 207–210.

Hsiao, K., Chapman, P., Nilsen, S., Eckman, C., Harigara Y., Younkin, S., et al. (1996). Correlative memory deficits, Aß elevation and amyloid plaques in transgenic mice. *Science, 274,* 99–102.

Khachaturian, Z. S. (1985). Diagnosis of Alzheimer's disease. *Archives of Neurology, 42,* 1097–1105.

Knapp, M. J., Knopman, D. S., Solomon, P. R., Pendlebury, W. W., Davis, C. S., & Gracon, S. I. (1994). A 30-week randomized controlled trial of high-dose tacrine in patients with Alzheimer's disease. *Journal of the American Medical Association, 271,* 985–991.

Knopman, D. S., DeKosky, S. T., Cummings, J. L., Chui, H., Corey-Bloom, J., et al. (2001). Practice parameter: Diagnosis of dementia (an evidence-based review). *Neurology, 56,* 1143–1153.

Mayeux, R., & Sano, M. (1999). Treatment of Alzheimer's disease. *New England Journal of Medicine, 341,* 1670–1679.

McKeith, I. G., Galasko, D., Kosaka, K., Perry, E. K., Dickson, D. W., Hansen, L. A., et al. (1996). Clinical and pathological diagnosis of dementia with Lewy bodies (DLB): Report of the CDLB international workshop. *Neurology, 47,* 1113–1124.

McKeith, I. G., Perry, E. K., & Perry, R. H. (1999). Consortium on dementia with Lewy bodies. Report of the Second Dementia with Lewy Body International Workshop: Diagnosis and treatment. *Neurology, 53,* 902–905.

McKhann, G., Drachman, D., Folstein, M., Katzman, R., Price, D., & Stadlan, E. M. (1984). Clinical diagnosis of Alzheimer's disease: Report of the NINCDS-ADRDA Work Group under the auspices of Department of Health and Human Services Task Force on Alzheimer's disease. *Neurology, 34,* 939–944.

Mirra, S. S., Heyman, A., McKeel, D., Sumi, S. M., Crain, B. J., Brownlee, L. M., et al. (1991). The consortium to establish a registry for Alzheimer's disease (CERAD). Part II: Standardization of the neuropathologic assessment of Alzheimer's disease. *Neurology, 41,* 479–486.

National Institute on Aging and Reagan Institute Working Group on Diagnostic Criteria for the Neuropathologic Assessment of Alzheimer's Disease. (1997). Consensus recommendations for the postmortem diagnosis of Alzheimer's disease. *Neurobiology and Aging, 18,* S1–S2.

Neary, D., Snowden, J. S., Gustafson, L., Passant, U., Stuss, D., Black, S., et al. (1998). Frontotemporal lobar degeneration: A consensus on clinical diagnostic criteria. *Neurology, 51,* 1546–1554.

Petersen, R. C., Stevens, J. C., Ganguli, M., Tangalos, E. G., Cummings, J. L., & DeKosky, S. T. (2001). Practice parameter: Early detection of dementia: Mild cognitive impairment (an evidence-based review). *Neurology, 56,* 1133–1142.

Reaume, A. G., Howland, D. S., Trusko, S. P., Savage, M. J., Lang, D. M., Greenberg, B. D., et al. (1996). Enhanced amyloidogenic processing of the ß-amyloid precursor protein in gene-targeted mice bearing the Swedish familial Alzheimer's disease mutations and a "humanized" Aß sequence. *Journal of Biological Chemistry, 271,* 23380–23388.

Rogers, S. L., & Friedhoff, L. T. (1996). The efficacy and safety of donepezil in patients with Alzheimer's disease: Results of a U.S. multicenter, randomized, double-blind, placebo-controlled trial. The Donepezil Study Group. *Dementia, 7,* 293–303.

The Ronald and Nancy Reagan Research Institute of the Alzheimer's Association and the National Institute on Aging Working Group. (1998). Consensus report of the working group on: Molecular and biochemical markers of Alzheimer's disease. *Neurobiology and Aging, 19,* 109–116.

Rosen, W. G., Terry, R. D., Fuld, P. A., Katzman, R., & Peck, A. (1980). Pathological verification of ischemic score in differentiation of dementias. *Annals of Neurology, 7,* 486–488.

Sano, M., Ernesto, C., Thomas, R. G., Klauber, M. R., Schafer, K., Grundman, M., et al. (1997). A controlled trial of selegiline, α-tocopherol, or both as treatments for Alzheimer's disease. The Alzheimer's Disease Cooperative Study. *New England Journal of Medicine, 336,* 1216–1222.

Schenk, D., Barbour, R., Dunn, W., Gordon, G., Grajeda, H., Guido, T., et al. (1999). Immunization with amyloid-ß attenuates Alzheimer-disease-like pathology in the PDAPP mouse. *Nature, 400,* 173–177.

Selkoe, D. J. (2001). Alzheimer's disease: Genes, proteins, and therapy. *Physiological Reviews, 81,* 741–766.

Snowdon, D. A., Kemper, S. J., Mortimer, J. A., Greiner, L. H., Wekstein, D. R., & Markesberry, W. R. (1996). Linguistic ability in early life and cognitive function and Alzheimer's disease in late life: Findings from the Nun Study. *Journal of the American Medical Association, 275,* 528–532.

Stock, G., & Campbell, J. (Eds.). (2000). *Engineering the human germline: An exploration of the science and ethics of altering the genes we pass to our children.* New York: Oxford University Press.

Strittmatter, W. J., Saunders, A. M., Schmechel, D., Pericak-Vance, M., Enghild, J., Salvesen, G. S., et al. (1993). Apoliproprotein E—high avidity binding to ß-amyloid and increased frequency of type-4 allele in late-onset Alzheimer's disease. *Proceedings of the National Academy of Sciences, USA, 90,* 1977–1981.

Sutor, B., Rummans, T. A., & Smith, G. E. (2001). Assessment and management of behavioral disturbances in nursing home patients with dementia. *Mayo Clinic Proceedings, 76,* 540–550.

Tangalos, E. G., Smith, G. E., Ivnik, R. J., Petersen, R. C., Kokmen, E., Kurland, L. T., et al. (1996). The Mini-Mental State Examination in general medical practice: Clinical utility and acceptance. *Mayo Clinic Proceedings, 71,* 827–829.

Turner, R. S. (2001). Alzheimer's disease in man and transgenic mice: Females at higher risk. *American Journal of Pathology, 158,* 797–801.

CHAPTER 2

Psychological Evaluation and Nonpharmacologic Treatment and Management of Alzheimer's Disease

Mary Sano and Christine Weber

Alzheimer's disease (AD), the most common form of dementia, is estimated to affect 4 million people in the United States and up to 15 million people worldwide. This neurodegenerative disorder is characterized by progressive loss of memory and other cognitive functions, which impairs social and occupational functioning. AD is the number one cause of disability in the elderly because it is not directly fatal and survival is long (about 10 years from diagnosis). Over the past decade, most medications approved for the treatment of AD work via cholinergic stimulation and target the symptoms of attention and memory. These treatments are not thought to affect the progression of disease, and current research for new drugs focuses on agents that target the characteristic neuropathological features of neuritic plaques composed of amyloid and neurofibrillary tangles composed of tau protein. While significant effort from the public sector and industry is focused on the biological aspects of the disease, there is a growing awareness of the social and psychological impact of this disease on patients and those who care for them. This chapter describes risk factors associated with the disease, describes aspects of the clinical diagnostic evaluation, and examines nonpharmacological interventions that may maintain function and ameliorate some of the psychological distress associated with this disease.

The authors are supported in this work in part by Federal Grants RO1AG 15922, UO1 AG 10483, and P50 AG08702.

RISK FACTORS

Alzheimer's disease is most commonly seen after the age of 60 years. As such, age is the most prominent risk factor for AD, and both incidence and prevalence increase dramatically after the sixth decade. For example, prevalence rates increase from 3 percent at age 65 years to 47 percent after the age of 85 years (Hebert, Scherr, Beckett, Albert, & Pilgrim, 1995), and incidence increases from 0.5 percent per year at the age of 65 years to 8 percent per year after the age of 85 years (Evans, 1990). Most studies suggest only minimal influence of gender on incidence; however, the prevalence tends to be higher in women because of greater longevity.

Other factors consistently reported to increase risk of AD include a family history of AD in a first-degree relative, which has been suggested to provide a two- to threefold increased risk, and the presence of an epsilon4 allele of apolipoprotein E, which appears to be a separate but not additive risk (Blacker et al., 1997). More controversial as risks but possible are head injury, either alone or in combination with other risk factors, low education, and cigarette smoking. The biological basis of head injury as a risk factor is supported by data suggesting its association with increased beta amyloid accumulation, which may exacerbate the amyloid accumulation seen in AD (Nicoll, Roberts, & Graham, 1996; Roberts, Allsop, & Bruton, 1990).

The concept of cognitive reserve has been hypothesized as an explanation for the education effect. Stern et al. (2000) demonstrated that AD patients with high education who were matched for cognitive performance to AD patients with low education actually had more brain pathology as measured by regional cerebral blood flow. The explanation offered is that among those with high education, cognitive performance may appear better while disease pathology advances at least as rapidly as those with low education. Alternately, education may be a surrogate for another variable including better lifetime health care or other unknown biological predisposition against cognitive deterioration.

Several variables have been suggested as protective against AD, including antioxidant exposure through vitamins or diet, the use of anti-inflammatory drugs, the use of estrogens, and the use of lipid lowering agents. However, none of these have been demonstrated as effective preventative agents in well-controlled clinical trials, although many trials are ongoing and should provide an answer over the next few years.

DIAGNOSTIC ASSESSMENT OF ALZHEIMER'S DISEASE

There are currently no guidelines to suggest routine screening of the elderly for dementia, and the clinical evaluation usually begins with a complaint either from the patient or from an observer. Because changes in cognition and memory, which are the most common early signs of AD, can be caused by many medical conditions, especially in the elderly, it is critical that such complaints be evaluated by a medical professional. For the diagnosis of AD, two broad areas must be evaluated: cognition and functioning. History, one of the most important tools of evaluation, should focus on characterizing the nature of the cognitive change, the rapidity with which it occurs, and the presence of important medical or life events occurring in proximity to the cognitive change. The other area to assess is functional ability, particularly function impaired by cognitive loss. Areas to address include difficulty handling financial matters, instrumental tasks such as shopping, chores, food preparation, and personal hygiene.

In general, slow, gradual cognitive change is the most common pattern observed in AD while more rapid change is associated with a range of medical conditions such as stroke or encephalopathy associated with medications and conditions such as viral or bacterial disease. The supporting observation from a relevant informant such as a family member or close friend is also critical in evaluating complaints. It has often been observed that the deficit may be minimized by the patient and usually it is at the behest of another that an evaluation is initiated.

ASSESSING COGNITION: MENTAL STATUS EXAMINATIONS AND NEUROPSYCHOLOGICAL EVALUATION

Mental status examination is a major part of the evaluation of cognitive complaint. One of the most commonly used instruments is the Mini-Mental State Examination (MMSE; Folstein, Folstein, & McHugh, 1975). The most common clinically useful version is a 30-item structured assessment of memory orientation, concentration, language, and constructional ability. Other screening tests are described briefly in Table 2.1. Among nonminority populations of average education, scores below 27 suggest dementia. When mental status is impaired and there is a reliable informant to confirm functional change, further neuropsychological testing may not be necessary.

Table 2.1 Cognitive Screening Measures for Alzheimer's Disease

	Score Range	Description	Comments
Mini Mental State Examination (MMSE)[a]	0–30	Well known. Quick.	Not sensitive to high premorbid function.
Clock Drawing[b]	1–10	Brief and easy to administer. Low cost. Appropriate for clinical settings.	Difficult to standardize scoring.
Blessed Information, Memory, Concentration[c]	0–28	Appropriate for clinical settings.	Minimal sensitivity for mild disease.
7-Minute Screen[d]	Categorical: Probability of dementia: high versus low	Appropriate for primary care setting. Easy to administer.	Little normative data. Testing materials required.
Modified Mini Mental State Examination (3MS)[e]	0–100	Sensitive to minimal change in high premorbid function.	Lengthy administration. Primarily used in research setting.

[a] "Mini-Mental State Examination (MMSE)," by J. R. Cockrell and M. F. Folstein, 1988, *Psychopharmacology Bulletin, 24,* pp. 689–692; and M. F. Folstein, S. E. Folstein, and P. R. McHugh, 1975, "Mini-Mental State: A Practical Method for Grading the Cognitive State of Patients for the Clinician," *Journal of Psychiatry Res., 12,* pp. 189–198.

[b] "Clock Drawing in Alzheimer's Disease: A Novel Measure of Dementia Severity," by T. Sunderland et al., 1989, *Journal of the American Geriatric Association, 37,* pp. 725–729; and "Screening for Alzheimer's Disease by Clock Drawing," by G. P. Wolf-Klein, F. A. Silverstone, A. P. Levy, and M. S. Brod, 1989, *Journal of the American Geriatric Association, 37,* pp. 730–734.

[c] "The Association between Quantitative Measures of Dementia and of Senile Change in the Cerebral Gray Matter of Elderly Subjects," by G. Blessed, B. E. Tomlinson, and M. Roth, 1968, *British Journal of Psychiatry, 114,* pp. 797–811.

[d] "Recognition of Alzheimer's Disease: The 7 Minute Screen," by P. R. Solomon and W. W. Pendlebury, 1998, *Family Medicine, 30,* pp. 265–271; and "A 7-Minute Neurocognitive Screening Battery Highly Sensitive to Alzheimer's Disease," by P. R. A. Solomon et al., 1998, *Archives of Neurology, 55,* pp. 349–355.

[e] "The Modified Mini-Mental State (3MS) Examination," by E. L. Teng and H. C. Chui, 1987, *Journal of Clinical Psychiatry, 48,* pp. 314–318.

However, certain conditions make it difficult to assess mental status with only a brief examination. Very highly educated individuals may perform well on mental status testing because it is not sufficiently challenging for them. The presence of premorbid or comorbid conditions might lower performance, making it difficult to determine if there is further decline. These could include depression, learning disability, prior CNS injury or disease, specific language deficit, or sensory deficit, which can compromise assessment. In such cases, more comprehensive neuropsychological assessment may be useful.

Neuropsychological evaluations assess memory, executive function, orientation, abstract reasoning, visual spatial abilities, and language. A review of assessments for these domains can be found elsewhere (Schmitt & Sano, 1994).

Deficits in learning and memory are the hallmark of AD, and normative data permits relatively sensitive evaluation of specific types of memory. Recall after a delay is one of the most sensitive measures for detection of dementia; among those who have no other deficit, it has been shown to predict rapid onset of dementia. This predictive value is so great that it has been used to define a prodrome to AD known as mild cognitive impairment (MCI). MCI refers to memory deficits with relatively minimal deficit in other cognitive areas and few functional consequences.

In the earliest stages of AD, working memory is impaired as measured by inefficient learning over time as well as poor recall after a delay. Typically, this is observable in both verbal and visual material. Executive function, the ability to plan and execute tasks, is often impaired even in mild AD. Deficits in executive function can be formally assessed with a task such as the Wisconsin Card Sort Test and can be observed in other cognitive tests such as verbal fluency and trails (Army Individual Test Battery, 1944; Benton & Hamsher, 1976; Heaton, 1981). Other cognitive domains that may be impaired early in the disease include visual spatial ability and naming. Orientation to time and place are often also impaired, which may be a result of both memory and visual spatial deficits as well as a specific deficit in orientation.

The availability of appropriate norms against which to compare performance is critical to the usefulness of a neuropsychological evaluation. This type of evaluation can be particularly helpful when the patient is highly educated because normative data for such individuals is readily available, particularly in the area of memory (Ivnik et al., 1990). Neuropsychological measures for these individuals can uncover significant memory impairment that may go undetected by brief mental status examinations.

Nonnative English speakers may have insufficient knowledge of the language to be accurately assessed. However, a growing number of tests can be used with Spanish speakers for whom there are reasonable amounts of normative data (Hohl, Grundman, Salmon, Thomas, & Thal, 1999; LaRue, Romero, Ortiz, Liang, & Lindeman, 1999; Loewenstein, Arguelles, Barker, & Duara, 1993; Mungas, Marshall, Weldon, Haan, & Reed, 1996; Ownby, Harwood, Acevedo, Barker, & Duara, 2001; Stricks, Pittman, Jacobs, Sano,

& Stern, 1998; Taussig, Mack, & Henderson, 1996). The presence of sensory loss or premorbid conditions can challenge the neuropsychologist because no appropriate normative data may be available. An alternative approach to evaluation in such cases is to demonstrate relative strengths in old knowledge and skills in the presence of specific deficits in areas that are most often deficient in AD as described previously.

ASSESSING FUNCTION: EVALUATION OF INSTRUMENTAL AND BASIC ACTIVITIES OF DAILY LIVING

There are many instruments that capture functional deterioration. However, most are too cumbersome for use in clinical evaluation, and an open, but focused, interview is the usual method for collecting this information. Two domains of function need to be considered: instrumental activities of daily living (ADL) and basic ADL. Instrumental ADL refers to the cognitive aspects of function, including the planning of activities to accomplish basic needs. These include activities such as shopping, chores, handling financial matters, and meal preparation. Basic ADL typically refers to eating, grooming, and toileting. Accurate functional assessment usually requires an observant other and usually cannot depend on the patient alone. Because many functional abilities are compromised by aging, it can be difficult to identify functional deficits due to dementia, especially in the earliest stages. Inquiring about subtle changes by asking about how much supervision and physical assistance is needed to accomplish an ADL can be a useful approach to assessment. If time permits, several instruments can be used (see Table 2.2).

ASSESSING BEHAVIORAL AND PSYCHIATRIC SYMPTOMS

While behavioral disturbances are not part of the diagnostic symptomatology, they are very common in AD, particularly as the disease progresses. Early in the disease, depression is noted, which may be minimally disturbing to patients and family. Later symptoms such as agitation, psychosis, and wandering can be disturbing and threaten patient safety. While clinicians often deal with these symptoms, there is less information on how to assess, prepare patient and family members, and treat in the earliest stages. Tools found useful for assessing behavioral and psychiatric disturbances in patients with AD are summarized in Table 2.3. While they may be burdensome

Table 2.2   Functional Assessments for Patients with Alzheimer's Disease

	Score Range	Description	Comments
Blessed Functional Assessment Scale[a]	0–17	Brief and easy to administer. Scores correlate with neuropathological findings.	Minimal sensitivity for mild disease.
Physical Self Maintenance Scale (PSMS)[b]	6–30	Widely used in demented and nondemented population.	Lengthy administration. Training required.
Alzheimer's Disease Cooperative Study-Activities of Daily Living (ADCS-ADL)[c]	0–52	Tailored to specific level of disease. Captures changes in functional ability.	Long form requires the informant to be well acquainted with the patient.

[a] "The Association between Quantitative Measures of Dementia and of Senile Change in the Cerebral Gray Matter of Elderly Subjects," by G. Blessed, B. E. Tomlinson, and M. Roth, 1968, *British Journal of Psychiatry, 114*, pp. 797–811.

[b] "Assessment of Older People: Self-Maintaining and Instrumental Activities of Daily Living," by M. P. Lawton and E. M. Brody, 1969, *Gerontologist, 9*, pp. 179–186.

[c] "An Inventory to Assess Activities of Daily Living for Clinical Trials in Alzheimer's Disease," by D. Galasko et al., 1997, *Alzheimer Disease and Associated Disorders, An International Journal, 11*(Supp. 2), S33–S39.

to use in clinical practice, they can provide important guidelines for assessing behavioral symptoms via clinical interview. For example, it is important to ask about specific behavioral and psychiatric disturbances, encouraging reporting of even mild symptoms. In a cohort of longitudinally followed patients with AD, symptoms were likely to persist even with medication once they appear (Devanand et al., 1992). Given this finding, clinicians may choose to provide education to caregivers and to assess their ability and preparedness for coping with these problems. The Neuropsychiatric Inventory, a tool often used in research, has been adapted for use by clinicians (Kaufer et al., 2000). This instrument, which is administered to an informant (usually a family member or someone else providing care and supervision), consists of questions about a wide range of behavioral and psychiatric symptoms and assesses how disturbing each symptom is. This may provide an introduction into assessing the caregiver's ability to handle these behavioral disturbances.

In the earliest stages of disease, patients may experience depression. This can result from awareness of cognitive loss or of growing dependence. Alternately, cognitive loss can be the source of reduced initiative perhaps in response to difficulties planning and executing activities. This lack of

Table 2.3   Behavioral Assessments for Patients with Alzheimer's Disease

	Score Range	Description	Comments
Neuropsychiatric inventory-Q (NPI-Q)[a]	0–250	Clinician's brief version of NPI.[b] Assesses psychiatric and behavioral disturbances and caregiver distress.	Requires minimal training.
Geriatric Depression Scale (GDS)[c]	0–30	Measures depression in the elderly.	Instrument is specific to depression.
Brief Psychiatric Rating Scale (BPRS)[d]	0–168	Used in a wide range of psychiatric illnesses, including dementia.	Requires experienced interviewer.

[a] "Validation of the NPI-Q: A Brief Clinical Form of the Neuropsychiatric Inventory, by D. I. Kaufer et al., 2000, *Journal of Neuropsychiatry and Clinical Neurosciences, 12,* pp. 233–239.

[b] "The Neuropsychiatric Inventory: Comprehensive Assessment of Psychopathology in Dementia," by J. L. Cummings, M. Mega, K. Gray, S. Rosenberg-Thompson, D. A. Carusi, and J. Gornbein, 1994, *Neurology, 44,* pp. 2308–2314.

[c] "Screening Test for Geriatric Depression" by J. A. Yesavage, T. L. Brink, T. S. Rose, O. Lum, P. H. Heersema, and M. Adey, 1982, *Clinical Gerontologist, 1,* pp. 37–43; and "Development and Validation of a Geriatric Depression Rating Scale: A Preliminary Report," by J. A. Yesavage et al., 1982–1983, *Journal of Psychiatric Research, 17,* pp. 37–49.

[d] "The Brief Psychiatric Rating Scale," by J. E. Overall and D. R. Gorham, 1962, *Psychological Reports, 10,* pp. 799–812.

initiative may be interpreted as withdrawal or depression even in the absence of depressed mood on the part of the patient. Several studies have suggested that depressive symptoms may be responsive to pharmacologic intervention but that they have no effect on cognition (Lyketsos et al., 2000). As the disease progresses, agitation or psychotic features such as hallucinations or delusions may occur. These symptoms can also arise from cognitive compromise and can be disturbing, challenging the coping strategies of the patient and family (Raskind, 1999).

Wandering is likely to occur at some point during the course of the disease. While definitive studies as to the cause are difficult to conduct, several causal factors have been proposed, including medication side effects; stress; confusion related to time; inability to recognize familiar people, places, and objects; fear arising from the misinterpretation of sights and sounds; or desire to fulfill former obligations, such as going to work or looking after a child. The need to address this behavioral problem is great because it causes worry to family members, impedes providing care to the patient, and can be a source of significant danger to the patient.

THE CAREGIVER ROLE IN MANAGING AD

The efficient diagnosis and successful management of AD depends on identifying a caregiver. Typically, family members and friends take on some part of the role and self-identify at the time of the initial presentation by providing a history of the cognitive problem. At this early stage, it is important to establish permission to speak openly with the caregiver to acknowledge and reinforce the notion that the caregiver is the advocate for the patient. Caregivers may be spouses of affected individuals; however, in many instances, they are other family members or friends. Because AD is a long, progressive illness, many may be unprepared for the difficulties associated with caring for the demented patient. In addition, because many caregivers maintain and implement interventions for patients, their health status can become the concern of the patient's doctor (Lucero, Pearson, Hutchinson, Leger-Krall, & Rinalducci, 2001). Caregiver burden can be described in emotional, physical, and social terms. Help for caregivers may be offered in a variety of ways, including offering education and training, caregiver support groups, and counseling. Providing information and education serve to decrease depression and caregiver burden and increase coping skills (Hepburn, Tornatore, Center, & Ostwald, 2001; Logsdon, McCurry, Moore, & Teri, 1997). Mittelman et al. (1993) reported that when caregivers and their families were offered a comprehensive intervention, including family counseling sessions and caregiver support groups tailored for individualized needs, time to nursing home placement was significantly postponed or reduced as compared to caregivers in a control group. Counseling sessions should attempt to provide education and information to family members for the behavioral symptoms present in AD patients and emphasize skills and techniques that may be used in the home. Increasing communication and understanding between family members and the caregiver may alleviate family conflicts. Providing increased support is a way of mitigating the emotional burden of caregivers and families and can help reduce stress and depression in caregivers (Mittelman et al., 1995).

The Alzheimer's Association is a national organization that offers education, support, and information to caregivers and patients. Many states have local chapters, which offer a variety of information and services to families. Brochures are available on AD diagnosis and treatment, and services available include caregiver support groups, early stage patient support groups,

Table 2.4   Internet Resources for Alzheimer's Disease Information

Name	Web Site	Description
National Alzheimer's Association	www.alz.org	Information about AD for caregivers and professionals.
Alzheimer's Disease Education and Referral Service	www.alzheimers.org	NIA Site—Information about AD and related disorders.
ElderCare Online	www.ec-online.net	Caregiver support and information.
Alzheimer's Disease Centers	www.alzheimers.org/pubs /adcdir.html	Directory of U.S. AD Centers.
Ageless Design	www.agelessdesign.com	Caregiver support and information.
Children of Aging Parents	www.caps4caregivers.org	Caregiver support and information.
National Alliance for Caregiving	www.Caregiving.org	Caregiver support and information.
National Hispanic Council on Aging	www.nhcoa.org	A variety of information and support for the Latino/Latina community.

workshops, and educational meetings. Workshops and educational meetings are available on topics such as understanding and coping with stress, Medicaid services, legal/financial issues, anticipatory grief, and end-of-life issues. The Alzheimer's Association offers a service called ASafe Return@, a national identification registry that assists in locating missing AD patients. With the ever-growing number of individuals who have access to computers and the World Wide Web, a number of Internet sites provide information and support to caregivers. Resources available through the Internet include listserve support groups, access to information in English and Spanish, and information for ethnic minorities. A full range of materials, which includes aspects of diagnosis, treatment, and clinical trials, is available. Select local and national sites that provide helpful resources are listed in Table 2.4.

MULTICULTURAL ISSUES IN ASSESSING AND MANAGING AD

There are a number of multicultural issues in dementia care and the AD patient, including cultural differences in disease presentation and the caregiver experience. Disease presentation may vary according to race. In a large observational study, Shadlen, Larson, Gibbons, McCormick, and Teri

(1999) found that African American patients had significantly lower MMSE test scores as compared with Caucasians and were more impaired upon disease recognition. The difference in scores was not attributable to gender, level of education, or income. African American patients had significantly higher rates of hypertension compared to Caucasians; however, measures of cerebrovascular comorbidity did not differ. Differences in groups in this study address the need for normative data for minority populations.

Studies suggest cultural variations in the role of the caregiver. Questions arise as to whether the needs of minority populations are similar to Caucasian populations. A recent review article by Janevic and Connell (2001) compared 20 studies involving ethnic minorities and Caucasians on a number of variables, including caregiver demographics and psychosocial factors. Many of the studies reviewed were interviews or self-report formats, and minority populations were African American, Asian, and Latino. In African Americans and Latino populations, caregivers were more likely to be family members other than a spouse, such as a daughter or son. A similar finding was seen in Korean caregivers. These individuals often provide care for multiple generations, including children, grandchildren, and parents. Education and support services need to be tailored to meet these varied needs, suggesting that development of education and support programs must consider cultural norms and the needs of younger individuals. Because caregiver characteristics may be different in an ethnic minority, differences in the use of long-term care may also be seen.

NONPHARMACOLOGICAL APPROACHES TO TREATING ALZHEIMER'S DISEASE

Nonpharmaceutical approaches for AD examine managing behavioral and cognitive symptoms without the use of medication. A secondary goal is to lessen caregiver burden. Nonpharmcological treatment approaches may be advantageous when medications are unavailable, the patient cannot tolerate the side effects of medications or does not comply with medication labeling instructions, or medications are contraindicated. These approaches may also supplement pharmacological treatment for the optimal patient management. Behavioral disturbances often lead to earlier placement of individuals in nursing homes and long-term care facilities. When caregivers can effectively manage behaviors at home, time to nursing home placement may be delayed (Mittelman, Ferris, Shulman, Steinberg, & Levin, 1996). This suggests that finding ways to manage difficult behaviors allows individuals to remain at home longer. Aggression is often seen in the later stages of AD and is a primary reason that individuals are placed in long-term care facilities (Raskind, 1999).

Behavioral/cognitive disturbances may result from a number of factors including cognitive change and neurobiological and environmental factors. Behavioral symptoms associated with dementia and AD are vast and include wandering, aggression, agitation, illusions, delusions, hallucinations, sleep disturbances, suspiciousness, paranoia, tearfulness, verbal outbursts, and mood disturbances. Common cognitive symptoms associated with AD include memory loss, confusion, spatial disorientation, thinking deficits, and reasoning difficulties. To determine the best technique, it is important to consider stage of disease and specific behavioral symptoms. Certain behaviors may be more amenable to change than others without the use of medication.

BEHAVIORAL MANAGEMENT TECHNIQUES

Literature that compares drug treatment to behavior management therapy (BMT) indicates that, in some instances, BMT can be as effective in managing symptoms as pharmaceutical interventions. Teri et al. (2000) compared pharmacological and nonpharmacological treatments in managing agitation and depressive symptoms for AD patients.

In this study, no significant differences were found among treatment with haloperidol, trazodone, BMT, or placebo, and results indicated that behavioral changes were seen in all groups, with modest reductions in agitation. Interestingly, results indicated that behavior therapy was as effective in this study population as compared to groups that received active drugs.

Behavioral therapy has demonstrated efficacy in managing difficult behaviors, agitation, and aggression, and mood can be elevated through identification and involvement in pleasant activities, while matching activities to the individual's cognitive status (Holmberg, 1997; Teri, 1994). In a comparison of behavioral management strategies, Teri, Logsdon, Uomoto, and McCurry (1997) examined behavioral treatments for depressive symptoms of AD patients. Two behavioral treatments, one emphasizing maximizing pleasant events and the other emphasizing caregiver problem solving, were compared to two control conditions, standard care and wait-list. Two active treatment groups involved identifying pleasant activities for the AD patient to participate in and allowed caregivers more flexibility and input in the treatment. The Pleasant Events Schedule (PES) AD (Teri & Logsdon, 1991) was created to help caregivers identify activities that AD patients would enjoy, based on the stage of the disease. A progressive course of therapy consisted of nine 60-minute sessions in which patient and caregiver would participate in a pleasant activity at varying degrees, as identified through the PES. Results indicated that patients in the active treatment groups demonstrated significant differences in level of depression. Additionally, caregivers who participated in the study and received behavioral treatment in either a pleasant event or problem-solving group demonstrated reductions in their level of depressive symptoms. This suggests that behavioral interventions may be considered to manage depressive symptoms in AD patients.

A number of behavioral symptoms are amenable to psychotherapy. For the AD patient, therapy early in the course of the disease may be more beneficial than later because of increased memory problems in later stages and problems with insight. Psychotherapy for the early stage patient can help alleviate symptoms of depression, anger, denial, and anxiety. Early stage patients may also benefit from the increased support offered in group therapy (Bonder, 1994; Goldsilver & Gruneir, 2001; Haggerty, 1990). Approaches to psychotherapy vary, and traditional outcomes for nondemented patients attempt to enhance daily functioning by providing insight, leading to an expression of emotion. Data on individual and group therapy for AD patients suggest both alleviate behavioral symptoms of demented patients in the early stages; however, developing insight is not thought to be successful or a helpful goal with these patients (Haggerty, 1990; Miller, 1989).

Early stage AD support groups are gaining popularity, and patients are benefiting from early diagnosis of their illness. These groups can offer support and coping skills to patients. Snyder, Quayhagen, Shepherd, and Bower (1995) found that individuals participating in group therapy reported positive themes of purposefulness, gratification belonging, and surviving. While negative themes were reported, which included helplessness, devaluation, and unpredictability, they were not the focus of discussion in group therapy.

Safety and comfort are essential in the group format, and the group experience helps individuals understand their illness, connect with others who have the disease, and develop better coping strategies. Goldsilver and

Gruneir (2001) posit an early disease-stage therapy model, called the *mainstream model*, which has four interrelated components—the member, group, worker, and group activity. The model can serve to enhance coping skills and help individuals develop understanding of their illness. In later stages of AD, psychotherapy may not be an effective strategy, particularly for behavioral symptoms, and later stages of the disease may be best served by other therapeutic methods, including expressive arts, music, theatre, and physical movement.

Music therapy is employed with a wide range of populations, and a considerable body of literature exists on the effects of music therapy in mediating AD symptoms. Music therapy is an allied health profession, and individuals are formally trained in this therapeutic method. In the therapeutic relationship, music is used as the medium to address psychological, cognitive, social, and physical needs of a patient (American Music Therapy Association). Music therapy techniques vary and include using musical instruments, singing, and improvisation. Positive effects of music therapy include alleviating behavioral symptoms and improving quality of life (Kydd, 2001). Music therapy is also associated with enhanced interactions with family and social skill improvement (Johnson, Cotman, Tasaki, & Shaw, 1998; Smith-Marchese, 1994). Music can also be used to facilitate reminiscence and stimulate long-term memory. Therapy can improve recognition after singing and improve verbalization of thoughts (Carruth, 1997; Kovach & Henschel, 1996).

Music has been shown to enhance spatial-temporal reasoning. Johnson et al. (1998) attempted to see whether spatial-temporal reasoning could be enhanced by an AD patient listening to a Mozart piano sonata. In a study of monozygotic twins, one AD twin demonstrated considerable improvement in a spatial-temporal reasoning task, suggesting functional plasticity in individuals with AD.

Kydd (2001) examined the effects of music therapy in helping an AD patient adjust to a long-term care facility. The patient, who had a music background, had been taught by a parent to read music and play instruments. On entry into a long-term care facility, he was given a diagnosis of probable AD; he was depressed, reclusive, and appeared angry at being sent to a home, displaying antisocial behavior. Music therapy was instituted once a week for two hours, and the patient was allowed to choose a preferred song. After an initial preference for private sessions, the patient began to join group sessions. Staff members noted a more positive affect, and group interaction became more appropriate. Overall, music was found to be an effective therapy for alleviating behavioral symptoms associated with transferring an individual from a home setting to a long-term care facility.

Exercise therapy programs may mediate physical problems occurring in AD, such as preventing falls and frailty by encouraging individuals to move their bodies. In general, physical activity is associated with improved mental health. Teri et al. (1998) studied the effects of exercise on AD patients, attempting to increase physical fitness, including balance, flexibility, strength, and endurance by training caregivers in appropriate methodology. Study participants were between 60 and 90 years of age, and exercise consisted of aerobic/endurance activities, strength, balance, and flexibility training. Researchers attempted to motivate sedentary individuals to engage in regular exercise. The model used was based on previous programs studied by Pate et al. (1995) and a program devised for older adults (Teri, 1994), which may be useful in ameliorating falls, physical health, and frailty (intervention and prevention). An indirect result of the study was comments by caregivers that patients' mood and behavior improved on days when exercise was instituted and that patients enjoyed the exercise.

ENVIRONMENTAL STRATEGIES/MODIFICATIONS

Another approach to modifying behavioral disturbances is modification of the environment to accommodate the AD patient. Products may focus on alleviating difficult behaviors, such as wandering, as well as provide opportunities for enjoyable activities for patients. Activities that naturally serve as recreational activities may also provide sensory stimulation, for example, the game Bingo (Sobel, 2001). The therapeutic kitchen has been used to support day programs in residential facilities (Marsden, Meehan, & Calkins, 2001). The "kitchen" is a supportive environment for the patient where safety is a main concern. Potentially dangerous items, such as cleaning agents, food processors, and utensils are stored in locked cabinets, and access is restricted. Cabinets are lower for easier access, countertop corners are rounded, cabinets are labeled, floors are nonslip, and lighting is ample. A five-session home environment program investigated by Gitlin, Corcoran, Winter, Boyce, and Hauck (2001) attempted to assist patients, as well as improve caregiver efficacy. Family caregivers were instructed by occupational therapists in ways to simplify the home environment, such as eliminating clutter, breaking down tasks into component parts, and educating the caregiver about dementia and behavioral management. For example, clothing may be laid out according to the order in which it is placed on the body, resulting in reduced anxiety and agitation in patients. A modest effect was seen in patient dependency over time, and caregivers reported improved self-efficacy and reduced disturbance during caregiving activities.

Modifying the patient's environment may include using devices to assist with behavioral symptoms such as wandering and forgetfulness. Products can be purchased at specialty stores via the World Wide Web (agelessdesign.com). To prevent and deter wandering, murals can disguise a door, and siren alarms can emit sound when a door is opened. Specialized telephones have large preset buttons, and pictures on buttons identify an individual's telephone number. In a nursing home setting, large print signs with residents' names and photographs have been found to help AD residents locate their rooms (Nolan, Mathews, & Harrison, 2001). However, care should be taken to consider the stage of the patient when considering environmental modification because patients' needs may change according to the degree of illness.

OTHER THERAPIES

Many other therapies have been studied to help AD patients, and a select few are briefly outlined in Table 2.5. Some of these methods have limited usefulness and are minimally developed. Use of other therapies may vary according to environmental setting and degree of behavioral symptoms present.

CONCLUSION

Alzheimer's disease represents a major health care challenge of the new millennium. Because of the growth of the aging population, even idealized estimates of successful prevention do not project a reduction in prevalence over the next 50 years. While basic scientists are developing targeted intervention, it is important to face the reality of this epidemic with clinical awareness, diagnostic acumen, and strategies for the delivery of care needed to

Table 2.5 Selected Behavioral Therapies for Alzheimer's Disease

Therapy	Description	Outcome
Animal Assisted Therapy[a]	Animals are employed as therapeutic agents. The model emphasizes contact with animals, including holding and petting them.	Animals provide psychosocial and physical benefits. Increased enjoyment, independence, and quality of life. A reduction of behavioral symptoms such as aggressiveness and rage. Delusions may occur.
Morning Bright Light Therapy[b]	Daily light therapy was given to patients in an attempt to improve sleep, wandering, violent outbreaks, restlessness, and delirium related behavior.	A reduced amplitude of sleep-wake schedule. In the dementia group, serum melatonin levels were significantly lower than controls.
ECT[c]	Useful in treating demented patients suffering from depression.	Scores on a depression rating scale declined significantly on discharge as compared to hospital admission scores. Improvements in cognition and mood were seen.

[a] "A Day Care Program and Evaluation of Animal Assisted Therapy (AAT) for the elderly with Senile Dementia," by M. Kanamori et al., 2001, *American Journal of Alzheimer's Disease and Other Dementias, 16,* pp. 234–239.
[b] "Morning Bright Light Therapy for Sleep and Behavior Disorders in Elderly Patients with Dementia," by K. Mishima, M. Okawa, Y. Hishikawa, S. Hozumi, H. Hori, and K. Takahashi, 1994, *Acta Psychiatrica Scandinavica, 89,* pp. 1–7.
[c] "The Benefits and Risks of ECT for Patients with Primary Dementia Who Also Suffer from Depression," by V. Rao and C. G. Lyketsos, 2000, *International Journal of Geriatric Psychiatry, 15,* pp. 729–735.

address the breadth of symptoms associated with this disease. Use of currently available pharmacologic agents is evidence of progress but remains inadequate. Nonpharmaceutical treatments are potentially powerful approaches to alleviate behavioral symptoms and assist in the daily care of the demented patient. Many methods serve to instruct and educate the caregiver, thus decreasing the burdens faced by these individuals. This is critical because the impact on caregivers is likely to be magnified as those younger and healthier become a progressively smaller portion of the population. While it is difficult to quantify any method as superior to another, interventions may be used according to the symptom presenting and illness stage. Best management of this disease should include psychotherapeutic techniques, environmental modification, and prudent use of pharmacology.

REFERENCES

American Music Therapy Association: Available from the World Wide Web: http://www.musictherapy.org.

Army Individual Test Battery. (1944). *Manual of directions and scoring.* Washington, DC: War Department, Adjutant General's Office.

Benton, A. L., & Hamsher, K. S. (1976). *Multilingual Aphasia Examination.* Iowa City: University of Iowa.

Blacker, D., Haines, J. L., Rodes, L., Terwedow, H., Go, R. C., Harrell, L. E., et al. (1997). ApoE-4 and age at onset of Alzheimer's disease: The NIMH genetics initiative. *Neurology, 48*(1), 139–147.

Blessed, G., Tomlinson, B. E., & Roth, M. (1968, July). The association between quantitative measures of dementia and of senile change in the cerebral gray matter of elderly subjects. *British Journal of Psychiatry, 114*(512), 797–811.

Bonder, B. R. (1994). Psychotherapy for individuals with Alzheimer's disease. *Alzheimer Disease and Associated Disorders, 8*(Suppl. 3), 75–81.

Carruth, E. (1997). The effects of singing and the spaced retrieval technique on improving face-name recognition in nursing home residents with memory loss. *Journal of Music Therapy, 34*(3), 165–186.

Cockrell, J. R., & Folstein, M. F. (1988). Mini-Mental State Examination (MMSE). *Psychopharmacology Bulletin, 24,* 689–692.

Cummings, J. L., Mega, M., Gray, K., Rosenberg-Thompson, S., Carusi, D. A., & Gornbein, J. (1994). The Neuropsychiatric Inventory: Comprehensive assessment of psychopathology in dementia. *Neurology, 44,* 2308–2314.

Devanand, D. P., Brockington, C. D., Moody, B. J., Brown, R. P., Mayeux, R., Endicott, J., et al. (1992). Behavioral syndromes in Alzheimer's disease. *International Psychogeriatrics, 4*(Suppl. 2), 161–184.

Evans, D. A. (1990). Estimated prevalence of Alzheimer's disease in the US. *Milbank Quarterly, 68,* 267–289.

Folstein, M. F., Folstein, S. E., & McHugh, P. R. (1975). Mini-Mental State: A practical method for grading the cognitive state of patients for the clinician. *Journal of Psychiatry Research, 12,* 189–198.

Galasko, D., Bennett, D., Sano, M., Ernesto, C., Thomas, R., Grundman, M., et al. (1997). An inventory to assess activities of daily living for clinical trials in Alzheimer's disease. *Alzheimer Disease and Associated Disorders, 11*(Suppl. 2), S33–S39.

Gitlin, L. N., Corcoran, M., Winter, L., Boyce, A., & Hauck, W. W. (2001). A randomized controlled trial of a home environmental intervention: Effect on efficacy and upset in caregivers and on daily function of persons with dementia. *Gerontologist, 41*(1), 4–14.

Goldsilver, P. M., & Gruneir, M. R. (2001, March/April). Early stage dementia group: An innovative model of support for individuals in the early stages of dementia. *American Journal of Alzheimer's Disease and Other Dementias, 16*(2), 109–113.

Haggerty, A. D. (1990). Psychotherapy for patients with Alzheimer's disease. *Advances, 7*(1), 55–60.

Heaton, R. K. (1981). *Wisconsin Card Sorting Test manual.* Odessa, FL: Psychological Assessment Resources.

Hebert, L. E., Scherr, P. A., Beckett, L. A., Albert, M. S., & Pilgrim, D. M. (1995). Age-specific incidence of Alzheimer's disease in a community population. *Journal of the American Medical Association, 273,* 1354–1359.

Hepburn, K. W., Tornatore, J., Center, B., & Ostwald, S. W. (2001). Dementia family caregiver training: Affecting beliefs about caregiving and caregiver outcomes. *Journal of the American Geriatrics Society, 49*(4), 450–457.

Hohl, U., Grundman, M., Salmon, D. P., Thomas, R. G., & Thal, L. J. (1999). Mini-Mental State Examination and Mattis Dementia Rating Scale performance differs in Hispanic and non-Hispanic Alzheimer's disease patients. *Journal of the International Neuropsychological Society, 5*(4), 301–307.

Holmberg, S. K. (1997). A walking program for wanderers: Volunteer training and development of an evening walker's group. *Geriatric Nursing, 18*(4), 160–165.

Ivnik, R., Malec, J. F., Tangalos, E. G., Petersen, R. C., Kokmen, S., & Kurkland, L. T. (1990). The Auditory-Verbal Learning Test (AVLT): Norms for ages 55 years and older. *Psychological Assessment, 2,* 304–312.

Janevic, M. R., & Connell, C. M. (2001). Racial, ethnic, and cultural differences in the dementia caregiving experience: Recent findings. *Gerontologist, 41*(3), 334–347.

Johnson, J. K., Cotman, C. W., Tasaki, C. S., & Shaw, G. L. (1998). Enhancement of spatial-temporal reasoning after a Mozart listening condition in Alzheimer's disease: A case study. *Neurological Research, 20,* 666–672.

Kanamori, M., Suzuki, M., Yamamoto, K., Kanda, M., Matsui, Y., Kojima, E., et al. (2001, July/August). A day care program and evaluation of animal assisted therapy (AAT) for the elderly with senile dementia. *American Journal of Alzheimer's Disease and Other Dementias, 16*(4), 234–239.

Kaufer, D. I., Cummings, J. L., Ketchel, P., Smith, V., MacMillan, A., Shelley, T., et al. (2000, Spring). Validation of the NPI-Q, a brief clinical form of the Neuropsychiatric Inventory. *Journal of Neuropsychiatry and Clinical Neurosciences, 12*(2), 233–239.

Kovach, C., & Henschel, H. (1996). Planning activities for patients with dementia. *Journal of Gerontological Nursing, 22*(9), 33–38.

Kydd, P. (2001). Using music therapy to help a client with Alzheimer's disease adapt to long-term care. *American Journal of Alzheimer's Disease and Other Dementias, 16*(2), 103–108.

LaRue, A., Romero, L. J., Ortiz, I. E., Liang, H. C., & Lindeman, R. D. (1999). Neuropsychological performance of Hispanic and non-Hispanic older adults: An epidemiologic survey. *Clinical Neuropsychologist, 13*(4), 474–486.

Lawton, M. P., & Brody, E. M. (1969). Assessment of older people: Self-maintaining and instrumental activities of daily living. *Gerontologist, 9,* 179–186.

Lee, H., Swanwick, G. R., Coen, R. F., & Lawlor, B. A. (1996, Fall). Use of the clock drawing task in the diagnosis of mild and very mild Alzheimer's disease. *International Psychogeriatrics, 8*(3), 469–476.

Loewenstein, D. A., Arguelles, T., Barker, W. W., & Duara, R. (1993). A comparative analysis of neuropsychological test performance of Spanish-speaking and English-speaking patients with Alzheimer's disease. *Journal of Gerontology, 48*(3), P142–P149.

Logsdon, R. G., McCurry, S. M., Moore, A. L., & Teri, L. (1997). Family and caregiver issues in the treatment of patients with Alzheimer's disease. *Seminars in Clinical Neuropsychiatry, 2*(2), 138–151.

Lucero, M., Pearson, R., Hutchinson, S., Leger-Krall, S., & Rinalducci, E. (2001). Products for Alzheimer's self-stimulatory wanderers. *American Journal of Alzheimer's Disease and Other Dementias, 16*(1), 43–50.

Lyketsos, C. G., Sheppard, J. M., Steele, C. D., Kopunek, S., Steinberg, M., Baker, A. S., et al. (2000). A randomized, placebo-controlled, double-blind clinical trial of sertraline in the treatment of depression complicating Alzheimer's disease: Initial results from the Depression in Alzheimer's Disease study. *American Journal of Psychiatry, 157*(10), 1686–1689.

Marsden, J. P., Meehan, R. A., & Calkins, M. P. (2001). Therapeutic kitchens for residents with dementia. *American Journal of Alzheimer's Disease and Other Dementias, 1695,* 303–311.

Miller, M. D. (1989). Opportunities for psychotherapy in the management of dementia. *Journal of Geriatric Psychiatry Neurology, 2*(1), 11–17.

Mishima, K., Okawa, M., Hishikawa, Y., Hozumi, S., Hori, H., & Takahashi, K. (1994). Morning bright light therapy for sleep and behavior disorders in elderly patients with dementia. *Acta Psychiatrica Scandinavica, 89,* 1–7.

Mittelman, M. S., Ferris, S. H., Shulman, E., Steinberg, M. A., Ambinder, A., Mackell, J. A., et al. (1995). A comprehensive support program: Effect on depression in spouse-caregivers of AD patients. *Gerontologist, 35*(6), 792–802.

Mittelman, M. S., Ferris, S. H., Shulman, E., Steinberg, G., & Levin, B. (1996). A family intervention to delay nursing home placement of patients with Alzheimer's disease: A randomized controlled trial. *Journal of the American Medical Association, 276,* 1725–1731.

Mittelman, M. S., Ferris, S. H., Steinberg, G., Shulman, E., Jackell, J. A., Ambinder, A., et al. (1993). An intervention that delays institutionalization of Alzheimer's disease patients: Treatment of spouse-caregivers. *Gerontologist, 33*(6), 730–740.

Mungas, D., Marshall, S. C., Weldon, M., Haan, M., & Reed, B. R. (1996). Age and education correction of Mini-Mental State Examination for English and Spanish-speaking elderly. *Neurology, 46*(3), 700–706.

Nicoll, J. A., Roberts, G. W., & Graham, D. I. (1996). Amyloid beta-protein, APOE genotype and head injury. *Annals of the New York Academy of Sciences, 777,* 271–275.

Nolan, B. A., Mathews, R. M., & Harrison, M. (2001). Using external memory aids to increase room finding by older adults with dementia. *American Journal of Alzheimer's Disease and Other Dementias, 16*(4), 251–254.

Overall, J. E., & Gorham, D. R. (1962). The Brief Psychiatric Rating Scale. *Psychological Reports, 10,* 799–812.

Ownby, R. L., Harwood, D. G., Acevedo, A., Barker, W., & Duara, R. (2001). Factor structure of the Cornell Scale for Depression in dementia for Anglo and Hispanic patients with dementia. *American Journal of Geriatric Psychiatry, 9*(3), 217–224.

Pate, R. R., Pratt, M., Blair, S. N., Haskell, W. L., Macera, C. A., Bouchard, C., et al. (1995). Physical activity and public health. *Journal of the American Medical Association, 273,* 402–407.

Rao, V., & Lyketsos, C. G. (2000). The benefits and risks of ECT for patients with primary dementia who also suffer from depression. *International Journal of Geriatric Psychiatry, 15*(8), 729–735.

Raskind, M. (1999). Evaluation and management of aggressive behavior in the elderly demented patient. *Journal of Clinical Psychiatry, 60*(Suppl. 15), 45–49.

Roberts, G. W., Allsop, D., & Bruton, C. (1990). The occult aftermath of boxing. *Journal of Neurology, Neurosurgery, and Psychiatry, 53*(5), 373–378.

Schmitt, F. A., & Sano, M. (1994). Neuropsychological approaches to the Study of Dementia. In J. C. Morris (Ed.), *Handbook of dementing illnesses* (pp. 89–124). New York: Marcel Dekker.

Shadlen, M. F., Larson, E. B., Gibbons, L., McCormick, W. C., & Teri, L. (1999). Alzheimer's disease symptom severity in Blacks and Whites. *Journal of the American Geriatric Society, 47*(4), 482–486.

Smith-Marchese, M. (1994). The effects of participatory music on the reality orientation and sociability of Alzheimer's residents in a long term care setting. *Activities, Adaptation & Aging, 8*(2), 101–110.

Snyder, L., Quayhagen, M. P., Shepherd, S., & Bower, D. (1995). Supportive seminar groups: An intervention for early stage dementia patients. *Gerontologist, 35*(5), 691–695.

Sobel, B. P. (2001). Bingo vs. physical intervention in stimulating short-term cognition in Alzheimer's disease patients. *American Journal of Alzheimer's Disease and Other Dementias, 16*(2), 115–120.

Solomon, P. R., Hirschoff, A., Kelly, B., Relin, M., Brush, M., DeVeaux, R. D., et al. (1998, March). A 7-minute neurocognitive screening battery highly sensitive to Alzheimer's disease. *Archives of Neurology, 55*(3), 349–355.

Solomon, P. R., & Pendlebury, W. W. (1998, April). Recognition of Alzheimer's disease: The 7 Minute Screen. *Family Medicine, 30*(4), 265–271.

Stern, Y., Moeller, J. R., Anderson, K. E., Luber, B., Zubin, N., Dimauro, A., et al. (2000). Different brain networks mediate task performance in normal aging and AD: Defining compensation. *Neurology, 55,* 1291–1297.

Stricks, L., Pittman, J., Jacobs, D. M., Sano, M., & Stern, Y. (1998). Normative data for a brief neuropsychological battery administered to English and Spanish-speaking community-dwelling elders. *Journal of the International Neuropsychological Society, 4,* 311–318.

Sunderland, T., Hill, J. L., Mellow, A. M., Lawlor, B. A., Gundersheimer, J., Newhouse, P. A., et al. (1989). Clock drawing in Alzheimer's disease: A novel measure of dementia severity. *Journal of the American Geriatric Society, 37,* 725–729.

Taussig, I. M., Mack, W. J., & Henderson, V. W. (1996). Concurrent validity of Spanish-language versions of the Mini-Mental State Examination, Mental Status Questionnaire, Information-Memory-Concentration test, and Orientation-Memory-Concentration test: Alzheimer's disease patients and nondemented elderly comparison subjects. *Journal of the International Neuropsychological Society, 2*(4), 286–298.

Teng, E. L., & Chui, H. C. (1987). The Modified Mini-Mental State (3MS) Examination. *Journal of Clinical Psychiatry, 48,* 314–318.

Teri, L. (1994). Behavioral treatment of depression in patients with dementia. *Alzheimer's Disease and Associated Disorders, 8*(Suppl. 3), 66–74.

Teri, L., & Logsdon, R. G. (1991). Identifying pleasant activities for Alzheimer's disease patients: The Pleasant Events Schedule-AD. *Gerontologist, 31*(1), 124–127.

Teri, L., Logsdon, R. G., Peskind, E., Raskind, M., Weiner, M. F., Tractenberg, R. E., et al. (2000, February). Treatment of agitation in AD: A randomized, placebo-controlled clinical trial. *Neurology, 56*(3), 1271–1278.

Teri, L., Logsdon, R. G., Uomoto, J., & McCurry, S. M. (1997). Behavioral treatment of depression in dementia patients: A controlled clinical trial. *Journals of Gerontology: Series B, Psychological Sciences and Social Sciences, 52B*(4), 159–166.

Teri, L., McCurry, S. M., Buchner, D. M., Logsdon, R. G., LaCroix, A. Z., Kukull, W. A., et al. (1998, October). Exercise and activity level in Alzheimer's disease: A potential treatment focus. *Journal of Rehabilitation Research and Development, 35*(4), 411–419.

Wolf-Klein, G. P., Silverstone, F. A., Levy, A. P., & Brod, M. S. (1989). Screening for Alzheimer's disease by clock drawing. *Journal of the American Geriatric Society, 37,* 730–734.

Yesavage, J. A., Brink, T. L., Rose, T. L., Lum, O., Huang, V., Adey, M. B., et al. (1982). Development and validation of a geriatric depression rating scale: A preliminary report. *Journal of Psychiatric Research, 17,* 37–49.

CHAPTER 3

Neurologic Aspects of Dementia with Lewy Bodies and Parkinson's Disease with Dementia

Donna Masterman and Margaret Swanberg

The two most common neurodegenerative disorders in the elderly are Alzheimer's disease (AD) and Parkinson's disease (PD). While each has well-defined clinical and pathologic features and specific criteria for clinical and pathological diagnosis, some degree of overlap between these two disorders exists. Some AD patients develop extrapyramidal signs and symptoms characteristic of PD, some patients with typical PD develop a dementia, and both disorders can co-occur in the same individual. This, however, does not explain all or even most of the cases of PD with dementia. Another entity known as dementia with Lewy bodies (DLB) has been estimated to account for 15% to 20% of late-onset dementias and has been only more recently recognized as the second most common cause of dementia after AD (McKeith, Perry, & Perry, 1999; McKeith et al., 1996). In this chapter, we focus on the dementias associated with both DLB and PD with dementia.

DEMENTIA WITH LEWY BODIES

Historical Perspective

In 1961, Okazaki, Lipkin, and Aronson, published the first case reports of two individuals who presented at ages 69 and 70 with dementia and severe extrapyramidal rigidity who, on autopsy, demonstrated diffuse Lewy body (LB) pathology in the cerebral cortex. Between the early 1960s and 1984, 34 similar cases were reported in Japan by Dr. Kosaka, who coined the term *DLB* in 1978. The term was used to describe the typical distribution of LB in the cortex and subcortical regions (Kosaka, Yoshimura, Ikeda, & Budka, 1984). In subsequent reports over the next decade, many more cases were recognized at autopsy. DLB is not a new disorder, but it has only recently been recognized due largely to the improvement in tissue staining techniques, which allowed for enhanced visualization of the LB in the cortex. On reexamination of postmortem material collected in Newcastle-upon-Tyne during the 1960s, it was revealed that 17% had cortical LB. More recent reports have found that approximately 10% to 36% of patients who referred for postmortem examination for dementia have Lewy body disease (Del Ser et al., 2000; Knopman, 2001; R. H. Perry et al., 1996), with AD being the most common misdiagnosis. Although DLB is the preferred term, it has also been called by other names such as Lewy body dementia, cortical Lewy body disease, diffuse Lewy body disease, and Lewy body variant of Alzheimer's disease.

Pathophysiology

Lewy bodies are spherical, intracytoplasmic, eosinophilic, neuronal inclusions with a dense hyaline core and a halo of radiating filaments composed of abnormally truncated and phosphorylated intermediate neurofilament proteins, which also contain ubiquitin and associated enzymes (see Figure 3.1). LBs may be single or multiple in a given neuron, and their size can vary substantially. The LB was first described by the German neuropathologist Friederich Lewy, who worked in Alois Alzheimer's laboratory in Munich between 1910 and 1912. Subcortical LBs are easily seen using conventional hematoxylin and eosin; however, cortical LBs are much less eosinophilic and lack the characteristic core and halo appearance, which made them difficult to detect until the late 1980s with the development of antiubiquitin immunohistocytochemical staining methods (Lennox et al., 1989). The LB is thought to be the result of altered neurofilament metabolism and/or transport due to neuronal damage and degeneration, which causes an accumulation of the altered cytoskeletal proteins. A neuronal protein found to be a core element of the LB is alpha-synuclein, first discovered in the late 1980s as a neuronal protein of unknown function. It was later linked to idiopathic Parkinson's disease in 1997 through the detection of a rare form of autosomal dominant PD due to a mutation in the gene for alpha-synuclein. In 1998, it was found that the LB consisted in large part of alpha-synuclein and that this protein actually formed the backbone of the LB (Spillantini, Crowther, Jakes, Hasegawa, & Goedert, 1998).

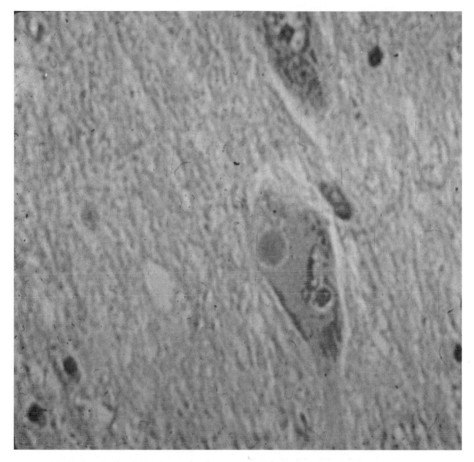

Figure 3.1 A typical subcortical Lewy body in the substantia nigra with hematoxylin and eosin staining. Photo compliments of Harry Vinters, MD, UCLA Medical Center.

DLB and AD Pathology

LBs are found in greater abundance in limbic cortical areas over neocortical and are also abundant in subcortical and brainstem nuclei—particularly the substantia nigra (although not as pronounced as in PD), as well as in basal forebrain and locus ceruleus. They are rare in occipital cortex. Lewy neurites are present in the hippocampus, amygdala, and nucleus basalis of Meynert.

Most cases with both brainstem and numerous neocortical and cortical LBs also have some degree of AD pathology. This includes diffuse plaques, neuritic plaques, and modest medial temporal neurofibrillary tangles (NFTs) present in sufficient numbers to meet accepted neuropathological criteria for AD (Hansen & Samuel, 1997; Hulette et al., 1995; McKeith et al., 1996). Fifteen percent have severe AD changes and 30% have concomitant microvascular or ischemic lesions, while hippocampal atrophy is greater in AD > DLB > control brains. In one series by Hansen et al. (1990), as many as 36% of patients clinically diagnosed as having AD in fact had LB at autopsy, and the term *Lewy body variant of Alzheimer's disease* was coined. However, pure diffuse Lewy body disease having no more AD changes than controls as described by Kosaka is rare. The apolipoprotein E4 allele encoded on chromosome 19 is known to be an established risk factor for developing AD. It appears that there is no such consistent association between Apo E4 and PD, but in DLB the ApoE4 allele frequencies are intermediate between AD and PD (Saitoh & Katzman, 1996).

The neuropathologic substrate underlying the dementia of DLB (or idiopathic PD) is controversial. Kosaka et al. (1984) suggested that in DLB, the dementia was primarily the result of cortical LB. Consistent correlations between severity of neuropsychiatric symptoms and LB density have not been established in many clinicopathological series (Gomez-Tortosa et al., 1999; Haroutunian et al., 2000; Samuel, Galasko, Masliah, & Hansen, 1996). The relative contribution to the clinical presentation of the different histopathologic changes remains unclear. Haroutunian et al. examined the degree to which LB burden contributes to dementia. Brain specimens were examined from 273 consecutive autopsies of elderly subjects between the ages of 60 and 107. Results indicated that the severity of dementia, as measured by the clinical dementia rating six months before death, correlated significantly and positively with the density of LBs. These correlations were independent of other neuropathological disorders commonly associated with dementia, including AD. The density of LBs correlated significantly with dementia severity whether the diagnostic criteria for AD were met or not met and after the contribution of classical AD lesions (neuritic plaques and neurofibrillary tangles) had been accounted for. It was concluded that the LB inclusions appear to contribute significantly to cognitive deficits in the elderly in a manner that is independent of other neuropathological disorders.

In addition, loss of choline acetyltransferase (ChAT) is profound in both AD and DLB. In fact, neurochemical analyses have found marked deficiencies in neocortical and neostriatal ChAT levels in DLB, which exceed those encountered in AD and loss of dopamine in the putamen comparable to that found in PD (Langlais et al., 1993; Samuel et al., 1996). ChAT depletion appears to contribute to the cognitive impairment and has been shown to correlate with degree of dementia (Samuel et al., 1996). Neocortical synapse loss has been shown to be a major correlate of AD dementia, and estimates of synapse loss are comparable in DLB and AD (Masliah, Mallory, De Teresa, Alford, & Hansen, 1993; Terry et al., 1991).

Clinical Presentation and Diagnosis of DLB

DLB has been recognized as a clinical entity that overlaps in clinical, pathological, and genetic features with AD and PD. Much of the literature describing the characteristic clinical profile of the DLB patient has come from evaluating patients presenting to memory disorders clinics, old age psychiatry clinics, or via retrospective chart review of autopsied confirmed cases. However, many patients with DLB present to movement disorders specialists, neurologists, and community physicians for symptoms of parkinsonism. In patients with PD, approximately 30% to 40% develop dementia; this risk increases with the patient's age. Many, but not all, will be found to have neuropathological changes consistent with a diagnosis of DLB, which is believed to be vastly underdiagnosed antemortem.

The key clinical features of DLB are shown in Table 3.1. Current consensus criteria for the clinical diagnosis of DLB require progressive cognitive decline and fluctuating cognition, recurrent visual hallucinations, or spontaneous motor features of parkinsonism. The specificity for the diagnosis of DLB using these criteria has been generally high (> 85%); however, sensitivity has been much lower and more variable (Hohl, Tiraboschi, Hansen, Thal, & Corey-Bloom, 2000; Litvan et al., 1998; McKeith et al., 1999; Mega et al., 1996). A more recent prospective validation of the consensus criteria for the diagnosis of DLB was found to have a sensitivity of 83% and a specificity of 91% (McKeith, Ballard, et al., 2000).

Development of dementia includes problems with memory and other areas of thinking such as language skills, visuospatial abilities, complex problem solving, and so on. Impairments of working memory and visuospatial functions, visual hallucinations, and depression have been identified as early indicators of DLB. Connor (2000) compared the cognitive profiles of patients with autopsy-confirmed AD with or without LB pathology on two dementia screening measures—the Mattis Dementia Rating Scale and component items of the Mini-Mental State Examination (MMSE). He found that although the groups did not differ significantly in age, education, total MMSE score, or Mattis Dementia Rating Scale (MDRS) score, the AD

Table 3.1   Consensus Diagnostic Criteria for Dementia with Lewy Bodies

1. "The central feature required for a diagnosis of DLB is progressive cognitive decline of sufficient magnitude to interfere with normal social or occupational function. Prominent or persistent memory impairment may not necessarily occur in the early stages, but is usually evident with progression. Deficits on tests of attention and of frontal-subcortical skills and visuospatial ability may be especially prominent."
2. Two of the following core features are *essential* for a diagnosis of *probable* DLB, and one is essential for *possible* DLB.
    a. Fluctuating cognition with pronounced variations in attention and alertness.
    b. Recurrent visual hallucinations which are typically well formed and detailed.
    c. Spontaneous motor features of parkinsonism.
3. Features supportive of the diagnosis of probable DLB include:
    • Repeated falls.
    • Syncope.
    • Transient loss of consciousness.
    • Neuroleptic sensitivity.
    • Systematized delusions.
    • Hallucinations in other modalities.
4. A diagnosis of DLB is less likely in the presence of:
    • Stroke disease evident as focal neurological signs or on brain imagining.
    • Any physical illness or other brain disorder evident on physical examination and investigation of any physical illness sufficient to account for the clinical picture.

Adapted from "Consensus Guidelines for the Clinical and Pathological Diagnosis of Dementia with Lewy Bodies (DLB): Report of the Consortium on DLB International Workshop," by I. G. McKeith et al., 1996, *Neurology,* pp. 1113–1124.

group performed significantly worse than the DLB group on the MDRS Memory subscale while the DLB group demonstrated poorer performance on the initiation/perseveration, attention, construction, or conceptualization subscales. The same overall pattern was observed in patients with mild to moderate disease severity and the moderate to severe cohort. The difference in pattern of deficits is similar to that seen between AD and more subcortical/frontal dementias, suggesting that the concomitant LB pathology significantly contributes to the presentation of the DLB cognitive dysfunction.

Features of Parkinson's disease include primarily bradykinesia (slowness of movement), rigidity, characteristic gait changes, and resting tremor. The typical 4 to 6 hertz resting tremor characteristic of idiopathic PD is unusual in the early stages of DLB (McKeith et al., 1996), and bradykinesia and rigidity are much more common. In addition, McKeith, Fairbairn, Perry, Thompson, and Perry (1992) reported 38% of patients with autopsy-proven DLB had a history of falls at initial presentation; however, an increase in fall-related injuries cannot entirely be accounted for by the presence of parkinsonism and may relate in part to cognitive fluctuations as well.

Fluctuations in Cognition

Fluctuations in the patient's mental abilities can be rather dramatic from one day to the next and may at times appear like episodic confusion or delirium. M. P. Walker et al. (2000) tried to better quantify and more clearly operationalize this core diagnostic feature of fluctuating cognition. The authors evaluated 15 DLB patients, 15 AD patients, and 10 elderly control subjects using a clinical Fluctuation Severity Scale (FC) as well as receiving measures of variability in attentional performance and slowing of the EEG across 90 sec epocs over one hour and one week. DLB patients had significantly more severe FC and more severe variability in attentional and slow EEG rhythms than either AD or normal controls in all periods.

Hallucinations

These are typically well-formed, visual hallucinations that are vivid. Less common are auditory or tactile hallucinations. The hallucinations tend to occur early in the course of the illness (33%) and may occur in the absence of medications or changes in Parkinson's medications, which are well known to cause these same symptoms. In addition, a two- to threefold increase in the rate of cognitive decline has been reported in some studies for patients experiencing visual hallucinations (Ballard et al., 2000).

Other Clinical Features of DLB

REM sleep behavior disorder can also be seen in association with DLB (Boeve et al., 1998; Turner, 2002), and some medical literature suggests that the pathologic substrate of idiopathic REM sleep behavior disorder may involve neuronal loss and LBs in the brainstem monoaminergic nuclei important in regulating sleep phenomena. *Neuroleptic supersensitivity* is another common feature in DLB. It is important to properly recognize DLB because patients with this disorder can be at high risk for developing serious side effects and potentially life-threatening reactions and supersensitivity to antipsychotic medications. *Olfactory function* is impaired in a number of neurodegenerative disorders including DLB. A study of olfactory function in 92 patients with dementia and 94 controls with neuropathological diagnoses found that subjects with LBs were more likely to be anosmic than those with AD or controls; and, among subjects with LBs, overall cortical LB scores and LB density in the cingulate were higher in those who were anosmic (McShane et al., 2001). There is also some difference with regard to prognosis (generally 6 to 8 years from the time of diagnosis) compared to 8 to 10 years for Alzheimer's disease and possibly a difference in treatment response to drugs (cholinesterase inhibitors) being more pronounced in those with DLB.

Diagnostic Accuracy

The current research criteria for diagnosing DLB was developed by the Consortium on DLB International Workshop (McKeith et al., 1996, 1999). To determine the validity of the international consensus criteria for the diagnosis of probable or possible DLB, McKeith et al. (1999) conducted a prospective clinical-pathological study of 50 dementia cases followed to autopsy. Twenty-six carried a clinical diagnosis of DLB, 19 with AD, and 5 with vascular dementia (VaD). The authors identified 29 cases at autopsy yielding a sensitivity and specificity of the clinical diagnosis of probable DLB of .83 and .95. They also reported no correlations between the distribution of LBs and any clinical features. Some studies have shown that when these criteria are applied, they show low sensitivity and high specificity due to high variability of symptoms: AD, 95%/79%; frontotemporal dementia (FTD), 97%/97%; progressive supranuclear palsy (PSP), 75%/98%; DLB, 34%/94%. Other studies of DLB show 22%/100% and 75%/79%.

Longitudinal Course

Some patients may first exhibit symptoms of short-term memory loss and are evaluated for possible AD; others first experience signs of PD and soon after develop problems with memory and other areas of thinking. Longitudinal and cross-sectional data are scant. In a recent study, McKeith, Ballard, et al. (2000) evaluated 261 subjects with DLB and found the primary presenting symptom was amnesia in one-third, orthostatic dizziness in one-third, visual hallucinations in one-fourth, and none presenting with extrapyramidal symptoms (EPS). Parkinsonism—primarily bradykinesia— was present in 43% early and in 77% later in the illness. About 25% of patients do not develop significant parkinsonism (McKeith, Ballard, et al., 2000). Fluctuating alertness and mentation was present in 58% early and 75% later in the course, recurrent falls occurred in 28% early and 37% later, and 61% developed neuroleptic sensitivity later in the illness. The core diagnostic features were also found consistently identified in a large multicenter study finding that features of parkinsonism (92.4%), cognitive fluctuations (89.1%), visual hallucinations (77.3%), delusions (46%), and repeated falls (42%) were all common.

Neuroimaging in DLB

Structural imaging using magnetic resonance imaging (MRI) has been used in AD to look particularly at hippocampal volume measurements as an early indicator of disease. O'Brien et al. (2001) looked at 28 patients with DLB, AD, VaD, and age-matched controls. The authors found accelerating atrophy with increasing severity of cognitive impairment, but there were no differences among the three dementia groups. Barber, Panikkar, and McKeith (2001) examined the relationship between white matter changes on MRI, brain atrophy, and ventricular dilation in 25 subjects with AD and 27 with DLB. Periventricular hyperintensities were found to independently correlate with advancing age and increasing ventricular dilatation in all subjects. In contrast, deep white matter hyperintensities did not correlate with measures of brain atrophy, ventricular dilatation, or age but were associated with a history of hypertension.

Minoshima et al. (2001) examined brain glucose metabolism in 11 DLB and 10 AD patients who had antemortem positron emission tomography (PET) imaging and autopsy confirmation. They also examined 53 clinically diagnosed probable AD patients, 13 of whom later filled clinical criteria for DLB. Significant reduction in metabolic activity involving the parietotemporal association and posterior cingulate and frontal association cortices were seen in autopsy-confirmed cases of AD and DLB. Only DLB patients showed significant metabolic reductions in the occipital cortex, particularly in the primary visual cortex, which distinguished DLB from AD with 90% sensitivity and 80% specificity. Similar findings on functional neuroimaging have been reported by other investigators (Lobotesis et al., 2001).

Treatment of DLB

There is pathological and biochemical data to suggest that the profound cholinergic deficit seen in DLB correlates with the cognitive symptoms as well as some of the neuropsychiatric disturbances (E. K. Perry, Marshall, Kerwin et al., 1990; R. H. Perry et al., 1996).

Several large, double-blind, placebo-controlled trials have been conducted for the treatment of AD. Cholinesterase inhibitors (ChEIs), the agents most widely used to treat AD, improve cognition and may have beneficial effects on behavioral disturbances and slow functional decline. Antioxidants including vitamin E and selegiline are being used based on the results of a single large randomized clinical trial indicating that these agents may slow the progression of the disease (Sano et al., 1997). There also is active research into disease-modifying therapies. Clinical trial data for treatment of the cognitive effects in DLB have been less well studied; however, several case reports and one randomized, double-blind, placebo-controlled trial suggests benefit of the ChEIs. Other treatment aims for patients with DLB include treatment of the marked neuropsychiatric manifestations, parkinsonism, and depression. Each of these types of therapy is considered in more detail later.

Cholinesterase Inhibitors

The Food and Drug Administration has approved four ChEIs for the treatment of AD: tacrine, donepezil, rivastigmine, and galantamine. These agents are being used for the behavioral and cognitive treatment of DLB (trials using galantamine have not been published). Patients with DLB may respond more favorably compared to those with AD. There is greater dysfunction of the cholinergic system in DLB, and the activity of choline acetyltransferase, the enzyme used to synthesize acetylcholine, is lower as well (Langlais et al., 1993; E. K. Perry, Marshall, Perry, et al., 1990; Shiozaki, Iseki, Hino, & Kosaka, 2001).

McKeith and colleagues (McKeith, Del Ser, et al., 2000) performed a randomized, placebo-controlled, double-blind trial using rivastigmine to treat behavioral disturbances in DLB. This was a large multicenter trial involving 120 patients. Nearly 63% in the treatment group showed at least a 30% improvement on the Neuropsychiatric Inventory (NPI; Cummings et al., 1994). Functionally, this equated to less apathy, less anxiety, and fewer delusions and hallucinations. Cognitive improvements, in particular, in measures of attention and memory also occurred. Cholinergic side effects (nausea, vomiting, and anorexia) were reported in some patients. Grace et al. (2001) reported on a smaller pilot trial of open-label treatment with rivastigmine in 29 DLB patients who were followed over a period of 96 weeks. No detectable declines in cognition as measured by the MMSE or of neuropsychiatric symptoms as measured by the NPI were seen, and scores were no worse than baseline. There was also no deterioration in parkinsonism over the treatment period.

Donepezil has been reported to be beneficial in DLB although no blinded studies have been reported. Several case series and reports have shown improvement in cognition using the MMSE (Folstein, Folstein, & McHugh, 1975), with scores increasing by up to four points. Neuropsychiatric improvement, particularly improvement in hallucinations, has been reported following treatment with donepezil (Rojas-Fernandez, 2001; Shea, MacKnight, & Rockwood, 1998). Agitation and delirium-like features common in DLB have likewise been shown to improve (Lanctot & Herrmann, 2000; Skjerve & Nygaard, 2000). Donepezil is generally well tolerated with only 3% of the patients published in the literature discontinuing the drug due to adverse events, which were predominantly gastrointestinal in nature. However, worsening of parkinsonism has been reported as a not uncommon side effect.

Querfurth, Allam, Geffroy, Schiff, and Kaplan (2000) examined the effects of the AChEI tacrine at 80 mg/day on cognitive task performance in six patients with a clinical diagnosis of DLB and six patients with AD. The MDRS, controlled Oral Word Association Test, and Boston naming tester were administered at baseline and at six months. Mild to moderate DLB responded favorably to tacrine through stabilization of global cognitive decline and specific cognitive areas.

Treatment of Motor Impairment

Parkinsonism frequently occurs in DLB (45% to 84%) and is one of the core clinical criteria. The symptoms of parkinsonism vary slightly in those with DLB compared to idiopathic PD with myoclonus being more frequent and the hallmark rest tremor being less frequent (Louis, Klatka, Liu, & Fahn, 1997). Parkinsonism and cognitive impairments typically begin in concert in DLB; in PD, cognitive impairment is usually delayed several years after the onset of motor symptoms. There is considerable debate regarding the utility of levodopa therapy in DLB; however, partial responses have been observed (Byrne, Lennox, Lowe, & Godwin-Austen, 1989; Hely, Reid, & Morris, 1996). Treatment studies consist of case reports and case series; large double-blind, controlled trials are lacking. The psychiatric effects of levodopa commonly limit the dose of dopaminergic agents that can be used in DLB patients, a population with an already high incidence of hallucinations and delusions.

Antipsychotic Agents

Neuroleptic sensitivity is one of the supportive features in the diagnosis of DLB. Neuropsychiatric symptoms such as delusions and hallucinations are core features and often require pharmacologic management. The combination of these neuropsychiatric symptoms and the exaggerated response to neuroleptics makes treatment of these features very challenging. McKeith et al. (1992) reported that 50% of DLB patients exposed to neuroleptics experienced a severe sensitivity with a threefold increase in mortality. These reactions were not dose-related, and most patients were taking typical neuroleptics. The newer atypical antipsychotics have the advantage of having a decreased propensity to cause EPS; however, sensitivity to these agents has also been described in patients with DLB (Ballard et al., 2000).

The atypical antipsychotics clozapine, olanzapine, and risperidone have been used to treat the neuropsychiatric aspects of DLB. Data using quetiapine and ziprasidone are not available.

Clozapine was the first atypical agent tried in an attempt to control neuropsychiatric features of DLB, and initial reports varied between dramatic efficacy (Chako, Hurley, & Jankovic, 1993) to worsening behavior and increasing confusion (Burke, Pfeiffer, & McComb, 1998). Some patients reported before the development of the diagnostic criteria had an unusual presentation and lacked pathologic confirmation, suggesting they may not have had DLB. The use of clozapine may be of particular benefit in DLB because, of all the antipsychotics, it has the lowest incidence of extrapyramidal side effects. Studies using clozapine in PD patients found it to be well tolerated and to have minimal effect on motor symptoms.

Success with risperidone has varied among the available case reports. In a series of 22 patients, Herrmann et al. (1998) reported nearly half had significant improvement and three-quarters of patients had at least minimal improvement. While 50% of those treated experienced some worsening of extrapyramidal symptoms, they were reported as mild—prompting discontinuation of the drug in only 3 of the 22 patients. Risperidone has been reported to induce neuroleptic malignant syndrome in DLB patients (Sechi et al., 2000). These studies, however, do not discourage the use of risperidone but recommend the need for increased vigilance for any evidence of extrapyramidal symptoms in those being treated.

The atypical antipsychotic olanzapine can be used in the behavioral management of DLB, but again with caution. Initial reports showed a variable response ranging from clear improvement, to no benefit, to intolerable side effects (Z. Walker et al., 1999). A post hoc analysis of DLB patients included in a larger study of olanzapine in AD found a significant reduction in hallucinations and delusions at 5 mg and 10 mg doses (Cummings, 1999). Higher doses did not confer any additional benefit and were not shown to be superior to placebo. There was no increase in parkinsonism among the patients receiving therapeutic doses.

Antidepressants

The reported frequency of depression in DLB varies between 30% and 50%. Rates may be slightly less frequent when *Diagnostic and Statistical Manual of Mental Disorders* fourth edition (*DSM-IV;* American Psychiatric Association, 1994) criteria for major depression are used and slightly higher if only depressive symptoms are assessed. The literature is also conflicting as to whether depression is more or less common in DLB when compared to AD or PD.

Randomized, placebo-controlled trials comparing the various classes of antidepressants in DLB are limited. While depression is a well-recognized feature of DLB, appropriate treatment is not well studied. The severity of the cholinergic deficit in DLB should make the family of tricyclic antidepressants (TCAs) a less than optimal choice because of their anticholinergic side effects. The selective serotonin reuptake inhibitors (SSRIs) and the multireceptor antidepressants venlafaxine, mirtazapine, and trazodone may be a better choice when efficacy and side-effect profiles are examined. These agents affect more specific brain receptor sites and generally do not target the histaminic or cholinergic sites.

PREVALENCE OF DEMENTIA IN IDIOPATHIC PD

Contrary to James Parkinson's initial impressions (1817) in his "Essay on the Shaking Palsy," he notes that *the senses and intellect are uninjured in PD,* and changes in cognitive function in PD are now accepted as an integral part of the clinical presentation of the disorder. Mild cognitive deficits are ubiquitous in PD; however, the incidence of frank dementia tends to be much lower. Prevalence rates of dementia reported in the literature range from 4% to 93%. Cummings (1988) calculated a mean prevalence of 39.9% based on 4,336 cases reported in the literature, whereas Brown and Marsden (1984) have suggested that 15% to 25% might be a more valid estimate. Prevalence figures must be viewed with caution and vary widely depending on what subpopulation is included (early versus late onset), what diagnostic criteria are used for dementia, and to what degree potential confounds of motor dysfunction are taken into account. Most studies examine heterogeneous PD samples, collapsing across disease duration, age, and motor symptom severity and treatment regimens. One factor that appears to be consistently important in determining which parkinsonian patients become demented is age.

Clinical Features of PD with Dementia

Age and Age at Onset

Celesia and Wanamaker's 1972 study was one of the first to show that older patients exhibit a higher incidence of cognitive impairment and overall dementia compared with younger parkinsonians, and they also exhibit a more rapid course of disease progression. This was subsequently supported by other investigators using standardized neuropsychological tests. Mayeux et al. (1988) found a 40% frequency of dementia in PD patients older than 65 years. Dubois, Pillon, Sternic, Lhermitte, and Agid (1990) studied a group of early-onset (< 45 years) and late-onset PD compared to age-matched controls. Early-onset PD exhibited mild memory problems and cognitive slowing, but late-onset exhibited more global cognitive dysfunction. But some have criticized these studies for examining only one point in time, thus bypassing the question of whether the older subjects were nondemented in their younger years and deteriorated with advancing age.

Biggins et al. in 1992 conducted serial assessments on 87 PD patients and 50 control subjects with 9- to 10-month intervals (cognition, mood, and motor symptoms). Initially, 6% were demented, but 54 months later, the cumulative incidence was 19% compared with none of the control subjects. They found the demented patients in this study were older, had PD longer, and had an older age of onset. In a prospective cohort study of 250 nondemented patients with idiopathic PD by Stern, Marder, Tang, and Mayeux (1993), the investigators looked at incidence of dementia over a five-year period. Seventy-four patients (30%) became demented during this period. The risk for developing dementia with PD was associated with age of onset over 70 years, history of depression, history of confusion or psychosis on L-dopa, an increased motor score, and presenting with facial masking.

Type of Motor Symptoms

Review of the literature with respect to subtype of PD and development of dementia has shown no relationship between the symptom of tremor and deterioration in any assessed cognitive domains. In contrast, bradykinesia, but not rigidity, consistently has been related to intellectual and cognitive deterioration in PD (Mayeux & Stern, 1983; Mortimer, Pirozzolo, Hansch, & Webster, 1982). Some investigators have found increased bradykinesia to be associated with specific cognitive impairment in constructional praxis and complex attention (Mayeux & Stern, 1983). It is common that early in the illness, PD patients exhibit unilateral motor symptoms. The study of asymmetries in cognitive deficits among patients with unilateral PD has shown mixed results (see review by Starkstein, 1992).

Medication Effects

There is lack of consensus concerning effects of pharmacotherapy on cognition in PD. L-dopa has been shown to result in improved performance on tasks of delayed verbal memory, choice reaction, and attention but may interfere with other tasks associated with frontal function. Cooper, Brotchie, Moser, Crossman, and Mitchell (1992) tested 82 newly diagnosed PD patients who had never been on medication with a full battery of neuropsychological testing. They were then randomly assigned to L-dopa, bromocriptine (a dopamine agonist), or anticholinergic medication and tested again after four months. Anticholinergic medications impaired short-term memory, and L-dopa improved a working memory task in that study.

Neuropsychological Characteristics of Dementia in PD

Cognitive disturbances may range from relative circumscribed deficits to global dementia. Mild cognitive deficits are common in idiopathic Parkinson's disease (IPD) and are characterized by impaired cognitive flexibility, psychomotor slowing, reduced ability to learn and retrieve new information, and impaired visuospatial skills. The concept of subdividing dementias on clinical grounds into cortical and subcortical dementias has been adapted by many in the field as a clinically useful concept, but others remain critical of this notion. The concept of subcortical dementia was originally based on an analysis of the pattern of personality and cognitive deficits in PSP (Albert, Fledman, & Willis, 1974) and Huntington's disease (HD; Folstein et al., 1975; see Table 3.2). The majority of studies addressing the concept of subcortical dementia have used PD as the prototypic subcortical dementia and AD as the prototypic cortical dementia. The term *subcortical dementia* originally applied to the constellation of cognitive deficits attributed to subcortical brain damage in humans and was initially characterized as including:

- Memory loss.
- Impaired manipulation of acquired knowledge (i.e., calculation and abstracting abilities).
- Personality changes marked by apathy and inertia.
- General slowness of thought processes (Albert et al., 1974).

Language

Aphasic disturbances are generally not part of PD dementia. Dysarthic disturbances are common, and there may be greater abnormalities in phrase-length speech melody, information content of spontaneous speech comprehension of written and spoken commands compared to PD without dementia.

Table 3.2   Common Medications Used in Treatment of LBD

Medication	Typical Starting Dose (mg/day)	Typical Maintenance Dose (mg/day)
Trazodone	25–50	200–300
Sertraline	25–50	100–150
Fluoxetine	10–20	20–40
Paroxetine	10	20–50
Citalopram	10–20	10–40
Mirtazapine		20–60
Buproprion		100–450
Venlafaxine		150–375
Nefazodone		200–600
Nortriptyline	25–50	75–100
Desipramine	25–50	25–200
Entacapone	200	200 each (1 dopa dose)
Pramipexole	.375	3.0–4.5

Memory

Explicit verbal memory (word lists, paired associate learning, brief prose passages) is disturbed in PD patients with dementia; however, the quality of this memory impairment is different from that seen in AD. Most often, the deficit is in memory retrieval (where patients are able to develop a normal learning curve but exhibit increased rates of forgetting on delayed recall and are much better at recognition). This differential recall/recognition is seen for PD patients over a broad range of mental status changes.

Explicit nonverbal memory (reproducing complex drawings, learning locations of places on maps) also is found to be impaired in Parkinson's disease with dementia (PDD). Remote memory is generally intact in the nondemented PD patient but impaired in PDD as is *implicit memory* (lexical priming and pursuit rotor learning) and *procedural memory* (perceptual or motor skills not readily accessible to conscious recollection but, when intact, can be executed with ease).

Bradyphrenia

The term *bradyphrenia* was coined by a French neurologist to describe a new psychiatric syndrome that was produced by encephalitis lethargica. The notion is one of lengthening of normal information processing time or "slowing of the thinking process," a concept that has been the subject of long standing. One way to address this is to compare performance on simple and choice reaction-timed tasks. The precise relationship between bradyphrenia and dementia remains unclear.

Visuospatial Skills

Deficits in this arena are among the most frequently reported cognitive changes accompanying PD, but the precise nature of these deficits and their relation to PD dementia remains incompletely understood. One of the confounds is the potential motor demands of certain tasks. Visual sensory function is normal in PD. Visual acuity, color perception, and depth perception are all unaffected, but visuoperceptual abilities are abnormal.

Higher Executive Function

The term *higher executive function* is generally used to refer to the concept of abstract thinking—planning ability to profit from feedback, judgment, and initiative. The frontal lobes are directly implicated because of the close linkage of the striatum and the frontal lobes by way of cortico-striato-thalamo-cortical circuits. The concept that the basal ganglia are involved in a form of higher motor control, as well as cognitive function per se, is gaining increasing acceptance. The pathophysiology of the intellectual impairment in PD is controversial and the subject of ongoing research. Whether extent and severity of executive deficits are predictive of dementia remains to be determined. PD nondemented differed significantly from control subjects on Raven's progressive matrices, Boston naming, Stroop color naming, picture arrangement, story recall after 10-minute delay, and Benton visual retention. While cognitive disturbances may range from relatively circumscribed deficits to global dementia, no clear evidence exists that these represent a continuum.

Mood/Affect

Major depression in PD and dementia is 30% as opposed to 6% in AD matched for dementia severity. Dysthymia was found in 27% PDD and 27% AD (Starkstein et al., 1996). A further complication is that the presence of dementing symptoms is often difficult to separate from affective changes seen in many patients with PD (20% to 60% of patients experience affective changes some time during the course of their illness; Cummings, 1986).

Pathologic/Anatomic Correlates of Cognitive/Behavioral Disturbances in PD

The classic neuropathologic findings of PD consist of degenerative lesions affecting the pigmented cells in the substantia nigra (SN) and other pigmented nuclei in the brain stem. Lewy bodies (eosinophilic cytoplasmic inclusions) in cells of the SN and locus ceruleus (LC) are present in almost all cases. There may also be cell loss in the nucleus basalis of Meynert, and some cases exhibit neurofibrillary tangles (NFT), senile plaques (SP), and granulovacuolar degeneration.

The nature of the histopathologic changes associated with PD with dementia continues to be debated. Although the dementia in PD might be explained by the co-occurrence of AD, mounting evidence argues against this as the sole explanation.

AD and PD frequently develop in the same age group. One large study looked at NFT/SP counts in PD patients at autopsy versus age-matched controls and demonstrated that AD changes were six times more frequent in the PD population (allowing for senile plaques only to make a diagnosis of AD; Boller, Mizutani, Roessmann, & Gambetti, 1980). Review of other studies reveals a co-occurrence rate of AD to be about 5% to 20% with PD pathology. Furthermore, a study by Hughes, Daniel, and Lees (1993) examining pathologically verified cases of PD revealed that all had cortical Lewy bodies (LB), but not all had a sufficient quantity to be classified as DLB. When these investigators further examined just those PD patients with well-documented dementia (33%), they found that only one-third had additional pathological changes of coexisting AD. DLB was found in one-tenth, and a vascular cause was seen in one-fifteenth. Thus, half of the well-documented dementia patients had no pathologically identified cause. A more recent pathological series reported by Louis et al. in 1997 found a larger percentage of cortical LBs associated with PDD, but 10 of 23 cases of PDD could still not be explained by either the co-occurrence of AD changes in the brain or sufficient numbers of cortical LBs to be classified as DLB.

The specific neuropsychological deficits in attention, memory, visuospatial, or frontal lobe functions frequently encountered in patients with IPD appear to arise from degeneration of different cerebral structures. The frontal lobes are directly implicated in these complex cognitive activities, and flow of information through the striatum from the frontal lobes by way of cortico-striato-thalamo-cortical circuits is believed to subserve many of these complex functions. However, the precise pathophysiological underpinnings of the intellectual impairment in IPD are controversial and the subject of ongoing research. Complex transmitter interactions are also undoubtedly important elements. In one study by Pisani, Bonsi, Centonze, Bernardi, and Calabresi (2001), electrophysiological experiments in vivo from behaving monkeys identified the cholinergic interneurons as being tonically active neurons (TANs). They appear to be activated by presentation of sensory stimuli of behavioral significance or linked to reward. Experimental evidence shows that integrity of the nigrostriatal dopaminergic system is essential for the TANs to express learned activity.

A number of attempts have been made to correlate the degree of neuronal loss in SN and dopamine (DA) depletion with cognitive changes without effect. More recent work by Rinne et al. (1989) revealed a significant association between the degree of dementia and neuronal loss in the medial portion of SN that projects to the medial frontal lobes. The authors concluded, based on the topographical organization of neurons in the SN, that intact projections to the caudate nucleus and limbic cortical areas are required for normal cognitive performance.

It is thought that neuronal loss of approximately 80% takes place before PD motor symptoms appear and that only DA neurons are affected early in the disease. The role of DA in dementia is supported by:

- Consistent correlation between dementia and akinesia.
- An association between cell loss in medial portion of SN and degree of dementia.
- 1-Methyl-4-phenyl-1,2,3,6-tetrahydropyridine (MPTP) patients who have selective disruption of the DA system also show cognitive abnormalities.
- The ability to partially improve some cognitive aspects with L-dopa.

On the other hand, the observation that little or no dementia is seen with Hoen and Yahr (H&R) stage I raises the possibility that the clinical expression of PDD in the later stages of the disease requires the involvement of additional neurotransmitter (NT) systems and neuronal circuits.

Loss of neurons in nucleus basalis of Meynert, an area rich in cholinergic cell bodies, was first described by Lewy in 1912. The pathology in this area, in fact, was described before the neuronal loss in the SN was fully appreciated. In addition, the degree of cell loss in the nucleus basalis in PD often exceeds that seen in AD. Cholinergic depletion in the nucleus basalis of Meynert is much higher in patients with PDD than in PD patients without dementia and may have implications for therapy. There have been a couple of small clinical series suggesting a benefit of cholinesterase inhibitor therapy on cognition in PDD, but large-scale, placebo-controlled studies are lacking. However, this deficiency also does not entirely explain the dementia seen in these patients. For example, Whitehouse (1986) showed that neuronal loss in the nucleus basalis is seen in PD patients with and without dementia, and, interestingly, postencephalitic PD patients did not have significant loss in the nucleus basalis but did show comparable rates of dementia and depression to idiopathic PD.

Other neurotransmitter system abnormalities may contribute to the cognitive dysfunction seen in some PD patients. The locus ceruleus (LC), an area rich in noradrenergic cells, is severely affected in PD, and changes in this subcortical region can be substantial in the absence of cortical pathology. This structure has been postulated to play an important role in cognition (particularly learning and memory) and may be important in PDD. For example, norepinephrine metabolism has been shown to be significantly lower in PDD patients compared to nondemented PD patients. Similarly, neuropeptides may also play an important role in the dementias of Parkinson's disease. In a few recent findings:

- Somatostatin is reduced in the frontal cortex, hippocampus, and entorhinal cortex of demented PD patients.
- Galanin coexists with ChAT in the nucleus basalis and is preserved in PD dementia.
- Neuropeptide Y coexists with catecholamines, especially norepinephrine, and may be differentially affected in PDD.

So much more needs to be learned regarding the neuroanatomical and neurochemical relationships with respect to cognitive dysfunction in PD.

The effects of pallidotomy and deep brain stimulation on cognitive function in IPD have now been looked at in a number of studies from different centers (Ghika et al., 1998; Krack et al., 1998; Kumar, Lozano, Montgomery, & Lang, 1998; Tronnier et al., 1997; Troster et al., 1997, 1998). Some have found modest declines in semantic verbal fluency and visuoconstructional tasks, but overall, no significant change in cognition has been consistently reported and fewer symptoms of anxiety and depressive symptoms have been described.

Alegret et al. (2001) examined MRI scans of 14 patients with advanced PD and correlated the scans with cognitive performance. They found that ventricular enlargement was negatively correlated with the performance on Rey Auditory Verbal Learning Test and Stroop Test, but no relationship was found between caudate atrophy and cognitive deficits. Degeneration of putamen nucleus was found to be associated with motor deficit.

Depression in PD

Depression is the most common neuropsychiatric disturbance in IPD. A comprehensive review of the literature by Cummings (1992) found rates of depression to average 40% with the range being 4% to 70% depending on the specific population assessed and the rating scales used. Of these, approximately half met criteria for major depression and the other half had chronic dysthymia. Another recent literature review between 1922 and 1998 by Slaughter, Slaughter, Nichols, and Martens (2001) found an overall prevalence of depression of 31% in patients with IPD. Between 20% and 60% of patients with IPD experience affective changes sometime during the course of their illness. Santamaria and Valles (1986) found that in 50% of the cases, depression preceded the motor manifestations by an average of five years. In general, depressed patients had a younger age of onset and were less physically disabled. Starkstein (1992) found depression to be more common in IPD with onset before age 55. Depressed patients with IPD have greater frontal lobe dysfunction and greater involvement of dopaminergic and noradrenergic systems than nondepressed patients with PD (Cummings, 1992). Although depression is more common among those with greater cognitive impairment, depression is equally frequent in IPD patients with and without overt dementia. In a paper by Starkstein et al. (1996), the presence of affective symptoms was compared in patients with IPD and dementia and AD. Major depression in IPD with dementia was 30% as opposed to 6% of AD patients matched for dementia severity. Dysthymia, however, was found in 27% PDD and 27% AD.

Treatment of depression in IPD includes the use of a wide range of antidepressants, only a few of which have been shown to be effective in this population in controlled studies. Selection of which antidepressant to use should be based on side effect profile of the drug and potential drug interactions. Antidepressants with more anticholinergic properties such as amitriptyline can produce cognitive disturbances in the elderly and should generally be avoided. Tricyclic antidepressants with fewer anticholinergic properties and cardiovascular side effects such as nortryptiline are generally better tolerated in the elderly population. The serotonin reuptake inhibitors have little effect on the cholinergic system and only minor action on norepinephrine and dopamine. They have few side effects and may offer some advantage in the treatment of depression in this patient population. A few relatively small-scale studies have shown them to be effective in this patient population. In a recent study of paroxetine (Ceravolo et al., 2000), six months of treatment with 20 mg was found to be effective in treating depression without worsening the parkinsonian motor symptoms. Extrapyramidal side effects, however, have been described as adverse events, and worsening of PD

Table 3.3   Contrasting Features of the Subcortical Dementia of
PD and AD

Feature	AD	PD
Language	Aphasia	Motor speech problems
Memory	Amnestic	Retrieval deficit
Visuospatial	Severe	Mild impairment
Processing speed	Normal	Slowed
Executive skills	Proportionate	Greater difficulty
Insight	Lacks insight	Preserved
Personality/mood	Unconcerned	Depression

symptoms have been reported in a few cases. Moreover, there is the potential of developing a serotonin syndrome if these drugs are used in conjunction with selegiline, an MAO-B inhibitor commonly used in the treatment of PD. Although this has only rarely been described in the literature, concurrent administration of selegiline and a selective serotonin reuptake inhibitor should be avoided. Bupropion is an antidepressant with indirect dopamine agonist effects and, therefore, may offer some additional advantage when treating depression. Data on the newer class of combined serotonin and norepinephrine reuptake inhibitors in treating depression specifically in PD are not available. Klaassen et al. (1995) published a meta-analysis of treatment of depression in PD and found that despite the abundance of literature on PD and depression, there was a paucity of well-controlled studies on the treatment of depression in this population. Electroconvulsive therapy is effective treatment for major depression in PD patients. In the majority of cases, improvements are seen in both the depression and in the extrapyramidal motor symptoms (Burke et al., 1998). These improvements in motor symptoms tend to be short-lived but may persist for weeks in some cases (Table 3.3).

Anxiety in PD

There is a significant interaction between anxiety and depression in IPD with 92% of anxiety disorder patients also manifesting depression. In one study (Menza, Robertson-Hoffman, & Bonapace, 1993), patients with IPD had significantly more anxiety than medical controls, with 28% of the IPD patients having an anxiety disorder diagnosis compared to 5% of controls. Another 40% of the patients with IPD exhibited more minor anxiety symptoms. These investigators also found that 43% of IPD patients had a depressive disorder; an additional 14% had depressive symptoms. It has been suggested that anxiety may be secondary in part to the antiparkinsonian medications. A study by Maricle, Nutt, and Carter (1995) investigated mood and anxiety fluctuations associated with L-dopa infusion therapy in a small series of patients and found that mood and anxiety symptoms slightly preceded but temporarily paralleled fluctuations in motor tapping scores. The effects of L-dopa on mood and anxiety were not related to relief of parkinsonism. Mood change preceded changes in tapping scores and started dropping before tapping scores deteriorated. There was no relationship between the amount of mood change, severity of parkinsonism, and the extent to which IPD improved during L-dopa infusion.

Psychosis in IPD

L-dopa and all dopamine agonists can induce adverse psychiatric effects. The mechanisms responsible for these symptoms are unknown, but mesolimbic dopaminergic and central serotoninergic systems are likely to be involved. Cummings (1991), in a review of the literature, summarized the neuropsychiatric adverse effects of dopaminergic agents in patients with IPD as follows: 30% develop visual hallucinations, 10% delusions, 15% confusion, 10% anxiety, 10% euphoria, and 1% mania.

Abnormal dreaming and increased sleep disruption may precede the development of psychotic symptoms by weeks to months and provide an important early clue to their potential occurrence. Visual hallucinations are the most common manifestation of the drug-induced psychosis. These hallucinations are usually well-formed, nonthreatening images of people or animals and tend to be nocturnal, recurrent, and stereotyped for each patient (Cummings, 1991). They typically occur on a background of a clear sensorium and may not be particularly troublesome to the patient if insight is retained. However, more disabling symptoms such as delusional thinking (which is frequently paranoid), confusion, and even frank delirium may develop and require immediate intervention (Holroyd, Currie, & Wooten, 2001). In a prospective study of hallucinations and delusions in PD, of 102 consecutive patients with strictly diagnosed PD, 26.5% had psychosis unrelated to delirium. Visual hallucinations occurred most commonly. Psychosis correlated with (1) disease severity, (2) dementia, (3) depression, and (4) worse visual acuity.

The treatment of drug-induced psychosis generally begins with reduction in the antiparkinsonian medication beginning first with adjunctive agents followed by lowering the levodopa dosage. After decreasing these agents, it may take several days for the psychosis to resolve, and sometimes significant worsening in the patient's motor symptoms precludes further lowering of the antiparkinsonian medications. In these cases, addition of an antipsychotic agent is warranted. Most standard neuroleptics can lead to worsening of the parkinsonian motor symptoms, making it difficult to achieve an effective therapeutic balance. Atypical antipsychotic agents offer a promising new avenue of treatment for these difficult cases.

Clozapine was the first medication in the class of atypical antipsychotic agents to be used in PD and has demonstrated favorable effects in the control of psychotic symptoms without compromising motor performance (Musser & Akil, 1996; the Parkinson's Study Group, 1999; Ruggieri, De Pandis, Bonamartini, Vacca, & Stocchi, 1997; Wolters, 1990). Doses as low as 6.25 mg have been effective, and most patients respond to doses under 100 mg (Ruggieri et al., 1997). Despite this benefit, drug toxicity even with low doses remains a serious potential problem. Agranulocytosis is the most worrisome potential side effect, and weekly blood monitoring is required.

Risperidone, another atypical antipsychotic agent, has not been studied in detail for treatment of drug-induced psychosis in PD, but reports in the literature on a small number of patients have found that this agent may exacerbate the parkinsonian motor symptoms (Rich, Friedman, & Ott, 1995).

Olanzapine (Zyprexa) is another new atypical antipsychotic agent. Use of olanzapine in the treatment of psychosis in PD has yet to be studied in detail, but this drug may offer another potential treatment option (Cummings et al., 2002; Marsh, Lyketsos, & Reich, 2001).

Quetiapine (Seroquel) is the latest atypical antipsychotic agent released in the United States; there was one report of its effectiveness in controlling psychosis in PD without exacerbating parkinsonian symptoms (Dewey & O'Suilleabhain, 2000; Parsa & Bastani, 1998).

Ondansetron is a $5HT_3$-receptor antagonist approved in 1991 for the treatment of nausea, but it has been investigated as a potential treatment of psychosis given the abundance of this receptor subtype in the limbic system. There have been some promising reports of its effectiveness in treating psychosis in advanced PD in some patients (Zoldan, Friedberg, Weizman, &

Melamed, 1996). Drug-induced psychiatric disturbances are not infrequent and remain important challenges in the management of the PD patient.

SUMMARY

While there remains considerable overlap between DLB and PDD, the progression, clinical presentation, and pathological findings point to these two entities being separate in many instances. A better understanding of the pathophysiology of both DLB and PD, as well as the genetics and risk factors related to these disorders, will aid in the development of better treatment approaches. In addition, novel compounds are continuing to be developed for the treatment of psychosis and may provide additional benefit in PD. Future directions in the treatment of DLB and PDD will undoubtedly involve a comprehensive, multifaceted treatment approach that uses disease-modifying agents together with safe and effective symptomatic treatments.

REFERENCES

Albert, M. L., Fledman, R. G., & Willis, A. L. (1974). The subcortical dementia of progressive supranuclear palsy. *Journal of Neurology, Neurosurgery, and Psychiatry, 37,* 121–130.

Alegret, M., Junque, C., Pueyo, R., Valldeoriola, F., Vendrell, P., Tolosa, E., et al. (2001, February). MRI atrophy parameters related to cognitive and motor impairment in Parkinson's disease. *Neurologia, 16*(2), 63–69.

American Psychiatric Association. (1994). *Diagnostic and statistical manual of mental disorders* (4th ed.). Washington, DC: Author.

Ballard, C. G., O'Brien, J. T., Swann, A., Neill, D., Lantos, P., Holmes, C., et al. (2000). One year follow-up of Parkinsonism in dementia with Lewy bodies. *Dementia and Geriatric Cognitive Disorders, 11*(6), 219–222.

Barber, R., Panikkar, A., & McKeith, I. G. (2001). Dementia with Lewy bodies: Diagnosis and management. *International Journal of Geriatrics Psychiatry, 16*(Suppl. 1), S12–S18.

Biggins, C. A., Boyd, J. L., Harrop, F. M., Madeley, P., Mindham, R. H., Randall, J. I., et al. (1992). A controlled, longitudinal study of dementia in Parkinson's disease. *Journal of Neurology, Neurosurgery, and Psychiatry, 55,* 566–571.

Boeve, B. F., Silber, M. H., Ferman, T. J., Kokmen, E., Smith, G. E., Ivnik, R. J., et al. (1998). REM sleep behavior disorder and degenerative dementia: An association likely reflecting Lewy body disease. *Neurology, 51*(2), 363–370.

Boller, F., Mizutani, T., Roessmann, V., & Gambetti, P. (1980). Parkinson disease, dementia, and Alzheimer disease: Clinicopathological correlations. *Annals of Neurology, 7,* 329–335.

Brown, R. G., & Marsden, C. D. (1984). How common is dementia in Parkinson's disease? *Lancet, 2,* 1262–1265.

Burke, W. J., Pfeiffer, R. F., & McComb, R. D. (1998). Neuroleptic sensitivity to clozapine in dementia with Lewy bodies. *Journal of Neuropsychiatry and Clinical Neuroscience, 10,* 227–229.

Byrne, E., Lennox, G., Lowe, J., & Godwin-Austen, R. B. (1989). Diffuse Lewy body disease: Clinical features in 15 cases. *Journal of Neurology, Neurosurgery, and Psychiatry, 52,* 709–717.

Celesia, G. G., & Wanamaker, W. M. (1972). Psychiatric disturbances in Parkinson's disease. *Diseases of the Nervous System, 9,* 577–583.

Ceravolo, R., Nuti, A., Piccinni, A., et al. (2000, October 24). Paroxetine in Parkinson's disease: Effects on motor and depressive symptoms. *Neurology, 55*(8), 1216–1218.

Chako, R. C., Hurley, R. A., & Jankovic, J. (1993). Clozapine use in diffuse Lewy body disease. *Journal of Neuropsychiatry and Clinical Neuroscience, 5,* 206–208.

Connor, D. J. (2000). *Dissertation Abstracts International, 61*(4), 2195B.

Cooper, A. J., Brotchie, J. M., Moser, B., Crossman, A. R., & Mitchell, I. J. (1992). Regional and temporal expression of the immediate early gene, c-fos in a rodent model of parkinsonism. *Neuroscience Letters, 42*(Suppl.), S35.

Cummings, J. L. (1986). Subcortical dementia. *British Journal of Psychiatry, 149,* 682–697.

Cummings, J. L. (1988). Intellectual impairment in Parkinson's disease: Clinical, pathologic and biochemical correlates. *Journal of Geriatric Psychiatry and Neurology, 1,* 24–36.

Cummings, J. L. (1991). Behavioral complications of drug treatment of Parkinson's disease. *Journal of the American Geriatrics Society, 39,* 708–716.

Cummings, J. L. (1992). Depression and Parkinson's disease: A review. *American Journal of Psychiatry, 149,* 443–454.

Cummings, J. L. (1999). Managing psychosis in patients with Parkinson's disease. *New England Journal of Medicine, 340,* 801–803.

Cummings, J. L., Mega, M., Gray, K., Rosenberg-Thompson, S., Carusi, D. A., & Gornbein, J. (1994). The neuropsychiatric inventory: Comprehensive assessment of psychopathology in dementia. *Neurology, 44,* 2308–2314.

Cummings, J. L., Street, J., Masterman, D., & Clark, W. S. (2002). Efficacy of olanzapine in the treatment of psychosis in dementia with Lewy bodies. *Dementia and Geriatric Cognitive Disorders, 13,* 67–73.

Del Ser, T., McKeith, I., Anand, R., Cicin-Sain, A., et al. (2000). Dementia with Lewy bodies: Findings from an international multicentre study. *International Journal of Geriatric Psychiatry, 15,* 1034–1045.

Dewey, R. B., & O'Suilleabhain, P. E. (2000). Treatment of drug-induced psychosis with quetiapine and clozapine in Parkinson's disease. *Neurology, 55,* 1753–1754.

Dubois, B., Pillon, B., Sternic, N., Lhermitte, F., & Agid, Y. (1990). Age-induced cognitive disturbances in Parkinson's disease. *Neurology, 40,* 38–41.

Folstein, M. F., Folstein, S. E., & McHugh, P. R. (1975). Mini-mental state: A practical method for grading the cognitive state of patients for the clinician. *Journal of Psychiatric Research, 12,* 189–198.

Ghika, J., Villemure, J. G., Fankhauser, H., Favre, J., Assal, G., & Ghika-Schmid, F. (1998, November). Efficiency and safety of bilateral contemporaneous pallidal stimulation (deep brain stimulation) in levodopa-responsive patients with Parkinson's disease with severe motor fluctuations: A 2-year follow-up review. *Journal of Neurosurgery, 89*(5), 713–718.

Gomez-Tortosa, E., Newell, K., Irizarry, M. C., et al. (1999). Clinical and quantitative pathological correlates of dementia with Lewy bodies. *Neurology, 53,* 1284–1291.

Grace, J., Daniel, S., Stevens, T., Shankar, K. K., Walker, Z., Byrne, E. J., et al. (2001). Long-term use of rivastigmine in patients with dementia with Lewy bodies: An open-label trial. *International Psychogeriatrics, 13,* 199–205.

Hansen, L., Salmon, D., Galasko, D., Masliah, E., Katzman, R., De Teresa, R., et al. (1990). The Lewy body variant of Alzheimer's disease: A clinical and pathologic entity. *Neurology, 40,* 1–8.

Hansen, L. A., & Samuel, W. (1997). Criteria for Alzheimer's disease and the nosology of dementia with Lewy bodies. *Neurology, 48,* 126–131.

Haroutunian, V., Serby, M., Purohit, D., Perl, D. P., Marin, D., Lantz, M., et al. (2000). Contribution of Lewy body inclusions to dementia in patients with and without Alzheimer disease neuropathological conditions. *Archives of Neurology, 57,* 1145–1150.

Hely, M. A., Reid, W. G., & Morris, J. G. (1996). Diffuse Lewy body disease: Clinical features in nine cases without coexistent Alzheimer's disease. *Journal of Neurology, Neurosurgery, and Psychiatry, 60,* 531–538.

Herrmann, N., Rivard, M. F., Flynn, M., Ward, C., Rabheru, K., & Campbell, B. (1998). Risperidone for the treatment of behavioral disturbances in dementia: A case series. *Journal of Neuropsychiatry and Clinical Neuroscience, 10,* 220–223.

Hohl, U., Tiraboschi, P., Hansen, L. A., Thal, L. J., & Corey-Bloom, J. (2000). Diagnostic accuracy of dementia with Lewy bodies. *Archives of Neurology, 57,* 347–351.

Holroyd, S., Currie, L., & Wooten, G. F. (2001, June). Prospective study of hallucinations and delusions in Parkinson's disease. *Journal of Neurology, Neurosurgery, and Psychiatry, 70*(6), 734–738.

Hughes, A. J., Daniel, S. E., & Lees, A. J. (1993). The clinical features of Parkinson's disease in 100 histologically proven cases. *Advances in Neurology, 60,* 595–599.

Hulette, C., Mirra, S., Wilkinson, W., Heyman, A., Fillenbaum, G., & Clark, C. M. (1995). The consortium to establish a registry for Alzheimer's disease (CERAD). Part IX: A prospective clinicopathological study of Parkinson's features in Alzheimer's disease. *Neurology, 45,* 1991–1995.

Klaassen, T., Verhey, F. R., Sneijders, G. H., Rozendaal, N., De Vet, H. C., & Van Praag, H. M. (1995). Treatment of depression in Parkinson's disease: A meta-analysis. *Journal of Neuropsychiatry and Clinical Neurosciences, 7,* 281–286.

Knopman, D. S. (2001). An overview of common non-Alzheimer dementias. *Clinics in Geriatric Medicine, 7,* 281–301.

Kosaka, K., Yoshimura, M., Ikeda, K., & Budka, H. (1984). Diffuse type of Lewy body disease: Progressive dementia with abundant cortical Lewy bodies and senile changes of varying degree: A new disease? *Clinical Neuropathology, 3,* 185–192.

Krack, P., Pollak, P., Limousin, P., Hoffmann, D., Xie, J., Benazzouz, A., et al. (1998). Subthalamic nucleus or internal pallidal stimulation in young onset Parkinson's disease. *Brain, 121*(Pt. 3), 451–457.

Kumar, R., Lozano, A. M., Montgomery, E., & Lang, A. E. (1998). Pallidotomy and deep brain stimulation of the pallidum and subthalamic nucleus in advanced Parkinson's disease. *Movement Disorders, 13*(Suppl. 1), 73–82.

Lanctot, K. L., & Herrmann, N. (2000, April). Donepezil for behavioural disorders associated with Lewy bodies: A case series. *International Journal of Geriatric Psychiatry, 15*(4), 338–345.

Langlais, P. J., Thal, L., Hansen, L., Galasko, D., Alford, M., & Masliah, E. (1993). Neurotransmitters in basal ganglia and cortex of Alzheimer's disease with and without Lewy bodies. *Neurology, 43,* 1927–1934.

Lennox, G., Lowe, J., Landon, M., Byrne, E. J., Mayer, R. J., & Godwin-Austen, R. B. (1989). Diffuse Lewy body disease: Correlative neuropathology using anti-ubiquitin immunocytochemistry. *Journal of Neurology, Neurosurgery, and Psychiatry, 52,* 1236–1247.

Lewy, F. H. (1912). Paralysis agitans. I: Pathologische Anatomie. In *Handbuch der Neurology III* (pp. 920–933). Berlin, Germany: Springer.

Litvan, I., MacIntyre, A., Goetz, C. G., Wenning, G. K., Jellinger, K., Verny, M., et al. (1998). Accuracy of the clinical diagnoses of Lewy body disease,

Parkinson's disease and dementia with Lewy bodies: A clinicopathologic study. *Archives of Neurology, 55,* 969–978.

Lobotesis, K., Fenwick, J. D., Phipps, A., Ryman, A., Swann, A., Ballard, C., et al. (2001). Occipital hypoperfusion on SPECT in dementia with Lewy bodies but not AD. *Neurology, 56,* 643–649.

Louis, E. D., Klatka, L., Liu, Y., & Fahn, S. (1997). Comparison of extrapyramidal features in 31 pathologically confirmed cases of diffuse Lewy body disease and 34 pathologically confirmed cases of Parkinson's disease. *Neurology, 48,* 376–380.

Maricle, R. A., Nutt, J. G., & Carter, J. H. (1995). Mood and anxiety fluctuation in Parkinson's disease associated with levodopa infusion: Preliminary findings. *Movement Disorders, 10,* 329–332.

Marsh, L., Lyketsos, C., & Reich, S. G. (2001, November/December). Olanzapine for the treatment of psychosis in patients with Parkinson's disease and dementia. *Psychosomatics, 42*(6), 477–481.

Masliah, E., Mallory, M., De Teresa, R., Alford, M., & Hansen, L. (1993). Differing patterns of aberrant neuronal sprouting in Alzheimer's disease with and without Lewy bodies. *Brain Research, 617,* 258–266.

Mayeux, R., & Stern Y. (1983). Intellectual dysfunction and dementia in Parkinson's disease. *Advances in Neurology, 38,* 211–227.

Mayeux, R., Stern, Y., Rosenstein, R., Marder, K., Hauser, A., Cote, L., et al. (1988). An estimate of the prevalence of dementia in idiopathic Parkinson's disease. *Archives of Neurology, 45,* 260–262.

McKeith, I. G., Ballard, C. G., Perry, R. H., Ince, P. G., O'Brien, J. T., Neill, D., et al. (2000). Prospective validation of consensus criteria for the diagnosis of dementia with Lewy bodies. *Neurology, 54,* 1050–1058.

McKeith, I. G., Del Ser, T., Spano, P., Emre, M., Wesnes, K., Anand, R., et al. (2000). Efficacy of rivastigmine in dementia with Lewy bodies: A randomized, double-blind, placebo-controlled international study. *Lancet, 356*(9247), 2031–2036.

McKeith, I. G., Fairbairn, A., Perry, R., Thompson, P., & Perry, E. (1992). Neuroleptic sensitivity in patients with senile dementia of Lewy body type. *British Medical Journal, 305,* 673–678.

McKeith, I. G., Galasko, D., Kosaka, K., Perry, E. K., Dickson, D. W., Hansen, L. A., et al. (1996). Consensus guidelines for the clinical and pathological diagnosis of dementia with Lewy bodies (DLB): Report of the consortium on DLB international workshop. *Neurology, 47,* 1113–1124.

McKeith, I. G., Perry, E. K., & Perry, R. H. (1999). For the consortium on dementia with Lewy bodies: Report of the second dementia with Lewy body international workshop. *Neurology, 53,* 902–905.

McShane, R. H., Nagy, Z., Esiri, M., King, E., Joachim, C., Sullivan, N., et al. (2001). Anosmia in dementia is associated with Lewy bodies rather than Alzheimer's pathology. *Journal of Neurology, Neurosurgery, and Psychiatry, 70,* 739–743.

Mega, M. S., Masterman, D. L., Benson, D. F., Vinters, H. V., Tomiyasu, U., Craig, A. H., et al. (1996). Dementia with Lewy bodies: Reliability and validity of clinical and pathologic criteria. *Neurology, 47,* 1403–1409.

Menza, M. A., Robertson-Hoffman, D. E., & Bonapace, A. S. (1993). Parkinson's disease and anxiety: Comorbidity with depression. *Biological Psychiatry, 24,* 465–470.

Minoshima, S., Foster, N. L., Sima, A., Frey, K. A., et al. (2001). Alzheimer's disease versus dementia with Lewy bodies: Cerebral metabolic distinction with autopsy confirmation. *Annals of Neurology, 50,* 358–365.

Mortimer, J. A., Pirozzolo, F. J., Hansch, E. C., & Webster, D. D. (1982). Relationship of motor symptoms to intellectual deficits in Parkinson's disease. *Neurology, 32,* 133–137.

Musser, W. S., & Akil M. (1996, Winter). Clozapine as a treatment for psychosis in Parkinson's disease: A review. *Journal of Neuropsychiatry and Clinical Neurosciences, 8*(1), 1–9.

O'Brien, J. T., Paling, S., Barber, R., Williams, E. D., Ballard, C., McKeith, I. G., et al. (2001, May 22). Progressive brain atrophy on serial MRI in dementia with Lewy bodies, AD, and vascular dementia. *Neurology, 56*(10), 1386–1388.

Okazaki, H., Lipkin, L. E., & Aronson, S. M. (1961). Diffuse intracytoplasmic ganglionic inclusions (Lewy type) associated with progressive dementia and quadriparesis in flexion. *Journal of Neuropathology and Experimental Neurology, 20,* 237–244.

Parkinson, J. (1817). *Essay on the shaking palsy.* London: Sherwood, Neely, and Jones.

The Parkinson Study Group. (1999). Low-dose clozapine for the treatment of drug-induced psychosis in Parkinson's disease. *New England Journal of Medicine, 340,* 757–763.

Parsa, M. A., & Bastani, B. (1998, Spring). Quetiapine (Seroquel) in the treatment of psychosis in patients with Parkinson's disease. *Journal of Neuropsychiatry and Clinical Neurosciences, 10*(2), 216–219.

Perry, E. K., Haroutunian, V., Perry, R. H., et al. (1994). Neocortical cholinergic activities differentiate Lewy body dementia from classical Alzheimer's disease. *Neuroreport, 5,* 747–749.

Perry, E. K., Marshall, E., Kerwin, J. M., et al. (1990). Evidence of a monoaminergic: Cholinergic imbalance related to visual hallucinations in Lewy body dementia. *Journal of Neurochemistry, 55*(4), 1454–1456.

Perry, E. K., Marshall, E., Perry, R. H., et al. (1990). Cholinergic and dopamin-ergic activities in senile dementia of Lewy body type. *Alzheimer Disease and Associated Disorders, 4,* 87–95.

Perry, R. H., Jaros, E. B., Irving, D., et al. (1996). What is the neuropathological basis of dementia associated with Lewy bodies? In R. Perry, I. Mckeith, & E. Perry (Eds.), *Dementia with Lewy bodies* (pp. 212–224). New York: Cambridge University Press.

Pisani, A., Bonsi, P., Centonze, D., Bernardi, G., & Calabresi, P. (2001, March). Functional coexpression of excitatory mGluR1 and mGluR5 on striatal cholinergic interneurons. *Clinical Neuropharmacology, 40*(3), 460–463.

Querfurth, H. W., Allam, G. J., Geffroy, M. A., Schiff, H. B., & Kaplan, R. F. (2000). Acetylcholinesterase inhibition in dementia with Lewy bodies: Results of a prospective pilot trial. *Dementia and Geriatric Cognitive Disorders, 11*(6), 314–321.

Rich, S. S., Friedman, J. H., & Ott, B. R. (1995). Risperidone versus clozapine in the treatment of psychosis in six patients with Parkinson's disease and other akine-tic-rigid syndromes. *Journal of Clinical Psychiatry, 56,* 556.

Rinne, J. O. (1989). Dementia in Parkinson's disease is related to neuronal loss in the medial substantia nigra. *Annals of Neurology, 26,* 47–50.

Rojas-Fernandez, C. (2001). Successful use of donepezil for the treatment of dementia with Lewy bodies. *Annals of Pharmacotherapy, 35,* 202–205.

Ruggieri, S., De Pandis, M. F., Bonamartini, A., Vacca, L., & Stocchi, F. (1997, June). Low dose of clozapine in the treatment of dopaminergic psychosis in Parkinson's disease. *Clinical Neuropharmacology, 20*(3), 204–209.

Saitoh, T., & Katzman, R. (1996). Genetic correlations in Lewy body disease. In R. G. Perry, I. G. McKeith, & E. K. Perry (Eds.), *Dementia with Lewy bodies* (pp. 336–349). New York: Cambridge University Press.

Samuel, W., Galasko, D., Masliah, E., & Hansen, L. A. (1996). Neocortical Lewy body counts correlate with dementia in the Lewy body variant of Alzheimer's disease. *Journal of Neuropathology and Experimental Neurology, 55,* 44–52.

Sano, M., Ernesto, C., Thomas, R. G., Klauber, M. R., Schafer, K., Grundman, M., et al. (1997). A controlled trial of selegiline, alpha-tocopherol, or both as treatment for Alzheimer's disease. *New England Journal of Medicine, 336,* 1216–1222.

Santamaria, J. T. E., & Valles, A. (1986). Parkinson's disease with depression: A possible subgroup of idiopathic parkinsonism. *Neurology, 36,* 1130–1133.

Sechi, G., Agnetti, V., Masuri, R., Deiana, G. A., Pugliatti, M., Paulus, K. S. M., et al. (2000). Risperidone, neuroleptic malignant syndrome and probable dementia with Lewy bodies. *Progress in Neuro-Psychopharmacology and Biological Psychiatry, 24,* 1043–1051.

Shea, C., MacKnight, C., & Rockwood, K. (1998). Donepezil for treatment of dementia with Lewy bodies: A case series of nine patients. *International Psychogeriatrics, 10,* 229–238.

Shiozaki, K., Iseki, E., Hino, H., & Kosaka, K. (2001). Distribution of m1 muscarinic acetylcholine receptors in the hippocampus of patients with alzheimer's disease and dementia with Lewy bodies: An immunohistochemical study. *Journal of the Neurological Sciences, 193*(1), 23–28.

Skjerve, A., & Nygaard, H. A. (2000, December). Improvement in sundowning in dementia with Lewy bodies after treatment with donepezil. *International Journal of Geriatric Psychiatry, 15*(12), 1147–1151.

Slaughter, J. R., Slaughter, K. A., Nichols, D., & Martens, M. P. (2001, Spring). Prevalence, clinical manifestations, etiology, and treatment of depression in Parkinson's disease. *Journal of Neuropsychiatry and Clinical Neurosciences, 13*(2), 187–196.

Spillantini, M. G., Crowther, R. A., Jakes, R., Hasegawa, M., & Goedert, M. (1998). Alpha-synuclein in filamentous inclusions of Lewy bodies from Parkinson's disease and dementia with Lewy bodies. *Proceedings of the National Academy of Sciences, USA, 95,* 6469–6473.

Starkstein, S. E. (1992). Cognition and Hemiparkinsonism. In S. J. Huber & J. L. Cummings (Eds.), *Parkinson's disease: Neurobehavioral aspects* (pp. 107–116). New York: Oxford University Press.

Starkstein, S. E., Sabe, L., Petracca, G., Chemerinski, E., Kuzis, G., Merello, M., et al. (1996). Neuropsychological and psychiatric differences between Alzheimer's disease and Parkinson's disease with dementia. *Journal of Neurology, Neurosurgery, and Psychiatry, 61,* 381–387.

Stern, Y., Marder, K., Tang, M. X., & Mayeux R. (1993). Antecedent clinical features associated with dementia in Parkinson's disease. *Neurology, 43,* 1690–1692.

Terry, R. D., Masliah, E., Salmon, D. P., Butters, N., De Teresa, R., Hill, R., et al. (1991). Physical basis of cognitive alterations in Alzheimer's disease: Synapse loss is the major correlate of cognitive impairment. *Annals of Neurology, 30,* 572–580.

Tronnier, V. M., Fogel, W., Kronenbuerger, M., et al. (1997). Is the medial globus pallidus a site for stimulation or lesioning in the treatment of Parkinson's disease? *Stereotactic and Functional Neurosurgery, 69*(1/4, Pt. 2), 62–68.

Troster, A. I., Fields, J. A., Wilkinson, S. B., Pahwa, R., Miyawaki, E., Lyons, K. E., et al. (1997, October). Unilateral pallidal stimulation for Parkinson's disease: Neurobehavioral functioning before and 3 months after electrode implantation. *Neurology, 49*(4), 1078–1083.

Troster, A. I., Wilkinson, S. B., Fields, J. A., et al. (1998, November). Chronic electrical stimulation of the left ventrointermediate (Vim) thalamic nucleus for the treatment of pharmacotherapy-resistant Parkinson's disease: A differential impact on access to semantic and episodic memory? *Brain and Cognition, 38*(2), 125–149.

Turner, R. S. (2002). Idiopathic rapid eye movement sleep behavior disorder is a harbinger of dementia with Lewy bodies. *Journal of Geriatric Psychiatry and Neurology, 15*(4), 195–199.

Walker, M. P., Ayre, G. A., Perry, E. K., Wesnes, K., McKeith, I. G., Tovée, M. J., et al. (2000, November/December). Quantification and characterisation of fluctuating cognition in dementia with Lewy bodies and Alzheimer's disease. *Dementia and Geriatric Cognitive Disorders,* 327–335.

Walker, Z., Grace, J., Overshot, R., Satarasinghe, S., Swan, A., et al. (1999, June). Olanzapine in dementia with Lewy bodies: A clinical study. *International Journal of Geriatric Psychiatry, 14*(6), 459–466.

Whitehouse, P. J. (1986). Clinical and neurochemical consequences of neuronal loss in the Nucleus Basalis of Meynert in Parkinson's disease and Alzheimer's disease. *Advances in Neurology, 45,* 393–397.

Wolters, E. C. (1999). Dopaminomimetic psychosis in Parkinson's disease patients: Diagnosis and treatment. *Neurology, 52*(Suppl. 3), S10–S13.

Zoldan, J., Friedberg, G., Weizman, A., & Melamed, E. (1996). Ondansetron, a 5-HT3 antagonist for visual hallucinations and paranoid delusional disorder associated with chronic L-DOPA therapy in advanced Parkinson's disease. *Advances in Neurology, 69,* 541–544.

CHAPTER 4

Neurologic Aspects of Prion Diseases and Frontotemporal Dementias

Daniel L. Murman

The degenerative dementias discussed in this chapter are the human prion diseases and the frontotemporal dementias (FTDs). These dementias are often termed *atypical* dementias because of their unique clinical and pathological features when compared to more common causes of dementia such as Alzheimer's disease and vascular dementia. Both prion diseases and FTD are rare, but as a group, these atypical degenerative dementias are frequently encountered in clinical practice. Practitioners need to be knowledgeable of the unique issues that arise in the diagnosis and management of patients' suffering from these dementias. There have been significant advances in our understanding of pathophysiology of these diseases in the past 10 years, and there is hope that effective disease-modifying treatments can be developed in the future. This chapter reviews these developments and our current understanding of how to diagnose and treat patients suffering from these unusual dementias.

EPIDEMIOLOGY

Prion Diseases

The most common human prion disease is Creutzfeldt-Jakob Disease (CJD). Death rates for CJD have been estimated from vital statistics in the United States. From 1979 to 1998, 4,751 deaths due to CJD were reported in the United States, resulting in an average annual death rate of 0.97 deaths per million persons (Gibbons, Holman, Belay, & Schonberger, 2000). Mortality data analysis is an efficient way of monitoring CJD incidence because CJD is invariably fatal within a short period (almost always within two years) and readily identifiable clinically. The incidence of CJD has not changed significantly during this period. In addition to CJD, other human prion diseases include kuru, fatal familial insomnia (FFI), and Gerstmann-Sträussler-Scheinker disease (GSS). Kuru was transmitted by ritualistic cannibalism among the Fore people of New Guinea, with no new cases reported since this practice was stopped. FFI and GSS, rare prion diseases caused by mutations in the prion protein gene, are discussed later in this chapter.

CJD has sporadic, familial (i.e., genetic), and transmissible (i.e., infectious) forms. This section focuses on sporadic and transmissible forms. Genetic forms of prion diseases are discussed in the next section. Sporadic CJD accounts for at least 85% of human prion disease cases. A review of 230 consecutive cases of sporadic CJD revealed that the disease affects men and women approximately equally with a majority of cases occurring between the ages of 55 and 75 years (range 19 to 83 years, average age of onset 61.5 years; Brown, Cathala, Castaigne, & Gajdusek, 1986). Cognitive decline was the earliest neurologic symptom in two-thirds of cases; however, one-third presented with noncognitive neurologic symptoms such as gait disturbances or, less commonly, changes in vision. Rapidly progressive dementia, myoclonus, extrapyramidal signs, and periodic EEG activity were seen in a majority of cases during their disease course. The mean duration of illness before death was 7.6 months.

Studies of the epidemiology of CJD have failed to identify consistent risk factors for sporadic CJD other than a family history of CJD or other non-CJD dementias (van Duijn et al., 1998; Wientjens et al., 1996). Wientjens et al. reported an increase in risk of sporadic CJD in those with a family history of CJD, and van Duijn et al. reported an increased risk of sporadic CJD in those with a family history of non-CJD dementias. The odds ratio for having a family history of non-CJD dementia in those with sporadic CJD was 2.26 (95% Confidence Interval [CI] 1.31 to 3.90) in the 1993 to 1995 European Union Collaborative Study. Consumption of meat, contact with blood and blood products, occupational exposure including work in a health profession, and prior surgery involving the central nervous system were not significant risk factors for sporadic CJD. One explanation for the increased risk of sporadic CJD in those with a family history of CJD or other dementias is the possibility that some of these cases represented unrecognized familial CJD because these studies did not include genetic testing. However, a genetic risk factor for CJD, including sporadic and iatrogenic forms, has been identified in other research and may account for some of these findings. Whether this risk factor applies to other causes of dementia is not known.

A naturally occurring polymorphism in the prion protein gene has been identified that can modify the risk of developing a prion disease and alter the phenotype of that prion disease. The polymorphism consists of either carrying a methionine (Met) or valine (Val) at codon 129 of the prion protein gene. Neither amino acid is sufficient to cause disease; however, individuals that are homozygous at this codon (i.e., either Met/Met or Val/Val) are at increased risk of sporadic CJD. Case control studies suggest the 82% to 96% of patients with sporadic CJD are homozygous at codon 129 compared to 49% in the normal populations (Alperovitch et al., 1999; Palmer, Dryden, Hughes, & Collinge, 1991). The impact of this polymorphism on risk of other prion diseases and the influence of this polymorphism on the phenotype of prion diseases are discussed in other sections of this chapter.

Cases of prion diseases transmitted from one person to another and, more recently, from one species to another (i.e., transmissible or *infectious* form of CJD) have been documented. Person-to-person transmission has been termed *iatrogenic CJD*. Cases have been reported after receiving pituitary growth hormone therapy derived from human cadavers, dura mater grafts, corneal transplants, and after neurosurgery and epilepsy monitoring that used contaminated surgical instruments and depth electrodes (Brown et al., 2000). In the 267 cases of iatrogenic CJD that have been documented worldwide, the majority of cases have been caused by receiving cadaveric human growth hormone (139 cases, 52%) and dura mater grafting (114 cases, 43%). The median incubation periods for these types of iatrogenic CJD are between 6 and 12 years. The proportion of recipients acquiring CJD from growth hormone varies from 0.3% to 4.4%, and the proportion acquiring CJD from dura mater grafts range from 0.02% to 0.05%. Cerebellar symptoms at the onset of clinical presentation predominate in these iatrogenic causes of CJD. The incidence of these iatrogenic causes of CJD is expected to dramatically decrease in the future due to awareness of these high-risk sources of contamination, changes in treatment methods (e.g., use of human growth hormone produced by bacteria using recombinant DNA technology instead of use of human cadavers), and new methods to prevent contamination of materials with prions.

In 1996, the United Kingdom's national CJD surveillance unit described a new phenotype of CJD they termed *new variant CJD* (vCJD; Will et al., 1996). Ten cases were described that had a very early age at onset (mean age of 29 years), prominent psychiatric or sensory symptoms as the presenting symptoms, and more prolonged course than sporadic CJD (mean duration 14 months). In addition, these cases had numerous prion protein amyloid plaques surrounded by a halo of intense spongiform degeneration that is not seen in sporadic CJD. These cases occurred at a time when the country was experiencing an epidemic of bovine spongiform encephalopathy (BSE), also called *mad cow disease*. The occurrence of these cases at the height of the BSE epidemic, when more than 175,000 cattle were known to be affected, raised the possibility that these cases of vCJD may have resulted from human consumption of BSE-infected beef. Gel electrophoresis of the prion proteins from BSE and vCJD victims and transmission studies in mice and primates support strongly the possibility that BSE was transmitted to humans and resulted in vCJD. At the end of 2001, 111 cases of vCJD had been diagnosed, with 107 occurring in the United Kingdom, three in France, one in the Republic of Ireland, and one in Italy.

The evidence that vCJD may have resulted from contamination of the human food supply with BSE-infected beef has raised fears of BSE and vCJD worldwide. Intense efforts are underway around the world to identify BSE-infected animals and prevent BSE-infected products from being consumed by humans as food, medications, biological products, or cosmetics. Risk of contracting vCJD from cattle with BSE in the United States is thought to be very low because no known cases of BSE have occurred in the United States and a ban on entry of foreign sources of BSE is in place. In addition, there is a belief that adequate guidelines exist to prevent similar outbreaks of BSE in cattle in the United States and that appropriate guidelines are in place to monitor cattle for BSE and prevent the human consumption of BSE-infected materials if an outbreak were to occur (Tan, Williams, Khan, Champion, & Nielsen, 1999).

As in sporadic CJD, people are at increased risk of infectious CJD if they are homozygous at codon 129 of the prion protein gene. Between 71% and 89% of patients that developed CJD from cadaver-derived human growth factor were homozygous at codon 129, and nearly 100% of patients who developed CJD from dura mater grafts or consumption of BSE-infected materials were homozygous at codon 129 (Alperovitch et al., 1999; Brown et al., 1994;

Collinge, Palmer, & Dryden, 1991). The reproducible association of codon 129 genotype and risk of sporadic and transmissible CJD suggests that the codon 129 genotype must play an important role in the pathophysiology of prion disease in humans.

Frontotemporal Dementia

Our understanding of the epidemiology of frontotemporal dementia (FTD) has been limited by confusion and controversy in what constitutes FTD both clinically and pathologically. The original descriptions of the prototypic FTD, Pick's disease, occurred in a series of papers between 1892 and 1906 by Arnold Pick. Pick described several patients with prominent behavioral disturbances and expressive language impairments that had very circumscribed atrophy of the frontal lobes. Alois Alzheimer described the histopathology in 1911, identifying swollen achromatic cells (Pick cells) and argyrophilic inclusions (Pick bodies). However, by the 1970s neuropathologists had established that some cases resembling Pick's disease clinically did not have Pick cells and Pick bodies at autopsy (Constantinidis, Richard, & Tissot, 1974).

It is now clear that many patients with clinical symptoms resembling Pick's disease lack classic Pick's disease pathology. Multiple names have been used to describe such cases, including frontal lobe degeneration of the non-Alzheimer's type, frontotemporal lobar degeneration, dementia lacking distinct histopathologic features, progressive subcortical gliosis, primary progressive aphasia, and semantic dementia. Consensus groups chose the name *frontotemporal dementia* (FTD) to describe patients that present with early and prominent changes in personality and control of behavior or early and progressive change in expressive language (Lund and Manchester Groups, 1994; Neary et al., 1998). Most of these patients have selective functional and pathologic involvement of the frontal and temporal lobes. Consensus criteria for the pathological classification of FTD cases have been published recently (McKhann et al., 2001). In addition, based on the recent discovery that mutations in the tau protein gene can produce a variety of clinical phenotypes, including cases closely resembling Pick's disease, FTD without classic Pick's disease pathology, and corticobasal degeneration, some have suggested the concept of Pick's complex that would include these three phenotypes and others that share similar pathologic findings (Hutton, 2001; Kertesz, 1997).

Because of the historical lack of consensus on how to diagnose FTD either clinically or pathologically, reliable estimates of the prevalence of FTD are not available. Some autopsy series of patients with dementia have recorded the prevalence of FTD pathology as low as 3% while others have described the autopsy prevalence as high as 10% (Gustafson, Brun, & Passant, 1992; Massoud et al., 1999). One large autopsy series of patients diagnosed with Alzheimer's disease ($n = 650$) demonstrated that 15 (2%) had Pick's disease at autopsy and 25 (4%) had nonspecific degenerations (Mendez, Mastri, Sung, & Frey, 1992). Many of these nonspecific cases may have met current criteria for FTD pathologically given the advances in immunohistochemical and biochemical classification of FTD that were not available at the time of the study. Recently, some have suggested that 12% to 20% of presenile dementia cases (i.e., onset before age 65) are caused by FTD (Morris et al., 2001). Thus, the age of the dementia patients being studied, the influence of unknown referral biases of FTD to or away from these dementia clinics where autopsies are facilitated, and prior lack of consensus on pathologic classification of FTD all influence these autopsy estimates of the prevalence of FTD. With these limitations acknowledged, a recent review article estimates 40,000 prevalent cases of FTD in the United States in year 2000 or 14 cases per 100,000 population (Prusiner, 2001). This estimate is higher than the individual prevalences of Huntington's disease, amyotrophic lateral sclerosis, and the spinocerebellar ataxias at the same time.

The literature provides summaries of typical characteristics of FTD patients based on large clinic samples (Binetti, Locascio, Corkin, Vonsattel, & Growdon, 2000; Gustafson, 1993; Pasquier, Lebert, Lavenu, & Guillaume, 1999). FTD commonly starts before age 65 and typically between the ages of 35 and 75 years. Men and women appear to be affected equally. Clinical onset is insidious, followed by slow progression of changes in behavior and language. Personality changes with disinhibition, lack of insight, and lack of judgment are predominant early in the course. As the disease progresses, progressive loss of speech is seen with stereotyped phrases and late mutism. The mean duration of clinically evident disease is 7.5 years with a range of 3 to 17 years. It has been estimated that between 20% and 40% of patients have a family history of FTD or other dementia affecting their relatives (Rizzu et al., 1999; Stevens et al., 1998). Thus, genetic factors appear to play a strong role in the risk of developing FTD in many cases. In familial cases of FTD, the disease is usually inherited in an autosomal dominant pattern (Chow, Miller, Hayashi, & Geschwind, 1999). Families with autosomal dominant inheritance of FTD account for about 10% of cases of FTD. Other epidemiologic studies investigating potential nongenetic risk factors have not been performed in FTD.

GENETICS

Prion Diseases

Point mutation and insertions in the prion protein gene on chromosome 20 can produce autosomal dominantly inherited prion diseases. Approximately 10% of prion diseases are inherited in this way. At least 23 different mutations have been found to segregate with inherited prion diseases (Collins, Boyd, Fletcher, Byron, et al., 2000; Prusiner & Hsiao, 1994). Three major phenotypes are seen in inherited prion diseases, specifically GSS, CJD, and FFI. GSS is characterized by progressive ataxia and dysarthria followed by the late appearance of decline in cognitive function. The most common presentation of GSS is the onset of disease between ages 30 and 40 years, and the average duration of illness is seven years. Neuropathologically, GSS is characterized by the presence of multicentric prion protein amyloid plaques localized predominantly in the cerebellum. GSS is seen only in an inherited form. Point mutations at codons 102, 105, 117, 198, 212, 217, and an insert mutation (eight octapeptide repeat) segregate with GSS. Patients with mutations at codon 117 have an early dementing or telencephalic form of GSS. The point mutations at codons 198 and 217 are found in patients with GSS who have prion protein amyloid plaques and neocortical neurofibrillary tangles that stain with antibodies to the tau protein.

The familial occurrence of CJD has been recognized since the 1930s, but it wasn't until 1991 that the first mutations were identified that segregated with familial CJD cases. Since that time, 12 mutations have been identified that produce an autosomal dominant inheritance of a CJD phenotype (Collins, Boyd, Fletcher, Byron, et al., 2000; Prusiner & Hsiao, 1994). These mutations include point mutations at codons 178, 180, 200, 208, 210, 232 and 1, 2, 4, 5, 6, and 7 octapeptide repeat insert mutations. In general, patients with familial CJD have a rapidly progressive dementia resulting in death within two years. Widespread spongiform degeneration, neuronal loss, and gliosis are seen in the cortex and basal ganglia, but prion protein amyloid plaques are not seen. The penetrance, age of onset, and clinical phenotype depends in part on the specific prion protein gene mutation. One of the most common familial CJD mutations is a mutation at codon 200. The inheritance of the codon 200 mutation has explained the unusually high incidence of CJD in Israeli Jews of Libyan origin and Slovaks in northern Czechoslovakia.

The same point mutation at codon 178, which substitutes an asparagine for an aspartic acid, can result in two distinct phenotypes. The first phenotype associated with the codon 178 mutation was a form of familial CJD. The clinical course and pathology was similar to sporadic CJD, except that it had a younger mean age of onset (46 versus 62 years), longer average duration (23 versus 6 months), and absence of periodic electroencephalographic activity (Brown et al., 1992). Soon after this association was found, it was discovered that the same codon 178 mutation could cause FFI (Medori et al., 1992). FFI is characterized clinically by untreatable insomnia, dysautonomia, and motor signs and pathologically by selective degeneration of the anterior ventral and mediodordal thalamic nuclei. This paradox of the same point mutation causing two very distinct phenotypes was solved when it was determined that the genotype at the codon 129 polymorphism determines whether patients with codon 178 mutation develop a CJD or FFI phenotype (Goldfarb et al., 1992). If the allele with the codon 178 mutation has a methionine at codon 129, FFI develops; if it has a valine at codon 129, CJD develops. It is unknown how the codon 129 polymorphism determines the specific patterns of pathology seen in the brains of patients with codon 178 mutations.

Frontotemporal Dementia

The finding of linkage of familial FTD to chromosome 17 and subsequent identification of mutations in the tau protein gene in these families has enhanced our understanding of FTD considerably. In 1996, a consensus conference reviewed the clinical, pathological, and genetic characteristics of a group of families with autosomal dominantly inherited neurodegenerative diseases that were genetically linked to a region of chromosome 17 (Foster et al., 1997). Although some of these families were recognized to have familial FTD, many others had been described in the literature with complicated and diverse names, including Pallido-Ponto-Nigral degeneration

(PPND), familial multiple system tauopathy with presenile dementia (FMST), hereditary dysphasic disinhibition dementia (HDDD), and familial progressive subcortical gliosis (FPSG). Common clinical manifestations of these families were changes in behavior—including apathy, disinhibition, repetitive behavior, and loss of personal awareness—and cognition—including early impairment of executive cognitive function with relative preservation of memory, orientation, and visuospatial function. Motor features such as parkinsonism, dystonia, upper and lower motor neuron signs (i.e., spasticity and amyotrophy), and oculomotor disturbances were common during the course of disease. Review of autopsy material from these families demonstrated that frontotemporal atrophy, neuronal or glial tau inclusions, and ballooned cells (Pick cells) were seen in most, but not all, families. The consensus conference recommended these and other families linked to this region be named *frontotemporal dementia and parkinsonism linked to chromosome 17* (FTDP-17).

Beginning in 1998, a series of mutations in the gene encoding the microtubule-associated protein tau on chromosome 17 has been found in families with FTDP-17 and is thought to be the cause of their disease (Clark et al., 1998). These findings have established that tau dysfunction can cause neurodegeneration and have brought together diverse neurodegenerative syndromes with distinct clinical and pathologic features, because of their similar genetic causes. To date, 16 mutations in more than 50 families have been identified. These include nine missense mutations and one deletion mutation in exons 9, 10, 12, and 13 of the tau protein gene and five mutations that are close to the 5' splice site of exon 10. Although there are general similarities in the features of FTDP-17 families with tau mutations as described in the FTDP-17 consensus conference, there is considerable intrafamilial and interfamilial differences in phenotype explained only partially by the unique tau mutations (Bird et al., 1999; Bugiani et al., 1999; van Swieten et al., 1999). In support of the concept of *Pick's Complex* proposed by Dr. Kertesz, tau protein gene mutations have resulted in phenotypes resembling Pick's disease, FTD without classic Pick bodies or Pick cells, corticobasal degeneration, FPSG, HDDD, and PPND (Kertesz, 1997).

Not all familial FTDs are caused by mutations in the tau protein gene. In two large studies of familial FTD, only 40% to 50% of the cases were found to have mutations in the tau protein gene (Morris et al., 2001; Rizzu et al., 1999). Thus, other mutations are likely to cause FTD in these families. One such family is a family with FTD that lacks distinctive pathologic features, including lack of tau or ubiquitin-positive inclusions. This family has been linked to chromosome 3 (Ashworth et al., 1999). The search for the genes and mutations causing this and other forms of FTD continues. Finally, in addition to the disease causing mutations in the tau protein gene described previously for FTDP-17, there is evidence that inheritance of unique "benign" polymorphisms in the tau protein gene is associated with an increased risk of developing progressive supranuclear palsy and corticobasal degeneration, two diseases with tau pathology related to FTDP-17 (Baker et al., 1999; Houlden et al., 2001). Similar associations of these polymorphisms with FTD have not been reported at this time.

PATHOPHYSIOLOGY

Prion Diseases

Despite debate and controversy, it is now generally accepted that prion diseases are caused by infectious proteins that are devoid of nucleic acids. In 1982, Dr. Stanley Prusiner derived the word *prion* from *pro*teinaceous and *inf*ectious to describe the agent and diseases caused by these infectious particles. Since that time, a tremendous amount of data has been collected that support the hypothesis of infectious proteins (Prusiner, 1998). The normal cellular form of the prion protein (PrP) is encoded by the prion protein gene on chromosome 20 and is designated PrP^C. The cellular function of PrP^C is not known. Prion diseases are caused by the development and spread of an abnormal form of PrP term PrP^{Sc}. In sporadic and infectious forms of prion disease, the primary structures (i.e., amino acid composition) of PrP^C and PrP^{Sc} do not differ. However, they do differ in their three-dimensional, folded structures (conformations). PrP^C is rich in α-helixes and has little ß-sheet conformation. In contrast, PrP^{Sc} has a greater amount of ß-sheet formation. This change in conformation in PrP is thought to be the fundamental event in the development of prion disease (Prusiner, 2001).

The differences in PrP^C and PrP^{Sc} confirmational structures result in unique biochemical properties, including the resistance of PrP^{Sc} to protease degradation (Prusiner, 1998). Proteolysis of PrP^{Sc} produces a protease-resistant molecule of approximately 131 amino acids designated PrP 27-30. Under similar conditions, PrP^C is completely hydrolyzed. PrP 27-30 can polymerize and form amyloid rods. These polymerized, prion amyloid rods make up PrP amyloid plaques in the brains of some patients with prion diseases, and the presence of PrP^{Sc} can be identified by limited proteolysis and immunohistochemical identification of PrP 27-30.

PrP^{Sc} replicates by causing the conversion of normal PrP^C into new PrP^{Sc} particles. PrP^C and PrP^{Sc} are hypothesized to come in physical contact with each other during this process and are facilitated by one or more molecular chaperones (e.g., protein X; Cohen, 1999). The rate of conversion of the normal conformation to the abnormal conformation is influenced by the quality of the physical association between the PrP^C and PrP^{Sc} molecules. The unique conformational properties of the PrP^{Sc} particle are reproduced in this conversion process. PrP^{Sc} can arise spontaneously, as in sporadic CJD, can be introduced into the organism, as in infectious CJD, or can result from destabilization of the normal secondary structure of PrP, as in the genetic form of CJD. If PrP^{Sc} is present and if the replication process is efficient, sufficient PrP^{Sc} accumulates and causes disease.

How PrP^{Sc} particles move within the nervous system, why there is selective vulnerability of neuronal populations in prion diseases resulting in phenotypic diversity, and how prions cause neuronal degeneration are not completely understood. It is suspected that prions are transported along axons in a pattern consistent with retrograde transport of other cellular proteins. The conformation structure and glycosylation of the PrP^{Sc} particle are felt to be important in determining the pattern and type of neuropathological changes in the brain and resulting clinical phenotype. For example, the conformation structure differences in PrP^{Sc} that result from mutations in the prion protein gene can result in phenotypes as different as FFI, GSS, and CJD. Similarly, studies show that two different types of PrP^{Sc} that differ in their molecular mass and glycosylation are associated with unique phenotypes in sporadic CJD (Parchi et al., 1996). These phenotypes are further modified by the codon 129 polymorphism, resulting in six distinct clinicopathological variants of sporadic CJD (Parchi et al., 1999). Neurodegenerative mechanisms such as apoptosis, excitotoxicity, and oxidative stress have all been implicated as potential mechanisms of neuronal loss caused by the accumulation of PrP^{Sc} (Muller, Laplanche, Ushijima, & Schroder, 2000).

Frontotemporal Dementia

The finding of tau protein gene mutations in FTDP-17 families has launched the search for the pathophysiologic mechanisms that lead to the unique and selective neurodegeneration seen in FTDP-17 patients. It is unclear if all FTD patients have disruptions in tau function, but it is felt that a better understanding of the mechanisms of neurodegeneration in FTDP-17 will have wider application to understanding and treating FTD and other neurodegenerative diseases. Thus, basic findings on the relationship between mutations in the tau protein gene and tau structure and function are reviewed next.

The primary function of the tau protein in the central nervous system is to assist in the assembly and organization of microtubules in neurons. Microtubules form the cytoskeleton of neurons and are crucial for axonal transport. Tau is a soluble protein with six major isoforms. Alternate splicing of exon 10 gives rise to isoforms with three or four microtubule-binding domains (3R and 4R tau; Hutton, 2001). Neurodegenerative diseases with tau inclusions differ in the composition of these tau isoforms. For example, Alzheimer's disease neurofibrillary tangles contain the normal ratio of both 3R and 4R isoforms, Pick's disease inclusions contain predominantly 3R tau, while progressive supranuclear palsy and corticobasal degeneration inclusions contain only 4R tau (Buee & Delacourte, 1999). Mutations in the tau protein gene causing FTDP-17 demonstrate that some mutations result in inclusions with the normal ratio of 3R and 4R tau as seen in Alzheimer's disease, while other mutations result in increased 4R isoforms as seen with progressive supranuclear palsy (PSP) and corticobasal degeneration (CBD).

In a recent review article, Dr. Hutton summarizes potential pathogenic mechanisms produced by the known tau mutations (Hutton, 2001). The majority of missense mutations disrupt normal tau-microtubule interactions, which results in higher levels of unbound tau in neurons and disrupts the normal cytoskeletal structure. Other mutations alter tau self-interaction and increase the likelihood of polymerization into tau filaments. Some mutations have both pathogenic mechanisms present, resulting in reduced microtubule binding by tau and a corresponding increase in unbound tau that has greater tendency to polymerize into insoluble filaments. Finally, mutations that alter the alternative splicing of tau exon 10 result in overproduction of the 4R tau isoforms. It is unclear how the increase in 4R tau leads to neurodegeneration, but one hypothesis is that 4R binding sites on microtubules become saturated with 4R tau. This could then result in elevated levels of unbound 4R tau available for incorporation into insoluble tau filaments. The pathogenic mechanism that occurs downstream of these alterations in tau biology and the development of insoluble tau filaments is unknown but likely shares basic cellular pathogenic mechanisms as other neurodegenerative diseases caused by the abnormal accumulation of insoluble proteins, including Alzheimer's disease, Parkinson's disease, and prion diseases (Prusiner, 2001).

DIAGNOSIS

Prion Diseases

The dramatic and atypical features of human prion diseases can be recognized readily in classic presentations of the common phenotypes. However, there is a wide range of clinical presentations and prion phenotypes that can make antemortem diagnosis very difficult in some patients. Clinical features that suggest prion disease, ancillary tests that can be of value in supporting a diagnosis of a prion dementia, and pathologic findings that confirm a diagnosis of a prion disease are discussed next.

In sporadic, infectious, and familial CJD, the clinical feature that is most characteristic of a diagnosis of a prion dementia is the rapidly progressive nature of the disorder. Within three to eight months of a patient's first symptoms, most patients develop severe dementia that results in their death in less than 1.5 years (Parchi et al., 1999). In a majority of patients, the initial symptoms are some type of cognitive impairment (e.g., memory loss, confusion, disorientation, intellectual decline), but, commonly, initial symptoms can be changes in vision, balance and gait, movement disorders, or psychiatric symptoms. At some point during the disease course, severe dementia, gait impairment or ataxia, hyperkinetic movement disorders including myoclonus, and behavioral symptoms are seen in most cases. Startle myoclonus is a classic clinical feature often seen in sporadic CJD and is very rare in other common causes of dementia. The average age of onset in sporadic CJD is approximately 61 (onset range 40 to 90 years), but familial CJD, some iatrogenic CJD, and vCJD cases present at a younger age. New variant CJD (vCJD) has been limited to cases in Europe so far, but may spread to other countries. These cases have had a very early age of onset (mean age of onset is 29 years) and frequently have presented with psychiatric symptoms and early sensory symptoms that were often painful (Zeidler et al., 1997).

Few conditions mimic the classic "cortical" presentation of CJD; however, the possibility of viral encephalitis, paraneoplastic limbic encephalitis, and Hashimoto's encephalitis needs to be considered in the right clinical situation because each of these conditions is potentially treatable (Seipelt et al., 1999). While these conditions can resemble CJD clinically, they can be diagnosed by looking for antibodies to thyroglobulin, thyroid peroxidase, or paraneoplastic antigens (e.g., antineuronal nuclear antibodies types 1 and 2) and by cerebral spinal fluid (CSF) analysis. Viral encephalitis can be distinguished from CJD by an inflammatory pleocytosis and the detection of viral nucleic acid by polymerase chain reaction in the CSF. Hashimoto's encephalitis patients have antibodies against thyroglobulin and thyroid peroxidase in addition to normal CSF, including 14-3-3 protein analysis. Patients with paraneoplastic limbic encephalitis can be diagnosed by identifying paraneoplastic antibodies.

A familial prion disease is suggested by a family history consistent with autosomal dominant inheritance of an atypical dementia and/or ataxia. However, some patients with familial prion diseases do not have an informative family history (e.g., adopted patient without knowledge of biologic family). The non-CJD presentations of familial prion disease (e.g., GSS and FFI) are difficult to diagnose without prior tissue confirmation of other family members. When patients present with slowly progressive ataxia without dementia (e.g., GSS), the variety of diseases that cause progressive cerebellar dysfunction need to be considered in the differential diagnosis, including the spinocerebellar atrophies. FFI or thalamic forms of CJD are suspected if intractable insomnia and dysautonomia develop, especially if there is a family history of similar cases. If a familial form of CJD is suspected, prion protein gene analysis is available in research laboratories to look for pathogenic mutations.

Several minimally invasive ancillary tests can provide supportive evidence of prion disease, including electroencephalograms (EEG), spinal fluid analysis for the 14-3-3 protein, and magnetic resonance imaging (MRI) imaging. The classic EEG pattern seen in CJD is periodic sharp wave complexes (PSWCs). This EEG pattern is present after approximately 12 weeks of symptoms in those who develop the EEG pattern. In late stages of the disease, the pattern may be lost. In sporadic CJD, PSWCs are seen in 60% to 80% of cases (Brown et al., 1986; Zerr et al., 2000). However, in many iatrogenic CJD, vCJD, and genetic CJD cases, PSWCs are absent. Detection of the 14-3-3 proteins in CSF has been described as a useful test to support a diagnosis of a prion disease. In studies of patients with suspected CJD, the test was positive in 93% of probable cases and 95% of definite cases (Zerr et al., 1998). The 14-3-3 proteins are a group of proteins involved in the regulation of protein phosphorylation and are found in the CSF of patients with conditions where significant brain injury is occurring. False positive results have been reported in herpes simplex encephalitis or other viral causes of encephalitis, acute stroke, subarachnoid hemorrhage, and meningeal carcinomatosis due to small cell lung cancer. As with EEG finding, vCJD and genetic forms of prion disease may be less likely to have 14-3-3 proteins in CSF. Finally, MRI imaging of the brain can show two characteristic abnormalities in the brains of patients with prion diseases (Collins, Boyd, Fletcher, Gonzales, et al., 2000). One is symmetric increased signal in the basal ganglia on T-2 and proton-density weighted images. These findings can be asymmetric in some patients and involve other structures including the thalamus, white matter, or cortex. The second MRI finding is high signal changes on diffusion-weighted imaging that may involve deep gray matter structures such as the thalamus and basal ganglia or the cortex, with cortical signal changes often having an asymmetric pattern.

Diagnostic criteria for making a clinical diagnosis of sporadic CJD have been proposed using clinical features and the results of the noninvasive ancillary tests. These criteria are shown in Table 4.1. MRI findings are not included in the diagnostic criteria at this time because the specificity and sensitivity of these imaging abnormalities are not well understood. The clinical phenotype expected in sporadic CJD and the likelihood of noninvasive ancillary tests being positive can be predicted by knowing patients' geno type at codon 129 of the prion protein gene and knowing whether they have type 1 or type 2 PrP^{Sc} as determined by the size and glycosylation of the

Table 4.1 Diagnostic Criteria for Sporadic CJD

Definite CJD	Neuropathological confirmation at postmortem or by brain biopsy (ideally by confirming the presence of PrP^{Sc} in the brain immunochemically).
Probable CJD	1. Progressive dementia of less than 2 years duration with at least two of these four features: myoclonus, visual or cerebellar signs, pyramidal or extrapyramidal signs, or akinetic mutism.
	2. Typical periodic sharp wave complexes (PSWCs) on EEG *or* 14-3-3 proteins detectable in the CSF.
Possible CJD	Clinical features as those for probable CJD, but no PSWCs and CSF negative for 14-3-3 proteins.

From "Recent Advances in the Pre-Mortem Diagnosis of Creutzfeldt-Jakob Disease," by S. Collins et al., 2000, *Journal of Clinical Neurosciences, 7,* pp. 195–202.

protease-resistant fragment of PrP^{Sc} (Parchi et al., 1999; Zerr et al., 2000). Six subtypes are found using this classification. This type of subtyping is not available for most clinicians; however, these results provide insights into which diagnostic tests may be of value in which clinical phenotype. Although data is limited on some of the rare subtypes, at least one of the three noninvasive tests (EEG, 14-3-3 protein, MRI) is expected to support a diagnosis of sporadic CJD in the majority of cases from all subtypes. In general, the presence of type 2 PrP^{Sc} makes it unlikely to have PSWCs on EEG (4% versus 78%), less likely to have 14-3-3 proteins in the CSF (75% versus 96%), but similarly likely to have MRI abnormalities (71% versus 68%).

The definitive diagnosis of a prion protein disease requires a tissue diagnosis. The classic histopathologic autopsy findings of prion diseases are spongiform degeneration, gliosis, and neuronal loss. In some prion diseases, prion protein amyloid plaques are seen, especially in the cerebellum. Prion diseases with prion protein amyloid plaques include Kuru, GSS, vCJD, and sporadic CJD patients that are heterozygous at codon 129 of the prion protein gene (i.e., Met/Val) and have type 2 PrP^{Sc}. Most cases of sporadic CJD have diffused pathologic changes in the cortex and subcortical structures such as the basal ganglia and cerebellum. However, the pathology of prion disease can be very focal, including cases with FFI and thalamic variants of sporadic CJD that preferentially and, at times, exclusively involve thalamic nuclei, GSS, and ataxic variants of sporadic CJD with preferential involvement of the cerebellum.

The pathologic diagnosis of a prion disease is aided and confirmed by the identification of the protease-resistant portion of PrP^{Sc} (i.e., PrP 27-30) by immunohistochemical techniques or Western blot. In the past, brain biopsies were performed more frequently in patients with suspected prion disease. However, brain biopsies in patients with suspected prion diseases are uncommon presently because of lack of effective treatments for prion diseases, the difficulty in decontaminating surgical equipment, and the availability of helpful, minimally invasive ancillary tests. It has been found that patients with vCJD have detectable PrP 27-30 in lymphoid tissue, including the tonsils, spleen, and lymph nodes even at early stages of their disease (Collins, Boyd, Fletcher, Gonzales, et al., 2000). Prospective studies of tonsil biopsies in vCJD have found PrP 27-30 in all technically adequate specimens of patients that later were confirmed to have vCJD. Interestingly, similar findings of PrP 27-30 in lymphoid tissue have not been found in any other prion diseases, including sporadic, iatrogenic, and genetic forms of CJD. Thus, tonsil biopsies may play a role in the early and definitive diagnosis of vCJD, but not other forms of prion diseases. Such timely and precise diagnostic procedures may become more important if effective, but potentially toxic, treatments for prion diseases become available.

Frontotemporal Dementia

FTD should be considered in patients who present with prominent changes in personality and behavior or isolated impairments of language early in the course of their dementia. Patients with FTD are much more likely to have a younger age of onset of symptoms and frequently have a family history of relatives that have suffered from a similar type of dementia. In the evaluation of FTD, it is important to perform a detailed assessment of noncognitive behavioral symptoms in addition to assessment of cognitive function to come to an accurate diagnosis. Although there is overlap between the behavioral and cognitive features of FTD and other causes of dementia, specific behavioral and neuropsychological features help in differentiating FTD from other causes. Evidence of frontal and temporal lobe atrophy on structural imaging (i.e., computed tomography [CT] or MRI) and evidence of decreased perfusion or metabolism in these brain regions on functional imaging (i.e., single photon emission computed tomography [SPECT] or positron emission tomography [PET]) are supportive of a diagnosis of FTD. As in other degenerative dementia, a definitive diagnosis of FTD requires pathological confirmation. The pathology underlying FTD is diverse and results in at least five pathological subtypes. In this section, each of these aspects of the diagnosis of FTD is reviewed in more detail.

Three common clinical presentations of FTD are observed. In a consensus statement on clinical diagnostic criteria for FTD, these three clinical presentations have been labeled as *frontotemporal dementia* (also designated as frontal variant of FTD by others), *semantic dementia* (also called the temporal variant of FTD by others), and *progressive nonfluent aphasia* (also termed primary progressive aphasia by others). This consensus classification outlines clinical features that are required for a clinical diagnosis, that are supportive of a diagnosis, that exclude a diagnosis of FTD (Neary et al., 1998), and are an extension of the original consensus criteria for the diagnosis of FTD that are referred to as the *Lund-Manchester research criteria* (Lund and Manchester Groups, 1994). Recent modifications of these consensus criteria have made them more general, but they are similar to previous criteria (McKhann et al., 2001). These criteria, shown in Table 4.2, are supplemented by core features of the three common presentations of FTD outlined by Neary et al. All presentations of FTD have an insidious onset and gradual progression. Onset is frequently before age 65, and a family history of FTD is common. Features of motor neuron disease or parkinsonism can been seen during the course of FTD, but hyperkinetic movement disorders (e.g., myoclonus, chorea) are not seen. Clinical features that would suggest an alternative cause of dementia are used to exclude FTD, including evidence of vascular dementia, HIV-associated dementia, multiple sclerosis, chronic alcoholism, herpes simplex encephalitis, or dementia due to closed head injury.

The most common presentation of FTD is the frontal variant of FTD, characterized by prominent noncognitive behavioral symptoms (Hodges, 2001; Neary et al., 1998). Patients with the frontal variant of FTD present with an early decline in social interpersonal conduct. This is manifested as a decline in manners and social graces, including disinhibited comments and actions or antisocial behavior such as criminal acts (e.g., shoplifting). There is also a change in the regulation of personal conduct that often produces passivity or inertia but can produce overactivity and aggression. These changes in social and personal conduct are associated with a loss of insight and emotional blunting with evidence of emotional shallowness and

Table 4.2   Clinical Criteria for Diagnosing Frontotemporal Dementia

1. The development of behavioral or cognitive deficits manifested by either:
   a. Early and progressive change in personality, characterized by difficulty in modulating behavior, often resulting in inappropriate responses or activities.
   b. Early and progressive change in language, characterized by problems with expression of language or severe naming difficulties, and problems with word meaning.
2. The deficits in 1a and 1b cause significant impairment in social and occupational functioning and represent a decline from a previous level of functioning.
3. The course is characterized by gradual onset and continuing decline in function.
4. The deficits in 1a and 1b are not due to other nervous system conditions, do not occur exclusively during delirium, and are not better accounted for by a psychiatric diagnosis.

From "Clinical and Pathological Diagnosis of Frontotemporal Dementia," Report of a Work Group on Frontotemporal Dementia and Pick's Disease, by G. M. McKhan et al., 2001, *Archives of Neurology, 58,* pp. 1803–1809.

lack of empathy for others. Supportive behavioral features include a decline in personal hygiene, mental inflexibility, distractibility, hyperorality, stereotyped behavior, and stimulus-bound utilization behavior. Cognitively, FTD patients have impairments of executive cognitive function including difficulties with planning, sequencing, and set shifting. However, early in the disease course, orientation, memory, and visual-spatial skills are preserved. Typically, these behavioral and cognitive symptoms are associated with decreased speech output, characterized by FTD patients not initiating conversation as often; when they do respond to questions, they often reply only in short phrases or stereotyped utterances. Rarely, the opposite can occur and patients may monopolize conversations. Decreased speech output progresses to mutism over time in most patients. Incontinence and primitive reflexes, such as grasp, snout, and sucking reflexes, are common.

Focal and asymmetric presentations of FTD are observed, resulting in progressive nonfluent aphasia and semantic dementia (Hodges, 2001; Neary et al., 1998). In primary nonfluent aphasia, patients present with hesitant, effortful speech output that is associated with agrammatism, phonemic paraphasias, and/or anomia. Other common features include stuttering, impaired repetition, and alexia. The meaning of words is preserved, as are memory and visual-spatial abilities. The language disorder is the most prominent feature of primary nonfluent aphasia and should not be associated with significant behavioral symptoms early in the course of the dementia. However, the behavioral changes observed in the frontal variant of FTD can be seen later in the disease course. In semantic dementia, speech production is effortless and without hesitancies, but the content of the words conveys little precise information. This is due to reduced use of precise terms for naming objects and increased use of general terms (e.g., using the term *animal* instead of *dog* or using a term such as *that thing*). Semantic dementia patients have a selective and progressive loss of semantic memory, described as the component of long-term memory that contains the permanent representation of our knowledge about things in the world and their interrelationships (Hodges et al., 1999). This loss of semantic memory results in impairment of naming and word comprehension as tested by word definition tests and object-pointing tests. Orientation, memory, and visual-spatial abilities are relatively spared as in primary nonfluent aphasia. Behavioral changes similar to those seen in the frontal variant of FTD may appear late in the disease course as can parkinsonism. Patients with semantic dementia that involves the right temporal lobe display prosopagnosia (i.e., inability to recognize and name familiar faces).

Neuropsychological testing can aid in the diagnosis of FTD. On neuropsychological testing, patients with FTD demonstrate impairments on frontal lobe tests in the absence of severe amnesia or visuospatial impairments (Neary et al., 1998). Specific language and semantic impairments can be measured with neuropsychological testing in progressive nonfluent aphasia and semantic dementia (Hodges, 2001; Hodges et al., 1999). Early in the disease course, most patients with FTD perform poorly on frontal lobe tests such as the Wisconsin Card Sort, Stroop Test, verbal fluency tests, and the Trail Making tests. At the same time, orientation and memory test performance are relatively intact and visuospatial abilities are normal. However, in some patients, behavioral symptoms may be severe at a time when objective cognitive deficits are minimal. In addition, the typical pattern of cognitive deficits seen in FTD can overlap with other more common causes of dementia, including vascular dementia and focal presentations of Alzheimer's disease (Cherrier et al., 1997; JAGS, 1997). Bedside screening tests of cognition such as the Mini-Mental State Examination are unreliable for the detection and monitoring of FTD because they underestimate the degree of cognitive impairment. Table 4.3 lists ancillary tests used in the diagnosis of prion disease and frontotemporal dementia.

Standardized evaluations of noncognitive behavioral symptoms and use of the proposed clinical criteria for FTD are important aids in the clinical diagnosis of FTD. For example, the Neuropsychiatric Inventory has been used to systematically quantify behavioral abnormalities in FTD. When compared to AD, FTD patients exhibited more severe apathy, disinhibition, euphoria, and aberrant motor behavior (Levy, Miller, Cummings, Fairbanks, & Craig, 1996). Similarly, the Frontal Behavioral Inventory has been purposed as an instrument useful in documenting and quantifying behavioral changes characteristic of FTD (Kertesz, Nadkarni, Davidson, & Thomas, 2000). Perseveration, indifference, inattention, inappropriateness, and loss of insight were rated significantly higher in FTD patients than in non-FTD patients. In a study of the Lund-Manchester research criteria for FTD, the behavioral and clinical features that most clearly differentiated FTD from AD were loss of personal awareness, hyperorality, perseverative behavior, and progressive reduction of speech (Miller et al., 1997). Use of the National Institute of Neurological and Communicative Disorders and Stroke-AD and

Table 4.3   Useful Ancillary Tests in Prion Disease and Frontotemporal Dementia

Disease	Ancillary Test	Findings
Prion diseases	Prion protein gene analysis.	Mutations in familial CJD, GSS, and FFI.
		Increased risk if homozygous at codon 129.
	EEG.	Periodic sharp wave complexes.
	14-3-3 proteins in CSF.	Elevated levels in CSF.
	MRI.	Symmetric increased signal in the basal ganglia on T-2 images and increased signal in cortical and subcortical structures on diffusion-weighted images.
	Tonsil biopsy.	PrP^{Sc} detected (in vCJD patients only).
Frontotemporal dementia	Neuropsychological tests.	Impairment on frontal-lobe tests with relative sparing of memory, orientation, and visuospatial skills.
	Behavioral inventories.	Presence of apathy, disinhibition, euphoria, perseveration, inappropriateness, and loss of insight.
	Structural brain imaging.	Selective frontal and temporal lobe atrophy.
	Functional brain imaging.	Decreased blood flow or metabolism in frontal and/or temporal lobes.

Related Disorders Association (NINCDS-ADRDA) criteria for AD in the diagnosis of dementia fails to accurately distinguish AD from FTD, resulting in many patients with FTD being diagnosed with AD (Varma et al., 1999). A lack of awareness of the main cognitive and behavioral symptoms of Pick's disease has been found to be the major cause of underrecognition of Pick's disease clinically and would apply to FTD in general (Litvan et al., 1997). Thus, use of standardized evaluations of noncognitive behavioral symptoms and use of consensus clinical criteria for FTD can improve significantly the sensitivity and specificity of the clinical diagnosis of FTD.

Structural and functional abnormalities can be detected in the frontal and temporal lobes of patients with FTD using brain imaging. Functional abnormalities precede structural changes in most patients with FTD, and PET has greater sensitivity in detecting subtle changes than does SPECT imaging. However, both SPECT and PET can assist in the diagnosis of FTD by demonstrating objective functional impairment in the frontal and temporal lobes, evaluating the degree of asymmetry of abnormalities, and ruling out significant posterior temporal and parietal lobe involvement. Initially, structural changes in FTD may be subtle and overlooked, especially in the frontal variant of FTD. However, as FTD progresses, frontal and temporal lobe atrophy becomes apparent. Voxel-based morphometry of MRI images in FTD patients has been compared to control subjects and reveals significant atrophy in FTD patients in the ventromedial frontal cortex, posterior orbital frontal cortex, the insula, and anterior cingulate cortex. In patients with the frontal variant of FTD, additional areas of atrophy were seen in the dorsolateral frontal cortex and premotor cortex, while patients with the temporal variant of FTD (i.e., semantic dementia) showed additional involvement of the anterior temporal cortex and amygdala/anterior hippocampal region (Rosen et al., 2002).

Pathologic evaluation of the brain is required to confirm the diagnosis of FTD. Recent criteria have been proposed to aid in classification of the pathology of the FTDs and describe five pathological subtypes (McKhann et al., 2001). Clinical subtypes of FTD do not correlate with specific pathological subtypes. At autopsy, gross pathology reveals selective atrophy of the frontal and temporal lobes in patients with FTD. Light microscopic findings of FTD include microvacuolation and astrocytic gliosis of the involved cortices, especially superficial cortical layers, as well as Pick cells and Pick bodies in some patients. The use of immunohistochemical techniques with antibodies against tau, ubiquitin, and crystalline has improved the categorization of FTD pathology (Cooper, Jackson, Lennox, Lowe, & Mann, 1995). In addition, biochemical analysis of insoluble tau inclusions (e.g., three or four microtubule-binding domains) is used to further categorize FTD pathology.

TREATMENT

Prion Diseases

There are no treatments available that have been shown to alter the course of prion diseases in humans. Currently, medical treatment is directed at controlling the neurologic and psychiatric symptoms, providing palliative care for patients and support for their families. For example, myoclonus and seizures can be controlled with anticonvulsant medications such as valproic acid and benzodiazepines. Severe hyperkinetic movement disorders such as chorea or dyskinesias and psychotic behavioral symptoms can be controlled with neuroleptic medications. Other psychiatric symptoms can be improved with medications that are used for behavioral symptoms in other patients with dementia. Quality nursing care is very important and can limit pain and the complications of being bedridden. Finally, and most importantly, patients and their families need a tremendous amount of emotional and social support to cope with these devastating diseases.

One goal of medical management is to prevent the infectious spread of prion diseases. Prions can be transmitted from one organism to another if nervous system tissue containing PrP^{Sc} from an infected patient is transferred to another patient. Thus, the equipment used in neurosurgery, corneal transplants, and depth electrodes must be decontaminated by methods that inactivate prions if they have come in contact with a patient with a prion disease. Procedures for decontaminating operating and autopsy rooms have been developed and are unique for prions (Committee on Health Care Issues, American Neurological Association, 1986; Steelman, 1999) Universal precautions should be used when handling cerebrospinal fluid, optic tissue, blood, and urine. Cerebrospinal fluid and optic tissue have the highest titers of infectious prions, but small amounts of infectious prions have been found in other tissues, blood, and urine (Committee on Health Care Issues, American Neurological Association, 1986). Secretory and excretory products such as saliva, sweat, and stool have not been found to contain infectious prions. Procedures for handling and deactivating tissue from patients with prion disease have been developed for pathologists (Committee on Health Care Issues, American Neurological Association, 1986). Patients with known prion disease are prevented from donating blood or other tissue although there have been no documented cases of the spread of prion disease by blood transfusions. Brown et al. suggests that transmission of prion diseases via blood transfusion is unlikely because of the absence of significant infectivity until symptomatic disease, a reduction of infectivity during plasma processing, and a need for the presence of five to seven times more infectious prions to transmit disease by the intravenous route as compared to the intracerebral route (Brown et al., 1999).

In the past several years, tremendous advances have been made in developing disease-altering therapies for prion diseases (Korth, May,

Cohen, & Prusiner, 2001; Perrier et al., 2000; Priola, Raines, & Caughey, 2000; Supattapone, Nguyen, Cohen, Prusiner, & Scott, 1999). This research suggests PrP^{Sc} production can be blocked at multiple steps, including stabilizing the PrP^{C} molecule to prevent the conformational change to PrP^{Sc}, destabilizing PrP^{Sc} so that it becomes protease sensitive, preventing PrP^{Sc} from serving as a template for replication, and blocking the interaction of protein X with PrP^{C} in the process of forming a complex with PrP^{Sc} (Perrier et al., 2000). Using scrapie-infected neuroblastoma cells to screen for inhibition of formation of PrP^{Sc} and clearance of preexisting PrP^{Sc}, researchers have found two effective antiprion compounds that have been used in humans for many years (Korth et al., 2001). The two compounds—chlorpromazine, an antipsychotic agent, and quinacrine, an antimalarial drug—were effective in inhibiting the accumulation of PrP^{Sc}. The mechanism by which these and related compounds are effective as antiprion agents is unclear. However, because both agents have been used safely in humans for more than 50 years, development of human trials is underway. Dosage required to produce antiprion effects and whether one agent will be more effective or better tolerated at therapeutic doses in humans is unknown. However, identification of these agents and development of the in vitro methods used to screen for antiprion agents are tremendous breakthroughs in the search for safe and effective treatments for the prion diseases.

Frontotemporal Dementia

Disease-modifying treatments are not available for FTD. However, development of transgenic mouse models of tauopathies is expected to quickly increase the speed of discovery of effective treatments for FTD (Lee & Trojanowski, 2001). In addition to the lack of disease-modifying treatments for FTD, controlled clinical trials of symptomatic treatments for the cognitive and behavioral manifestations of FTD have not occurred. This is due in part to the rarity of the disorder, which results in a need for a very large number of study sites to recruit enough patients for controlled clinical trials. Similarly, underrecognition of FTD and lack of consensus on how to diagnose FTD have hindered studies of symptomatic therapeutics for patients with FTD.

There is neurochemical evidence of a serotonergic deficit in FTD in addition to possible cholinergic and dopaminergic deficits, although the last two neurotransmitter deficits are controversial (Francis et al., 1993; Litvan, 2001; Sparks & Markesbery, 1991). An open label trial of serotonin selective reuptake inhibitors (SSRIs; fluoxetine, sertraline, paroxetine) in patients with FTD has demonstrated improvement of behavioral symptoms in some patients (Swartz, Miller, Lesser, & Darby, 1997). Specifically, SSRI treatment improved disinhibition, depression, carbohydrate craving, and compulsions in at least half of the subjects tested. Trials of cholinesterase inhibitors in FTD have not been reported. Although not tested specifically in FTD, some have speculated that dopamine agonists such as bromocriptine may improve executive cognitive function in FTD as has been shown in patients with closed head injuries (McDowell, Whyte, & D'Esposito, 1998). Treatment of psychosis, agitation, sexually inappropriate behavior, and aggression has not been studied in FTD specifically, but medications used in patients with these behaviors caused by other forms of dementia are recommended. As in all forms of dementia, providing families and caregivers information, emotional support, and respite are invaluable in dementia patient care.

NEW DIRECTIONS

Tremendous advances have been made in our understanding of prion diseases and FTDs. There is hope that with this growing understanding of the pathophysiology of these diseases, effective disease-altering treatments will be developed. If such treatments are developed, it will become vital to accurately diagnose patients with prion diseases and FTD, so that disease-specific treatments can be initiated. The information reviewed in this chapter should help practicing clinicians recognize and diagnose prion diseases and FTDs. Being able to better diagnose these atypical degenerative dementias is invaluable for providing patients and their families accurate information about prognosis, risk, and treatment options. In addition, our improved understanding of prion diseases and FTDs will serve as a foundation for future scientific advances in each of the areas discussed in this chapter.

REFERENCES

Alperovitch, A., Zerr, I., Pocchiari, M., Mitrova, E., de Pedro Cuesta, J., Hegyi, I., et al. (1999). Codon 129 prion protein genotype and sporadic Creutzfeldt-Jakob disease. *Lancet, 353*(9165), 1673–1674.

Ashworth, A., Lloyd, S., Brown, J., Gydesen, S., Sorensen, S. A., Brun, A., et al. (1999). Molecular genetic characterisation of frontotemporal dementia on chromosome 3. *Dementia and Geriatric Cognitive Disorders, 10,* 193–201.

Baker, M., Litvan, I., Houlden, H., Adamson, J., Dickson, D., Perez Tur, J., et al. (1999). Association of an extended haplotype in the tau gene with progressive supranuclear palsy. *Human Molecular Genetics, 8*(4), 711–715.

Binetti, G., Locascio, J. J., Corkin, S., Vonsattel, J. P., & Growdon, J. H. (2000). Differences between Pick disease and Alzheimer disease in clinical appearance and rate of cognitive decline. *Archives of Neurology, 57*(2), 225–232.

Bird, T. D., Nochlin, D., Poorkaj, P., Cherrier, M., Kaye, J., Payami, H., et al. (1999). A clinical pathological comparison of three families with frontotemporal dementia and identical mutations in the tau gene (P301L). *Brain, 122* (Pt. 4), 741–756.

Brown, P., Cathala, F., Castaigne, P., & Gajdusek, D. C. (1986). Creutzfeldt-Jakob disease: Clinical analysis of a consecutive series of 230 neuropathologically verified cases. *Annals of Neurology, 20*(5), 597–602.

Brown, P., Cervenakova, L., Goldfarb, L. G., McCombie, W. R., Rubenstein, R., Will, R. G., et al. (1994). Iatrogenic Creutzfeldt-Jakob disease: An example of the interplay between ancient genes and modern medicine. *Neurology, 44*(2), 291–293.

Brown, P., Cervenakova, L., McShane, L. M., Barber, P., Rubenstein, R., & Drohan, W. N. (1999). Further studies of blood infectivity in an experimental model of transmissible spongiform encephalopathy, with an explanation of why blood components do not transmit Creutzfeldt-Jakob disease in humans. *Transfusion, 39*(11/12), 1169–1178.

Brown, P., Goldfarb, L. G., Kovanen, J., Haltia, M., Cathala, F., Sulima, M., et al. (1992). Phenotypic characteristics of familial Creutzfeldt-Jakob disease associated with the codon 178Asn PRNP mutation. *Annuals of Neurology, 31*(3), 282–285.

Brown, P., Preece, M., Brandel, J. P., Sato, T., McShane, L., Zerr, I., et al. (2000). Iatrogenic Creutzfeldt-Jakob disease at the millennium. *Neurology, 55*(8), 1075–1081.

Buee, L., & Delacourte, A. (1999). Comparative biochemistry of tau in progressive supranuclear palsy, corticobasal degeneration, FTDP-17, and Pick's disease. *Brain Pathology, 9*(4), 681–693.

Bugiani, O., Murrell, J. R., Giaccone, G., Hasegawa, M., Ghigo, G., Tabaton, M., et al. (1999). Frontotemporal dementia and corticobasal degeneration in a family with a P301S mutation in tau. *Journal of Neuropathology and Experimental Neurology, 58,* 667–677.

Cherrier, M. M., Mendez, M. F., Perryman, K. M., Pachana, N. A., Miller, B. L., & Cummings, J. L. (1997). Frontotemporal dementia versus vascular dementia:

differential features on mental status examination. *Journal of the American Geriatric Society, 45*(5), 579–583.

Chow, T. W., Miller, B. L., Hayashi, V. N., & Geschwind, D. H. (1999). Inheritance of frontotemporal dementia. *Archives of Neurology, 56*(7), 817–822.

Clark, L. N., Poorkaj, P., Wszolek, Z., Geschwind, D. H., Nasreddine, Z. S., Miller, B., et al. (1998). Pathogenic implications of mutations in the tau gene in pallido-ponto-nigral degeneration and related neurodegenerative disorders linked to chromosome 17. *Proceedings of the National Academy of Sciences, USA, 95*(22), 13103–13107.

Cohen, F. E. (1999). Protein misfolding and prion diseases. *Journal of Molecular Biology, 293*(2), 313–320.

Collinge, J., Palmer, M. S., & Dryden, A. J. (1991). Genetic predisposition to iatrogenic Creutzfeldt-Jakob disease. *Lancet, 337*(8755), 1441–1442.

Collins, S., Boyd, A., Fletcher, A., Byron, K., Harper, C., McLean, C. A., et al. (2000). Novel prion protein gene mutation in an octogenarian with Creutzfeldt-Jakob disease. *Archives of Neurology, 57*(7), 1058–1063.

Collins, S., Boyd, A., Fletcher, A., Gonzales, M. F., McLean, C. A., & Masters, C. L. (2000). Recent advances in the premortem diagnosis of Creutzfeldt-Jakob disease. *Journal of Clinical Neurosciences, 7*(3), 195–202.

Committee on Health Care Issues, American Neurological Association. (1986). Precautions in handling tissues, fluids, and other contaminated materials from patients with documented or suspected Creutzfeldt-Jakob disease. *Annals of Neurology, 19*(1), 75–77.

Constantinidis, J., Richard, J., & Tissot, R. (1974). Pick's disease. Histological and clinical correlations. *European Neurology, 11*(4), 208–217.

Cooper, P. N., Jackson, M., Lennox, G., Lowe, J., & Mann, D. M. (1995). Tau, ubiquitin, and alpha B-crystallin immunohistochemistry define the principal causes of degenerative frontotemporal dementia. *Archives of Neurology, 52*(10), 1011–1015.

Foster, N. L., Wilhelmsen, K., Sima, A. A., Jones, M. Z., D'Amato, C. J., & Gilman, S. (1997). Frontotemporal dementia and Parkinsonism linked to chromosome 17: A consensus conference. *Annals of Neurology, 41*(6), 706–715.

Francis, P. T., Holmes, C., Webster, M. T., Stratmann, G. C., Procter, A. W., & Bowen, D. M. (1993). Preliminary neurochemical findings in non-Alzheimer dementia due to lobar atrophy. *Dementia, 4*(3/4), 172–177.

Gibbons, R. V., Holman, R. C., Belay, E. D., & Schonberger, L. B. (2000). Creutzfeldt-Jakob disease in the United States: 1979–1998. *Journal of the American Medical Association, 284*(18), 2322–2323.

Goldfarb, L. G., Petersen, R. B., Tabaton, M., Brown, P., LeBlanc, A. C., Montagna, P., et al. (1992). Fatal familial insomnia and familial Creutzfeldt-Jakob disease: Disease phenotype determined by a DNA polymorphism. *Science, 258*(5083), 806–808.

Gustafson, L. (1993). Clinical picture of frontal lobe degeneration of non-Alzheimer type. *Dementia, 4*(3/4), 143–148.

Gustafson, L., Brun, A., & Passant, U. (1992). Frontal lobe degeneration of non-Alzheimer type. *Baillière's Clinical Neurology, 1*(3), 559–582.

Hodges, J. R. (2001). Frontotemporal dementia (Pick's disease): Clinical features and assessment. *Neurology, 56*(11, Suppl. 4), S6–S10.

Hodges, J. R., Patterson, K., Ward, R., Garrard, P., Bak, T., Perry, R., et al. (1999). The differentiation of semantic dementia and frontal lobe dementia (temporal and frontal variants of frontotemporal dementia) from early Alzheimer's disease: A comparative neuropsychological study. *Neuropsychology, 13*(1), 31–40.

Houlden, H., Baker, M., Morris, H. R., MacDonald, N., Pickering Brown, S., Adamson, J., et al. (2001). Corticobasal degeneration and progressive supranuclear palsy share a common tau haplotype. *Neurology, 56*(12), 1702–1706.

Hutton, M. (2001). Missense and splice site mutations in tau associated with FTDP-17: Multiple pathogenic mechanisms. *Neurology, 56*(11, Suppl. 4), S21–S25.

Kertesz, A. (1997). Frontotemporal dementia, Pick disease, and corticobasal degeneration. One entity or 3? *Archives of Neurology, 54,* 1427–1429.

Kertesz, A., Nadkarni, N., Davidson, W., & Thomas, A. W. (2000). The Frontal Behavioral Inventory in the differential diagnosis of frontotemporal dementia. *Journal of the International Neuropsychological Society, 6*(4), 460–468.

Korth, C., May, B. C., Cohen, F. E., & Prusiner, S. B. (2001). Acridine and phenothiazine derivatives as pharmacotherapeutics for prion disease. *Proceedings of the National Academy of Sciences, USA, 98*(17), 9836–9841.

Lee, V. M., & Trojanowski, J. Q. (2001). Transgenic mouse models of tauopathies: Prospects for animal models of Pick's disease. *Neurology, 56*(11, Suppl. 4), S26–S30.

Levy, M. L., Miller, B. L., Cummings, J. L., Fairbanks, L. A., & Craig, A. (1996). Alzheimer disease and frontotemporal dementias: Behavioral distinctions. *Archives of Neurology, 53*(7), 687–690.

Litvan, I. (2001). Therapy and management of frontal lobe dementia patients. *Neurology, 56*(11, Suppl. 4), S41–S45.

Litvan, I., Agid, Y., Sastry, N., Jankovic, J., Wenning, G. K., Goetz, C. G., et al. (1997). What are the obstacles for an accurate clinical diagnosis of Pick's disease? A clinicopathological study. *Neurology, 49*(1), 62–69.

Lund and Manchester Groups. (1994). Clinical and neuropathological criteria for frontotemporal dementia. The Lund and Manchester Groups. *Journal of Neurology, Neurosurgery, and Psychiatry, 57*(4), 416–418.

Massoud, F., Devi, G., Stern, Y., Lawton, A., Goldman, J. E., Liu, Y., et al. (1999). A clinicopathological comparison of community-based and clinic-based cohorts of patients with dementia. *Archives of Neurology, 56*(11), 1368–1373.

McDowell, S., Whyte, J., & D'Esposito, M. (1998). Differential effect of dopaminergic agonists on prefrontal function in traumatic brain injury patients. *Brain, 121*(6), 1155–1164.

McKhann, G. M., Albert, M. S., Grossman, M., Miller, B., Dickson, D., & Trojanowski, J. Q. (2001). Clinical and pathological diagnosis of frontotemporal dementia: Report of the Work Group on Frontotemporal Dementia and Pick's Disease. *Archives of Neurology, 58*(11), 1803–1809.

Medori, R., Tritschler, H. J., LeBlanc, A., Villare, F., Manetto, V., Chen, H. Y., et al. (1992). Fatal familial insomnia, a prion disease with a mutation at codon 178 of the prion protein gene. *New England Journal of Medicine, 326*(7), 444–449.

Mendez, M. F., Mastri, A. R., Sung, J. H., & Frey, W. H., III. (1992). Clinically diagnosed Alzheimer disease: Neuropathologic findings in 650 cases. *Alzheimer Disease and Associated Disorders, 6*(1), 35–43.

Miller, B. L., Ikonte, C., Ponton, M., Levy, M., Boone, K., Darby, A., et al. (1997). A study of the Lund-Manchester research criteria for frontotemporal dementia: Clinical and single-photon emission CT correlations. *Neurology, 41*, 1374–1382.

Morris, H. R., Khan, M. N., Janssen, J. C., Brown, J. M., Perez-Tur, J., Baker, M., et al. (2001). The genetic and pathological classification of familial frontotemporal dementia. *Archives of Neurology, 58*(11), 1813–1816.

Muller, W. E., Laplanche, J. L., Ushijima, H., & Schroder, H. C. (2000). Novel approaches in diagnosis and therapy of Creutzfeldt Jakob disease. *Mechanisms of Ageing and Development, 116*(2/3), 193–218.

Neary, D., Snowden, J. S., Gustafson, L., Passant, U., Stuss, D., Black, S., et al. (1998). Frontotemporal lobar degeneration: A consensus on clinical diagnostic criteria. *Neurology, 51*, 1546–1554.

Palmer, M. S., Dryden, A. J., Hughes, J. T., & Collinge, J. (1991). Homozygous prion protein genotype predisposes to sporadic Creutzfeldt-Jakob disease. *Nature, 352*(6333), 340–342.

Parchi, P., Castellani, R., Capellari, S., Ghetti, B., Young, K., Chen, S. G., et al. (1996). Molecular basis of phenotypic variability in sporadic Creutzfeldt-Jakob disease. *Annals of Neurology, 39*(6), 767–778.

Parchi, P., Giese, A., Capellari, S., Brown, P., Schulz Schaeffer, W., Windl, O., et al. (1999). Classification of sporadic Creutzfeldt-Jakob disease based on molecular and phenotypic analysis of 300 subjects. *Annals of Neurology, 46*(2), 224–233.

Pasquier, F., Lebert, F., Lavenu, I., & Guillaume, B. (1999). The clinical picture of frontotemporal dementia: Diagnosis and follow-up. *Dementia and Geriatric Cognitive Disorders, 10,* 110–114.

Perrier, V., Wallace, A. C., Kaneko, K., Safar, J., Prusiner, S. B., & Cohen, F. E. (2000). Mimicking dominant negative inhibition of prion replication through structure-based drug design. *Proceedings of the National Academy of Sciences, USA, 97*(11), 6073–6078.

Priola, S. A., Raines, A., & Caughey, W. S. (2000). Porphyrin and phthalocyanine antiscrapie compounds. *Science, 287*(5457), 1503–1506.

Prusiner, S. B. (1998). Prions. *Proceedings of the National Academy of Sciences, USA, 95*(23), 13363–13383.

Prusiner, S. B. (2001). Shattuck lecture: Neurodegenerative diseases and prions. *New England Journal of Medicine, 344*(20), 1516–1526.

Prusiner, S. B., & Hsiao, K. K. (1994). Human prion diseases. *Annals of Neurology, 35*(4), 385–395.

Rizzu, P., van Swieten, J. C., Joosse, M., Hasegawa, M., Stevens, M., Tibben, A., et al. (1999). High prevalence of mutations in the microtubule-associated protein tau in a population study of frontotemporal dementia in the Netherlands. *American Journal of Human Genetics, 64*(2), 414–421.

Rosen, H. J., Gorno-Tempini, M. L., Goldman, W. P., Perry, R. J., Schuff, N., Weiner, M., et al. (2002). Patterns of brain atrophy in frontotemporal dementia and semantic dementia. *Neurology, 58*(2), 198–208.

Seipelt, M., Zerr, I., Nau, R., Mollenhauer, B., Kropp, S., Steinhoff, B. J., et al. (1999). Hashimoto's encephalitis as a differential diagnosis of Creutzfeldt-Jakob disease. *Journal of Neurology, Neurosurgery, and Psychiatry, 66*(2), 172–176.

Sparks, D. L., & Markesbery, W. R. (1991). Altered serotonergic and cholinergic synaptic markers in Pick's disease. *Archives of Neurology, 48,* 769–799.

Steelman, V. M. (1999). Prion diseases: An evidence-based protocol for infection control. *Association of Registered Nurses Journal, 69*(5), 946–954, 956–967.

Stevens, M., van Duijn, C. M., Kamphorst, W., de Knijff, P., Heutink, P., van Gool, W. A., et al. (1998). Familial aggregation in frontotemporal dementia. *Neurology, 50*(6), 1541–1545.

Supattapone, S., Nguyen, H. O., Cohen, F. E., Prusiner, S. B., & Scott, M. R. (1999). Elimination of prions by branched polyamines and implications for therapeutics. *Proceedings of the National Academy of Sciences, USA, 96*(25), 14529–14534.

Swartz, J. R., Miller, B. L., Lesser, I. M., & Darby, A. L. (1997). Frontotemporal dementia: Treatment response to serotonin selective reuptake inhibitors. *Journal of Clinical Psychiatry, 58*(5), 212–216.

Tan, L., Williams, M. A., Khan, M. K., Champion, H. C., & Nielsen, N. H. (1999). Risk of transmission of bovine spongiform encephalopathy to humans in the United States: Report of the Council on Scientific Affairs, American Medical Association. *Journal of the American Medical Association, 281*(24), 2330–2339.

van Duijn, C. M., Delasnerie Laupretre, N., Masullo, C., Zerr, I., de Silva, R., Wientjens, D. P., et al. (1998). Case-control study of risk factors of Creutzfeldt-Jakob disease in Europe during 1993–95. European Union (EU) Collaborative Study Group of Creutzfeldt-Jakob disease (CJD). *Lancet, 351*(9109), 1081–1085.

van Swieten, J. C., Stevens, M., Rosso, S. M., Rizzu, P., Joosse, M., de Koning, I., et al. (1999). Phenotypic variation in hereditary frontotemporal dementia with tau mutations. *Annals of Neurology, 46,* 617–626.

Varma, A. R., Snowden, J. S., Lloyd, J. J., Talbot, P. R., Mann, D. M., & Neary, D. (1999). Evaluation of the NINCDS-ADRDA criteria in the differentiation of Alzheimer's disease and frontotemporal dementia. *Journal of Neurology, Neurosurgery, and Psychiatry, 66*(2), 184–188.

Wientjens, D. P., Davanipour, Z., Hofman, A., Kondo, K., Matthews, W. B., Will, R. G., et al. (1996). Risk factors for Creutzfeldt-Jakob disease: A reanalysis of case-control studies. *Neurology, 46*(5), 1287–1291.

Will, R. G., Ironside, J. W., Zeidler, M., Cousens, S. N., Estibeiro, K., Alperovitch, A., et al. (1996). A new variant of Creutzfeldt-Jakob disease in the U.K. *Lancet, 347*(9006), 921–925.

Zeidler, M., Stewart, G. E., Barraclough, C. R., Bateman, D. E., Bates, D., Burn, D. J., et al. (1997). New variant Creutzfeldt-Jakob disease: Neurological features and diagnostic tests. *Lancet, 350*(9082), 903–907.

Zerr, I., Bodemer, M., Gefeller, O., Otto, M., Poser, S., Wiltfang, J., et al. (1998). Detection of 14-3-3 protein in the cerebrospinal fluid supports the diagnosis of Creutzfeldt-Jakob disease. *Annals of Neurology, 43*(1), 32–40.

Zerr, I., Schulz Schaeffer, W. J., Giese, A., Bodemer, M., Schroter, A., Henkel, K., et al. (2000). Current clinical diagnosis in Creutzfeldt-Jakob disease: Identification of uncommon variants. *Annals of Neurology, 48*(3), 323–329.

CHAPTER 5

Psychological and Neuropsychological Aspects of Lewy Body and Frontal Dementia

Margaret P. Norris and Mary E. Haines

Recognition of non-Alzheimer's dementias has become essential for experts in geriatrics. Unfortunately, many laypersons and even general practitioners equate the terms *Alzheimer's* and *dementia*. In fact, as many as two-thirds of Alzheimer's disease (AD) patients have a coexisting condition (Lim et al., 1999), making pure AD far less common than was once thought. This chapter reviews the more common other dementia, including mixed dementia, which is the co-occurrence of AD and vascular dementia; Lewy body dementia, which most often occurs in conjunction with AD pathology; and frontotemporal dementia, a group of non-Alzheimer pathologies with focal atrophy of the frontotemporal areas. Within each of these dementias, we review the literature on the epidemiology, diagnostic standards, clinical diagnostic practices, symptoms, and interventions of these dementias. Accurate differential diagnosis of dementia is critical for discerning its pathophysiology, understanding the relationship between coexisting dementia, and developing disease-specific treatments for distinct forms of dementia.

LEWY BODY DEMENTIA

In 1961, Okazaki and colleagues first described diffuse Lewy bodies in two demented patients with parkinsonism and psychiatric symptoms. Lewy body dementia may rarely occur as a pure disease or, more commonly, in combination with AD or Parkinson's disease. Numerous terms have been used, including *diffuse Lewy body dementia, Lewy body variant of AD,* and

Parkinson's disease with dementia (Drachman & Swearer, 1998). The generic term, dementia with Lewy bodies (LBD), is recommended by the Consortium on Dementia with Lewy bodies (McKeith et al., 1996) and is used in this chapter. The pure form of diffuse Lewy body dementia is rare (Holmes, Cairns, Lantos, & Mann, 1999; Mega et al., 1996) because the majority of cases with LBD have significant number of plaques that are morphologically indistinguishable from those found in AD cases. Mild to severe AD pathology was found in 81% of clinical LBD cases (Londos, Passant, Brun, & Gustafson, 2000). It is not understood whether these cases represent a variant of AD or concurrent AD and Lewy body pathology. The heterogeneity of Lewy body disease is further complicated by coexisting vascular pathology, which has been reported in 4% (Holmes et al., 1999) to 30% of cases at autopsy (McKeith, Perry, & Perry, 1999). The etiology of LBD remains unknown. A genetic cause has been hypothesized but not yet identified, and Brown (1999) has speculated that Parkinson's disease and LBD may be genetically heterogeneous. For a detailed description of the pathological distinctions of Lewy body disease, see Hansen et al. (1990), Lennox and Lowe (1998), and McKeith et al. (1996).

Epidemiology

In a review of pathology studies based on patients with clinical signs of dementia, rates of observed Lewy bodies ranged from 7% to 36%, with the majority of the studies reporting 16% to 28% rates (Lennox & Lowe, 1998). Among autopsy studies, few account for multiple etiologies, although some evidence suggests dementia associated with Lewy bodies may be more common than vascular disease. For example, among 146 cases with pathological confirmation of AD, 26% also had Lewy bodies, compared to 18% that also had infarcts (Galasko et al., 1994). However, using a broader definition of infarcts, mixed dementia (MD) was observed in 16% of autopsied cases compared to 11% of LBD cases (Homes et al., 1999).

Age of onset for LBD and AD are similar with a range of 50 to 85 years old (Brown, 1999). LBD may be twice as high in males than females. LBD usually has a more rapid course than AD, often with severe disability in only five years (Drachman & Swearer, 1998). Lewy body and AD patients do not appear to differ on most other characteristics such as education, age of onset, age at death, and survival time from first evaluation (Weiner et al., 1996).

Diagnostic Standards

Several clinical diagnostic criteria have been proposed and revised in recent years. Currently, the most widely accepted criteria were developed at the First International Workshop of the Consortium of Dementia with Lewy Bodies (McKeith et al., 1996). These criteria for probable LBD include progressive cognitive decline and two of the following: fluctuating cognition with variations in alertness and attention, recurrent visual hallucinations that are usually well formed and detailed, or spontaneous motor symptoms of parkinsonism. The consortium cautions that many patients with other forms of dementia also have some of these symptoms. Other criteria symptoms that further indicate LBD are repeated falls, syncope, transient loss of consciousness, neuroleptic sensitivity, systematized delusions, and hallucinations in modalities other than visual. These clinical diagnostic criteria do not exclude a concomitant diagnosis of AD because many patients meet criteria for both forms of dementia (McKeith et al., 1999). Because the diagnostic criteria is recent, few autopsy studies have investigated the accuracy of the standards, which are reviewed next.

The interrater reliability and validity of these consensus diagnostic standards for LBD were evaluated in 40 patients with numerous dementias confirmed at autopsy (Lopez et al., 1999). Reliability and validity were based on information obtained at the first evaluation of eight LBD patients and subsequently rated by only four clinicians. The kappa for LBD was .37 (compared to .73 for AD), the sensitivity for LBD was .34 (compared to .95 for AD), and the specificity for LBD was .94 (compared to .79 for AD). These results suggest the consensus diagnostic criteria for LBD are not reliably rated across clinicians and produce few false positives but many false negatives. Hence, there is a tendency to underdiagnose LBD, which the authors attribute to the nonspecific features of LBD and the coexistence of the two diseases. They conclude that the consensus standards for diagnosing LBD are suboptimal.

Clinical Diagnosis

Numerous differential diagnoses should be considered—especially Parkinson's disease with dementia, pure AD, vascular dementia (VaD), or MD. As with VaD and AD, the clinical distinction between LBD and

AD is inherently complex because the two conditions frequently coexist. Prospective studies that compare pure cases of LBD and AD are rare. Some researchers have argued that neuropsychological and neuroimaging studies have not been successful in distinguishing LBD and AD (Miller, 1997); others have argued that there is considerable evidence that these forms of dementia are distinguishable. As reviewed later, a large body of literature points to similarities and differences in the cognitive deficits associated with LBD and AD.

The potential fallacy of clinical diagnosis is well illustrated by Magnuson, Keller, and Roccaforte (2000), who described a case of a patient with a proto-typical LBD presentation. The patient had variable cognitive performance, vivid visual hallucinations of animate figures, delusions, apathy, and depression. Parkinsonian signs were present two years before cognitive decline. The use of haloperidol led to increased agitation and physical aggression, and cognitive dysfunction slowed down with use of donepezil. Despite this seemingly prototypical LBD presentation, postmortem examination revealed multiple lacunar infarcts and hemorrhages in subcortical white matter, basal ganglia, pons, and cerebellum. There were few neurofibrillary tangles and no Lewy bodies.

Autopsy Studies

Definitive diagnosis requires postmortem pathological examination. As with MD, there is some discordance between clinical diagnoses and definitive pathology examination at autopsy. The sensitivity and specificity of the current diagnostic criteria, established by the consortium (McKeith et al., 1996), appear superior to other clinical criteria proposed before the consortium (Mega et al., 1996). Nevertheless, in a review of autopsy studies examining the accuracy of the current diagnostic criterion for DLB, sensitivity rates ranged from .22 to .83, and specificity rates ranged from .87 to 1.0 (McKeith & Burn, 2000), indicating underdiagnosis of true cases of DLB is more common than false positive cases of DLB. Most errors are clinical diagnoses of AD in patients who are later found at autopsy to have LBD with AD (Salmon et al., 1996). In addition, as many as one-third of clinically diagnosed cases of MD are later found to be LBD at autopsy (Galasko et al., 1994). Thus, rates obtained from clinical studies are generally lower than those found in autopsy studies.

Symptoms

Cognitive Deficits

A growing body of literature examines the symptoms that may distinguish LBD from pure Parkinson's disease and AD. In addition, the differential diagnosis between LBD and pure Parkinson's disease can be ambiguous because the latter is also associated with cognitive changes. Between 20% and 40% of patients with Parkinson's disease develop dementia (Brown, 1999; Drachman & Swearer, 1998). Mental slowing, visuospatial problems, and minor deficits in set shifting, retrieval, verbal fluency, and effortful cognitive processing are common in patients with Parkinson's disease (McKeith & Burn, 2000; Small & Mayeux, 2000). Parkinson's disease may also accompany psychiatric disturbances including depression, apathy, hallucinations, and delusions. As many as 44% of individuals with Parkinson's disease in clinics report visual hallucinations (McKeith & Burn, 2000). McKeith and Burn conclude that the deficits associated with Parkinson's disease, although measurable on neuropsychological tests, are unlikely to be severe enough to interfere with daily functioning. Significant impairments in orientation, memory, and other cognitive abilities are suggestive of coexisting AD or LBD. According to consensus (McKeith et al., 1996), Parkinson's disease with dementia should be diagnosed rather than LBD if there is a minimum of 12 months of only motor symptoms; however, this time period is recognized as arbitrary and subject to revision as more longitudinal data is acquired.

The fluctuations in cognitive abilities, considered characteristic signs of LBD, occur in approximately 75% of cases (McKeith & Burn, 2000). Unfortunately, fluctuating activities of daily living (ADLs) and test performance appear to have low interrater reliability compared to other symptoms of frontotemporal dementias (FTD; Mega et al., 1996). In addition, fluctuations in level of alertness, resulting in confusional states or transient reduction in level of consciousness may lead to incorrect diagnoses of vascular dementia or delirium (Brown, 1999). Findings further suggest that disturbed consciousness may also be exhibited in irregularities of REM sleep (McKeith et al., 1999). Lennox and Lowe (1998) suggest the basis for these deficits may be frontal-subcortical connections that control alertness and attention. There is a trend for these fluctuations to decrease as the disease progresses.

Because pure Lewy body disease is rare, only limited research is available that describes the cognitive deficits specific to this pathology. In comparing a small number of cases of pure Lewy body to pure AD cases, only two differences emerged: DLB patients performed worse on measures of construction, and AD patients performed worse on memory tests (Salmon et al., 1996). However, all patients had global cognitive impairment. While it has been speculated that LBD/AD should cause more clinical impairment than pure Lewy body disease or pure Alzheimer's disease (Drachman & Swearer, 1998), limited research has not yet supported this hypothesis.

Several neuropsychology studies have found that patients with LBD, compared to AD, exhibit greater impairment in attention, fluency, visuospatial and constructional abilities, psychomotor speed, and frontal symptoms such as mental inflexibility, deficits in forming concepts, and problems with decision making, problem solving, planning, and execution (Brown, 1999; Lennox & Lowe, 1998; McKeith & Burn, 2000). Measures that commonly show these impairments include digit span, reaction time tests, vigilance tests, verbal fluency tasks, similarities, Wisconsin Card Sorting test, block design, and clock drawing (Lennox & Lowe, 1998; McKeith & Burn, 2000). AD and LBD may also result in subtle differences in memory functioning. Patients with LBD may have more problems with retrieval compared to the acquisition impairment seen in AD patients. In addition, memory impairment may not be present in initial stages but will eventually develop (McKeith & Burn, 2000). Poor attention, personality changes, and executive functioning are more likely to be the first signs in LBD (Drachman & Swearer, 1998). It is important to recognize, however, that these distinctive patterns are less likely to be true among patients with coexisting AD pathology. In these more common cases, a more typical presentation of AD symptoms is often seen at onset with later development of extrapyramidal rigidity and visual hallucinations.

Many studies suggest that LBD and AD patients have more overlapping cognitive deficits than divergence (Brown, 1999). For example, patients with clinical diagnoses of LBD AD were compared on 16 psychometric measures covering a broad range of cognitive abilities (Walker, Allen, Shergill, & Katona, 1997). Their performance significantly differed on only two measures: Lewy body patients had greater impairment on visuospatial measure (copying of geometric designs and clock), and AD patients had greater impairment on delayed recall. Lambon Ralph et al.'s (2001) summary of studies comparing cognitive impairments in those with LBD versus AD revealed more similarities than differences. Like AD patients, the LBD patients were impaired across all areas of cognition. Lewy body patients consistently showed more visuospatial impairments than AD patients. Studies were inconsistent as to verbal fluency and attention, some showing equivalent performances and others showing worse performance in LBD patients. Contrary to the assumption of greater frontal deficits in LBD, they performed at the same level as AD patients on category fluency, similarities, motor sequencing tasks, but worse on Trails A. Lambon Ralph et al. compared the performance of AD and Lewy body patients on a variety of semantic memory and executive functioning tests and found mostly equivalent performance. Lewy body patients performed worse on measures of visuospatial ability, and AD patients performed worse on measures of delayed recall.

Important cautions are necessary before conclusions from this literature are finalized. Very few studies are prospective comparisons followed by postmortem confirmation of diagnoses. Hence, we should assume that inaccurate clinical diagnoses exaggerate overlapping symptoms. In addition, many of these studies are based on small sizes, and poor replication across studies is relatively common. This problem is exacerbated by differences in measures used across studies. Despite these caveats, even the few longitudinal studies with postmortem follow up indicate Lewy body patients and AD patients do not significantly differ on cognitive deficits, perhaps with the exception of attention, fluency, and visuospatial processing (Hansen et al., 1990; Heyman et al., 1999; Weiner et al., 1996). These areas are also often impaired in pure AD patients, however, reducing the clinical utility of these differences across groups. The overall similarity in cognitive deficits between LBD and AD patients certainly reflects the overlapping pathology of the diseases. In summary, in a review of studies examining the accuracy of diagnoses of LBD, the American Academy of Neurology concluded that neuropsychological tests do not reliably distinguish LBD from AD or VaD (Knopman et al., 2001).

Mood and Behavioral Disturbances

Psychiatric symptoms such as depression, delusions, and recurrent and vivid visual hallucinations are prominent features of LBD (Brown, 1999). Visual hallucinations are complex and highly detailed and form animate images. Delusions may also be thematically connected with the content of the hallucinations (McKeith et al., 1996). Hallucinations in other modalities may occur but, typically, not in the absence of visual hallucinations (Lennox & Lowe, 1998). Hallucinations and delusions may be the most discriminating symptoms of LBD (Hirono et al., 1999). However, Ballard et al. (1995) noted that although roughly 90% of patients with LBD experience psychotic symptoms, this sign is not pathognomonic because 65% to 70% of patients with AD and vascular dementia also experience psychotic symptoms. Their findings suggest that patients with LBD may experience more frequent and variable psychotic symptoms than other dementia patients. Transient visual hallucinations are common in other forms of dementia and delirium. McKeith and Burn (2000) argue that the persistence, rather than merely the presence of visual hallucinations, is a diagnostic indicator.

Some research suggests depression occurs at a higher rate in LBD (approximately 38%) than in AD cases (approximately 16%; McKeith & Burn, 2000). However, this finding was not replicated by Hirono and colleagues (1999), who found similar rates of depression in LBD, AD, and frontotemporal dementia patients. More research is needed to investigate the efficacy of antidepressant medications for Lewy body patients with depressive symptomatology.

Motor Impairments

There are important differences in the development of motor symptoms among patients with LBD compared to Parkinson's patients. In Parkinson's patients, the extrapyramidal symptoms are resting tremor, cogwheel rigidity of limbs, increased axial tone, masked facial expression, and impairment of gait, posture, and equilibrium. Among Lewy body patients, parkinsonian symptoms were observed in only 24% of cases at initial presentation but in 77% of cases over the full course of the disorder (McKeith & Burn, 2000). The parkinsonian symptoms of LBD tend to be milder and more symmetrical than in idiopathic Parkinson's disease (Brown, 1999; Lennox & Lowe, 1998). Tremor is the least common motor symptom, and resting tremor is especially rare. In addition, myoclonus is more frequent, falls are more common, and parkinsonian symptoms may develop only following neuroleptic treatment and may be severe, prolonged, and even fatal (see later discussion). Motor abnormalities such as bradykinesia, rigidity, masked facies, and parkinsonian gait may be helpful is distinguishing LBD patients from AD patients (Galasko, Katzman, Salmon, & Hansen, 1996; Hansen et al., 1990).

Interventions

The vast majority of the treatment literature focuses on pharmaceutical interventions. Drug therapy is especially critical in treating patients with LBD primarily because of the serious iatrogenic effects that can occur. Two of the primary sets of symptoms—motor disturbance and psychosis—are typically treated by drugs that exacerbate the other set of primary symptoms. First, dopamine-blocking neuroleptics used to treat psychosis are likely to seriously worsen the extrapyramidal symptoms. Traditional neuroleptic medications such as haloperidol and phenothiazines may produce irreversible parkinsonism, impair consciousness level, and induce autonomic distubances. Hypersensitive responses to neuroleptic drugs in LBD patients may also occur among patients without a history of previous parkinsonian symptoms (Brown, 1999). McKeith and Burn (2000) recommend the cautious use of clozapine, an atypical antipsychotic agent, although further research is needed. The second complication in symptom management occurs when trying to minimize the motor symptoms. The response to antiparkinsonian medications such as levodopa is complicated by worsened psychotic symptoms, for example, exacerbating hallucinations, psychotic symptoms, and confusion. Given the grave and simultaneously counterindications of antipsychotic and antiparkinsonian medications, research on nonpharmacological behavioral treatment strategies seems imperative.

A positive finding from the pharmacological treatment literature is the discovery that patients with LBD may have a better response to acetylcholinesterase inhibitors than AD patients (Brown, 1999; Drachman & Swearer, 1998). Donepezil is most often used when dementia is the prominent symptom (Drachman & Swearer, 1998). Early evidence suggests cholinesterase inhibitors may improve somnolence, hallucinations and delirium, cognition, and attention.

Summary of Lewy Body Dementia

Although pathologically distinct from Alzheimer's disease, LBD usually occurs in combination with the neurofibrillary tangles and plagues of AD, suggesting an etiological connection between these two forms of dementia that has not yet been discovered. Epidemiological characteristics such as the low rate of pure LBD cases, the higher rate of LBD in males than females, and the more rapid course of LBD compared to pure AD, may provide clues into the risk and etiological factors of LBD.

The most widely accepted criteria for LBD (McKeith et al., 1996) are progressive cognitive decline and two of the following: fluctuating cognition with variations in alertness and attention, recurrent well-formed and detailed visual hallucinations, or spontaneous motor symptoms of parkinsonism. Other criteria symptoms suggestive of LBD are repeated falls, syncope, transient loss of consciousness, neuroleptic sensitivity, systematized delusions, and hallucinations in modalities other than visual. Postmortem studies indicate these criteria are highly specific but not particularly sensitive to identifying true cases of LBD. Missed cases are most often diagnosed either pure AD or VaD. The lack of distinction between LBD and AD is certainly complicated by their frequent co-occurrence and their similarly affected brain regions. On the other hand, misdiagnosed cases of LBD as MD may, in part, reflect clinicians' being less aware of the need to consider LBD as a rule-out dementia diagnosis, particularly in the presence of symptoms such as variations in alertness, visual hallucinations, and motor impairments.

Studies that compare pure LBD to pure AD remind us that the cognitive symptoms of these dementias share far more similarities than differences (Salmon et al., 1996). Several neuropsychology studies have found greater impairment among patients with LBD, compared to AD, in the areas of attention, fluency, visuospatial and constructional abilities, psychomotor speed, and frontal symptoms. However, it must be recognized that a statistically significant difference in average scores across groups does not always lead to accurate classification of individuals. Thus far, the literature suggests that the differential diagnosis of LBD and AD cannot be based on distinct patterns of cognitive deficits in either group. Several factors may be masking their distinction. First, they most often coexist and, even in their pure forms, they affect the same regions of the brain, rendering them less likely to produce distinctive clinical indicators. Second, few studies are prospective comparisons with postmortem confirmation of diagnoses; hence, we must assume that inaccurate clinical diagnoses exaggerate overlapping symptoms. Finally, many of these studies are based on small sizes, and measures used across studies are not standardized. These factors certainly thwart efforts to produce replication across studies.

While LBD and AD appear to share many cognitive impairments, psychiatric and motor disturbances may have greater utility in differentiating LBD from AD. Recurrent, complex, and vivid visual hallucinations are prominent features of LBD, as are delusions. Again, these symptoms are not pathognomonic of LBD because they also are present in other forms of dementia and delirium. Further research should examine the hypothesis that the persistence and predominance of these symptoms, rather than merely their presence, are diagnostic indicators. In addition, more studies are needed to discern if the motor abnormalities such as bradykinesia, rigidity, masked facies, and parkinsonian gait may be helpful in distinguishing LBD from AD patients (Galasko et al., 1996; Hansen et al., 1990).

The importance of accurate diagnosis is perhaps most apparent in consideration of the possible iatrogenic effects of treating patients with LBD with neuroleptics or antiparkinsonian medications. While these treatment strategies may initially seem appropriate, the misdiagnosed LBD patient treated with neuroleptics may face irreversible parkinsonism, impaired consciousness, and autonomic disturbances; or if treated with antiparkinsonian medication, the patient may face worsening psychotic symptoms. Given the serious limitations on using antipsychotic and antiparkinsonian medications, research on nonpharmacological behavioral treatment strategies is imperative.

FRONTOTEMPORAL DEMENTIA

Frontotemporal dementia is among the most recently recognized dementia syndromes, first described in the 1980s by Brun (1987) in Sweden and Neary and Snowden (1988) in England. Frontotemporal dementia is a broad term that refers to a group of non-Alzheimer's dementias with focal atrophy of the frontotemporal areas. The nomenclature of frontotemporal dementia has been modified by various investigators, resulting in controversy and confusion (Rosen, Legenfelder, & Miller, 2000). Subsyndromes include frontal lobe dementia (FLD), Pick's disease, motor neuron disease with dementia, progressive nonfluent aphasia, and semantic aphasia. FLD is the most common of these disorders. McKhann et al. (2001) recommend that these clinical syndromes be collectively referred to as *frontotemporal dementia* (FTD), whereas more precise names were suggested to describe neuropathological findings. Although these subsyndromes of FTD can be distinguished pathologically, their clinical presentations have much overlap, reflecting the same affected region of the brain. The etiological distinctions of these pathologies remain unknown (Neary & Snowden, 1996), although genetics is strongly indicated because 38% to 50% of FTD patients have an affected first-degree relative (Brun & Gustafson, 1998; Rosen et al., 2000). For a detailed description of their pathologies, see Brun et al. (1994), Brun and Gustafson (1999), and McKhann et al. (2001).

Although Pick's disease and FTD are pathologically distinguishable, they are not clinically distinctive. Pick's disease is distinguished by the histological change of astrocytic gliosis and neuronal inclusion bodies, accounting for only a minority of cases (Neary & Snowden, 1996). Most of the literature, particularly clinical studies, examines samples that consist primarily of FTD but presumably also a small number of Pick's (e.g., Johanson & Hagberg, 1989; Pachana, Boone, Miller, Cummings, & Berman, 1996).

Onset of FTD is typically in the fifties with deterioration of personality, behavior, and speech, and the course is an insidious and slow progression. Motor neuron disease with dementia (MNDD) also has an insidious start, usually in the sixth decade, but the mean duration of MNDD is only 30 months before death. Also similar to FTD and Pick's, early presentation of MNDD typically includes changes in personality and behavior and stereotyped perseverative speech developing into echolalia and mutism. The diagnosis of MNDD is based on the rapidly aggressive course and signs of anterior horn involvement. MNDD may also be distinguished from FTD by dysarthria, dysphagia, fasciculations, and muscular wasting.

Progressive nonfluent aphasia results from primarily left asymmetric degeneration and is characterized by expressive aphasia. Language impairments include agrammatism, phonemic paraphasias, and anomia (Rosen et al., 2000). In contrast, semantic aphasia, which primarily results from temporal lobe degeneration, is evidenced by loss of semantic knowledge (Rosen et al., 2000). Speech becomes increasingly devoid of content with relatively intact flow of speech (e.g., prosody, phonology, syntax). As both progressive nonfluent aphasia and semantic aphasia progress, the behavioral abnormalities associated with FTD emerge.

Epidemiology

Large autopsy studies suggest FTD makes up approximately 8% to 10% of cases of dementia (Brun & Gustafson, 1998), although the rate may be as low as 3% in samples of older age (Hooten & Lyketsos, 1996; Knopman, Mastri, Frey, Zung, & Rustan, 1990). There is a 38% to 50% co-occurrence rate of dementia in first-degree relatives of FTD patients, suggesting a likely genetic etiology (Brun & Gustafson, 1998; Stevens et al., 1998). The presenium onset distinguishes FTD from most other dementias. The male to female ratio was 3:5 in a Dutch population study (Stevens et al., 1998), and most consider it to approach an even distribution in males and females (Brun & Gustafson, 1998).

Mean age of onset in 30 postmortem-verified cases was 56 ±7.6 years, and mean duration was 8.1 ±3.4 years (Brun & Gustafson, 1999). These figures are similar to cases based on clinical diagnoses, described as having a mean age of onset at 54.8 ±8.5 years and a mean duration of 5.9 ±2.9 years (Stevens et al., 1998).

Diagnostic Standards

Two international conferences on frontotemporal dementia culminated in clinical and neuropathological diagnostic criteria for frontotemporal dementia (Brun et al., 1994), often referred to as the *Lund-Manchester criteria* in the literature. Using the broad term *frontotemporal dementia* (FTD), the clinical criteria of FTD include core diagnostic features, which include behavioral disturbances, affective symptoms, speech disturbance, intact spatial orientation and praxis, physical signs, and laboratory tests, including brain imaging and neuropsychological test results. Supportive diagnostic features such as presenile onset and positive family history, as well as diagnostic exclusion features, are also delineated. The consensus group also outlined the neuropathological features that are distinctive of frontal lobe degeneration type, Pick's disease, and MNDD. A subsequent update of the criteria included consensus criteria for progressive nonfluent aphasia and semantic dementia (Neary et al., 1998).

The National Institute of Neurologic, Communicative Disorders and Stroke-AD and Related Disorders Association (NINCDS-ADRDA) diagnostic criteria were evaluated in a prospective longitudinal study of dementia, including 30 AD and 25 FTD patients with postmortem confirmation of diagnoses (Varma et al., 1999). Twenty-eight of the 30 AD patients had fulfilled NINCDS-ADRDA criteria for AD, resulting in a high sensitivity of .93. However, 20 of the 26 FTD patients also met NINCDS-ADRDA criteria for AD, resulting in a low specificity of .23. Hence, the NINDCS-ADRDA criteria appear to be poor at discriminating between AD and FTD. This problem results from related symptoms of dementia, not coexisting pathologies, because FTD, by definition, exists in the absence of AD pathology. As pointed out by the authors, when the NINCDS-ADRDA criteria were originally developed, the need to distinguish between AD and FTD was not yet recognized. Varma and colleagues recommended that diagnoses be considered tentative when patients meet criteria for both AD and FTD.

The interrater reliability and validity of the NINCDS-ADRDA criteria for AD and the Lund-Manchester criteria were evaluated in 40 patients with numerous dementias confirmed at autopsy (Lopez et al., 1999). Reliability and validity were based on information obtained at the first evaluation and rated by only four clinicians. The kappa for FTD was .75 (compared to .73 for AD), the sensitivity for FTD was .97 (compared to .95 for AD), and the specificity for FTD was .97 (compared to .79 for AD). These results suggest the Lund-Manchester diagnostic criteria for FTD are reliably rated by different clinicians and produce few false positives and false negatives, which the authors attribute to the unique cognitive and psychiatric features of FTD. Studies comparing a larger number of clinicians and patients are still needed.

Clinical Diagnosis

Diagnosis of FTD is usually based on use of the Lund-Manchester clinical criteria and brain imaging (Brun & Gustafson, 1998). Hallmark behavioral and cognitive symptoms are reviewed later. CT and MRI scans eventually show focal frontal atrophy although greater utility in making differential diagnoses comes from SPECT scans showing decreased blood flow in the frontotemporal regions and PET scans showing decreased cerebral metabolism (Drachman & Swearer, 1998; Rosen et al., 2000). Among 26 autopsy-confirmed cases of FTD, 25 had been accurately diagnosed as FTD by focal frontal blood flow decreases, and only three cases with FTD diagnoses based on regional blood flow were found at autopsy to have predominantly frontal mixed dementia pathology (Risberg, Passant, Warkentin, & Gustafson, 1993).

The clinical presentations of FTD and AD are fairly distinct, particularly at the early stage of the diseases, because these dementias are anatomically selective. The pathological changes of FTD primarily occur in the frontal and anterior temporal regions, whereas the pathological changes of AD begin in the hippocampus and posterior temporal and parietal regions. The initial stage of FTD is characterized by changes in personality and behavior, affective symptoms, and progressive speech impairment. As FTD and AD progress and spread, the clinical dissimilarities between them are blurred (Rosen et al., 2000), a critical issue for comparative investigations because the patient groups will appear less distinctive in the later stages.

Although the clinical diagnosis of FTD is typically clearer than MD or Lewy body disease, some particular differential diagnoses can be difficult (Brun & Gustafson, 1998). FTD may be clinically indistinguishable from AD with a predominantly frontal degeneration (approximately 5% of AD cases), vascular dementia occurring selectively in the frontal lobes, Huntington's disease, progressive supranuclear palsy, corticobasal ganglionic degeneration, Creutzfeldt-Jakob disease, subcortical ischemic white matter disease, and frontal lobe tumors. Rosen et al. (2000) summarized some of these distinguishing presentations. FTD is also often mistaken for psychiatric disturbances because it most commonly affects people in midlife and the first symptoms are often in the domains of personality and behavior (McKhann et al., 2001).

Autopsy Studies

More longitudinal studies that follow diagnosed cases to autopsy are awaited. Compared to AD, MD, and Lewy body disease, there are fewer autopsy studies in the literature reporting the rates of FTD confirmed by pathological examination, presumably reflecting the very recent recognition of FTD. Although considered a relatively rare form of dementia, Gustafson (1993) reported frontal lobe dementia accounts for approximately 8% of cases of dementia, and only 2% are identified as Pick's dementia. The rate of FTD varies by age of sample. Separating FTD from Pick's cases, 3% of a large sample of dementia cases at autopsy had FTD, and another 3% of cases had Pick's disease (Knopman et al., 1990). In a subsample of these cases that were under age 70, a 10% rate of FTD was observed and 6.8% made up Pick's disease.

Symptoms

Cognitive Deficits

The dissimilarities of the cognitive deficits associated with FTD and AD reflect their distinct pathologies. AD affects the limbic system and parieto-temporal association cortex, causing characteristic signs of amnesia, visuospatial impairment, apraxia, and aphasia. In contrast, the regional specificity of FTD is not manifested with these global cognitive deficits (Neary & Snowden, 1996). The most commonly documented cognitive impairments of FTD include progressive expressive aphasia seen as word-finding difficulty, reduction of speech, slow verbal production, frequent use of stereotyped responses and phrases, imitating speech such as echolalia, and eventually mutism. Receptive language skills such as comprehension tend to remain intact, as do structural components of language such as phonology, morphology, and syntax. Pick's patients may, however, have both expressive and receptive language deficits (Johanson & Hagberg, 1989). Memory impairment may occur early in Pick's disease because of the hippocampal involvement (Brun & Gustafson, 1999). Impaired executive functions such as poor organization, planning, sequencing, and ability to shift sets are also hallmark signs of FTD. Cognitive and motor slowing and mental rigidity are also commonly observed. FTD patients are often thought to have better visuospatial, orientation, memory, and reasoning abilities than AD patients (Lindau et al., 2000). Spatial disorientation was absent in all FTD patients at the time of their initial evaluation, in contrast to 75% of AD patients who were disoriented (Frisoni et al., 1995). In general, testing FTD patients may be complicated, or even precluded, by expressive speech impairment and disturbed behavior such as distractibility, poor cooperation, and poor test strategies (Brun & Gustafson, 1999). One-third of FTD patients were not able to complete neuropsychological testing because of restlessness, perseveration, stereotyped behavior, and stimulus boundedness (Smeding & deKoning, 2000).

Interestingly, a number of studies have not documented worse memory and constructional abilities in AD compared to FTD patients (Boone et al., 1999; Pachana et al., 1996; Razani, Boone, Miller, Lee, & Sherman, 2001). For example, in a comparison of 11 neuropsychological variables, only one, Rey-Osterrieth recall, showed significant group differences with FTD patients scoring better than AD patients (Pachana et al., 1996). There were no significant differences on other measures of memory, executive, language, attention, and constructional functioning. Many researchers have emphasized the important differences in the nature of the failures between the two groups, rather than the performance level per se (Neary & Snowden, 1996; Pachana et al., 1996; Varma et al., 1999). For example, FTD patients' constructional impairments may result from poor planning and strategic organization rather than the spatial deficits characteristic of AD. Similarly, memory failures in FTD patients may not result from amnesia per se but lack of effortful strategies and initiation. This distinction may explain why FTD patients are not observed to have the same degree of memory impairment in daily functioning as AD patients (Frisoni et al., 1995). In addition, it must be kept in mind that as patients progress further into the illnesses, the impairments of the two groups will have more overlap; for example, executive dysfunction will become increasingly less specific to FTD over time.

The importance of the complete neuropsychological profiles rather than individual measures or functions was illustrated in two comparisons of FTD and AD, first in a sample of cases with diagnoses verified at autopsy and then in an independent patient sample with clinical diagnoses (Elfgren et al., 1994). Only better visuospatial skills in FTD than AD were replicated in the clinical sample. Comparisons of vocabulary ability and verbal memory were not consistent across samples. Nevertheless, results of the combined tests correctly classified 89% of the autopsy sample and 84% of the clinical sample. Other attempts to identify distinctive group profiles have not been successful. The rank order of the test scores were compared in FTD and AD patients (Pachana et al., 1996). The authors concluded that FTD patients performed better on memory tests and worse on executive tests, and the opposite pattern occurred in the AD patients. In fact, inspection of the rankings reveals that two of the three best and worst tests were the same for both patient groups. Best scores were on Digit Span and Rey Auditory Verbal Learning recognition, and worst scores were on Stroop time and Rey-Osterrieth copy.

The heterogeneous cognitive profiles of FTD patients may be due, in part, to hemispheric asymmetry (Boone et al., 1999; Lindau et al., 2000; Razani et al., 2001). Based on SPECT scans, patients were classified as bilateral FTD, right-sided, or left-sided FTD, and their deficits were compared to AD patients (Lindau et al., 2000; Razani et al., 2001). Language impairment was significantly more frequent in FTD than AD patients and more frequent in left FTD than the other FTD groups (Lindau et al., 2000; Razani et al., 2001). Loss of executive functions was more common in bilateral FTD than the other groups (Lindau et al., 2000), whereas more perseverative errors were observed in right FTD patients compared to left FTD and AD patients (Razani et al., 2001). Visuospatial impairment occurred in roughly the same frequency as first symptoms in AD and FTD (Lindau et al., 2000), although looking at relative scores, rather than absolute scores, left FTD patients performed worse on Verbal Intelligence Quotient (VIQ) minus Performance Intelligence Quotient (PIQ) compared to AD and right FTD patients (Razani et al., 2001).

Caution in the use of cognitive screening measures for detecting FTD is especially realized from a number of studies. Using the consortium to establish a registry in AD (CERAD) battery, FTD patients scored better than AD patients on construction tests and calculations, but language, abstract reasoning, and memory scores were similar (Mendez et al., 1996). Mathuranath and colleagues (Mathuranath, Nestor, Berrios, Rakowicz, & Hodges, 2000) developed a cognitive screening measure that expanded the Mini-Mental State Examination (MMSE) by adding additional memory, language, and visuospatial components. FTD patients scored better than AD patients on orientation, attention, and memory, and they scored worse than AD patients on letter fluency, language, and naming. Nevertheless, false classifications remained a significant problem because of overlapping distributions. Screening measures may not be precise enough to offer acceptable classification rates. In addition, cognitive screening measures that do not include data on behavior may not be able to distinguish AD from FTD. As described in the following section, evaluation of mood and behavior is critical in the assessment of FTD.

Mood and Behavioral Disturbances

Personality changes are often the earliest and most prominent symptoms of FTD (Knopman et al., 1990; Miller et al., 1991). Mood problems typically include apathy, emotional aloofness, lack of empathy, and lability. Personality and behavior changes may include impersistence without purpose or directed goals, impaired judgment, self-centeredness, socially inappropriate behavior, neglect of personal hygiene, poor insight and awareness, inflexible and rigid routines, perseverative responses, excessive oral stimulation and consumption, and elaborate rituals (Brun & Gustafson, 1999; Neary & Snowden, 1996). FTD patients are also described as disinhibited, restless, impulsive, irritable, aggressive, easily provoked, and sexually inappropriate (Brun & Gustafson, 1999; Neary & Snowden, 1996).

The differential diagnosis between FTD and affective disorders can be difficult. Symptoms such as lack of concern, withdrawal, lability, impulsiveness, irritability, aspontaneity, poor planning and judgment, and disinhibition can be easily misinterpreted as either unipolar or bipolar mood disorders. One-third to two-thirds of FTD patients referred to specialty dementia clinics were tentatively diagnosed with a psychiatric disturbance by their general physicians (Gregory & Hodges, 1996; Pasquier, Lebert, Lavenu, & Guillaume, 1999). According to Brun and Gustafson (1999), the majority of FTD and Pick's disease patients are initially treated with antidepressant medications.

Only a few empirical studies have compared the behavior and mood problems seen in FTD patients to other dementia groups. Behavioral disturbances (personality change, disinhibition, irritability, euphoria, aggression, lability, and changes in oral/dietary behavior) were present in all FTD patients but only 19% of AD patients at the time of their first evaluation (Frisoni et al., 1995). Clinically diagnosed AD patients were observed to have more psychotic symptoms than FTD, and FTD patients had more depression, lability of mood, anxiety, agitation, disinhibition, and social withdrawal (Lopez et al., 1996). In contrast, among nine psychiatric symptoms, FTD patients had higher rates only on disinhibition and euphoria ratings than AD and LBD patients (Hirono et al., 1999). Barber, Snowden, and Craufurd (1995) developed a questionnaire given to informants of FTD and AD patients with pathological confirmation of diagnoses. Timing the symptom to early, middle, or late aided the distinction, as did specific content rather than general content (e.g., losing objects versus memory problems). The absence of symptoms also proved to be highly discriminating. Many symptoms were rarely, if ever, present in FTD patients: losing objects, getting lost when wandering, disorientation, and visual hallucinations. Personality changes were highly discriminating, which were uniformly reported as early symptoms in FTD patients but occurred at various stages in AD. In addition, AD patients reacted to their changes with anxiety, distress, and loss of confidence, whereas FTD patients did not. The total questionnaire scores resulted in no overlapping scores between the groups. As with neuropsychological tests, no one indicator is pathognomonic; rather, the overall pattern is discriminating, and information about the reason for impairment (e.g., organization versus memory problems) gleaned from specific questions may be more useful than general statements of failure. Further research on this questionnaire is needed because interrater reliability was modest, and it remains unknown whether the questionnaire is effective during the course of the illness because interviews were done years after patient death.

Motor Impairments

In a small sample of autopsied confirmed cases, motor impairments were not part of the initial presentation in any of the cases (Knopman et al., 1990). However, as the disease progressed, most patients developed rigidity, masked facies, gait disturbance, dysarthria, and dysphagia. Only two of these cases were diagnosed with MNDD, whose clinical presentation varied from other cases only in having a substantially more rapid progression of deterioration. As noted previously, dysarthria, dysphagia, fasciculations, and muscular wasting may distinguish MNDD (Brun & Gustafson, 1998), and these symptoms may appear early in the disease.

Although minor differences in reflexes and motor function were observed between AD and FTD patients, Lopez and colleagues (1996) concluded that these symptom differences are not distinctive markers between AD and FTD.

Interventions

Data on treatment strategies for FTD are scarce because this group of dementias has only recently been recognized. Theoretical bases for developing treatments may progress with the discovery of mutations of the tau gene in FTD and mouse models of FTD (Perry & Miller, 2001). The site of action with acetylcholinesterase drug therapies for AD remains unknown; hence, there is no theoretical rationale for the application of these drugs to FTD patients (Lebert & Pasquier, 1999; Litvan, 2001). Unlike AD patients, FTD patients do not show sensitivity to anticholinergic medications, further suggesting that cholinesterase inhibitors are not implicated for treatment of FTD (Duara, Barker, & Luis, 1999).

Selective serotonin reuptake inhibitor (SSRI) treatment has been hypothesized to improve the behavioral disturbances because serotonin receptor binding is reduced in FTD patients (Lebert & Pasquier, 1999; Swartz, Miller, Lesser, & Darby, 1997). In a small preliminary study, 11 FTD patients were administered SSRIs and four behavioral symptoms were rated for signs of improvement three months later (Swartz et al., 1997). Depression, carbohydrate craving, compulsions, and disinhibition improved in slightly more than half the patients exhibiting each of these symptoms. In another small study, trazadone was effective in reducing delusions, aggression, anxiety, and irritability; and a higher dosage produced further gains in these symptoms and also in depression, disinhibition, and aberrant motor behavior (Lebert & Pasquier, 1999). These studies have several limitations including small sample sizes, use of different SSRIs, uncontrolled and unblinded designs, and lack of detail in the behavioral ratings. Nevertheless, they establish a basis for more methodologically sound SSRI treatment outcome research.

Very few studies have investigated behavioral treatments of FTD (Litvan, 2001). As with other dementias, FTD behavioral intervention studies emphasize individualized programs based on patient needs but are not specific to the cause of dementia (e.g., Robinson, 2001; Talerico & Evans, 2001).

Summary of Frontotemporal Dementia

The database and knowledge of FTD that has accumulated in only 20 years of research is impressive. Unlike MD and LBD, FTD does not occur concurrently with AD pathology. Rather, it is defined as a group of non-Alzheimer's dementias with focal atrophy of the frontotemporal areas. Subsyndromes include frontal lobe dementia (FLD), Pick's disease, motor neuron disease with dementia, progressive nonfluent aphasia, and semantic aphasia. Important characteristics of FTD make these dementias more dissimilar from AD than are MD and LBD. First, the pathological changes of FTD more focally affect the frontal and anterior temporal regions, whereas the pathological changes of AD typically begin in the hippocampus and posterior temporal and parietal regions and eventually may nonselectively impair much of the subcortical and cortical areas of the brain. FTD may also affect the brain asymmetrically, unlike more global dementias such as AD, VaD, MD, and LBD. Second, a genetic etiology of FTD is more strongly implicated by the roughly 50% co-occurrence rate of dementia in first-degree relatives. Third, average age of onset is in the fifties; this presenium onset also distinguishes FTD from most other dementias.

The Lund-Manchester diagnostic criteria for FTD have demonstrated high reliability and sensitivity rates comparable to those obtained for AD and even higher specificity rates compared to AD. These impressive results are probably attributable to the unique cognitive and psychiatric features of FTD. In contrast, investigations of the NINCDS-ADRDA diagnostic standards for AD have found that most FTD patients also meet

NINCDS-ADRDA criteria for AD. This is not surprising given that the NINCDS-ADRDA criteria were originally developed when the need to distinguish between AD and FTD was not yet recognized.

In addition to relatively precise diagnostic criteria for FTD, diagnosis may be aided by functional imaging techniques such as SPECT scans, which show decreased blood flow, and PET scans, which may reveal decreased cerebral metabolism in the frontotemporal regions. Unfortunately, these highly specialized and costly procedures are not available to all clinicians. The anatomically selective pathology of FTD results in a more distinct clinical presentation of FTD, particularly at the early stage of the diseases. The initial stage of FTD is characterized by changes in personality, behavior, and mood and progressive expressive aphasia. Although FTD may be clinically distinguishable from AD, other differential diagnoses that are challenging include AD and VaD with predominately frontal degeneration, Huntington's disease, progressive supranuclear palsy, corticobasal ganglionic degeneration, Creutzfeldt-Jakob disease, subcortical ischemic white matter disease, and frontal lobe tumors. FTD is more often mistaken for psychiatric disturbances than these other relatively rare conditions.

FTD patients are often thought to have better visuospatial and constructional, attention, orientation, memory, and reasoning abilities than AD patients. Nevertheless, investigations have documented that FTD and AD patients may perform similarly on measures of these cognitive skills. While quantitative scores between the two groups may be roughly equivalent, some researchers have argued that qualitative differences in error analysis distinguish these patient groups. More systematic research is needed to test this hypothesis. Furthermore, many studies have been remiss in documenting the duration of illness, a critical problem because FTD and AD clinical dissimilarities become blurred as the diseases progress and spread in the later stages.

The earliest and predominant symptoms of FTD are more often in the areas of mood, personality, and behavior than cognition. These may include apathy, lack of empathy, lability, irritability, impersistence, purposeless behavior, impaired judgment, socially inappropriate behavior, neglect of personal hygicnc, poor insight and awareness, inflexibility, perseverative responses, excessive oral stimulation and consumption, elaborate rituals, and disinhibition. The early onset of these may be particularly telling of FTD, as is the absence of deficits in orientation, memory, and spatial skills that are severe enough to interfere with daily functioning. These behavioral and cognitive distinctions may be difficult for caregivers (not to mention patients) to discern. For example, family members may interpret inactivity and withdrawal as forgetting to attend to daily tasks rather than apathy and neglect. Not surprisingly, research suggests that better discrimination may be achieved from questions that solicit specific and detailed information than from general and broad information (Barber et al., 1995).

FTD treatment research lags far behind other dementias. Drug therapies for slowing the progression of FTD, comparable to acetylcholinesterase drug therapies for AD, have not yet been developed. Given the predominance of mood and behavior symptoms of FTD, it is disappointing that only a handful of studies have investigated the use of psychotropic medications for FTD. Psychosocial interventions for the behavioral disturbances of dementia have been shown to be effective but have not been differentially applied to the various types of dementia.

CONCLUSIONS

Although autopsy studies are regarded as the most definitive way to estimate the rate of brain disorders and evaluate the validity of clinical diagnoses, some limitations should be noted. The first problem is verification bias in autopsy findings; that is, since autopsies are performed only on those who have died, it eliminates patients in the early stages of the illness when the dementia diagnosis may be less accurate (Bowler et al., 1998). The consequence is that autopsy comparisons may artificially raise the apparent accuracy of the clinical diagnoses. In particular, the results of autopsy studies have limited generalization to the large number of cases of depression or drug toxicity and other causes of delirium, which are initially misdiagnosed as dementia. Second, autopsy studies inevitably find variable rates of these dementias due to differences in sample sources. Only a few epidemiology studies stem from community-based samples. Most prevalence figures are established in specialty clinics where rates of rare forms of dementia or complicated cases are likely to be higher than those obtained from the general population. Rates may also vary because of nonstandard definitions of diseases, which is particularly problematic for MD and VaD. Finally, autopsy investigations typically focus on only one or a small number of dementias. Thus, studies that estimate rates of only AD and MD (e.g., Bowler et al., 1998) inevitably find higher rates than studies that calculate rates of AD, VaD, MD, and LBD (e.g., Holmes et al., 1999).

Given these caveats, this literature collectively points to some general conclusions about the rate of these dementias; however, precise comparisons remain unknown. First, pure AD is far less common than has been recognized. Perhaps making up only one-third to one-half of AD cases (Holmes et al., 1999; Lim et al., 1999), it is imperative that etiology and treatment research recognize the high rates of coexisting MD and LBD. Second, MD appears to be more common than pure AD, particularly given the high rate of coexisting white matter lesions and neurofibrillary tangles and plaques (Rockwood, 1997). Third, although some researchers have identified higher rates of Lewy bodies than infarcts in Alzheimer-confirmed cases (Galasko et al., 1994), this comparison is likely based on a narrow definition of MD. Using a broader definition of infarcts, the coexistence of AD with infarcts is perhaps two to three times more frequent than concomitant AD with LBD (Holmes et al., 1999). Fourth, pure cases of VaD are not common but are more frequent than pure LBD cases. Finally, FTD appears to be the least common among these diseases; however, there are many other causes of dementia that are rare, such as Creutzfeldt-Jakob disease, Huntington's disease, progressive supranuclear palsy, and corticobasal ganglionic degeneration.

The poor recognition of nonpure cases of AD has certainly impeded our accrued knowledge of the etiology of dementia. For example, as many as half of patients with pure AD identified at autopsy did not have a history of clinical dementia (Snowdon et al., 1997), suggesting the expression of dementia per se is closely tied to the additive effects of dual brain diseases. Unlike MD, the risk factors for LBD are unknown, presumably because LBD has only recently been recognized and researched. As genetic research advances our knowledge of the cause(s) of FTD, new information may shed light on the causes of other dementias.

The accuracy of clinical diagnoses is determined by two factors—the base rate of the disorder and the utility of the indicators. Hence, AD and MD diagnostic accuracy should be superior to rarer diseases such as LBD and FTD. However, diagnostic standards are poorly developed for MD compared to LBD and FTD. Inadequate criterion for MD results from lack of agreement in defining VaD and infarcts contributing to dementia (Roman et al.,

1993). In addition, the NINCDS-ADRDA criteria are highly accurate in identifying AD; however, accuracy declines for nonpure cases such as LBD and MD (Galasko et al., 1994). Unfortunately, many general physicians overlook causes of dementia other than AD and fail to consider that more than one brain abnormality is likely to contribute to dementia. The literature implies that clinicians should simultaneously use diagnostic criteria for AD, VaD, LBD, and FTD. Specificity figures reviewed previously suggest MD, LBD, and FTD are likely to be underdiagnosed when relying only on NINCDS-ADRDA criteria.

Several implications and recommendations are gleaned from the neuropsychology literature. Looking for statistical differences on single cognitive measures has been the primary approach in neuropsychological investigations; however, this strategy is not likely to be fruitful for two reasons. First, cognitive measures administered to numerous dementia patients usually have much dispersion (i.e., large standard deviations), reflecting the large individual differences within diagnostic groups. This creates overlapping distributions across groups and, thus, poor discrimination. Second, virtually every neuropsychological measure taps multiple cognitive skills. Thus, patients may perform poorly on the same measure, for example, Rey Complex Figure, for a host of different reasons—poor memory, impaired spatial skills, inadequate organizational strategies, impaired concentration, and so on. Results of the FTD literature suggest that individual test comparisons fail to detect differences in the cognitive functioning of AD and FTD patients that are otherwise apparent in daily functioning. Research is needed to develop systematic ways to compare profile patterns and to analyze failure systems. These approaches, which have been longstanding principles of leaders in the field of clinical neuropsychology (e.g., Lezak, 1995), need to be more commonly adopted in research arenas. It must also be kept in mind that the primary function of neuropsychological assessments is to describe the cognitive deficits and strengths of individual patients, information that is not provided by other laboratory tests such as imaging techniques. While the neuropsychological evaluation may not provide definitive diagnostic information, it will provide critical information for patient management by depicting how the dementia is impacting the patient's mental functioning.

The literature describing the symptomatology of FTD and LBD highlights the prevalence of noncognitive deficits associated with dementia. The neuropsychology field has established solid psychometric standards for developing cognitive tests. Unfortunately, these scientific standards have not been applied to the measurement of behavioral deficits. The most fundamental foundation of neuropsychology lies in normative data, which provides a basis for evaluating an individual's test score. Although behavior questionnaires are abundant, there is a critical need in the field of neuropsychology to standardize behavioral measures that are normed on various dementia groups. Such measures would likely increase the diagnostic process, allowing individual behavioral analyses that could be compared to norms obtained from AD, MD, LBD, and FTD patients.

A final comment about neuropsychological assessment of dementia patients concerns the use of screening measures. Screening tests are appropriately used to detect a small number of false negatives and a moderate number of false positives. This process should be used for determining the possible presence of dementia, but it is not acceptable for evaluation of the differential diagnosis of type of dementia. Differential assessments, by definition, examine more precise, detailed, and subtle indicators and, thus, require more extensive approaches than can be offered by screening measures.

The differentiation of various causes of dementia is not simply an academic process but has important implications for treatment and patient management planning. Treatment outcome studies, in general, must meet the challenges of sound methodological standards (e.g., adequate sample sizes, inclusion of control groups, clear divisions among treatments under study, placebo effects). In the treatment of dementia, these challenges are especially complicated because dementia-specific treatment effects cannot be determined if differential diagnoses are not clearly established. Counterindications of certain pharmacological treatments for LBD emphasize the dire need for accurate diagnosis before iatrogenic effects of treatments are risked. In addition, the hereditary component of FTD indicates that genetic counseling should be considered an important part of treatment (Hooten & Lyketsos, 1996).

The treatment literature reviewed in this chapter reveals two serious shortfalls. First, treatment of specific dementias has largely been ignored. Unlike psychosocial interventions, pharmacological treatments will require individually developed treatments for various dementias with distinct pathophysiologies. For example, the acetylcholinesterase inhibitor medications originally developed for slowing the progression of AD appear to be more effective for LBD but not efficacious in treating FTD. In contrast, behavioral programs are typically generic as to cause of dementia but highly individualized in developing interventions that are patterned for each patient. Because the psychosocial interventions are not specific to type of dementia, important findings from this literature are briefly reviewed in this conclusion section rather than in the previous individual sections.

Psychosocial interventions of dementia include a variety of techniques focused on demented patients and family or professional caregivers. Techniques include behavioral approaches targeting behavior excesses (e.g., agitation) and deficits (e.g., withdrawal); emotion-oriented approaches such as supportive psychotherapy, reminiscence therapy, life review, and validation therapy; cognitive remediation therapies such as reality orientation and skills training; and stimulation-oriented approaches such as recreational and activity therapies.

Given the deficits of demented individuals, psychological interventions for dementia patients are often targeted at caregivers and staff or altering the physical environment to promote safety and structure (Talerico & Evans, 2001). Behavioral management training for staff of extended care facilities has been shown to reduce behavior problems. For example, Moniz-Cook et al. (1998) discovered that the behavior problems of residents declined in facilities where staff received behavior management training. However, the effects were not long lasting; within one year, the rate of problem behaviors in the facilities was back to the pretraining level. It seems apparent that refresher courses are needed on a routine basis to maintain consistency in ability to manage problem behaviors.

Based on a large literature review, behavioral and environmental strategies for reducing behavioral problems have solid empirical support (Gatz et al., 1998; Kasl-Godley & Gatz, 2000). In another review of 11 treatment studies, 9 showed intervention was better than placebo (Rabins et al., 2000). Both educational and emotional support therapies were effective, but emotional support was more effective than education and the combination was better than either one alone. In contrast, there is cautious support for life review and reminiscence therapy for relieving depression and increasing life satisfaction in dementia patients (Kasl-Godley & Gatz, 2000). Finally, the limitation of cognitive remediation training for patients with progressive dementias, regardless of etiology, is widely acknowledged (Beck, Heacock, Mercer, Thatcher, & Sparkman, 1988). Even among studies that show improvements in the experimental group, gains appear to be minimal, are likely to fade over time, and do not tend to generalize beyond the specific treatment conditions (Kasl-Godley & Gatz, 2000). Furthermore, these efforts may produce iatrogenic effects including agitation, anxiety, and depression.

Psychological/behavioral studies are often conducted in institutional settings, where large numbers of participants are readily available. However, these samples of convenience leave a gap in our knowledge about the treatment effects with mildly impaired individuals who are more often residing at home—a serious limitation because these patients may be the most likely to benefit from such interventions. Management of behavioral disturbances is critical because these often cause more problems than reduced intellectual capacity. Estimates of the proportion of demented individuals who exhibit behavioral problems are as high as 93% (Moniz-Cook et al., 1998). Much of the stress experienced by caregivers stems from their attempts to manage behavior (Purandare, Allen, & Burns, 2000), and behavioral problems may play a significant role in caregivers' decisions to place their loved ones in nursing facilities (Balestreri, Grossberg, & Grossberg, 2000).

In conclusion, our current scientific knowledge base and clinical services are stymied by various dementias that are difficult to distinguish because they have symptoms that are not uniform either within or across patient groups. This review highlights the necessity to cultivate greater attention to the dementias caused by diseases other than or in addition to Alzheimer's disease. With this recognition, research on the pathophysiology, etiology, and treatment of dementias is likely to flourish.

REFERENCES

Balestreri, L., Grossberg, A., & Grossberg, G. T. (2000). Behavioral and psychological symptoms of dementia as a risk factor for nursing home placement. *International Psychogeriatrics, 12,* 59–62.

Ballard, C. G., Saad, K., Patel, A., Gahir, M., Solis, M., Cooper, B., et al. (1995). The prevalence and phenomenology of psychotic symptoms in dementia sufferers. *International Journal of Geriatric Psychiatry, 10,* 477–485.

Barber, R., Snowden, J. S., & Craufurd, D. (1995). Frontotemporal dementia and Alzheimer's disease: Retrospective differentiation using information from informants. *Journal of Neurology, Neurosurgery, and Psychiatry, 59,* 61–70.

Beck, C., Heacock, P., Mercer, S., Thatcher, R., & Sparkman, C. (1988). The impact of cognitive skills remediation training on persons with Alzheimer's disease or mixed dementia. *Journal of Geriatric Psychiatry, 21,* 73–88.

Boone, K. B., Miller, B. L., Lee, A., Berman, N., Sherman, D., & Stuss, D. T. (1999). Neuropsychological patterns in right versus left frontotemporal dementia. *Journal of the International Neuropsychological Society, 5,* 616–622.

Bowler, J. V., Munoz, D. G., Mersky, H., & Hachinski, V. (1998). Fallacies in the pathological confirmation of the diagnosis of Alzheimer's disease. *Journal of Neurology, Neurosurgery, and Psychiatry, 64,* 18–24.

Brown, D. F. (1999). Lewy body dementia. *Annals of Medicine, 31,* 188–196.

Brun, A. (1987). Frontal lobe degeneration of the non-Alzheimer type. I. Neuropathology. *Archives of Gerontology and Geriatrics, 6,* 193–208.

Brun, A., Englund, B., Gustafson, L., Passant, U., Mann, D. M., Neary, D., et al. (1994). Clinical and neuropathological criteria for frontotemporal dementia. *Journal of Neurology, Neurosurgery, and Psychiatry, 57,* 416–418.

Brun, A., & Gustafson, L. (1998). Frontal lobe degeneration of the non-Alzheimer type and dementia in motor neuron disease. In W. R. Markesbery (Ed.), *Neuropathology of dementing disorders* (pp. 158–169). London: Arnold.

Brun, A., & Gustafson, L. (1999). Clinical and pathological aspects of frontotemporal dementia. In B. L. Miller & J. L. Cummings (Eds.), *The human frontal lobes* (pp. 349–369). New York: Guilford Press.

Drachman, D. A., & Swearer, J. M. (1998). Cognitive disorders: Degenerative dementias. In J. Bogousslavsky & M. Fisher (Eds.), *Textbook of neurology* (pp. 389–414). Boston: Butterworth Heinemann.

Duara, R., Barker, W., & Luis, C. A. (1999). Frontotemporal dementia and Alzheimer's disease: Differential diagnosis. *Dementia and Geriatric Cognitive Disorders, 10,* 37–42.

Elfgren, C., Brun, A., Gustafson, L., Johanson, A., Minthon, L., Passant, U., et al. (1994). Neuropsychological tests as discriminators between dementia of Alzheimer type and frontotemporal dementia. *International Journal of Geriatric Psychiatry, 9,* 635–642.

Frisoni, G. B., Pizzolato, G., Geroldi, C., Rossato, A., Bianchetti, A., & Trabucchi, M. (1995). Dementia of the frontal type: Neuropsychological and (^{99}Tc)-HMPAO SPET features. *Journal of Geriatric Psychiatry and Neurology, 8,* 42–48.

Galasko, D., Hansen, L. A., Katzman, R., Wiederholt, W., Masliah, E., Terry, R., et al. (1994). Clinical-neuropathological correlations in Alzheimer's disease and related dementias. *Archives of Neurology, 51,* 888–895.

Galasko, D., Katzman, R., Salmon, D. P., & Hansen, L. A. (1996). Clinical and neuropathological findings in Lewy body dementias. *Brain and Cognition, 31,* 166–175.

Gatz, M., Fiske, A., Fox, L. S., Kaskie, B., Kasl-Godley, J. E., McCallum, T. J., et al. (1998). Empirically validated psychological treatments for older adults. *Journal of Mental Health and Aging, 4,* 9–46.

Gregory, C. A., & Hodges, J. R. (1996). Frontotemporal dementia: Use of consensus criteria and prevalence of psychiatric disorders. *Neuropsychiatry, Neuropsychology, and Behavioral Neurology, 9,* 145–153.

Gustafson, L. (1993). Clinical picture of frontal lobe degeneration of non-Alzheimer type. *Dementia, 4,* 143–148.

Hansen, L., Salmon, D., Galasko, D., Masliah, E., Katzman, R., DeTeresa, R., et al. (1990). The Lewy body variant of Alzheimer's disease: A clinical and pathological entity. *Neurology, 40,* 1–8.

Heyman, A., Fillenbaum, G. G., Gearing, M., Mirra, S. S., Welsh-Bohmer, K. A., Peterson, B., et al. (1999). Comparison of Lewy body variant of Alzheimer's disease with pure Alzheimer's disease. *Neurology, 52,* 1839–1844.

Hirono, N., Mori, E., Tanimukai, S., Kazui, H., Hashimoto, M., Hanihara, T., et al. (1999). Distinctive neurobehavioral features among neurodegenerative dementias. *Journal of Neuropsychiatry and Clinical Neuroscience, 11,* 498–503.

Holmes, C., Cairns, N., Lantos, P., & Mann, A. (1999). Validity of current clinical criteria for Alzheimer's disease, vascular dementia and dementia with Lewy bodies. *British Journal of Psychiatry, 174,* 45–50.

Hooten, W. M., & Lyketsos, C. G. (1996). Frontotemporal dementia: A clinico-pathological review of four postmortem studies. *Journal of Neuropsychiatry and Clinical Neuroscience, 8,* 10–19.

Johanson, A., & Hagberg, B. (1989). Psychometric characteristics in pts with frontal lobe degeneration of non-Alzheimer type. *Archives of Gerontology and Geriatrics, 8,* 129–137.

Kasl-Godley, J. E., & Gatz, M. (2000). Psychosocial interventions for individuals with dementia: An integration of theory, therapy, and a clinical understanding of dementia. *Clinical Psychology Review, 20,* 755–782.

Knopman, D. S., DeKosky, S. T., Cummings, J. L., Chui, H., Corey-Bloom, J., Relkin, N., et al. (2001). Practice parameter: Diagnosis of dementia (an evidence-based review). Report of the quality standards subcommittee of the American Academy of Neurology. *Neurology, 56,* 1143–1153.

Knopman, D. S., Mastri, A. R., Frey, W. H., Zung, J. H., & Rustan, T. (1990). Dementia lacking distinctive histological features: A common non-Alzheimer degenerative dementia. *Neurology, 40,* 251–256.

Lambon Ralph, M. A., Powell, J., Howard, D., Whitworth, A. B., Garrard, P., & Hodges, J. R. (2001). Semantic memory is impaired in both dementia with Lewy bodies and dementia of Alzheimer's type. A comparative neuropsychological study and literature review. *Journal of Neurology, Neurosurgery, and Psychiatry, 70,* 149–156.

Lebert, F., & Pasquier, F. (1999). Trazadone in the treatment of behavior in frontotemporal dementia. *Human Psychopharmacology, 14,* 279–281.

Lennox, G. G., & Lowe, J. S. (1998). Dementia with Lewy bodies. In W. R. Markesbery (Ed.), *Neuropathology of dementing disorders* (pp. 181–192). London: Arnold.

Lezak, M. D. (1995). *Neuropsychological Assessment* (3rd ed.). New York: Oxford University.

Lim, A., Tsuang, D., Kukull, W., Nochlin, D., Leverenz, J., McCormick, W., et al. (1999). Clinico-neuropathological correlation of Alzheimer's disease in a community-based sample. *Journal of the American Geriatrics Society, 47*(5), 564–569.

Lindau, M., Almkvist, O., Kushi, J., Boone, K., Johansson, S. E., Wahlund, L. O., et al. (2000). First symptoms: Frontotemporal dementia versus Alzheimer's disease. *Dementia and Geriatric Cognitive Disorders, 11*, 286–293.

Litvan, I. (2001). Therapy and management of frontal lobe dementia patients. *Neurology, 56*(Suppl. 4), 41–45.

Londos, E., Passant, U., Brun, A., & Gustafson, L. (2000). Clinical Lewy body dementia and the impact of vascular components. *International Journal of Geriatric Psychiatry, 15*, 40–49.

Lopez, O. L., Gonzales, M. P., Becker, J. T., Reynolds, C. F., Sudilovsky, A., & DeKosky, S. T. (1996). Symptoms of depression and psychosis in Alzheimer's disease and frontotemporal dementia. *Neuropsychiatry, Neuropsychology, and Behavioral Neurology, 9*, 154–161.

Lopez, O. L., Litvan, I., Catt, K. E., Stowe, R., Klunk, W., Kaufer, D. I., et al. (1999). Accuracy of four clinical diagnostic criteria for the diagnosis of neuro-degenerative disorders. *Neurology, 53*, 1292–1299.

Magnuson, T. M., Keller, B. K., & Roccaforte, W. (2000). Vascular dementia presenting as Lewy-body dementia. *Journal of the American Geriatrics Society, 48*, 1348.

Mathuranath, P. S., Nestor, P. J., Berrios, G. E., Rakowicz, W., & Hodges, J. R. (2000). A brief cognitive test battery to differentiate Alzheimer's disease and frontotemporal dementia. *Neurology, 55*, 1613–1620.

McKeith, I. G., & Burn, D. (2000). Spectrum of Parkinson's disease, Parkinson's dementia, and Lewy body dementia. *Neurologic Clinics, 18*, 865–883.

McKeith, I. G., Galasko, D., Kosaka, K., Perry, E. K., Dickson, D. W., Hansen, L. A., et al. (1996). Consensus guidelines for the clinical and pathologic diagnosis of Lewy bodies (DLB): Report of the consortium on DLB international workshop. *Neurology, 47*, 1113–1124.

McKeith, I. G., Perry, E. K., & Perry, R. H. (1999). Report of the second dementia with Lewy body international workshop. *Neurology, 53*, 902–905.

McKhann, G. M., Albert, M. S., Grossman, M., Miller, B., Dickson, D., & Trojanowski, J. Q. (2001). Clinical and pathological diagnosis of frontotemporal dementia. *Archives of Neurology, 58*, 1803–1809.

Mega, M. S., Masterman, D. L., Benson, D. F., Vinters, H. V., Tomiyasu, U., Craig, A. H., et al. (1996). Dementia with Lewy bodies: Reliability and validity of clinical and pathologic criteria. *Neurology, 47,* 1403–1409.

Mendez, M. F., Cherrier, M., Perryman, K. M., Pachana, N., Miller, B. L., & Cummings, J. L. (1996). Frontotemporal dementia versus Alzheimer's disease: Differential cognitive features. *Neurology, 47,* 1189–1194.

Miller, B. L. (1997). Clinical advances in degenerative dementias. *British Journal of Psychiatry, 171,* 1–3.

Miller, B. L., Cummings, J. L., Villaneuva-Meyer, J., Boone, K., Mehringer, C. M., Lesser, I. M., et al. (1991). Frontal lobe degeneration: Clinical, neuropsychological, and SPECT characteristics. *Neurology, 41,* 1374–1382.

Moniz-Cook, E., Agar, S., Silver, M., Woods, R., Wang, M., Elston, C., et al. (1998). Can staff training reduce behavioral problems in residential care for the elderly mentally ill? *International Journal of Geriatric Psychiatry, 13,* 149–158.

Neary, D., & Snowden, J. (1996). Fronto-temporal dementia: Nosology, neuropsychology, and neuropathology. *Brain and Cognition, 31,* 176–187.

Neary, D., Snowden, J. S., Gustafson, L., Passant, U., Stuss, D., Black, S., et al. (1998). Frontotemporal lobar degeneration: A consensus on clinical diagnostic criteria. *Neurology, 51,* 1546–1554.

Neary, D., Snowden, J. S., Northen, B., & Goulding, P. J. (1988). Dementia of frontal lobe type. *Journal of Neurology, Neurosurgery, and Psychiatry, 51,* 353–361.

Okazaki, H., Lipkin, L. E., & Aronson, S. M. (1961). Diffuse intracytoplasmic ganglionic inclusions (Lewy type) associated with progressive dementia and quadriparesis in flexion. *Journal of Neuropathology and Experimental Neurology, 20,* 237–244.

Pachana, N. A., Boone, K. B., Miller, B. L., Cummings, J. L., & Berman, N. (1996). Comparison of neuropsychological functioning in Alzheimer's disease and frontotemporal dementia. *Journal of the International Neuropsychological Society, 2,* 505–510.

Pasquier, F., Lebert, F., Lavenu, I., & Guillaume, B. (1999). The clinical picture of frontotemporal dementia: Diagnosis and follow up. *Dementia and Geriatric Cognitive Disorders, 10,* 10–14.

Perry, R. J., & Miller, B. L. (2001). Behavior and treatment in frontotemporal dementia. *Neurology, 56*(Suppl. 4), 46–51.

Purandare, N., Allen, N. H., & Burns, A. (2000). Behavioral and psychological symptoms of dementia. *Reviews in Clinical Gerontology, 10,* 245–260.

Rabins, P., Blacker, D., Bland, W., Bright-Long, L., Cohen, E., Katz, I., et al. (2000). Practice guidelines for the treatment of patients with Alzheimer's disease and other dementias of late life. In *Practice Guidelines for the Treatment of Psychiatric Disorders* (pp. 69–137). Washington DC: American Psychiatric Association.

Razani, J., Boone, K. B., Miller, B. L., Lee, A., & Sherman, D. (2001). Neuropsychological performance of right- and left-frontotemporal dementia compared to Alzheimer's disease. *Journal of International Neuropsychological Society, 7,* 468–480.

Risberg, J., Passant, U., Warkentin, S., & Gustafson, L. (1993). Regional blood flow in frontal lobe dementia of non-Alzheimer type. *Dementia, 4,* 186–187.

Robinson, K. M. (2001). Rehabilitation applications in caring for patients with Pick's disease and frontotemporal dementias. *Neurology, 56*(Suppl. 4), 56–58.

Rockwood, K. (1997). Lessons from mixed dementia. *International Psychogeriatrics, 9,* 245–249.

Roman, G. C., Tatemichi, T. K., Erkinjuntti, T., Cummings, J. L., Masdeu, J. C., Garcia, J. H., et al. (1993). Vascular dementia: Diagnostic criteria for research studies. *Neurology, 43,* 250–260.

Rosen, H. J., Legenfelder, J., & Miller, B. (2000). Frontotemporal dementia. *Neurologic Clinics, 18,* 979–992.

Salmon, D. P., Galasko, D., Hansen, L. A., Masliah, E., Butters, N., Thal, L. J., et al. (1996). Neuropsychological deficits associated with diffuse Lewy body disease. *Brain and Cognition, 31,* 148–165.

Small, S. A., & Mayeux, R. (2000). Alzheimer disease and related dementias. In L. P. Rowland (Ed.), *Merritt's neurology* (10th ed., pp. 633–641). Baltimore: Lippincott Williams & Wilkins.

Smeding, H. M., & deKoning, I. (2000). Frontotemporal dementia and neuropsychology: The value of missing values. *Journal of Neurology, Neurosurgery, and Psychiatry, 68,* 726–730.

Snowdon, D. A., Greiner, L. H., Mortimer, J. A., Riley, K. P., Greiner, P. A., & Markesberry, W. R. (1997). Brain infarction and the clinical expression Alzheimer's disease: The nun study. *Journal of the American Medical Association, 277,* 813–817.

Stevens, M., van Duijn, C. M., Kamphorst, W., de Knijff, P., Heutink, P., van Gool, W. A., et al. (1998). Familial aggregation in frontotemporal dementia. *Neurology, 50,* 1541–1545.

Swartz, J. R., Miller, B. L., Lesser, I. M., & Darby, A. L. (1997). Frontotemporal dementia: Treatment response to serotonin selective reuptake inhibitors. *Journal of Clinical Psychiatry, 58,* 212–216.

Talerico, K. A., & Evans, L. K. (2001). Responding to safety issues in frontotemporal dementias. *Neurology, 56*(Suppl. 4), 52–55.

Varma, A. R., Snowden, J. S., Lloyd, J. J., Talbot, P. R., Mann, D. M., & Neary, D. (1999). Evaluation of the NINCDS-ADRA criteria in the differentiation of Alzheimer's disease and frontotemporal dementia. *Journal of Neurology, Neurosurgery, and Psychiatry, 66,* 184–188.

Walker, Z., Allen, R. L., Shergill, S., & Katona, C. L. E. (1997). Neuropsychological performance in Lewy body dementia and Alzheimer's disease. *British Journal of Psychiatry, 170,* 156–158.

Weiner, M. F., Risser, R. C., Cullum, C. M., Honig, L., White, C., Speciale, S., et al. (1996). Alzheimer's disease and its Lewy body variant: A clinical analysis of postmortem verified cases. *American Journal of Psychiatry, 153,* 1269–1273.

CHAPTER 6

Neurologic Aspects of Vascular Dementia: Basic Concepts, Diagnosis, and Management

Gustavo C. Román

Vascular dementia (VaD) is the second most common form of dementia in the elderly after Alzheimer's disease (AD; Geldmacher & Whitehouse, 1996). This high frequency is consistent with the fact that stroke and ischemic heart disease are two leading causes of morbidity and mortality in the elderly. However, the deleterious effects of cerebrovascular and cardiovascular disease on cognitive function in the aged are only beginning to be recognized. For instance, in a recent study, Zuccalà et al. (2001) found vascular cognitive impairment in 26% of patients discharged from the hospital after treatment of congestive heart failure (CHF). Therefore, the potential number of cases of VaD of cardiogenic origin in the United States is very high, given that there are about 4.5 million patients with CHF. Cognitive dysfunction correlates inversely with left ventricular ejection fraction and systolic blood pressure. Thus, cerebral hypoperfusion appears to be a critical factor in cardiogenic VaD, although CHF is also a potential source of embolic stroke.

In addition, around one-third of stroke survivors ages 65 and older develop VaD (range: 25% to 41%) within three months following the ictus (Pohjasvaara, Erkinjuntti, Vataja, & Kaste, 1997; Tatemichi et al., 1990; Tatemichi, Desmond, Stern, et al., 1992). Therefore, in the United States alone, approximately 125,000 new cases of VaD after ischemic stroke occur every year (about one-third of the estimated 360,000 incident cases of AD). Based on these figures, more than one million elderly people are currently affected by poststroke VaD, and as many as another million, by cardiogenic VaD from CHF. However, the large majority of cases of VaD remain undiagnosed and untreated. It has been postulated that cardiogenic and poststroke VaD will become the most common form of dementia in the elderly (Román, 2002a).

DEFINITION

Vascular dementia is an etiologic category of the dementia syndrome that includes several clinical forms of dementia caused by ischemic or hemorrhagic cerebrovascular disease or by ischemic-hypoperfusive brain lesions of cardiovascular origin. VaD is more than multiinfarct dementia (MID) because it may be produced by a single, strategically located lacunar stroke or by periventricular white matter lesions with incomplete ischemia (Román et al., 1993).

EVOLUTION OF THE CONCEPT OF VAD

In 1910, Emil Kraepelin formulated the initial concept of *arteriosclerotic dementia,* a denomination that encompassed all cases of dementia in old age (senile dementia) and remained practically unchallenged for the next 60 years. VaD was originally called *arteriosclerotic insanity* by Otto Binswanger and Alois Alzheimer, who separated VaD from syphilitic dementia paralytica and from other forms of senile and presenile dementia (Mast, Tatemichi, & Mohr, 1995). Alzheimer and Binswanger were the first to underline the large clinicopathological spectrum of VaD.

Arteriosclerotic dementia incorrectly became synonymous with senile dementia, and it was widely held that cortical atrophy in the elderly resulted from progressive strangulation of blood flow leading to hypoxic neuronal death. This idea prevailed until 1974 when Hachinski, Lassen, and Marshall proposed the name *multiinfarct dementia* (MID), based on the findings of Tomlinson, Blessed, and Roth (1970), who were able to correlate dementia with volume of brain tissue lost to infarctions (i.e., patients with > 50 to 100 ml of tissue loss were more likely to develop VaD). Concurrently, it became clear that AD was the main cause of cerebral atrophy and senile dementia (Katzman, 1976).

With the development of brain imaging, in particular, computerized tomography (CT) and magnetic resonance imaging (MRI), the role of ischemic lesions of the cerebral white matter and lacunar strokes was recognized; and the all-inclusive term *vascular dementia* was introduced.

Lack of a clear definition of VaD and appropriate operational diagnostic criteria hampered studies on the frequency of VaD. In 1991, a workshop convened at the U.S. National Institutes of Health provided diagnostic criteria for VaD for use in neuroepidemiological studies and for controlled clinical trials (Román et al., 1993). The development of these criteria also contributed to reawaken research interest on VaD.

THE NINDS-AIREN CRITERIA

The diagnosis of VaD according to the consensus criteria of the National Institute of Neurological Disorders and Stroke (NINDS) and the Association Internationale pour la Recherche et l'Ensignement en Neurosciences (AIREN); (see Table 6.1) requires three basic elements:

1. Dementia, that is, impairment of memory and two other cognitive domains, such as executive function, attention, or orientation. The deficit should be severe enough to interfere with activities of daily living and not be explained solely by the motor consequences of the stroke.

2. Cerebrovascular lesions, demonstrated by brain imaging, including multiple strokes, a single strategic stroke, or extensive periventricular ischemia. By definition, absence of vascular lesions by brain imaging excludes VaD.

3. A link between dementia and vascular lesions, usually defined by onset of dementia within three months following a stroke.

However, Binswanger's disease and lacunar state resulting from multiple lacunes—two types of VaD associated with small vessel disease—may present as a slowly progressive subcortical-type dementia syndrome. Onset of the disease in these patients is often difficult to determine. In these two instances, the link between imaging and dementia is provided not by a temporal link but by the location and extent of the lesions.

EPIDEMIOLOGY

The high prevalence of vascular pathologies capable of producing VaD in the elderly is directly related to the progressive aging of the population. In Europe and North America, people 85 years old and older are the fastest

Table 6.1   NINDS-AIREN Diagnostic Criteria for Vascular Dementia*

I. The criteria for the diagnosis of *probable* VaD include *all* of the following:
  A. *Dementia:* Impairment of memory and two or more cognitive domains (including executive function), interfering with ADLs and not due to physical effects of stroke alone. *Exclusion criteria:* Alterations of consciousness, delirium, psychoses, severe aphasia or deficits precluding testing, systemic disorders, Alzheimer's disease or other forms of dementia.
  B. *Cerebrovascular disease:* Focal signs on neurological examination (hemiparesis, lower facial weakness, Babinski sign, sensory deficit, hemianopia, dysarthria) consistent with stroke (with or without history of stroke), *and* evidence of relevant CVD by brain CT or MRI including *multiple large-vessel infarcts* or a *single strategically placed infarct* (angular gyrus, thalamus, basal forebrain, or PCA or ACA territories), as well as *multiple basal ganglia* and *white matter lacunes* or *extensive periventricular white matter lesions,* or combinations thereof. *Exclusion criteria:* Absence of cerebrovascular lesions on CT or MRI.
  C. *A Relationship between the two disorders:* Manifested or inferred by the presence of one or more of the following:
    1. Onset of dementia within 3 months following a recognized stroke.
    2. Abrupt deterioration in cognitive functions; or fluctuating, stepwise progression of cognitive deficits.
II. Clinical features *consistent* with the diagnosis of *probable* VaD include the following:
  A. Early presence of gait disturbances (small-step gait or marche à petits pas or magnetic, apraxic-ataxic, or parkinsonian gait).
  B. History of unsteadiness and frequent, unprovoked falls.
  C. Early urinary frequency, urgency, and other urinary symptoms not explained by urologic disease.
  D. Pseudobulbar palsy.
  E. Personality and mood changes, abulia, depression, emotional incontinence, or other deficits including psychomotor retardation and abnormal executive function.
III. Features that make the diagnosis of VaD uncertain or unlikely include:
  A. Early onset of memory deficit and progressive worsening of memory and other cognitive functions such as language (transcortical sensory aphasia), motor skills (apraxia), and perception (agnosia), in the absence of corresponding focal lesions on brain imaging.
  B. Absence of focal neurological signs, other than cognitive disturbances.
  C. Absence of CVD on CT or MRI.

ACA = Anterior cerebral artery; ADLs = Activities of daily living; CT = Computerized tomography; CVD = Cerebrovascular disease; MRI = Magnetic resonance imaging; PCA = Posterior cerebral artery; VaD = Vascular dementia.

* From "Vascular Dementia: Diagnostic Criteria for Research Studies," Report of the NINDS-AIREN International Work Group, by G. C. Román, T. K. Tatemichi, T. Erkinjuntti, et al., 1993, *Neurology, 43,* pp. 250–260.

growing segment of the population and will number nearly 19 million by the year 2050. In addition, after age 85, close to 50% of the population has some form of cognitive impairment (Evans, 1990). Likewise, the incidence of stroke rises exponentially with age, increasing 100-fold from age 30 to 40 (3/10,000) to age 80 to 90 (300/10,000; Bonita, 1992).

PREVALENCE

A meta-analysis of 47 international studies on the prevalence of VaD by Jorm and Jolley (1998) found a number of consistent trends, as follows:

1. *Age-specific rates.* VaD prevalence increases exponentially with age, up to 95 years of age. The exponential rise is steeper for AD than for VaD; for the latter, prevalence rates double every 5.3 years, compared with 4.5 years for AD. Prevalence rates range from about 1.5 per 100 at ages 70 to 75 years to 14 to 16.3 per 100 at age 80 and older. VaD had higher prevalence than AD in 85-year-olds in Italy and Gothenburg (Sweden).

2. *Sex distribution.* VaD appears to be more common in men, especially before age 75, in contrast with AD, which predominates in women.

3. *Geographic (racial) variation.* VaD is more prevalent in Asian, Blacks, and Hispanics than in Caucasian populations. Stroke is the leading cause of death in Asian countries, compared with a third place in industrial countries. For instance, the number of strokes in China equals those of all developed countries combined (Bonita, 1992). Hypertensive small-vessel disease causing intracerebral hemorrhages, lacunar strokes, and white matter ischemia are particularly common in these racial groups.

INCIDENCE

Incidence data for VaD from longitudinal cohort studies are rather limited. Dubois and Herbert (2001) used age-standardized incidence ratios (SIRs) to analyze data from 10 incidence studies of VaD in comparison with the Canadian Study of Health and Aging. SIRs ranged from 0.42 to 2.68, confirming the geographical and racial variation of VaD.

CLINICAL DIAGNOSIS OF VAD

A number of ischemic and hemorrhagic neuropathological lesions may result in VaD (see Table 6.2). However, despite the anatomic and pathophysiological complexity of VaD, the clinical diagnosis of VaD may be simplified in two major groups, *acute* and *subacute,* according to the temporal profile of presentation.

ACUTE VAD

This group includes patients with new onset of dementia after an ictal event, such as a cerebral hemorrhage or, more often, a "strategic stroke" resulting

Table 6.2 Pathological Lesions Capable of Producing Vascular Dementia*

1. Multi-Infarct Dementia.
   Multiple large complete infarcts, cortico-subcortical in location, usually with perifocal incomplete infarction involving the white matter.
2. Strategic Infarct Dementia.
   A single brain infarct, often lacunar in size, damages functionally critical areas of the brain (angular gyrus, thalamus, basal forebrain, posterior cerebral artery and anterior cerebral artery territories).
3. Small-Vessel Disease with Dementia.
   Subcortical:
       Binswanger disease.
       CADASIL (Cerebral Autosomal Dominant Arteriopathy with
           Subcortical Infarcts and Leukoencephalopathy) .
       Lacunar dementia or lacunar state *(état lacunaire).*
       Multiple lacunes with extensive perifocal incomplete infarctions.
   Cortical and Subcortical:
       Hypertensive and arteriolosclerotic angiopathy.
       Amyloid angiopathies (including British dementia).
       Collagen-vascular disease with dementia.
4. Ischemic-Hypoxic Dementia (Hypoperfusive).
   Diffuse anoxic-ischemic encephalopathy.
   Restricted injury due to selective vulnerability.
   Incomplete white-matter infarction.
   Border-zone infarction.
5. Hemorrhagic Dementia.
   Traumatic subdural hematoma.
   Subarachnoid hemorrhage.
   Cerebral hematoma.
   Venous thrombosis.
6. Other mechanisms.

*Modified from "Pathology and Pathophysiology of Cerebrovascular Dementia: Pure Subgroups of Obstructive and Hypoperfusive Etiology," by A. Brun, 1994, *Dementia, 5,* pp. 145–147.

from occlusion of a large-size vessel or from a lacunar stroke due to small-vessel disease.

Dementia Due to Large-Vessel Infarction

Large ischemic strokes in three possible locations (so-called *strategic* strokes) may produce VaD:

1. A posterior form, with infarction in the territory of the posterior cerebral artery (PCA), involving ventral-medial temporal lobe, occipital structures, and thalamus. Brandt, Steinke, Thie, and Pessin (2000) found that about 25% of patients with infarctions in the PCA territory present with amnesia as a result of damage to the hippocampus, isthmus, entorhinal and perirhinal cortex, and parahippocampal gyrus. More limited lesions may occur with territorial infarctions of the anterior or posterior choroidal arteries. Unilateral lesions verbal amnesia with left-sided lesions and loss of visuospatial memory and memory for locations with lesions on the right side; bilateral damage gives rise to global amnesia. In some patients with mesial temporal lobe lesions (hippocampus and its projections), episodic anterograde amnesia—similar to that of AD—may be observed, resulting in difficulties for the differential diagnosis (Sarangi et al., 2000).

2. An anterior form, with infarction in the anterior cerebral artery (ACA) territory and medial frontal lobe lesions. Direct ischemic injury of the cholinergic nuclei in the basal forebrain has been documented in patients with subarachnoid hemorrhage from ruptured aneurysms of the anterior communicating artery (AComA), usually after surgical repair (von Cramon & Markowitsch, 2000). The damage results from sacrifice of perforating branches of the AComA or proximal ACA at the time of surgery, and patients present with severe anterograde amnesia for verbal or visuospatial material, along with severe apathy, lack of initiative and spontaneity, and executive dysfunction (Phillips, Sangalang, & Sterns, 1987). Postmortem neuropathological lesions were found in midline basal areas, rostral to the anterior commisure and lamina terminalis, destroying the medial septal nuclei (Ch1), the vertical portion (Ch2) of the nucleus of the diagonal band of Broca (ndbB), the nucleus accumbens, and adjacent areas. Damage to the cholinergic neurons in the septal nucleus and

ndbB appears to determine the persistence of the amnesia (Gade & Mortensen, 1990; Phillips et al., 1987).

3. A basal form, with bilateral involvement of the basal ganglia and thalamus, more correctly classified under the small-vessel type of acute VaD (see, thalamic dementia section later).

Poststroke Dementia

In addition to the previous forms of strategic single-stroke dementia, the most common form of *poststroke VaD* is MID, occurring when dementia develops after multiple strokes. The incidence of poststroke dementia is ascertained by performing cognitive tests after stroke (typically, at three months postictus).

According to Tatemichi et al. (1990), Pohjasvaara et al. (1997), and Barba et al. (2000), the most important risk factors for poststroke VaD are older age, lower educational level, recurrent stroke, left hemisphere stroke (associated with a fivefold increase in risk of developing poststroke dementia, an effect not explained by aphasia), as well as presence of dysphagia, gait limitations, and urinary impairment. Patients with poststroke VaD are more often current smokers and have lower blood pressure and orthostatic hypotension. Larger periventricular white matter ischemic lesions by MRI are also predictive of poststroke dementia. Moroney and colleagues (1996) observed that hypoxic and ischemic complications of acute stroke (e.g., seizures, cardiac arrhythmias, aspiration pneumonia) increase more than fourfold the risk of developing poststroke dementia.

Lacunar Dementia ("Inferior Genu" Dementia)

The clinical picture is characterized by sudden change in cognition, associated with fluctuating attention, memory loss, confusion, abulia, psychomotor retardation, inattention, and other features of frontal lobe dysfunction but with mild focal findings such as hemiparesis or dysarthria (Pantoni et al., 2001; Tatemichi, Desmond, Prohovnik, et al., 1992; Tatemichi, Desmond, & Prohovnik, 1995). Lacunar dementia is usually due to a single lacunar stroke involving the inferior genu of the internal capsule, causing ipsilateral blood flow reduction to the inferomedial frontal cortex by a mechanism of diaschisis (Chukwudelunzu, Meschia, Graff-Radford, & Lucas, 2001; Mori, 1998). This lesion in the genu of the inferior capsule may sever corticothalamic and thalamocortical fibers in the thalamic peduncles that detach from the internal capsule to enter the thalamus at its rostral and caudal poles and along its dorsal surface. Lacunar strokes of the inferior genu of the internal capsule result from involvement of anterior perforators arising from the internal carotid artery (ICA) or from the ACA. These arteries are frequently affected by hypertension and other forms of small-vessel SIVD and could be an unrecognized cause of cognitive deficits. For instance, Ghika et al. (1989) found neuropsychological deficits in up to 34% of patients with lacunes in the territory of deep perforators of the ICA system identified by brain CT.

Thalamic Dementia

A mechanism similar to the one mentioned previously probably underlies the so-called "thalamic dementia of vascular origin" (Castaigne et al., 1966) caused by large bilateral paramedian thalamic polar infarcts (Bogousslavsky, 1995) and some cases of caudate stroke (Caplan et al., 1990). Lesions involve the anterior (polar) thalamus in territories irrigated by the polar thalamic artery, a branch of the posterior communicating artery; or, the medial and central thalamus involving the dorsomedial nucleus and the mamillothalamic tract (Van der Werf, Witter, Uylings, & Jolles, 2000). These last two structures are irrigated by the paramedian thalamic artery, a branch of the basilar-PCA. The critical lesion in the production of thalamic amnesia is the damage of the mamillothalamic tract that projects into the anterior nuclei of the thalamus, and then to the cingulate cortex (Bogousslavsky, Regli, & Uske, 1988; Van der Werf et al., 2000).

All patients present with depressed level of consciousness that gradually improves over days to weeks to reveal impairments in attention, motivation, initiative, executive functions, memory, as well as dramatic verbal and motor slowness and apathy (Ghika-Schmid & Bogousslavsky, 2000; Katz, Alexander, & Mandell, 1987). Gaze abnormalities are common and include vertical gaze paresis, medial rectus paresis, and absent convergence (Bogousslavsky et al., 1988). Dysarthria and mild hemiparesis may be present when the lesions extend to the subthalamic and midbrain tegmentum in the territory of the superior paramedian mesencephalic artery. Left thalamic lesions have memory deficits more often than right-sided lesions; verbal and sometimes visual memory loss is present with left-sided lesions and visual amnesia with right-sided ones. Global amnesia occurs with bilateral lesions or in those with simultaneous damage to the mamillothalamic tract and the inferior thalamic peduncle (Graff-Radford, Damasio, Yamada, Eslinger, & Damasio, 1985).

SUBACUTE VAD

The main forms of subacute VaD are *Binswanger's disease, CADASIL (cerebral autosomal dominant arteriopathy with subcortical infarcts and leukoencephalopathy)*, and some types of *cerebral amyloid angiopathy*. The temporal profile of presentation of these conditions is typically subacute, with a chronic course marked by fluctuations and progressive worsening. This group is characterized clinically by a subcortical dementia with frontal lobe deficits, depressive mood changes, motor involvement, parkinsonian features, pseudobulbar palsy, and urinary urgency.

Binswanger's Disease

In 1894, Binswanger described as the hallmark of this condition the presence of an ischemic periventricular leukoencephalopathy that typically spares the arcuate subcortical U fibers (as cited in Blass, Hoyer, & Nitsch, 1991; Brun, Fredriksson, & Gustafson, 1992). These periventricular, distal-territory, white matter lesions in the elderly brain are due to chronic ischemia with incomplete infarction (Erkinjuntti et al., 1996; Pantoni & García, 1995, 1997; Román, 1987, 1988; van Gijn, 1998; van Swieten et al., 1991). Small-vessel disease and multiple lacunes often coexist in Binswanger's disease (Román, 1985a, 1985b). This combination of lacunes and white matter lesions is called *subcortical ischemic VaD* (SIVD) and is currently considered one of the most common forms of VaD (Román, Erkinjuntti, Wallin, Pantoni, & Chui, 2002).

The clinical manifestations of Binswanger's disease include a cognitive and motor syndrome with characteristics of subcortical dementia including executive dysfunction, loss of verbal fluency, slowing of motor function with perseveration, impersistence, inattention, difficulties with set shifting, and abnormal Luria's kinetic melody tests. Memory loss is characterized by poor retrieval and intact recognition. Apathy, depression, and behavioral problems are common. Mild residual hemiparesis or other discrete focal findings are often found, as well as a peculiar short-stepped gait *(marche à petits pas)*, dysarthria, pseudobulbar palsy, and, in some cases, astasia-abasia. Extrapyramidal features, such as inexpressive facies, slowness of movement, axial rigidity, and loss of postural reflexes, frequent falls, increased urinary frequency, and nocturia are also common findings (Babikian & Roper, 1987; Caplan, 1995; Fredriksson, Brun, & Gustafson, 1992; Román, 1987).

CADASIL

The first genetic form of VaD to be clearly identified (Bousser & Tournier-Lasserve, 1994; Tournier-Lasserve, Iba-Zizen, Romero, & Bousser, 1991; Tournier-Lasserve et al., 1993) was CADASIL, a systemic autosomal dominant arteriopathy mapped to chromosome 19 as a mutation of the *Notch 3* gene (Tournier-Lasserve et al., 1993). Onset of the disease is in early adulthood (mean age: 46 years), leading to VaD and death about 20 years after onset. The underlying vascular lesion is a nonamyloid, nonatherosclerotic microangiopathy with thickening, reduplication and fragmentation of the internal elastic lamella of small arteries and arterioles, and presence of deposits of eosinophilic, periodic acid Schiff (PAS)-positive material in the arterial media. On electron microscopy, these deposits consist of typical granular osmiophilic material present in the basement membranes of vascular smooth muscle cells of arterioles (100 to 400 mm in diameter) and capillaries, primarily in the brain but also in other organs. The diagnosis may be established by skin biopsy (Ruchoux et al., 1995) with confirmation by immunostaining with a *Notch 3* monoclonal antibody (Joutel et al., 2001). Neuropathology examination shows lacunar strokes localized in basal ganglia, thalamus, centrum ovale, and pons, associated with extensive, confluent areas of frontal ischemic leukoencephalopathy, particularly in periventricular regions.

Clinically, CADASIL is a subcortical form of VaD that begins in early adulthood with recurrent ischemic episodes, usually transient ischemic attacks (TIAs) or lacunar strokes, in the absence of risk factors for vascular disease, culminating in VaD and death usually about 20 years after onset of symptoms. Migraine with aura and depression are also common. The dementia is subcortical, frontal in type, accompanied by gait disturbances, urinary incontinence, and pseudobulbar palsy, clinically identical to that of sporadic Binswanger's disease. Striking white matter changes and lacunar strokes can be demonstrated by brain CT and MRI in symptomatic and asymptomatic members of families affected by CADASIL.

SEPARATING AD FROM VAD

The Nun Study (Snowdon et al., 1997) reported that in very old subjects, lacunes are an important factor in the clinical expression of AD. The difficulties in separating VaD from AD have been stressed, and the names *mixed dementia* or *AD plus CVD* have been used for cases combining vascular and degenerative pathologies. In addition, patients with anterior choroidal artery stroke may fulfill criteria for AD (Sarangi et al., 2000).

As mentioned before, the prevalence of cerebrovascular and cardiovascular diseases increases steeply with age; therefore, histological changes of AD in the elderly often coexist with stroke and vascular pathology (Galasko et al., 1994; Lim et al., 1999). Lacunar strokes appear to multiply the effect of AD lesions, whereby, in elderly subjects with presence of one or two lacunar strokes, the likelihood of clinically manifesting a dementia is increased 20-fold (Snowdon et al., 1997). Also, a lesser amount of senile plaques and neurofibrillary tangles are required for the subject to manifest signs of dementia.

The instruments used to separate AD from VaD include the following:

1. The *ischemic score:* This score may provide additional elements for the diagnosis of the multiinfarct form of VaD (Moroney et al., 1996). A score of 7 or greater is consistent with MID, a score of 4 is consistent with AD, and a score of 5 to 6 is suggestive of AD plus CVD. Moroney et al. found the following features more often in VaD than in AD: stepwise deterioration, fluctuating course, history of hypertension, history of stroke, and focal neurological symptoms.

2. The *prestroke dementia interview* (Hénon et al., 2001): By means of a careful interview of relatives and caregivers, it is possible to successfully diagnose prestroke dementia because, in most instances, probable AD is a likely etiology for progressive memory loss occurring before the ictus. This is found in about one-third of poststroke dementia patients (Hénon et al., 2001; Jagust, 2001).

3. *Mild cognitive impairment* (MCI): The amnestic form of MCI is readily identifiable and carries a risk of conversion to clinically probable AD at a rate of 10% to 15% per year, compared with 1% to 2% per year in healthy age-matched control subjects (Petersen et al., 2001). Vascular risk factors may predispose not only to VaD, but also to the development of AD.

PATHOGENESIS OF VAD

Fisher (1965) remarked that lacunar strokes typically do not cause disturbances in higher cerebral functions and, when present, "always exclude a lacunar diagnosis." Although the vast majority of lacunes in the aged population are silent (Longstreth et al., 1998), hospital-based lacunar infarction series show that about 30% of these patients develop dementia (Babikian, Wolfe, Linn, Knoefel, & Albert, 1990; Tatemichi et al., 1993; Wolfe, Linn, Babikian, Knoefel, & Albert, 1990). In our own clinicopathological review of 100 consecutive autopsies of patients with lacunar strokes at the Hôpital de La Salpêtrière (Román, 1975, 1985b), we found 72 cases with multiple lacunes, but only 36% of these were clinically demented. In 6 cases, AD was responsible for the dementia (AD plus CVD). In 16 of these cases of *état lacunaire,* appropriate celloidin-embedded coronal sections stained for myelin were available; in these, the number and location of the lacunes were similar to those of nondemented controls. However, in demented patients, dilatation of the lateral ventricles was present, suggesting that advanced white matter lesions from Binswanger's disease were causing the cognitive decline; another possible explanation was undiagnosed normal-pressure hydrocephalus (Román, 1991). In CADASIL, a direct relationship exists between white matter lesions load and degree of cognitive deterioration (Chabriat et al., 1998), and, in general, the same is true of sporadic Binswanger's disease. Recently, Kramer et al. (2002) demonstrated decline in executive function in *nondemented* patients with subcortical lacunes. Of interest, the executive function measures were correlated with the extent of white matter abnormalities but not with the number of lacunes.

Population-based MRI data (Longstreth et al., 1996, 1998) indicate that lacunes and white matter changes are common lesions, found in about one in four people older than 65 years. Most lacunes (89%) are silent, associated with increasing age, hypertension, higher creatinine level, smoking, carotid disease, and diabetes (Longstreth et al., 1998). The apolipoprotein Eε 2/3 genotype has also been associated with microangiopathic brain lesions (Schmidt et al., 1997). Multivariate models (Longstreth et al., 1996, 1998) suggest that white matter lesions of increasing severity are associated more strongly than lacunes with cognitive impairment and lower limb dysfunction. The clinical manifestations of evolving white matter lesions and most lacunes are not recognized as strokes by patients or physicians and, to be detected, require specific and sensitive tests of executive function. Unfortunately, widely used bedside tests for dementia screening such as the Mini-Mental State Examination (MMSE) and the cognitive portion of the CAMDEX (Cambridge Mental Disorders of the Elderly Examination [CAMCOG]), target only posterior cortical areas and overlook executive functions (Román & Royall, 1999).

FRONTAL EXECUTIVE FUNCTION

VaD is characterized clinically by executive dysfunction, that is, the prominent loss of executive function (Cummings, 1994). This is a major component of the cognitive disability and the dementia and explains the loss of planning capacity, working memory, attention and concentration, stimuli discrimination, abstraction, conceptual flexibility, and self-control (Fuster, 2000; Royall et al., 2002). Frontal executive functions control volition, planning, programming, and monitoring of complex goal-directed activities such as cooking, dressing, shopping, and housework. Patients with executive dysfunction are often capable of performing individual steps of a complex problem but are unable to provide a correct strategy to solve it. In contrast with AD, memory loss is not an early feature of VaD and is never as profound as in AD. Tests for instrumental activities of daily living are a good surrogate of executive function control.

Executive dysfunction, as well as other subcortical features of VaD, including mood and personality changes, gait, and urinary control problems, are due to interruption of frontal cortico-subcortical pathways. Alexander et al. (1986) demonstrated the existence of five parallel anatomic circuits that link regions of the frontal cortex to the striatum (caudate nucleus), globus pallidus-substantia nigra, and thalamus, with thalamo-cortical connections closing the loop. These independent frontal circuits originate in the supplementary motor area, frontal eye fields, dorsolateral prefrontal region, lateral orbitofrontal area, and anterior cingulate cortex (Masterman & Cummings, 1997; Mega & Cummings, 1994). The last three are the principal behaviorally-relevant circuits, and identifiable symptoms are produced by interruption at any point of each loop by lacunar strokes or by white matter lesions:

1. Disconnection of the dorsolateral prefrontal-subcortical circuit results in executive dysfunction.

2. Orbito-frontal-subcortical circuit lesions preclude frontal inhibition of the limbic system and are manifested by uninhibited behaviors, impulsivity, and personality change.

3. The anterior cingulate (medial frontal) cortex mediates motivation; thus, lesions of this circuit often result in apathy, abulia, and even akinetic mutism.

Each segment of the circuit has different neurotransmitters, modulators, and receptor subtypes that may provide the basis for future pharmacological intervention.

EXECUTIVE FUNCTION TESTS

A few bedside tests are available for the evaluation of executive dysfunction, including the CLOX test, a brief measure of executive control based on a clock drawing task (Royall, Cordes, & Polk, 1998); the trail making test, part B; Luria's kinetic melody tests (Luria, 1966) and the behavioral dyscontrol scale (Grigsby, Kaye, & Robbins, 1992); the EXIT-25, a structured interview for clinical assessment of frontal symptoms (Royall, Mahurin, & Gray, 1992); and STEP, a method for evaluation of cognitive, psychiatric, and neurological frontal subcortical symptoms and signs (Wallin et al., 1996). In addition, Román and Royall (1999) emphasized that gait, balance, micturition control, and manual dexterity should be evaluated in patients with VaD to determine their functional status. A depression scale should also be used routinely to diagnose and treat vascular depression (Alexopoulos, Kiosses, Klimstra, Kalayam, & Bruce, 2002).

DRUG TREATMENTS FOR VAD

Relatively few medications for VaD have been tested in controlled clinical trials (Román, 2000a). The purported efficacy of *vasodilators* such as nicotinic acid, cyclandelate, and papaverine, among others, is based on uncontrolled open-label trials. Other drugs with modest efficacy in VaD, demonstrated in randomized controlled clinical trials (Class I evidence) include calcium channel blockers, piracetam, oxiracetam, nicergoline, citicoline, memantine, pentoxifylline and propentofylline, aspirin, triflusal, and Ginkgo biloba.

CHOLINESTERASE INHIBITORS

The cholinergic agents approved for the treatment of AD, including donepezil hydrochloride (Aricept®), rivastigmine tartrate (Exelon®), and galantamine hydrobromide (Reminyl®), have been used in patients with AD plus CVD. Only donepezil has been used in cases with VaD after excluding AD patients.

Rivastigmine in doses of 1 to 12 mg/day was evaluated in 700 patients with mild to moderate AD with or without vascular risk factors according to the modified ischemic score. Cognitive function, measured by the ADAS-cog test, was significantly improved versus placebo, particularly in patients with vascular risk factors (Kumar, Anand, Messina, Hartman, & Veach, 2000). Galantamine (24 mg/day) was evaluated in 537 patients with AD plus CVD or with VaD according to NINDS/AIREN criteria. After six months, ADAS-cog scores were better in the treated group compared with placebo. The Clinician's Interview-based Impression of Change plus caregiver input (CIBIC-plus), the behavioral measures (Neuropsychiatric Inventory [NPI]), and the activities of daily living (Disability Assessment in Dementia [DAD]) improved or remained stable in the treated group (Erkinjuntti et al., 2002).

Two large ($n = 1,200$) donepezil trials are the only ones to have included pure cases of probable and possible VaD, recruited according to the NINDS/AIREN criteria. Results of Trial 307 are yet to be published. Trial 308 included 616 patients randomized to low-dose donepezil 5 mg/day ($n = 208$), high-dose 10 mg/day ($n = 215$), or placebo ($n = 193$) for 24 weeks. The population selected was clearly different from cases of AD plus CVD, in that it showed less cognitive decline in the placebo group than AD cases and an overall higher frequency of cardiovascular and cerebrovascular pathology. The two treated groups showed significant improvement in cognitive scores (ADAS-cog, MMSI) and global scores (CIBIC-plus) compared to placebo (Pratt et al., 2002).

PUBLIC HEALTH ASPECTS OF VAD

Of major public health interest are the results of treatment trials of hypertension and use of statins in the elderly showing decreased incidence of dementia. Treatment of other risk factors for VaD is also indicated, including smoking, hyperfibrinogenemia, orthostatic hypotension, cardiac arrhythmias, congestive heart failure, and obstructive sleep apnea. Blood glucose control in patients with diabetes and lowering of fibrinogen and lipids should be beneficial. Food supplementation with folic acid has been recently implemented in an effort to reduce effects of hyperhomocysteinemia on vascular disease. Other preventable factors should be determined in an effort to decrease the risk of dementia and disabling stroke with appropriate preventive treatment (Román, 2002b).

REFERENCES

Alexander, G. E., DeLong, M. R., & Strick, P. L. (1986). Parallel organization of functionally segregated circuits linking basal ganglia and cortex. *Annual Review of Neurosciences, 9,* 137–181.

Alexopoulos, G. S., Kiosses, D. N., Klimstra, S., Kalayam, B., & Bruce, M. L. (2002). Clinical presentation of the depression-executive dysfunction syndrome of late life. *American Journal of Geriatric Psychiatry, 10,* 98–106.

Babikian, V. L., & Ropper, A. H. (1987). Binswanger's disease: A review. *Stroke, 18,* 2–12.

Babikian, V. L., Wolfe, N., Linn, R., Knoefel, J. E., & Albert, M. L. (1990). Cognitive changes in patients with multiple cerebral infarcts. *Stroke, 21,* 1013–1018.

Barba, R., Martinez-Espinosa, S., Rodriguez-Garcia, E., Pondal, M., Vivancos, J., & Del Ser, T. (2000). Poststroke dementia: Clinical features and risk factors. *Stroke, 31,* 1494–1501.

Blass, J. P., Hoyer, S., & Nitsch, R. (1991). A translation of Otto Binswanger's article: The delineation of the generalized progressive paralyses. *Archives of Neurology, 48,* 961–972.

Bogousslavsky, J. (1995). Thalamic infarcts. In G. Donnan, B. Norrving, J. Bamfortd, & J. Bogousslavsky (Eds.), *Lacunar and other subcortical infarctions* (pp. 149–170). Oxford, England: Oxford University Press.

Bogousslavsky, J., Regli, F., & Uske, A. (1988). Thalamic infarcts: Clinical syndromes, etiology, and prognosis. *Neurology, 38,* 837–848.

Bonita, R. (1992). Epidemiology of stroke. *Lancet, 339,* 342–344.

Bousser, M.-G., & Tournier-Lasserve, E. (1994). Summary of the Proceedings of the First International Workshop on CADASIL (cerebral autosomal dominant arteriopathy with subcortical infarcts and leukoencephalopathy), Paris, May 19–21, 1993. *Stroke, 25,* 704–707.

Brandt, T., Steinke, W., Thie, A., & Pessin, M. S. (2000). Posterior cerebral artery territory infarcts: Clinical features, infarct topography, causes and outcome.

Multicenter results and a review of the literature. *Cerebrovascular Diseases,* *10,* 170–182.

Brun, A., Fredriksson, K., & Gustafson, L. (1992). Pure subcortical arteriosclerotic encephalopathy (Binswanger's disease): A clinicopathological study. Part II: Pathologic features. *Cerebrovascular Diseases, 2,* 87–92.

Caplan, L. R. (1995). Binswanger's disease–revisited. *Neurology, 45,* 253–262.

Caplan, L. R., Schmahmann, J. D., Kase, C. S., Feldmann, E., Baquis, G., Greenberg, J. P., et al. (1990). Caudate infarcts. *Archives of Neurology, 47,* 133–143.

Castaigne, P., Buge, A., Cambier, J., Escourolle, R., Brunet, P., & Degos, J. D. (1996). Démence thalamique d'origine vasculaire par ramollissement bilatéral, limité au territoire du péduncule retromamillaire. A propos de deux observations anatomo-cliniques. *Revue Neurologique (Paris), 114,* 89–107.

Chabriat, H., Levy, C., Taillia, M.-T., Iba-Zizen, M. T., Vahedi, K., Joutel, A., et al. (1998). Patterns of MRI lesions in CADASIL (cerebral autosomal dominant arteriopathy with subcortical infarcts and leukoencephalopathy). *Neurology, 51,* 452–457.

Chukwudelunzu, F. E., Meschia, J. F., Graff-Radford, N. R., & Lucas, J. A. (2001). Extensive metabolic and neuropsychological abnormalities associated with discrete infarction of the genu of the internal capsule. *Journal of Neurology, Neurosurgery, and Psychiatry, 71,* 658–662.

Cummings, J. L. (1994). Vascular subcortical dementias: Clinical aspects. *Dementia, 5,* 177–180.

Dubois, M. F., & Herbert, R. (2001). The incidence of vascular dementia in Canada: A comparison with Europe and East Asia. *Neuroepidemiology, 20,* 179–187.

Erkinjuntti, T., Benavente, O., Eliasziw, M., Munoz, D. G., Sulkava, R., Haltia, M., et al. (1996). Diffuse vacuolization (spongiosis) and arteriolosclerosis in the frontal white matter occurs in vascular dementia. *Archives of Neurology, 53,* 325–332.

Erkinjuntti, T., Kurz, A., Gauthier, S., Bullock, R., Lilienfeld, S., & Damaraju, C. V. (2002). Efficacy of galantamine in probable vascular dementia and Alzheimer's disease combined with cerebrovascular disease: A randomised trial. *Lancet, 359,* 1283–1290.

Evans, D. A. (1990). Estimated prevalence of Alzheimer's disease in the United States. *Milbank Quarterly, 68,* 267–289.

Fisher, C. M. (1965). Lacunes: Small deep cerebral infarcts. *Neurology, 15,* 774–784.

Fredriksson, K., Brun, A., & Gustafson, L. (1992). Pure subcortical arteriosclerotic encephalopathy (Binswanger's disease): A clinicopathological study. Part I: Clinical features. *Cerebrovascular Diseases, 2,* 82–86.

Fuster, J. M. (2000). Executive frontal functions. *Experimental Brain Research, 133,* 66–70.

Gade, A., & Mortensen, E. L. (1990). Temporal gradient in the remote memory impairment of amnesic patients with lesions in the basal forebrain. *Neuropsychologia, 28,* 985–1001.

Galasko, D., Hansen, L. A., Katzman, R., Wiederholt, W., Masliah, E., Terry, R., et al. (1994). Clinical-neuropathological correlations in Alzheimer's disease and related dementia. *Archives of Neurology, 51,* 888–895.

Geldmacher, D. S., & Whitehouse, P. J. (1996). Evaluation of dementia. *New England Journal of Medicine, 335,* 330–336.

Ghika, J., Bogousslavsky, J., & Regli, F. (1989). Infarcts in the territory of the deep perforators from the carotid system. *Neurology, 39,* 507–512.

Ghika-Schimid, F., & Bogousslavsky, J. (2000). The acute behavioral syndrome of anterior thalamic infarction: A prospective study of 12 cases. *Annals of Neurology, 48,* 220–227.

Graff-Radford, H. B., Damasio, H., Yamada, T., Eslinger, P. J., & Damasio, A. R. (1985). Nonhaemorrhagic thalamic infarction: Clinical, neuropsychological and electrophysiological findings in four anatomical groups defined by computerized tomography. *Brain, 108,* 485–516.

Grigsby, J., Kaye, K., & Robbins, L. J. (1992). Reliabilities, norms and factor structure of the Behavioral Dyscontrol Scale. *Perceptual and Motor Skills, 74,* 883–892.

Hachinski, V., Lassen, N., & Marshall, J. (1974). Multiinfarct dementia: A cause of mental deterioration in the elderly. *Lancet, 14,* 207–210.

Hénon, H., Durieu, I., Guerouaou, D., Lebert, F., Pasquier, F., & Leys, D. (2001). Poststroke dementia: Incidence and relationship to prestroke cognitive decline. *Neurology, 57,* 1216–1222.

Jagust, W. (2001). Untangling vascular dementia. *Lancet, 358,* 2097–2098.

Jorm, A. F., & Jolley, D. (1998). The incidence of dementia: A meta-analysis. *Neurology, 51,* 728–733.

Joutel, A., Favrole, P., Labauge, P., Chabriat, H., Lescoat, C., Andreux, F., et al. (2001). Skin biopsy immunostaining with a Notch 3 monoclonal antibody for CADASIL diagnosis. *Lancet, 358,* 2049–2051.

Katz, D. I., Alexander, M. P., & Mandell, A. M. (1987). Dementia following strokes in the mesencephalon and diencephalon. *Archives of Neurology, 44,* 1127–1133.

Katzman, R. (1976). The prevalence and malignancy of Alzheimer's disease, a major killer. *Archives of Neurology, 33,* 217–218.

Kramer, J. H., Reed, B. R., Mungas, D., Weiner, M. W., & Chui, H. C. (2002). Executive dysfunction in subcortical ischemic vascular disease. *Journal of Neurology, Neurosurgery, and Psychiatry, 72,* 217–220.

Kumar, V., Anand, R., Messina, J., Hartman, R., & Veach, J. (2000). An efficacy and safety analysis of Exelon in Alzheimer's disease patients with concurrent vascular risk factors. *European Journal of Neurology,* 159–169.

Lim, A., Tsuang, D., Kukull, W., Nochlin, D., Leverenz, J., McCormick, W., et al. (1999). Clinico-neuropathological correlation of Alzheimer's disease in a community-based case series. *Journal of American Geriatrics Society, 47,* 564–569.

Longstreth, W. T., Jr., Bernick, C., Manolio, T. A., Bryan, N., Jungreis, C. A., & Price, T. R. (1998). Lacunar infarcts defined by magnetic resonance imaging of 3,660 elderly people: The Cardiovascular Health Study. *Archives of Neurology, 55,* 1217–1225.

Longstreth, W. T., Jr., Manolio, T. A., Arnold, A., Burke, G. L., Bryan, N., Jungreis, C. A., et al. (1996). Clinical correlates of white matter findings on cranial magnetic resonance imaging of 3,301 elderly people. The Cardiovascular Health Study. *Stroke, 27,* 1274–1282.

Luria, A. R. (1996). *Higher cortical functions in man.* New York: Basic Books.

Mast, H., Tatemichi, T. K., & Mohr, J. P. (1995). Chronic brain ischemia: The contributions of Otto Binswanger and Alois Alzheimer to the mechanisms of vascular dementia. *Journal of the Neurological Sciences, 132,* 4–10.

Masterman, D. L., & Cummings, J. L. (1997). Frontal-subcortical circuits: The anatomic basis of executive, social and motivated behaviors. *Journal of Psychopharmacology, 11,* 107–114.

Mega, M. S., & Cummings, J. L. (1994). Frontal-subcortical circuits and neuropsychiatric disorders. *Journal of Neuropsychiatry and Clinical Neurosciences, 6,* 358–370.

Mori, E. (1998). Acute behavioral derangement: Impairments of awareness, attention, emotion, and motivation. In M. Ginsberg & J. Bogousslavsky (Eds.), *Cerebrovascular disease* (pp. 1145–1148). Cambridge, MA: Blackwell.

Moroney, J. T., Bagiella, E., Desmond, D. W., Paik, M. C., Stern, Y., & Tatemichi, T. K. (1996). Risk factors for incident dementia after stroke: Role of hypoxic ischemic disorders. *Stroke, 27,* 1283–1289.

Pantoni, L., Basile, A. M., Romanelli, M., Piccini, C., Sarti, C., Nencini, P., et al. (2001). Abulia and cognitive impairment in two patients with capsular genu infarct. *Acta Neurologica Scandinavica, 104,* 185–190.

Pantoni, L., & García, J. H. (1995). The significance of cerebral white matter abnormalities 100 years after Binswanger's report: A review. *Stroke, 26,* 1293–1301.

Pantoni, L., & García, J. H. (1997). Cognitive impairment and cellular/vascular changes in the cerebral white matter. *Annals of the New York Academy of Sciences, 826,* 92–102.

Petersen, R. C., Doody, R., Kurz, A., Mohs, R. C., Morris, J. C., Rabins, P. V., et al. (2001). Current concepts in mild cognitive impairment. *Archives of Neurology, 58,* 1985–1992.

Phillips, S., Sangalang, V., & Sterns, G. (1987). Basal forebrain infarction. A clinicopathologic correlation. *Archives of Neurology, 44,* 1134–1138.

Pohjasvaara, T., Erkinjuntti, T., Vataja, R., & Kaste, M. (1997). Dementia three months after stroke. Baseline frequency and effect of different definitions of dementia in the Helsinki Stroke Aging Memory Study (SAM) cohort. *Stroke, 28,* 785–792.

Pratt, R. D., Perdomo, C. A., & The 308 Study Group. (2002). Results of clinical studies with donepezil in vascular dementia. *American Journal of Geriatric Psychiatry, 10*(Suppl. 1), 44.

Román, G. C. (1975). *Les Lacunes Cérébrales: Étude Clinique et Neuropathologique de 100 Cas* Mémoire pour le Titre d'Assistant Étranger, Travail du Service de Neurologie et Neuropsychologie, Hôpital de la Salpêtrière, (Professeur François Lhermitte). Paris: Université de Paris.

Román, G. C. (1985a). The identity of lacunar dementia and Binswanger disease. *Medical Hypothesis, 16,* 389–391.

Román, G. C. (1985b). Lacunar dementia. In J. T. Hutton & A. D. Kenny (Eds.), *Senile dementia of the Alzheimer type* (pp. 131–151). New York: Alan R. Liss.

Román, G. C. (1987). Senile dementia of the Binswanger type: A vascular form of dementia in the elderly. *Journal of the American Medical Association, 258,* 1782–1788.

Román, G. C. (1988). Why not Binswanger's disease? *Archives of Neurology, 45,* 141–142.

Román, G. C. (1991). White matter lesions and normal-pressure hydrocephalus: Binswanger disease or Hakim syndrome. *American Journal of Neuroradiology, 12,* 40–41.

Román, G. C. (2000). Perspectives in the treatment of vascular dementia. *Drugs of Today, 36,* 641–653.

Román, G. C. (2002a). Vascular dementia may be the most common form of dementia in the elderly. *Journal of the Neurological Sciences, 203–204,* 7–10.

Román, G. C. (2002b). Vascular dementia revisited: Diagnosis, pathogenesis, treatment and prevention. *Medical Clinics of North America, 86,* 477–499.

Román, G. C., Erkinjuntti, T., Wallin, A., Pantoni, L., & Chui, H. C. (2002). Subcortical ischaemic vascular dementia. *Lancet Neurology, 1,* 426–436.

Román, G. C., & Royall, D. R. (1999). Executive control function: A rational basis for the diagnosis of vascular dementia. *Alzheimer Disease and Associated Disorders, 13*(Suppl. 3), S69–S80.

Román, G. C., Tatemichi, T. K., Erkinjuntti, T., Cummings, J. L., Masdeu, J. C., Garcia, J. H., et al. (1993). Vascular dementia: Diagnostic criteria for research studies. Report of the NINDS-AIREN International Work Group. *Neurology, 43,* 250–260.

Royall, D. R., Cordes, J. A., & Polk, M. (1998). CLOX: An executive drawing task. *Journal of Neurology, Neurosurgery, and Psychiatry, 64,* 588–594.

Royall, D. R., Lauterbach, E. C., Cummings, J. L., Reeve, A., Rummans, T. A., Kaufer, D. I., et al. (2002). Executive Control Function: A review of its promise and challenges to clinical research. *Journal of Neuropsychiatry and Clinical Neurosciences, 14,* 377–405.

Royall, D. R., Mahurin, R. K., & Gray, K. F. (1992). Bedside assessment of executive cognitive impairment: The executive interview. *Journal of American Geriatrics Society, 40,* 1221–1226.

Ruchoux, M. M., Guerouaou, D., Vandenhaute, B., Pruvo, J. P., Vermersch, P., & Leys D. (1995). Systemic vascular smooth muscle impairment in cerebral autosomal dominant arteriopathy with subcortical infarcts and leukoencephalopathy. *Acta Neuropathol (Berl), 89,* 500–512.

Sarangi, S., San Pedro, E. C., & Mountz, J. M. (2000). Anterior choroidal artery infarction presenting as a progressive cognitive deficit. *Clinics in Nuclear Medicine, 25,* 187–190.

Schmidt, R., Schmidt, H., Fazekas, F., Schumacher, M., Niederkorn, K., Kapeller, P., et al. (1997). Apolipoprotein E polymorphism and silent microangiopathy-related cerebral damage. Results of the Austrian Stroke Prevention Study. *Stroke, 28,* 951–956.

Snowdon, D. A., Greiner, L. H., Mortimer, J. A., Riley, K. P., Greiner, P. A., & Markesbery, W. R. (1997). Brain infarction and the clinical expression of Alzheimer's disease. The Nun Study. *Journal of the American Medical Association, 277,* 813–817.

Tatemichi, T. K., Desmond, D. W., Paik, M., Figueroa, M., Gropen, T. I., Stern, Y., et al. (1993). Clinical determinants of dementia related to stroke. *Annals of Neurology, 33,* 568–575.

Tatemichi, T. K., Desmond, D. W., & Prohovnik, I. (1995). Strategic infarcts in vascular dementia. A clinical and imaging experience. *Arzneimittelforschung [Drug Research], 45,* 371–385.

Tatemichi, T. K., Desmond, D. W., Prohovnik, I., Cross, D. T., Gropen, T. I., Mohr, J. P., et al. (1992). Confusion and memory loss from capsular genu infarction: A thalamocortical disconnection syndrome? *Neurology, 42,* 1966–1979.

Tatemichi, T. K., Desmond, D. W., Stern, Y., Sano, M., Mayeux, R., & Andrews, H. (1992). Prevalence of dementia after stroke depends on diagnostic criteria. *Neurology, 42,* 413.

Tatemichi, T. K., Foulkes, M. A., Mohr, J. P., Hier, D. B., Price, T. R., & Wolf, P. A. (1990). Dementia in stroke survivors in the Stroke Data Bank cohort: Prevalence, incidence, risk factors, and computed tomographic findings. *Stroke, 21,* 858–866.

Tomlinson, B., Blessed, G., & Roth, M. (1970). Observations on the brains of demented old people. *Journal of the Neurological Sciences, 11,* 205–242.

Tournier-Lasserve, E., Iba-Zizen, M. T., Romero, N., & Bousser, M.-G. (1991). Autosomal dominant syndrome with stroke-like episodes and leukoencephalopathy. *Stroke, 22,* 1297–1302.

Tournier-Lasserve, E., Joutel, A., Melki, J., Weissenbach, J., Lathrop, G. M., Chabriat, H., et al. (1993). Cerebral autosomal dominant arteriopathy with subcortical infarcts and leukoencephalopathy maps to chromosome 19q12. *Nature Genetics, 3,* 256–259.

Van der Werf, Y., Witter, M. P., Uylings, H. B., & Jolles, J. (2000). Neuropsychology of infarctions in the thalamus: A review. *Neuropsychologia, 38,* 613–627.

van Gijn, J. (1998). Leukoaraiosis and vascular dementia. *Neurology, 51*(Suppl. 3), S3–S8.

van Swieten, J. C., van den Hout, J. H., van Kettel, B. A., Hijdra, A., Wokke, J. H., & van Gijn, J. (1991). Periventricular lesions in the white matter on magnetic resonance imaging in the elderly: A morphometric correlation with arteriolosclerosis and dilated perivascular spaces. *Brain, 114,* 761–774.

von Cramon, D. Y., & Markowitsch, H. J. (2000). Human memory dysfunctions due to septal lesions. In R. Numan (Ed.), *The behavioral neuroscience of the septal region* (pp. 380–413). New York: Springer.

Wallin, A., Edman, A., Blennow, K., Gottfries, C. G., Karlsson, I., Regland, B. et al. (1996). Stepwise comparative status analysis (STEP): A tool for the identification of regional brain syndromes in dementia. *Journal of Geriatric Psychiatry Neurology, 4,* 185–199.

Wolfe, N., Linn, R., Babikian, V. L., Knoefel, J. E., & Albert, M. L. (1990). Frontal systems impairment following multiple lacunar infarcts. *Archives of Neurology, 47,* 129–132.

Zuccalà, G., Onder, G., Pedone, C., Carosella, L., Pahor, M., Bernabei, R., et al. (2001). Hypotension and cognitive impairment: Selective association in patients with heart failure. *Neurology, 57,* 1986–1992.

CHAPTER 7

Psychological and Neuropsychological Aspects of Vascular and Mixed Dementia

Margaret P. Norris, Susan E. MacNeill, and Mary E. Haines

Vascular dementia (VaD) has been estimated to range from the second to the fourth most common form of dementia. Similar to Alzheimer's disease (AD), VaD is a clinical diagnosis that is confirmed only on autopsy. Unlike the clinical criteria for AD, however, there is wide variability in the clinical criteria established to diagnose VaD. Coupling that with autopsy studies showing that most clinical cases of VaD turn out to be mixed dementias or even AD (Nolan, Lino, Seligman, & Blass, 1998), it is clear that VaD is an area full of controversy. This chapter reviews the clinical criteria for VaD, explores the relationship between stroke and dementia and the relationship between cognitive deficits and vascular disease, and then delves into the area of mixed dementia.

STROKE AND DEMENTIA

Stroke, the interruption of blood supply carrying oxygen and nutrients to the brain, is the proximal cause of VaD. There are two major types of stroke: ischemic (thrombic or embolic) and hemmorhagic. Stroke is the leading cause of adult disability, the third-leading cause of death; there are more than 4 million stroke survivors in the United States. Age is the greatest risk factor for stroke. Other risk factors include sociodemographic variables such as being male or belonging to a minority group. Modifiable risk factors include hypertension, cigarette smoking, transient ischemic attacks, heart disease, and diabetes mellitus.

Several studies have linked stroke to dementia onset. Tatemichi et al. (1992) studied 251 hospital patients with ischemic stroke, as well as a group of medical controls. Twenty-six percent of the stroke patients became demented within three months as compared to only 5% of the medical controls. Correlates of dementia onset included age, lower levels of education, and African American race. Censori et al. (1996) studied 304 consecutive stroke admissions, of which 146 individuals met the criteria for first stroke. Twenty-five percent of the sample became demented within three months. The strongest predictors of dementia onset in this sample were presence of diabetes, atrial fibrillation, aphasia, and middle cerebral artery infarcts.

Findings from the nun study, however, give pause as to whether infarcts cause the dementia or whether the infarct uncovered or accentuated an already-existing neuropathological condition (Snowdon et al., 1997). Snowdon hypothesized that members of the neuropathological group (i.e., on autopsy, plaques and tangles consistent with AD) who also had a brain infarct would have a history of poorer cognition and a higher prevalence of dementia. Indeed, the group of nuns with an infarct had lower Mini-Mental State Examination (MMSE) scores than those without an infarct. In addition, whereas 88% of the nuns with at least one infarct in the neuropathological group were demented, only 57% of the nuns without an infarct were demented, despite having neuropathological conditions consistent with AD. Thus, the relation of stroke and its causal role in dementia remains unclear.

DIAGNOSTIC CRITERIA FOR VASCULAR DEMENTIA

Four major clinical criteria are used in the diagnosis of VaD. The National Institute of Neurological Disorders and Stroke Association Internationale de Recherche et l'Ensignement en Neurosciences (NINDS-AIREN) criteria contain explicit statements about the diagnosis of dementia, the evidence for stroke, and the relationship between stroke and dementia (Román et al., 1993). Dementia, using this criteria, is defined as memory impairment and impairment in two other cognitive domains (i.e., language, attention, visuospatial skills, executive functioning). Cerebrovascular disease is defined by focal signs on neurological exam and evidence of stroke by brain imaging. Finally, there must be a relationship between the dementia and the vascular disease. The second clinical criteria in use are the California Alzheimer's Disease Diagnostic and Treatment Center (ADDTC) criteria for ischemic VaD (Chui et al., 1992). *Dementia* is defined as a deterioration from a prior level of functioning, and there must be evidence of two or more ischemic strokes. In comparing and contrasting these two clinical criteria, many differences are noted. The ADDTC group sought to clinically define only ischemic VaD, whereas the NINDS group sought to define all VaD. The ADDTC group defined dementia only as a deterioration of cognitive functioning, whereas the NINDS group defined dementia as memory impairment plus two other areas of cognitive impairment. The ADDTC group also required evidence of two ischemic strokes, whereas the NINDS group required evidence of only one stroke (ischemic or hemorrhagic).

The two other major criteria used to clinically define VaD include the *Diagnostic and Statistical Manual of Mental Disorders,* Fourth Edition (*DSM-IV*; American Psychiatric Association, 1994), and Hachinski Ischemia Scale. The *DSM-IV* criteria define dementia as impairment in memory and in one other domain of cognitive functioning. Stroke is defined by focal signs and/or symptoms or by laboratory evidence. Unlike the ADDTC and the NINDS criteria, the *DSM-IV* criteria does not require evidence of stroke via brain imaging. The *DSM-IV* criteria for dementia are the same for vascular and AD memory impairment plus impairment in one other area of cognition. This differs from both the ADDTC and the NINDS.

The Hachinski Ischemia Scale was developed originally to differentiate vascular from Alzheimer's dementia (Hachinski, 1975). It uses a combination of history and signs and symptoms of vascular events. Speed of onset, presence of certain comorbid diseases, personality factors, and focal signs or symptoms make up the scale. The scale is now used to determine if there is a vascular component to the dementia rather than differentiating it from AD. The Hachinski Ischemia Scale is unique in its criteria relative to the other three.

Several studies have noted problems in clinical accuracy and reliability due to the preponderance of accepted clinical criteria for VaD. Wetterling, Kanitz, and Borgis (1996) noted that of 167 older demented patients, only 5 met the standards for 3 of the clinical criteria used to diagnose VaD. Forty-five of the patients met the *DSM-IV* criteria for VaD, 23 met the ADDTC criteria, and 12 met the NINDS criteria. Gold et al. (1997) studied the clinical utility of the NINDS and ADDTC using neuropathological data as the gold standard for diagnosis. The NINDS had a sensitivity of .58 and a specificity of .80, whereas the ADDTC had a sensitivity of .63 and a specificity of .64. A high percentage of cases had both AD and VaD.

In sum, Knopman et al. (2001) concluded from studies that compared various clinical criteria with neuropathological findings, that clinical diagnoses have high specificity but very low sensitivity.

COGNITIVE DIFFERENTIATION OF VASCULAR AND ALZHEIMER'S DEMENTIA

The most common studies of cognition in VaD have been attempts to distinguish it from AD. This line of research has most often investigated whether semantic abilities in AD are worse than in those with VaD and whether the deficits noted in VaD cases are consistent with a frontal-subcortical dementia (Mast, MacNeill, & Lichtenberg, 2002). A number of studies have attempted to differentiate dementia groups via cognitive patterns and overall abilities. These are reviewed more thoroughly in the Mast et al. study. Overall, the studies suffer from several methodological deficiencies. First, most of the studies use small sample sizes and, therefore, are underpowered. Second, and perhaps most importantly, the MMSE is used as a control for overall levels of dementia. The use of a screening measure to control for overall level of impairment is problematic. It is no surprise, then, that the results of the studies reviewed by Mast and colleagues exhibit no clear pattern.

Mast et al. (2002) demonstrated a new methodology for neuropsychological differential diagnosis research and applied this methodology to investigating for differences between those with dementia and stroke and those with dementia and no stroke. The MIMIC model (multiple indicators, multiple causes) is an extension of confirmatory factor analysis and a specific application of structural equation modeling. The model contains one or more latent variables, which are simultaneously identified by multiple endogenous indicators and multiple exogenous variables. Thus, in their study, the unique contributions of stroke to dementia is measured by controlling the latent variable of global impairment as calculated across a variety of neuropsychological tests. In their study of 217 persons with dementia, stroke did not exhibit unique effects on cognition. Given the overlap between AD and VaD, this finding was not surprising.

MIXED DEMENTIA

Recognition of non-Alzheimer's dementias has become essential for experts in geriatrics. Unfortunately, many laypersons and even general practitioners equate the terms *Alzheimer's* and *dementia*. In fact, as many as two-thirds of Alzheimer's patients have a coexisting condition (Lim et al., 1999), making pure Alzheimer's far less common than was once thought. This section reviews the more common *other* dementias, including mixed dementia, which is the co-occurrence of Alzheimer's and VaD. Within mixed dementia, we review the literature on the epidemiology, diagnostic standards, clinical diagnostic practices, symptoms, and interventions of these dementias. Accurate differential diagnosis of dementia is critical for discerning their pathophysiology, understanding the relationship between coexisting dementia, and developing disease-specific treatments for distinct forms of dementia.

Definition

There is increasing recognition that AD and VaD often coexist (De Deyn et al., 1999). The term *mixed dementia* (MD) specifically refers to the combination of AD and VaD. Although other dementias may coexist, they are more accurately referred to by their combined names or termed *nonspecific dementias*. Mixed dementia has had a fairly recent but poorly recognized status in the dementia lexicon (Rockwood, Bowler, Erkinjuntti, Hachinski, & Wallin, 1999).

Detection of MD has primarily grown out of neuropathological studies demonstrating that the demarcation between AD and VaD is not as sharp as has been previously presumed (Rockwood et al., 1999). At autopsy, as many as 28% to 35% of dementia cases were more accurately classified as MD (Bowler, Munoz, Merskey, & Hachinski, 1998). Further, the prevalence rate appears to be substantially underestimated as the proportion of AD patients with white matter lesions range from 44% to 76% (Rockwood, 1997). If white matter lesions are deemed ischemic, as reviewed later, the true rate of MD increases substantially, making it among the most common causes of dementia. As a result, researchers have questioned the use of the terms *Alzheimer's dementia* and *vascular dementia* based on evidence that many cases are, in fact, mixed dementia (Gorelick, Nyenhuis, Garron, & Cochran, 1996). The association between stroke and AD is far greater than chance, suggesting common underlying mechanisms (Rockwood, 1997). As reviewed later, MD, VaD, and AD share overlapping risk factors and similar clinical presentations (Rockwood et al., 1999). However, the complex relationship among MD, AD, and VaD is not yet well understood.

Several risk factors for MD have been examined, including cerebrovascular disease, white matter lesions, lacunar infarcts, and traumatic brain injury.

Although the link between cerebrovascular disease and VaD is fairly clear and has been well investigated, only recently have studies investigated whether vascular disease is also a risk factor for the development of AD. A review of the recent literature led Kalaria (2000) to suggest that vascular risk factors (e.g., atherosclerosis, atrial fibrillation, coronary artery disease, hypertension, and diabetes mellitus) significantly increase the risk of AD. In the large population-based Rotterdam study, atherosclerosis was associated with both AD and VaD; furthermore, participants with atherosclerosis and the apoE4 genotype had an increased risk for both AD and VaD (Hofman et al., 1997). Lacunar infarcts, primarily resulting from moderate to severe atherosclerosis in the arteries of the circle of Willis, were highly predictive of cognitive impairment, suggesting a critical role in the development of MD (Snowdon et al., 1997). Several questions about the link between AD and cerebrovascular disease remain unanswered, for example, whether the vascular lesions seen in individuals with AD are incidental or causal in the development of AD, and what threshold for cerebrovascular disease might be related to AD dementia.

One of the most critical features of MD is white matter lesions; it is commonly reported that at least one-third to one-half of cases of AD have a large number of white matter lesions (De Deyn et al., 1999; Rockwood, 1997). In cases reclassified after neuroimaging results were taken into account, 90% of those reclassified as MD had leukaraiosis (Frisoni et al., 1995). It has further been speculated that the mechanism of lacunar infarcts in dementia is through the resulting periventricular ischemic white matter disease (Román, 1997). White matter volume was significantly correlated with cognitive functioning in patients who subsequently had postmortem examinations, and white matter volume was substantially lower in demented patients than in nondemented patients (C. D. Smith, Snowdon, Wang, & Markesberry, 2000). Pasquier and Leys (1997) conclude that dementia is often the result of the additive effects of cerebrovascular lesions, Alzheimer pathology, and white matter changes.

Neuropathological evidence suggests that the location of infarcts may also be critical in producing MD (Snowdon et al., 1997). Impaired performance on neuropsychological tests was present in 75% of the AD patients with infarcts in the lobes of the neocortex, compared to 93% of AD patients with lacunar infarcts in the basal ganglia, thalamus, or deep white matter. In contrast, only 57% of those without these infarcts showed clinical signs of dementia. Furthermore, dementia may also be an interactive function of the extent of neurofibrillary tangles and the presence of lacunar infarcts (Snowdon et al., 1997). At a mean of 1.9 or more neurofibrillary tangles in the neocortex, 100% of those with one or more lacunar infarcts in the basal ganglia, thalamus, and deep white matter were demented. In contrast, among those without lacunar infarcts, 100% rate of dementia was observed only in those with 15.7 or more neurofibrillary tangles.

One of the posited environmental risk factors for the development of AD is traumatic brain injury (TBI). While mild TBI does not seem to pose a major risk for the development of later AD (Mehta et al., 1999), animal research points to a connection between moderate to severe TBI and neurodegeneration (D. H. Smith et al., 1999). The neurodegeneration in this particular study took the form of the accumulation of proteins that are the precursors necessary for the development of plaques, which are the hallmark of AD. These findings have tentatively been confirmed in humans; these same proteins are increased in the cerebrospinal fluid of patients following severe TBI (Emmerling et al., 2000). However, it remains unknown whether these individuals are those who would be at risk for the development of later AD regardless of whether they had incurred a TBI or not. Another study indicates that individuals who possess the APOE epsilon 4 allele are those who have the deposits of the proteins subsequent to TBI (Teasdale, Nicoll, Murray, & Fiddes, 1997). There is also some evidence that sustaining a TBI later in life may increase the risk of the development of AD (Mortimer, van Duijn, & Chandra, 1991). Certainly, the ability for neuronal repair, which is compromised in both older individuals and those with the APOE epsilon 4 allele, seems to play a part (Jorm, 2000). While there is no evidence to date for a correlation between TBI and the later development of MD, certainly risky behaviors that can predispose a person to sustain a TBI may also correlate with risk factors for developing VaD (e.g., excessive alcohol use). If a person also possesses a genetic predisposition to AD, the risk for MD may be increased as well.

Epidemiology

MD was historically thought to be the third most prevalent form of dementia, falling behind AD and VaD (Seno, Ishino, Inagaki, Iijima, Kaku, & Inata, 1999; Seno, Ishino, Inagaki, Iijima, Kaku, Inata, & Hirai, 1999; Wang et al., 2000). However, neuropathological studies suggest MD is far more common than pure VaD. Snowdon and colleagues (1997) observed 47% of demented cases with neuropathological evidence of both AD had at least one brain infarct. Others have also observed that the majority of cases clinically diagnosed as VaD also had evidence of AD at autopsy, consistent with a diagnosis of MD (Gorelick et al., 1996). The American Academy of Neurology concluded that MD exists in 29% to 41% of dementia cases coming to autopsy, whereas pure VaD accounted for only 9% to 10% of cases (Knopman et al., 2001). Incidence rates of MD in elderly samples from the general population are estimated to range from 0.55% in Western countries (Skoog, Nilsson, Palmertz, Andreasson, & Svanborg, 1993) to 0.27% in Japan and China (Wang et al., 2000).

Although the prevalence of AD seems to increase with age and female gender, VaD and MD do not appear to increase as rapidly with these factors; rather, the rates of VaD, and MD by extension, increase with male gender (Manubens et al., 1995). This latter finding seems to be consistent internationally (Wang et al., 2000). VaD or MD was present in 50% of demented males, as determined by autopsy results (Tomlinson, Blessed, & Roth, 1970).

Diagnostic Standards

Diagnosis of MD is inherently linked to diagnostic criteria for AD and VaD. The National Institute of Neurologic Communicative Disorders and Stroke-Alzheimer Disease and Related Disorders Association (NINDS-ADRDA) established a consensus for the neuropathological diagnosis of AD by quantifying the neuritic or senile plaques in a given anatomical region for specific age groups. However, such consensus for the diagnosis of VaD does not exist. Thus, much of the confusion in the definition of MD and, therefore, prevalence rates of MD stems from the evolving, yet unresolved, definition of VaD. Two widely recognized diagnostic standards for VaD and MD have been established, one by NINDS-AIREN and the other by the State of California ADDTC.

The NINDS-AIREN diagnostic criteria recommend that the term *mixed dementia* be discouraged from epidemiological studies because the vascular contribution to the dementia is ill defined, whereas the role of neuronal depopulation is clear (Román et al., 1993). Hence, they view the diagnosis of AD as taking precedence over VaD, even when there is clear evidence of a stroke accompanied by worsening cognition. Rather than using the term *mixed dementia,* they recommend a diagnosis of Alzheimer's dementia with cerebrovascular disease. In contrast, the ADDTC criteria for mixed dementia are the presence of one or more systemic or brain disorders that are thought to be *causally* related to the dementia (Chui et al., 1992). They recommend that the degree of confidence in the diagnosis of VaD be specified as possible, probable, or definite, and other disorder(s) contributing to the dementia should be listed. The ADDTC is ambiguous about primacy, whereas the NINDS-AIREN guidelines are clear that AD is the primary diagnosis.

Recognizing the lack of consensus of a single diagnostic method for VaD, one study compared the ADDTC and NINDS-AIREN criteria for MD to neuropathological analyses (Gold et al., 1997). Of the 41 MD cases verified by pathological report but clinically diagnosed as VaD, 54% were misdiagnosed using the ADDTC criteria while 29% were misdiagnosed using the NINDS-AIREN criteria, suggesting both criteria need modification.

In trying to reconcile differences in diagnostic standards, C. I. Cohen, Araujo, Guerrier, and Henry (1997) recommend the more specific dual diagnoses of AD and VaD when both criteria are met and that terminology suggesting primacy be avoided because evidence for this distinction is typically not clear. They further suggest the use of the modifiers of *probable* or *possible* mixed dementia be used when full criteria for either AD or VaD are not met. Tomlinson et al. (1970) pointed out that neuropathological standards for both AD and VaD may be subclinical, that is, in the lower range of normal; however, the combination of both is likely to result in significant brain damage and cognitive impairment. Dementia may be present in patients before stroke, but cognitive impairment may be mild and unrecognized until the additive effect of the stroke occurs (De Deyn et al., 1999).

Clinical Diagnosis

Despite the apparent inaccuracy of clinical diagnosis of MD, as reviewed later, it is important to examine how the clinical diagnosis of MD is most often reached. The Hachinski Ischemia Scale (HIS), originally developed to diagnose VaD, has also been used to classify MD. The presence of dementia and low scores on this scale (4 or lower) are classified as AD and high scores (7 or higher) as VaD (Hachinski et al., 1975). However, the validity of using intermediate scores from this scale to diagnose MD has been questioned by neuropathological studies. Only 18% of verified MD cases had HIS scores of 5 to 6 (Gold et al., 1997). In addition, HIS scores do not distinguish VaD from MD cases (Rosen, Terry, Fuld, Katzman, & Peck, 1980). All AD cases had scores of 5 or lower, but VaD and MD cases ranged from 7 to 14. The mean ranks were 3, 9.25, and 10.6 for AD, VaD, and MD, respectively. The features observed only in VaD and MD cases (and thus, helpful in ruling out AD) included abrupt onset, stepwise deterioration, history of stroke, focal neurological signs, and somatic complaints. Features common to all groups were fluctuating course, nocturnal confusion, depression, hypertension, and atherosclerosis. Despite the evidence that AD and VaD are typically distinguished by the HIS (Hachinski et al., 1974), it does not appear to differentiate VaD from MD.

Similar results were reported in an autopsy study that compared HIS scores in cases of AD, VaD, and MD and examined whether unique features are associated with individual groups (Moroney et al., 1997). The HIS cutoffs were most accurate for classifying VaD cases: 84% of VaD had scores of 7 or higher, 76% of AD cases had scores of 4 or less, but only 12% of MD cases had scores of 5 or 6. The MD cases were misdiagnosed as VaD (58%) more often than as AD (29%). The most common features in MD cases were focal neurological symptoms, atherosclerosis, focal neurological signs, and fluctuating course, but these were all also common features in the VaD cases. Stepwise deterioration and emotional incontinence significantly distinguished MD from VaD, but these symptoms existed in only 32% and 12% of MD cases, respectively. Fluctuating course and history of stroke distinguished MD from AD, but again, the overlapping occurrence of these symptoms in AD cases underscores that these are not pathognomonic markers. These authors also conclude that HIS scores are highly accurate in distinguishing VaD from AD, but not in distinguishing MD from either VaD or AD.

Clinical diagnosis is often made based on medical history, physical examination, brief rating scales such as the MMSE and the Blessed Dementia Rating Scale, full neuropsychological batteries, blood tests, and neuroimaging results. The value of adding the more expensive procedures, that is, neuropsychological tests, blood work, and neuroimaging tests was examined (Chui & Zhang, 1997). Customary procedures were medical history from the patient and family, assessment of activities of daily living using the Blessed Dementia Rating Scale, physical and neurological exam, and a mental status exam. Additional diagnostic procedures were blood tests, MRI and/or CT scans, neuropsychological assessments, lumbar puncture, EEG, and SPECT studies, resulting in a change of diagnosis in a subset of patients. Using these additional procedures, AD cases dropped from 50% to 41%. There was a 6% increase in MD cases (from 16% to 22%), due largely to lab tests showing positive MHATP, low T_4, high TSh, or low B12, and a 4% increase in VaD cases, due mostly to neuroimaging results. The results of neuropsychological testing changed the diagnosis in 11% of the cases—mostly as to whether cognitive symptoms were severe enough to warrant a dementia diagnosis. In total, patient management was modified in 13% of the cases due to the change in diagnosis (e.g., treatment of vascular risk factors or depression). Similar results also confirmed the important role of radiograph findings in accurately diagnosing cases of MD (Frisoni et al., 1995). Based on CT scans, rates of pure AD were reduced from 82% to 61% by identifying 21% of patients with MD. Further, probable VaD was disconfirmed in 41% of the cases previously diagnosed as VaD by clinical history and examination.

The evidence for diagnosis of MD based on neuropsychological tests is lacking. There is an astonishing dearth of investigations comparing the cognitive deficits of MD to AD or VaD. In contrast, a great deal of neuropsychology research examines whether a pattern of cognitive deficits reliably discriminates AD from VaD patients (e.g., Looi & Sachdev, 1999; Villardita, 1993). As reviewed by Mast et al. (2002), this research has not yielded a consistent pattern of neuropsychological deficits that distinguish VaD from AD. If cognitive variables do not distinguish AD from VaD, there is little reason to expect accurate identification of MD using neuropsychological assessments. On the other hand, this literature is based almost exclusively on cases with unconfirmed diagnoses. If the nonsignificant differences are assumed to be an artifact of misdiagnosed cases, the implication for MD remains inconclusive because misplacement of AD and VaD in diagnostic groups would inevitably result in similarities rather than differences between these groups. Regardless of which conclusion is adopted, little evidence exists to currently support the use of neuropsychological results to differentially diagnose MD.

Not surprisingly, clinical history obtained from family also appears to be inadequate for making an accurate diagnosis of mixed dementia. Relatives of deceased dementia patients gave retrospective reports on the patients' symptoms, course, and features of cognitive impairment using the

Dementia Questionnaire (Li et al., 1997). Compared to autopsy diagnoses, sensitivity of pure AD was .71 and specificity of pure AD was also .71. However, sensitivity of pure VaD was only .41 and specificity was .84. Accuracy of MD diagnoses based on clinical history was poor; 43% of MD cases were misclassified as AD and 31% were misclassified as VaD. The imprecise diagnostic information provided by symptom review is likely a result of the overlapping symptoms in AD, VaD, and MD.

Autopsy Studies

Autopsy studies provide the most accurate information about the true rate of MD, as well as a gold standard for evaluating the accuracy of clinical diagnosis of MD. Collectively, studies comparing rates of AD, VaD, and MD report approximately one-third of cases have MD. Gold et al. (1997) observed 36% of autopsy cases were MD, and the seminal work by Tomlinson et al. (1970) observed 36% of autopsied cases were MD. Lower rates, approximately 13% to 15%, are noted when VaD and MD are more narrowly defined by multiinfarcts (Moroney et al., 1997) or when samples include other forms of dementia such as AD with Lewy bodies and Parkinson's disease (Galasko et al., 1994; Holmes, Cairns, Lantos, & Mann, 1999). Prevalence rates may also vary depending on sample source.

The NINCDS-ADRDA clinical diagnoses of MD predicted AD lesions reasonably well (79% had AD lesions at autopsy) and substantially better than VaD (only 53% had coexisting infarcts; Galasko et al., 1994). The most common false positive errors of MD cases were those incorrectly diagnosed by clinical criteria as AD with Lewy body dementia. Approximately 16% of the patients with neuropathological diagnosis of AD with Lewy body dementia were clinically diagnosed as MD, indicating that these conditions are difficult to distinguish. False negative errors were the rule, not the exception, with 64% of the MD cases identified at autopsy having clinical diagnoses of AD. The authors conclude that the major strength of the NINCDS-ADRDA guidelines is in identifying AD cases, but the guidelines fare worse in identifying cases of MD.

In a comparison of the two major diagnostic criteria of MD, both were moderately accurate in predicting postmortem diagnosis (Gold et al., 1997). The sensitivity of the NINDS-AIREN and ADDTC criteria was only .58 and .63, respectively. The specificity of the NINDS-AIREN (.80) fared better than the specificity of the ADDTC criteria (.64). As stated previously, these results indicate better diagnostic criteria for MD are needed.

A problem in autopsy studies is that the pathological diagnoses of VaD and MD are more subjective than they are for other diseases such as AD, Lewy body, or Parkinson's disease. The positive predictive power of AD was 81% when standard criteria for VaD and MD were used, but fell to 44% when cases with any amount of infarct were classified as MD (Bowler et al., 1998). Because there is no agreement on the minimum volume of infarcts that should change a case from AD to MD, rates of MD cases may vary across autopsy studies.

Symptoms

The rate of cognitive decline was examined in a longitudinal study that investigated the differences among the progression of AD, VaD, and MD. Cognitive functions evolved similarly in the three diseases with the exception of memory (Bowler et al., 1997). In the early stages of the disease, the memory impairments were more significant in AD than MD patients, but that impairment caught up in MD and VaD in the moderate and late stages of the diseases. The rate of decline did not differ across groups in most areas of cognitive functioning including language, arithmetic, reasoning, praxis, orientation, attention, and visuoconstructional skills. However, this study included 129 probable AD, but only 12 probable VaD and 36 probable MD, and diagnoses were based on clinical presentations; therefore, their findings may be contaminated by misclassifications of some cases. In a larger study involving 443 MD, 291 possible AD, and 967 probable AD, there was a trend for a consistent decline for both AD and MD (Corey-Bloom, Galasko, Hofstetter, Jackson, & Thal, 1993).

Mood and Behavioral Disturbances

Overall, the behavioral and psychological symptoms of dementia are such a salient feature of the disease that there is now a push to include this as a diagnosis or syndrome in the International Classification of Diseases (ICD; Zaudig, 2000). Depression and anxiety are common in dementia, and these can be the first symptoms of a dementia in the absence of initial cognitive deficits (Reding, Haycox, & Blass, 1985). The clinician should suspect a mood or anxiety disorder in individuals presenting with possible dementia, most particularly in persons who are aware of their memory and cognitive failings, compared to patients whose relative or caregiver is noticing the cognitive difficulties (U.S. Department of Health and Human Services, 1996). An individual in the early stages of dementia is more likely to experience a mood or anxiety disorder than one in the moderate or later stage (Merriam, Aronson, Gaston, Wey, & Katz, 1988). The clinical interview is a necessity in ruling out a mood disturbance and, because of the cognitive deficits that are present in dementia, collateral information as to the patient's mood is necessary.

The clinical presentations of depression and anxiety are not often distinguishable between dementias, further clouding the picture among AD, VaD, and MD. In addition, mood disturbances can range from major depressive disorder to mild depression symptoms. However, studies suggest that the presence of ischemic disease seems to be positively correlated with the presence of depressed mood and psychomotor slowing (e.g., Corey-Bloom et al., 1993; Hargrave, Geck, Reed, & Mungas, 2000). In a study of 256 individuals with AD and 36 with ischemic vascular disease or MD, not only was depression more frequent in the latter group, but also it was more severe (Hargrave, Geck, et al., 2000). In another study of three large groups of patients (possible AD, probable AD, and MD), a trend toward a greater frequency of depressed mood was found in the MD group (Corey-Bloom et al., 1993). Therefore, it appears to be critical for the clinician to assess for mood disturbance in individuals presenting with MD.

Apathy also seems to afflict a significant proportion of demented individuals (Corey-Bloom et al., 1993). It can present by itself or, less commonly, as a combination of periods of agitation and periods of passivity (U.S. Department of Health and Human Services, 1996). Much of the initiation and motivation to complete even simple tasks dwindles as the disease progresses. In contrast to the slightly higher rate of depression in MD patients cited previously, apathy was observed less frequently in MD than in AD patients (Kunik et al., 2000). In addition to interdementia differences, there may be ethnic differences. For example, the risk of anxiety and depression concomitant with dementia (not specific to MD) was lower for African Americans and Hispanics than for White individuals (Hargrave, Geck, et al., 2000), whereas the risk of apathy was lower for Hispanic individuals with MD (Hargrave, Stoeklin, Haan, & Reed, 2000).

Apathy can be a burden to caregivers because they must work all that much harder to get the individual to initiate behavior. In addition, indifference to a person's own deficits can be a significant safety risk. Anosagnosia, or an unawareness of deficits, is a common sequela of right hemisphere lesions and may lead to patients' engaging in activities that they cannot safely perform (Hoffman & Platt, 2000). Because of their apathetic behavior, demented individuals also tend to interact less frequently and withdraw from social situations. In a study that compared individuals with AD to those who had either ischemic vascular disease or MD (the authors combined these two groups), decreased affect and withdrawal were more prevalent and more severe in the vascular disease/MD group (Hargrave, Geck, et al., 2000).

In contrast to apathy and withdrawal, some individuals exhibit agitation, aggression, or sexually inappropriate behavior (Hermann & Black, 2000). Psychotic symptoms may include a wide variety of delusions, hallucinations (usually visual), and nocturnal agitation (Eker & Ertan, 2000). Studies report contradictory findings on the comparative rates of behavioral disturbances across dementia groups. For example, the frequency and severity of behavioral disturbances did not differ across patients with MD, VaD, and AD (Swearer, Drachman, O'Donnell, & Mitchell, 1988). Yet, others have reported that behavioral disturbances were more common in MD than AD or MID patients, which the authors interpret as the synergistic effect of two brain diseases on behavior (D. Cohen et al., 1993). Another study compared the differences in cognitive and behavioral problems exhibited by AD, VaD, dementia due to alcohol, and MD (Kunik et al., 2000). On the Cohen-Mansfield Agitation Inventory, the MD individuals had significantly more frequent episodes of agitation and verbal aggression than did the individuals with dementia due to alcohol abuse; however, there was no significant difference in the character or severity of agitation among the four groups. In a longitudinal study, the rate of deteriorating behavior was similar in AD, VaD, and MD patients (Barclay, Zemcov, Blass, & Sansone, 1985). Importantly, at 30 months after the initial evaluation, all groups had higher scores on the Haycox, a behavioral rating scale, and equivalent proportions of patients from all groups required institutional care.

Motor Impairments

The vascular component of MD also appears to produce psychomotor slowing. More severe psychomotor slowing was observed in a vascular disease/ MD group of individuals compared to AD individuals (Hargrave, Geck, et al., 2000), which is consistent with the more frequent white matter changes observed in MD and VaD. Subcortical areas are affected; therefore, extrapyramidal signs can also be present in MD (Schaufele, Bickel, & Weyerer, 1999). Individuals with VaD, and thereby extending to individuals with MD, may present with physical impairments that are the evidence of vascular lesions: hemiplegia, visual deficits, dysphagia, gait disturbances, fine-motor dyscoordination, reduced sensation, difficulties with proprioception, or dysarthria (Hoffman & Platt, 2000). Motor disability can have a significant impact on demented individuals and their caregivers because the physically debilitated individual is less capable of assisting with the completion of activities of daily living.

Interventions

Limitations in this area of research are noteworthy. Few pharmacological or psychological intervention studies compare MD patients to AD or VaD patients; therefore, there is not enough empirical evidence to draw solid conclusions. Pharmacological agents include those used to treat specific behavioral disturbances including depression, psychosis, and agitation and those used to directly attenuate the progression of the dementia. Unfortunately, studies that examine the efficacy of drugs in treating psychiatric symptoms in demented patients rarely distinguish MD from AD or VaD. When patients with MD are included in treatment studies, they are usually combined with other dementia groups. There are exceptions; for example, the efficacy of resperidone in treating psychotic behavior and agitation was compared across diagnostic groups and the improvements did not vary in AD, VaD, or MD patients (Katz et al., 1999). Nevertheless, diagnoses were based on clinical criteria, rendering the results about treatment effects specific to MD somewhat inconclusive. For a review of pharmacological treatment of depression, psychosis, and other behavioral disturbances, see Chapters 9, 10, and 12 of this handbook, Rabins et al. (2000), and Salzman (2001).

Similar methodological problems exist in studies examining the efficacy of drugs developed to directly treat dementia. Treatment studies rely on clinical diagnosis, and strict exclusion standards may be used that eliminate patients with MD (Forstl, 2000). Hence, knowledge of the benefit of drug therapies for MD remains tied to the VaD and AD literature. According to the American Academy of Neurology, there are no adequately controlled trials supporting the use of any pharmacological agents to treat the cognitive deterioration in either MD or VaD (Doody et al., 2001). For general reviews, see De Deyn et al. (1999), Rabins et al. (2000), Salzman (2001), as well as Chapter 14 of this handbook.

As with pharmacological studies, cognitive and behavioral intervention studies have almost exclusively studied AD patients or unspecified dementia patients. These findings may at least represent a starting point for application to MD. Because these treatment studies are not specific to MD, they are briefly reviewed in the summary section of this chapter.

SUMMARY

The clinical picture of vascular dementia has become more clear and more cloudy in recent years. As we described, while there is agreement that stroke often immediately precedes dementia, the criteria for a clinical diagnosis of VaD are widely variable. In addition, the relationship of stroke to Alzheimer's disease is also unclear. Thus, VaD is viewed today as being much less common than was originally thought. Instead, mixed dementia appears far more common than VaD.

Clinical awareness of MD lags far behind the fairly recent gains in our scientific knowledge of this common cause of dementia. Clearly, neuropathological studies identify a substantially higher rate of mixed dementia cases than clinical diagnoses suggest (Gold et al., 1997; Snowdon et al., 1997; Tomlinson et al., 1970). Collectively, studies suggest that one-third to one-half of dementia cases are not pure cases, but rather are caused by the presence of both Alzheimer and vascular pathologies. The low rate of accurate clinical diagnoses of MD appears to be largely a function of the absence of diagnostic markers, unclear diagnostic standards for VaD, and the inevitable complications of clinical diagnoses when more than one etiology is present. Although HIS scores and patterns of cognitive deficits do not reliably support clinical diagnosis of MD, accuracy does seem to improve with neuroimaging techniques.

The coexistence of AD and VaD is higher than chance, suggesting shared risk factors. Cerebrovascular disease increases the risk for not only VaD, but also AD. Furthermore, autopsy studies following antemortem data suggest that the interactive effects of these two disease processes are likely to result in the clinical expression of dementia. Debilitating cognitive impairment appears to result from the presence of multiple factors, for example, neurofibrillary tangles, as well as lacunar infarcts in subcortical regions (Snowdon et al., 1997). Further prospective studies that include both cognitive measures and neuropathological analyses at autopsy are necessary to understand this interactive process of AD and VaD.

The commonalities of these brain disorders are further evidenced by the overlapping symptomatology in MD, AD, and VaD. With both cortical and subcortical lesions, areas of impairment are widespread, including cognitive, affective, behavioral, and motor functioning. Some investigations have observed higher rates of depression, behavioral disturbance, and motor impairments in VaD and MD, which may reflect the additive component of subcortical damage. Nevertheless, distinctive symptom patterns are not obvious, and certainly there are no pathognomonic markers of MD. Rate of decline also appears more similar than distinct in these diseases, with the important caveat that mortality rates for VaD and MD are higher than for AD.

Greater recognition of MD will advance scientific knowledge of both AD and VaD. As we gain insight into the pathophysiology of these disease processes, this knowledge base will shed light on the expression and etiology of the diseases. Future research will address important unanswered questions such as identifying genetic and environmental risk factors, distinguishing the degree of incidental versus causal connections between AD and VaD, ascertaining the physiological threshold tolerance of MD that triggers the clinical expression of dementia, and identifying laboratory tests with satisfactory diagnostic accuracy.

REFERENCES

American Psychiatric Association. (1994). *Diagnostic and statistical manual of mental disorders* (4th ed.). Washington, DC: Author.

Barclay, L. L., Zemcov, A., Blass, J. P., & Sansone, J. (1985). Survival in Alzheimer's disease and vascular dementia. *Neurology, 35,* 834–840.

Bowler, J. V., Eliasziw, M., Steenhuis, R., Munoz, D. G., Fry, R., Merskey, H., et al. (1997). Comparative evolution of Alzheimer disease, vascular dementia, and mixed dementia. *Archives of Neurology, 54,* 697–703.

Bowler, J. V., Munoz, D. G., Merskey, H., & Hachinski, V. (1998). Fallacies in the pathological confirmation of the diagnosis of Alzheimer's disease. *Journal of Neurology, Neurosurgery, and Psychiatry, 64,* 18–24.

Censori, B., Manara, O., Agostinis, C., Camerlingo, M., Casto, L., Galavotti, B., et al. (1996). Dementia after first stroke. *Stroke, 27,* 1205–1210.

Chui, H., Victoroff, J. I., Margolin, D., Jagust, W., Shankle, R., & Katzman, R. (1992). Criteria for the diagnosis of ischemic vascular dementia proposed by the state of California Alzheimer's Disease Diagnostic and Treatment Centers. *Neurology, 42,* 473–480.

Chui, H., & Zhang, Q. (1997). Evaluation of dementia: A systematic study of the usefulness of the American Academy of Neurology's Practice Parameters. *Neurology, 49,* 925–935.

Cohen, C. I., Araujo, L., Guerrier, R., & Henry, K. A. (1997). Mixed dementia: Adequate or antiquated? A critical review. *American Journal of Geriatric Psychiatry, 5,* 279–283.

Cohen, D., Eisdorfer, C., Gorelick, P., Paveza, G., Luchins, D. L., Freels, S., et al. (1993). Psychopathology associated with Alzheimer's disease and related disorders. *Journal of Gerontology, 48,* M255–M260.

Corey-Bloom, J., Galasko, D., Hofstetter, C. R., Jackson, J. E., & Thal, L. J. (1993). Clinical features distinguishing large cohorts with possible AD, probable AD, and mixed dementia. *Journal of the American Geriatrics Society, 41,* 31–37.

De Deyn, P. P., Goeman, J., Engelborghs, S., Hauben, U., D'Hooge, R., Baro, F., et al. (1999). From neuronal and vascular impairment to dementia. *Pharmacopsychiatry, 32*(1), 17–24.

Doody, R. S., Stevens, J. C., Beck, C., Dubinsky, R. M., Kaye, J. A., Gwyther, L., et al. (2001). Practice parameter: Management of dementia (an evidence-based review). Report of the quality standards subcommittee of the American Academy of Neurology. *Neurology, 56,* 1154–1166.

Eker, E., & Ertan, T. (2000). Behavioral and psychological symptoms of dementia in eastern and southeastern Europe and the Middle East. *International Psychogeriatrics, 12,* 409–413.

Emmerling, M. R., Morganti-Kossman, M. C., Kossman, T., Stahel, P. F., Watson, M. D., Evans, L. M., et al. (2000). Traumatic brain injury elevates the Alzheimer's amyloid peptide A beta 42 in human CSF. A possible role for nerve cell injury. *Annals of the New York Academy of Sciences, 903,* 118–122.

Forstl, H. (2000). Clinical issues in current drug therapy for dementia. *Alzheimer Disease and Associated Disorders, 14*(1), S103–S108.

Frisoni, G. B., Beltramello, A., Binetti, G., Bianchetti, A., Weiss, C., Scuratti, A., et al. (1995). Computed tomography in the detection of the vascular component in dementia. *Gerontology, 41,* 121–128.

Galasko, D., Hansen, L. A., Katzman, R., Wiederholt, W., Masliah, E., Terry, R., et al. (1994). Clinical-neuropathological correlations in Alzheimer's disease and related dementias. *Archives of Neurology, 51,* 888–895.

Gold, G., Giannakopoulas, P., Montes-Paixao, C., Herrmann, F. R., Mulligan, R., Michel, J. P., et al. (1997). Sensitivity and specificity of newly proposed clinical criteria for possible vascular dementia. *Neurology, 49,* 690–694.

Gorelick, P. B., Nyenhuis, D. L., Garron, D. C., & Cochran, E. (1996). Is vascular dementia really Alzheimer's disease or mixed dementia? *Neuroepidemiology, 15,* 286–290.

Hachinski, V. C., Illif, L. D., Zilkha, E., Du Boulay, G. H., McAllister, V. L., Marshall, J., et al. (1975). Cerebral blood flow in dementia. *Archives of Neurology, 32,* 632–637.

Hargrave, R., Geck, L. C., Reed, B., & Mungas, D. (2000). Affective behavioral disturbances in Alzheimer's disease and ischemic vascular disease. *Journal of Neurology, Neurosurgery, and Psychiatry, 68,* 41–46.

Hargrave, R., Stoeklin, M., Haan, M., & Reed, B. (2000). Clinical aspects of dementia in African American, Hispanic, and White patients. *Journal of the National Medical Association, 92,* 15–21.

Hermann, N., & Black, S. E. (2000). Behavioral disturbance in dementia: Will the real treatment please stand up? *Neurology, 55,* 1247–1248.

Hoffman, S. B., & Platt, C. A. (2000). *Comforting the confused* (2nd ed.). New York: Springer.

Hofman, A., Ott, A., Breteler, M. M. B., Bots, M. L., Slooter, A. J. C., van Harskamp, F., et al. (1997). Atherosclerosis, apolipoprotein E, and prevalence of dementia and Alzheimer's disease in the Rotterdam study. *Lancet, 349,* 151–154.

Holmes, C., Cairns, N., Lantos, P., & Mann, A. (1999). Validity of current clinical criteria for Alzheimer's disease, vascular dementia and dementia with Lewy bodies. *British Journal of Psychiatry, 174,* 45–50.

Jorm, A. (2000). Risk factors for Alzheimer's disease. In J. O'Brien, D. Ames, & A. Burns (Eds.), *Dementia* (2nd ed.) London: Arnold.

Kalaria, R. N. (2000). The Blood-brain barrier and cerebrovascular pathology in Alzheimer's disease. *Annals of the New York Academy of Sciences, 893,* 113-125.

Katz, I. R., Jeste, D. V., Mintzer, J. E., Clye, C., Napolitano, J., & Brecher, M. (1999). Comparison of resperidone and placebo for psychosis and behavioral disturbances associated with dementia: A randomized, double-blind trial. *Journal of Clinical Psychiatry, 60,* 107–115.

Knopman, D. S., DeKosky, S. T., Cummings, J. L., Chui, H., Corey-Bloom, J., Relkin, N., et al. (2001). Practice parameter: Diagnosis of dementia (an evidence-based review). Report of the quality standards subcommittee of the American Academy of Neurology. *Neurology, 56,* 1143–1153.

Kunik, M. E., Huffman, J. C., Bharani, N., Hillman, S. L., Molinari, V. A., & Orengo, C. A. (2000). Behavioral disturbances in geropsychiatric inpatients across dementia types. *Journal of Geriatric Psychiatry and Neurology, 13,* 49–52.

Li, G., Aryan, M., Silverman, J. M., Haroutunian, V., Perl, D. P., Birstein, S., et al. (1997). The validity of the family history method for identifying Alzheimer disease. *Archives of Neurology, 54,* 634–640.

Lim, A., Tsuang, D., Kukull, W., Nochlin, D., Leverenz, J., McCormick, W., et al. (1999). Clinico-neuropathological correlation of Alzheimer's disease in a community-based sample. *Journal of the American Geriatrics Society, 47*(5), 564–569.

Looi, J. C. L., & Sachdev, R. S. (1999). Differentiation of vascular dementia from AD on neuropsychological tests. *Neurology, 53,* 670–678.

Manubens, J. M., Martinez-Lage, J. M., Lacruz, F., Muruzabal, J., Larumbe, R., Guarch, C., et al. (1995). Prevalence of Alzheimer's disease and other dementing disorders in Pamplona, Spain. *Neuroepidemiology, 14,* 155–164.

Mast, B. T., MacNeill, S. E., & Lichtenberg, P. A. (2002). A MIMIC model approach for neuropsychological research: The case of vascular dementia. *Aging, Neuropsychology, and Cognition, 9,* 21–37.

Mehta, K. M., Ott, A., Kalmijn, S., Slooter, A. J. C., van Duijn, C. M., Hofman, A., et al. (1999). Head trauma and risk of dementia and Alzheimer's disease. *Neurology, 53,* 1959–1962.

Merriam, A. E., Aronson, M. K., Gaston, P., Wey, S. L., & Katz, I. (1988). The psychiatric symptoms of Alzheimer's disease. *Journal of the American Geriatrics Society, 36,* 7–12.

Moroney, J. T., Bagiella, E., Desmond, D. W., Hachinski, V. C., Molsa, P. K., Gustafson, L., et al. (1997). Meta-analysis of the Hachinski Ischemic Score in pathologically verified dementias. *Neurology, 49,* 1096–1105.

Mortimer, J. A., van Duijn, C. M., & Chandra, V. (1991). Head trauma as a risk factor for Alzheimer's disease: A collaborative re-analysis of case-control studies. *International Journal of Epidemiology, 20,* S28–S35.

Nolan, K. A., Lino, M. M., Seligman, A. W., & Blass, J. P. (1998). Absence of vascular dementia in an autopsy series from a dementia clinic. *Journal of the American Geriatric Society, 46,* 596–604.

Pasquier, F., & Leys, D. (1997). Why are stroke patients prone to develop dementia? *Journal of Neurology, 244,* 135–142.

Rabins, P., Blacker, D., Bland, W., Bright-Long, L., Cohen, E., Katz, I., et al. (2000). Practice guidelines for the treatment of patients with Alzheimer's disease and other dementias of late life. In *Practice guidelines for the treatment of psychiatric disorders* (pp. 69–137). Washington, DC: American Psychiatric Association.

Reding, M., Haycox, J., & Blass, J. (1985). Depression in patients referred to a dementia clinic: A three-year prospective study. *Archives of Neurology, 42,* 894–896.

Rockwood, K. (1997). Lessons from mixed dementia. *International Psychogeriatrics, 9,* 245–249.

Rockwood, K., Bowler, J., Erkinjuntti, T., Hachinski, V., & Wallin, A. (1999). Subtypes of vascular dementia. *Alzheimer Disease and Associated Disorders, 13*(3), S59–S65.

Román, G. C. (1997). Brain infarction and the clinical expression of Alzheimer disease. *Journal of the American Medical Association, 278,* 113–114.

Román, G. C., Tatemichi, T. K., Erkinjuntti, T., Cummings, J. L., Masdeu, J. C., Garcia, J. H., et al. (1993). Vascular dementia: Diagnostic criteria for research studies. *Neurology, 43,* 250–260.

Rosen, W. G., Terry, R. D., Fuld, P. A., Katzman, R., & Peck, A. (1980). Pathological verification of ischemic score in differentiation of dementias. *Annals of Neurology, 7,* 486–488.

Salzman, C. (2001). *Psychiatric medications for older adults: The concise guide.* New York: Guilford Press.

Schaufele, M., Bickel, H., & Weyerer, S. (1999). Predictors of mortality among demented elderly in primary care. *International Journal of Geriatric Psychiatry, 14,* 946–956.

Seno, H., Ishino, H., Inagaki, T., Iijima, M., Kaku, K., & Inata, T. (1999). A neuropathological study of dementia in nursing homes over a 17-year period, in Shimane Prefecture, Japan. *Gerontology, 45,* 44–48.

Seno, H., Ishino, H., Inagaki, T., Iijima, M., Kaku, K., Inata, T., et al. (1999). A neuropathological study of dementia in nursing homes in Shimane Prefecture, Japan: Evaluation of the age and gender effect. *Journals of Gerontology: Series A, Biological Sciences and Medical Sciences, 54,* M312–M314.

Skoog, I., Nilsson, L., Palmertz, B., Andreasson, L. A., & Svanborg, A. (1993). A population-based study of dementia in 85-year-olds. *New England Journal of Medicine, 328,* 153–158.

Smith, C. D., Snowdon, D. A., Wang, H., & Markesberry, W. R. (2000). White matter volumes and periventricular white matter hypersensitivities in aging and dementia. *Neurology, 54,* 838–842.

Smith, D. H., Chen, X.-H., Nonaka, M., Trojanowski, J. Q., Lee, V. M., Saatman, K. E., et al. (1999). Accumulation of amyloid beta and tau and the formation of neurofilament inclusions following diffuse brain injury in the pig. *Journal of Neuropathology and Experimental Neurology, 58,* 982–992.

Snowdon, D. A., Greiner, L. H., Mortimer, J. A., Riley, K. P., Greiner, P. A., & Markesberry, W. R. (1997). Brain infarction and the clinical expression Alzheimer's disease: The Nun Study. *Journal of the American Medical Association, 277,* 813–817.

Swearer, J. M., Drachman, D. A., O'Donnell, B. F., & Mitchell, A. L. (1988). Troublesome and disruptive behavior in dementia: Relationship to diagnosis and disease severity. *Journal of the American Geriatrics Society, 36,* 784–790.

Tatemichi, T. K., Desmond, D. W., Mayeux, R., Paik, M., Stern, Y., Sano, M., et al. (1992). Dementia after stroke: Baseline frequency, risks, and clinical features in a hospitalized cohort. *Neurology, 42,* 1185–1193.

Teasdale, G. M., Nicoll, J. A. R., Murray, G., & Fiddes, M. (1997). Association of apolipoprotein E polymorphism with outcome after head injury. *Lancet, 350,* 169–171.

Tomlinson, B. E., Blessed, G., & Roth, M. (1970). Observations on the brains of demented old people. *Journal of Neurological Sciences, 11,* 205 242.

U.S. Department of Health and Human Services. (1996). Recognition and initial assessment of Alzheimer's disease and related dementias. In *Clinical practice guideline.* Rockville, MD: Agency for Health Care Policy and Research.

Villardita, C. (1993). Alzheimer's disease compared with cerebrovascular dementia: Neuropsychological similarities and differences. *Acta Neurologica Scandinavica, 87,* 299–308.

Wang, W., Wu, S., Cheng, X., Dai, H., Ross, K., Du, X., et al. (2000). Prevalence of Alzheimer's disease and other dementing disorders in an urban community of Beijing, China. *Neuroepidemiology, 19,* 194–200.

Wetterling, T., Kanitz, R. D., & Borgis, K. J. (1996). Comparison of different diagnostic criteria for vascular dementia (ADDTC, *DSM-IV,* ICD-10, NINDS-AIREN). *Stroke, 27,* 30–36.

Zaudig, M. (2000). Behavioral and psychological symptoms of dementia in the International Classification of Diseases (ICD-10) and beyond (ICD-11). *International Psychogeriatrics, 12,* 29–40.

CHAPTER 8

Neurologic Aspects of Nondegenerative, Nonvascular Dementias

Judith L. Heidebrink

EPIDEMIOLOGY

Although dementia is most often the result of a degenerative or vascular disease, there are almost innumerable other causes of dementia. These other dementias, albeit less common, are important because many may be improved or stabilized with early recognition and treatment. This chapter highlights some of the infectious, toxic/metabolic, hydrocephalic, neoplastic, traumatic, and demyelinating etiologies of dementia.

Epidemiological studies provide varying estimates for the relative frequency of specific dementias. Frequency estimates may be influenced dramatically by the characteristics of the population studied (age, geographic location, community vs. referral basis) and the diagnostic methods employed (clinical vs. pathologic). Sultzer and Cummings (1994) compiled data from 34 studies of dementia in 3,587 patients. As shown in Table 8.1, the conditions discussed in this chapter, when combined, may explain fewer than 15% of all cases of dementia. In certain populations, however, one condition alone may account for more than 15% of dementia.

Infectious

Dementia may be the major sequela of an acute, encephalitic process or a minor component of a chronic, meningeal process. Infections in which dementia is often the presenting neurologic feature include human immunodeficiency virus (HIV) dementia, progressive multifocal encephalopathy (PML), neurosyphilis, and Whipple's disease.

Unheard of more than 20 years ago, HIV now infects an estimated 40 million persons worldwide. Dementia due to HIV has been termed *HIV*

Table 8.1   Frequency of Specific Dementias from 34 Studies of
3,587 Patients

Cause of Dementia	Overall Frequency (%)	Maximum Frequency in Any Study (%)
Toxic/Metabolic		
Alcoholism	3.7	20.8
Medications	1.2	8.3
Anoxia	0.2	3.2
Other metabolic	1.5	7.7
Hydrocephalic	1.5	11.7
Neoplastic	1.5	7.7
Traumatic		
Subdural hematoma	0.4	2.7
Other head trauma	0.5	4.7
Infectious	0.6	3.8

Adapted from "Seconary Dementias in the Elderly," in *Clinical Neurology of Aging*
(2nd ed.), by M. L. Albert and J. E. Knoefel (eds.), 1994, New York: Oxford University Press.

*encephalopathy, acquired immune deficiency syndrome (AIDS) dementia
complex, HIV-associated dementia complex,* and the term used in this chapter, *HIV dementia.* The incidence of HIV dementia in the United States may
be declining following introduction of highly active antiretroviral therapy.
In contrast, its prevalence may rise because of enhanced survival. Currently, an estimated 15% of individuals with AIDS will develop HIV dementia (McArthur, 2000). The likelihood of developing HIV dementia
increases with increasing viral load and decreasing CD4+ lymphocyte
count.

PML is almost exclusively a disease of immunocompromised individuals. It was initially described in older patients with lymphoproliferative
disorders. Now the overwhelming majority of cases of PML occur in the
HIV-positive population. As with HIV dementia, PML occurs late in the
course of HIV infection and is rarely the AIDS-defining illness. The AIDS
epidemic has also led to a resurgence of neurosyphilis. Overall, though, the
incidence of syphilis is declining in the United States and remains high
in only a few midwestern and southern regions (St Louis & Wasserheit,
1998). As a result, in the absence of a specific risk factor (e.g., HIV positivity, prior history of syphilis, or residence in a high-risk region), the
American Academy of Neurology no longer recommends serologic testing
for syphilis in the routine evaluation of dementia (Knopman et al., 2001).

The first case of Whipple's disease was described nearly 100 years ago, yet it remains an exceedingly rare cause of dementia. There are fewer than 1,000 reports of the disease in the published literature. Most come from North America or Europe, and it is unknown whether this represents an identification bias or true geographic association. The mean age of onset of Whipple's disease is close to 50, and men outnumber women by more than 4:1 (Anderson, 2000).

Toxic/Metabolic

Toxins and metabolic abnormalities should be considered in all cases of dementia, but especially in the elderly, who have a higher prevalence of systemic illness and medication use. The list of toxic/metabolic causes of dementia is extensive (see Table 8.2). Many of these conditions produce an acute confusional state more often than a dementia. Nonetheless, they are not infrequently identified in epidemiological studies of dementia. In 200 elderly patients with symptoms for three or more months, medications (9.5%) and hypothyroidism (3%) were the leading toxic/metabolic causes of dementia (Larson, Reifler, Suni, Canfield, & Chinn, 1986). Features that favored a toxic/metabolic cause were a higher number of prescription medications and a shorter duration and lesser severity of dementia. This chapter reviews the toxic/metabolic dementias associated with alcoholism, thyroid disease, and

Table 8.2   Toxic/Metabolic Causes of Dementia

Exogenous Toxins
    Alcohol
    Medications
    Brain radiation
    Organic solvents
    Heavy metals
    Carbon monoxide
Metabolic Abnormalities
    Endocrine imbalance
    Pulmonary insufficiency
    Cardiac failure
    Hematological disorders
    Renal dysfunction
    Hepatic failure
    Electrolyte derangement
    Nutritional deficiency

vitamin B12 deficiency. Details of other toxic/metabolic causes of dementia may be found in a review by Feldmann and Plum (1993).

Neuropsychological impairment may be detected in nearly half of individuals who drink excessive alcohol daily. Women and the elderly are particularly susceptible (Cummings & Benson, 1983). The prevalence of overt dementia is lower but may approach 25% in elderly alcoholics (Finlayson, Hurt, Davis, & Morse, 1988). Pellagra as a cause of dementia in alcoholics has diminished greatly since the institution of grain products fortified with niacin. Degeneration of the corpus callosum, Marchiafava-Bignami disease, is a rare complication of chronic alcohol consumption. It was first described in red wine-drinking Italian men, but has since been reported with many other forms of alcohol and in multiple locations worldwide. Hypothyroidism and vitamin B12 deficiency are both common in the elderly, but B12 deficiency is much rarer as a cause of dementia.

Hydrocephalic

Normal pressure hydrocephalus (NPH) is primarily a disorder of older adults. Even so, it typically accounts for less than 10% of dementia in the elderly. In a multicenter study, the annual incidence of shunt-responsive NPH was found to be only 2.2 per million persons (Vanneste, Augustijn, Dirven, Tan, & Goedhart, 1992). The majority of cases of NPH arise secondary to a central nervous system (CNS) insult or structural abnormality. Risk factors include subarachnoid hemorrhage, head injury, obstructive intraventricular lesions, craniotomy, meningitis, and aqueductal stenosis. In 914 cases of NPH reviewed by Katzman (1977), 314 were idiopathic.

Neoplastic

Neoplasms account for roughly 1% of dementia. A variety of tumor types are responsible, including astrocytomas, meningiomas, and intracranial metastases from lung or breast cancer. The incidence of both primary and metastatic brain tumors rises with age, peaking near age 70. In the elderly, 60% of intracranial tumors are metastatic (A. E. Walker, Robins, & Weinfeld, 1985).

Traumatic

Head trauma is the leading cause of neurologic impairment in the young. In 1995, the annual incidence of hospitalization in the United States for traumatic brain injury was 98 per 100,000 population (Thurman & Guerrero, 1999). The rate for males was nearly twice that of females. Mechanisms of traumatic cognitive dysfunction range from focal, penetrating injuries to global effects of closed head injury. When coma persists more than 24 hours after closed head injury, cognitive recovery is almost uniformly incomplete (Bond, 1986). Milder head injuries, when repetitive, can also lead to irreversible dementia. Such is the case in dementia pugilistica or the "punch-drunk" syndrome observed in boxers. The risk of dementia pugilistica is related more closely to the number of blows resulting in brain rotation than to the number of knockout blows (Unterharnscheidt, 1975). In the elderly, a subdural hematoma producing dementia may develop following minimal head injury or in the absence of antecedent trauma.

Demyelinating

Multiple sclerosis (MS), like head trauma, is more frequently encountered as a cause of dementia when younger populations are studied. MS has its peak onset in the third and fourth decades of life and is more common in women than men by 2:1. The risk of MS is significantly higher among those raised in latitudes farther from the equator, particularly for the Northern Hemisphere (Kurtzke, 1985). As with alcoholism, neuropsychological impairment may be detected in 50% of persons with MS, but fewer than 10% have frank dementia (Halligan, Reznikoff, Friedman, & LaRocca, 1988).

GENETICS

Alcoholism and MS have genetic influences that are well described and are not reviewed here. Whether genetics plays a role in the development of dementia in these disorders is unknown. Individuals who inherit an abnormality in the thiamine-dependent enzyme transketolase may be predisposed to the cognitive effects of thiamine deficiency, Wernicke-Korsakoff syndrome (Blass & Gibson, 1977). The apolipoprotein epsilon 4 allele (apo E4) has gained significant attention as a risk factor for Alzheimer's disease (AD). It has been studied in sporadic AD, late-onset familial AD, and in AD that arises following head trauma (see Chapter 1). Preliminary evidence suggests that it may also influence acute recovery from traumatic brain injury (Lichtman, Seliger, Tycko, & Marder, 2000; Teasdale, Nicoll, Murray, & Fiddes, 1997). In addition, apo E4 may increase susceptibility to dementia pugilistica. Jordan et al. (1997) evaluated 30 professional boxers for evidence of brain injury. Among those with the greatest number of professional bouts, the boxers possessing at least one apo E4 allele had more severe impairment. Apo E polymorphism did not alter the risk of cognitive impairment in 89 subjects with MS studied by Oliveri et al. (1999). Little is known about the role of genetics in the other acquired dementias discussed in this chapter.

PATHOPHYSIOLOGY

Infectious

The pathogen in HIV dementia is the RNA retrovirus itself. HIV penetrates the CNS at or near the time of seroconversion, likely through infected mononuclear cells. Productive infection occurs much later, when the host is immunosuppressed (McArthur, 2000). The pathologic hallmark of HIV infection is the multinucleated giant cell. The periphery of this cell is ringed with nuclei and has vacuolated cytoplasm. The multinucleated giant cell contains HIV nucleic acids and may reflect viral replication. Other pathologic findings include perivascular inflammatory infiltrates and microglial nodules. The latter contain microglia, macrophages, and lymphocytes. Both multinucleated giant cells and microglial nodules are widely distributed in the brain but are more apparent in white matter, basal ganglia, and thalamus (Budka, 1991). White matter often demonstrates diffuse pallor. Cortical atrophy, gliosis, and neuronal loss are observed with a frontotemporal predisposition. Surviving neurons have reduced dendritic and synaptic density. The mechanism for these neuronal changes is unclear because direct neuronal infection is not evident. Specific HIV proteins and/or cytokine products of macrophage activation may be neurotoxic. Severity of cognitive impairment parallels the intensity of macrophage activation (Glass, Fedor, Wesselingh, & McArthur, 1995).

The JC virus, a member of the papova virus family, causes PML. Antibodies to this ubiquitous virus can be detected in most adults, suggesting that PML is a disease of viral reactivation in the CNS of an immunocompromised host. Punctate areas of grayish discoloration at the gray/white junction are early macroscopic changes. With progression, large areas of white matter become grossly softened and necrotic. Posterior brain regions are particularly affected. Microscopically, there is extensive demyelination with foamy macrophages and a marked astrocytic reaction. Surrounding oligodendrogliocytes have enlarged nuclei and intranuclear inclusions containing the JC virus. Adjacent regions of gray matter may also be affected, particularly in the HIV-positive population (Scaravilli & Harrison, 1997).

Neurosyphilis is a late consequence of infection with the spirochete *Treponema pallidum*. Like HIV, this organism invades the CNS within months of exposure. The resultant meningeal inflammation is usually asymptomatic, but clinical features of aseptic meningitis may occur. Untreated, the meningeal inflammation persists in approximately 30% of individuals, who remain at risk for subsequent neurologic complications (Merritt, Adams, & Solomon, 1946). Before the age of antibiotics, dementia developed in an estimated 5% of cases of syphilis, ensuing 5 to 25 years after initial exposure (Merritt et al., 1946). This form of neurosyphilis has been termed *paretic neurosyphilis, general paralysis of the insane,* or *dementia paralytica.* Gross pathologic findings include leptomeningeal thickening and cortical atrophy. Neuronal degeneration, gliosis, and perivascular inflammation are seen microscopically. Silver stains confirm the presence of the spirochete in gray matter.

Tropheryma whippelii is the causative organism in Whipple's disease. This rod-shaped bacillus is periodic acid Schiff (PAS) dye positive, weakly gram positive, but not acid fast. The natural reservoir for this organism is unknown, and humans are its only known host. Because gastrointestinal symptoms are prominent in Whipple's disease, ingestion of the bacillus is presumed. Dissemination may be widespread, including involvement of heart, lungs, skin, and CNS. Neuropathological changes include cerebral atrophy and irregularly distributed granulomas in the cerebral and cerebellar cortices and periaqueductal gray matter. The granulomas contain PAS-positive macrophages, in which bacillary debris may be detected by electron microscopy.

Toxic/Metabolic

Alcoholism can indirectly cause dementia through nutritional deficiency. The most widely recognized example is the Wernicke-Korsakoff syndrome, a result of thiamine deficiency. Thiamine is a critical cofactor in cerebral glucose metabolism. Wernicke's encephalopathy is an acute presentation of thiamine deficiency and is often followed by the chronic amnesia of Korsakoff psychosis. The pathological substrates of Wernicke's encephalopathy and

Korsakoff psychosis are identical. Petechial hemorrhages, neuronal loss, and gliosis affect the diencephalon and brainstem. Principal sites are the mamillary bodies, dorsal medial nucleus of the thalamus, and periaqueductal gray matter. No distinct cortical pathology is uniformly seen (Victor, 1994). A deficiency of niacin leads to pellagra. The large pyramidal cells of the cerebral cortex are disproportionately affected. They appear swollen with cytoplasmic clearing due to loss of Nissl substance, and their nuclei are shrunken and eccentric.

It is unknown whether Marchiafava-Bignami disease results from a direct or indirect effect of chronic alcoholism. The pathologic hallmarks are demyelination of the corpus callosum, especially the genu, and the anterior commissure. Replacement of cortical neurons with gliosis is seen in the third layer of the frontal and temporal lobes.

The term *primary alcoholic dementia* has been used to imply that alcohol acts as a direct toxin and causes a dementia whose pathophysiology is distinct from the aforementioned disorders. However, it is not clear that a primary alcoholic dementia truly exists (Victor, 1994). In their review of 711 brain autopsies, Torvik, Lindboe, and Rodge (1982) found that nearly all cases of alcoholic dementia had neuropathologic findings of Wernicke-Korsakoff disease. Well-nourished rodents exhibit cognitive deficits and hippocampal pathology with alcohol exposure, but extraordinary doses are required (D. W. Walker, Hunter, & Abraham, 1981). In humans with alcoholism apparently uncomplicated by nutritional deficiency, there have been varying reports of neuronal loss or morphologic changes in the frontal cortex. Cerebral atrophy from white matter loss is also described. However, rigorous clinicopathologic correlations in uncomplicated alcoholics are lacking.

Despite its wide-ranging neurologic manifestations, hypothyroidism has no definitive neuropathology.

Vitamin B12 is essential as an enzymatic cofactor in the synthesis of myelin. Deficiency leads to demyelination in both the central and peripheral nervous systems. Cerebral demyelination occurs in a patchy, perivascular distribution. There is minimal axonal degeneration or reactive gliosis.

Hydrocephalic

Cerebrospinal fluid (CSF) normally circulates out the ventricular system to the subarachnoid space, flowing over the cerebral convexities before being absorbed into the venous sinus system. When there is an impediment to CSF flow, intraventricular pressure rises above convexity pressure and results in ventricular enlargement. Over time, the ventricular and convexity pressures equilibrate, and a chronic state of ventricular dilatation with "normal" pressure develops. Although opening pressure is normal when measured randomly by lumbar puncture, sophisticated continuous pressure monitoring reveals mild, episodic elevations in intraventricular pressure (Crockard, Hanlon, Duda, & Mullan, 1977). These episodic pressure elevations and a decrease in ventricular compliance may contribute to the maintenance of ventricular enlargement. Nerve fibers mediating cognition, lower extremity motor function, and bladder control surround the frontal horns of the lateral ventricles. The clinical symptoms of NPH are due to either stretching of these fibers or their vascular supply.

Secondary NPH arises from a known impediment to CSF flow. Subarachnoid hemorrhage and head trauma are the most common antecedent events (Katzman, 1977). The initial trigger for ventricular dilatation in idiopathic NPH remains elusive. Not surprisingly, the only consistent neuropathologic finding in NPH is severe hydrocephalus. This is categorized as either communicating or noncommunicating, depending on the patency of ventricular connections. Obstructive masses may be apparent in CSF pathways. Leptomeningeal thickening ranges from absent to marked, and leptomeningeal discoloration indicates prior subarachnoid hemorrhage.

Neoplastic

Neoplastic disease can produce dementia via at least three distinct mechanisms. First, the mass effect of a tumor or its associated edema may disrupt cognitive function. Tumors located in the frontal lobe, temporal lobe, or diencephalon are most likely to produce dementia in this manner. Second, metastatic seeding of the meninges can cause dementia. Malignancies associated with leptomeningeal metastases include lymphoproliferative disorders and metastatic melanoma, breast cancer, and small cell lung cancer. The affected meninges become clouded, thickened, and nodular. Third, the paraneoplastic syndrome of limbic encephalitis may ensue from the immune response to certain neoplasms. This rare disorder is characterized pathologically by a perivascular infiltrate of lymphocytes and macrophages in limbic structures. The amygdala and hippocampus exhibit neuronal loss with gliosis and microglial nodules (Gultekin et al., 2000). Small cell lung cancer is the associated tumor in the majority of cases of limbic encephalitis.

Traumatic

Head trauma can also effect dementia through numerous mechanisms. Subdural hematoma results when the veins that bridge the dural sinuses and cortical surface are sheared. Older adults are particularly susceptible because cerebral atrophy already stretches these veins. Closed head injury from a linear force is associated with coup and contrecoup contusions. Orbital and temporal poles are injured by contact with adjacent bony surfaces. Rotational forces shear axons in the subcortical white matter, brainstem, and corpus callosum. In dementia pugilistica, several unique pathologic alterations accompany the white matter injury. These include a cavum septum pellucidum that is often fenestrated, Purkinje cell loss and tonsillar injury, neurofibrillary tangles and depigmentation in the substantia nigra, and diffuse beta amyloid deposition and neurofibrillary tangles in the cerebral cortex. Neuritic amyloid plaques and Lewy bodies are not seen (Corsellis, Bruton, & Freeman-Browne, 1973). In the series of boxers examined by Corsellis and colleagues, memory loss correlated with the extensive tangle deposition in medial temporal lobes. At the cellular level, head trauma results in a cascade of biochemical processes, including ion flow, excitatory amino acid release, free radical production, and inflammation, culminating in apoptotic or necrotic cell death (Faden, 2001).

Demyelinating

Cognitive symptoms in MS depend on the number and location of cerebral demyelinating lesions. Frontal subcortical, diffuse periventricular, and gray matter plaques have all been associated with cognitive impairment (Mendez & Frey, 1992). Disease burden, as measured by magnetic resonance imaging (MRI), also correlates with cognitive dysfunction in MS (Comi et al., 1999). The degree of correlation varies with the precise imaging and neuropsychological measures used. Specific MRI correlates of cognitive dysfunction include corpus callosum atrophy, T1 or T2 total lesion load, and frontal lobe lesion load (Comi et al., 1999; Franklin, Heaton, Nelson, Filley, & Seibert, 1988; Rao, Leo, Haughton, St. Aubin-Faubert, & Bernardin, 1989).

DIAGNOSIS

A careful history, physical examination, and mental status assessment serve as the cornerstone of a specific diagnosis of dementia. Diseases with identical sites of CNS pathology often produce similar cognitive deficits, but may be distinguished by patient risk factors, rate of progression, or accompanying noncognitive or extraneural findings. In addition, many of the conditions reviewed in this chapter have supportive findings on laboratory and imaging evaluations.

Infectious

HIV dementia is rarely the AIDS-defining illness, but should be considered in any individual with risk factors for HIV. Symptoms begin insidiously and progress over months. Early symptoms may mimic depression or medication effects and include apathy, poor concentration, and short-term memory difficulties. Mania and agitation can also be seen (Navia, Jordan, & Price, 1986). In contrast to depression, HIV dementia is associated with early motor abnormalities, such as unsteady gait, slowed limb/eye movements, and tremor. Formal neuropsychological testing helps to objectify nonspecific cognitive and motor complaints. Deficits are observed earliest on tasks of delayed free recall, psychomotor speed (finger tapping, grooved pegboard), visuospatial skills, and frontal lobe function. Language, attention, and recognition memory are initially spared (McArthur, Sacktor, & Selnes, 1999). Over time, cognitive deficits become widespread with aphasia progressing to frank mutism. Additional examination findings include limb hyperreflexia, spasticity, and frontal release signs. There may also be accompanying features of an HIV myelopathy, with spastic paraparesis but no sensory level (McArthur, 2000).

Because the early features of HIV dementia may go unrecognized, some have advocated cognitive screening of individuals with CD4 counts below 200. An HIV Dementia Scale created for this purpose consists of three measures:

1. Recall of four words.
2. Speed of printing the upper case alphabet.
3. Speed of copying a cube (McArthur et al., 1999).

HIV dementia must be distinguished from opportunistic infections, which often have a more rapid course and characteristic CSF or imaging findings (see also Special Populations section). CSF findings in HIV dementia are nonspecific and include elevated protein (65%), a mild lymptocytic pleiocytosis (25%), increased immunoglobulins (80%), oligo-clonal bands (35%), but negative myelin basic protein (McArthur, Roos, & Johnson, 1993). HIV-positive individuals without cognitive impairment may have an identical CSF profile. Neuroimaging findings in HIV demen-tia are also nonspecific and include atrophy and ill-defined, nonenhancing signal changes in deep white matter.

PML is diagnosed by clinical and radiologic findings and by detection of JC virus DNA in CSF. PML produces a rapidly progressive dementia with multifocal symptoms that mirror the areas of demyelination. Hemiparesis, aphasia, visual field defects, and ataxia are common. With involvement of gray matter, seizures, visual agnosias, apraxia, and neglect are also ob-served. Neuroimaging reveals single, multiple, or confluent areas of signal change in white matter, particularly in parieto-occipital regions. These typically do not enhance or have mass effect but are better defined than the changes seen with HIV dementia. Routine CSF studies are normal. How-ever, polymerase chain reaction (PCR) analysis can detect JC virus DNA in CSF with good sensitivity and excellent specificity. In a study of 23 pa-tients with confirmed PML and 48 controls, PCR sensitivity was 74% and specificity 96% (Fong, Britton, Luinstra, Toma, & Mahony, 1995).

Dementia paralytica has been dubbed the "great imitator," given its clin-ical resemblance to many other mental disorders. Early symptoms include forgetfulness and changes in personality. Progression to dementia occurs over months or longer. The dementia may mimic AD in its impairment of memory and other cortical functions. Psychiatric symptoms are common and range from depression to psychosis to mania with delusions of grandeur. With evolution, seizures, incontinence, and immobility develop. Abnormalities on general neurologic examination include intention tremors of the face or hands and pupil abnormalities such as the classic Argyll Robertson pupil: a small, irregular pupil that accommodates but does not constrict to light or dilate with painful stimuli.

Laboratory testing for neurosyphilis begins with serology. Treponemal tests (FTA, MHATP) are more sensitive than nontreponemal tests (RPR, VDRL) in neurosyphilis. A negative treponemal blood test virtually ex-cludes neurosyphilis (Simon, 1985). A positive treponemal blood test in an individual with dementia is an indication to pursue lumbar puncture. In the neurosyphilis cases reported by Merritt and colleagues (1946), the CSF exhibited a lymphocytic pleiocytosis of 10 to 100 cells (90%), elevated protein of up to 100 (75%), and positive nontreponemal Wasserman serology (100%). However, currently available nontreponemal tests have a lower CSF sensitivity at 30% to 70% (Hart, 1986). Thus, a negative CSF VDRL does not exclude neurosyphilis, unless protein level and white blood cell (WBC) count are also normal.

CSF results are difficult to interpret in the patient with HIV, who may have elevations in protein and white cell count from HIV itself. However, a protein greater than 65 or WBC higher than 20 cells/cubic mm is atypical for HIV alone, and treatment for neurosyphilis should be considered (Simpson & Berger, 1996).

When CSF VDRL is negative and protein or cell count elevations have multiple potential etiologies, a negative CSF FTA can exclude neurosyphilis (Jaffe et al., 1978). Due to false positives, a reactive CSF FTA is not definitive for neurosyphilis. Imaging studies in dementia paralytica are usually normal or reveal nonspecific atrophy.

The diagnosis of Whipple's disease requires a high index of suspicion. This rare systemic illness is characterized by symptoms of malabsorption (steatorrhea, abdominal pain, and weight loss), intermittent fever, migratory arthralgias, and lymphadenopathy. Neurologic symptoms arise in 5% to 50% of cases, and isolated nervous system involvement may occur in up to 5% of cases (Anderson, 2000). Cognitive impairment is the most common neurologic manifestation (71%), followed by supranuclear gaze palsy and altered level of consciousness (Louis, Lynch, Kaufmann, Fahn, & Odel, 1996). Hypothalamic involvement leads to hypersomnia and hyperphagia. Ataxia, seizures, and myoclonus are also observed. Oculomasticatory myorhythmia (OMM) and oculofacial-skeletal myorhythima (OFSM) are pathognomonic for CNS Whipple's disease, but either is present in only 20% of cases (Louis et al., 1996). OMM consists of synchronous 1 hertz movements of ocular and masticatory muscles. More widespread involvement of facial and limb muscles is termed *OFSM*.

Cerebral imaging and routine CSF studies are nondiagnostic in Whipple's disease. Imaging may reveal atrophy, enhancing mass lesions, white matter signal changes, or no abnormalities. Likewise, spinal fluid may be normal or have an elevated protein or white cell count. CSF can be centrifuged and stained for PAS-positive cells, but more often, duodenal biopsy is required to identify PAS-positive macrophages containing bacillary debris. PCR technology is now available to detect a portion of the *Tropheryma whippelii* gene sequence. PCR analysis can be performed on CSF, duodenal tissue, or other affected tissue/fluid and has a greater accuracy than PAS-staining or electron microscopy (Ramzan et al., 1997). Testing should be performed in individuals with unexplained systemic symptoms and at least one neurologic finding indicative of Whipple's disease: dementia with psychiatric symptoms, supranuclear vertical gaze palsy, hypothalamic manifestations, or rhythmic myoclonus (Louis et al., 1996).

Toxic/Metabolic

Wernicke's encephalopathy should be suspected when an acute confusional state is accompanied by ophthalmoplegia and ataxia or occurs in an individual at risk for thiamine deficiency. MRI reveals increased T2 signal in mamillary bodies, medial thalamus, and periaqueductal gray matter. Diffusion-weighted imaging shows high signal intensity in corresponding regions, which is reversible with treatment (Chu, Kang, Kim, Lee, & Park, 2002). Despite treatment of Wernicke's encephalopathy, a chronic amnestic syndrome, Korsakoff psychosis, may result. The amnesia can also develop insidiously and without other neurologic findings. Patients are typically apathetic and have little insight into their memory deficit. Confabulation, once felt to be a consistent feature of Korsakoff psychosis, often diminishes over time or is absent entirely (Victor, Adams, & Collins, 1989). Formal neuropsychological testing in Korsakoff psychosis confirms the marked deficit in memory. Additionally, impairments are observed on measures of visual-spatial function (block design, object assembly) and executive function (Wisconsin card sort, trails test). Cerebral imaging in alcoholics often reveals reduced brain volume. The degree of atrophy is mild and is reversible with abstinence (Ron, Acker, Shaw, & Lishman, 1982; Victor, 1994).

Pellagra classically causes the triad of dermatitis, dementia, and diarrhea. However, neurologic symptoms may occur in isolation, and early diagnosis is hindered by clinical overlap with depression. Over time, psychosis, pyramidal findings, and myoclonus develop. The clinical features of Marchiafava-Bignami disease are variable but often suggest frontal lobe dysfunction. Mentation and gait are slowed, apathy and incontinence are seen, and frontal release signs are prominent. MRI imaging reveals the characteristic corpus callosum degeneration.

Hyperthyroidism may cause subtle difficulties with attention and memory, but rarely frank dementia. Weight loss, tremor, heat intolerance, tachycardia, or exophthalmos should suggest the diagnosis. In the elderly, hyperthyroidism more often presents with fatigue. Cognitive deficits in hypothyroidism range from mild inattention to overt dementia or a florid psychosis. A profound alteration in consciousness, myxedema coma, is rare. Noncognitive features include weight gain, cold intolerance, coarse hair/skin, and delayed muscle relaxation with limb reflex examination. Thyroid dysfunction is confirmed with thyroid function tests. A thyroid stimulating hormone (TSH) assay is the most useful single test to detect thyroid dysfunction (Ross, 2001). In general, elevated TSH levels indicate hypothyroidism and depressed levels suggest hyperthyroidism. Exceptions arise in the setting of hypothalamic or pituitary disease, and a simultaneous free T4 level may help to clarify thyroid status.

As with hypothyroidism, Vitamin B12 deficiency has been associated with a variety of cognitive and psychiatric symptoms. However, myelopathy and neuropathy are much more common neurologic findings. In 143 patients with documented B12 deficiency and neurologic symptoms, only 17 had dementia. In only one patient was dementia the sole clinical manifestation (Healton, Savage, Brust, Garrett, & Lindenbaum, 1991). Hematologic findings of B12 deficiency include megaloblastic anemia, hypersegmented neutrophils, and macrocytosis. The diagnosis is confirmed by a low serum B12 level. An elevated homocysteine or methylmalonic acid level establishes the diagnosis when serum B12 levels are borderline.

Hydrocephalic

The diagnosis of NPH traditionally relies on:

1. The clinical triad of gait disturbance, dementia, and urinary incontinence.
2. Imaging evidence of hydrocephalus.
3. A normal pressure at lumbar puncture.

Unfortunately, many patients respond poorly to shunting if shunting is delayed until the full clinical triad appears. Gait disturbance is typically the initial manifestation of NPH. Alterations in gait may range from a wide-based, unsteady gait to a "magnetic" gait with impaired initiation and small, shuffling steps. Postural instability is common, as are falls. Mild pyramidal findings (leg spasticity, plantar extensor responses) are also observed. Although the gait disturbance may resemble that of Parkinson's disease, lack of response to dopaminergic therapy distinguishes NPH from Parkinson's disease.

Cognitive deficits in NPH are mild in comparison to the gait disturbance. The presence of early or severe dementia should dissuade the clinician from a diagnosis of NPH. Inattention and lack of initiative are common. Mental processes are slowed (bradyphrenia) but may be insufficiently impaired to meet strict criteria for dementia. Formal neuropsychological testing may reveal difficulties on tasks of frontal lobe or visual-spatial function. Delayed free recall is often affected, whereas recognition memory is substantially preserved. In contrast to AD, aphasia, apraxia, and agnosia are notably absent in NPH (Gustafson & Hagberg, 1978). The absence of urinary incontinence should not prevent a diagnosis of NPH because frank incontinence may not occur until late in the course. Urinary frequency arises much earlier. Fecal incontinence may arise late.

Neuroimaging in NPH reveals ventricular enlargement that is disproportionate to any cerebral atrophy that is present. The frontal horns of the lateral ventricles take on a bowed appearance. Transependymal migration of CSF may be seen in periventricular regions. MRI imaging is preferable to computerized tomography (CT) because MRI can assess better the patency of ventricular connections and presence of obstructive lesions. MRI is also very sensitive in detecting ischemic white matter signal changes, which can cause a clinical syndrome that mimics NPH. In the presence of moderate cerebral atrophy, a determination of "disproportionate" ventricular enlargement may be difficult. The frontal horn ratio can be used to quantify the degree of hydrocephalus. This is calculated as the maximum width of the frontal horns divided by the inner skull diameter at the same level. It has been proposed that a minimum frontal horn ratio of 0.32 be present to consider NPH (Gyldensted, 1977).

The circulatory properties of CSF can be assessed via cisternography. Classically, NPH is associated with delayed ventricular clearance of the injected radioisotope. However, this finding has little predictive value in determining shunt responsiveness (Benzel, Pelletier, & Levy, 1990); thus, cisternography has been abandoned by many clinicians in the diagnosis and management of NPH. Lumbar puncture is used to confirm a normal opening pressure and to assess for clinical improvement following removal of 30 to 50 ml CSF. Improvement, when seen, begins as early as

30 minutes after CSF removal and may persist for months (Wikkelso, Andersson, Blomstrand, Lindqvist, & Svendsen, 1986).

Neoplastic

An intracranial neoplasm should be considered as a cause of dementia when there are symptoms or signs of raised intracranial pressure, seizures, or focal examination findings. Neuroimaging and biopsy are confirmatory. Leptomeningeal metastases are a diagnostic consideration in any rapidly progressive dementia. The presence of cranial or spinal nerve abnormalities or a known history of malignancy should increase suspicion. Meningeal enhancement on cerebral imaging is supportive but lacks sensitivity and specificity. CSF studies are nearly always abnormal and often show dramatic increases in protein (up to 2,500 mg/dL) and cell count (up to 1,800 mononuclear cells/cubic mm; Balm & Hammack, 1996; Wasserstrom, Glass, & Posner, 1982). Opening pressure is high and glucose is low in up to one-half of cases. Multiple lumbar punctures are often required to identify malignant cells. With a single tap, cytology is positive in 55% to 75% of cases of known leptomeningeal metastases. This rises to 90% by the third lumbar puncture (Balm & Hammack, 1996; Wasserstrom et al., 1982).

Limbic encephalitis also has a rapid presentation, and symptoms include amnesia, emotional lability, personality change, confabulation, hallucinations, and seizures. In addition, patients often have limb dysesthesias, proprioceptive loss, and gait impairment due to an accompanying paraneoplastic sensory neuronopathy. A history of malignancy is often lacking, as the neurologic symptoms predate other tumor manifestations (Dropcho, 2002). Brain MRI may be normal in limbic encephalitis but typically reveals increased T2 signal in the medial temporal lobes, amygdala, and occasionally in the hypothalamus (Dirr, Elster, Donofrio, & Smith, 1990; Gultekin et al., 2000). CSF protein and lymphocyte count are usually mildly elevated, but can also be normal. Paraneoplastic antibody testing should be performed, but negative assays do not exclude an associated neoplasm. Imaging for underlying malignancies is often required. Anti-Hu antibodies (also termed type 1 antineuronal nuclear antibodies) strongly suggest a small cell lung cancer. Anti-Ta antibodies have been detected in limbic encephalitis associated with testicular or breast cancer. Other associated tumors include thymoma and Hodgkin's lymphoma.

Traumatic

A history of head trauma coincident with the onset of dementia makes the diagnosis of a traumatic dementia straightforward. Acute brain imaging may reveal regions of contusion, hemorrhage, or edema. MRI is superior to CT in detecting diffuse axonal injury from shearing forces. Neuropsychological symptoms of closed head injury reflect the predominant frontotemporal pathology. The most common cognitive impairments are memory loss, inattention, slowed processing, and altered judgment and planning (Capruso & Levin, 1996). Behavioral disturbances range from impulsivity to apathy. Aphasia, agnosia, and apraxia are unusual in the absence of focal injury. Dementia pugilistica has similar clinical features, except symptoms develop after a series of head blows, rather than after a single trauma. Moreover, dementia pugilistica is unique in its prominent parkinsonian features, including resting tremor. Dysarthria and ataxia are also part of the punch-drunk syndrome. Subdural hematomas can arise in the absence of significant head trauma, particularly in the elderly. The diagnosis is confirmed by CT or MRI.

Demyelinating

Demyelinating disease should be considered in any young patient with dementia. However, dementia is rarely the presenting symptom in MS because the disease burden is usually substantial by the time dementia arises. Nonetheless, patients with demyelinating disease may not have sought medical attention for prior neurologic symptoms. Demyelinating dementia is characterized by slowed mental processing. Performance IQ is typically lower than verbal IQ, though aphasia may occur (Rao, Leo, Bernardin, & Unverzagt, 1991). Recall is worse than recognition memory. Poor insight and impaired frontal abilities (attention, set shifting, verbal fluency) are common. MS, dementia pugilistica, and NPH can all have similar cognitive profiles. All three can also affect gait, but MS can produce a multitude of additional examination abnormalities, reflecting multifocal involvement of the CNS. A careful examination often reveals findings suggestive of demyelinating disease, such as an afferent pupillary defect or internuclear ophthalmoplegia. Radiologically, multiple periventricular white matter lesions with variable enhancement are visible.

TREATMENT

Infectious

A decade ago, patients with HIV dementia had a median survival of less than six months (Bouwman et al., 1998). Antiretroviral therapy has dramatically enhanced survival in HIV and also improved cognition in HIV dementia. Early monotherapy trials with zidovudine demonstrated that it could improve neuropsychological performance (Schmitt et al., 1988; Yarchoan et al., 1987). Combination therapy appears even more efficacious. Combination therapy that uses at least three agents or includes a protease inhibitor is termed *highly active antiretroviral therapy* (HAART). HAART can improve both the neuropsychological and the radiological abnormalities of HIV dementia (Sacktor, Skolasky, & Esposito, 1999). HAART reduces CSF viral RNA load to undetectable levels, but RNA load rises over time when there is antiretroviral resistance. The optimal components of HAART for HIV dementia are not known. There are currently more than two dozen reverse transcriptase inhibitors and protease inhibitors. Agents with higher CSF penetration are logical choices and include the reverse transcriptase inhibitors zidovudine, stavudine, abacavir, and nevirapine (Enting et al., 1998). Indinavir has the best CSF penetration of the protease inhibitors, which otherwise have poor penetration. Sacktor et al. (2001) demonstrated improved psychomotor speed in patients receiving HAART regimens containing at least one CSF-penetrating drug. Interestingly, regimens with multiple CSF-penetrating drugs had no advantage over those with only a single CSF-penetrating drug. Both types of regimens significantly reduced plasma viral load. Unfortunately, HAART is unaffordable or otherwise unavailable to the vast majority of those affected with HIV worldwide.

There is currently no definitive therapy specifically for PML. However, HAART regimens that include a protease inhibitor have altered survival in PML. Prior to HAART, individuals with PML rarely survived more than one year after diagnosis. Only on an exceptional basis was prolonged survival or even recovery reported (Berger & Mucke, 1988). Cytarabine showed promise in case reports but did not produce a consistent benefit to survival (Enting & Portegies, 2000). With the introduction of HAART containing a protease inhibitor, median survival extending beyond two years has been demonstrated in PML (Dworkin, 2002). This is despite concerns that HAART may make latent JC virus infection symptomatic by facilitating an immune system inflammatory response (Razonable, Aksamit, Wright, & Wilson, 2001). Even with prolonged survival, neurologic status does not always improve with HAART (Gasnault et al., 1999). Cidofovir, a nucleotide antiviral, may a useful adjunctive therapy to HAART, though preliminary studies have not consistently shown a survival benefit (Razonable et al., 2001).

Standard therapy for neurosyphilis is intravenous crystalline penicillin G at 3 to 4 million units every four hours for 10 to 14 days. An alternative regimen is intramuscular procaine penicillin at 2.4 million units a day plus oral probenicid 500 mg four times a day, together for 10 to 14 days. In addition, some experts follow either of these courses with intramuscular benzathine penicillin 2.4 million units weekly for three doses (Centers for Disease Control and Prevention, 1998). For persons with serious penicillin allergy, intravenous or intramuscular ceftriaxone 1 to 2 grams daily for 10 to 14 days is an option, though efficacy studies are limited. Treatment halts progression and, if initiated early, may improve symptoms. Without treatment, average survival after diagnosis is 2.5 years (Merritt et al., 1946).

CSF abnormalities resolve slowly with treatment of neurosyphilis. In immunocompetent patients, CSF should be reexamined at three months, six months, and every additional six months after therapy until cell count and protein are normal and CSF-VDRL is nonreactive. Retreatment is indicated if white cell count has not improved at six months or normalized at one year, protein has not normalized at one year, or CSF VDRL titer has not dropped fourfold by one year (Marra, 2000). Relapse rate is higher in patients with HIV because of their impaired cellular immune response. A similar schedule for CSF reexamination is recommended. However, a persistent mild protein elevation may be from HIV itself and would not constitute an indication for retreatment or additional lumbar punctures if cell count and CSF VDRL are negative (Marra, 2000).

Long-term antibiotic therapy is required to treat Whipple's disease. Oral trimethoprim-sulphamethoxazole (one double strength tablet b.i.d.) for at least one year is the mainstay of therapy. Some advocate an initial two-week course of parenteral penicillin and streptomycin followed by one month of parenteral ceftriaxone before beginning cotrimazole (Anderson, 2000). Chloramphenicol and tetracycline have also been used. Success of therapy is monitored by clinical measures and PCR analysis.

CSF and duodenal PCR should be negative before antibiotic therapy is discontinued. Despite appropriate therapy, neurological recovery may be incomplete, and relapses off therapy are common.

Toxic/Metabolic

Prompt administration of intravenous thiamine in Wernicke's encephalopathy reverses the symptoms and helps prevent development of Korsakoff psychosis. The amnesia of Korsakoff psychosis can also improve with intervention, and this improvement may account for the loss of confabulation over time. Established memory deficits rarely disappear, but many improve within months (Victor et al., 1989). The early effects of pellagra respond to niacin administration. A dose of 300 to 500 mg per day is given until symptoms resolve, usually within weeks, followed by maintenance dosing. Abstinence and adequate nutrition may ameliorate deficits in Marchiafava-Bignami disease, but some degree of dementia usually persists. Hypothyroidism responds well to treatment with exogenous thyroid hormone. TSH levels are used to guide replacement. Initial therapy of symptomatic B12 deficiency is at least 100 micrograms parenterally per day for one week, followed by 1,000 micrograms injected monthly (Healton et al., 1991). Rapid neurologic improvement begins within days, though full recovery often takes months.

Hydrocephalic

Once NPH is diagnosed, clinicians face the greater challenge of determining which patients will benefit from ventricular shunting. Roughly one-half of patients with NPH improve after shunting. However, estimates range as high as 70% in cases of secondary NPH to as low as 30% in idiopathic cases (Vanneste, 2000). Gait disturbances respond most dramatically, and cognitive improvement may be limited. The potential benefits of shunting must be weighed against a 30% to 40% long-term risk of postsurgical complications (Vanneste et al., 1992).

There is no single clinical, radiological, or physiological parameter that identifies the best candidates for ventricular shunting. Although the CSF tap test (see Diagnosis section) has strong prima facie support and may be helpful when positive, it is limited by its low predictive value when negative (Malm et al., 1995; Wikkelso et al., 1986). More extensive or invasive CSF tests have been proposed. For example, patients may be monitored for

Table 8.3   Predictors of a Favorable Shunt Response in NPH

Short duration of symptoms (less than 2 years).

Gait disturbance that predates cognitive decline.

Cognitive decline of mild severity and short duration (less than 6 months).

Hydrocephalus secondary rather than idiopathic.

Cerebral atrophy and white matter lesions limited on cerebral imaging.

Significant clinical improvement with large volume CSF tap(s) or continuous CSF drainage.

B-waves present at least 50 percent of the recorded time during intracranial pressure monitoring.

clinical improvement over a period of three to five days of continuous lumbar CSF drainage. Alternatively, continuous intracranial pressure monitoring can be performed to assess for episodic increases in intracranial pressure (B waves). Neither procedure is widely available, and correlations with shunt responsiveness are scarce. Ultimately, any recommendation as to shunting in NPH relies on the combination of available clinical and ancillary data. Putative predictors of shunt responsiveness are listed in Table 8.3.

Neoplastic

The treatment of intracranial neoplasms varies with tumor site and histology and may involve a combination of surgery, radiation, and chemotherapy. Prognosis varies by tumor type and patient characteristics. Leptomeningeal metastases are treated with radiation, intrathecal, and intravenous chemotherapy. Untreated, survival is less than two months (Balm & Hammack, 1996). With treatment, neurologic symptoms may stabilize or remit, but long-term survival is rare. Limbic encephalitis improves roughly half of the time when the underlying neoplasm is treated (Gultekin et al., 2000). The absence of anti-Hu antibodies in the presence of small cell lung cancer increases the likelihood of recovery with treatment (Dropcho, 2002). A discussion of individual therapies is beyond the scope of this chapter.

Traumatic

Acute interventions for head trauma include surgical evacuation of hematomas, administration of prophylactic anticonvulsants, and optimization of cerebral perfusion pressure. In severe head injury, recovery is heralded by emergence from coma into a state of posttraumatic amnesia

(Capruso & Levin, 1996). Disorientation and an inability to register or retrieve ongoing events characterize posttraumatic amnesia. The duration of posttraumatic amnesia is highly predictive of long-term recovery. In a study by Oddy, Humphrey, and Uttley (1978), the majority (71%) of patients with posttraumatic amnesia lasting fewer than seven days were able to resume employment within six months after head injury. More significant head trauma is associated with residual deficits in memory, attention, processing speed, and problem solving. Cognitive rehabilitation facilitates recovery, the bulk of which occurs over the first six months following injury.

Because even minor head trauma, when repetitive, carries the risk of significant cognitive deficits, careful assessment is necessary after any head injury. The American Academy of Neurology (1997) has published guidelines for the management of concussion in sports. The guidelines include recommendations for sideline mental status assessment. Athletes sustaining a Grade I concussion, defined as no loss of consciousness and resolution of all symptoms (confusion, headache, dizziness, etc.) within 15 minutes, may return to competition. However, if a second Grade I concussion is sustained in the same contest, the athlete should be removed from competition until asymptomatic for one week both at rest and with exertion. If an initial head injury causes confusion for greater than 15 minutes, no return to play that day is allowed, and a neurologic evaluation is required to determine whether the athlete may return to play after one week without symptoms. Any concussion involving loss of consciousness, even if brief, requires emergent neurologic evaluation and at least one week of abstinence from competition.

Demyelinating

In the past decade, several immunomodulatory therapies have become available for the treatment of relapsing, remitting MS. As a group, these therapies prevent relapses and limit disability. Surprisingly little information is currently available as to their impact on cognitive impairment in MS. However, because trials have shown impressive radiologic results and cognition correlates with radiologic burden, a benefit to cognition is likely. In a small one-year trial, interferon-beta-1b therapy improved attention and visual recall, whereas control patients demonstrated significant declines in these same areas (Barak & Achiron, 2002). A two-year, placebo-controlled trial of glatiramer acetate showed no effect on cognition, but subjects had limited neuropsychological deficits at baseline (Weinstein et al., 1999).

Fatigue in MS may respond to amantadine, pemoline, or modafinil, but cognitive benefits of these agents are unproven. Geisler et al. (1996) found that neither amantidine nor pemoline was better than placebo in enhancing cognition in MS.

SPECIAL POPULATIONS

Determining the cause of cognitive impairment in a patient with HIV can be a diagnostic challenge. Such patients are at risk for opportunistic infections, CNS lymphoma, and dementia from HIV itself. Many opportunistic infections present as an encephalopathy, with altered level of consciousness, rather than as a dementia. Time course and noncognitive symptoms can help distinguish specific etiologies. In most cases, MRI imaging is necessary. If nondiagnostic, a lumbar puncture is usually required. Features that can distinguish causes of cognitive impairment in the patient with HIV are summarized in Table 8.4.

When following a patient with dementia, it is important to determine whether the clinical course is consistent with the diagnosed etiology. In many instances, a toxic or metabolic cause may be contributory, but not the sole cause of dementia. Thus, continued evaluation is necessary when a reversible etiology has been discovered. For example, if B12 deficiency or hypothyroidism is discovered, cognition should be reassessed following appropriate therapy. Continued progression warrants further evaluation for an alternate cause of dementia.

FUTURE DEVELOPMENTS

The future treatment of HIV dementia will likely involve a combination of antiretroviral and neuroprotective therapies. Antiretroviral drugs with good CSF penetration continue to be developed and will provide alternatives when resistance arises to current therapies. Neuroprotective strategies target the inflammatory and neurotoxic responses to viral penetration of the CNS. Compounds under investigation include calcium channel blockers, antioxidants, and antagonists of platelet activating factor, glutamate, and tumor necrosis factor. Similarly, future therapies for PML may

Table 8.4   Causes of Cognitive Impairment in the Patient with HIV

Cause	Noncognitive Symptoms	Time Course	CD 4 Count	MRI Findings	Other Tests
HIV dementia	Motor slowing, unsteady gait.	Several months.	< 200	Atrophy, ill-defined. White matter hyperintensity.	
PML	Visual loss, hemiparesis, or other focal signs.	Weeks to months.	< 100	Patchy to confluent white matter lesions.	CSF PCR + 60%.
Neurosyphilis	Pupil changes, psychiatric symptoms.	Several months.	Any	Nonspecific.	CSF + VDRL, elevated protein and/or WBCs.
CNS lymphoma	Seizures, focal signs.	Weeks to months.	< 100	Solitary, deep enhancing lesion.	
Toxoplasma encephalitis	Seizures, focal signs, fever.	Days to weeks.	< 200	Multiple ring-enhancing lesions.	+ Serum antibodies.
CMV encephalitis	Seizures.	Days to weeks.	< 100	Periventriculitis.	CSF PCR + 90%
Cryptococcal meningitis	Fever, headache.	Weeks to months.	< 200	Nonspecific.	CSF + antigen, India ink.

combine antiviral and anti-inflammatory agents. Negative trials of cytarabine in PML have been attributed to inadequate CNS drug penetration (Levy, Major, Ali, Cohen, & Groothius, 2001). Techniques to improve intraparenchymal delivery of cytarabine are being developed and tested in clinical trials. Although progress in the treatment of HIV and associated illnesses has been considerable, the lack of worldwide availability of therapies will continue to limit the impact of future advances.

In traumatic brain injury, neuroprotective strategies have shown promise in experimental animal models. However, results of clinical trials using agents ranging from antioxidants to calcium channel and glutamate antagonists have been disappointing. The limited therapeutic time window following head injury presents a formidable challenge. Treatment "in the field" with compounds that intervene at multiple sites in the postinjury cascade may be required.

The cognitive benefits of immunomodulatory therapy in MS require further study. Cholinesterase inhibitors, a standard treatment for the dementia of AD, are also under investigation in MS.

REFERENCES

American Academy of Neurology. (1997). Practice parameter: The management of concussion in sports (summary statement). Report of the Quality Standards Subcommittee. *Neurology, 48,* 581–585.

Anderson, M. (2000). Neurology of Whipple's disease. *Journal of Neurology, Neurosurgery, and Psychiatry, 68,* 2–5.

Balm, M., & Hammack, J. (1996). Leptomeningeal carcinomatosis: Presenting features and prognostic factors. *Archives of Neurology, 53,* 626–632.

Barak, Y., & Achiron, A. (2002). Effect of interferon-beta-1b on cognitive functions in multiple sclerosis. *European Neurology, 47,* 11–14.

Benzel, E. C., Pelletier, A. L., & Levy, P. G. (1990). Communicating hydrocephalus in adults: Prediction of outcome after ventricular shunting procedures. *Neurosurgery, 26,* 655–660.

Berger, J. R., & Mucke, L. (1988). Prolonged survival and partial recovery in AIDS-associated progressive multifocal leukoencephalopathy. *Neurology, 38,* 1060–1065.

Blass, J. P., & Gibson, G. E. (1977). Abnormality of a thiamine-requiring enzyme in patients with Wernicke-Korsakoff syndrome. *New England Journal of Medicine, 297,* 1367–1370.

Bond, M. R. (1986). Neurobehavioral sequelae of closed head injury. In I. Grant & K. H. Adams (Eds.), *Neuropsychological assessment of neuropsychiatric disorders* (pp. 348–373). New York: Oxford University Press.

Bouwman, F. H., Skolasky, R. L., Hes, D., Selnes, O. A., Glass, J. D., Nance-Sproson, T. E., et al. (1998). Variable progression of HIV-associated dementia. *Neurology, 50,* 1814–1820.

Budka, H. (1991). Neuropathology of human immunodeficiency virus infection. *Brain Pathology, 1,* 163–175.

Capruso, D. X., & Levin, H. S. (1996). Neurobehavioral outcome of head trauma. In R. Evans (Ed.), *Neurology and trauma* (pp. 201–221). Philadelphia: Saunders.

Centers for Disease Control and Prevention. (1998). Guidelines for treatment of sexually transmitted diseases. *Morbidity and Mortality Weekly Report, 47,* 1–128.

Chu, K., Kang, D. W., Kim, H. J., Lee, Y. S., & Park, S. H. (2002). Diffusion-weighted imaging abnormalities in Wernicke encephalopathy: Reversible cytotoxic edema? *Archives of Neurology, 59,* 123–127.

Comi, G., Rovaris, M., Falautano, M., Santuccio, G., Martinelli, V., Rocca, M. A., et al. (1999). A multiparametric MRI study of frontal lobe dementia in multiple sclerosis. *Journal of the Neurological Sciences, 171,* 135–144.

Corsellis, J. A., Bruton, C. J., & Freeman-Browne, D. (1973). The aftermath of boxing. *Psychological Medicine, 3,* 270–303.

Crockard, H. A., Hanlon, K., Duda, E. E., & Mullan, J. F. (1977). Hydrocephalus as a cause of dementia: Evaluation of computerized tomography and intracranial pressure monitoring. *Journal of Neurology, Neurosurgery, and Psychiatry, 40,* 736–740.

Cummings, J. L., & Benson, D. F. (1983). *Dementia: A clinical approach.* Boston: Butterworth.

Dirr, L. Y., Elster, A. D., Donofrio, P. D., & Smith, M. (1990). Evolution of brain MRI abnormalities in limbic encephalitis. *Neurology, 40,* 1304–1306.

Dropcho, E. J. (2002). Remote neurologic manifestations of cancer. *Neurologic Clinics, 20,* 85–122.

Dworkin, M. S. (2002). A review of progressive multifocal leukoencephalopathy in persons with and without AIDS. *Current Clinical Topics in Infectious Diseases, 22,* 181–195.

Enting, R. H., Hoetelmans, R. M., Lange, J. M., Burger, D. M., Beijnen, J. H., & Portegies, P. (1998). Antiretroviral drugs and the central nervous system. *AIDS, 12,* 1941–1955.

Enting, R. H., & Portegies, P. (2000). Cytarabine and highly active antiretroviral therapy in HIV-related progressive multifocal leukoencephalopathy. *Journal of Neurology, 247,* 134–138.

Faden, A. I. (2001). Neuroprotection and traumatic brain injury: The search continues. *Archives of Neurology, 58,* 1553–1555.

Feldmann, E., & Plum, F. (1993). Metabolic dementia. In P. J. Whitehouse (Ed.), *Dementia* (pp. 307–336). Philadelphia: Davis.

Finlayson, R. E., Hurt, R. D., Davis, L. J., & Morse, R. M. (1988). Alcoholism in elderly persons: A study of the psychiatric and psychosocial features of 216 inpatients. *Mayo Clinic Proceedings, 63,* 761–768.

Fong, I. W., Britton, C. B., Luinstra, K. E., Toma, E., & Mahony, J. B. (1995). Diagnostic value of detecting JC virus DNA in cerebrospinal fluid of patients with progressive multifocal leukoencephalopathy. *Journal of Clinical Microbiology, 33,* 484–486.

Franklin, G. M., Heaton, R. K., Nelson, L. M., Filley, C. M., & Seibert, C. (1988). Correlation of neuropsychological and MRI findings in chronic progressive multiple sclerosis. *Neurology, 38,* 1826–1829.

Gasnault, J., Taoufik, Y., Goujard, C., Kousignian, P., Abbed, K., Boue, F., et al. (1999). Prolonged survival without neurological improvement in patients with AIDS-related progressive multifocal leukoencephalopathy on potent combined antiretroviral therapy. *Journal of Neurovirology, 5,* 421–429.

Geisler, M. W., Sliwinski, M., Coyle, P. K., Masur, D. M., Doscher, C., & Krupp, L. B. (1996). The effects of amantadine and pemoline on cognitive functioning in multiple sclerosis. *Archives of Neurology, 53,* 185–188.

Glass, J. D., Fedor, H., Wesselingh, S. L., & McArthur, J. C. (1995). Immunocytochemical quantification of HIV in the brain: Correlations with HIV-associated dementia. *Annals of Neurology, 38,* 755–762.

Gultekin, S. H., Rosenfeld, M. R., Voltz, R., Eichen, J., Posner, J. B., & Dalmau, J. (2000). Paraneoplastic limbic encephalitis: Neurological symptoms, immunological findings and tumour association in 50 patients. *Brain, 123,* 1481–1494.

Gustafson, L., & Hagberg, B. (1978). Recovery in hydrocephalic dementia after shunt operation. *Journal of Neurology, Neurosurgery, and Psychiatry, 41,* 940–947.

Gyldensted, C. (1977). Measurements of the normal ventricular system and hemispheric sulci of 100 adults with computerized tomography. *Neuroradiology, 14,* 183–192.

Halligan, F. R., Reznikoff, M., Friedman, H. P., & LaRocca, N. G. (1988). Cognitive dysfunction and change in multiple sclerosis. *Journal of Clinical Psychology, 44,* 540–548.

Hart, G. (1986). Syphilis tests in diagnostic and therapeutic decision making. *Annals of Internal Medicine, 104,* 368–376.

Healton, E. B., Savage, D. G., Brust, J. C., Garrett, T. J., & Lindenbaum, J. (1991). Neurologic aspects of cobalamin deficiency. *Medicine, 70,* 229–245.

Jaffe, H. W., Larsen, S. A., Peters, M., Jove, D. F., Lopez, B., & Schroeter, A. L. (1978). Tests for treponemal antibody in CSF. *Archives of Internal Medicine, 138,* 252–255.

Jordan, B. D., Relkin, N. R., Ravdin, L. D., Jacobs, A. R., Bennett, A., & Gandy, S. (1997). Apolipoprotein E epsilon4 associated with chronic traumatic brain injury in boxing. *Journal of the American Medical Association, 278,* 136–140.

Katzman, R. (1977). Normal pressure hydrocephalus. In C. E. Wells (Ed.), *Dementia* (2nd ed., pp. 69–92). Philadelphia: Davis.

Knopman, D. S., DeKosky, S. T., Cummings, J. L., Chui, H., Corey-Bloom, J., Relkin, N., et al. (2001). Practice parameter: Diagnosis of dementia (an evidence-based review). Report of the quality standards subcommittee of the American Academy of Neurology. *Neurology, 56,* 1143–1153.

Kurtzke, J. F. (1985). Epidemiology of multiple sclerosis. In P. J. Vinken, G. W. Bruyn, & H. L. Klawans (Eds.), *Handbook of clinical neurology* (Vol. 47, pp. 259–287). New York: Elsevier.

Larson, E. B., Reifler, B. V., Suni, S. M., Canfield, C. G., & Chinn, N. M. (1986). Features of potentially reversible dementia in elderly outpatients. *Western Journal of Medicine, 145,* 488–492.

Levy, R. M., Major, E., Ali, M. J., Cohen, B., & Groothius, D. (2001). Convection-enhanced intraparenchymal delivery (CEID) of cytosine arabinoside (AraC) for the treatment of HIV-related progressive multifocal leukoencephalopathy (PML). *Journal of Neurovirology, 7,* 382–385.

Lichtman, S. W., Seliger, G., Tycko, B., & Marder, K. (2000). Apolipoprotein E and functional recovery from brain injury following postacute rehabilitation. *Neurology, 55,* 1536–1539.

Louis, E. D., Lynch, T., Kaufmann, P., Fahn, S., & Odel, J. (1996). Diagnostic guidelines in central nervous system Whipple's disease. *Annals of Neurology, 40,* 561–568.

Malm, J., Kristensen, B., Karlsson, T., Fagerlund, M., Elfverson, J., & Ekstedt, J. (1995). The predictive value of cerebrospinal fluid dynamic tests in patients with idiopathic adult hydrocephalus syndrome. *Archives of Neurology, 52,* 783–789.

Marra, C. M. (2000). Neurosyphilis. In L. E. Davis & P. G. Kennedy (Eds.), *Infectious diseases of the nervous system* (pp. 373–400). Boston: Butterworth-Heinemann.

McArthur, J. C. (2000). HIV-associated dementia. In L. E. Davis & P. G. Kennedy (Eds.), *Infectious diseases of the nervous system* (pp. 165–213). Boston: Butterworth-Heinemann.

McArthur, J. C., Roos, R. P., & Johnson, R. T. (1993). Viral dementias. In P. J. Whitehouse (Ed.), *Dementia* (pp. 237–275). Philadelphia: Davis.

McArthur, J. C., Sacktor, N., & Selnes, O. (1999). Human immunodeficiency virus-associated dementia. *Seminars in Neurology, 19,* 129–150.

Mendez, M. F., & Frey, W. H., II. (1992). Multiple sclerosis dementia. *Neurology, 42,* 696.

Merritt, H. H., Adams, R. D., & Solomon, H. C. (1946). *Neurosyphilis.* New York: Oxford University Press.

Navia, B. A., Jordan, B. D., & Price, R. W. (1986). The AIDS dementia complex. I: Clinical features. *Annals of Neurology, 19,* 517–524.

Oddy, M., Humphrey, M., & Uttley, D. (1978). Subjective impairment and social recovery after closed head injury. *Journal of Neurology, Neurosurgery, and Psychiatry, 41,* 611–616.

Oliveri, R. L., Cittadella, R., Sibilia, G., Manna, I., Valentino, P., Gambardella, A., et al. (1999). APOE and risk of cognitive impairment in multiple sclerosis. *Acta Neurologica Scandinavica, 100,* 290–295.

Ramzan, N. N., Loftus, E., Burgart, L. J., Rooney, M., Batts, K. P., Wiesner, R. H., et al. (1997). Diagnosis and monitoring of Whipple disease by polymerase chain reaction. *Annals of Internal Medicine, 126,* 520–527.

Rao, S. M., Leo, G. J., Bernardin, L., & Unverzagt, F. (1991). Cognitive dysfunction in multiple sclerosis. I: Frequency, patterns, and prediction. *Neurology, 41,* 685–691.

Rao, S. M., Leo, G. J., Haughton, V. M., St. Aubin-Faubert, P., & Bernardin, L. (1989). Correlation of magnetic resonance imaging with neuropsychological testing in multiple sclerosis. *Neurology, 39,* 161–166.

Razonable, R. R., Aksamit, A. J., Wright, A. J., & Wilson, J. W. (2001). Cidofovir treatment of progressive multifocal leukoencephalopathy in a patient receiving highly active antiretroviral therapy. *Mayo Clinic Proceedings, 76,* 1171–1175.

Ron, M. A., Acker, W., Shaw, G. H., & Lishman, W. A. (1982). Computerized tomography of the brain in chronic alcoholism: A survey and follow-up study. *Brain, 105,* 497–514.

Ross, D. S. (2001). Serum thyroid-stimulating hormone measurement for assessment of thyroid function and disease. *Endocrinology and Metabolism Clinics of North America, 30,* 245–264.

Sacktor, N. C., Skolasky, R. L., & Esposito, D. (1999). Combination antiretroviral therapy including protease inhibitors improves HIV-associated cognitive impairment. *Neurology, 53,* 391–396.

Sacktor, N. C., Tarwater, P. M., Skolasky, R. L., McArthur, J. C., Selnes, O. A., Becker, J., et al. (2001). CSF antiretroviral drug penetrance and the treatment of HIV-associated psychomotor slowing. *Neurology, 57,* 542–544.

Scaravilli, F., & Harrison, M. J. (1997). Infectious diseases causing dementia. In M. M. Esiri & J. H. Morris (Eds.), *The neuropathology of dementia* (pp. 357–384). Cambridge, England: Cambridge University Press.

Schmitt, F. A., Bigley, J. W., Mckinnis, R., Logue, P. E., Evans, R. W., & Drucker, J. L. (1988). Neuropsychological outcome of zidovudine (AZT) treatment of patients with AIDS and AIDS-related complex. *New England Journal of Medicine, 319,* 1573–1578.

Simon, R. P. (1985). Neurosyphilis. *Archives of Neurology, 42,* 606–613.

Simpson, D. M., & Berger, J. R. (1996). Neurologic manifestations of HIV Infection. *Medical Clinics of North America, 80,* 1363–1394.

St Louis, M. E., & Wasserheit, J. N. (1998). Elimination of syphilis in the United States. *Science, 281,* 353–354.

Sultzer, D. L., & Cummings, J. L. (1994). Secondary dementias in the elderly. In M. L. Albert & J. E. Knoefel (Eds.), *Clinical neurology of aging* (2nd ed., pp. 379–395). New York: Oxford University Press.

Teasdale, G. M., Nicoll, J. A., Murray, G., & Fiddes, M. (1997). Association of apolipoprotein E polymorphism with outcome after head injury. *Lancet, 350,* 1069–1071.

Thurman, D., & Guerrero, J. (1999). Trends in hospitalization associated with traumatic brain injury. *Journal of the American Medical Association, 282*, 954–957.

Torvik, A., Lindboe, C. F., & Rodge, S. (1982). Brain lesions in alcoholics: A neuropathological study and clinical correlations. *Journal of the Neurological Sciences, 56*, 233–248.

Unterharnscheidt, F. J. (1975). Injuries due to boxing and other sports. In P. J. Vinken & G. W. Bruyn (Eds.), *Handbook of clinical neurology* (Vol. 23, pp. 531–567). New York: Elsevier.

Vanneste, J. A. (2000). Diagnosis and management of normal-pressure hydrocephalus. *Journal of Neurology, 247*, 5–14.

Vanneste, J. A., Augustijn, P., Dirven, C., Tan, W. F., & Goedhart, Z. D. (1992). Shunting normal pressure hydrocephalus: Do the benefits outweigh the risks? A multicenter study and literature review. *Neurology, 42*, 54–59.

Victor, M. (1994). Alcoholic dementia. *Canadian Journal of Neurological Sciences, 21*, 88–99.

Victor, M., Adams, R. D., & Collins, G. H. (1989). *The Wernicke-Korsakoff syndrome: A clinical and pathological study of 245 patients, 82 with postmortem examinations* (2nd ed.). Philadelphia: Davis.

Walker, A. E., Robins, M., &Weinfeld, F. D. (1985). Epidemiology of brain tumors: The national survey of intracranial neoplasms. *Neurology, 35*, 219–226.

Walker, D. W., Hunter, B. E., & Abraham, W. C. (1981). Neuroanatomical and functional deficits subsequent to chronic ethanol administration in animals. *Alcoholism Clinical and Experimental Research, 5*, 267–282

Wasserstrom, W. R., Glass, J. P., & Posner, J. B. (1982). Diagnosis and treatment of leptomeningeal metastases from solid tumors: Experience with 90 patients. *Cancer, 49*, 759–772.

Weinstein, A., Schwid, S. I., Schiffer, R. B., McDermott, M. P., Giang, D. W., & Goodman, A. D. (1999). Neuropsychologic status in multiple sclerosis after treatment with glatiramer. *Archives of Neurology, 56*, 319–324.

Wikkelso, C., Andersson, H., Blomstrand, C., Lindqvist, G., & Svendsen, P. (1986). Normal pressure hydrocephalus. Predictive value of the cerebrospinal fluid tap-test. *Acta Neurologica Scandinavica, 73*, 566–573.

Yarchoan, R., Berg, G., Brouwers, P., Fischl, M. A., Spitzer, A. R., Wichman, A., et al. (1987). Response of human-immunodeficiency-virus-associated neurological disease to 3'-azido-3'deoxythymidine. *Lancet, 1*, 132–135.

CHAPTER 9

Psychiatric Diagnosis and Management of Psychosis in Dementia

Gregory H. Pelton

Alzheimer's disease (AD), the predominant form of dementia, comprises 60% to 80% of all cases of dementia (Stoppe et al., 1999). The number of patients with AD represents a growing public health problem that may reach crisis proportions in the future. In 1993, the estimated AD population in the United States was approximately 4 million, and it is estimated to reach 14 million by the year 2050 (Tariot, Podgorski, Blazina, & Leibovici, 1993). AD has been defined as the neurodegenerative illness with the most neuropsychiatric sequelae, including behavioral dyscontrol and psychosis. Behavioral complications and psychosis during AD constitute a tremendous burden to caregivers and are common precipitants of institutionalization (Burns, Jacoby, & Levy, 1990; Cohen et al., 1993; Deimling & Bass, 1986; Weiner, Alexander, & Shortell, 1996). Antipsychotic medications are the treatment of choice for psychosis or behavioral complications associated with dementia (Helms, 1985; Schneider, Pollock, & Lyness, 1990), with drug utilization studies showing that antipsychotics are used in 35% to 51% of elderly institutionalized patients (Avorn, Dreyer, Connelly, & Soumerai, 1989; Giron et al., 2001; Lantz, Louis, Lowenstein, & Kennedy, 1990).

Before any drug therapy is initiated, however, the clinician needs to determine if the psychosis or behavioral disturbance is due to other causes such as an underlying medical condition, comorbid psychiatric condition, drug effects and interactions, infections, sensory disturbances, and unmet care needs. Any secondary medical conditions should be treated and problematic medications adjusted or discontinued. Alternatively, nonpharmacologic interventions may be effective: change in room, reduction in noise level, brief periodic nursing contacts, behavior modification, or family education (Holm et al., 1999; Leibovici & Tariot,1988; Mintzer et al., 1993; Rovner, 1996). If these interventions fail, pharmacologic treatment may be necessary.

The majority of early clinical treatment trials, conducted mainly in the 1970s and 1980s, used conventional antipsychotics as the mainstay of pharmacotherapy. The results of meta-analyses of placebo-controlled treatment trials indicated that conventional antipsychotic treatment in dementia was significantly more efficacious than placebo but that the magnitude of the advantage over placebo averaged only 18% (Lanctot, Best, & Mittmann, 1998; Schneider et al., 1990). Most studies were largely uncontrolled with high side effect and high dropout rates, and the few placebo-controlled trials conducted had several methodological flaws (Barnes, Veith, Okimoto, Raskind, & Gumbreck, 1982; Petrie et al., 1982; Rada & Kellner, 1976).

Despite limitations of these early studies, conventional antipsychotics continued to be the mainstay of treatment for hallucinations and delusions in the nursing home setting. Unfortunately, their nonjudicious use to manage unspecified behavioral symptoms in older nursing home patients (Thapa, Meador, Gideon, Fought, & Ray, 1994) led to the promulgation of the Omnibus Budget Reconciliation Act (OBRA) of 1987 (Elon & Pawlson, 1992), which became effective in 1990. OBRA required identification of target symptoms, justification for use of antipsychotics, and mandatory attempts to decrease or stop the antipsychotic medication every three months. During this time, several other medications were reported to be effective, primarily in uncontrolled studies or in controlled studies with relatively small samples: trazodone (Lawlor et al., 1994; Lebert, Pasquier, & Petit, 1994), selective serotonin reuptake inhibitors (Burke, Folks, Roccaforte, & Wengel, 1994; Geldmacher, Waldman, Doty, & Heilman, 1994; Pollock et al., 1997), lithium (Holton & George, 1985), carbamazepine (Tariot et al., 1998), valproate (Porsteinsson et al., 2001), buspirone (Lawlor et al., 1994), and propranolol (Weiler, Mungas, & Bernick, 1988). Thus, contrary to the new governmental mandates, a consensus statement by the American Association of Geriatric Psychiatry, the Alzheimer's Association, and the American Geriatric Society noted that antipsychotic drugs were a critical pharmacological agent with established efficacy to treat psychotic symptoms, and their use was important in the armamentarium of treatment options for psychosis and agitation in dementia (Small, Rabins, & Barry, 1997). Unfortunately, it remained unclear what the appropriate antipsychotic dose should be or what the appropriate duration of antipsychotic treatment should be to ensure quality of care (Elon & Pawlson, 1992; Sweet & Pollock, 1995) and to guide the clinicians treating patients with dementia and psychosis.

With respect to long-term outcome, there have been very few placebo-controlled treatment trials on continuation (or discontinuation) treatment in AD patients with behavioral complications. In one controlled study of patients with dementia whose antipsychotics were discontinued in accordance with OBRA regulations, 50% were rated as much worse (largely due to verbal and physical aggression) by blinded raters and needed to resume psychotropic medication, in contrast to 5% of a comparison patient group in the same setting (Horwitz, Tariot, Mead, & Cox, 1995). In three other studies involving psychotropic medication withdrawal in dementia, the primary intervention was an educational program or alteration of nursing home structure with psychotropic medication withdrawal a secondary feature, making it difficult to evaluate the impact of psychotropic medication withdrawal in isolation (Avorn et al., 1992; Fitz & Mallya, 1992). In another uncontrolled two-year follow-up study of 38 diagnostically heterogeneous geriatric inpatients receiving antipsychotics, when their medication was withdrawn, the results were mixed (Connelly, 1993). A major limitation of this study was that patients on psychotropics were withdrawn without determining whether the patients had target symptoms warranting the use of such medications in the first place. One placebo controlled study examined both antipsychotic and benzodiazepine discontinuation. Cohen-Mansfield et al. (1999) reported that withdrawing haloperidol, thioridazine, or lorazepam in 58 nursing home patients (of whom 35 completed the trial) did not lead to worsening of behavioral symptoms during a six-week, placebo-controlled discontinuation trial. Important methodological issues may help explain these divergent results. In the Cohen-Mansfield et al. study, patients were not required to have target symptoms of psychosis or behavioral dyscontrol that warranted treatment with psychotropic medications, and "responder" status was never established. Therefore, it is possible that patients without behavioral complications received antipsychotics (and benzodiazepines), and, not surprisingly, discontinuation of these medications did not lead to the emergence of symptoms because such symptoms were not present in the first place. In the only other controlled antipsychotic discontinuation study (Horwitz et al., 1995), patients were required to have behavioral dyscontrol or psychosis, and discontinuation of antipsychotics was associated with high relapse rates. In summary, the limited literature suggests a high risk of worsening of symptoms and relapse in medication-responsive patients who are discontinued from antipsychotic medication. However, there are no large-scale, systematic studies on this issue.

With the introduction of atypical antipsychotics, the use of conventional antipsychotics in geriatric patients is becoming more limited. The limiting factors in the use of conventional neuroleptics are the high incidence of serious cardiovascular and anticholinergic symptoms with the low potency antipsychotics (e.g., chlorpromazine, thioridazine) and extrapyramidal symptoms (EPS) and tardive dyskinesia (TD) with the high potency antipsychotics (e.g., haloperidol). In addition, even though conventional antipsychotics were endorsed as effective clinical management tools in the treatment of psychosis in dementia, in a meta-analysis of the controlled and uncontrolled studies using conventional antipsychotics and examining their efficacy, the risk-to-benefit ratio associated with conventional antipsychotics was questionable (Schneider, 1993).

More recently, the atypical antipsychotics have provided new options in the treatment of psychosis of dementia, particularly AD. Clozapine was first available in the United States in 1990, with risperidone, olanzapine, and quetiapine introduced later in the 1990s. Atypical antipsychotics are now widely used because of their favorable neurological side effect profile compared to conventional antipsychotics (Casey, 1991; Glazer & Morgenstern, 1988; Jeste, Lacro, et al., 1999); for example, in a series of 255 AD patients treated with risperidone for one year, the cumulative incidence of persistent emergent TD was only 2.6% (Jeste, Rockwell, et al., 1999). Atypical antipsychotics are in the process of replacing conventional antipsychotics and are a primary treatment option in clinical practice.

The completion of several large, double-blind placebo-controlled clinical trials (De Deyn et al., 1999; Devanand et al., 1998; Katz et al., 1999; Street et al., 2000) supports the effectiveness of antipsychotics in general in treating psychotic and behavioral disturbances in dementia. While these antipsychotic medication trials have demonstrated efficacy, a narrow therapeutic dosing window has been identified for both the conventional and newer atypical antipsychotics. Thus, lower doses of either conventional or atypical antipsychotics than those used in schizophrenic patients afford an acceptable side effect profile in the treatment of psychosis and behavioral dyscontrol of dementia. At the lower dosing schedules, atypical antipsychotics are better tolerated than conventional antipsychotics, particularly with respect to the risk of EPS and TD (De Deyn et al., 1999; Jeste,

Rockwell, et al., 1999). The propensity of the atypical antipsychotics to be well tolerated, effective, and to produce a low side effect profile has been shown most clearly with risperidone. In more than 1,000 patients in placebo-controlled trials, risperidone has consistently shown efficacy with a benign side-effect profile (Brodaty et al., 2001; De Deyn et al., 1999; Katz et al., 1999). The other atypical antipsychotics may show a similar efficacy and low side-effect profile. In the ongoing National Institute of Mental Health (NIMH) Clinical Antipsychotic Treatment Intervention Effectiveness (CATIE) multicenter medication trial, a parallel-group comparison of three atypical antipsychotics (risperidone, olanzapine, quetiapine) and placebo (with citalopram as a second phase treatment) is ongoing; on its completion, more answers will be available to the treating clinician (Schneider et al., 2001).

Psychotic and behavioral disturbances are associated with all dementing disorders, including frontal lobe dementia, basal ganglia diseases with dementia, vascular dementias, traumatic brain injury, multiple sclerosis, central nervous system (CNS) infections, and Huntington's disease (Ballard, Gray, & Ayre, 1999; Binetti et al., 1993; Sultzer, Levin, Mahler, High, & Cummings, 1993). However, this review focuses predominantly on clinical treatment trials of psychosis in AD patients. The safety and efficacy in the treatment of psychosis of AD is presumed to be similar to that in other dementia diagnoses. These diseases and their associated risks from antipsychotic treatments are discussed only briefly. Controlled treatment trials in other specific dementia diagnostic groups are still needed; thus, recommendations in their management are limited.

EPIDEMIOLOGY AND PREVALENCE

In AD, psychotic and behavioral complications are common and heterogeneous in their presentation (Reisberg et al., 1987; Rubin, Morris, & Berg, 1987). Psychotic symptoms are very common, with the prevalence, depending on the study, ranging from 10% to 73% (Cohen et al., 1993; Cummings, Miller, Hill, & Neshkes, 1987; Gormley & Rizwan, 1998; Mega, Cummings, Fiorello, & Gornbein, 1996; Wragg & Jeste, 1989). The prevalence of delusions has been reported to range from 0% to 40% in AD (Bucht & Adolfsson, 1983; Devanand, 1997; Devanand, Jacobs, & Tang, 1997; Lyketsos et al., 2000; Reisberg et al., 1989), but isolated psychotic symptoms may be two to three times as common as diagnosable psychotic disorders (Wragg &

Jeste, 1989). Hallucinations are also common in dementia, with a prevalence between 21% and 49% in different studies (Burns et al., 1990; Mega et al., 1996). Visual and auditory hallucinations are most common. Varying degrees of agitation occur in one-third to one-half of AD patients (Cohen-Mansfield, Marx, & Rosenthal, 1989; Devanand et al., 1997), with aggressive behavior being less common (Swearer, Drachman, O'Donnell, & Mitchell, 1988). The large ranges in prevalence rates may be explained, in part, by the various settings where the information was gathered (e.g., outpatient, assisted living, nursing home) and differing methods of assessment. Delusions are most prevalent during the middle phase of illness (Cummings et al., 1987; Mega et al., 1996; Wragg & Jeste, 1989) and are a common precipitant of institutionalization (Stern et al., 1997). The informant (e.g., direct clinical interview with the patient, interview with the caregiver, or chart review), criteria for diagnosis of psychosis or psychotic disorder (Wragg & Jeste, 1989), and the prevalence of concurrent psychopathology (e.g., agitation, aggression) all affect identification of symptoms.

It is uncommon for patients with dementia to have a typical, sustained, and well-developed delusional syndrome. More often, delusional processes are chronic and intermittent. Cummings et al. (1987) noted that 30% of moderately advanced AD patients were delusional at the time of their cross-sectional study, but 50% had exhibited delusions at some point in the course of their illness. Drevets and Rubin (1989) showed that delusions were more common in the middle stages of the illness (63%) than in the first stage (30%) or the third stage (52%). In a prospective follow-up study, Zubenko et al. (1991) reported that psychosis emerged in 7% of mildly demented patients, 43% of moderately demented patients, and 50% of those with severe dementia. Even though most studies find that delusional patients have greater cognitive deficits than nondelusional patients (Flynn, Cummings, & Gornbein, 1991; Jeste, Wragg, Salmon, Harris, & Thal, 1992; Lopez et al., 1991), no consistent relationships between disturbances in specific cognitive domains and the occurrence of delusions have been identified. Therefore, delusions do not necessarily indicate the severity of cognitive impairment. However, several investigators have found a more rapid decline in cognitive functioning among delusional patients with AD (Drevets & Rubin, 1989; Lopez et al., 1991; Stern et al., 1987).

In a naturalistic longitudinal follow-up study examining the course of psychopathology in AD, Devanand et al. (1997) examined the long-term clinical course of AD by following AD patients at the mild to moderate stage of illness over time. They recruited 235 AD patients with early, probable AD at three sites and followed up at six-month intervals. Trained research technicians established reliability and gave the Columbia University Scale for Psychopathology in Alzheimer's Disease (CUSPAD; Devanand et al., 1992) to informants. Using dichotomous ratings (present or absent) for each symptom category on the CUSPAD, Markov analyses were used to predict the probability of developing or maintaining the specific type of psychopathology at the next visit. In these analyses, behavioral dyscontrol (defined as wandering or agitation or physical aggression) was the most frequent and highly persistent category. Paranoid delusions and hallucinations were moderately persistent, and about 50% of patients with one of these symptoms were likely to manifest the same symptom six months later. Paulsen et al. (2000) computed the cumulative four-year incidence of new-onset psychosis of AD to be 51%. Other studies have shown that behavioral complications, particularly agitation and aggression, become more frequent with illness progression (McShane et al., 1997; Reisberg et al., 1989; Rubin et al., 1987; Wragg & Jeste, 1989). These data also show that symptoms of psychopathology fluctuate over time to varying degrees depending on the type of symptom.

Overall, these naturalistic studies indicate psychotic symptoms (paranoid delusions and hallucinations) are intermediate in persistence, suggesting that the need for long-term antipsychotic treatment of these symptoms may require periodic reevaluation. Agitation, on the other hand, is highly persistent, indicating that treatment of this target behavior may need to be relatively prolonged. This treatment model is further supported by the results from the Newcastle-upon-Tyne group, showing that 53% of AD patients with psychotic symptoms no longer had psychotic symptoms at one-year follow up (Ballard et al., 2001).

DIAGNOSTIC CRITERIA

In the report "Mental Health: A Report of the Surgeon General" (U.S. Department of Health and Human Services, 1999), the surgeon general expressed concern for the lack of information about treatment of symptoms of dementia such as psychosis and agitation, particularly in the late stages of the disease. In March 2000, the Food and Drug Administration (FDA) held a meeting of the Psychopharmacological Drugs Advisory Committee (PDAC) in an attempt to build consensus on how to reliably diagnose and treat patients with psychotic and behavioral disturbances related to dementia. The PDAC identified the frequently used term *Behavioral and Psychological Symptoms of Dementia* (BPSD), which includes psychosis and agitation/aggression, as too broad to be considered a diagnostic entity. From an epidemiological, clinical, and regulatory perspective, it was too difficult to define reliable outcome criteria with such a diverse set of signs and symptoms of dementia (Laughren, 2001). Rather, specific diagnostic criteria for psychosis or agitation/aggression of AD, in a manner analogous to the *Diagnostic and Statistical Manual of Mental Disorders,* fourth edition (*DSM-IV*; American Psychiatric Association, 1994) criteria for psychosis during schizophrenia were needed (Jeste & Finkel, 2000).

At the PDAC meeting, *Psychosis of AD* criteria defined by Jeste and Finkel (2000; see Table 9.1) were provisionally accepted by the FDA (Laughren, 2001). The criteria include a primary diagnosis of AD, the presence of either hallucinations or delusions that have an onset subsequent to the onset of dementia, but are present for at least one month, and which are associated with disruption in the patient's and/or other's functioning. In addition, other causes for psychosis were exclusion criteria (e.g., schizophrenia, delirium, or other general medical condition). Unfortunately, a similar consensus was not reached on how to best define *agitation* in association with AD (Laughren, 2001).

Irrespective of how the FDA and other consensus organizations ultimately categorize the psychopathological symptoms of AD, the clinician is left with the fact that in dementia, psychotic symptoms and agitated and aggressive behaviors often coexist and substantially overlap (Lyketsos et al., 2000). In the Devanand et al. (1998) study, of the 71 AD patients, 51 (71.8%) met criteria for psychosis and all 71 patients met criteria for behavioral dyscontrol; the breakdown is comparable in other trials of this type (De Deyn et al., 1999; Katz et al., 1999; Street et al., 2000). Several studies addressing neuropsychiatric symptom patterns in AD have identified phenomenological subgroups of patients from among those with AD. Lyketsos et al. (1999) found that physical aggression is linked with delusions and depression, Klein et al. (1999) found that wandering was associated with sleep disorders, and Tariot et al. (1995) found in a large factor-analytic study that the neuropsychiatric symptoms of AD occur in eight clusters: depression, psychosis, defective self-regulation, irritability/agitation, vegetative features, apathy, aggression,

Table 9.1   Diagnostic Criteria for Psychosis of Alzheimer's Disease

A. Characteristic symptoms.
   Presence of one (or more) of the following symptoms:
   1. Visual or auditory hallucinations.
   2. Delusions.
B. Primary diagnosis.
   All the criteria for dementia of the Alzheimer type are met.*
C. Chronology of the onset of symptoms of psychosis versus onset of symptoms of dementia.
   There is evidence from the history that the symptoms in Criterion A have not been present continuously since prior to the onset of the symptoms of dementia.
D. Duration and Severity.
   The symptoms(s) in Criterion A have been present, at least intermittently, for 1 month or longer. Symptoms are severe enough to cause some disruption in the patients and/or others functioning.
E. Exclusion of schizophrenia and related psychotic disorders.
   Criteria for Schizophrenia, Schizoaffective Disorder, Delusional Disorder, or Mood Disorder with Psychotic Features have never been met.
F. Relationship to delirium.
   The disturbance does not occur exclusively during the course of a delirium.
G. Exclusion of other causes of psychotic symptoms.
   The disturbance is not better accounted for by another general medical condition or direct physiological effects of a substance (e.g., a drug of abuse, a medication).

Associated features: (*Specify* if associated)
   With agitation: when there is evidence, from history of examination, of prominent agitation with or without physical or verbal aggression.
   With negative symptoms: when prominent negative symptoms, such as apathy, affective flattening, avolition, or motor retardation, are present.
   With depression: when prominent depressive symptoms, such as depressed mood, insomnia or hypersomnia, feelings of worthlessness or excessive or inappropriate guilt, or recurrent thoughts of death, are present.

*Published from "Psychosis of Alzheimer's Disease and Related Dementias: Diagnostic Criteria for a Distinct Syndrome," by D. V. Jeste and S. I. Finkel, 2000," *American Journal of Geriatric Psychiatry, 8,* pp. 29–34.

and affective lability. These clusters of clinical features have come under several terms, as mentioned earlier, including *Behavioral and Psychological Signs and Symptoms of Dementia* (BPSSD) and *Noncognitive Symptoms of dementia* (Finkel et al., 1996). Further, the *DSM* approach to classify these symptoms of dementia is still evolving. Thus, in the absence of consensus in the field and a better understanding of the pathoetiology of these symptoms, the treatment of psychosis and agitation/aggression of dementia frequently needs to be considered together (Edell & Tunis, 2001; Lyketsos, Breitner, & Rabins, 2001; Lyketsos, Sheppard, et al., 2001; Madhusoodanan, 2001; Madhusoodanan, Suresh, Brenner, & Pillai, 1999; Rapoport et al., 2001). From a practical standpoint, the decision to use a psychotropic medication, typically an antipsychotic medication, is dependent on the balance between how to safely treat a mix of target symptoms in dementia patients and the knowledge that no medication has been specifically approved by the FDA for this purpose. Clinically and in research studies, it has been found that the diverse psychotic and disruptive symptoms of AD often respond to similar treatment modalities (Aarsland, Cummings, Yenner, & Miller, 1996; Devanand et al., 1998; Katz et al., 1999; Street et al., 2000; Tariot et al., 1995).

Clinical Characteristics in *Psychosis of AD*

Psychotic signs associated with dementia include delusions, hallucinations, and misperceptions. As noted previously, the vast majority of patients with dementia are likely to develop psychosis, agitation, aggression, or disruptive behavior over the course of their illness. There have been many attempts to biologically and psychologically link psychotic symptoms to agitation and aggression. In schizophrenia, antipsychotics are often assumed to be specific for the treatment of psychosis, and improvement in symptoms of behavioral dyscontrol is believed to be secondary to improvement in psychosis. Unfortunately, this close association in schizophrenia does not appear to apply to patients with dementia. In fact, in a double-blind placebo-controlled trial that compared risperidone, haloperidol, and placebo, there were no differences among active medications for psychosis (both were effective), but aggression was reduced both in severity and frequency to a greater extent on risperidone compared to either haloperidol or placebo (De Deyn et al., 1999). The reason for improvement in behavioral dyscontrol on one antipsychotic versus another remains unclear in patients with dementia. It is, however, a logical speculation that either the pathophysiology of AD or mechanism of action of antipsychotics in AD, or both, are different from that in schizophrenia.

Because of the difficulty in disentangling the various neuropsychiatric symptoms of AD, a number of efforts have been put forth to identify and quantify specific target symptoms. The common psychotic symptoms of AD are delusions, illusions, and visual hallucinations. *Delusions* are defined as false beliefs that are out of context with the person's social and cultural background and that the patient will not accept as false. The delusions of AD are typically of the paranoid type, nonbizarre, and simple. In AD, common delusions include the following: others are stealing from the patient, a person's spouse is having an affair, and family members plan to abandon the patient despite evidence to the contrary (Reisberg et al., 1987). Reisberg et al. reported that 48% of 33 delusional AD patients manifested delusions of theft, 21% believed their house was not their home, and 9% believed their spouse had been replaced by an imposter. Complex or bizarre delusions (e.g., religious or grandiose delusions) commonly observed in schizophrenia or mania are distinctly unusual in AD.

Even though misperceptions are very prevalent in dementia (ranging from 1% to 50% in different studies), these symptoms are not considered delusions because they are a type of cognitive deficit. Examples of misperceptions are the inability to recognize themselves in the mirror, the belief that television characters are real, and the misidentification of objects. Hence, misperceptions are not viewed as psychotic features, often do not disrupt behavior, and are often not treated.

Hallucinations are defined as false sensory perceptions that are not distortions or illusions (misinterpretation of a sensory stimulus). Visual and auditory hallucinations are most common with varied prevalence between 5% and 20% in different studies. Hallucinations in AD are more frequently visual than auditory (Holroyd, 1996); the reverse is true for schizophrenia. Typical schizophrenia delusions (e.g., hearing multiple voices speaking at once or hearing one voice with a running commentary on the patient's actions) are rare in AD. A number of groups have found that delusions or hallucinations are commonly associated with aggression, agitation, and disruptive behavior (Flynn et al., 1991; Rabins, Mace, & Lucas, 1982; Rockwell, Krull, Dimsdale, & Jeste, 1994). Often, however, patients do not seem to change their behavior because the delusions or hallucinations are not upsetting. Family members are, however, often very upset by having a loved one with delusions or hallucinations, and sometimes treatment is initiated to reduce symptoms and caregiver burden.

Assessment of Psychosis in Alzheimer's Disease

Using one of the neuropsychiatric batteries to help determine target symptoms should occur after reversible medical conditions (e.g., occult infection, metabolic imbalance) and iatrogenic or medication-induced symptom production are ruled out. Several assessment batteries are available to identify and reliably quantify target symptoms for treatment.

The most common rating scales available to measure neuro-psychiatric symptoms of AD include the Neuropsychiatric Inventory (NPI; Cummings et al., 1994), NPI/NH (Wood et al., 2000), Behavioral Pathology in Alzheimer's Disease (BEHAVE-AD; Reisberg, 1984), the Gottfries-Brane-Steen Scale (Gottfries, Brane, & Steen, 1982), CERAD Behavior Rating Scale (Tariot et al., 1995), the Cohen-Mansfield Agitation Inventory (Cohen-Mansfield et al., 1989), and the Columbia University Scale for Psychopathology (CUSPAD) (Devanand et al., 1992).

The NPI is a caregiver-based instrument (Cummings et al., 1994) that has become widely used in the research setting. The NPI is a valid and reliable means of assessing neuropsychiatric symptoms (e.g., agitation, apathy, depression, anxiety, delusions, hallucinations, irritability, and delusions) in patients with dementia, with a decision tree approach making it very useful (Cummings & McPherson, 2001). The NPI's psychometric properties include strong reliability and validity established in a number of studies and a variety of settings and demonstrated sensitivity to change in several clinical trials evaluating psychopharmacologic approaches to treat behavioral complications in dementia or AD (McKeith, Fairbairn, Perry, & Thompson, 1994; Street et al., 2000, 2001; Tariot, Solomon, et al., 2000). The NPI can be administered at every visit by a trained evaluator, monitoring for symptom improvement.

The *Neuropsychiatric Inventory/Nursing Home Version* (NPI/NH) is a caregiver-rated scale administered in nursing home patients. The NPI/NH, like the NPI, is a structured interview with a few minor modifications assessing the frequency and severity of 12 psychobehavioral symptoms associated with dementia (Wood et al., 2000). The NPI/NH allows professional staff of the care facility to act as the informant, rather than obtaining information from the caregiver of a community-dwelling elderly person as required to complete the NPI.

The BEHAVE-AD (Reisberg et al., 1987) is a caregiver-rated instrument based on a 25-item scale that measures behavioral disturbances in seven major categories (delusions, hallucinations, activity disturbances, aggressiveness, sleep disturbance, affective disturbance, and anxiety). Each symptom is scored on a four-point scale of severity, where 0 = not present to 4 = most severe. The BEHAVE-AD scale specifically measures the occurrence and severity of behavioral problems in patients with AD and has been found to be a reliable scale that has been used in clinical trials (De Deyn et al., 1999; Katz et al., 1999; Montaldi, Brooks, & McColl, 1990; Sclan, Saillon, Franssen, Hugonot-Diener, & Saillon, 1996).

The Gottfries Scale is a caregiver-completed scale that measures behavioral disturbances, cognitive disturbances, and some functional impairment (Gottfries et al., 1982). This scale is not very specific in terms of the nature of behavioral disturbances, has some features that may make it difficult to train raters, and has rarely been used in the United States.

The Behavioral Rating Scale for Dementia (BRSD) of the *Consortium to Establish a Registry for Alzheimer's Disease* (CERAD; Tariot et al., 1995) scale derives target symptoms; it is comprehensive, specifically measuring the occurrence and severity of behavioral problems in patients with AD. Unfortunately, it is very long (48 questions), requires training to administer, and is impractical compared to the NPI.

The Cohen-Mansfield Agitation Inventory (CMAI) is excellent for detailing patterns of agitation in nursing home patients with AD, but it cannot be used in outpatients because of the intensive observation by an informant that is required (Cohen-Mansfield et al., 1989; Koss et al., 1997). This assessment tool focuses only on agitation and does not assess psychosis.

The CUSPAD is useful to assess psychopathology, but it does not have quantitative ratings for items and, hence, is not appropriate for repeated testing to monitor efficacy of a treatment (Devanand et al., 1992). The CUSPAD criteria provide for the definition of a delusion as "broad" (does not accept caregiver's correction of the false belief) and "narrow" (does not accept caregiver's correction of the false belief, and occurs more than three times per week). Hallucinations are defined as "vague" or "clear." The presence of either a delusion (narrow definition) or hallucination (clear) on the CUSPAD is required for a person to have "psychosis."

Neurobiological Mechanisms of Psychosis in Dementia

Based on neuroimaging studies, an association between delusions in dementia and dysfunction in the paralimbic area of the frontal cortex has been found (Sultzer, 1996). Using neuropathological and neuochemical investigations in patients with primary dementia, those with psychosis have been found to have significantly more plaques and tangles in the medial temporal-prosubicular area and the middle frontal cortex (Zubenko et al., 1991) and four to five times higher levels of abnormal paired helical filament (PHF)-tau protein in the entorhinal and temporal cortices (Mukaetova-Ladinska, Harrington, Roth, & Wischik, 1993). A decrease in serotonin in the prosubiculum of the cerebral cortex was found in psychotic versus nonpsychotic dementia patients (Lawlor, Ryan, & Bierrer, 1995; Zubenko et al., 1991). Acetylcholine decreases in function have been correlated with increased thought disorders (Sunderland et al., 1997), and cholinergic agents have been observed to decrease the emergence of psychotic symptoms (Bodick, Offen, & Shannon, 1997; Cummings, Gorman, & Shapiro, 1993; Kaufer, Cummings, & Christine, 1996; Raskind, 1999). Higher levels of norepinephrine in the substantia nigra (Zubenko et al., 1991) and higher levels of beta-adrenergic receptors (Russo-Neustadt & Cotman, 1997) in multiple brain regions in psychotic versus nonpsychotic AD patients have also been observed. These data support the clinical finding of an enhanced responsiveness of the norepinephrine system and increased psychosis in AD patients (Peskind et al., 1995; Raskind & Peskind, 1994).

As the technology of our field advances, our understanding of the pathophysiology of psychosis will improve. For example, it has been posited that an interaction of cholinergic deficiency, particularly severe in the limbic system structures of the AD brain (Proctor, Palladino, & Fillipo, 1988), and the relatively preserved dopaminergic system may produce regional functional changes leading to the occurrence of psychosis. This is supported by some data suggesting acetylcholinesterase inhibitors (Cummings et al., 1993; Kaufer et al., 1996) as well as medications that block dopamine function (e.g., antipsychotic agents; Daniel, 2000) can ameliorate the psychosis of AD. Recent work, however, has shown that a variation in dopamine receptor (DR) gene subtypes exists between nonpsychotic AD patients and psychotic AD patients. The investigators found homozygosity of the B2 allele of DR1 in the nonpsychotics versus homozygosity of the 1 and 2 alleles of DR3 in the psychotic AD patients (Holmes et al., 2001; Sweet et al., 1998). Likewise, in 275 subjects with AD, it has been shown that 52% of AD patients with psychotic symptoms were homozygous for the C102 allele for the serotonin 2A receptor gene, as compared with 6.9% of AD patients without psychosis (Nacmias, Tedde, Forleo, Piacentini, Latoracca, et al., 2001; Nacmias, Tedde, Forleo, Piacentini, Guarnieri, et al., 2001). Even though an answer to the neuropathological basis of psychosis in AD has not been established, these types of results yield confirmatory data that a histopathological underpinning exists to the psychotic symptoms associated with dementia (Bondareff, 1996).

Location of Patient Being Treated

The location of the patient (nursing home, assisted living, or outpatient) does not alter the choice or dose of medication to be considered in treating psychotic symptoms in dementia. The residential status of a patient is partly dependent on the patient's clinical state and partly on the ability of the caregiver to manage the patient at home. Whether and when the patient is admitted to a nursing home are highly variable factors that may depend as much on the caregiver's tolerance threshold and available resources as the patient's clinical state. Furthermore, the range of semi-independent, assisted living, intermediate nursing care, and specialized dementia facilities has created a spectrum of caregiving that defies simple categorizations and overlaps with intensive in-home services. In both outpatients and nursing home patients, the results of trials comparing antipsychotic medications in AD (De Deyn et al., 1999) and dose-comparison studies of individual antipsychotic medications (Devanand et al., 1998; Katz et al., 1999; Street et al., 2000) have been similar, regardless of whether the study was conducted in outpatients (Devanand et al., 1998), nursing homes (Katz et al., 1999; Street et al., 2000), or other institutionalized settings (De Deyn et al., 1999), even though the severity of symptoms has been shown to vary according to site. The one exception is the trial that found no significant differences among haloperidol, trazodone, and placebo in treating agitation in 149 outpatients with AD (Jeste & Finkel, 2000). In that study, a fourth subgroup received behavior management based on the choice of individual sites participating in the study, thereby creating issues in the design and statistical analysis, besides compromising blindness to some degree. The results of that study need to be placed in the context of the large number of other studies showing superiority for antipsychotics over placebo in a variety of settings.

CURRENT TREATMENT

Conventional Antipsychotics

Uncontrolled reports suggest that 25% to 75% of demented patients with behavioral complications respond to antipsychotics (Carlyle, Ancill, & Sheldon, 1993; Kral, 1961; Reisberg et al., 1987; Tewfik et al., 1970). During the past two decades, only a handful of random assignment, double-blind, placebo-controlled trials of antipsychotics in dementia have been conducted and published. Most studies were conducted in inpatient units or in nursing homes. In a four-week trial, thiothixene ($\leq$ 15 mg/day) demonstrated marginal superiority over placebo in the treatment of 42 patients with organic brain syndrome (Rada & Kellner, 1976). Limited information about diagnosis, nonstratified assignment of psychotic patients to the treatment groups, short trial duration, and a high placebo response rate (55%) were problematic. In another study of 61 patients with dementia (30 AD and 26 vascular), global clinical improvement was significantly greater with haloperidol (35%, mean daily dose 4.6 mg) or loxapine (32%, mean daily dose 21.9 mg) compared to placebo (9%). A large proportion had vascular dementia (42.6%), and the use of antiparkinsonian agents and chloral hydrate were limitations (Petrie et al., 1982). In another study of 53 patients, loxapine and thioridazine showed a small advantage over placebo but led to more side effects (Barnes et al., 1982). Diagnostic heterogeneity (55% AD, 38% vascular dementia), the use of concomitant sedative and anticholinergic medications, and the high placebo response rate limited these findings.

These studies had several methodological flaws, including diagnostic heterogeneity and the permitted use of other psychotropics. Schneider et al. (1990) conducted a meta-analysis of placebo-controlled trials of antipsychotics in agitated patients with any form of organic brain syndrome. Clinical worsening, dropout, and side effects were not accounted for in this meta-analysis. Antipsychotics were moderately superior to placebo (one-tailed $p = .004$), with effect size reduced by the high placebo response rate in some studies (Barnes et al., 1982; Rada & Kellner, 1976). These high placebo response rates indirectly suggest that patients with very mild symptoms were included to enhance sample size, thereby increasing Type II error, that is, finding no difference when, in fact, there was a "true" difference.

In 33 demented patients in a nursing home, thiothixene (variable dose, 0.25 mg to 18 mg daily) was superior to placebo in the treatment of agitation (Finkel et al., 1995). In a more recent report, haloperidol 2 mg to 3 mg daily and 0.5 mg to 0.75 mg daily were compared in a randomized, double-blind, six-week placebo-controlled trial in the treatment of psychosis and disruptive behaviors in 71 AD outpatients (Devanand et al., 1998). Haloperidol 2 mg to 3 mg daily was efficacious and superior to both low dose and placebo on the Brief Psychiatric Rating Scale (BPRS) psychosis factor ($p < .03$ and $p < .05$, respectively) and psychomotor agitation ($p < .03$ and $p < .04$, respectively). There were less robust effects on other outcome measures. Response rates using three sets of criteria were greater for haloperidol 2 mg to 3 mg daily (55% to 60%) compared to haloperidol 0.5 mg to 0.75 mg daily (25% to 35%) or placebo (25% to 30%). Extrapyramidal signs (EPS) tended to be greater for haloperidol 2 mg to 3 mg daily than for the other two conditions, primarily because of a subgroup (20%) that developed moderate to severe EPS. Other somatic side effects, cognitive performance, and daily functioning did not differ among the three treatment conditions. Low-dose haloperidol did not differ from placebo on any measure of efficacy or side effects. The results indicated a favorable therapeutic profile for haloperidol in doses of 2 mg to 3 mg daily, although a subgroup did develop moderate to severe EPS. Based on these results, a starting dose of haloperidol of 1 mg daily with gradual, upward dose titration was recommended, with the suggestion that the narrow therapeutic window observed with haloperidol may also apply to the use of other antipsychotics in AD patients with psychosis and disruptive behaviors (Devanand et al., 1998).

Comparisons among Conventional Antipsychotics

Earlier studies comparing low-potency to high-potency antipsychotics did not show consistent differences in efficacy (Barnes et al., 1982; Carlyle et al., 1993; Cowley & Glen, 1979; Petrie et al., 1982; Rosen, 1979; Smith, Taylor, & Linkous, 1974; Tsuang, Lu, Stotsky, & Cole, 1971). These studies were often limited by the lack of a placebo control and diagnostic heterogeneity in sample selection. Overall, there is little evidence to indicate superior efficacy for a specific class of conventional antipsychotic in the treatment of neuropsychiatric disturbances in dementia (Devanand, 1995; Salzman, 1987).

Conventional Antipsychotics versus Benzodiazepines

The few studies that compared antipsychotics to benzodiazepines suffered from methodological flaws, particularly with respect to sample selection and study design (Burgio et al., 1992; Covington, 1975; Kirven & Montero, 1973; Stotsky, 1984; Tewfik et al., 1970). The limited data available do not indicate superiority for benzodiazepines over antipsychotics in the treatment of behavioral complications in demented patients.

Benzodiazepines can lead to tolerance and dependence, and worsening of cognition is a concern. Despite the known deleterious effects of benzodiazepines on learning and memory in normal subjects (Ghoneim, Mewaldt, Berie, & Hinrichs, 1981; Jones, Lewis, & Spriggs, 1978; Liljequist, Linnoila, & Mattila, 1978), particularly in the elderly (Pomara et al., 1990), side effect comparison studies of antipsychotics and benzodiazepines in demented patients have not been conducted.

Conventional Antipsychotic Side Effects

Older patients are more sensitive to the side effects of neuroleptics. At comparable doses, low potency antipsychotics such as thioridazine and chlorpromazine are less likely to cause EPS than high potency antipsychotics such as haloperidol, but as many as 50% of all patients between 60 and 80 years of age receiving conventional antipsychotic medication develop either EPS or tardive dyskinesia (Jeste et al., 1995). Low potency antipsychotics are more likely to cause orthostatic hypotension, which increases the risk of falls and fractures (Ray, Federspiel, & Schaffner, 1980). Sedation is one of the most common side effects of antipsychotic drugs, with low potency antipsychotics being potent inducers. In addition, low potency antipsychotics have a greater propensity for anticholinergic side effects; thus, sleep may be induced but daytime confusion and disorientation may also ensue. Unfortunately, little work has been done on the effects of antipsychotics on cognition and activities of daily life in AD, and it remains unclear if the anticholinergic effects of low-potency antipsychotics (e.g., thioridazine) impact negatively on cognitive function to a greater extent than high-potency antipsychotics (e.g., haloperidol).

Atypical Antipsychotics

Recently developed atypical antipsychotics—that is, clozapine, risperidone, olanzapine, and quetiapine—are considered, by a majority of geriatric psychiatrists and other physicians, as a better and safer choice than the conventional antipsychotics, particularly in the geriatric population. Since the marketing of clozapine, the first atypical neuroleptic, in 1990, there have been a number of clinical trials, both uncontrolled and controlled, in the use of these medications in psychosis and behavioral dyscontrol in AD. The choice of drug depends on the patient's clinical profile and the drug's side-effect profile. However, more head-to-head comparison studies between conventional antipsychotics and atypical antipsychotics (De Deyn et al., 1999) and head-to-head comparisons among atypical antipsychotics are still needed (the CATIE trial is currently in progress).

Clozapine

Clozapine has substantial serotonergic blockade, as well as antiadrenergic and stimulation of histaminergic activity. It is also a potent muscarinic acetylcholine receptor antagonist (Lieberman, 1998; Tandon et al., 1998). Clozapine may be more efficacious than other antipsychotics in schizo- phrenia, and the risk of developing tardive dyskinesia (TD) is virtually nil (Kane, Honigfeld, Singer, & Meltzer, 1988). However, in the elderly with dementia and psychosis, several considerations need to be kept in mind. First, circulating levels of clozapine rise with dose and age, may be slightly higher in women then in men, sedation is high, and seizure potential is ele- vated (Centorrino et al., 1994; Kurz et al., 1998). Second, the sedative and orthostatic side effects may be substantial. The use of clozapine has been shown to lead to orthostatic hypotension in AD, which increases the risk of falls and fractures (Chengappa, Baker, & Kreinbrook, 1995). Third, there is a need for intensive monitoring for blood dyscrasias, which is reported to occur in 0.38% of patients (Kane et al., 1988). These safety issues are of major importance in elderly demented patients. There have been no pub- lished double-blind controlled trials using clozapine to treat psychosis or behavioral complications in demented patients. The few retrospective re- views and case reports indicate moderate efficacy but with significant ad- verse events (Oberholzer, Hendriksen, Monsch, Heierli, & Stahelin, 1992; Pitner, Mintzer, Pennypacker, & Jackson, 1995; Salzman, 1995).

Risperidone

Risperidone has a higher serotonin 5-HT2 than dopamine D2 blocking prop- erty, alph1 and alpha2 adrenergic blocking properties, and minimal hista- minergic H1 blocking properties, and practically no affinity for cholinergic receptors (Janssen et al., 1988; Madhusoodanan et al., 1999). Its elimination half-life has been reported to be between 20 and 22 hours, allowing once-a- day dosing if indicated (Byerly & DeVane, 1996). Risperidone has a de- creased propensity for EPS, and a 6 mg daily dose appears to be optimal in schizophrenia (Chouinard, Jones, & Remington, 1993). However, the opti- mal risperidone dose range in elderly demented patients with psychosis and/or behavioral dyscontrol is far lower and time to response significantly different (Katz et al., 1999).

Open-Label Studies

In a series of 109 nursing home patients with dementia and behavioral dyscontrol, risperidone was significantly more effective in the 0.5 mg to 1 mg/day dose. No notation of improvement in psychotic symptoms was made, and 29 of the patients (27%) discontinued treatment because of lack of efficacy and 17 (16%) because of adverse effects (Goldberg & Goldberg, 1997). Similar results were found in a small series of 15 patients treated with risperidone 0.5 mg/day in a nine-week trial (Lavretsky & Sultzer, 1998). In a chart review of 122 hospital records of patients newly treated with risperidone, 56 were demented with psychosis or behavioral dyscontrol. Eighty-two percent responded to risperidone as measured by the Clinical Global Impression scale; adverse events included hypotension in 29% and EPS in 11% (Zarate et al., 1997).

Controlled Clinical Trials

A large-scale multicenter study showed efficacy for risperidone in the 1 mg to 2 mg daily dose range, with 0.5 mg being essentially equivalent to placebo (Katz et al., 1999). In that study, 625 demented patients living in nursing homes (73% AD, 15% vascular, 12% mixed), with psychosis and behavioral disturbance (mean age 83 years old, mean 30-item Mini-Mental State Examination [MMSE] 6.6), were randomized to receive either risperidone 0.5 mg/day, risperidone 1 mg/day, risperidone 2 mg/day, or placebo for 12 weeks. To be included in the study, patients had to have a score on the BEHAVE-AD of 8 or greater, and a 50% reduction in the BEHAVE-AD score was the categorical primary outcome measure. The 12-week course of treatment was completed by 435 (70%) patients, with discontinuations primarily due to adverse events (12% placebo, 8%, 16%, and 24% of patients receiving 0.5, 1, and 2 mg/day of risperidone, respectively). At endpoint, placebo and 0.5 mg daily were similar (33%) in response, with 1 mg (45%) and 2 mg (50%) showing significantly superior response to either placebo or 0.5 mg. Patients receiving risperidone 2 mg daily were more likely to develop EPS and sedation than the patients receiving risperidone 0.5 mg or 1 mg daily, suggesting a relatively narrow therapeutic window for this atypical antipsychotic in elderly patients with dementia. Orthostatic hypotension was a relatively infrequent side effect in this study (Katz et al., 1999).

Olanzapine

Olanzapine blocks multiple receptor sites, including 5-HT2A/2C and dopamine D4/3/2/1, with a serotonin to dopamine receptor binding ratio of 8 : 1, histaminergic H1 receptors, muscarinic acetylcholine receptors, and noradrenergic alpha1 receptors (Bymaster et al., 1996; Tamminga et al., 1987). Olanzapine is well absorbed, is unaffected by food, and, with a mean half-life of 30 hours, can be used once a day (Fulton & Goa, 1997).

Open Label

In a retrospective chart review of 998 patients (mean age 81 years old) admitted to a hospital with psychotic or behavioral dyscontrol and dementia, the authors examined change in these psychopathological problems on discharge, after physician's choice of antipsychotic (Edell & Tunis, 2001). Primary outcome measure was the change in 16 subitems of the Psychogeriatric Dependency Rating Scale (PDRS; Wilkinson & Graham-White, 1980), which represent psychotic and behavioral dyscontrol symptoms. On discharge, 289 patients were prescribed haloperidol, 209 patients were prescribed olanzapine, and 500 were prescribed risperidone. An analysis of change in overall PDRS score showed olanzapine producing a significantly greater improvement (decrease in PDRS) as compared to haloperidol ($p < .01$) or risperidone ($p < .001$). An analysis of change in specific PDRS items associated with psychosis found olanzapine significantly reduced symptom severity when compared to risperidone ($p < .005$) and haloperidol ($p < .01$). Likewise, a significant reduction in aggression/agitation factors of PDRS was found for olanzapine versus haloperidol ($p < .001$) and risperidone ($p < .001$). No significant differences were noted when risperidone and haloperidol were compared. No data was presented on the dose of each antipsychotic medication administered at discharge. Side effects were comparable for the three treatments (Edell & Tunis, 2001).

Controlled-Treatment Trials

In an eight-week, double-blind, placebo-controlled dose-finding treatment trial of 238 elderly outpatients (mean age 78.6 years) who had AD and psychosis, patients were randomized to a flexible olanzapine dosage (1 mg to 8 mg/day) or placebo for eight weeks. Olanzapine was initiated at a dose of 1 mg/day, with a 1 mg to 2 mg/day increase every 14 days (mean dose 2.4 mg/day). On the primary outcome measures, there were no significant differences on efficacy measures (BEHAVE-AD rating scale) or on adverse events for EPS, EKG, weight changes, or laboratory alterations. The lack of efficacy, however, may have been because of too low a dose of olanzapine (Satterlee & Sussman, 1998).

In a second multicentered, double-blind, placebo-controlled clinical trial, 206 nursing home patients (mean age 83 years old and mean MMSE 6.9) with psychosis and behavioral dyscontrol during AD were treated. Patients were randomized to either a fixed dose of olanzapine 5 mg/day, 10 mg/day, 15 mg/day, or placebo for six weeks. All patients treated with olanzapine were begun on 5 mg/day, which increased by 5 mg/day every seven days for the patients randomized to receive 10 mg or 15 mg/day. On the primary outcome measure (NPI), olanzapine was found to be efficacious. A dose of 5 mg was significantly more effective than placebo, but 10 mg to 15 mg/day was not. The prominent side effects of sedation and weight gain were limiting factors for the use of higher doses (Street et al., 2000).

Quetiapine

Quetiapine acts as an antagonist at multiple neurotransmitter receptors in the brain, including D1, D2, serotonin 5HT-1A and 5HT-2, Histamine H1, and adrenergic alpha1 and alpha2 receptors. D2 receptor affinity is less than that for 5HT-2 receptors. Quetiapine has no appreciable binding affinity to cholinergic muscarinic or benzodiazepine receptors (Casey, 1996; Goldstein, 1995). It has a short half-life (approximately three to six hours; Fulton & Goa, 1997), but, despite this, efficacy has been documented with twice-daily administration (Fleischhacker, 1998; McManus, Arvanitis, & Kowalcyk, 1999). There have been no controlled treatment trials published using quetiapine in patients with psychosis or behavioral dyscontrol in dementia.

In an open-label multicenter efficacy study of psychosis in the elderly (including idiopathic psychosis, e.g., schizophrenia, bipolar, major depression [40%]; psychosis of AD [50%]; and psychosis of Parkinson's disease [10%]), 151 patients (mean age 77 years old) were treated. Median quetiapine dose was 100 mg/day (range 100 mg to 400 mg/day). Significant improvement was seen in the primary outcome measure of psychosis as measured by BPRS ($p < .0001$) and CGI ($p < .01$). The significant side effects included somnolence in 32%, dizziness/postural hypotension in 13%, and EPS in 6% (McManus et al., 1999). Clinical experience in these patients suggests that relatively high doses (100 mg to 600 mg daily) can be used with few side effects (Tariot, Salzman, Yeung, Pultz, & Rak, 2000). This allows for raising the upper limit of the therapeutic window for quetiapine compared to other antipsychotics, and this may confer an advantage in those patients who cannot tolerate moderate doses of other antipsychotics because of side effects. The incidence of EPS is very low, and the risk of a rare lenticular and corneal opacity has been reported in predrug release studies. However, with no placebo-controlled treatment trials with quetiapine, in the elderly dementia patient with psychosis, recommendations for its use are lacking.

Dose-Finding Studies

Although antipsychotics have been widely used since the 1950s, only recently has it become clear that relatively low doses are sufficient for both acute and maintenance treatment for most patients with schizophrenia (Stone, Garve, Griffith, Hirschowitz, & Bennett, 1995; Van Putten, Marder, Mintz, & Poland, 1992). It is clearly important to avoid the problem of using excessive antipsychotic doses in elderly demented patients who are particularly prone to side effects (e.g., EPS). On the other hand, using too low a dose may reduce efficacy. As already described, there have been two published placebo-controlled studies comparing different doses of the same antipsychotic medication (Devanand et al., 1998; Katz et al., 1999). These studies with haloperidol and risperidone, respectively, produced similar results, in that very low doses were ineffective while high doses led to side effects, suggesting that a relatively narrow therapeutic window exists for the use of these medications in patients with dementia who develop psychosis and behavioral complications. Alternatively, when three doses of olanzapine were compared in the same controlled study (5 mg, 10 mg, 15 mg) to placebo, the 5 mg and 10 mg treatment conditions were superior to placebo (Street et al., 2000). Even though quetiapine has not been studied adequately in placebo-controlled trials, in a one-year, multicenter, open-label trial, a wide dose range of quetiapine was studied (25 mg/day to 800 mg/day). The results showed a progressive improvement in psychosis observed during the course of the trial (measured by reduction in BPRS and CGI severity of illness scale) and few side effects (Tariot, Salzman, et al., 2000).

Optimal Duration of Antipsychotic Treatment

The need for continuation antipsychotic treatment in dementia, and the optimal duration of such treatment, remains to be evaluated in empirical research. In addition, potential predictors of both response and relapse remain to be established.

Choice of Conventional versus Atypical Antipsychotic

The propensity for conventional antipsychotics to cause EPS in dementia and to increase the risk of tardive dyskinesia in elderly psychotic patients (Jeste, Lacro, et al., 1999) has led to a growing preference for atypical antipsychotics in the treatment of patients with dementia who develop psychosis or behavioral dyscontrol. However, it is important to note that there is no evidence of superior efficacy for any atypical antipsychotic compared to any conventional antipsychotic in the treatment of psychosis in dementia. In the only controlled treatment trial comparing an atypical antipsychotic to a conventional antipsychotic, De Deyn et al. (1999) compared the effects of risperidone, haloperidol, and placebo in a double-blind placebo-controlled flexible-dose study for behavioral dysregulation of dementia (not psychosis of dementia). They used a 30% reduction from baseline to endpoint in BEHAVE-AD total score as responder criteria. They found in 344 patients with dementia and behavioral dyscontrol that risperidone (average dose 1.1 mg/day), haloperidol (average dose 1.2 mg/day), and placebo had 54%, 63%, and 47% improvement rates, respectively, at week 12 ($p = .25$). Likewise, no significant differences in improvement were seen between any groups on psychosis factor scores. In post hoc analysis, both haloperidol and risperidone were significantly better than placebo at reducing the absolute BEHAVE-AD score and aggression cluster score ($p = .01$), and risperidone was more effective than haloperidol ($p = .05$). Again, no post hoc tests were significantly different on psychosis factor scores. Haloperidol had a significantly greater EPS score at endpoint than either risperidone or placebo, and no difference was noted between risperidone and placebo (De Deyn et al., 1999).

As in the treatment of schizophrenia, it is the differential side-effect profile rather than efficacy that should help determine the choice of antipsychotic medication. Patients prone to orthostatic hypotension (e.g., patients receiving beta blockers) may develop this side effect on risperidone or olanzapine, and weight gain can be a problem with olanzapine. As already noted, clozapine is associated with many side effects, requires extensive monitoring, and should be reserved for those patients who do not respond to the other available agents. Quetiapine is surprisingly well tolerated, though the research database on this medication is not as extensive as it is with the other antipsychotics. Likewise, the incidence of TD after the conventional antipsychotic haloperidol has been shown to be significantly higher than that seen with atypical neuroleptics (Jeste, Lacro, et al., 1999). Overall, the decreased likelihood for neurologic side effects, both short term and long term, are likely to make atypical antipsychotics the treatment of choice in many patients. In general, it is felt that when treating psychosis of AD, risperidone can be started at 0.25 mg/day or twice a day dosing, with a 0.5 mg increase per week, to a maximum of 2 mg to 3 mg a day. Olanzapine dosing should start at 2.5 mg/day or 5 mg/day and slowly increase to a targeted daily dosing between 5 mg and 10 mg/day. Seroquel should be started at 25 mg twice daily, with dose increases as tolerated up to 300 mg twice daily.

If a conventional antipsychotic is used, a starting dose of haloperidol 1 mg daily equivalent is suggested, with subsequent individualized titration to achieve an optimal trade-off between efficacy and side effects. Anticholinergic agents to treat EPS should be avoided, particularly in AD where the cholinergic deficit is believed to underlie much of the cognitive picture. In some patients, the concomitant use of a hypnotic (e.g., chloral hydrate at low dose) may be required. Nonresponse after 6 to 12 weeks or intolerable side effects should lead to consideration of another class of antipsychotic or an alternative type of medication.

SUMMARY

These limited data indicate that antipsychotics, both conventional and atypical, are efficacious in the treatment of psychotic features in some demented patients. It remains unclear if some delusions that are clearly secondary to cognitive impairment (e.g., the belief that deceased parents are alive) are less likely to respond to antipsychotics. Antipsychotics have also been shown to be efficacious in the treatment of behavioral problems such as agitation and catastrophic reactions. The relative efficacy of antipsychotics in different subtypes of dementia (e.g., AD and vascular dementia) has not been adequately studied. In the five placebo-controlled clinical trials using conventional or atypical antipsychotics, the response rates varied between 45% and 60% for active medication and 20% and 45% for placebo (De Deyn et al., 1999; Devanand et al., 1998; Edell & Tunis, 2001; Katz et al., 1999; Street et al., 2000), resulting in an 18% to 26% improvement over placebo (Lanctot et al., 1998). The magnitude of response has been moderate at best, with a "cure" of the target psychotic or behavioral symptom relatively uncommon.

Before starting antipsychotics in the demented elderly, a careful evaluation of the estimated trade-off between efficacy and side effects is advised. The choice of medication depends more on likely side effects than differential efficacy. While antipsychotics have demonstrated efficacy for psychosis, aggression, and psychomotor agitation in dementia, conventional antipsychotics have a narrow therapeutic index, are poorly tolerated, and have frequent treatment emergent side effects, including worsening of cognition and the emergence of EPS and TD. Atypical antipsychotics, on the other hand, are better tolerated than conventional antipsychotics, particularly with respect to the risk of EPS and TD (De Deyn et al., 1999; Jeste, Lacro, et al., 1999) and are now considered the appropriate first choice agent to be used in most cases of psychosis in AD, where longer term treatment may be necessary.

Specific target symptoms should be identified and monitored during antipsychotic treatment. Besides potential neurologic side effects, cognition and activities of daily living should be monitored. In patients maintained for extended periods on antipsychotics, assessment for TD should be conducted at regular intervals. Periodic attempts should be made to taper or discontinue the antipsychotic, though the optimal period of continuation antipsychotic treatment in demented patients is currently not known.

REFERENCES

Aarsland, D., Cummings, J. L., Yenner, G., & Miller, B. (1996). Relationship of aggressive behavior to other neuropsychiatric symptoms in patients with Alzheimer's disease. *American Journal of Psychiatry, 153*(2), 243–247.

Avorn, J., Dreyer, P., Connelly, K., & Soumerai, S. B. (1989). Use of psychotropic medication and the quality of care in rest homes. *New England Journal of Medicine, 320,* 227–232.

Avorn, J., Soumerai, S. B., Everitt, D. E., Ross-Degnan, D., Beers, M. H., Sherman, D., et al. (1992). A randomized trial of a program to reduce the use of psychoactive drugs in nursing homes. *New England Journal of Medicine, 327,* 168–173.

Ballard, C., Gray, A., & Ayre, G. (1999). Psychotic symptoms, aggression and restlessness in dementia. *Rev Neurol, 155*(Suppl. 4), S44–S52.

Ballard, C. G., Margallo-Lana, M., Fossey, J., Reichelt, K., Myint, P., Potkins, D., et al. (2001). A 1-year follow-up study of behavioral and psychological symptoms in dementia among people in care environments. *Journal of Clinical Psychiatry, 62*(8), 631–636.

Barnes, R., Veith, R., Okimoto, J., Raskind, M., & Gumbreck, G. (1982). Efficacy of antipsychotic medications in behaviorally disturbed dementia patients. *American Journal of Psychiatry, 139,* 1170–1174.

Binetti, G., Bianchetti, A., Padovani, A., Lenzi, G. L., de Leo, D., & Trabucchi, M. (1993). Delusions in Alzheimer's disease and multiinfarct dementia. *Acta Neurologica Scandinavica, 88*(1), 5–9.

Bodick, N. C., Offen, W. W., Shannon, H. E., et al. (1997). The selective muscarinic agonist xanomeline improves both the cognitive deficits and behavioral symptoms of Alzheimer disease. *Alzheimer Disease and Associated Disorders, 11*(Suppl. 4), S16–S22.

Bondareff, W. (1996). Neuropathology of psychotic symptoms in Alzheimer's disease. *International Psychogeriatrics, 8*(Suppl. 3), 233–237, 269–272.

Brodaty, H., Draper, B., Saab, D., Low, L. F., Richards, V., Paton, A. H., et al. (2001). Psychosis, depression and behavioral disturbances in Sydney nursing home residents: Prevalence and predictors. *International Journal of Geriatric Psychiatry, 16*(5), 504–512.

Bucht, G., & Adolfsson, R. (1983). The comprehensive psychopathological rating scale in patients with dementia of Alzheimer type and multiinfarct dementia. *Acta Psychiatrica Scandinavica, 68,* 263–270.

Burgio, L. D., Reynolds, C. F., Janosky, J. E., Perel, J., Thornton, J. E., & Hohman, M. J. (1992). A behavioral microanalysis of the effects of haloperidol and oxazepam in demented psychogeriatric inpatients. *International Journal of Geriatric Psychiatry, 7,* 253–262.

Burke, W. J., Folks, D. G., Roccaforte, W. H., & Wengel, S. P. (1994). Serotonin reuptake inhibitors for the treatment of coexisting depression and psychosis in dementia of the Alzheimer type. *Journal of American Geriatric Psychiatry, 2*(4), 352–354.

Burns, A., Jacoby, R., & Levy, R. (1990). Psychiatric phenomena in Alzheimer's disease. II: Disorders of perception. *British Journal of Psychiatry, 157,* 76–81.

Byerly, M. J., & DeVane, C. L. (1996). Pharmacokinetics of clozapine and risperidone: A review of recent literature. *Journal of Clinical Psychopharmacology, 16*(2), 177–187.

Bymaster, F. P., Calligaro, D. O., Falcone, J. F., Marsh, R. D., Moore, N. A., Tye, N. S., et al. (1996). Radioreceptor binding profile of the atypical antipsychotic olanzapine. *Neuropsychopharmacology, 14*(2), 87–96.

Carlyle, W., Ancill, R. J., & Sheldon, L. (1993). Aggression in the demented patient: A double-blind study of loxapine versus haloperidol. *Journal of Clinical Psychopharmacology, 8*(2), 103–108.

Casey, D. (1991). Neuroleptic-induced extrapyramidal syndromes and tardive dyskinesia. *Schizophrenia Research, 4*, 109–120.

Casey, D. E. (1996). Extrapyramidal syndromes and new antipsychotic drugs: Findings in patients and nonhuman primate models. *British Journal of Psychiatry, 168*(Suppl. 29), 32–39.

Centorrino, F., Baldessarini, R., Kando, J., Frankenburg, F. R., Volpicelli, S. A., & Flood, J. G. (1994). Clozapine and metabolites: Concentrations in serum and clinical findings during treatment of chronically psychotic patients. *Journal of Clinical Psychopharmacology, 14*(2), 119–125.

Chengappa, K. N., Baker, R. W., & Kreinbrook, S. B. (1995). Clozapine use in female geriatric patients with psychosis. *Journal of Geriatric Psychiatry and Neurology, 8*, 12–15.

Chouinard, G., Jones, B., & Remington, G. I. (1993). A Canadian multicenter placebo-controlled study of fixed doses of risperidone and haloperidol in the treatment of chronic schizophrenic patients. *Journal of Clinical Psychopharmacology, 13*(1), 25–40.

Cohen, D., Eisdorfer, C., Gorelick, P., Paveza, G., Luchins, D. J., Freels, S., et al. (1993). Psychopathology associated with Alzheimer's disease and related disorders. *Journals of Gerontology: Series A, Biological Sciences and Medical Sciences, 48*(6), M255–M260.

Cohen-Mansfield, J., Lipson, S., Werner, P., Billig, N., Taylor, L., & Woosley, R. (1999). Withdrawal of haloperidol, thioridazine, and lorazepam in the nursing home. *Archives of Internal Medicine, 159*, 1733–1740.

Cohen-Mansfield, J., Marx, M. S., & Rosenthal, A. S. (1989). A description of agitation in a nursing home. *Journals of Gerontology: Series A, Biological Sciences and Medical Sciences, 3*, M77–M84.

Connelly, P. J. (1993). Antipsychotic drugs in continuing care: A 2-year follow-up audit. *International Journal of Geriatric Psychiatry, 8*(3), 261–264.

Covington, J. S. (1975). Alleviating agitation, apprehension, and related symptoms in geriatric patients. *Southern Medical Journal, 58*, 719–724.

Cowley, L. M., & Glen, R. S. (1979). Double-blind study of thioridazine and haloperidol in geriatric patients with a psychosis associated with organic brain syndrome. *Journal of Clinical Psychiatry, 40,* 411–419.

Cummings, J. L., Gorman, D. G., & Shapiro, J. (1993). Physostigmine ameliorates the delusions of Alzheimer's disease. *Biological Psychiatry, 33*(7), 536–541.

Cummings, J. L., & McPherson, S. (2001). Neuropsychiatric assessment of Alzheimer's disease and related dementias. *Aging, 13*(3), 240–246.

Cummings, J. L., Mega, M. S., Gray, K., Rosemberg-Thompson, S., & Gornbein, T. (1994). The Neuropsychiatric Inventory: Comprehensive assessment of psychopathology in dementia. *Neurology, 44*(12), 2308–2314.

Cummings, J. L., Miller, B., Hill, M. A., & Neshkes, R. (1987). Neuropsychiatric aspects of multi-infarct dementia and dementia of the Alzheimer type. *Archives of Neurology, 44,* 389–393.

Daniel, D. G. (2000). Antipsychotic treatment of psychosis and agitation in the elderly. *Journal of Clinical Psychiatry, 61*(Suppl. 14), 49–52.

De Deyn, P. P., Rabheru, K., Rasmussen, A., Bocksberger, J. P., Dautzenberg, P. L., Eriksson, S., et al. (1999). A randomized trial of risperidone, placebo, and haloperidol for behavioral symptoms of dementia. *Neurology, 53*(5), 946–955.

Deimling, G. T., & Bass, D. M. (1986). Symptoms of mental impairment among elderly adults and their effects on family caregivers. *Journals of Gerontology: Series A, Biological Sciences and Medical Sciences, 41,* M778–M784.

Devanand, D. P. (1995). *Role of neuroleptics in treatment of behavioral complications* (pp. 131–151). B. A. Lawlor. Washington, DC: American Psychiatric Press.

Devanand, D. P. (1997). Use of the Columbia University Scale to assess psychopathology in Alzheimer's disease. *International Psychogeriatrics, 9*(Suppl. 1), 137–142, 143–150.

Devanand, D., Jacobs, D., & Tang, M. (1997). The course of psychopathologic features in mild to moderate Alzheimer's disease. *Archives of General Psychiatry, 54,* 257–263.

Devanand, D. P., Marder, K., Michaels, K. S., Sackeim, H. A., Bell, K., Sullivan, M. A., et al. (1998). A randomized, placebo-controlled dose-comparison trial of haloperidol for psychosis and disruptive behaviors in Alzheimer's disease. *American Journal of Psychiatry, 155*(11), 1512–1520.

Devanand, D. P., Miller, L., Richards, M., Marder, K., Bell, K., Mayeux, R., et al. (1992). The Columbia University Scale for Psychopathology in Alzheimer's disease. *Archives of Neurology, 49,* 371–376.

Drevets, W. C., & Rubin, E. H. (1989). Psychotic symptoms and the longitudinal course of dementia of the Alzheimer type. *Biological Psychiatry, 25,* 39–48.

Edell, W. S., & Tunis, S. L. (2001). Antipsychotic treatment of behavioral and psychological symptoms of dementia in geropsychiatric inpatients. *American Journal of Geriatric Psychiatry, 9*(3), 289–297.

Elon, R., & Pawlson, L. G. (1992). The impact of OBRA on medical practice within nursing facilities. *Journal of American Geriatrics Society, 40*(9), 958–963.

Finkel, S. I., Costa e Silva, J., Cohen, G., Miller, S., & Sartorius, N. (1996). Behavioral and psychological signs and symptoms of dementia: A consensus statement on current knowledge and implications for research and treatment. *International Psychogeriatrics, 8*(Suppl. 3), 497–500.

Finkel, S. I., Lyons, J. S., Anderson, R. L., Sherrell, K., Davis, J., Cohen-Mansfield, J., et al. (1995). A randomized, placebo-controlled trial of thiothixene in agitated, demented nursing home patients. *International Journal of Geriatric Psychiatry, 10,* 129–136.

Fitz, D., & Mallya, A. (1992). Discontinuation of a psychogeriatric program for nursing home residents: Psychotropic medication changes and behavioral reactions. *Journal of Applied Gerontology, 11*(1), 50–63.

Fleischhacker, W. W. (1998). Problems in evaluating new antipsychotic drugs. *Wiener Medizinische Wochenschrift, 148*(11/12), 266–272.

Flynn, F. G., Cummings, J. L., & Gornbein, J. (1991). Delusions in dementia syndromes: Investigation of behavioral and neuropsychological correlates. *Journal of Neuropsychiatry Clinical Neurosciences, 3*(4), 364–370.

Fulton, B., & Goa, K. L. (1997). Olanzapine: A review of its pharmacological properties and therapeutic efficacy in the management of schizophrenia and related psychoses. *Drugs, 53*(2), 281–298.

Geldmacher, D. S., Waldman, A. J., Doty, L., & Heilman, K. M. (1994). Fluoxetine in dementia of the Alzheimer's type: Prominent adverse effects and failure to improve cognition. *Journal of Clinical Psychiatry, 2*(2), 161.

Ghoneim, M. M., Mewaldt, S. P., Berie, J. L., & Hinrichs, J. V. (1981). Memory and performance effects of single and three-week administration of diazepam. *Psychopharmacology, 73,* 147–151.

Giron, M. S., Forsell, Y., Bernsten, C., Thorslund, M., Winblad, B., & Fastbom, J. (2001). Psychotropic drug use in elderly people with and without dementia. *International Journal of Geriatric Psychiatry, 16*(9), 900–906.

Glazer, W., & Morgenstern, H. (1988). Predictors of occurrence, severity and course of tardive dyskinesia in an outpatient population. *Journal of Clinical Psychopharmacology, 8,* 10S–16S.

Goldberg, R. J., & Goldberg, J. (1997). Risperidone for dementia-related disturbed behavior in nursing home residents: A clinical experience. *International Psychogeriatrics, 9*(1), 65–68.

Goldstein, J. M. (1995). Pharmacotherapy of schizophrenia. *Lancet, 346*(8972), 450.

Gormley, N., & Rizwan, M. R. (1998). Prevalence and clinical correlates of psychotic symptoms in Alzheimer's disease. *International Journal of Geriatric Psychiatry, 13*(6), 410–414.

Gottfries, C. G., Brane, G., & Steen, G. (1982). A new rating scale for dementia syndromes. *Archives of Gerontology and Geriatrics, 1,* 311–330.

Helms, P. (1985). Efficacy of antipsychotics in the treatment of the behavioral complications of dementia. *Journal of the American Geriatrics Society, 33,* 206–209.

Holm, A., Michel, M., Stern, G. A., Hung, T., Klein, T., Flaherty, L., et al. (1999). The outcomes of an inpatient treatment program for geriatric patients with dementia and dysfunctional behaviors. *Gerontologist, 39*(6), 668–676.

Holmes, C., Smith, H., Ganderton, R., Arranz, M., Collier, D., Powell, J., et al. (2001). Psychosis and aggression in Alzheimer's disease: The effect of dopamine receptor gene variation. *Journal of Neurology, Neurosurgery, and Psychiatry, 71,* 777–779.

Holroyd, S. (1996). Visual hallucinations in a geriatric psychiatry clinic: Prevalence and associated diagnoses. *Journal of Geriatric Psychiatry and Neurology, 9*(4), 171–175.

Holton, A., & George, K. (1985). The use of lithium carbonate in severely demented patients with behavioral disturbance. *British Journal of Psychiatry, 146,* 99–100.

Horwitz, G. J., Tariot, P. N., Mead, K., & Cox, C. (1995). Discontinuation of antipsychotics in nursing home patients with dementia. *American Journal of Geriatric Psychiatry, 3,* 290–299.

Janssen, P. A. J., Niemegeers, C. J. E., Awouters, F., Schellekens, K. H. L., Megens, A. A. H., & Meert, T. F. (1988). Pharmacology of risperidone (R 64 766), a new antipsychotic with serotonin-S2 and dopamine-D2 antagonistic properties. *Journal Pharmacol Exp Ther, 244*(2), 685–693.

Jeste, D. V., Caligiuri, M. P., Paulsen, J. S., Heaton, R. K., Lacro, J. P., Harris, M. J., et al. (1995). Risk of tardive dyskinesia in older patients. A prospective longitudinal study of 266 outpatients. *Archives of General Psychiatry, 52*(9), 756–765.

Jeste, D. V., & Finkel, S. I. (2000). Psychosis of Alzheimer's disease and related dementias. Diagnostic criteria for a distinct syndrome. *American Journal of Geriatric Psychiatry, 8*(1), 29–34.

Jeste, D. V., Lacro, J. P., Bailey, A., Rockwell, E., Harris, M. J., & Caligiuri, M. P. (1999). Lower incidence of tardive dyskinesia with risperidone compared with haloperidol in older patients. *Journal of American Geriatrics Society,* *47*(6), 716–719.

Jeste, D. V., Lacro, J. P., Palmer, B., Rockwell, E., Harris, M. J., & Caligiuri, M. P. (1999). Incidence of tardive dyskinesia in early stages of low-dose treatment with typical neuroleptics in older patients. *American Journal of Psychiatry, 156*(2), 309–311.

Jeste, D. V., Rockwell, E., Harris, M. J., Lohr, J. B., & Lacro, J. P. (1999). Conventional vs. newer antipsychotics in elderly patients. *American Journal of Geriatric Psychiatry, 7*(1), 70–76.

Jeste, D. V., Wragg, R. E., Salmon, D. P., Harris, M. J., & Thal, L. J. (1992). Cognitive deficits of patients with Alzheimer's disease with and without delusions. *American Journal of Psychiatry, 149,* 184–189.

Jones, D. M., Lewis, M. J., & Spriggs, T. L. B. (1978). The effects of low doses of diazepam on human performance in group administered tasks. *British Journal of Clinical Pharmacology, 6,* 333–337.

Kane, J., Honigfeld, G., Singer, J., & Meltzer, H. (1988). Clozapine for the treatment-resistant schizophrenic. A double-blind comparison with chlorpromazine. *Archives of General Psychiatry, 45*(9), 789–796.

Katz, I. R., Jeste, D. V., Mintzer, J. E., Clyde, C., Napolitano, J., & Brecher, M. (1999). Comparison of risperidone and placebo for psychosis and behavioral disturbances associated with dementia: A randomized, double-blind trial. Risperidone Study Group. *Journal of Clinical Psychiatry, 60*(2), 107–115.

Kaufer, D. I., Cummings, J. L., & Christine, D. (1996). Effect of tacrine on behavioral symptoms in Alzheimer's disease: An open-label study. *Journal of Geriatric Psychiatry and Neurology, 9*(1), 1–6.

Kirven, L. G., & Montero, E. F. (1973). Comparison of thioridazine and diazepam in the control of nonpsychotic symptoms associated with senility: Double-blind study. *Journal of American Geriatrics Society, 21,* 546–551.

Klein, D. A., Steinberg, M., Galik, E., et al. (1999). Wandering behavior in community-residing persons with dementia. *International Journal of Geriatric Psychiatry, 14*(4), 272–279.

Koss, E., Weiner, M., Ernesto, C., Cohen-Mansfield, J., Ferris, S. H., Grundman, M., et al. (1997). Assessing patterns of agitation in Alzheimer's disease patients with the Cohen-Mansfield Agitation Inventory. The Alzheimer's Disease Cooperative Study. *Alzheimer Disease and Associated Disorders, 11*(Suppl. 2), S45–S50.

Kral, V. A. (1961). The use of thioridazine (Mellaril) in aged people. *Canadian Medical Association Journal, 84,* 152–154.

Kurz, M., Hummer, M., Kemmler, G., Kurzthaler, I., Saria, S., & Fleischhacker, W. W. (1998). Long-term pharmacokinetics of clozapine. *British Journal of Psychiatry, 173,* 341–344.

Lanctot, K., Best, T., & Mittmann, N. (1998). Efficacy and safety of neuroleptics in behavioral disorders associated with dementia. *Journal of Clinical Psychiatry, 59*(10), 550–561, 562–563.

Lantz, M. S., Louis, A., Lowenstein, G., & Kennedy, G. J. (1990). A longitudinal study of psychotropic prescriptions in a teaching nursing home. *American Journal of Psychiatry, 147*(12), 1637–1639.

Laughren, T. (2001). A regulatory perspective on psychiatric syndromes in Alzheimer disease. *American Journal of Geriatric Psychiatry, 9*(4), 340–345.

Lavretsky, H., & Sultzer, D. (1998). A structured trial of risperidone for the treatment of agitation in dementia. *American Journal of Geriatric Psychiatry, 6*(2), 127–135.

Lawlor, B. A., Radcliffe, J., Molchan, S. E., Martinez, R. A., Hill, J. L., & Sunderland, T. (1994). A pilot placebo-controlled study of trazodone and buspirone in Alzheimer's disease. *International Journal of Geriatric Psychiatry, 9*(1), 55–59.

Lawlor, B. A., Ryan, T. M., Bierer, L. M., et al. (1995). Lack of association between clinical symptoms and postmortem indices of brain serotonin function in Alzheimer's disease. *Biological Psychiatry, 37*(12), 895–896.

Lebert, F., Pasquier, F., & Petit, H. (1994). Behavioral effects of trazodone in Alzheimer's disease. *Journal of Clinical Psychiatry, 55*(12), 536–538.

Leibovici, A., & Tariot, P. N. (1988). Agitation associated with dementia: A systematic approach to treatment. *Psychopharmacology Bulletin, 24,* 39–42.

Lieberman, J. A. (1998). Maximizing clozapine therapy: Managing side effects. *Journal of Clinical Psychiatry, 59*(Suppl. 3), 38–43.

Liljequist, R., Linnoila, M., & Mattila, M. J. (1978). Effect of diazepam and chlorpromazine on memory functions in man. *European Journal of Clinical Pharmacology, 13,* 339–343.

Lopez, O. L., Becker, J. T., Brenner, R. P., Rosen, J., Bajulaiye, O., & Reynolds, C. (1991). Alzheimer's disease with delusions and hallucinations: Neuropsychological and electroencephalographic correlates. *Neurology, 41*(6), 906–912.

Lyketsos, C. G., Breitner, J. C., & Rabins, P. V. (2001). An evidence-based proposal for the classification of neuropsychiatric disturbance in Alzheimer's disease. *International Journal of Geriatric Psychiatry, 16*(11), 1037–1042.

Lyketsos, C. G., Sheppard, J. M., Steinberg, M., Tschanz, J. A., Norton, M. C., Steffens, D. C., et al. (2001). Neuropsychiatric disturbance in Alzheimer's disease clusters into three groups: The Cache County Study. *International Journal of Geriatric Psychiatry, 16*(11), 1043–1053.

Lyketsos, C. G., Steele, C., Galik, E., Rosenblatt, A., Steinberg, M., Warren, A., et al. (1999). Physical aggression in dementia patients and its relationship to depression. *American Journal of Psychiatry, 156*(1), 66–71.

Lyketsos, C. G., Steinberg, M., Tschanz, J. T., Norton, M. C., Steffens, D. C., & Breitner, J. C. S. (2000). Mental and behavioral disturbances in dementia: Findings from the Cache County Study on Memory in Aging. *American Journal of Psychiatry, 157*(5), 708–714.

Madhusoodanan, S. (2001). Introduction: Antipsychotic treatment of behavioral and psychological symptoms of dementia in geropsychiatric patients. *American Journal of Geriatric Psychiatry, 9*(3), 283–288.

Madhusoodanan, S., Suresh, P., Brenner, R., & Pillai, R. (1999). Experience with the atypical antipsychotics—risperidone and olanzapine in the elderly. *Annals of Clinical Psychiatry, 11*(3), 113–118.

McKeith, I. G., Fairbairn, A. F., Perry, R. H., & Thompson, P. (1994). The clinical diagnosis and misdiagnosis of senile dementia of Lewy body type (SDLT). *British Journal of Psychiatry, 165*(3), 324–332.

McManus, D. Q., Arvanitis, L. A., & Kowalcyk, B. B. (1999). Quetiapine, a novel antipsychotic: Experience in elderly patients with psychotic disorders. Seroquel Trial 48 Study Group. *Journal of Clinical Psychiatry, 60*(5), 292–298.

McShane, R., Keene, J., Fairburn, C., et al. (1997). Issues in drug treatment for Alzheimer's disease. *Lancet, 350*(9081), 886–887.

Mega, M. S., Cummings, J. L., Fiorello, T., & Gornbein, J. (1996). The spectrum of behavioral changes in Alzheimer's disease. *Neurology, 46*(1), 130–135.

Mintzer, J. E., Lewis, L., Pennypaker, L., Simpson, W., Bachman, D., Wohlreich, G., et al. (1993). Behavioral Intensive Care Unit (BICU): A new concept in the management of acute agitated behavior in elderly demented patients. *Gerontologist, 33*(6), 801–806.

Montaldi, D., Brooks, D. N., & McColl, J. H. (1990). Measurements of regional cerebral blood flow and cognitive performance in Alzheimer's disease. *Journal of Neurology, Neurosurgery, and Psychiatry, 53*, 33–38.

Mukaetova-Ladinska, E. B., Harrington, C. R., Roth, M., & Wischik, C. M. (1993). Biochemical and anatomical redistribution of tau protein in Alzheimer's disease. *American Journal of Pathology, 143*(2), 565–578.

Nacmias, B., Tedde, A., Forleo, P., Piacentin, S., Guarnieri, B. M., Bartoli, A., et al. (2001). Association between 5-HT(2A) receptor polymorphism and psychotic symptoms in Alzheimer's disease. *Biological Psychiatry, 50*(6), 472–475.

Nacmias, B., Tedde, A., et al. (2001). Psychosis, serotonin receptor polymorphism and Alzheimer's disease. *Archives of Gerontology and Geriatrics, 33*(Suppl. 1), 279–283.

Oberholzer, A., Hendriksen, C., Monsch, A., Heierli, B., & Stahclin, H. (1992). Safety and effectiveness of low-dose clozapine in psychogeriatric patients: A preliminary study. *International Psychogeriatrics, 4*(2), 187–195.

Paulsen, J. S., Salmon, D. P., Thal, L. J., Romero, R., Weisstein-Jenkins, C., Galasko, D., et al. (2000). Incidence of and risk factors for hallucinations and delusions in patients with probable Alzheimer's disease. *Neurology, 54*(10), 1965–1971.

Peskind, E. R., Raskind, M. A., Wingerson, D., Pascualy, M., Thal, L. J., Dobie, D. J., et al. (1995). Enhanced hypothalamic-pituitary-adrenocortical axis responses to physostigmine in normal aging. *Journals of Gerontology: Series A, Biological Sciences and Medical Sciences, 50*(2), M114–M120.

Petrie, W. M., Ban, T. A., Berney, S., Fujimori, M., Guy, W., Ragheb, M., et al. (1982). Loxapine in psychogeriatrics: A placebo and standard controlled clinical investigation. *Journal of Clinical Psychopharmacology, 2,* 122–126.

Pitner, J. K., Mintzer, J. E., Pennypacker, L. C., & Jackson, C. W. (1995). Efficacy and adverse effects of clozapine in four elderly psychotic patients. *Journal of Clinical Psychiatry, 56*(5), 180–185.

Pollock, B. G., Mulsant, B. H., Sweet, R., Burgio, L. D., Kirshner, M. A., Shuster, K., et al. (1997). An open pilot study of citalopram for behavioral disturbances of dementia: Plasma levels and real-time observations. *American Journal of Geriatric Psychiatry, 5*(1), 70–78.

Pomara, N., Deptula, D., Singh, R., et al. (1990). *Cognitive toxicity of benzodiazepines in the elderly, in anxiety in the elderly: Treatment and research* (pp. 175–196). New York: Springer.

Porsteinsson, A. P., Tariot, P. N., Erb, R., et al. (2001). Placebo-controlled study of divalproex sodium for agitation in dementia. *American Journal of Geriatric Psychiatry, 9*(1), 58–66.

Proctor, H. J., Palladino, G. W., & Fillipo, D. (1988). Failure of autoregulation after closed head injury: An experimental model. *Journal of Trauma and Dissociation, 28*(3), 347–352.

Rabins, P. V., Mace, N. L., & Lucas, M. J. (1982). The impact of dementia on the family. *Journal of the American Medical Association, 248*(3), 333–335.

Rada, R. T., & Kellner, R. (1976). Thiothixene in the treatment of geriatric patients with chronic organic brain syndrome. *Journal of American Geriatrics Society, 24,* 105–107.

Rapoport, M. J., van Reekum, R., Freedman, M., Streiner, D. L., Simard, M., Clarke, D., et al. (2001). Relationship of psychosis to aggression, apathy and function in dementia. *International Journal of Geriatric Psychiatry, 16*(2), 123–130.

Raskind, M. A. (1999). Evaluation and management of aggressive behavior in the elderly demented patient. *Journal of Clinical Psychiatry, 60*(Suppl. 15), 45–49.

Raskind, M. A., & Peskind, E. R. (1994). Neurobiologic bases of noncognitive behavioral problems in Alzheimer disease. *Alzheimer Disease and Associated Disorders, 8*(Suppl. 3), 54–60.

Ray, W. A., Federspiel, C. F., & Schaffner, W. (1980). A study of antipsychotic drug use in nursing homes: Epidemiologic evidence suggesting misuse. *American Journal of Public Health, 70,* 485–491.

Reisberg, B. (1984). Alzheimer's disease: Stages of cognitive decline. *American Journal of Nurses, 84*(2), 225–228.

Reisberg, B., Borenstein, J., Salob, S. P., Ferris, S. H., Franssen, E., & Georgotas, A. (1987). Behavioral symptoms in Alzheimer's disease: Phenomenology and treatment. *Journal of Clinical Psychiatry, 48*(Suppl. 5), 9–15.

Reisberg, B., Ferris, S. H., et al. (1989). Clinical features of a neuropathologically verified familial Alzheimer's cohort with onset in the fourth decade: Comparison with senile onset Alzheimer's disease and etiopathogenic implications. *Prog Clinical Biol Res, 317,* 43–54.

Rockwell, E., Krull, A. J., Dimsdale, J., & Jeste, D. V. (1994). Late-onset psychosis with somatic delusions. *Psychosomatics, 35*(1), 66–72.

Rosen, J. H. (1979). Double-blind comparison of haloperidol and thioridazine in geriatric outpatients. *Journal of Clinical Psychiatry, 40,* 17–20.

Rovner, B. W. (1996). Behavioral disturbances of dementia in the nursing home. *International Psychogeriatrics, 8*(Suppl. 3), 435–437.

Rubin, E., Morris, J. C., & Berg, L. (1987). The progression of personality changes in senile dementia of the Alzheimer's type. *Journal of American Geriatrics Society, 35* 721–725.

Russo-Neustadt, A., & Cotman, C. W. (1997). Adrenergic receptors in Alzheimer's disease brain: Selective increases in the cerebella of aggressive patients. *Journal of Neurosciences, 17*(14), 5573–5580.

Salzman, C. (1987). Treatment of agitation in the elderly. In H. Y. Meltzer (Ed.), *Psychopharmacology: The third generation of progress* (pp. 1167–1176). New York: Raven Press.

Salzman, C. (1995). Medication compliance in the elderly. *Journal of Clinical Psychiatry, 56*(Suppl. 1), 18–22, 23.

Satterlee, J. S., & Sussman, M. R. (1998). Unusual membrane-associated protein kinases in higher plants. *Journal of Membrane Biology, 164*(3), 205–213.

Schneider, L. S. (1993). Efficacy of treatment for geropsychiatric patients with severe mental illness. *Psychopharmacology Bulletin, 29*(4), 501–524.

Schneider, L. S., Pollock, V. E., & Lyness, S. A. (1990). A meta-analysis of controlled trials of neuroleptic treatment in dementia. *Journal of American Geriatrics Society, 28,* 553–563.

Schneider, L. S., Tariot, P. N., Lyketsos, C. G., Dagerman, K. S., Davis, K. L., Davis, S., et al. (2001). National Institute of Mental Health Clinical Antipsychotic Trials of Intervention Effectiveness (CATIE): Alzheimer disease trial methodology. *American Journal of Geriatric Psychiatry, 9*(4), 346–360.

Sclan, S. G., Saillon, A., Franssen, E., Hugonot-Diener, L., & Saillon, A. (1996). The behavior pathology in Alzheimer's disease rating scale (BEHAVE-AD): Reliability and analysis of symptom category scores. *International Journal of Geriatric Psychiatry, 2,* 1–12.

Small, G. W., Rabins, P. V., & Barry, P. P. (1997). Diagnosis and treatment of Alzheimer disease and related disorders. Consensus statement of the American Association for Geriatric Psychiatry, the Alzheimer's Association, and the American Geriatrics Society. *Journal of the American Medical Association, 278*(16), 1363–1371.

Smith, G., Taylor, C., & Linkous, P. (1974). Haloperidol versus thioridazine for the treatment of psychogeriatric patients: A double-blind clinical trial. *Psychosomatics, 15,* 134–138.

Stern, Y., Mayeux, R., Hauswer, W. A., Bush, R., Sano, M., Hauser, W. A., et al. (1987). Predictors of disease course in patients with probable Alzheimer's disease. *Neurology, 37,* 1649–1653.

Stern, Y., Tang, M. X., Albert, M., Brandt, J., Jacobs, D. M., Bell, K., et al. (1997). Predicting time to nursing home care and death in individuals with Alzheimer disease. *Journal of the American Medical Association, 277*(10), 806–812.

Stone, C. K., Garve, D. L., Griffith, J., Hirschowitz, J., & Bennett, J. (1995). Further evidence of a dose-response threshold for haloperidol in psychosis. *American Journal of Psychiatry, 152*(8), 1210–1212.

Stoppe, G., Koller, M., Hornig, C., Lund, I., et al. (1999). Gerontopsychiatric treatment in comparison between integrated management at a university and separated management at a district hospital. II: Diagnoses and treatment. *Psychiatr Prax, 26*(6), 283–288.

Stotsky, B. (1984). Multicenter studying thioridazine with diazepam and placebo in elderly, nonpsychotic patients with emotional and behavioral disorders. *Clinical Therapy, 6,* 546–559.

Street, J. S., Clark, W. S., Gannon, K. S., Cummings, J. L., Bymaster, F. P., Tamura, R. N., et al. (2000). Olanzapine treatment of psychotic and behavioral symptoms in patients with Alzheimer disease in nursing care facilities: A double-blind, randomized, placebo-controlled trial. *Archives of General Psychiatry, 57*(10), 968–976.

Street, J. S., Clark, W. S., Kadam, D. L., Mitan, S. J., Juliar, B. E., Feldman, P. D., et al. (2001). Long-term efficacy of olanzapine in the control of psychotic and behavioral symptoms in nursing home patients with Alzheimer's dementia. *International Journal of Geriatric Psychiatry, 16*(Suppl. 1), S62–S70.

Sultzer, D. L. (1996). Behavioral syndrome in dementia: Neuroimaging insights. *Semin Clinical Neuropsychiatry, 1*(4), 261–271.

Sultzer, D. L., Levin, H. S., Mahler, M. E., High, W. M., & Cummings, J. L. (1993). A comparison of psychiatric symptoms in vascular dementia and Alzheimer's disease. *American Journal of Psychiatry, 150*(12), 1806–1812.

Sunderland, T., Molchan, S. E., Little, J. T., Bahro, M., Putnam, K. T., & Weingartner, H. (1997). Pharmacologic challenges in Alzheimer disease and normal controls: Cognitive modeling in humans. *Alzheimer Disease and Associated Disorders, 11*(Suppl. 4), S23–S26.

Swearer, J. M., Drachman, D. A., O'Donnell, B. F., & Mitchell, A. L. (1988). Troublesome and disruptive behaviors in dementia. *Journal of American Geriatrics Society, 36,* 784–790.

Sweet, R. A., Nimgaonkar, V. L., Kamboh, M. I., Lopez, O. L., Zhang, F., & DeKosky, S. T. (1998). Dopamine receptor genetic variation, psychosis, and aggression in Alzheimer's disease. *Archives of Neurology, 55,* 1335–1340.

Sweet, R. A., & Pollock, B. G. (1995). Neuroleptics in the elderly: Guidelines for monitoring. *Harv Rev Psychiatry, 2*(6), 327–335.

Tamminga, C. A., Foster, N. L., et al. (1987). Alzheimer's disease: Low cerebral somatostatin levels correlate with impaired cognitive function and cortical metabolism. *Neurology, 37*(1), 161–165.

Tandon, S. K., Prasad, S., et al. (1998). Efficacy of amphipathic dithiocarbamates in intracellular cadmium mobilization and in modulation of hepatic and renal metallothionein in cadmium preexposed rat. *Chem Biol Interact, 114*(3), 161–175.

Tariot, P. N., Erb, R., Podgorski, C. A., Cox, C., Patel, S., Jakimovich, L., et al. (1998). Efficacy and tolerability of carbamazepine for agitation and aggression in dementia. *American Journal of Psychiatry, 155*(1), 54–61.

Tariot, P. N., Mack, J. L., Patterson, M. B., Edland, S. D., Weiner, M. F., Fillenbaum, G., et al. (1995). The Behavior Rating Scale for Dementia of the Consortium to Establish a Registry for Alzheimer's Disease. *American Journal of Psychiatry, 152,* 1349–1357.

Tariot, P. N., Podgorski, C. A., Blazina, L., & Leibovici, A. (1993). Mental disorders in the nursing home: Another perspective. *American Journal of Psychiatry, 150*(7), 1063–1069.

Tariot, P. N., Salzman, C., Yeung, P. P., Pultz, J., & Rak, I. W. (2000). Long-term use of quetiapine in elderly patients with psychotic disorders. *Clinical Therapy, 22*(9), 1068–1084.

Tariot, P. N., Solomon, P. R., Morris, J. C., Kershaw, P., Lilienfeld, S., & Ding, C. (2000). A 5-month, randomized, placebo-controlled trial of galantamine in AD. The Galantamine United States-10 Study Group. *Neurology, 54*(12), 2269–2276.

Tewfik, G. I., Jain, V. K., Harcup, M., et al. (1970). Effectiveness of various tranquilizers in the management of senile restlessness. *Gerontol Clin, 12,* 351–359.

Thapa, P. B., Meador, K. G., Gideon, P., Fought, R. L., & Ray, W. A. (1994). Effects of antipsychotic withdrawal in elderly nursing home residents. *Journal of American Geriatrics Society, 42*(3), 280–286.

Tsuang, M. M., Lu, L. M., Stotsky, B. A., & Cole, J. O. (1971). Haloperidol versus thioridazine for hospitalized psychogeriatric patients: Double-blind study. *Journal of American Geriatrics Society, 19,* 593–600.

U.S. Department of Health and Human Services. (Ed.). (1999). *Mental health: A report of the Surgeon General.* Rockville, MD: U.S. Department of Health and Human Services, Substance Abuse and Mental Health Services Administration, Center for Mental Health Services.

Van Putten, T., Marder, S. R., Mintz, J., & Poland, R. E. (1992). Haloperidol plasma levels and clinical response: A therapeutic window relationship. *American Journal of Psychiatry, 149*(4), 500–505.

Weiler, P. G., Mungas, D., & Bernick, C. (1988). Propranolol for the control of disruptive behavior in senile dementia. *Journal of Geriatric Psychiatry and Neurology, 1*(4), 226–230.

Weiner, B. J., Alexander, J. A., & Shortell, S. M. (1996). Leadership for quality improvement in health care: Empirical evidence on hospital boards, managers, and physicians. *Medical Care Research and Review, 53*(4), 397–416.

Wilkinson, I. M., & Graham-White, J. (1980). Psychogeriatric Dependency Rating Scales (PGDRS): A method of assessment for use by nurses. *British Journal of Psychiatry, 137,* 558–565.

Wood, S., Cummings, J. L., Hsu, M. A., Barclay, T., Wheatley, M. V., Yarema, K. T., et al. (2000). The use of the neuropsychiatric inventory in nursing home residents: characterization and measurement. *American Journal of Geriatric Psychiatry, 8,* 75–83.

Wragg, R. E., & Jeste, D. V. (1989). Overview of depression and psychosis in Alzheimer's disease. *American Journal of Psychiatry, 146,* 577–587.

Zubenko, G. S., Moossy, J., Marinez, A. J., et al. (1991). Neuropathologic and neurochemical correlates of psychosis in primary dementia. *Archives of Neurology, 48*(6), 619–624.

CHAPTER 10

Psychiatric Assessment and Treatment of Depression in Dementia

Helen C. Kales and Alan M. Mellow

The interface of depression and dementia is a challenging but critical area in the assessment and treatment of dementia. The traditional focus of this interface has been an emphasis on avoiding the misdiagnosis of dementia in elderly patients having depression with associated cognitive impairment, so-called *pseudodementia*. However, it is increasingly recognized that a more common and often more difficult clinical quandary is accurately diagnosing depression in existing dementia (Draper, 1999). Depressive symptoms and syndromes are frequent in already-established cases of dementia, complicating clinical management, exacerbating functional difficulties, and creating other negative outcomes. Recent studies have also investigated whether depression may be a prodromal symptom of or an independent risk factor for the development of dementia. This chapter focuses on depression occurring in the three most common types of dementia—Alzheimer's dementia (AD), vascular dementia (VaD), and diffuse Lewy body dementia (DLBD).

THE ISSUE OF PSEUDODEMENTIA

Historically, much emphasis has been given to the distinction of depression from dementia in late life. The term *pseudodementia* has long been used to denote the cognitive impairment that occurs with depression which reverses with adequate treatment of mood symptoms. However, more recent studies have revealed that many cases of so-called pseudodementia either have cognitive deficits that do not remit despite clinical recovery (Abas, Sahakian, & Levy, 1990) or are found to have irreversible cognitive impairment on follow-up. In one study, up to 50% of geriatric patients with *reversible dementia* were found to have irreversible dementia at five-year follow-up (Alexopoulos, Meyers, Young, Mattis, & Kakuma, 1993). In another study, depressed mood in elderly community-dwelling residents without dementia was associated with a significantly increased risk of dementia diagnosis at follow-up of one to five years (Devanand et al., 1996). Butters et al. (2000) found that elderly nondemented subjects with depression and mild cognitive impairment improved cognitively with remission of mood symptoms but remained mildly cognitively impaired. These authors noted that this subgroup of late-life depression patients is likely at high risk of developing progressive dementia.

These findings have led some to suggest that pseudodementia may in fact be *predementia* (Reifler, 2000), although a small study of subjects who died during a major depressive episode did not confirm that cognitive impairment during a depressive episode was related to AD- or VaD-type neuropathological change on autopsy (O'Brien et al., 2001). In a recent small single photon emission computed tomography (SPECT) study of depressive pseudodementia subjects compared to healthy controls, depressed subjects and AD subjects found decreased cerebral blood flow in the pseudodementia group in the temporoparietal region, similar to that of the AD group and different from that of the depression group (Cho et al., 2002). Taking into account the studies to date suggests that, in a subset of elderly patients (perhaps up to half), depression heralds a dementia syndrome. These lines of evidence have led investigators to study the question of whether depression is a prodromal symptom of dementia or whether it might be an actual risk factor for dementia.

IMPORTANCE OF DIAGNOSIS AND TREATMENT

Once a diagnosis of dementia is established, the clinical picture often remains complex. The diagnosis of depression in dementia is made challenging by *overlap* symptoms common to the two disorders. Communication difficulties in later stages of dementia as well as increasing reliance on caregiver reports may also increase the difficulty of diagnosis of depression (Thorpe & Groulx, 2001). However, although difficult, accurate diagnosis of depression in dementia is of clinical importance. Diagnosis and treatment of depression is worthwhile in any individual in an attempt to alleviate individual suffering. Additional multiple other benefits of treatment of depression in dementia are possible and include removal of any depressive contribution to memory problems, improving functional status, potential cost savings of excess health care utilization due to depression, and reducing caregiver burden.

Impact on Functional Status

Depression in dementia is known to cause reduction in functional status at any stage of dementia. Pearson, Teri, Reifler, and Raskind (1989) demonstrated that patients with Mini-Mental State Scores (Folstein, Folstein, & McHugh, 1975) of 16 to 19 were unable to perform instrumental activities of daily living (IADLs) in the presence of depression, whereas those at the same cognitive level without depression could do so. A later study extended this finding, reporting that the presence of depression was predictive of functional status in AD, with mildly cognitively impaired subjects less able to perform IADLs and moderately cognitively impaired subjects less able to perform activities of daily living (ADLs; Fitz & Teri, 1994). Hargrave, Reed, and Mungas (2000) also found a link between depression in dementia and functional impairment. This diminished function as well as aggression (Lyketsos et al., 1999) and other behavioral difficulties such as vocal disruption (Dwyer & Byrne, 2000), which have also been linked to depression in dementia, may lead to premature nursing home placement in some patients with dementia.

Health Care Utilization

Patients with coexisting depression and dementia were found by our group to use inpatient health care and nursing home care at a significantly higher rate than patients with either condition alone (Kales, Blow, Copeland, Bingham, & Kammerer, 1999). From a health services perspective, the combined comorbidity appeared to function as the "worst of both worlds" with high inpatient medical and psychiatric and nursing home utilization and low outpatient utilization. It was our hypothesis that there might be barriers to effective outpatient care in these patients, such as low rates of depression detection and treatment in primary care and the impact of caregiver issues such as caregiver burden and prioritization of "medical" issues by the caregiver.

Depression in dementia has been linked to nursing home placement both indirectly and directly. Steele, Rovner, Chase, and Folstein (1990) found higher Hamilton Rating Scale for Depression (Ham-D; Hamilton, 1960) scores in patients with AD placed in nursing homes than in those patients maintained in the community. Preliminary data from a prospective one-year study of outcomes and health service utilization by our group suggest that patients with depression and dementia are significantly more likely to be placed in nursing homes by one-year follow-up than patients with either depression or dementia alone (Kales, Blow, Roberts, Visnic, & Mellow, 2001). Preliminary data from our study also indicates that depression was significantly less detected in patients with dementia than in patients with depression alone by nonstudy providers.

Caregiver Burden

Caregiver burden is well described in dementia in general. Several studies illustrate, however, that caregiver burden and depression may be amplified when caregivers care for patients who have both dementia and depression (Donaldson, Tarrier, & Burns, 1998; Teri, 1997). However, as it has been shown that even slight improvements in patients' function can enhance quality of life for the caregiver, diagnosis and treatment of depression in dementia can make a clear impact.

Depression in dementia may lead patients more quickly down the road to nursing home placement. A hypothetical sequence such as that depicted in Figure 10.1 may occur in some patients.

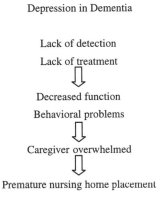

Depression in Dementia

Lack of detection
Lack of treatment

Decreased function
Behavioral problems

Caregiver overwhelmed

Premature nursing home placement

Figure 10.1   Hypothesized relationship of depression to nursing home placement in some patients with dementia.

Thus, the diagnosis and treatment of depression in dementia is not only worthwhile, it is an area where physicians and health care providers in a variety of disciplines can make a clear difference in quality of life for the patient as well as the caregiver.

PATHOPHYSIOLOGY

Neurotransmitter Abnormalities

Several groups have hypothesized a neurological basis for depression in AD in the locus ceruleus (Forstl et al., 1992; Zubenko & Mossy, 1988; Zweig et al., 1988). These studies reported that the antemortem development of depression in patients with AD was found to be associated with degenerative changes in the locus ceruleus, substantia nigra, dorsal raphe, and basal nucleus of Meynert on autopsy. However, a more recent study (Hoogendijk et al., 1999) refuted these earlier results, finding no supplementary loss of pigmented neurons in the locus ceruleus in patients with depression and AD. These authors suggested that the findings of the earlier studies may be explained by the fact that patients with depression in AD in those studies may have been at more advanced stages of dementia.

Neuroendocrine Theories

Hypercortisolemia associated with late life depression has been found to be associated with neuronal degeneration in the rat as well as human hippocampus (Sapolsky, 2000; Sheline, Wang, Gado, Csernansky, & Vannier, 1996). Thus, a neuroendocrine hypothesis for depression as a risk factor for dementia holds that late-life depression-induced cortisolemia could cause hippocampal degeneration and eventual cognitive decline. Lupien et al. (1994) found that aged subjects showing significantly increased cortisol levels with age and with high basal cortisol levels had impaired cognitive performance compared to aged controls without those abnormalities. Katona and Aldridge (1985) found failure of suppression on the Dexamethasone Suppression Test (DST) in 10 of 20 patients with dementia; nonsuppressors had significantly higher depression scores on the Depressive Signs Scale (DSS) than suppressors. Following antidepressant treatment, three of eight nonsuppressors reverted to normal suppression, but this was not associated with clinical improvement.

Circadian rhythm disturbance has been hypothesized to contribute to mental decline and depressive mood in AD (Moe, Vitello, Larsen, Larsen, & Prinz, 1995). Liu et al. (2000) investigated the expression of neuropeptide vasopressin (AVP) mRNA in the human suprachiasmatic nucleus of AD patients with and without depression as well as age-matched controls. No significant differences were found in amount of AVP mRNA between AD patients with and without depression.

A link between estrogen replacement therapy and upregulation of serotonin and acetylcholine has been noted in healthy women (Toran-Allerand et al., 1992). One clinical trial found that female AD patients using estrogen replacement had better cognitive response to the cholinesterase inhibitor tacrine (Schneider & Farlow, 1997). The relationship between mood and estradiol levels has been studied in women with AD (Carlson, Sherwin, & Chertkow, 2000). Compared to healthy elderly controls, depression ratings were highest in AD women who were nonestrogen users. The authors suggested that women with AD who are not taking estrogen replacement may be especially vulnerable to depression.

Apolipoprotein E

Genetic risk is thought to be important to the expression of major depression in AD. AD patients with a positive family history of depression have been reported to be twice as likely to develop depression in the context of AD as those without such a family history (Lyketsos, Tune, Pearlson, & Steele, 1996; Pearlson et al., 1990). The apolipoprotein E (APOE) locus on chromosome 19 has been shown to modify risk and age of onset of AD, leading investigators to study whether it is also associated with depression in AD. Lyketsos, Baker, et al. (1997) found that the prevalence of various psychiatric disturbances, including depression, did not differ significantly in AD patients with different APOE genotypes. Cantillon et al. (1997) also found that APOE4 allele frequency was not increased in subjects with late-onset depression in AD. Scarmeas et al. (2002) also found no significant associations between APOE genotype and the incidence of depression in AD patients.

Cerebral Imaging and Blood Flow Correlates

Extrapolating from studies of poststroke depression, depression in vascular dementia is thought to be associated with left frontal or subcortical lesions

(Robinson, Kubos, Starr, Rao, & Price, 1984; Robinson, Starkstein, & Price, 1988; Starkstein, Robinson, & Price, 1987; Starkstein, Robinson, & Price, 1988). Lyketsos, Treisman, Lipsey, Morris, and Robinson (1998) noted that while cognitive deficits in VaD are a function of both the location and the amount of brain tissue affected, depressive features appear to occur equally in all stages of VaD. This suggests that depression in VaD is not the consequence of additive tissue loss but instead the result of cerebrovascular pathology in particular brain areas, such as frontal and subcortical lesions (Lyketsos et al., 1998; Rao & Lyketsos, 2000b).

The increase in depressive symptoms in VaD with subcortical impairment may relate to pathology of frontostriatal circuits (Austin & Mitchell, 1995). Starkstein et al. (1996) found evidence for more severe frontal lobe dysfunction using SPECT scanning in VaD than AD patients. Using positron emission tomography (PET) scanning techniques, investigators also found that depression in AD was significantly associated with frontal hypometabolism, supporting frontal involvement (especially left-sided) in depression, regardless of disease etiology (Hirono et al., 1998). Another cerebral blood flow study found that over time, elderly AD subjects with dementia and depression exhibited fewer affective/reactive symptoms and greater agitation/motor slowing, which paralleled significant reductions in left temporal regional cerebral blood flow compared to nondepressed AD subjects (Ritchie, Gilham, Ledesert, Touchon, & Kotzki, 1999).

A magnetic resonance imaging (MRI) study found no relationship between the clinical diagnosis of major depression in AD patients and white matter hyperintensities (WMH); however, clinician-rated depressive symptoms were higher in subjects with large anterior WMH (Clark et al., 1998). In the early AD group, MRI abnormalities were related to greater premorbid depression and to less depressive symptom increase after AD onset.

EPIDEMIOLOGY

The overall prevalence rate for major depression in dementia is approximately 20% (Ballard, Bannister, Solis, Oyebode, & Wilcock, 1996). Depressive symptoms are even more prevalent; the Cache County Study found that 24% of subjects with dementia had depressive symptoms (Lyketsos, Steinberg, et al., 2000).

Depression is thought to occur in all stages of dementia (Emery & Oxman, 1992; McAllister & Price, 1982), but there is controversy about the relationship between the prevalence of depression and dementia severity (Rosen & Zubenko, 1991). The degree of cognitive impairment may affect the clinical expression and frequency of depressive symptoms (Cummings, Ross, Absher, Gornbein, & Hadjiaghai, 1995; Migliorelli et al., 1995; Moye, Robiner, & Mackenzie, 1993; Reisberg et al., 1989; Troisi et al., 1993). Some have suggested that the prevalence of major depression is unrelated to the severity of dementia (Allen, Jolley, Comish, & Burns, 1997; Fischer, Simanyi, & Danielczyck, 1990; Fitz & Teri, 1994; Lazarus, Newton, Cohler, Lesser, & Schweon, 1987; Reding, Haycox, & Blass, 1985; Swearer, Drachman, O'Donnell, & Mitchell, 1988; Teri & Wagner, 1991; Verhey, Jolles, Ponds, & Vreeling, 1993), while others found that it is an inverse relationship (Burns, Jacoby, & Levy, 1990; Cooper, Mungas, & Weiler, 1990; Lopez, Boller, Becker, Miller, & Reynolds, 1990; Reifler, Larson, & Hanley, 1982; Reifler et al., 1989). Still other investigators have found increased depression with dementia severity (Greenwald et al., 1989; Rovner, Broadhead, Spencer, Carson, & Folstein, 1989). A recent study examining the prevalence of depression among dementia patients and normal controls in chronic care facilities in the last six months of life found that major depression was highly prevalent regardless of cognitive status (Evers et al., 2002).

Alzheimer's Dementia

There is wide variation in prevalence estimates for major depression in AD, ranging from 0% to 86% (Burns, Jacoby, & Levy, 1990; Wragg & Jeste, 1989). This variation likely reflects several factors: population studied (lower in community and neurological settings than psychiatric inpatient or nursing home settings), diagnostic approaches (*Diagnostic and Statistical Manual of Mental Disorders [DSM]* criteria, rating scales, caregiver report, etc.), dementia stage, exclusion of patients with prior depression, as well as symptom overlap between depression and dementia (Lazarus et al., 1987; Meyers, 1998).

Most studies have shown prevalence rates in the range of 10% to 25% (Migliorelli et al., 1995; Rovner et al., 1989; Teri & Wagner, 1992) and greater than 40% for depressive symptoms (Weiner, Edland, & Lusczynska, 1994; Wragg & Jeste, 1989). In examining outpatients with AD, Lyketsos, Steele, et al. (1997) found that 51% of patients had very few depressive symptoms, 27% had minor depression, and 22% were diagnosed with major depression.

Depression in AD has been associated with a prior history of depression (Harwood, Barker, Ownby, & Duara, 1999; Pearlson et al., 1990; Rovner et al., 1989; Strauss & Ogrocki, 1996), family history of depression (Pearlson et al., 1990; Rovner et al., 1989), younger age at AD onset (O'Connor, Pollitt, & Roth, 1990; Rovner et al., 1989; Zubenko, Rifai, Mulsant, Sweet, & Pasternak, 1996), and female gender (Lazarus et al., 1987; Reifler, Larson, & Hanley, 1982).

Some (Pearlson et al., 1990; Rovner et al., 1989) but not all (Migliorelli et al., 1995) investigators have found an association of depression in dementia with a positive family history of depression. Lyketsos et al.'s (Lyketsos et al., 1996) study reported this association, but only in women, and found no relationship between risk for depression in AD and younger age at AD onset or personal history of depression. Other studies found personal histories of depression to be significantly associated with depression in AD (Harwood et al., 1999; Pearlson et al., 1990; Rovner et al., 1989; Strauss & Ogrocki, 1996). However, a recent study found that while family history of major depression significantly predicted major depression in AD, personal history of depression did not (Butt & Strauss, 2001). The authors also noted that most depressed patients in the sample were experiencing their first lifetime episode of depression, with neither prior personal histories of depressive episodes nor family histories of depression.

The risk of developing depression in AD may be associated with level of education; however, the two existing studies each report different conclusions with regard to educational level. Geerlings et al. (2000) reported that depressed mood was strongly associated with AD in persons with more than eight years of education, while Hargrave, Reed, et al. (2000) found depression in dementia (AD and VaD) associated with lower education levels.

Prodrome or Risk Factor?

Questions have been raised as to whether depression in late life is linked to an increased risk of dementia or whether a *lifetime* history of depression might also increase dementia risk. Jorm's (2001) meta-analysis found evidence to support an association between a prior history of depression and dementia from both case-control studies and prospective studies, but the author stated that the evidence did not clearly support any one hypothesis as an explanation. The study by Speck et al. (1995) suggested that a lifetime history of depression might be associated with an increased risk of AD, but another study linked the increased risk of AD only with late-onset depression (Jorm et al., 1991). Steffens et al. (1997) indicated that the risk of AD was associated with *any* lifetime history of prior depression, but that the risk was strongest when the depression onset was within two years of the onset of dementia. The most recent study in clergy members by Wilson et al. (2002) found that baseline depression rating in cognitively intact subjects was associated with both risk of AD and rate of cognitive decline over a seven-year follow-up period; for each depressive symptom, the risk of developing AD increased by an average of 19%, and annual decline on a global cognitive measure increased by an average of 24%.

Vascular Dementia

Prevalence rates for depression are reported to be higher in VaD than in AD (Ballard et al., 2000; Hargrave, Geck, Reed, & Mungas, 2000; Payne et al., 1998; Reichman & Coyne, 1995; Rovner, Kafonek, Filipp, Lucas, & Folstein, 1986; Sultzer, Levin, Mahler, High, & Cummings, 1993), although some studies disagree (Ballard, Cassidy, Bannister, & Mohan, 1993; Molsa, Martitila, & Rinne, 1995; Reding, Haycox, & Blass, 1985). Newman (1999) noted that in many of the studies indicating higher prevalence rates, subjects were recruited from clinical settings, thus raising the question of sampling bias; the community sample of those authors showed a prevalence rate for major depression of only 3.2% for AD but 21.2% for VaD. Depressive symptoms were also more common in Cache County subjects with VaD (32%) than with AD (20%) (Lyketsos, Steinberg, et al., 2000).

Diffuse Lewy Body Dementia (DLBD)

Prevalence rates for depression in DLBD are less studied. Depression may be more common in DLBD than in AD (Ballard et al., 2002). Rates of depressive symptoms have been reported to be up to 50% of DLBD patients (Klatka, Louis, & Schiffer, 1996) with the proportion of major depression estimated at 14% to 33% (Ballard et al., 1995; McKeith, Perry, Fairbairn, Jabeen, & Perry, 1992). A study comparing clinical and neuropathological cohorts using *Diagnostic and Statistical Manual of Mental Disorders,* third edition, revised (*DSM-III-R*; American Psychiatric Association, 1987) criteria for major depression found that depression was more common in DLBD than in AD (clinical cohort: DLBD 19% vs. 8% AD; neuropathological cohort: 32% DLBD and 12.5% AD; Ballard et al., 1999).

ASSESSMENT

The diagnosis of depression in dementia is complicated by several factors: overlap symptoms, the question of symptom persistence, cohort effect, ageist myths, communication difficulties in later stages of dementia, agnosonosia, and reliability of caregiver reports (Thorpe & Groulx, 2001).

Overlap Symptoms

The overlap of symptoms of depression and dementia are listed in Table 10.1.

Because of symptoms in common, depression can be misdiagnosed as dementia (pseudodementia) and dementia misdiagnosed as depression (pseudodepression). These overlap symptoms are generally more chronic and slowly developing in dementia and more subacute in depression. Depression and apathy/lack of motivation associated with dementia may also be difficult to distinguish in some cases from depression. It is estimated that apathy is experienced by 40% to 50% of AD patients in early or intermediate stages of the disease (Rubin, Morris, & Berg, 1987), by 10% of patients with left-hemisphere stroke, and by 25% of patients with right-hemisphere stroke (Marin, Firinciogullari, & Biedrzycki, 1994; Starkstein, Federoff, Price, Leiguarda, & Robinson, 1993). Apathy and depression often coexist; one study found that 37% of AD patients studied had apathy—24% had depression and 13% had no depression (Starkstein, Petracca, Chemerinski, & Kremer, 2001).

Table 10.1   The Overlap Symptoms of Depression and Dementia

Loss of interest/amotivation/apathy.
Appetite changes.
Sleep changes.
Psychomotoric changes (agitation or retardation).
Fatigue/lack of energy.
Difficulty concentrating/thinking.

The possibility of a superimposed depression in dementia should be considered when chronic symptoms associated with dementia progression such as weight loss, sleep changes due to loss of diurnal rhythms, or amotivation become more severe over the course of a few weeks (Thorpe & Groulx, 2001). In terms of specific symptoms seen in major depression in dementia, depressed patients with dementia have been found to have symptom profiles similar to patients without dementia (Chemerinski, Petracca, Sabe, Kremer, & Starkstein, 2001; Cummings, 1988), especially in mild dementia (Draper, 1999).

The Question of Symptom Persistence

Some have suggested that many depressive symptoms are largely transient, mild, shallower, or self-limited in patients with dementia (Devanand et al., 1997; Katz, 1998). O'Connor, Pollitt, and Roth (1990) and Forsell, Jorm, and Winblad (1994) found remissions of depression in all of their subjects with depression in dementia at baseline. However, other studies have found evidence for the persistence of depressive symptoms/syndromes. Janzing, Teunisse, and Bouwens (2000) reported that both syndromal and subsyndromal depression were highly persistent in nursing home residents with dementia, few of whom were treated with antidepressants. Another study demonstrated a recurrence rate of 85% for depressive symptoms in dementia (Levy et al., 1996). In terms of major depression, there is evidence for a chronic course of depression in dementia, with one study reporting that 58% of subjects with major depression in dementia still had depression at 16-month follow-up (Starkstein et al., 1997).

Cohort Effect/Ageism

The cohort effect concerning late-life depression also applies to patients with depression in dementia. Elders raised in the time of the Great Depression may be more stoic and less psychologically minded than previous or subsequent cohorts. Sadness may be described less in some patients with major depression due to this effect. Ageism may also hinder the diagnosis of depression in dementia with some family members, patients, or providers assuming it is "natural" to be depressed secondary to cognitive declines (Thorpe & Groulx, 2001) or that "I would be depressed, too, if I had dementia and other medical problems."

Aphasia/Agnosonosia

In late dementia, communication of depressive mood states may be difficult secondary to aphasia. Here, making a diagnosis of depression may depend more on caregiver reporting (see later discussion) as well as careful observation. Behavioral disturbances including aggression, vocal disruption, as well as food refusal can all represent depressive equivalents and should prompt the search for other depressive symptoms. Additionally, some patients with dementia experience agnosonosia (denial of disability), which may further complicate self-reports of depressive symptoms (Burke et al., 1998).

Caregiver Issues

The use of caregiver informants can aid, as well as complicate, the diagnosis of depression in dementia. Caregivers themselves are prone to high levels of burden and depression. Depression related behaviors may be among the most distressing to caregivers of patients with dementia (Donaldson et al., 1998). The occurrence of depression in dementia patients has been found to correlate strongly with caregiver burden and their own depression (Donaldson et al., 1998; Shua-Haim, Haim, Shi, Kuo, & Smith, 2001; Teri, 1997).

There is some suggestion that some caregivers may overstate mood symptoms in the patients they are caring for secondary to their own issues of burden and depression, "carrying their own baggage" into the interview room (Schulz & Williamson, 1990; Schulz, O'Brien, Bookwala, & Fleissner, 1995). Teri and Truax (1994) found significant correlations between caregiver Ham-D and Ham-D ratings of their impaired relatives; however, no association of caregiver depression with videotaped ratings of anonymous patients was found. Moye, Robiner, and Mackenzie (1993) found that caregivers' responses as to patients' depression were not associated with caregiver depression. Burke et al. (1998) reported that increased caregiver burden was associated with a larger discrepancy with patient reports in both AD and control subjects; this symptom gap was increased in subjects with AD and agnosonosia. Given the conflicting reports concerning caregiver input, Katz (1998) has noted increased variability in mood and associated symptoms of depression in patients with dementia could lead to both overreporting of depression by caregivers and underrecognition by clinicians observing patient behavior for limited periods of time.

Making the Diagnosis

Taking all of the factors complicating the diagnosis of depression in dementia into account, how should diagnosis best be approached? In early dementia, assessment of depression is similar to that of elderly patients without cognitive impairment. However, in some cases (especially in the later stages of dementia) spotting depression in dementia might require more detective work.

Alexopoulos (1996) and others (Nahas, Kunik, Orengo, Molinari, & Workman, 1997) have suggested that given the complicating factors hindering the diagnosis of depression in dementia, an all-inclusive approach is often best to identify patients who may benefit from antidepressant treatment. Given the potential concerns for caregiver overreporting, as well as patient underreporting of depression, it is recommended that providers take into account and weigh and balance both patient self-reports and caregiver reports as well as their own observations (Mackenzie, Robiner, & Knopman, 1989; Moy, Robiner, & Mackenzie, 1993). This information can then be integrated to make the diagnosis of depression in dementia.

Table 10.2 lists elements of the history and observation of the patient that may be helpful.

Two of the items listed in Table 10.2 merit special mention due to their importance in patients with dementia: suicidal ideation and impact of the stage of dementia on diagnosis of depression.

Table 10.2 Clues toward Diagnosing Depression in Dementia

Acute/subacute changes of symptoms: (e.g., acute weight loss over several weeks).

Intrapsychic features: hopelessness, worthlessness, despair, suicidal ideation.

Signs (advanced dementia): crying, sad appearance, acute changes in affective reactivity or motor activity.

Depressive equivalents (advanced dementia).

Agitation with depressive themes.

Screaming with depressive content ("I'm no good!").

Vocal disruption.

Food refusal.

Mood-congruent depressive delusions: themes of guilt, sin, punishment.

Family history of depression.

Prior history of depression.

Suicidal Ideation

Suicidal ideation should be taken very seriously in any patient. The risk of suicide has been thought to be of less concern in patients with dementia due in part to ageism and the fact that most studies of attempted and completed suicide in the elderly (Catell & Jolley, 1995; Lyness, Conwell, & Nelson, 1992) have reported few cases associated with dementia. However, when studies include comorbid diagnoses, dementia has been found in 14% of elderly completed suicides (Carney, Rich, Burke, & Fowler, 1994) as well as 8% to 26% of elderly suicide attempts (Draper, 1995; Frierson, 1991; Schmid, Manjee, & Shah, 1994). In most of these cases, depression was regarded as the primary diagnosis. Draper, MacCuspie-Moore, and Brodaty (1998) noted suicidal ideation and/or the "wish to die" in 4% of patients attending a memory disorders clinic. These symptoms were significantly associated with comorbid depression, especially in AD.

Advanced Dementia

Studies have found associations between depression and aggression (Lyketsos et al., 1999; Menon et al., 2001), disruptive vocalization (Dwyer & Byrne, 2000), and food refusal (Volicer, Rheume, & Cyr, 1994). Thus, in advanced dementia, these symptoms can be interpreted as *depressive equivalents* in the presence of other symptoms of major depression (e.g., agitation with acute changes in sleep pattern, appetite, interest).

Provisional Diagnostic Criteria

Recently, a group of investigators with extensive research and clinical experience related to late-life depression and AD proposed provisional diagnostic criteria for depression in AD for the purpose of (a) facilitating hypothesis-driven research in this area and (b) providing a consistent target for treatment research (Olin, Schneider, et al., 2002). These authors noted in particular the widely varying prevalence estimates for depression in AD as part of the background and rationale for the criteria (Olin, Katz, Meyers, Schneider, & Lebowitz, 2002). The authors also acknowledged that the criteria are broad, rely on clinical judgment, and reflect both the overlap between the two syndromes and the state of knowledge in the area. Unlike the criteria for a major depressive episode, the provisional diagnostic criteria for depression in AD require the presence of three or more symptoms (vs. five for a major depressive episode), do not require the presence of the symptoms every day, include added criteria for irritability and social isolation, and incorporate criteria for loss of interest revised to reflect decreased positive affect in response to social contact/activities.

Further Workup

In addition to history, physical examination, review of systems, and laboratory testing to rule out other medical causes of symptoms such as sleep changes or amotivation are useful. This workup should be keyed to the patient's comorbid illnesses and other symptoms identified on review of systems. Common medical triggers for acute behavioral changes include medical conditions such as thyroid disease or urinary tract infections and medication changes/side effects (Teri & Logsdon, 2000).

Rating Scales

While standard depression scales have been used in the assessment of depression in dementia, difficulties in their application (Burke, Houston, Boust, & Roccaforte, 1989; Gilley & Wilson, 1997; Knesevich, Martin, Berg, & Danziger, 1983; Wagle, Ho, Wagle, & Berrios, 2000) have led to the development of several scales designed specifically for use in this population (Thorpe & Groulx, 2001). The most widely used scales for depression in dementia are the Cornell Scale for Depression in Dementia (CSDD; Alexopoulos, Abrams, Young, & Shamoian, 1988a) and the Dementia Mood Assessment Scale (DMAS; Sunderland et al., 1988). These scales were designed for use as screening tools and not as a replacement for thorough diagnostic assessment (Alexopoulos, 1996). However, they are useful adjuncts to prompt identification of depressive symptoms in patients with dementia.

The CSDD, a 19-item instrument incorporating information from both patient and caregiver interview, is thought to be the most comprehensive measure of depressive symptoms of dementia (Ownby, Harwood, Acevedo, Barker, & Duara, 2001). The CSDD has been shown to be more reliable than several other commonly used scales such as the Ham-D or DMAS. CSDD items were selected based on expert recommendations about depression in dementia as well as a literature review. Ratings on the CSDD have been found to be significantly related to clinical diagnoses of depression in elderly patients with or without dementia (Alexopoulos, Abrams, Young, & Shamoian, 1988a, 1988b; Vida, Des Rosiers, Carrier, & Gauthier, 1994). Scores greater than 12 on the CSDD are strongly correlated with a psychiatric diagnosis of a major depressive episode (Lyketsos, Steele, et al., 1997; Vida et al., 1994).

SETTINGS

Patients with depression in dementia can be encountered in any clinical or community setting. A national database study of elderly veterans with depression in dementia, depression alone, and dementia alone by our group examined the health service utilization of these categories (Kales, Blow, Copeland, Bingham, & Kammerer, 1999). We found that patients with depression in dementia were high users of inpatient services (inpatient medical and psychiatric care and nursing home care). These patients also used significantly fewer outpatient resources than the group with depression alone. Based on these results, we hypothesized that there might be barriers to effective outpatient treatment in patients with depression in dementia, perhaps prompting inpatient or nursing home admission in more acute/crisis situations. Our group recently completed a prospective one-year study of patients with depression in dementia compared to either group alone. Preliminary results indicate that patients with depression in dementia have significantly higher rates of nursing home placement at one-year follow-up than patients with depression or dementia alone (Kales et al., 2001).

PHARMACOLOGIC TREATMENTS

Antidepressants

Many of the treatment studies of depression in dementia are difficult to compare given varying diagnostic categories (symptoms vs. depressive syndromes) and types of studies performed (case reports, case series, chart reviews, open trials). Results of the four placebo-controlled outcome trials of antidepressants in patients with AD who met criteria for major depression are shown in Table 10.3.

Current expert recommendations (DeKosky, 1997; Katz, 1998; Lebowitz et al., 1997) describe serotonin reuptake inhibitors (SSRIs) as first-line agents for depression in dementia. Given the limited data available, this recommendation is based largely on more benign side-effect profiles than on an evidence base. As noted in the first two trials listed in Table 10.3, there is

Table 10.3   Placebo-Controlled Outcomes Trials for Depression Dementia

Author	Antidepressant	Method	Outcomes	Comments
Reifler et al. (1989)	Imipramine (TCA)	8-week trial. Ham-D, MMSE, DRS, OARS ratings. Therapeutic imipramine levels.	Significant but comparable improvement in imipramine and placebo groups.	Worsened cognition (DRS scores) in imipramine group possibly because of anti-cholinergic effect of imipramine.
Petracca et al. (1996)	Clomipramine (TCA)	Ham-D , MMSE, FIM.	Significant improvement in clomipramine and placebo groups. Significantly greater mood improvement with clomipramine.	MMSE score improved more during clomipramine crossover to placebo (more adverse cognitive effects of clomipramine).
Roth et al. (1996)	Moclobemide (reversible MAOI)	6-week trial. Ham-D , MMSE, SCAG, GDS.	Significant improvement in moclobemide and placebo groups. Significantly greater mood improvement with moclobemide.	No cognitive effects of moclobemide noted.
Lyketsos et al. (2000)	Sertraline	12-week DBPC trial. CSDD, Ham-D, MMSE.	Significantly more clinical improvement in sertraline group. Significantly more partial responders in sertraline group.	No cognitive effects of sertraline noted.

concern that the tricyclic antidepressants (TCAs) increase vulnerability to anticholinergic effects, including cognitive decrements, by blocking brain muscarinic cholinergic receptors. TCAs have been noted to cause cognitive changes with even low doses (such as imipramine 25 mg/day) in depressed AD patients (Teri, 1991). Although the SSRIs are not free of side effects, anticholinergic effects are considerably less problematic.

As shown in Table 10.3, only one placebo-controlled trial has addressed the use of an SSRI in major depression in dementia; this trial found significantly greater antidepressant effect (Lyketsos, Sheppard, et al., 2000). Taragano, Lyketsos, Mangone, Allegri, and Comesana-Diaz (1997) examined the use of fluoxetine versus amitryptyline in a double-blind fixed dose treatment trial of major depression in AD and found that both treatments were effective, while fluoxetine was much better tolerated. Nyth and Gottfries' (1990) double-blind placebo-controlled study of citalopram in dementia patients with depressive symptoms also found significant improvement with few/mild side effects. Magai, Kennedy, Cohen, and Gomberg (2000) studied late-stage AD nursing home patients with depressive symptoms in a double-blind trial of sertraline and found no significant benefits over placebo, although they hypothesized that a trend effect on a "knit brow" facial measure might be more sensitive to signs of depression in their population. A study of patients with dementia and major or minor depression with a double-blind parallel design of paroxetine versus imipramine found both drugs were effective, although there was a suggestion that paroxetine was better tolerated (Katona, Hunter, & Bray, 1998). There are also uncontrolled studies finding SSRIs to be effective and well tolerated in patients with co-morbid dementia, depression, and psychosis (Burke et al., 1997) and in AD and a possible depressive equivalent, food refusal (Volicer et al., 1994).

Experts contend that given the more benign side-effect profile, a trial of an SSRI in cases of possible sustained depression in dementia is often warranted (Raskind & Peskind, 2001). Successful treatment of depression in dementia might decrease individual suffering, improve function at a given level of cognition (Fitz & Teri, 1994), remove depressive contribution to memory problems (Cole, 1983), reduce caregiver burden, and potentially delay nursing home placement.

The significant placebo response noted in three of the four trials of treatment of depression in AD indicates that this response may be frequent in dementia patients who may show wide fluctuations in depressive symptomatology (Alexopoulos, 1996); thus, early improvement of depression in dementia should be viewed with caution. Alexopoulos has pointed out that such patients are prone to early relapse and should have careful follow-up.

Cholinesterase Inhibitors

There is a paucity of data as to the effect of cognitive enhancers on depression in dementia. There is some suggestion that these medications may reduce anxiety and apathy in AD patients (Levy, Cummings, & Kahn-Rose, 1999), leading to conjecture that these medications could be ameliorating subsyndromal depression in some cases. Kaufer, Cummings, and Christine (1996) conducted an open-label study of tacrine on behavioral symptoms in subjects with AD and found marked decreases in Neuropsychiatric Inventory scores, with symptoms of anxiety, apathy, hallucinations, aberrant motor behaviors, and disinhibition most responsive. In an open-label study of donepezil in AD patients with low levels of behavioral disturbance, reduction in behavioral dysregulation and depression ratings were noted but were significant only up to four months (Weiner et al., 2000). The authors concluded that donepezil has a "mildly positive effect" on emotional/behavioral symptoms of AD in addition to cognitive effect.

NONPHARMACOLOGICAL TREATMENTS

Electroconvulsive Therapy (ECT)

The data on ECT and depression in dementia are limited. However, among patients with severe or medication-refractory depression, ECT should be considered. Limited data suggest that the outcome may be similar to elderly patients without dementia, however, with increased post-ECT confusion likely in patients with dementia (Nelson & Rosenberg, 1991). A retrospective study of ECT in depressed elderly patients with AD, VaD, or other types of dementia found significant discharge improvements in both mood and cognition, although 49% of patients developed a delirium during the ECT course (Rao & Lyketsos, 2000a). The authors of this study suggest that the confusion seen during ECT could be minimized by decreasing the frequency of treatment to one to two times per week.

Interpersonal/Behavioral Approaches

As noted in Table 10.3, significant placebo response has been found in three of the four placebo-controlled trials. Katz (1998) noted that the pronounced improvement of depressive symptoms in placebo groups in those trials suggests that interpersonal or behavioral approaches might be effective in the treatment of depression in dementia. Teri, Logsdon, Uomoto, and McCurry (1997) studied two types of behavioral interventions—the use of pleasant events for patients living in the community and teaching problem solving for their caregivers—compared to a control wait-list condition in depressed patients with AD. Both approaches were associated with significant improvement in depressive symptoms in both patients and caregivers, and the improvement was maintained for six months. These results suggest that treatment of the caregiver may be an important factor in the treatment of the patient or providing some type of supportive intervention with the patient-caregiver dyad.

MULTICULTURAL ISSUES

It is likely that many of the issues complicating the diagnosis of depression in dementia are magnified when it comes to diagnosing depression in dementia patients of differing ethnicities or cultures. Factors that have been hypothesized to affect the diagnosis of depression itself in different ethnocultural groups include sociocultural differences between patients and clinicians, differences in symptom presentations, sensitivity of screening instruments for diverse populations, and differences in biological vulnerabilities (Adebimpe, 1994; Adebimpe, Hedlund, Cho, & Wood, 1982; Bell & Mehta, 1980; Brown, Schulberg, & Madonia, 1996; Fabrega, Mezzich, & Ulrich, 1988; Jones & Gray, 1986; Mukherjee et al., 1983; Simon, Fleiss, Gurland, Stiller, & Sharpe, 1973; Strakowski, McElroy, Keck, & West, 1996).

Prior studies of rates of clinical diagnosis of late-life depression have found significantly lower rates of depression diagnoses and higher rates of psychotic disorder diagnoses in African American elderly patients compared to Caucasians (Fabrega et al., 1994; Kales et al., 2000; Leo, Narayan, Sherry, Michalek, & Pollack, 1997; Mulsant et al., 1993). These findings in clinical settings contrast with the lack of differences found in epidemiological surveys or studies that used research criteria to diagnose depression (e.g., Epidemiological Catchment Area [ECA] data). However, others have noted that ECA data as to racial differences should be interpreted with caution due to the small number of African American respondents.

Prevalence rates of depression in dementia in African American patients have been estimated at 12% to 16% (Cohen, Hyland, & Magai, 1998; Gurland et al., 1999; Yeo, Gallagher-Thompson, & Lieberman, 1996), which is similar to rates in Caucasian patients. A study of African American AD patients diagnosed neuropsychiatric symptoms with a semistructured interview with patient and caregiver; the authors diagnosed major depression in 20% of the sample (Harwood, Barker, Ownby, & Duara, 2000).

However, given the general difficulty in diagnosing depression in dementia, this has led to the study of potential racial differences in clinical diagnostic rates of depression in dementia. Our earlier retrospective national database study found racial differences in both rates of the clinical diagnosis of depression and depression in dementia among elderly veterans; African American veterans had significantly lower rates of both depression alone and depression in dementia diagnoses (Kales et al., 1999). Cohen, Hyland, and Magai (1998) studied this issue in nursing home patients with dementia and found no racial differences in levels of depression as measured by study investigators; however, they did find that White dementia patients had significantly higher rates of study-diagnosed *possible major/minor depression* (34% vs. 19%). The authors reviewed Minimum Data Set notation of recognition and treatment of depression by nursing home staff and found that depression was both underrecognized and undertreated in *both* African American and Caucasian patients. Hargrave, Stoeklin, Haan, and Reed (2000) found no association between rates of major or minor depression and ethnicity.

One study examined the hypothesis that the APOE4 allele would be associated with increased frequency of depression in a community sample of African American elderly (Class et al., 1997); no such association was found.

Harwood, Barker, Ownby, Bravo, et al. (2000) found depression diagnosed on CSDD (score > 7) in almost 40% of Cuban American AD patients residing in the community, higher than the cited 10% to 20% prevalence rates for the non-Hispanic AD sample. The authors noted that the prevalence might be an overestimate of depression in dementia in Hispanics because the study was based on a clinic sample; in addition, because Hispanics have consistently been shown to underuse mental health services (Hough et al., 1987), the study sample was likely a more symptomatic group. Further, depression classification was based on rating scale cutoff and not on a clinical diagnosis.

There is a paucity of data concerning the rate of depression in dementia among Asian patients. Liu et al. (1999) studied consecutive patients in a Chinese memory clinic and found a rate of 5% for major depression and 11% for dysthymia/other depression. The authors noted that the lower prevalence than seen in many U.S. studies might have been due to the study setting. It was also noted that the prevalence of depression in Chinese AD patients is likely higher than that of the Chinese geriatric population but that no such applicable community estimates were available.

NEW DIRECTIONS

A most exciting area of new research on the interface between depression and dementia is the concept of *vascular depression*. Depression often develops not only in VaD, but also in patients with vascular disease or risk factors who may not have the full dementia syndrome. The *vascular depression hypothesis* (Alexopoulos, Meyers, Young, Campbell, et al., 1997; Krishnan, Hays, & Blazer, 1997) describes a depressive syndrome occurring after the age of 65 in the context of cerebrovascular disease.

Vascular depression may explain the frequent association of late-life depression with white matter hyperintensities seen on magnetic resonance imaging (Zubenko et al., 1990), which, in turn, have been found to be associated with poorer treatment response (Hickie et al., 1995; Simpson, Baldwin, Jackson, & Burns, 1998; Simpson, Jackson, Baldwin, & Burns, 1997). This frequent association has led some investigators to suspect that in a subset of elderly patients, cerebrovascular disease is more germane to late-life depression than genetic or psychological factors.

The vascular depression hypothesis may also help to explain why late-life depression seems to increase the risk of dementia in that the two disorders may be linked through the common mechanism of vascular disease. It may also explain the occurrence of prestroke depression in which silent cerebrovascular pathology manifests as depression before the onset of cognitive dysfunction in both lacunar and cortical stroke (Colantonio, Kasl, Ostfeld, & Berkman, 1993). A Canadian population-based study found that a history of depression was a significant risk factor for subsequent vascular dementia (Hebert et al., 2000). The authors noted that depression might be a premonitory syndrome for VaD in stroke patients or a marker of cerebral damage.

Studies of patients with vascular depression have found that it is often associated with more subtle cognitive abnormalities in sequencing, planning, and decision making—executive dysfunction—in patients *without* overt cognitive impairment. Executive dysfunction may result from vascular or degenerative disruption of cortical-striato-pallido-thalamo-cortical (CSPTC) pathways (Alexopoulos, Meyers, Young, Kakuma, et al., 1997; Dolan et al., 1992; Krishnan, 1993).

Patients with executive dysfunction have been found to be less responsive to antidepressant medications (Kalayam & Alexopoulos, 1999), and elderly depressed nonresponders to fluoxetine were found to score significantly lower on measures of executive functioning (Dunkin et al., 2000). A subsequent study by Alexopoulos, Meyers, Young, Kalayam, Kakuma, et al. (2000) found that patients with depression and executive dysfunction were more likely to relapse or have residual depressive symptoms. These observations have led to the question as to whether patients with vascular depression need new types of pharmacological or other types of interventions.

Alexopoulos, Meyers, Young, Kakuma, et al. (1997) noted that, assuming vascular lesions promote depression resulting in a vascular depression syndrome, research on interventions and agents used in the prevention and treatment of cerebrovascular disease may be relevant for treatment of such patients. This could include the cessation of smoking as well as limited alcohol intake, prevention and treatment of cerebrovascular disease (lipid lowering agents, antiplatelet agents, free radical scavengers, calcium channel blockers, NMDA receptor agonists, gangliosides and aminosteroids), and modification of CSPTC pathways (agents affecting the neurotransmitters dopamine, acetylcholine, and enkephalin). Forthcoming research in the area of the treatment of vascular depression is likely to shed new light on the complex relationship between depression and dementia in late life.

REFERENCES

Abas, M. A., Sahakian, B. J., & Levy, R. (1990). Neuropsychological deficits and CT scan changes in elderly depressives. *Psychological Medicine, 20,* 507–520.

Adebimpe, V. R. (1994). Race, racism, and epidemiological surveys. *Hospital Community Psychiatry, 45,* 27–31.

Adebimpe, V. R., Hedlund, J. L., Cho, D. W., & Wood, J. B. (1982). Symptomatology of depression in Black and White patients. *Journal of National Medicine Association, 74,* 185–190.

Alexopoulos, G. S. (1996). The treatment of depressed demented patients. *Journal of Clinical Psychiatry, 57*(Suppl. 14), 14–20.

Alexopoulos, G. S., Abrams, R. C., Young, R. C., & Shamoian, C. A. (1988a). Cornell Scale for Depression in Dementia. *Biological Psychiatry, 23,* 271–284.

Alexopoulos, G. S., Abrams, R. C., Young, R. C., & Shamoian, C. A. (1988b). Use of the Cornell Scale in nondemented patients. *Journal of American Geriatrics Society, 36,* 230–236.

Alexopoulos, G. S., Meyers, B. S., Young, R. C., Campbell, S., Silbersweig, D., & Charlson, M. (1997). "Vascular depression" hypothesis. *Archives of General Psychiatry, 54,* 915–922.

Alexopoulos, G. S., Meyers, B. S., Young, R. C., Kakuma, T., Silbersweig, D., & Charlson, M. (1997). Clinically defined vascular depression. *American Journal of Psychiatry, 154,* 562–565.

Alexopoulos, G. S., Meyers, B. S., Young, R. C., Kalayam, B., Kakuma, T., Gabrielle, M., et al. (2000). Executive dysfunction and long-term outcomes of geriatric depression. *Archives of General Psychiatry, 57,* 285–290.

Alexopoulos, G. S., Meyers, B. S., Young, R. C., Mattis, S., & Kakuma, T. (1993). The course of geriatric depression with "reversible dementia": A controlled study. *American Journal of Psychiatry, 150,* 1693–1699.

Allen, H., Jolley, D., Comish, J., & Burns, A. (1997). Depression in dementia: A study of mood in a community sample and referrals to a community service. *International Journal of Geriatric Psychiatry, 12,* 513–518.

Austin, M. P., & Mitchell, P. (1995). The anatomy of melancholia: Does frontal-subcortical pathophysiology underpin its psychomotor and cognitive manifestations? *Psychological Medicine, 25,* 665–672.

Ballard, C., Bannister, C., Solis, M., Oyebode, F., & Wilcock, G. (1996). The prevalence, associations and symptoms of depression amongst dementia sufferers. *Journal of Affective Disorders, 36,* 135–144.

Ballard, C. G., Cassidy, G., Bannister, C., & Mohan, R. N. (1993). Prevalence, symptom profile, and aetiology of depression in dementia sufferers. *Journal of Affective Disorders, 29,* 1–6.

Ballard, C., Holmes, C., McKeith, I., Neill, D., O'Brien, J., Cairns, N., et al. (1999). Psychiatric morbidity in dementia with Lewy bodies: A prospective clinical and neuropathological comparative study with Alzheimer's disease. *American Journal of Psychiatry, 156,* 1039–1045.

Ballard, C., Johnson, M., Piggott, M., Perry, R., O'Brien, J., Rowan, E., et al. (2002). A positive association between 5HT re-uptake binding sites and depression in dementia with Lewy bodies. *Journal of Affective Disorders, 69,* 219–223.

Ballard, C., Neill, D., O'Brien, J., McKeith I. G., Ince, P., & Perry, R. (2000). Anxiety, depression, psychosis in vascular dementia: Prevalence and associations. *Journal of Affective Disorders, 59,* 97–106.

Ballard, C. G., Saad, K., Patel, A., Gahir, M., Solis, M., Coope, C., et al. (1995). The prevalence and phenomenology of psychotic symptoms in dementia sufferers. *International Journal of Geriatric Psychiatry, 10,* 477–486.

Bell, C. C., & Mehta, H. (1980). The misdiagnosis of Black patients with manic-depressive illness. *Journal of National Medical Association, 72,* 141–145.

Brown, C., Schulberg, H. C., & Madonia, M. J. (1996). Clinical presentations of major depression by African Americans and Whites in primary care medical practice. *Journal of Affective Disorders, 41,* 181–191.

Burke, W. J., Dewan, V., Wengel, S. P., Roccaforte, W. H., Nadolny, G. C., & Folks, D. G. (1997). The use of selective serotonin reuptake inhibitors for depression and psychosis complicating dementia. *International Journal of Geriatric Psychiatry, 12,* 519–525.

Burke, W. J., Houston, M. J., Boust, S. J., & Roccaforte, W. H. (1989). Use of the Geriatric Depression Scale in dementia of the Alzheimer type. *Journal of American Geriatrics Society, 37,* 856–860.

Burke, W. J., Roccaforte, W. H., Wengel, S. P., McArthur-Miller, D., Folks, D. G., & Potter, J. F. (1998). Disagreement in the reporting of depressive symptoms between patients with dementia of the Alzheimer type and their collateral sources. *American Journal of Geriatric Psychiatry, 6,* 308–319.

Burns, A., Jacoby, R., & Levy, R. (1990). Psychiatric phenomena in Alzheimer's disease. III: Disorders of mood. *British Journal of Psychiatry, 157,* 92–94.

Butt, Z. A., & Strauss, M. E. (2001). Relationship of family and personal history to the occurrence of depression in persons with Alzheimer's disease. *American Journal of Geriatric Psychiatry, 9,* 249–254.

Butters, M. A., Becker, J. T., Nebes, R. D., Zmuda, M. D., Mulsant, B. H., Pollack, B. G., et al. (2000). Changes in cognitive functioning following treatment of late-life depression. *American Journal of Psychiatry, 157,* 1949–1954.

Cantillon, M., Harwood, D., Barker, W., St. George-Hyslop, P., Tsuda, T., Ekatarina, R., et al. (1997). No association between apolipoprotein E genotype and late-onset depression in Alzheimer's disease. *Biological Psychiatry, 41* 246–248.

Carlson, L. E., Sherwin, B. B., & Chertkow, H. M. (2000). Relationships between mood and estradiol (E2) levels in Alzheimer's disease (AD) patients. *Journals of Gerontology: Series B., Psychological Sciences and Social Sciences, 55,* 47–53.

Carney, S. S., Rich, C. L., Burke, P. A., & Fowler, R. C. (1994). Suicide over 60: The San Diego study. *Journal of American Geriatric Society, 42,* 174–180.

Catell, H., & Jolley, D. J. (1995). One hundred cases of suicide in elderly people. *British Journal of Psychiatry, 166,* 451–477.

Chemerinski, E., Petracca, G., Sabe, L., Kremer, J., & Starkstein, S. E. (2001). The specificity of depressive symptoms in patients with Alzheimer's disease. *American Journal of Psychiatry, 158,* 68–72.

Cho, M. J., Lyoo, I. K., Lee, D. W., Kwon, J. S., Lee, J. S., Lee, D. S., et al. (2002). Brain single photon emission computed tomography findings in depressive pseudodementia patients. *Journal of Affective Disorders, 69,* 159–166.

Clark, L. M., McDonald, W. M., Welsh-Bohmer, K. A., Siegler, I. C., Dawson, D. V., Tupler, L. A., et al. (1998). Magnetic resonance imaging correlates of depression in early- and late-onset Alzheimer's disease. *Biological Psychiatry, 44,* 592–599.

Class, C. A., Unverzagt, F. W., Gao, S., Sahota, A., Hall, K. S., & Hendrie, H. C. (1997). The association between Apo E genotype and depressive symptoms in elderly African American subjects. *American Journal of Geriatric Psychiatry, 5,* 339–343.

Cohen, C. I., Hyland, K., & Magai, C. (1998). Depression among African American nursing home patients with dementia. *American Journal of Geriatric Psychiatry, 6,* 162–175.

Colantonio, A., Kasl, S. V., Ostfeld, A. M., & Berkman, L. F. (1993). Psychosocial predictors of stroke outcomes in an elderly population. *Journal of Gerontology, 48,* S261–S268.

Cole, M. G. (1983). Age, age of onset and course of primary depressive illness in the elderly. *Canadian Journal of Psychiatry, 28,* 102–104.

Cooper, J. K., Mungas, D., & Weiler, P. G. (1990). Relation of cognitive status and abnormal behaviors in Alzheimer's disease. *Journal of American Geriatrics Society, 38,* 867–870.

Cummings, J. (1988). Depression in vascular dementia. *Journal of Clinical Psychiatry, 10,* 209–231.

Cummings, J. L., Ross, W., Absher, H., Gornbein, J., & Hadjiaghai, L. (1995). Depressive symptoms in Alzheimer disease: Assessment and determinants. *Alzheimer Disease and Associated Disorders, 9,* 87–93.

DeKosky, S. T. (1997). Managing Alzheimer's disease. *Neurology, 48*(Suppl. 5), S1–S41.

Devanand, D. P., Jacobs, D. M., Tang, M. X., Del Castillo-Castaneda, C., Sano, M., Marder, K., et al. (1997). The course of psychopathological features in mild to moderate Alzheimer disease. *Archives of General Psychiatry, 54,* 257–263.

Devanand, D. P., Sano, M., Tang, M. X., Taylor, S., Gurland, B. J., Wilder, D., et al. (1996). Depressed mood and the incidence of Alzheimer's disease in the elderly living in the community. *Archives of General Psychiatry, 53,* 175–182.

Dolan, R. J., Bench, C. J., Brown, R. G., Scott, L. C., Friston, K. J., & Frackowiak, R. S. (1992). Regional cerebral blood flow abnormalities in depressed patients with cognitive impairment. *Journal of Neurology, Neurosurgery, and Psychiatry, 55,* 768–773.

Donaldson, C., Tarrier, N., & Burns, A. (1998). Determinants of caregiver stress in Alzheimer's disease. *International Journal of Geriatric Psychiatry, 13* 248–256.

Draper, B. (1995). Prevention of suicide in old age. *Medical Journal of Australia, 162,* 533–534.

Draper, B. (1999). The diagnosis and treatment of depression in dementia. *Psychiatric Services, 50,* 1151–1153.

Draper, B., MacCuspie-Moore, C., & Brodaty, H. (1998). Suicidal ideation and the "wish to die" in dementia patients: The role of depression. *Age and Ageing 27,* 503–507.

Dunkin, J. J., Leuchter, A. F., Cook, I. A., Kasl-Godley, J. E., Abrams, M., & Rosenberg-Thompson, S. (2000). Executive dysfunction predicts nonresponse to fluoxetine in major depression. *Journal of Affective Disorders, 60,* 13–23.

Dwyer, M., & Byrne, G. J. (2000). Disruptive vocalization and depression in older nursing home residents. *International Psychogeriatrics, 12,* 463–471.

Emery, V. O., & Oxman, T. E. (1992). Update on the dementia spectrum of depression. *American Journal of Psychiatry, 149,* 305–317.

Evers, M. M., Samuels, S. C., Lantz, M., Khan, K., Brickman, A. M., & Marin, D. B. (2002). The prevalence, diagnosis and treatment of depression in dementia patients in chronic care facilities in the last six months of life. *International Journal of Geriatric Psychiatry, 17,* 464–472.

Fabrega, H., Mezzich, J., & Ulrich, R. F. (1988). Black-White differences in psychopathology in an urban psychiatric population. *Comprehensive Psychiatry, 29,* 285–297.

Fabrega, H., Mulsant, B. M., Rifai, A. H., Sweet, R. A., Pasternak, R., Ulrich, R., et al. (1994). Ethnicity and psychopathology in an aging hospital-based population. *The Journal of Nervous and Mental Disease, 182,* 136–144.

Fischer, P., Simanyi, M., & Danielczyk, W. (1990). Depression in dementia of the Alzheimer type and in multiinfarct dementia. *American Journal of Psychiatry, 147,* 1484–1487.

Fitz, A. G., & Teri, L. (1994). Depression, cognition, and functional ability in patients with Alzheimer's disease. *Journal of American Geriatrics Society, 42,* 186–191.

Folstein, M. F., Folstein, S. E., & McHugh, P. R. (1975). Mini-mental state: A practical method for grading the cognitive state of patients for the clinician. *Journal of Psychiatric Research, 12,* 189–198.

Forsell, Y., Jorm, A. F., & Winblad, B. (1994). Association of age, sex, cognitive dysfunction, and disability with major depressive symptoms in an elderly sample. *American Journal of Psychiatry, 151,* 1600–1604.

Forstl, H., Burns, A., Luthert, P., Cairns, N., Lantos, P., & Levy, R. (1992). Clinical and neuropathological correlates of depression in Alzheimer's disease. *Psychological Medicine,* 877–884.

Frierson, R. L. (1991). Suicide attempts by the old and the very old. *Archives of Internal Medicine, 151,* 141–144.

Geerlings, M. I., Schmand, B., Braam, A. W., Jonker, C., Bouter, L. M., & van Tilburg, W. (2000). Depressive symptoms and risk of Alzheimer's disease in more highly educated older people. *Journal of the American Geriatrics Society, 48,* 1092–1097.

Gilley, D. W., & Wilson, R. S. (1997). Criterion-related validity of the Geriatric Depression Scale in Alzheimer's disease. *Journal of Clinical and Experimental Neuropsychology,* 489–499.

Greenwald, B. S., Kramer-Ginsberg, E., Marin, D. B., Laitman, L. B., Hermann, C. K., Mohs, R. C., et al. (1989). Dementia with coexistent major depression. *American Journal of Psychiatry, 146,* 1472–1478.

Gurland, B. J., Wilder, D. E., Lantigua, R., Stern, Y., Chen, J., Killeffer, E. H., et al. (1999). Rates of dementia in three ethnoracial groups. *International Journal of Geriatric Psychiatry, 14,* 481–493.

Hamilton, M. (1960). A rating scale for depression. *Journal of Neurology, Neurosurgery, and Psychiatry, 23,* 56–62.

Hargrave, R., Geck, L. C., Reed, B., & Mungas, D. (2000). Affective behavioral disturbances in Alzheimer's disease and ischemic vascular disease. *Journal of Neurology, Neurosurgery, and Psychiatry, 68,* 41–46.

Hargrave, R., Reed, B., & Mungas, D. (2000). Depressive syndromes and functional disability in dementia. *Journal of Geriatric Psychiatry and Neurology, 13,* 72–77.

Hargrave, R., Stoeklin, M., Haan, M., & Reed, B. (2000). Clinical aspects of dementia in African American, Hispanic, and White patients. *Journal of the National Medical Association, 92,* 15–21.

Harwood, D. G., Barker, W. W., Ownby, R. L., Bravo, M., Aguero, H. & Duara, R. (2000). Depressive symptoms in Alzheimer's disease: An examination among community-dwelling Cuban American patients. *American Journal of Geriatric Psychiatry, 8,* 84–91.

Harwood, D. G., Barker, W. W., Ownby, R. L., & Duara, R. (1999). Association between premorbid history of depression and current depression in Alzheimer's disease. *Journal of Geriatric Psychiatry and Neurology, 12,* 72–75.

Harwood, D. G., Barker, W. W., Ownby, R. L., & Duara, R. (2000). Clinical characteristics of community-dwelling Black Alzheimer's disease patients. *Journal of National Medical Association, 92,* 424–429.

Hebert, R., Lindsay, J., Verreault, R., Rockwood, K., Hill, G., & Dubois, M. F. (2000). Vascular dementia: Incidence and risk factors in the Canadian study of health and aging. *Stroke, 31,* 1487–1493.

Hickie, I., Scott, E., Mitchell, P., Wilhelm, K., Austin, M. P., & Bennett, B. (1995). Subcortical hyperintensities on magnetic resonance imaging: Clinical correlates and prognostic significance in patients with severe depression. *Biological Psychiatry, 37,* 151–160.

Hirono, N., Mori, E., Ishii, K., Ikejiri, Y., Imamura, T., Shimomura, T., et al. (1998). Frontal lobe hypometabolism and depression in Alzheimer's disease. *Neurology, 50,* 380–383.

Hoogendijk, W. J., Sommer, I. E., Pool, C. W., Kamphorst, W., Hofman, M. A., Eikelenboom, P., et al. (1999). Lack of association between depression and loss of neurons in the locus coeruleus in Alzheimer disease. *Archives of General Psychiatry, 56,* 45–51.

Hough, R. L., Landsverk, J. A., Karno, M., Burnam, M. A., Timbers, D. M., Escobar, J. I., et al. (1987). Utilization of health and mental health services by Los Angeles Mexican Americans and non-Hispanic Whites. *Archives of General Psychiatry, 44,* 702–709.

Janzing, J., Teunisse, R., & Bouwens, P. (2000). The course of depression in elderly subjects with and without dementia. *Journal of Affective Disorders, 57,* 49–54.

Jones, B. E., & Gray, B. A. (1986). Problems in diagnosing schizophrenia and affective disorders among Blacks. *Hospital Community Psychiatry, 37,* 61–65.

Jorm, A. F. (2001). History of depression as a risk factor for dementia: An updated review. *Australian and New Zealand Journal of Psychiatry, 35,* 776–781.

Jorm, A. F., van Duijn, C. M., Chandra, V., Fratiglioni, L., Graves, A. B., Heyman, A., et al. (1991). Psychiatric history and related exposures as risk factors for Alzheimer's disease: A collaborative re-analysis of case-control studies. Eurodem Risk Factors Research Group. *International Journal of Epidemiology, 20*(Suppl. 2), S43–S47.

Kalayam, B., & Alexopoulos, G. S. (1999). Prefrontal dysfunction and treatment response in geriatric depression. *Archives of General Psychiatry, 56,* 713–718.

Kales, H. C., Blow, F. C., Bingham, C. R., Copeland, L. A., & Mellow, A. M. (2000). Race and inpatient psychiatric diagnoses among elderly veterans. *Psychiatric Services, 51,* 795–800.

Kales, H. C., Blow, F. C., Copeland, L. A., Bingham, C. R., Kammerer, E. E., & Mellow, A. M. (1999). Health care utilization by older patients with coexisting depression and dementia. *American Journal of Psychiatry, 156,* 550–556.

Kales, H. C., Blow, F. C., Roberts, J. S., Visnic, S., & Mellow, A. M. (2001). Dementia, depression and coexisting dementia and depression: Detection of diagnoses and 12-month health care outcomes. *American Journal of Geriatric Psychiatry, 9,* 72.

Katona, C. L., & Aldridge, C. R. (1985). The dexamethasone suppression test and depressive signs in dementia. *Journal of Affective Disorders, 8,* 83–89.

Katona, C. L., Hunter, B. N., & Bray, J. (1998). A double-blind comparison of the efficacy and safety of paroxetine and imipramine in the treatment of depression with dementia. *International Journal of Geriatric Psychiatry, 13,* 100–108.

Katz, I. R. (1998). Diagnosis and treatment of depression in patients with Alzheimer's disease and other dementias. *Journal of Clinical Psychiatry, 59*(Suppl. 9), 38–44.

Kaufer, D. I., Cummings, J. L., & Christine, D. (1996). Effect of tacrine on behavioral symptoms in Alzheimer's disease: An open-label study. *Journal of Geriatric Psychiatry and Neurology, 9,* 1–6.

Klatka, L. A., Louis, E. D., & Schiffer, R. B. (1996). Psychiatric features in diffuse Lewy body disease: A clinicopathologic study using Alzheimer's disease and Parkinson's disease comparison groups. *Neurology, 47,* 1148–1152.

Knesevich, J. W., Martin, R. L., Berg, L., & Danziger, W. (1983). Preliminary report on the affective symptoms in the early stages of senile dementia of the Alzheimer type. *American Journal of Psychiatry, 140,* 233–235.

Krishnan, K. R. (1993). Neuroanatomic substrates of depression in the elderly. *Journal of Geriatric Psychiatry and Neurology, 6,* 39–58.

Krishnan, K. R., Hays, J. C., & Blazer, D. G. (1997). MRI-defined vascular depression. *American Journal of Psychiatry, 154,* 497–501.

Lazarus, L. W., Newton, N., Cohler, B., Lesser J., & Schweon, C. (1987). Frequency and presentation of depressive symptoms in patients with primary degenerative dementia. *American Journal of Psychiatry, 144,* 41–45.

Lebowitz, B. D., Pearson, J. L., Schneider, L. S., Reynolds, C. F., III, Alexopoulos, G. S., Bruce, M. L., et al. (1997). Diagnosis and treatment of depression in late-life. Consensus statement update. *Journal of the American Medical Association, 278,* 1186–1190.

Leo, R. J., Narayan, D. A., Sherry, C., Michalek, C., & Pollock, D. (1997). Geropsychiatric consultation for African Americans and Caucasian patients. *General Hospital Psychiatry, 19,* 216–222.

Levy, M. L., Cummings, J. L., Fairbanks, L. A., Bravi, D., Calvani, M., & Carta, A. (1996). Longitudinal assessment of symptoms of depression, agitation, and psychosis in 181 patients with Alzheimer's disease. *American Journal of Psychiatry, 153,* 1438–1443.

Levy, M. L., Cummings, J. L., & Kahn-Rose, R. (1999). Neuropsychiatric symptoms and cholinergic therapy for Alzheimer's disease. *Gerontologist, 45*(Suppl. 1), 15–22.

Liu, C. Y., Fuh, J. L., Teng, E. L., Wang, S. J., Wang, P. N., Yang, Y. Y., et al. (1999). Depressive disorders in Chinese patients with Alzheimer's disease. *Acta Psychiatrica Scandinavica, 100,* 451–455.

Liu, R. Y., Zhou, J. N., Hoogendijk, W. J., van Heerikhuize, J., Kamphorst, W., Unmehopa, U. A., et al. (2000). Decreased vasopressin gene expression in the biological clock of Alzheimer disease patients with and without depression. *Journal of Neuropathology and Experimental Neurology, 59,* 314–322.

Lopez, O. L., Boller, F., Becker, J. T., Miller, M., & Reynolds, C. F., III. (1990). Alzheimer's disease and depression: Neuropsychological impairment and progression of the illness. *American Journal of Psychiatry, 147,* 855–860.

Lupien, S., Lecours, A. R., Lussier, I., Schwartz, G., Nair, N. P., & Meaney, M. J. (1994). Basal cortisol levels and cognitive deficits in human aging. *Journal of Neuroscience, 14,* 2893–2903.

Lyketsos, C. G., Baker, L., Warren, A., Steele, C., Brandt, J., Steinberg, M., et al. (1997). Depression, delusions, and hallucinations in Alzheimer's disease: no relationship to apolipoprotein E genotype. *Journal of Neuropsychiatry and Clinical Neurosciences, 9,* 64–67.

Lyketsos, C. G., Sheppard, J. M., Steele, C. D., Kopunek, S., Steinberg, M., Baker, A. S., et al. (2000). A randomized, placebo-controlled, double-blind clinical trial of sertraline in the treatment of depression complicating Alzheimer's disease: Initial results from the Depression in Alzheimer's Disease Study. *American Journal of Psychiatry, 157*(10), 1686–1689.

Lyketsos, C. G., Steele, C., Baker, L., Galik, E., Kopunek, S., Steinburg, M., et al. (1997). Major and minor depression in Alzheimer's disease: Prevalence and impact. *Journal of Neuropsychiatry and Clinical Neurosciences, 9,* 556–561.

Lyketsos, C. G., Steele, C., Galik, E., Rosenblatt, A., Steinberg, M., Warren, A., et al. (1999). Physical aggression in dementia patients and its relationship to depression. *American Journal of Psychiatry, 156,* 66–71.

Lyketsos, C. G., Steinberg, M., Tschanz, J. T., Norton, M. C., Steffens, D. C., & Breitner, J. C. (2000). Mental and behavioral disturbances in dementia: Findings from the Cache County Study on Memory in Aging. *American Journal of Psychiatry, 157,* 708–714.

Lyketsos, C. G., Treisman, G. J., Lipsey, J. R., Morris, P. L., & Robinson, R. G. (1998). Does stroke cause depression? *Journal of Neuropsychiatry and Clinical Neurosciences, 10,* 103–107.

Lyketsos, C. G., Tune, L. E., Pearlson, G., & Steele C. (1996). Major depression in Alzheimer's disease: An interaction between gender and family history. *Psychosomatics, 37,* 380–384.

Lyness, J. M., Conwell, W., & Nelson, J. C. (1992). Suicide attempts in elderly psychiatric inpatients. *Journal of American Geriatrics Society, 40,* 320–324.

Mackenzie, T. B., Robiner, W. N., & Knopman, D. S. (1989). Differences between patient and family assessments of depression in Alzheimer's disease. *American Journal of Psychiatry, 146,* 1174–1178.

Magai, C., Kennedy, G., Cohen, C. I., & Gomberg, D. (2000). A controlled clinical trial of sertraline in the treatment of depression in nursing home patients with late-stage Alzheimer's disease. *American Journal of Geriatric Psychiatry, 8,* 66–74.

Marin, R. S., Firinciogullari, S., & Biedrzycki, R. C. (1994). Group differences in the relationship between apathy and depression. *Journal of Nervous and Mental Diseases, 182,* 235–239.

McAllister, T. W., & Price, T. R. (1982). Severe depressive pseudodementia with and without dementia. *American Journal of Psychiatry, 139,* 626–629.

McKeith, I. G., Perry, R. H., Fairbairn, A. F., Jabeen, S., & Perry, E. K. (1992). Operational criteria for senile dementia of Lewy body type (SLDT). *Psychological Medicine, 22,* 911–922.

Mcnon, A. S., Gruber-Baldini, A. L., Hebel, J. R., Kaup, B., Loreck, D., Itkin Zimmerman, S., et al. (2001). Relationship between aggressive behaviors and depression among nursing home residents with dementia. *International Journal of Geriatric Psychiatry, 16,* 139–146.

Meyers, B. S. (1998). Depression and dementia: Comorbidities, identification and treatment. *Journal of Geriatric Psychiatry Neurology, 11,* 201–205.

Migliorelli, R., Teson, A., Sabe, L., Petracchi, M., Leiguarda, R., & Starkstein, S. E. (1995). Prevalence and correlates of dysthymia and major depression among patients with Alzheimer's disease. *American Journal of Psychiatry, 152,* 37–44.

Moe, K. E., Vitello, M. V., Larsen, L. H., & Prinz, P. N. (1995). Symposium: Cognitive processes and sleep disturbances: sleep/wake patterns in Alzheimer's disease: relationships with cognition and function. *Journal of Sleep Research, 4,* 15–20.

Molsa, P. K., Martitila, R. J., & Rinne, U. K. (1995). Long-term survival and predictors of mortality in Alzheimer's disease and multiinfarct dementia. *Acta Neurologica Scandinavica, 91,* 159–164.

Moye, J., Robiner, W. N., & Mackenzie, T. B. (1993). Depression in Alzheimer patients: Discrepancies between patient and caregiver reports. *Alzheimer Disease and Associated Disorders, 7,* 187–201.

Mukherjee, S., Shukla, S., Woodle, J., Rosen, A. M., & Olarte, S. (1983). Misdiagnosis of schizophrenia in bipolar patients: A multiethnic comparison. *American Journal of Psychiatry, 140,* 1561–1574.

Mulsant, B. H., Stergiou, A., Keshavan, M. S., Sweet, R. A., Rifai, A. H., Pasternak, R., et al. (1993). Schizophrenia in late life: Elderly patients admitted to an acute-care psychiatric hospital. *Schizophrenia Bulletin, 19,* 709–721.

Nahas, Z., Kunik, M. E., Orengo, C. A., Molinari, V., & Workman, R. (1997). Depression in male geropsychiatric inpatients with and without dementia: A naturalistic study. *Journal of Affective Disorders, 46,* 243–246.

Nelson, J. P., & Rosenberg, D. R. (1991). ECT treatment of demented elderly patients with major depression: A retrospective study of efficacy and safety. *Convulsive Therapy, 7,* 157–165.

Newman, S. C. (1999). The prevalence of depression in Alzheimer's disease and vascular dementia in a population sample. *Journal of Affective Disorders, 52,* 169–176.

Nyth, A. L., & Gottfries, C. G. (1990). The clinical efficacy of citalopram in treatment of emotional disturbances in dementia disorders: A Nordic multicentre study. *British Journal of Psychiatry, 157,* 891–894.

O'Brien, J., Thomas, A., Ballard, C., Brown, A., Ferrier, N., Jaros, E., et al. (2001). Cognitive impairment in depression is not associated with neuropathologic evidence of increased vascular or Alzheimer-type pathology. *Biological Psychiatry, 49,* 130–136.

O'Connor, D. W., Pollitt, P. A., & Roth, M. (1990). Coexisting depression and dementia in a community survey of the elderly. *International Psychogeriatrics, 2,* 45–53.

Olin, J. T., Katz, I. R., Meyers, B. S., Schneider, L. S., & Lebowitz, B. D. (2002). Provisional diagnostic criteria for depression of Alzheimer disease: Rationale and background. *American Journal of Geriatric Psychiatry, 10,* 129–141.

Olin, J. T., Schneider, L. S., Katz, I. R., Meyers, B. S., Alexopoulos, G. S., Breitner, J. C., et al. (2002). Provisional diagnostic criteria for depression of Alzheimer disease. *American Journal of Geriatric Psychiatry, 10,* 125–128.

Ownby, R. L., Harwood, D. G., Acevedo, A., Barker, W., & Duara, R. (2001). Factor structure of the Cornell Scale for Depression in Dementia for Anglo and Hispanic patients with dementia. *American Journal of Geriatric Psychiatry, 9,* 217–224.

Payne, J. L., Lyketsos, C. G., Steele, C., Baker, L., Galik, E., Kopunek, S., et al. (1998). Relationship of cognitive and functional impairment to depressive features in Alzheimer's disease and other dementias. *Journal of Neuropsychiatry and Clinical Neurosciences, 10,* 440–447.

Pearlson, G. D., Ross, C. A., Lohr, W. D., Rovner, B. W., Chase, G. A., & Folstein, M. F. (1990). Association between family history of affective disorder and the depressive syndrome of Alzheimer's disease. *American Journal of Psychiatry, 147,* 452–456.

Pearson, J. L., Teri, L., Reifler, B. V., & Raskind, M. A. (1989). Functional status and cognitive impairment in Alzheimer's patients with and without depression. *Journal of American Geriatrics Society, 37,* 1117–1121.

Petracca, G., Teson, A., Chemerinski, E., Leiguarda, R., & Starkstein, S. E. (1996). A double-blind placebo-controlled study of clomipramine in depressed patients with Alzheimer's disease. *Journal of Neuropsychiatry and Clinical Neurosciences, 8,* 270–275.

Rao, V., & Lyketsos, C. G. (2000a). The benefits and risks of ECT for patients with primary dementia who also suffer from depression. *International Journal of Geriatric Psychiatry, 15,* 729–735.

Rao, V., & Lyketsos, C. G. (2000b). Neuropsychiatric sequelae of traumatic brain injury. *Psychosomatics, 41,* 95–103.

Raskind, M. A., & Peskind, E. R. (2001). Alzheimer's disease and related disorders. *Medical Clinics of North America, 85,* 803–817.

Reding, M., Haycox, J., & Blass, J. (1985). Depression in patients referred to a dementia clinic. A three-year prospective study. *Archives of Neurology, 42,* 894–896.

Reichman, W. E., & Coyne, A. C. (1995). Depressive symptoms in Alzheimer's disease and multiinfarct dementia. *Journal of Geriatric Psychiatry and Neurology, 8,* 96–99.

Reifler, B. V. (2000). A case of mistaken identity: Pseudodementia is really predementia. *Journal of American Geriatrics Society, 48,* 593–594.

Reifler, B. V., Larson, E., & Hanley, R. (1982). Coexistence of cognitive impairment and depression in geriatric outpatients. *American Journal of Psychiatry, 139,* 623–626.

Reifler, B. V., Teri, L., Raskind, M., Veith, R., Barnes, R., White, E., et al. (1989). Double-blind trial of imipramine in Alzheimer's disease patients with and without depression. *American Journal of Psychiatry, 146,* 45–49.

Reisberg, B., Ferris, S. H., de Leon, M. J., Kluger, A., Franssen, E., Borenstein, J., et al. (1989). The stage specific temporal course of Alzheimer's disease: Functional and behavioral concomitants based upon cross-sectional and longitudinal observation. *Progress in Clinical and Biological Research, 317,* 23–41.

Ritchie, K., Gilham, C., Ledesert, B., Touchon, J., & Kotzki, P. O. (1999). Depressive illness, depressive symptomatology and regional cerebral blood flow in elderly people with subclinical cognitive impairment. *Age and Ageing, 28,* 385–391.

Robinson, R. G., Kubos, K. L., Starr, L. B., Rao, K., & Price, T. R. (1984). Mood disorders in stroke patients. Importance in location of lesions. *Brain, 107,* 81–93.

Robinson, R. G., Starkstein, S. E., & Price, T. R. (1988). Poststroke depression and lesion location. *Stroke, 19,* 125–126.

Rosen, J., & Zubenko, G. S. (1991). Emergence of psychosis and depression in the longitudinal evaluation of Alzheimer's disease. *Biological Psychiatry, 29,* 224–232.

Roth, M., Mountjoy, C. Q., & Amrein, R. (1996). Moclobemide in elderly patients with cognitive decline and depression: An international double-blind, placebo-controlled trial. *British Journal of Psychiatry, 168,* 149–157.

Rovner, B. W., Broadhead, J., Spencer, M., Carson, K., & Folstein, M. F. (1989). Depression and Alzheimer's disease. *American Journal of Psychiatry, 146,* 350–353.

Rovner, B. W., Kafonek, S., Filipp, L., Lucas, M. J., & Folstein, M. F. (1986). Prevalence of mental illness in a community nursing home. *American Journal of Psychiatry, 143,* 1446–1449.

Rubin, E. H., Morris, J. C., & Berg, L. (1987). The progression of personality changes in senile dementia of the Alzheimer's type. *Journal of American Geriatrics Society, 35,* 721–725.

Sapolsky, R. (2000). The possibility of neurotoxicity in the hippocampus in major depression: A primer on neuron death. *Biological Psychiatry, 48,* 755–765.

Scarmeas, N., Brandt, J., Albert, M., Devanand, D. P., Marder, K., Bell, K., et al. (2002). Association between the APOE genotype and psychopathologic symptoms in Alzheimer's disease. *Neurology, 58,* 1182–1188.

Schmid, H., Manjee, K., & Shah, T. (1994). On the distinction of suicide ideation versus attempt in elderly psychiatric inpatients. *Gerontologist, 34,* 332–339.

Schneider, L. S., & Farlow, M. L. (1997). Combined tacrine and estrogen replacement therapy in patients with Alzheimer's disease. *Annals of the New York Academy of Sciences, 826,* 317–322.

Schulz, R., O'Brien, A. T., Bookwala, J., & Fleissner, K. (1995). Psychiatric and physical morbidity effects of dementia caregiving: Prevalence, correlates, and causes. *Gerontologist, 35,* 771–791.

Schulz, R., & Williamson, G. (1990). Biases in family assessments of depression in patients with Alzheimer's disease. *American Journal of Psychiatry, 147,* 377–378.

Sheline, Y. I., Wang, P. W., Gado, M. H., Csernansky, J. G., & Vannier, M. W. (1996). Hippocampal atrophy in recurrent major depression. *Proceedings of the National Academy of Sciences, USA, 93,* 3908–3913.

Shua-Haim, J. R., Haim, T., Shi, Y., Kuo, Y. H., & Smith, J. M. (2001). Depression among Alzheimer's caregivers: Identifying risk factors. *American Journal of Alzheimer's Disease and Other Dementias, 16,* 353–359.

Simon, R. J., Fleiss, J. L., Gurland, B. J., Stiller, P. R., & Sharpe, L. (1973). Depression and schizophrenia in hospitalized Black and White mental patients. *Archives of General Psychiatry, 28,* 509–512.

Simpson, S., Baldwin, R. C., Jackson, A., & Burns, A. S. (1998). Is subcortical disease associated with a poor response to antidepressants? Neurological, neuropsychological, and neuroradiological findings in late-life depression. *Psychological Medicine, 28,* 1015–1026.

Simpson, S. W., Jackson, A., Baldwin, R. C., & Burns, A. (1997). Subcortical hyperintensities in late-life depression: Acute response to treatment and neuropsychological impairment. *International Psychogeriatrics, 9,* 257–275.

Speck, C. E., Kukull, W. A., Brenner, D. E., Bowen, J. D., McCormick, W. C., Teri, L., et al. (1995). History of depression as a risk factor for Alzheimer's disease. *Epidemiology, 6,* 366–369.

Starkstein, S. E., Chemerinski, E., Sabe, L., Kuzis, G., Petracca, G., Teson, A., et al. (1997). Prospective longitudinal study of depression and anosognosia in Alzheimer's disease. *British Journal of Psychiatry, 171,* 47–52.

Starkstein, S. E., Federoff, J. P., Price, T. R., Leiguarda, R., & Robinson, R. G. (1993). Apathy following cerebrovascular lesions. *Stroke, 24,* 1625–1630.

Starkstein, S. E., Petracca, G., Chemerinski, E., & Kremer, J. (2001). Syndromic validity of apathy in Alzheimer's disease. *American Journal of Psychiatry, 158,* 872–877.

Starkstein, S. E., Robinson, R. G., & Price, T. R. (1987). Comparison of cortical and subcortical lesions in the production of poststroke mood disorders. *Brain, 110,* 1045–1059.

Starkstein, S. E., Robinson, R. G., & Price, T. R. (1988). Comparison of patients with and without poststroke major depression matched for size and location of lesion. *Archives of General Psychiatry, 45,* 247–252.

Starkstein, S. E., Sabe, L., Vazquez, S., Teson, A., Petracca, G., Chemerinski, E., et al. (1996). Neuropsychological, psychiatric, and cerebral blood flow findings in vascular dementia and Alzheimer's disease. *Stroke, 27,* 408–414.

Steele, C., Rovner, B., Chase, G. A., & Folstein, M. (1990). Psychiatric symptoms and nursing home placement of patients with Alzheimer's disease. *American Journal of Psychiatry, 147,* 1049–1051.

Steffens, D. C., Plassman, B. L., Helms, M. J., Welsh-Bohmer, K. A., Saunders, A. M., & Breitner, J. C. (1997). A twin study of late-onset depression and apolipoprotein E epsilon 4 as risk factors for Alzheimer's disease. *Biological Psychiatry, 41,* 851–856.

Strakowski, S. M., McElroy, S. L., Keck, P. E., & West, S. A. (1996). Racial influence on diagnosis in psychotic mania. *Journal of Affective Disorders, 39,* 157–162.

Strauss, M. E., & Ogrocki, P. K. (1996). Confirmation of an association between family history of affective disorder and the depressive syndrome of Alzheimer's disease. *American Journal of Psychiatry, 153,* 1340–1342.

Sultzer, D. L., Levin, H. S., Mahler, M. E., High, W. M., & Cummings, J. L. (1993). A comparison of psychiatric symptoms in vascular dementia and Alzheimer's disease. *American Journal of Psychiatry, 150,* 1806–1812.

Sunderland, T., Alterman, I. S., Yount, D., Hill, J. L., Tariot, P. N., Mueller, E. A., et al. (1988). A new scale for the assessment of depressed mood in demented patients. *American Journal of Psychiatry, 145,* 955–959.

Swearer, J. M., Drachman, D. A., O'Donnell, B. F., & Mitchell, A. L. (1988). Troublesome and disruptive behaviors in dementia. Relationships to diagnosis and disease severity. *Journal of American Geriatrics Society, 36,* 784–790.

Taragano, F. E., Lyketsos, C. G., Mangone, C. A., Allegri, R. F., & Comesana-Diaz, E. (1997). A double-blind randomized, fixed-dose trial of fluoxetine vs. amitriptyline in the treatment of major depression complicating Alzheimer's disease. *Psychosomatics, 38,* 246–252.

Teri, L. (1991). Imipramine in the treatment of depressed Alzheimer's patients: Impact on cognition. *Journal of Gerontology, 46,* 372–377.

Teri, L. (1997). Behavior and caregiver burden: Behavior problems in patients with Alzheimer disease and its association with caregiver distress. *Alzheimer Disease and Associated Disorders, 11*(Suppl. 1), S35–S38.

Teri, L., & Logsdon, R. G. (2000). Assessment and management of behavioral disturbances in Alzheimer disease. *Comprehensive Therapy, 26,* 169–175.

Teri, L., Logsdon, R. G., Uomoto, J., & McCurry, S. M. (1997). Behavioral treatment of depression in dementia patients: A controlled clinical trial. *Journals of Gerontology: Series B, Psychological Sciences and Social Sciences, 52,* 159–166.

Teri, L., & Truax, P. (1994). Assessment of depression in dementia patients: Association of caregiver mood with depression ratings. *Gerontologist, 34,* 231–234.

Teri, L., & Wagner, A. W. (1991). Assessment of depression in patients with Alzheimer's disease: Concordance among informants. *Psychology and Aging, 6,* 280–285.

Teri, L., & Wagner, A. W. (1992). Alzheimer's disease and depression. *Journal of Consulting and Clinical Psychology, 60,* 379–391.

Thorpe, L., & Groulx, B. (2001). Depressive syndromes in dementia. *Canadian Journal of Neurological Science, 28*(Suppl. 1), S83–S95.

Toran-Allerand, C. D., Miranda, R. C., Bentham, W. D., Sohrabji, F., Brown, T. J., Hochberg, R. B., et al. (1992). Estrogen receptors colocalize with low affinity nerve growth factor receptors in cholinergic neurons of the basal forebrain. *Proceedings of the National Academy of Sciences, USA, 89,* 4668–4672.

Troisi, A., Pasini, A., Gori, G., Sorbi, T., Biagini, C., Aulisi, A., et al. (1993). Assessment of depression in Alzheimer disease: Symptoms, syndrome, and computer tomography findings. *Dementia, 4,* 87–93.

Verhey, F. R., Jolles, J., Ponds, R. W., & Vreeling, F. W. (1993). Psychiatric disorders in patients of a memory outpatient clinic. *Nederlands Tijdschrift Voor Geneeskunde, 137,* 1054–1058.

Vida, S., Des Rosiers, P., Carrier, L., & Gauthier, S. (1994). Depression in Alzheimer's disease: Receiver operating characteristic analysis of the Cornell Scale for Depression in Dementia and the Hamilton Depression Scale. *Journal of Geriatric Psychiatry and Neurology, 7,* 159–162.

Volicer, L., Rheume, Y., & Cyr, D. (1994). Treatment of depression in advanced Alzheimer's disease using sertraline. *Journal of Geriatric Psychiatry and Neurology, 7,* 227–229.

Wagle, A. C., Ho, L. W., Wagle, S. A., & Berrios, G. E. (2000). Psychometric behavior of BDI in Alzheimer's disease patients with depression. *International Journal of Geriatric Psychiatry, 15,* 63–69.

Weiner, M. F., Edland, S. D., & Luszczynska, H. (1994). Prevalence and incidence of major depression in Alzheimer's disease. *American Journal of Psychiatry, 151,* 1006–1009.

Weiner, M. F., Martin-Cook, K., Foster, B. M., Saine, K., Fontaine, C. S., & Svetlik, D. A. (2000). Effects of donepezil on emotional/behavioral symptoms in Alzheimer's disease patients. *Journal of Clinical Psychiatry, 61,* 487–492.

Wilson, R. S., Barnes, L. L., Mendes de Leon, C. F., Aggarwal, N. T., Schneider, J. S., Bach, J., et al. (2002). Depressive symptoms, cognitive decline, and the risk of AD in older persons. *Neurology, 59,* 364–370.

Wragg, R. E., & Jeste, D. V. (1989). Overview of depression and psychosis in Alzheimer's disease. *American Journal of Psychiatry, 146,* 577–587.

Yeo, G., Gallagher-Thompson, D., & Lieberman, M. (1996). Variations in dementia characteristics by ethnic category. In G. Yeo & D. Gallagher-Thompson (Eds.), *Ethnicity and the dementias* (pp. 21–30). Washington, DC: Taylor & Francis.

Zubenko, G. S., & Mossy, J. (1988). Major depression in primary dementia. Clinical and neuropathologic correlates. *Archives of Neurology, 45,* 1182–1186.

Zubenko, G. S., Rifai, A. H., Mulsant, B. H., Sweet, R. A., Pasternak, R. E. (1996). Premorbid history of major depression and the depressive syndrome of Alzheimer's disease. *American Journal of Geriatric Psychiatry, 4,* 85–90.

Zubenko, G. S., Sullivan, P., Nelson, J. P., Belle, S. H., Huff, F. J., & Wolf, G. L. (1990). Brain imaging abnormalities in mental disorders in late life. *Archives of Neurology, 47,* 1107–1111.

Zweig, R. M., Ross, C. A., Hedreen, J. C., Steele, C., Cardillo, J. E., Whitehouse, P. J., et al. (1988). The neuropathology of aminergic nuclei in Alzheimer's disease. *Archives of Neurology, 24,* 233–242.

CHAPTER 11

Psychological and Nonpharmacological Aspects of Depression in Dementia

Peter A. Lichtenberg and Benjamin T. Mast

The relationship between depression and dementia has been one of intense scientific and clinical interest over the past twenty years. Raskind (1998) summarized the major ideas about how depression relates to dementia:

1. Depression is either a prodrome or a risk factor for dementia.
2. Depression complicates dementia through the direct contribution to excess disabilities.

By far, the most intense scientific attention is given these days to the debate as to whether depression is a prodrome of dementia, specifically Alzheimer's disease (AD), or whether depression is instead a risk factor for the development of AD or other forms of dementia.

This chapter is divided into five sections. In the first section, we explore the evidence for and against the question of depression as risk factor or prodrome. In addition to providing the empirical evidence and interpreting whether it supports either or both concepts, we present information on the vascular depression hypothesis and how this framework may shed light on the mechanisms involved in the depression-dementia debate. In the second section, we explore the notion that depression causes excess disability in those with dementia. We interpret the empirical evidence in the context of the *activity limitation* framework of depression. In the third section, we review the evidence concerning the phenomenology of depression in dementia. Assessment of depression in dementia is discussed in the fourth section. In the final section, we explore nonpharmacological treatments that are available for practitioners in treating depression and its symptomatology. Each section concludes with clinical implication highlights that are supported by the empirical literature.

DEPRESSION AS PRODROME OR RISK FACTOR

In conceptualizing depression as a prodrome for dementia, specifically for AD, depression is expressly viewed as an early expression of the underlying pathobiology of dementia. This is an important concept in AD because of the general knowledge that there is underlying pathology involved in Alzheimer's many years before symptoms are present and a full-blown clinical dementia syndrome is apparent (Bondi, Salmon, Galasko, Thomas, & Thal, 1999; Morris et al., 2001). There is great interest, therefore, in discovering dementia at its earliest stage of onset so that treatment can postpone and/or prevent symptoms.

Alexopoulos, Myers, Young, Mattis, and Kakuma (1993) and Devanand, Sano, and Tang (1996) presented data that could be used to support the prodrome idea. Alexopoulos and colleagues compared two groups of older depressives. One group had cognitive impairment ($n = 23$) that was reversible once antidepressant treatment was completed. The second group was also treated for depression but never displayed any cognitive impairment ($n = 34$). They then followed the groups yearly for a period of three years. The results were striking. In survivors, 10 of 15 (67%) with reversible dementia went on to have a diagnosed dementia by three-year follow-up, whereas only 4 of 26 (15%) in the cognitively intact group did so. The authors concluded that the reversible dementia group clearly contained a significant number of patients who were in the preclinical stage of dementia.

Devanand and colleagues (1996) followed more than 1,000 individuals age 60 and older on a yearly basis. Baseline mood disorder in the absence of cognitive impairment was associated with a moderately increased risk for incident dementia at follow-up. Zubenko (2000) addressed the notion of depression as a prodrome to dementia in a slightly different fashion. He investigated the evidence for the neurobiology of major depression in AD. Forty-three percent of his sample of those who had depression along with a diagnosis of AD came from a family where major depression occurred. In contrast, only 9% of the nondepressed demented individuals came from a family with a history of major depression. Zubenko postulated that early cholinergic loss in Alzheimer's dementia patients could be the cause of depression before the onset of clinically significant cognitive decline. He speculated that this finding is specific to AD and not generalizable to vascular dementia (VaD). The most widely accepted alternative interpretation to that of these data that are used to suggest depression as a prodrome to dementia, and most particularly AD, is to view depression as an independent risk factor for dementia.

The depression-as-a-risk-factor hypothesis suggests that the presence of depression somewhere along the life span puts individuals at higher risk for developing dementing disorders. The data from Speck et al. (1995) are intriguing in this regard. These authors took 294 individuals with AD from their registry and compared them with 300 randomly selected older adults of similar age and gender. After controlling for gender, age, education, and type of informant, the authors found evidence that the experience of depression was modestly associated with dementia onset. Of greater interest, however, was that the association was stronger (odds ratio of $2:0$) for those whose depressive episode occurred more than 10 years before their dementia onset than for those whose depressive episode occurred within 10 years of the dementia onset (odds ratio $0:9$). These data clearly do not support the notion of depression as prodrome to AD and would suggest that depression is at most a risk factor for the development of AD.

Visser, Verhey, Ponds, Kester, and Jolles (2000) investigated this issue by studying the relationship between depression and dementia onset in 111 individuals diagnosed with mild cognitive impairment. These nondemented, cognitively impaired individuals were screened at baseline, two years, and five years. At the five-year follow-up, 52 participants remained in the study. Of the 25 individuals who developed dementia within the five-year period, 15 (60%) were mildly depressed at baseline. Depression was also common, however, in those without dementia at the five-year point (37/73 original sample; 52%). The preclinical group (25 individuals who were diagnosed with dementia) was significantly older at baseline than was the nondemented group (63 vs. 71 years of age). Interestingly, and consistent with many preclinical studies, age and memory impairment (not depression) were the only significant baseline predictors of dementia.

Li, Meyer, and Thornby (2001a, 2001b) investigated the relationship among AD, VaD, mild cognitive impairment (MCI), normal aging, and depression in their 3.5-year follow-up study. They included 146 elders with normal cognition, 19 participants with MCI, 42 with AD, and 32 with VaD. At baseline, prevalence of depression among those with dementia was greater than in the normal group (AD 20%, VaD 34%, and 13% normal elders). Unique predictors included having either AD or VaD, heart disease, and a history of depression. The MCI group was then added for the longitudinal study. Nearly 80% of the sample was treated with serotonin selective reuptake inhibitors (SSRI) antidepressant medications during the study. At follow-up, 35 of the normals had become classified with MCI, 9 of the 16 MCI patients developed dementia, all of the AD patients demonstrated cognitive decline, whereas 25% of the VaD patients showed cognitive improvement. New-onset depression was significantly higher among VaD elders than the other groups (13/23). Those with AD had the highest depression rating scores at baseline, but these diminished over time. The VaD patients remained at higher levels of depression. Depression persisted in 60% of depressed MCI patients and 66% of VaD patients, whereas only 33% of AD patients had persistent depression. This was striking given that the AD group had the lowest rate of antidepressant treatment (50%). Depression in MCI individuals was more common in those who later became demented (57%) as compared to the nondemented (16%). The authors concluded that depression in the face of MCI should be considered a risk factor for preclinical dementia.

Vascular Depression Hypothesis

A conceptual framework for understanding the mechanisms at work with depression as a prodrome or risk factor for dementia may be the *vascular depression hypothesis* (Alexopoulos, Meyers, Young, Campbell, et al., 1997; Alexopoulos, Meyers, Young, Kakuma, et al., 1997). This hypothesis states that vascular risk factors and/or disease can predispose, precipitate, or perpetuate depressive disorders in older age. The authors speculate that specific disruption of the frontal-subcortical brain circuitry is responsible for the mood disorder.

Simpson, Allen, Tomenson, and Burns (1998) investigated neurological correlates and depression in patients with either AD ($n = 60$) or VaD ($n = 39$) and found evidence to support the vascular depression hypothesis. VaD patients had a higher prevalence rate of depression (50%) than did AD patients (28%). Predictors of depression included presence of VaD, older age, increased cognitive impairment, and extrapyramidal signs in

AD patients. The authors conclude that the findings of risk factors in both AD and VaD patients support the vascular depression hypothesis.

Neuroimaging studies have investigated the relationship between vascular brain changes and depression. Coffey, Figiel, Djang, and Weiner (1990) reported a finding that has since been replicated many times in nondemented depressed elders. He found that the presence of moderate to severe white matter hyperintensities on magnetic resonance imaging (MRI) was significantly related to the presence of depression. He noted that the simple presence of white matter changes on MRI was an age-related change and that it held clinical significance for depression only when the changes were moderate to severe.

O'Brien et al. (1996) investigated white matter changes in a group of normal adults age 55 years and older ($n = 40$), depressives age 55 years and older ($n = 61$), and a group of nondepressed Alzheimer's patients ($n = 68$). The authors confirmed Coffey's finding that white matter changes were common in 59% of normal elders. White matter changes were extremely common in depressives, with 85% having these changes and 30% showing severe changes. Overall, deep white matter changes appeared no different between the AD nondepressed and the depressed group. After controlling for differences in vascular risk factors and blood pressure, however, an association was found between white matter change severity and depressive disorders.

Barber et al. (1999) investigated white matter changes on MRI in AD ($n = 28$), VaD ($n = 25$), normal age (75), and those with Lewy body dementia (LBD; $n = 27$). White matter changes and periventricular changes were greater in all dementia groups as compared to controls. Those with white matter changes in the frontal area had significantly higher depression scores than did those without frontal lesions. The authors concluded that their data supported the possibility that frontal and subcortical white matter lesions are implicated in late life depression regardless of type of dementia. Ballard et al. (2000) furthered this line of research by investigating specific aspects of vascular aspects in depression among those with VaD. The authors studied 30 individuals with VaD and found that those individuals with small infarct volumes in the frontal subcortical areas were more likely to be depressed than were those with larger infarct volumes in other locations of the brain.

Clinical Implications

- Older depressives with cognitive impairment and/or moderate to severe white matter disease on MRI are at risk for conversion to dementia.
- Regular follow-up with at-risk depressives will enable dementia to be detected at an early stage.
- Older adults who are "vascularly burdened" are at higher risk for depression onset.

Summary

There is a convergence of evidence that, in many instances, depression and dementia are significantly related. The debate about whether depression is prodrome or risk factor takes a back seat in this discussion to the issue of whether the mechanisms of brain change that produce depression are understood. The most supported biomedical hypothesis to date is the vascular depression hypothesis. This hypothesis expands our conceptualization of VaD in depression and dementia because it allows for the influence of vascular risk factors on brain and behavior change, even in the absence of a stroke. Thus, MRI studies are consistently showing that vascular risk factors are related to white matter changes, which are related to depression in dementia no matter what the etiology. The overlapping of VaD and AD is an idea that has been embraced in other ways as well (Snowden et al., 1997). While the association of vascular risk factors and apparent brain changes to depression are powerful ideas, the exact mechanisms of how these changes take place and exactly how they influence depression is not understood at this time.

DEPRESSION AND EXCESS DISABILITY IN DEMENTIA— THE ACTIVITY LIMITATION FRAMEWORK

A major issue of scientific and clinical importance to understanding dementia is determining in what ways depression affects cognitive and noncognitive symptoms. Family caregivers report that the noncognitive symptoms of dementia (e.g., apathy, agitation) have greater impact on the family unit's day-to-day life than do the cognitive symptoms of dementia (Riley & Snowden, 1999). Of concern, then, is how depressive syndromes affect the behaviors of the person with dementia and whether depression should be an area of intense intervention, not only to remove the depressive symptoms but to forestall excess disabilities in persons with dementia. One conceptual framework to use in assessing these issues is the activity limitation framework.

The activity limitation framework was developed from research data that focused on medically ill elders (Williamson, 1992; Williamson & Schulz, 1995). Physical illness, pain, functional abilities, and depression were investigated cross-sectionally and longitudinally. The authors reported that it was only the changes in physical health such as pain that affected functional skills related to depression. Another way of stating this finding is to view activity limitation as a mediator of pain and depression. Thus, in extrapolating this to dementia, it is to the extent that functional skills are affected that depressive syndromes emerge and remain stable. This framework has some empirical support for it, both in general geriatric medical studies and in studies of demented elders.

Nanna, Lichtenberg, Abuda-Bella, and Barth (1997) reported on 423 cognitively impaired (56%) and intact (44%) medical rehabilitation patients. Both cognition and depression were independent predictors of functional recovery beyond initial level of function and demographic variables. Those with depression had less functional recovery than those without depression. A more recent study focused on the specific relationship between depression and functional abilities in primary care elders.

Stewart, Prince, Richards, Brayne, and Mann (2001) compared the relationships between depression and disablement and depression and cardiovascular risk factors in a sample of 287 primary care Caribbean-born elders. Nineteen percent of the sample was classified as depressed, 58% had hypertension, 29% had diabetes, and 16% had a Mini-Mental State Examination (MMSE) score of less than 20. Basic and advanced activities of daily living as well as mobility were also measured. The authors reported a strong association between depression and disablement but no association between CVRFs and depression. The authors used only measures of individual CVRFs and no cumulative vascular burden measure. Mast (2002) and Yochim and Lichtenberg (2002) have demonstrated that CVRFs and depression may be related only when there is cumulative vascular burden. Nevertheless, the results of the study supported the activity limitation framework.

Hargrave, Reed, and Mungas (2000) investigated depressive syndromes and functional disability in dementia among AD ($n = 582$), VaD ($n = 48$), and mixed AD and VaD patients ($n = 61$). Several interesting findings emerged from these data. First, depression was related to both demographic factors and type of dementia. Major and minor depression were more common in those with less education, and major but not minor depression was more common in those with VaD than with AD. In relation to the activity limitation framework, depression was significantly related to both cognition and functional abilities and was significantly more related to functional abilities than to cognition. These data provided support for the activity limitation framework in demented elders.

Espiritu et al. (2001) used slightly differing methodology but reported findings similar to the Hargrave study. The group investigated caregiver reports of functional abilities using self-reported depression and the MMSE in more than 200 demented elders. Whereas the Hargrave study used rate-based depressive determination, self-report depression was significantly related to ADL skills in the Espiritu sample beyond the effects of demographic and cognitive factors. Thus, the significant relationship between self-reported depression with caregiver reports of function provided further support for the activity limitation framework.

Starkstein et al. (1997) reported on a prospective study of depression in AD. These researchers categorized 62 patients as either not depressed, having minor depression, or having major depression at baseline and reexamined the groups at two-year follow-up. Nineteen percent of the sample had major depression at baseline, and half of this group remained depressed at follow-up regardless of whether they underwent antidepressant treatment. Thirty-four percent of the sample had minor depression at baseline, and at follow-up only 28% remained in the minor depressed group. Twenty-one percent of the nondepressed group at baseline had depression on follow-up. Both cognition and functional abilities declined at the same rate for each group regardless of depression status. In this sample, no support was found for the activity limitation framework, although the authors did not investigate the depression groups separately to see who remained depressed versus those whose depression remitted.

The presence and course of depression in long-term care residents is another important area of research and clinical practice. Janzig, Teunisse, Bouwens, Hof, and Zitman (2000) investigated depression in 91 demented and 110 nondemented long-term care residents at baseline and at 6- and 12-month follow-up. At baseline, 32% of dementia patients had major (12%) or minor (20%) depression, and 50% of nondemented residents had major (11%) or minor (39%) depression. Functional abilities and depression severity at baseline, and not dementia status, predicted depression persistence, thus supporting the activity limitation framework. These rates of depression in long-term care match those of many other researchers (Gerety et al., 1994; Lichtenberg, 1994).

Menon et al. (2001) investigated other noncognitive symptoms that are related to the presence of depression. They investigated 1,101 long-term care residents with dementia in a stratified random sample of 59 long-term care facilities. In those with a dementia diagnosis, verbal and physical aggression were more frequent. Twenty-one percent of the demented group was depressed and, as compared to the nondepressed dementia patients, the depressive had significantly more ADL limitations and psychiatric symptoms than did the nondepressive group. Specifically, those patients who were moderate to severely demented and had depression were more likely to be physically and verbally aggressive.

Depression in Dementia: Effects on Cognition

Our understanding of whether the presence of depression in persons with dementia, particularly in those with AD, is associated with excess cognitive disabilities is limited. Ross, Arnsberger, and Fox (1998) reported that although a group of depressive and nondepressive patients with AD had similar MMSE scores, cognition was significantly related to depression diagnosis beyond psychosocial and demographic predictors. Their study, from the California Alzheimer's Disease Cooperative, consisted of 183 patients with depression and 1,300 nondepressed patients. The authors concluded that depression contributes to cognitive excess disabilities. These findings have been reported by others as well (see Lichtenberg, Ross, Mills, & Manning, 1995, for a review). Of greater interest more recently has been whether there is a specific pattern of cognitive excess disability in depressed persons with dementia.

Wefel, Hoyt, and Massman (2000) compared 37 depressed Alzheimer's patients with 98 nondepressed Alzheimer's patients on 13 neuropsychological measures. The groups were matched on MMSE scores; and tests of general intellectual functioning, attention and concentration, memory functioning, language functioning, and psychomotor functioning were administered to both groups. A modified Bon Ferroni procedure was used for the multiple comparisons. The depressed group demonstrated significantly worse cognitive functioning than the nondepressed group only on tasks of complex attention and speeded motor programming. The authors concluded that these findings were consistent with cerebral dysfunction in the frontal-subcortical areas. This pattern of results has been found in a group of younger unipolar depressed individuals as well (Massman, Delis, Butters, Dupont, & Gillin, 1992).

Clinical Implications

- Depression is linked to cognitive and noncognitive excess disabilities.
- Interventions that focus on keeping persons with dementia functionally and physically active may prevent or postpone depressive reactions.
- There is a need for studies that investigate whether functionally based interventions reduce depression in persons with dementia.
- Aggressive and agitated long-term care residents are likely to have comorbid depression.

Summary

In contrast to the neurological approach to depression found in the vascular depression framework, the activity limitation framework focuses on the effects of functioning on the presence and persistence of depression. These frameworks are not mutually exclusive, but do indeed investigate different domains. The evidence for the activity limitation framework is fairly positive. Depression in those with dementia is significantly related to functional abilities. Indeed, those demented individuals with depression appear to suffer from excess disabilities in terms of self-care, independence, and, in nursing home settings, verbal and physical aggressiveness. By extension, maximizing independence should be integral to the reduction of depression in persons with dementia.

PHENOMENOLOGY OF DEPRESSION IN DEMENTIA

Understanding the unique aspects of depression in dementia can assist clinicians and researchers in the detection and treatment of this syndrome.

Lazarus, Newton, Cohler, Lesser, and Schweon (1987) were one of the earlier research groups to examine the phenomenology of depression in dementia. In their investigation of 44 persons with dementia, 18 participants were diagnosed as depressed via the Hamilton Rating Scale. Interrater reliability was .68 for this study. The authors reported that those items associated with inner states of despair were far more common than were vegetative symptoms. Thus, mood, anxiety, and hopelessness were noted to be particular aspects of depression in those with dementia. Much of the data following the Lazarus group's study has supported their initial findings.

Katz (1998) and Verhey and Visser (2000) have specified that mood disorders appear to be more prominent in those with preclinical and those with mild dementia. Verhey and Visser examined a group of 116 nondemented patients, of which 25 became demented after two years. Thirteen of the 25 individuals who became demented were depressed at baseline. Their depression was characterized by more minor depression symptoms, specifically mood disturbances, guilt, and suicidal thoughts. These authors advocated a term *emotional vulnerability syndrome* and urged clinicians to broaden the diagnostic criteria to allow for minor depression.

Chemerinski, Petracca, Sabe, Kremer, and Starkstein (2001) evaluated how well mood as rated by both caregiver and dementia patient accounted for depressive syndromes in 253 persons with AD, 47 persons with depression but no dementia, and 20 healthy controls. Depressed mood as rated by both caregivers and patients was a powerful predictor of a host of other depressive symptoms including apathy, anxiety, insomnia, loss of interest, agitation, and psychomotor retardation. These data further supported the importance of assessing mood in persons with dementia.

Patterson et al. (1990) investigated minor depression in 34 persons with AD and 21 spousal controls. Six (18%) of the patients had evidence of minor depression using the Cornell Scale versus two (10%) of the controls based on interviews. Sadness, lack of pleasure, and anxiety were the most common symptoms among those with depression and dementia, whereas vegetative signs were the least common in that group.

Apathy and social withdrawal have been the second area of focus in the phenomenology of depression studies. Starkstein (2000) reported on the prevalence of apathy in 301 individuals with probable AD, 106 with depression but no dementia, and 25 controls. Approximately one-quarter of those with depression and dementia had apathy symptoms compared to

14% of those with dementia only and 0% in the control group. Forsell, Jorm, Fratiglioni, Grut, and Winbald (1993) used a population-based sample to examine how depression phenomenology changed over time. Investigating 213 persons with possible dementia, 11% met the criteria of the *Diagnostic and Statistical Manual of Mental Disorders,* third edition, revised (*DSM-III-R*; American Psychiatric Association [APA], 1987) for major depressive disorder. A principal components analysis was carried out on nine categories of depressive symptoms. Mood disturbance was found to be the most prominent symptom in those with mild dementia and depression, whereas apathy was the most prominent symptom in those with moderate to severe dementia.

Mast (2002) performed a methodologically advanced analysis of the phenomenology of depression in dementia with the goal of identifying unique patterns of symptoms endorsement associated with cognitive impairment. A series of multiple indicators multiple causes (MIMIC) models were estimated from data for 580 geriatric rehabilitation patients with varying levels of cognitive impairment. The MIMIC model methodology combines confirmatory factor analysis with time response concepts and, in the current context, allows for examination of the impact of cognitive impairment at two distinct levels of analysis: the impact of cognitive impairment on global depression severity (i.e., second-order latent factor) and on the probability of endorsing specific symptom clusters (i.e., first-order latent factors; technical descriptions of the MIMIC model methodology can be found in Muthen, 1989; geriatric assessment applications of the MIMIC model can be found in Mast & Lichtenberg, 2000; Mast, MacNeill, & Lichtenberg, 2002). The results from these analyses indicted that greater cognitive impairment was associated with more severe depressive symptoms and was uniquely associated with symptoms of social withdrawal and apathy, even after controlling for the global depression severity effect.

Clinical Implications

- Depressive symptoms in persons with dementia are most likely to consist of mood and/or symptoms of apathy/withdrawal.

Summary

There is considerable evidence that mood and apathy/withdrawal are the most prominent symptoms in those with both depression and dementia. These findings have important implications. As demonstrated by many researchers (Chemerinski et al., 2001; Mast, 2002), mood is one area that persons with dementia self-report accurately. These findings support the notion of using both self-report and informant/observer-based report. In addition, the fact that mood and apathy/withdrawal are prominent symptoms in dementia is consistent with the vascular depression hypothesis. In our review of the data for that hypothesis earlier in the chapter, there was considerable evidence that white matter changes were disrupting the frontal subcortical circuitry of the brain. Sulzer, Levin, Mahler, High, and Cummings (1993) reported on data that was also consistent with the vascular depression hypothesis in that patients with VaD appear to have higher rates of depression than do patients with AD.

ASSESSMENT OF DEPRESSION IN DEMENTIA

Depression is a syndrome, a constellation of symptoms that potentially has many etiologies. In this chapter, we are focused on depression in persons with dementia and have discussed two conceptual frameworks that help explain depression onset—the vascular depression and activity limitation frameworks. The *Diagnostic and Statistical Manual of Mental Disorders,* fourth edition (*DSM-IV*; APA, 1994), codes depression in persons with dementia as 290.13—dementia with depressed mood, including those with major depressive disorder. Implicit in this diagnosis is the consideration of minor depressive disorder. Minor depression is listed in the *DSM-IV* appendix but is not currently a *DSM-IV*-coded diagnosis. Minor depression, however, is subsumed under 290.13, the code for dementia with depressed mood as defined previously. The major distinctions between major and minor depression are typically not found concerning mood but the number of vegetative symptoms that are experienced (sleep, appetite, psychomotor slowing, etc.). The scales discussed in the following sections were created to assess for depression severity in those with major depression. The scales, however, appear to be useful in detecting minor depression as well.

Clinician Rating Scales

Clinician rating scales are typically completed after interactions with persons with dementia, with family and/or professional caregivers, and after clinician observation of behavior. In many ways, then, these assessments may be the most complete and objective. Limitations of these scales, however, include:

- Trained raters are needed.
- Statements and views of the person with dementia are always overridden by caregiver report.
- The scales were created to assess severity of major depressive disorders.
- It has not yet been well articulated on how to use the scales to assess minor depression.

The two most commonly used rating scales are the Hamilton and the Cornell scales. We include a brief description of those, along with the Consortium to Establish a Registry for Alzheimer's Disease (CERAD) scale, which taps into a more focused domain of affective functioning.

Hamilton Rating Scale for Depression

The Hamilton Rating Scale for Depression (HRSD; Hamilton, 1967), the gold standard in most outcome research on depression in dementia, has been used the longest with older persons with dementia. Several versions of the HRSD have been used. The most common version is a 17-item scale on which each item is rated on a three- or five-point scale, with the total score resulting from summing the 17 items. Scores of 24 are indicative of a major depression. Williams (1988) developed the Structured Interview Guide for the HRSD to address noted reliability and validity problems. Although the scale was created to assess for change in severity of depression, it has commonly been used as a diagnostic tool with good clinical utility (Edelstein, Kalish, Drozdick, & McKee, 1999).

Cornell Scale for Depression in Dementia

The Cornell Scale is a 19-item measure whose items were constructed so that they could be completed based on interviews and direct observation (Alexopoulos, Abrams, Young, & Shamoian, 1988). This rating scale was created especially for assessment of depression severity in dementia patients. The authors examined the literature for depression phenomenology common in dementia patients and then elicited feedback from 11 experts on the categories they chose. The rater is to first interview the dementia patient's caregiver in an in-depth manner and then briefly interview the patient. Internal consistency and interrater reliability were reported as strong in the validation study and in several more recent studies. One final advantage of the Cornell Scale was its validation against the criteria for minor depression. Katz (1998) observed that almost all of the Cornell Scale items could be mapped onto the Hamilton Rating Scale items, thus making the instruments comparable in many ways. Specifically, he noted that 17 of the 19 items from the Cornell Scale can be mapped onto the Hamilton Scale.

Consortium to Establish a Registry for Alzheimer's Disease (CERAD) Behavioral Rating Scale

The caregiver informants of 303 persons with dementia from 16 medical centers across the nation were interviewed to establish a common behavioral rating scale for the Alzheimer's disease research centers (Tariot et al., 1995). Two raters evaluated 104 of these persons independently so that interrater reliability could be assessed. Mean MMSE scores for the demented participants was 15.5, and the mean duration of the dementia was almost six years. This effort was not directed at creating a depression scale but, rather, creating a scale that captured the wide range of behavioral problems exhibited by persons with dementia. Nevertheless, emerging from a factor analysis conducted on 34 of the original 55 items was a factor of depressive features. These included items of hopelessness, poor self-esteem, wish to die, sad appearance, guilt, and anxiety. Jacobs, Strauss, Patterson, and Mack (1998) investigated how well the CERAD Behavior Rating Scale characterized depression. In a sample of 29 depressed and 40 nondepressed persons with AD, the depression and anxiety items on the Behavioral Rating Scale were significantly different between the groups. Overall classification was 70%, with a 59% sensitivity and a 78% specificity. Thus, the scale appears useful as a brief screening device.

Cautionary Note

Katz (1998) urged clinicians and investigators to be aware of factors present in caregiver raters that may lessen the validity of depressive symptom reports. The bulk of this focus has been on how the caregiver's own depression affects his or her ratings of the person with dementia. This has been an area of substantial research in the caregiving literature, but it is only touched on here. Neundorfer et al. (2001) performed a seven-year longitudinal study of 353 caregivers of persons with dementia who remained in the community throughout the study. Sixty percent of the sample had between 2 and 10 data points on caregiver depression as measured by the

Center for Epidemiological Studies-Depression (CES-D), as well as the demented person's depression as measured by the mood-related scale, Behavior Rating Scale for Dementia. The authors reported that the mood of the person with dementia was modestly related to caregiver depression ($r = .16$, $p < .05$) and that caregiver increase in depression can increase the depression and instrumental activities of daily living (IADL) abilities of the person with dementia. Specifically, the acceleration or increase of the caregiver's depression was predicted by the acceleration in the dementia person's dependency in basic and advanced ADL abilities.

Teri and Truax (1994) used an experimental design to assess how well caregivers with depression could rate depression in persons with dementia. Caregiver depression was measured by the CES-D, and depression in persons with dementia was rated by the Hamilton Depression Rating Scale. Caregivers were also randomly assigned to watch a five-minute tape of actors simulating behaviors from either a depressed person with dementia or a nondepressed person with dementia. Caregivers were accurately able to rate the tapes, and their own level of depression did not correlate with their ratings. Similar to Neundorfer, caregivers' own depression was related to depression in persons with dementia ($r = .34$, $p < .05$). Although care recipient and caregiver depression are significantly related, it does not appear, in general, that this affects the accuracy of caregiver ratings. These findings were supported in another investigation of how well caregiver ratings matched diagnostic interviews by trained psychiatrists (Chemerinski et al., 2001).

Finally, Allen, Esser, Tyriver, and Striepling (2000) reported that when using Certified Nursing Assistant reports of depressive symptoms based on the Cornell Scale, no differences were noted between those carrying a diagnosis of depression and dementia and those simply having a diagnosis of dementia. This finding points out the importance of being aware of the level of training that raters have in administration and scoring for any rating scale.

Self-Report Measures: Geriatric Depression Scale (GDS)

While there are many self-report depression measures that have been used with older adults (e.g., CES-D, Zung, Beck), the Geriatric Depression Scale is by far the one with the most applicability to older persons with dementia. Historically, the usefulness of the GDS has been called into question. Burke, Houston, Boust, and Roccaforte (1989) and Kafonek et al. (1989)

reported that the clinical utility of the GDS was poor in long-term care residents with dementia. Lesher and Berryhill (1994) and Parmelee, Katz, and Lawton (1989) provided evidence that the GDS was both internally consistent and clinically valid in individuals with mild to moderate dementia.

Two more recent studies have provided further support for the importance and validity of using the report of persons with dementia in any evaluation of mood. In a study mentioned earlier (Espiritu et al., 2001), dementia patients' self-report of depression was a unique and significant predictor of the caregiver reports of patients' IADL scores. These findings held even when the sample was further divided into the more severely cognitively impaired (MMSE < 15). Perhaps the most intriguing findings about the GDS are the ones made by Mast (2002). The internal consistency of the GDS was examined among 580 geriatric patients with four levels of cognitive impairment as defined by the Mattis Dementia Rating Scale (Mattis, 1988): cognitively intact (DRS = 126+), mild cognitive impairment (DRS 103–125), moderate impairment (DRS 90–102), and severely impaired (DRS < 90). Surprisingly, the internal consistency did not decline as cognitive impairment increased. Conbach's alpha estimates were as follows: .86 (intact), .87 (mild), .87 (moderate), and .88 (severe). These findings support the reliability of the GDS among patients with severe cognitive impairment.

Chemerinski et al. (2001) investigated how well Alzheimer's patients themselves could report their own mood. Patients with dementia (both with and without depression) had a mean MMSE score of 19, although the standard deviation was large (6). The depressed patients (as diagnosed by psychiatrists) themselves rated their own mood as significantly worse than those persons with dementia but without depression ($t = 6$, $p < .00001$). This finding is consistent with Mast's (2002) and Espiritu et al.'s (2001) finding that self-report depression information offers unique and valuable clinical information.

Clinical Implications

- Self-report information concerning mood states is generally valid in persons with dementia.
- Family caregiver reports of depression in persons with dementia are typically valid, even when caregiver is depressed.
- It is recommended that both informant ratings/observer scales and self-report information on depression be gathered and used.

NONPHARMACOLOGICAL TREATMENT FOR DEPRESSION IN DEMENTIA

Nonpharmacological treatment for depression in dementia has focused on the dyad of both the caregiver and the person with dementia. In a randomized controlled trial of short-term supportive counseling aimed at reducing caregiver burden (not depression in persons with dementia), Mittelman, Ferris, Shulman, Steinberg, and Levin (1996) reported that the intervention led to delayed nursing home admissions for the person with dementia.

The most rigorous research on improving depression in persons with dementia through nonpharmacological treatments comes from Teri and colleagues at the University of Washington. This work is based heavily on Lewinsohn's behavioral theory of depression. Lewinsohn and Graf (1973) reported on cross-sectional data of younger, middle age, and older adults who kept a record of mood ratings and daily events. The authors noted that mood fluctuated widely and was significantly related to the number of pleasurable events that individuals engaged in. In summary, the behavioral theory of depression states that depression is caused by an excess of aversive events and a dearth of pleasant ones. Clarke and Lewinsohn (1989) published the "Coping with Depression Course," which focused on teaching individuals three basic facts. First, mood is not a stable experience, but it fluctuates. Second, the fluctuations in mood are largely directly under the control of the depressed individual. Third, when changes are made to incorporate more pleasure into life on a daily basis, mood improves and depression remits. Zeiss and Lewinsohn (1986) added some guidelines on how to adapt behavioral treatment for depression to meet the needs of older adults. They stressed the importance of providing a clear rationale for each task and to being sensitive to pleasant events for elders.

Teri and colleagues extended the work of behavioral treatment for depression by using it with Alzheimer's patients. Teri and Logsdon (1991) began by creating the Pleasant Events Schedule-AD, a specific set of potentially satisfying events of persons with AD. Teri and Uomoto (1991) then published some case studies demonstrating in an AB design that, both at baseline and at follow-up, depression in persons with dementia was related to number of events and length of time spent with pleasant events. The authors were encouraged by the fact that by working directly with caregivers, they could help increase the amount of pleasant events for persons with dementia.

Teri, Logsdon, Uomoto, and McCurry (1997) extended this research through a clinical intervention study, which compared behavioral treatment, support group intervention, and a wait-list control group. In all, 42 caregivers of depressed persons with dementia received one of two behavioral therapy groups (pleasant events focus or problem-solving focus), 10 caregivers were in the support group, and 20 were on the wait-list control group. Depression, as measured by the Hamilton Rating Scale, improved significantly for depressed persons with dementia in both of the behavior therapy groups, whereas it did not change in either the support or wait-list groups. Interestingly, there was a corresponding improvement in caregiver depression as well. Thirty-two of the 42 participants completed a six-month follow-up, and treatment gains were maintained.

A similar line of research has been conducted with cognitively intact and mild to moderately demented individuals in medical rehabilitation (Lichtenberg, Kimbarow, Wall, Roth, & MacNeil, 1998). This group adapted behavioral treatment techniques so that they could be incorporated into occupational therapy sessions or into psychotherapy sessions led by the psychologist. Mood ratings, relaxation, and engagement in a pleasant event activity were carried out for 30 to 45 minutes during each occupational therapy session. In all, 26 participants received behavioral treatment, and 13 individuals received standard care (no psychological services). Participants' depression was evaluated at baseline and at discharge. The treatment groups demonstrated significant improvements with depression, as measured by self-report Geriatric Depression Scale scores, whereas the no-treatment group did not.

Clinical Implications

- Nonpharmacological treatments for depression in dementia appear promising.
- Teaching behavioral therapy techniques to family or nonmental health caregivers appears an effective strategy for depression treatment of depressed persons with dementia.
- Effectiveness of nonpharmacological treatments, as with any treatment, requires longitudinal assessments.

REFERENCES

Alexopoulos, G., Meyers, B., Young, R., Campbell, S., Silbersweig, D., & Charlson, R. (1997). Vascular depression hypothesis. *Archives of General Psychiatry, 54,* 915–923.

Alexopoulos, G., Meyers, B., Young, R., Kakuma, T., Silbersweig, D., & Charlson, M. (1997). Clinically defined vascular depression. *American Journal of Psychiatry, 154*(4), 562–565.

Alexopoulos, G., Meyers, S., Young, R., Mattis, S., & Kakuma, T. (1993). The course of geriatric depression with "reversible dementia": A controlled study. *American Journal of Psychiatry, 150,* 1693–1699.

Alexopoulos, G. S., Abrams, R. C., Young, R. C., & Shamoian, C. A. (1988). Cornell Scale for Depression in Dementia. *Biological Psychiatry, 23,* 271–284.

Allen, B., Esser, W., Tyriver, C., & Striepling, A. (2000). The behavioral assessment of depression for people with dementia. *American Journal of Alzheimer's Disease and Other Dementias, 15,* 303–307.

American Psychiatric Association. (1994). *Diagnostic and statistical manual of mental disorders* (4th ed.). Washington, DC: Author.

Ballard, C., McKeith, I., O'Brien, J., Kalaria, R., Jaros, E., Ince, P., et al. (2000). Neuropathological substrates of dementia and depression in vascular dementia, with a particular focus on cases with small infarct volumes. *Dementia and Geriatric Cognitive Disorders, 11,* 59–65.

Ballard, C., Patel, A., Solis, M., & Wilcock, G. (1996). A one-year follow up study of depression in dementia sufferers. *British Journal of Psychiatry, 168,* 287–291.

Barber, R., Scheltens, P., Gholkar, A., Ballard, C., McKeith, I., Ince, P., et al. (1999). White matter lesions on magnetic resonance imaging in dementia with Lewy bodies, Alzheimer's disease, vascular dementia and normal aging. *Journal of Neurology, Neurosurgery, and Psychiatry, 67,* 66–72.

Bondi, M. W., Salmon, D. P., Galasko, D., Thomas, R. G., & Thal, L. J. (1999). Neuropsychological function and apolipoprotein E genotype in the preclinical detection of Alzheimer's disease. *Psychology and Aging, 2,* 295–303.

Burke, W. J., Houston, M. J., Boust, S. J., & Roccaforte, W. H. (1989). Use of the Geriatric Depression Scale in dementia of the Alzheimer type. *Journal of the American Geriatrics Society, 37,* 856–860.

Chemerinski, E., Petracca, G., Sabe, L., Kremer, J., & Starkstein, S. (2001). The specificity of depressive symptoms in patients with Alzheimer's disease. *American Journal of Psychiatry, 158,* 68–72.

Clarke, G., & Lewinsohn, P. (1989). The Coping with Depression Course: A group psychoeducational intervention for unipolar depression. *Behavior Change, 6*(2), 54–69.

Coffey, C., Figiel, G., Djang, W., & Weiner, R. (1990). Subcortical hyperintensity on magnetic resonance imaging: A comparison of normal and depressed elderly subjects. *American Journal of Psychiatry, 147*(2), 187–189.

Devanand, D., Sano, S., & Tang, M. (1996). Depressed mood and the incidence of Alzheimer's disease in the elderly living in the community. *Archives of General Psychiatry, 53,* 175–182.

Edelstein, B., Kalish, K. D., Drozdick, L. W., & McKee, D. R. (1999). Assessment of depression and bereavement in older adults. In P. A. Lichtenberg (Ed.), *Handbook of assessment in clinical gerontology* (pp. 11–58). New York: Wiley.

Espiritu, D. E., Rashid, H., Mast, B. T., Fitzgerald, J., Steinberg, J., & Lichtenberg, P. A. (2001). The relationship of self-reported depression and cognition to functional abilities in African American elders with Alzheimer's disease. *International Journal of Geriatric Psychiatry, 16,* 1098–1103.

Forsell, Y., Jorm, A., Fratiglioni, L., Grut, M., & Winbald, B. (1993). Application of *DSM-III-R* criteria for major depressive episode to elderly subjects with and without dementia. *American Journal of Psychiatry, 150*(8), 1199–1202.

Gerety, M. B., Williams, J. W., Mulrow, C. D., Cornell, J. E., Kadri, A. A., Rosenberg, J., et al. (1994). Performance of case-finding tools for depression in the nursing home: Influence of clinical and functional characteristics and selection of optimal threshold scores. *Journal of the American Geriatrics Society, 42,* 1103–1109.

Hamilton, M. (1967). Development of a rating scale for primary depressive illness. *British Journal of Social and Clinical Psychology, 6,* 278–296.

Hargrave, R., Reed, B., & Mungas, D. (2000). Depressive syndromes and functional disability in dementia. *Journal of Geriatric Psychiatry, 13,* 72–77.

Jacobs, M., Strauss, M., Patterson, M., & Mack, J. (1998). Characterization of depression in Alzheimer's disease by the CERAD Behavior Rating Scale for Dementia (BRSD). *American Journal of Geriatric Psychiatry, 6,* 53–58.

Janzig, J., Teunisse, R., Bouwens, P., Hof, M., & Zitman, F. (2000). The course of depression in elderly subjects with and without dementia. *Journal of Affective Disorders, 57,* 49–54.

Kafonek, S. K., Ettinger, W. H., Roca, R., Kittner, S., Taylor, N., & German, P. S. (1989). Instruments for screening for depression and dementia in a long term care facility. *Journal of the American Geriatrics Society, 37,* 29–34.

Katz, I. R. (1998). Diagnosis and treatment of depression in patients with Alzheimer's disease and other dementias. *Journal of Clinical Psychiatry, 59,* 38–44.

Lazarus, L., Newton, N., Cohler, B., Lesser, J., & Schweon, C. (1987). Frequency and presentation of depressive symptoms in patients with primary degenerative dementia. *American Journal of Psychiatry, 144*(1), 41–45.

Lesher, E. L., & Berryhill, J. S. (1994). Validation of the Geriatric Depression Scale—Short Form among inpatients. *Journal of Clinical Psychology, 50,* 256–260.

Lewinsohn, P., & Graf, M. (1973). Pleasant activities and depression. *Journal of Consulting and Clinical Psychology, 41*(2), 261–268.

Li, Y. S., Meyer, J., & Thornby, J. (2001a). Depressive symptoms among cognitively normal versus cognitively impaired elderly subjects. *International Journal of Geriatric Psychiatry, 16,* 455–461.

Li, Y. S., Meyer, J., & Thornby, J. (2001b). Longitudinal follow-up of depressive symptoms among normal versus cognitively impaired elderly. *International Journal of Geriatric Psychiatry, 16,* 718–727.

Lichtenberg, P. A. (1994). *A guide to psychological practice in geriatric long term care.* Binghamton, NY: Haworth Press.

Lichtenberg, P., Kimbarow, M., Wall, J., Roth, E., & MacNeil, S. (1998). *Depression in geriatric medical and nursing home patients: A treatment manual.* Detroit, MI: Wayne State University Press.

Lichtenberg, P., Ross, T., Mills, S., & Manning, C. (1995). The relationship between depression and cognition in older adults: A cross-validation study. *Journals of Gerontology: Series B, Psychological Sciences and Social Sciences, 50B*(1), P25–P32.

Massman, P., Delis, D., Butters, N., Dupont, R., & Gillin, J. C. (1992). The subcortical dysfunction hypothesis of memory deficits in depression: Neuropsychological validation in a subgroup of patients. *Journal of Clinical and Experimental Neuropsychology, 14*(5), 687–706.

Mast, B. T. (2002). *An examination of the post-stroke and vascular depression hypotheses among geriatric rehabilitation patients.* Doctoral dissertation, Wayne State University, Detroit, MI.

Mast, B. T., & Lichtenberg, P. A. (2000). Assessment of functional abilities among geriatric patients: A mimic model of the Functional Independence Measure. *Rehabilitation Psychology, 45,* 49–64.

Mast, B. T., MacNeill, S. E., & Lichtenberg, P. A. (2002). A MIMIC model approach to research in geriatric neuropsychology: The case of vascular dementia. *Aging, Neuropsychology, and Cognition, 9,* 21–37.

Mast, B. T., MacNeill, S. E., & Lichtenberg, P. A. (in press). Post stroke and vascular depression in geriatric rehabilitation patients. *American Journal of Geriatric Psychiatry.*

Mattis, S. (1988). *Dementia Rating Scale: Professional manual.* Odessa, FL: Psychological Assessment Resources.

Menon, A., Gruber-Baldini, A., Hebel, R., Kaup, B., Loreck, D., Zimmerman, S., et al. (2001). Relationship between aggressive behaviors and depression among nursing home residents with dementia. *International Journal of Geriatric Psychiatry, 16,* 139–146.

Mittelman, M., Ferris, S., Shulman, E., Steinberg, G., & Levin, B. (1996). A family intervention to delay nursing home placement of patients with Alzheimer disease. *Journal of the American Medical Association, 276*(21), 1725–1731.

Morris, J. C., Storandt, M., Miller, J. P., McKeel, D. W., Price, J. L., Rubin, E. H., et al. (2001). Mild cognitive impairment represents early-stage Alzheimer disease. *Archives of Neurology, 58,* 397–405.

Muthen, B. O. (1989). Latent variable modeling in heterogenous populations. *Psychometrika, 54,* 557–585.

Nanna, M., Lichtenberg, P. A., Abuda-Bella, D., & Barth, J. T. (1997). The role of cognition and depression in predicting functional outcome in geriatric medical rehabilitation patients. *Journal of Applied Gerontology, 16,* 120–132.

Neundorfer, M., McClendon, M., Smyth, K., Stuckey, J., Strauss, M., & Patterson, M. (2001). A longitudinal study of the relationship between levels of depression among persons with Alzheimer's disease and levels of depression among their family caregivers. *Journals of Gerontology: Series B, Psychological Sciences and Social Sciences, 56B,* P301–P313.

O'Brien, J., Desmond, P., Ames, D., Schweitzer, I., Harrigan, S., & Tress, B. (1996). A magnetic resonance imaging study of white matter lesions in depression and Alzheimer's disease. *British Journal of Psychiatry, 168,* 477–485.

Parmelee, P. A., Katz, I. R., & Lawton, M. P. (1989). Psychometric properties of the Geriatric Depression Scale among the institutionalized aged. *Psychological Assessment, 1,* 331–338.

Patterson, M., Schnell, A., Martin, R., Mendez, M., Smyth, K., & Whitehouse, P. (1990). Assessment of behavioral and affective symptoms in Alzheimer's disease. *Journal of Geriatric Psychiatry and Neurology, 3,* 21–30.

Raskind, M. A. (1998). The clinical interface of depression and dementia. *Journal of Clinical Psychiatry, 59,* 9–12.

Riley, K. P., & Snowden, D. A. (1999). The challenges and successes of aging: Findings from the Nun study. *Advances in Medical Psychotherapy, 10,* 1–12.

Ross, L. K., Arnsberger, P., & Fox, P. J. (1998). The relationship between cognitive functioning and disease severity with depression in dementia of the Alzheimer's type. *Aging and Mental Health, 2*(4), 319–327.

Simpson, S., Allen, H., Tomenson, B., & Burns, A. (1998). Neurological correlates of depressive symptoms in Alzheimer's disease and vascular dementia. *Journal of Affective Disorders, 53,* 129–136.

Snowden, D. A., Griner, L. H., Mortimer, J. A., Riley, K. P., Greiner, P. A., & Markesbery, W. R. (1997). Brain infarction and the clinical expression of Alzheimer disease. *Journal of the American Medical Association, 277,* 813–817.

Speck, C., Kukull, W., Brenner, D., Bowen, J., McCormick, W., Teri, L., et al. (1995). History of depression as a risk factor for Alzheimer's disease. *Epidemiology, 6,* 366–369.

Starkstein, S. (2000). Apathy and withdrawal. *International Psychogeriatrics, 12*(1), 135–137.

Starkstein, S., Chemerinski, E., Sabe, L., Kuzis, G., Petracca, G., Teson, A., et al. (1997). Prospective longitudinal study of depression and anosognosia in Alzheimer's disease. *British Journal of Psychiatry, 171,* 47–52.

Stewart, R., Prince, M., Richards, M., Brayne, C., & Mann, A. (2001). Stroke, vascular risk factors and depression. *British Journal of Psychiatry, 178,* 23–28.

Sulzer, D., Levin, H., Mahler, M., High, W., & Cummings, J. (1993). A comparison of psychiatric symptoms in vascular dementia and Alzheimer's disease. *American Journal of Psychiatry, 150*(12), 1806–1812.

Tariot, P., Mack, J., Patterson, M., Edland, S., Weiner, M., Fillenbaum, G., et al. (1995). The Behavior Rating Scale for Dementia of the Consortium to Establish a Registry for Alzheimer's Disease. *American Journal of Psychiatry, 152*(9), 1349–1357.

Teri, L., & Logsdon, R. (1991). Identifying pleasant activities for Alzheimer's disease patients: The Pleasant Events Schedule-AD. *Gerontologist, 31*(1), 124–127.

Teri, L., Logsdon, R., Uomoto, J., & McCurry, S. (1997). Behavioral treatment of depression in dementia patients: A controlled clinical trial. *Journals of Gerontology: Series B, Psychological Sciences and Social Sciences, 52B*(4), P159–P166.

Teri, L., & Truax, P. (1994). Assessment of depression in dementia patients: Association of caregivers mood with depression ratings. *Gerontologist, 34*(4), 231–234.

Teri, L., & Uomoto, J. (1991). Reducing excess disability in dementia patients: Training caregivers to manage patient depression. *Clinical Gerontologist, 10*(4), 49–63.

Verhey, F., & Visser, P. (2000). Phenomenology of depression in dementia. *International Psychogeriatrics, 12*(1), 129–134.

Visser, P. J., Verhey, F. R., Ponds, R., Kester, A., & Jolles, J. (2000). Distinction between preclinical Alzheimer's disease and depression. *Journal of the American Geriatrics Society, 48,* 479–484.

Wefel, J. S., Hoyt, B. D., & Massman, P. J. (2000). Neuropsychological functioning in depressed versus non-depressed participants with Alzheimer's disease. *Neuropsychology, 14,* 249–257.

Williams, J. B. (1988). A structured interview guide for the Hamilton Depression Rating Scale. *Archives of General Psychiatry, 45,* 742–747.

Williamson, G. (1992). Physical illness and symptoms of depression among elderly outpatients. *Psychology and Aging, 7*(3), 343–351.

Williamson, G., & Schulz, R. (1995). Activity restriction mediates the association between pain and depressed affect: A study of younger and older adult cancer patients. *Psychology and Aging, 10,*(3), 369–378.

Yochim, B., & Lichtenberg, P. A. (2002). Cerebrovascular risk factors and depressed mood in inner city older adults. *Clinical Psychologist.*

Zeiss, A., & Lewinsohn, P. (1986). Adapting behavioral treatment for depression to meet the needs of the elderly. *Clinical Psychologist, 39,* 98–100.

Zubenko, G. (2000). Neurobiology of major depression in Alzheimer's disease. *International Psychogeriatrics, 12*(1), 217–230.

CHAPTER 12

Psychiatric Assessment and Treatment of Nonpsychotic Behavioral Disturbances in Dementia

Anton P. Porsteinsson, J. Michael Ryan, M. Saleem Ismail, and
Pierre N. Tariot

In addition to core cognitive and functional deficits, neuropsychiatric
symptoms, emotional disorders, and behavioral alterations are ubiquitous
among patients with dementia syndromes. Clinicians should be concerned
with the behavioral signs and symptoms of Alzheimer's disease (AD) and
other dementias because they are prevalent, distressing to the patient, and
upsetting to caregivers. Often they contribute significantly to the need for
institutional care. A previous cross-sectional multicenter study of several
hundred outpatients with AD found that no patient had been free of behavioral signs or symptoms in the preceding month (Tariot, Mack, et al.,
1995). A population-based study of dementia found a point prevalence of
psychopathology of more than 60% and asserted that the lifetime risk of
psychopathology for a patient with dementia approached 100% (Lyketsos
et al., 2000). These figures make clear that it is important to know how to
recognize and manage the behavioral manifestations of dementia.

Behavioral and psychological signs and symptoms of dementia are heterogeneous and can be difficult to categorize, even for the expert. However,
clinical experience and studies teach us that certain symptom patterns can
be discerned; a relatively recent consensus conference on the issue asserted
in a summary statement issued by the International Psychogeriatric Association that behavioral signs and symptoms occur commonly and can include
observable motor and verbal behaviors as well as psychological phenomena
(Finkel, Costa e Silva, Cohen, Miller, & Sartorius, 1996). These signs and
symptoms, summarized in Table 12.1, do not meet the usual criteria for

Table 12.1   Summary of Literature Regarding Psychopathology of Dementia*

	Range (%)	Median (%)
Disturbed affect/mood	0–86	19
Disturbed ideation	10–73	33.5
Altered perception		
Hallucinations	21–49	28
Misperceptions	1–49	23
Agitation		
Global	10–90	44
Wandering	0–50	18
Aggression		
Verbal	11–51	24
Physical	0–46	14.3
Resistive/uncooperative	27–65	44
Anxiety	0–50	31.8
Withdrawn/passive/behavior	21–88	61
Vegetative behaviors		
Sleep	0–47	27
Diet/appetite	12.5–77	34

*Percentage of patients affected among studies reviewed.

Adapted from "The Psychopathology of Dementia," by P. Tariot and L. Blazina, 1993. In *Handbook of Dementing Illnesses,* J. Morris, ed., New York: Marcel Dekker, pp. 461–475.

major psychiatric disorders and outside of psychosis or depression in AD, they tend to occur in a *subsyndromal* fashion. As our understanding of these phenomena improves, the language will sharpen. The figures in the table provide a rough estimate of the likelihood of a patient's experiencing a particular sign or symptom. These features tend to fluctuate in individuals over time, and there is tremendous heterogeneity among individuals. For instance, the study of Devanand et al. (1997) found that affective symptoms tend to fluctuate considerably over a year and psychotic symptoms somewhat less so, while agitation tends to emerge as the illness progresses and tends to persist once it has emerged. The main points, however, are that patterns of signs and symptoms can be predicted, and there is a significant degree of heterogeneity among and within patients.

While there is not a uniform relationship between severity of dementia and types of behavioral disturbance, some general trends can be discerned. Depressive and anxious symptoms are relatively common in the mild stages, as are social withdrawal and lack of initiative, which may be interpreted as manifestations of depression but actually might be better understood as apathy. Irritability, delusions (frequently paranoid in nature), wandering, and agitation are most common in moderate stages of illness. In advanced stages, socially inappropriate or disinhibited behavior, repetitive purposeless actions, aggression, or marked apathy can be seen (Jost & Grossberg, 1996). Longitudinal studies have suggested that depressive features tend to fluctuate over a period of months to years and psychotic features somewhat less so, whereas agitation tends to be linked with disease progression and persists once it has emerged (Devanand et al., 1997).

Although our understanding of the underlying neurobiology of AD is advancing rapidly, the etiology and pathophysiology of behavioral and psychological signs and symptoms is far less well understood. The literature is inconsistent most likely because of methodological problems, including qualification and quantification of the behavioral substrates and the fleeting nature of behavioral symptomatology. This suggests that the neurobiological changes of behavior are dynamic, involving biochemical, structural, genetic, and environmental factors rather than static causes alone. It is also highly likely that certain behaviors reflect unmet needs or emotions as well as misapprehension of the behavior of others or of the environment based on cognitive disturbance. Dementia diagnosis may also be an important factor, as evidence mounts that patients with AD, vascular dementia (VaD), dementia with Lewy bodies, dementia of Parkinson's disease, and frontotemporal dementia have varying clinical presentations. In conclusion, these complex behavioral phenomena will probably be understood best as multidetermined.

Agitation is the paradigm of psychopathology addressed in this chapter because the principles pertaining to treatment of agitation are easily applied to treatment of other behavioral signs and symptoms. In caring for a patient with dementia and agitation, we rely on a systematic approach to evaluation and management that has been articulated previously (Loy, Tariot, & Rosenquist, 1999; Rosenquist, Tariot, & Loy, 2000; Tariot, 1999). The key general elements in this approach are summarized in Table 12.2, which emphasizes clarification of target symptoms, ruling out delirium or occult major psychiatric diagnoses, and creatively addressing possible social, environmental, or behavioral remedies. There are excellent reviews of nonpharmacological interventions in other chapters in this book. Only in emergent situations or when these nonpharmacologic interventions have failed should medications be deployed.

Table 12.2   Summary of General Principles to the Approach of Agitation and Aggression in Patients with Dementia

1. Define target symptoms.
2. Establish or revisit medical diagnoses.
3. Establish or revisit neuropsychiatric diagnoses.
4. Assess and reverse aggravating factors.
5. Adapt to specific cognitive deficits.
6. Identify relevant psychosocial factors.
7. Educate caregivers.
8. Employ behavior management principles.
9. Use psychotropic medications for specific psychiatric syndromes.
10. For remaining problems, consider symptomatic pharmacotherapy:
    - Use psychobehavioral metaphor.
    - Use medication class relevant to metaphor and with empirical evidence of efficacy.
    - Start low, go slow.
    - Avoid toxicity.
    - Use lowest effective dose.
    - Withdraw after appropriate period, observe for relapse.
    - Serial trials sometimes needed.

Adapted from "Treatment of Agitation in Dementia," by P. N. Tariot, 1999, *Journal of Clinical Psychiatry, 60*(Suppl. 8), pp. 11–20.

SELECTING A MEDICATION

Because there is little empirical evidence to guide decision making in selecting a medication, we begin by formulating a working hypothesis as to the nature of the patient's psychopathology where the target symptom pattern is roughly analogous to a more typical drug-responsive syndrome. We have previously termed this the *psychobehavioral metaphor* (Leibovici & Tariot, 1988), a phrase that emphasizes the heuristic and tentative nature of the process. We then select a psychotropic to match the dominant target symptoms. In an effort to expand on this process, the following discussion provides examples of some typical psychobehavioral metaphors. If the agitation is associated with delusions of theft or harm, we might select an antipsychotic. If it is associated with tearfulness, social withdrawal, or preoccupation with themes of loss or death, we might consider an antidepressant first. If it is associated with impulsivity, aggression, lability of mood, and/or excessive motor activity, we might consider a mood stabilizer first.

While clinical studies have not validated this approach, two major practice guidelines for treatment of agitation rest on the assumption that matching target symptoms to drug class is, in fact, appropriate. One was based strictly on published data (American Psychiatric Association [APA], 1997), while the other was based on expert clinical consensus (Alexopoulos, Silver, Kahn, Frances, & Carpenter, 1998). After we select a class of medications, we choose from within it one for which there is reasonable evidence of efficacy and limited safety and tolerability problems. A simple dosing regimen is helpful; optimal dosing in general is kept to one or two times daily. After starting treatment, monitoring treatment effects is based on the clear baseline that has been established. Usually, the best we can hope for is a reduction in the frequency or severity of symptoms rather than a full resolution. It may be helpful to ask the caregiver to keep a record of the frequency and severity of target behaviors. Several scales are available for this purpose, which are reviewed in other chapters. A general principle is "Start low, go slow." Medication is generally started at low doses and gradually increased until there is evidence of either clear benefit or early toxicity. When a treatment trial is positive, it is reasonable to continue treatment for a period of weeks or months and at some point consider tapering the medication and reevaluating symptoms. Where a medication appears ineffective, it is reasonable to perform an empiric trial in reverse, tapering the medication and watching for problems during withdrawal. That may reveal behavioral problems that were actually better during the treatment period. Remember that no one medication or class is effective for every patient, and it is often difficult to find something that achieves complete remission for a particular patient. These tend to be the patients who undergo serial trials of increasingly unconventional therapies and who receive combination therapy.

MAJOR CLASSES OF PSYCHOTROPICS

Safety, tolerability, and efficacy are the major determinants for the selection of a specific medication for a specific patient; these issues are the focus of the rest of the chapter. We have previously written comprehensive reviews of the available literature, with complete tables and references (Loy et al., 1999; Rosenquist et al., 2000). The thrust here is to highlight the major points as we see them now. Bear in mind that the field is changing quickly and new studies are emerging regularly that may have the potential to alter our opinion of certain agents or classes.

Conventional Antipsychotics

Evidence from two meta-analytical studies of conventional antipsychotics illustrates that the effects of these agents were consistent and modest, that no single agent showed superiority, and that side effects tended to emerge in a predictable fashion and ultimately define selection of a particular agent. Both reviews examined the use of conventional antipsychotics for behavioral disturbance rather than for specific symptoms or psychoses. Schneider, Pollock, and Lyness (1990) reported the overall result that 59% of patients treated with a conventional antipsychotic showed categorical behavioral improvement versus 41% of those receiving placebo, an 18% drug-placebo difference. This difference is referred to as the *effect size,* that is, an objective measure of actual drug effect that factors in the effect of placebo. Remarkably, the figure of 18% tends to stand up across trials of most psychotropic agents conducted since that time, as becomes evident in this review. Placebo response rates in the Schneider et al. meta-analysis ranged from 20% to 65%. A more recent meta-analysis was conducted by Lanctot et al. (1998), which included several modern studies as well as earlier studies that Schneider et al. (1990) had excluded because of lack of methodological rigor. The conclusions were similar: The average effect size seen was 26%, with placebo response rates ranging from 19% to 50%. Both meta-analyses emphasized that side effects occurred significantly more often on drug than placebo (typically 25% more often, at least, for studies of fairly short duration). These side effects included akathisia, parkinsonism, tardive dyskinesia, sedation, peripheral and central anti-cholinergic effects, postural hypotension, cardiac conduction defects, and falls. Patients with extrapyramidal signs or symptoms are most vulnerable to the risk of extrapyramidal toxicity of older as well as newer antipsychotics, especially patients with Lewy body dementia (Ballard, Grace, McKeith, & Holmes, 1998). Long-term safety data are generally lacking. Bear in mind, however, that rates of tardive dyskinesia are at least fivefold greater in the elderly than in younger populations (Jeste et al., 1995). McShane et al. (1997) reported an association between the prescription of antipsychotics in patients with dementia and accelerated cognitive decline. The study made no conclusions as to a causal relationship, but the results emphasize the need for the careful scrutiny of the use of conventional antipsychotics in this patient population.

The meta-analyses cited previously did not include a major study by De-vanand et al. (1998) examining use of placebo versus low dose (0.5 to 0.75 mg/day) versus higher dose (2 to 3 mg/day) of haloperidol. Response rates were similar to the results of the previous meta-analyses. Subjects receiving 2 to 3 mg/day showed moderate to severe extrapyramidal signs and symptoms. This study provides the best illustration of the narrow therapeutic index of this type of agent in patients with dementia.

Atypical Antipsychotics

Recently, several trials have demonstrated that atypical antipsychotics are safer than the conventional antipsychotics in elderly patients with behavioral and psychological symptoms of dementia (BPSD) and ameliorate the symptoms of psychosis, aggression, and agitation. This section assesses the results of these trials for each individual agent.

Clozapine

This was the earliest atypical agent released, but there are only anecdotes addressing the use of this agent in patients with dementia. A typical starting dose tends to be 12.5 mg/day, with maintenance doses 12.5 to 50 mg/day. While pointing out occasional successes, the reports emphasize toxicity such as sedation, ataxia, falls, delirium, and suppression of bone marrow function. These toxicities, the need for monitoring of cell counts, and the lack of data indicating efficacy mean that most clinicians are likely to choose other agents first.

Risperidone

Two large multicenter trials have been completed in nursing home patients with fairly severe dementia (Mini-Mental State Examination [MMSE] 6 to 7). Both studies were three months in duration and included patients with AD and/or VaD who experienced agitation and/or psychotic features. The first study compared risperidone at doses of 0.5, 1, and 2 mg/day with placebo in 625 institutionalized subjects (Katz et al., 1999). Reasons for discontinuation included adverse events (15.4%), lack of efficacy (5%), and other causes (10.1%). Extrapyramidal features emerged in roughly one quarter of subjects at the 2 mg/day dose during this time, with good tolerability and safety otherwise. Using an a priori definition of clinical response, 33%

of patients in the placebo group were rated as improved, as were a similar percentage of patients in the 0.5 mg/day group, 45% of those receiving 1 mg/day, and 50% of patients receiving 2 mg/day. Subscale scores indicated beneficial effects on both measures of psychosis and aggression (verbal and/or motor). These response rates (i.e., 12% to 17%) are in the range of those previously reported by Schneider et al. (1990) for conventional antipsychotics, but the results suggest improved safety and tolerability of this agent compared to conventional agents.

A second trial compared placebo with flexible doses of risperidone or haloperidol (0.5 to 4 mg/day) in 344 nursing home residents with dementia accompanied by agitation and/or psychosis (De Deyn et al., 1999). The mean doses used were 1.2 and 1.1 mg/day, respectively. There were 18% dropouts due to adverse experiences, 15% due to lack of efficacy, and 6% for other reasons. Treatment response, defined as greater than 30% reduction in the BEHAVE-AD total score, was reported in 72%, 69%, and 61% of the risperidone, haloperidol, and placebo groups at 12 weeks, respectively. Secondary analyses showed an absence of effect of either active treatment relative to placebo on measures of psychosis, with a positive effect with both active treatments on measures of aggression. Incidence of extrapyramidal adverse events was 11% for patients on placebo, 15% for those on risperidone, and 22% for those on haloperidol—numbers generally consistent with prior studies. Sedation occurred more frequently on haloperidol (18.3%) and risperidone (12.2%) than placebo (4.4%).

Taken together, these risperidone studies comprised the largest placebo-controlled, multicenter studies ever conducted of any form of treatment for agitation associated with dementia. A conservative interpretation of the available evidence would be that the efficacy of risperidone is roughly equivalent to that of haloperidol, perhaps slightly better. The tolerability of risperidone appears to be better, with low-moderate risk of dose-related parkinsonism and sedation.

Olanzapine

Two studies address the use of this agent in patients with dementia. One was a placebo-controlled parallel group study in 238 outpatients with dementia and agitation and/or psychosis. The primary aim of the study was to address appropriate dosing as well as tolerability. The dose range used was 1 to 10 mg/day; the average dose at the end of the study was 2.7 mg/day.

This dose was not associated with either toxicity or efficacy (Satterlee et al., 1995). More recently, Street et al. (2000) reported results from a randomized, parallel group, multicenter study in 206 nursing home residents treated with placebo versus olanzapine in doses of 5, 10, and 15 mg/day, again including patients with dementia and agitation and/or psychosis. Approximately 5% of the placebo group dropped out due to adverse experiences, versus 10.7% of the 5 mg/day group and 17% of the 15 mg/day group. Low-dose olanzapine (5 and 10 mg/day) produced significant improvement compared with placebo on the Core Total sum of the agitation, delusions, and hallucinations items of the Neuropsychiatric Inventory, Nursing Home Version (NPI/NH). No difference was seen between olanzapine 15 mg/day and placebo. The proportion of patients exhibiting a response on the Core Total (> 50% reduction, baseline to endpoint) was significantly greater for the 5 mg (65.5%) and 10 mg (57.1%) olanzapine groups as compared to placebo (35.6%) but again not for the 15 mg group (43.1%). The chief side effects observed were apparently dose-related sedation (25% to 35.8%) and gait disturbance, occurring in roughly 20% of subjects.

Quetiapine Fumarate

There is one journal article and one published abstract on the use of this agent in patients with dementia. The article addresses a one-year open label study of flexible dose quetiapine in older patients with psychoses of multiple origins, of whom 101 had either VaD or AD (Tariot, Salzman, Ycunc, Pultz, & Rak, 2000). The starting dose was 25 mg/day; the median dose was roughly 100 mg/day. A total of 15% of subjects withdrew over one year because of adverse experiences or intercurrent illnesses. Side effects were typically mild and transient. At any point during the trial, 30% of subjects experienced sedation, 15% developed orthostatic hypotension, and 12% experienced dizziness, typically early in the trial and usually rated as mild. The incidence of extrapyramidal signs and symptoms was low. The open trial in patients with dementia suggested encouraging behavioral effects, which led to the implementation of a more definitive multicenter placebo-controlled trial of this agent in comparison with haloperidol and placebo in patients with dementia and psychosis—actually the first such study completed that we know of. The results have been presented only in abstract form thus far in the subset of subjects with AD. The mean dose of quetiapine was about 120 mg/day; that of haloperidol was about 2 mg/day. Neither antipsychotic improved psychotic symptoms to a greater extent than placebo, but both improved agitation. Quetiapine treatment was associated with better daily function than treatment with placebo or haloperidol. Quetiapine demonstrated better tolerability than haloperidol with extra pyramidal symptoms (EPS) and anticholinergic effects similar to placebo (Tariot, Schneider, Katz, & Mintzer, 2002). A better understanding of the study and its results will hinge on a full publication, which has not appeared at this point.

Other Atypical Antipsychotics

Ziprasidone has no published data on use in this patient population. Aripiprazole, a novel dopamine partial agonist, is undergoing two large phase III studies in this patient population.

Summary of Atypical Antipsychotics

The atypical antipsychotics as a class are very likely better tolerated than typical antipsychotics and at least as efficacious. Within the class of atypicals, there appear to be modest differences in terms of clinical effectiveness, but the significance of these differences is unclear. There are limited long-term data addressing either safety or efficacy of these agents in the elderly and even less in people with dementia. Jeste, Okamoto, Napolitano, Kane, and Martinez (2000) reported a cumulative incidence rate for tardive dyskinesia of 2.6% in 330 patients with dementia treated openly with risperidone (mean dose of about 1 mg/day) for a median of 273 days. This figure is considerably less than that reported in older subjects treated with conventional agents (Jeste et al., 1995) and is consistent with data reported in a prospective longitudinal study of risperidone and haloperidol in older subjects with mixed psychiatric disorders (Jeste et al., 1999). We are not aware of long-term data with olanzapine in patients with dementia. The available long-term data for quetiapine come from the one-year open trial mentioned previously. If better effectiveness is proven in comparison with conventional agents, it is likely that consensus guidelines will be developed rapidly that advocate routine preferential use of these agents instead of conventional agents.

One of the National Institute of Mental Health (NIMH)-funded Clinical Antipsychotic Trials of Intervention Effectiveness (CATIE) projects is a double-blind study of the clinical effectiveness of four commonly used medications—risperidone, olanzapine, quetiapine, and citalopram—in outpatients with AD and delusions, hallucinations, and/or clinically significant aggression or agitation. The goal is to use broader measures to examine the public health effectiveness of the interventions to demonstrate real-world outcomes in real-world people. It is hoped that this trial will provide data on the optimum choices of antipsychotics in different subgroups, appropriate dose range, and any unique safety issues in each group (Schneider et al., 2001).

BENZODIAZEPINES

Most studies with benzodiazepines generally showed an average reduction in agitation with short-term therapy, although few were placebo controlled. The study of Coccaro et al. (1990) is probably the most rigorous of the modern studies of this type of agent, in which oxazepam 10 to 60 mg/day was compared with low-dose haloperidol in patients with mixed dementia diagnoses. Five percent of patients in the benzodiazepine group were reported as improved versus 24% of those in the haloperidol group, a difference that appears large but did not reach statistical significance because of the small sample size. The most recent study of this class of agents compared alprazolam 0.5 mg/b.i.d. with haloperidol 0.6 mg/day in a crossover study (Christensen & Benfield, 1998). The doses of both agents used in this study were probably too low to expect an effect, and none was seen.

High rates of side effects with benzodiazepines such as ataxia, falls, confusion, anterograde amnesia, sedation, lightheadedness, and tolerance and withdrawal syndromes are reported (Patel & Tariot, 1991). Thus, we tend to reserve use of benzodiazepines for agitation associated with procedures or time-limited acute or as-needed use. Drugs with simpler metabolisms and relatively short half-lives, such as lorazepam 0.5 mg one to four times daily, are selected most often; long-acting agents such as flurazepam and nitrazepam are usually avoided.

BUSPIRONE

Buspirone has been shown to be effective in reducing agitation and aggression in animal models, and there are reports of benefits in patients with organic brain syndrome. Reports on use in patients with BPSD are limited and show no clear picture of benefits. The medication is generally well tolerated but may require several weeks to achieve maximum clinical benefit (Lawlor, 1994).

ANTIDEPRESSANTS

There are a number of case series and open trials suggesting benefit of trazodone in doses from 50 mg to 400 mg/day (Rosenquist et al., 2000). Symptoms of irritability, anxiety, restlessness, and depressed affect have been reported to improve in some cases, along with disturbed sleep. The main side effects have included sedation, orthostatic hypotension, and occasional delirium. In a nine-week crossover study, Sultzer, Gray, Gunay, Berisford, and Mahler (1997) compared trazodone at a mean dose of 220 mg/day with haloperidol at a mean dose of 2.5 mg/day in 28 patients. Agitation improved equally in both groups with better tolerability in the trazodone group. More recently, Teri, Logsdon, et al. (2000) reported negative results for all active treatments in a multicenter outpatient study contrasting trazodone, haloperidol, placebo, and caregiver training. The magnitude of placebo response in this study was consistent with other published reports on the treatment of agitation in patients with AD. Mean doses for haloperidol, 1.8 mg, and for trazodone, 200 mg, appear adequate. The patients in this study had broadly defined agitation, ranging from mildly disruptive behaviors to physical violence and aggression. The heterogeneity may have affected the results and highlights the importance of clearer definition of study participants. Nevertheless, the marginal efficacy of the active treatments suggests a prompt reevaluation of patients who do not respond to one of these agents and consideration of other treatment approaches. The Expert Consensus Guideline (Alexopoulos et al., 1998) favors trazodone for sleep disturbance primarily, relegating it to second-or-third-line use for mild agitation. A typical starting dose is 25 mg/day, with maximum doses usually 100 to 250 mg/day.

There are mixed results in clinical trials employing selective serotonin reuptake inhibitors for agitation in patients with dementia. A review of controlled studies of citalopram in patients with various dementia diagnoses was performed by Nyth and Gottfries (1990), suggesting some beneficial behavioral effects in nondepressed patients with AD but not VaD. This conclusion was supported by two open trials of this agent (Pollock et al., 1997;

Ragneskog, Eriksson, Karlsson, & Gottfries, 1996). Pollock et al. (2002) also reported on a controlled study, where perphenazine at a target dose of 0.1 mg/kg/day and citalopram 20 mg/day showed reduction in measures of agitation/aggression and/or psychosis in comparison with placebo during a 17-day treatment trial. More than 50% of subjects in each of the study arms withdrew from the study. The study patients were hospitalized because of the severity of their symptoms, which most likely explains the high attrition rate observed. The limited duration of the study reflects more what can be accomplished during a brief hospitalization versus outpatient settings, where the majority of these patients receive their treatment. As to other agents, no benefit has been reported yet for fluoxetine or fluvoxamine, and only anecdotes have been presented with respect to other serotonergic agents (reviewed in Loy et al., 1999). Use of serotonergic agents is fairly widespread despite limited data. This may be due in part to neurobiological data linking serotonergic dysfunction to behavior disturbance in dementia and the usually benign side effect profile of this class, which includes gastrointestinal symptoms, sedation or insomnia, sexual dysfunction, and, less commonly, paradoxical agitation.

ANTICONVULSANTS

Carbamazepine and valproate are the best-studied psychotropic agents in this class. The bulk of available evidence supports the conclusion that they are likely to have anti-agitation efficacy essentially equivalent to other "effective" psychotropics. Carbamazepine has been examined in four placebo-controlled studies. Chambers, Bain, Rosbottom, Ballinger, and McLaren (1982) performed an eight-week crossover study in 19 women with mild agitation who also received antipsychotics: This brief report was negative. Tariot et al. (1994) performed a 12-week placebo-controlled pilot crossover study in 25 patients, showing encouraging effects on agitation and not other aspects of psychopathology. A more recent confirmatory parallel group study of six-weeks' duration in 51 patients also found a significant reduction in agitation using a mean dose of 300 mg/day (Tariot et al., 1998). Tolerability in these studies was generally good, with evidence of sedation and ataxia (Tariot et al., 1998; Tariot, Frederiksen, et al., 1995); there was an 8% dropout due to side effects in the larger confirmatory carbamazepine study. Finally, Olin, Fox, Pawluczyk, Taggart, and Schneider (2001) performed a six-week controlled study in 21 outpatients with BPSD associated with severe AD, who were treatment resistant to antipsychotics. Greater improvement was seen on the Clinical Global Impression of Change (CGIC) and the Brief Psychiatric Rating Scale (BPRS) hostility item with a trend for the hallucination item for the carbamazepine group over placebo. It is likely that side effects seen in other populations, such as rashes, more serious sedation, hematologic abnormalities, hepatic dysfunction, and altered electrolytes, for example, would be more evident with widespread use of this agent in the elderly, which may limit its use (Tariot, Frederiksen, et al., 1995). Further, it has considerable potential for significant drug-drug interactions. The carbamazepine studies help provide proof-of-concept for the anti-agitation efficacy of anticonvulsants.

Valproic acid, which is also available as a significantly better tolerated enteric-coated derivative (divalproex sodium) has clinical effects generally similar to those achieved by carbamazepine in the treatment of mania. It is approved by the U.S. FDA for treatment of acute mania associated with bipolar disorder. Fourteen case reports or case series focus on use in patients with BPSD and describe a total of 202 subjects. In the aggregate, approximately two-thirds of these subjects were reported to show improved agitation, with valproate doses ranging from a general low of about 500 mg/day to a general maximal dose of 1,500 mg/day, with levels typically ranging from 20 to about 100 mcg/ml. Porsteinsson et al. (2001) reported on the first randomized, placebo-controlled, parallel group study of this agent, six weeks in length, in 56 nursing home residents who experienced dementia with agitation. The purpose of this study was not to prove efficacy but to establish effect size and clarify proper dosing to plan a larger definitive study. The average divalproex dose achieved in this study was 826 mg/day, resulting in an average level of about 46 mcg/ml. There was a 10% dropout rate due to adverse experiences. Despite the small sample size, the primary measure of agitation showed a near-significant reduction on valproate versus placebo, supported by similar results with CGIC. There were no changes in other behavioral measures. Tolerability was generally good: Serious adverse events occurred at a rate of 10% in both the drug and placebo groups, with milder side effects occurring more often in the drug group, chiefly consisting of sedation, mild gastrointestinal distress, mild ataxia, and expected mild (but not clinically significant) decrease in platelet count (about 20,000/mm^3).

A multicenter, randomized, placebo-controlled, six-week, parallel group study of divalproex sodium was conducted in patients with dementia and agitation who also met criteria for secondary mania (Tariot et al., 2001). This study was designed using an aggressive dosing and titration protocol, in which a target dose of 20 mg/kg/day was achieved in 10 days. This plan resulted in unacceptable sedation in roughly 25% of the drug-treated group and a relatively high dropout rate, leading to premature discontinuation of the study. The original sample size was 172 nursing home residents, with 100 completers at the time the study was suspended. While there was no significant drug-placebo effect on manic features, there was a significant effect of drug on agitation as measured by the Cohen-Mansfield Agitation Inventory (Cohen-Mansfield, 1986). Sedation occurred in 36% in the drug group versus 20% of the placebo group, and mild thrombocytopenia occurred in 7% of the drug group and none of the placebo-treated patients. There were no other drug-placebo differences in adverse effects. Side effects reported in the package insert include those described previously plus hair loss, mild thrombocytopenia, and hepatic or pancreatic dysfunction that can rarely be fatal. These more serious events have not been reported in the elderly and are more likely to be seen in children requiring multiple anticonvulsants. The available evidence would suggest use of a starting dose of about 125 mg p.o. b.i.d, increasing by 125 to 250 mg increments every five to seven days, with a maximal dose determined by clinical response, or where there is uncertainty, a serum level of about 60 to 90 mcg/ml.

There are no controlled studies of which we are aware of the newer anticonvulsants including lamotrogine, gabapentin, and topiramate, although at least two case reports and a retrospective case series suggest benefit with gabapentin (Hawkins, Tinklenberg, Sheikh, Peyser, & Yesavage, 2000; Regan & Gordon, 1997). Because anticonvulsants, as a class, are relatively well tolerated, based on years of experience in numerous clinical populations with other disorders, definitive trials showing efficacy and reasonable tolerability will very likely influence clinical practice in the future. Although beyond the scope of this chapter, there is considerable intriguing biological data addressing the mechanism of action of mood stabilizers, suggesting in particular that lithium and valproate, but not other agents, may have clinically relevant neuroprotective properties (Manji, Moore, & Chen, 2000). Further understanding of these issues may differentiate among available agents and also lead to the identification of new targets for therapy.

OTHER AGENTS FOR AGITATION

As summarized eloquently by Cummings (2000), considerable evidence suggests that cholinergic agents, especially cholinesterase inhibitors, may have psychotropic effects in patients with dementia. The most compelling data come from recent trials. A prospective clinical trial of metrifonate versus placebo found modest reduction in average neuropsychiatric symptoms in the drug group versus placebo group (Morris et al., 1998). Development of this drug, however, has been abandoned due to toxicity. Tariot, Logsdon, et al. (2000) showed reduced incidence of neuropsychiatric symptoms on drug versus placebo in outpatients who generally lacked psychopathology at baseline in a five-month study of galantamine. An exploratory 20-week placebo-controlled study of rivastigmine versus placebo in patients with Lewy body dementia showed that patients on the drug were significantly less apathetic and anxious and had fewer delusions and hallucinations than controls. Almost twice as many patients on rivastigmine were deemed responders, defined as at least 30% improvement from baseline on the four-item subscore calculated as the sum of scores for delusions, hallucinations, apathy, and depression items of the NPI (McKeith et al., 2000). In the only prospective study of cholinesterase inhibitors in an AD population with meaningful levels of behavioral disturbances at baseline, Feldman et al. (2001) reported that in a six-month trial of donepezil versus placebo in outpatients with moderate to severe AD, statistically significant benefits were seen not only on cognitive and functional measures. In this study, significant improvement was seen in the donepezil-treated group in the total NPI score. In addition, a trend across all items on the NPI favored donepezil, with significant benefits on apathy, depression, and anxiety. Less rigorous studies of cholinergic agents suggested similar effect (Cummings, 2000). It is possible that future trial data will clarify the extent to which cholinergic therapy given presymptomatically may delay or attenuate the emergence of agitation. Once behavioral symptoms are present, it appears that these agents as a class may have selective, clinically important behavioral effects at least in some patients with dementia, which are relatively modest on average. The role of cholinergic agents for agitation specifically is likely to be fairly limited.

Beta blockers have not been studied very extensively, with most evidence coming from older reports in patients with mixed organic brain syndromes (see, for review, Tariot, Schneider, & Katz, 1995). Shankle, Nielson, and

Cotman (1995) have published the most recent study, reporting that some measures of aggression improved in 8 of 12 patients with dementia who received low doses of propranolol (30 to 80 mg/day). The likelihood of adverse reactions in this population, including bradycardia, hypotension, worsening of congestive heart failure, or asthma, as well as others, is high. As there are no placebo-controlled, randomized studies of this class of agents, it probably is relegated to rare, unconventional use.

There are no definitive studies of either estrogenic or anti-androgenic approaches, although there are roughly a dozen published anecdotes at this point (see, for review, Rosenquist et al., 2000). The available evidence is provocative but by no means definitive—controlled studies will be extremely helpful.

Other rarely used or unconventional approaches have been summarized in our previous publications (Loy et al., 1999; Rosenquist et al., 2000; Tariot, 1999).

COMBINATION THERAPY

Partial resolution of symptoms is usually the best that can be expected when intervening pharmacologically in BPSD. Combination use of psychopharmacological agents is very common in this population, but very limited studies are available to date. There is a great public health need to explore this practice further in a controlled fashion.

SUMMARY

Clinicians attempt to treat agitation and other behavioral psychological symptoms associated with dementia as best they can. The clearest guidance as to use of medications comes from definitive clinical trials. At this point, evidence is mounting that certain treatment approaches make sense and can be roughly rank-ordered, although none have been proven beyond any doubt to dictate standard clinical practice. This state of affairs highlights the significance of available consensus statements to guide the practicing clinician in the meantime (Alexopoulos et al., 1998; APA, 1997).

Psychotropic medication should be used only after simpler nonpharmacologic interventions have been attempted. We, along with the consensus statement authors, adopt an approach toward drug selection that is based on matching target symptoms to the most relevant drug class. Most of the available clinical trial data indicate that antipsychotics as a group are likely to show benefit for agitation associated with psychotic features. Evidence is also substantial that this class of agents may show efficacy, for agitation, or aggression even in the absence of psychosis. The evidence is clear that the typical antipsychotics have a high risk of side effects in the short run and especially in the long term. The newer agents appear promising, at least in terms of tolerability relative to conventional agents; the returns are not all in yet concerning relative efficacy. The volume of studies addressing non-antipsychotic medications is less, chiefly addressing the potential role of anticonvulsants, antidepressants, and anxiolytics. Largely, evidence supports effectiveness of these agents at least in a substantial percentage of patients. Interestingly, available data as to effect size across all effective agents point toward an average drug group response rate of about 60% and a placebo response rate of about 40%. No one agent works for all patients, and we do not know yet whether someone who fails one agent is more or less likely to respond to another. Likewise, although combination therapy is widely used, there is remarkably limited data to guide the clinician in this respect. There is room for hope because a significant amount of data is on the horizon and improved definitions of the types of behavioral disturbances we deal with will allow for a clearer sense of exactly how and when therapy should be deployed.

REFERENCES

Alexopoulos, G. S., Silver, J. M., Kahn, D. A., Frances, A., & Carpenter, D. (1998, April). Treatment of agitation in older persons with dementia. *Postgraduate Medicine,* 1–88.

American Psychiatric Association. (1997). Practice guideline for the treatment of patients with Alzheimer's disease and other dementias of late life. *American Journal of Psychiatry, 154,* 1–39.

Ballard, C., Grace, J., McKeith, I., & Holmes, C. (1998). Neuroleptic sensitivity in dementia with Lewy bodies and Alzheimer's disease. *Lancet, 351,* 1032–1033.

Chambers, C. A., Bain, J., Rosbottom, R., Ballinger, B. R., & McLaren, S. (1982). Carbamazepine in senile dementia and overactivity: A placebo controlled double blind trial. *IRCS Medical Science 10,* 505–506.

Christensen, D. B., & Benfield, W. R. (1998). Alprazolam as an alternative to low-dose haloperidol in older, cognitively impaired nursing facility patients. *Journal of the American Geriatrics Society, 46,* 620–625.

Coccaro, E. F., Kramer, E., Zemishlany, Z., Thorne, A., Rice, C. M., Giordani, B., et al. (1990). Pharmacologic treatment of noncognitive behavioral disturbances in elderly demented patients. *American Journal of Psychiatry, 147,* 1640–1645.

Cohen-Mansfield, J. (1986). Agitated behaviors in the elderly. II: Preliminary results in the cognitively deteriorated. *Journal of the American Geriatrics Society, 34,* 722–727.

Cummings, J. L. (2000). Cholinesterase inhibitors: A new class of psychotropic compounds. *American Journal of Psychiatry, 157*(1), 4–16.

De Deyn, P. P., Rabheru, K., Rasmussen, A., Bocksberger, J. P., Dautzenberg, P. L., Eriksson, S., et al. (1999). A randomized trial of risperidone, placebo, and haloperidol for behavioral symptoms of dementia. *Neurology, 53,* 946–955.

Devanand, D. P., Jacobs, D. M., Tang, M. X., Castillo-Castaneda, C., Sano, M., Marder, K., et al. (1997). The course of psychopathologic features in mild to moderate Alzheimer disease. *Archives of General Psychiatry, 54,* 257–263.

Devanand, D. P., Marder, K., Michaels, K., Sackeim, H. A., Bell, K., Sullivan, M., et al. (1998). A randomized, placebo-controlled, dose-comparison trial of haloperidol for psychosis and disruptive behaviors in Alzheimer's disease. *American Journal of Psychiatry, 155,* 1512–1520.

Feldman, H., Gauthier, S., Hecker, J., Vellas, B., Subbiah, P., Whalen, E., et al. (2001). A 24-week, randomized, double-blind study of donepezil in moderate to severe Alzheimer's disease. *Neurology, 57,* 613–620.

Finkel, S. I., Costa e Silva, J., Cohen, G., Miller, S., & Sartorius, N. (1996). Behavioral and psychological signs and symptoms of dementia: A consensus statement on current knowledge and implications for research and treatment. *International Psychogeriatrics, 8*(Suppl. 3), 497–500.

Hawkins, J. W., Tinklenberg, J. R., Sheikh, J. I., Peyser, C. E., & Yesavage, J. A. (2000). A retrospective chart review of gabapentin for the treatment of aggressive and agitated behavior in patients with dementias. *American Journal of Geriatric Psychiatry, 8,* 221–225.

Jeste, D. V., Caligiuri, M. P., Paulsen, J. S., Heaton, R. K., Lacro, J. P., Harris, M. J., et al. (1995). Risk of tardive dyskinesia in older patients: A prospective longitudinal study of 266 outpatients. *Archives of General Psychiatry, 52,* 756–765.

Jeste, D. V., Lacro, J. P., Bailey, A., Rockwell, E., Harris, M. J., & Caligiuri, M. P. (1999). Lower incidence of tardive dyskinesia with risperidone compared with haloperidol in older patients. *Journal of American Geriatrics Society, 47,* 716–719.

Jeste, D. V., Okamoto, A., Napolitano, J., Kane, J. M., & Martinez, R. A. (2000). Low incidence of persistent tardive dyskinesia in elderly patients with dementia treated with risperidone. *American Journal of Psychiatry, 157,* 1150–1155.

Jost, B. C., & Grossberg, G. T. (1996). The evolution of psychiatric symptoms in Alzheimer's disease: A natural history study. *Journal of American Geriatrics Society, 44,* 1078–1081.

Katz, I. R., Jeste, D. V., Mintzer, J. E., Clyde, C., Napolitano, J., & Brecher, M. (1999). Comparison of risperidone and placebo for psychosis and behavioral disturbances associated with dementia: A randomized, double-blind trial (Risperidone Study Group). *Journal of Clinical Psychiatry, 60,* 107–115.

Lanctot, K. L., Best, T. S., Mittmann, N., Liu, B. A., Oh, P. I., Einarson, T. R., et al. (1998). Efficacy and safety of neuroleptics in behavioral disorders associated with dementia. *Journal of Clinical Psychiatry, 59,* 550–561.

Lawlor, B. A. (1994). A pilot placebo-controlled study of trazodone and buspirone in Alzheimer's disease. *International Journal of Geriatric Psychiatry, 9,* 55–59.

Leibovici, A., & Tariot, P. N. (1988). Agitation associated with dementia: A systematic approach to treatment. *Psychopharmacology Bulletin, 24,* 49–53.

Loy, R., Tariot, P. N., & Rosenquist, K. (1999). Alzheimer's disease: Behavioral management. In I. R. Katz, D. Oslin, & M. P. Lawton (Eds.), *Annual review of gerontology and geriatrics: Focus on psychopharmacologic interventions in late life* (pp. 136–194). New York: Springer.

Lyketsos, C. G., Steinberg, M., Tschanz, J. T., Norton, M. C., Steffens, D. C., & Breitner, J. C. (2000). Mental and behavioral disturbances in dementia: Findings from the Cache County Study on Memory in Aging. *American Journal of Psychiatry, 157,* 708–714.

Manji, H. K., Moore, G. J., & Chen, G. (2000). Lithium up-regulates the cytoprotective protein Bcl-2 in the CNS in vivo: A role for neurotrophic and neuroprotective effects in manic depressive illness. *Journal of Clinical Psychiatry, 61*(Suppl. 9), 82–96.

McKeith, I., Del Ser, T., Spano, P., Emrie, M., Wesnes, K., Anand, R., et al. (2000). Efficacy of rivastigmine in dementia with Lewy bodies: A randomized, double blind, placebo-controlled international study. *Lancet, 356,* 2031–2036.

McShane, R., Keene, J., Gedling, K., Fairburn, C., Jacoby, R., & Hope, T. (1997). Do neuroleptic drugs hasten cognitive decline in dementia? Prospective study with necropsy follow up. *British Medical Journal, 314,* 266–270.

Morris, J. C., Cyrus, P. A., Orazem, J., Mas, J., Bieber, F., Ruzicka, B. B., et al. (1998). Metrifonate benefits cognitive, behavioral, and global function in patients with Alzheimer's disease. *Neurology, 50,* 1222–1230.

Nyth, A. L., & Gottfries, C. G. (1990). The clinical efficacy of citalopram in treatment of emotional disturbances in dementia disorders: A Nordic multicenter study. *British Journal of Psychiatry, 157,* 894–901.

Olin, J. T., Fox, L. S., Pawluczyk, S., Taggart, N. A., & Schneider, L. S. (2001). A pilot randomized trial of carbamazepine for behavioral symptoms in treatment resistant outpatients with Alzheimer Disease. *American Journal of Geriatric Psychiatry, 9,* 400–405.

Patel, S., & Tariot, P. N. (1991). Pharmacologic models of Alzheimer's disease. *Psychiatric Clinics of North America, 14,* 287–308.

Pollock, B. G., Mulsant, B. H., Rosen, J., Sweet, R. A., Mazumdar, S., Bharucha, A., et al. (2002). Comparison of citalopram, perphenazine, and placebo for the acute treatment of psychosis and behavioral disturbances in hospitalized, demented patients. *American Journal of Psychiatry, 159,* 460–465.

Pollock, B. G., Mulsant, B. H., Sweet, R. A., Burgio, L. D., Kirshner, M. A., Shuster, K., et al. (1997). An open pilot study of citalopram for behavioral disturbances of dementia: Plasma levels and real-time observations. *American Journal of Geriatric Psychiatry, 5,* 70–78.

Porsteinsson, A. P., Tariot, P. N., Erb, R., Cox, C., Smith, E., Jakimovich, L., et al. (2001). Placebo-controlled study of divalproex sodium for agitation in dementia. *American Journal of Geriatric Psychiatry, 9,* 58–66.

Ragneskog, H., Eriksson, S., Karlsson, I., & Gottfries, C. G. (1996). Long-term treatment of elderly individuals with emotional disturbances: An open study with citalopram. *International Psychogeriatrics, 8,* 659–668.

Regan, W. M., & Gordon, S. M. (1997). Gabapentin for behavioral agitation in Alzheimer's disease. *Journal of Clinical Psychopharmacology, 17,* 59–60.

Rosenquist, K., Tariot, P. N., & Loy, R. (2000). Treatments for behavioral and psychological symptoms in Alzheimer's disease and other dementias. In J. O'Brien, D. Ames, & A. Burns (Eds.), *Dementia* (2nd ed., pp. 571–601). London: Arnold.

Satterlee, W. G., Reams, S. G., Burns, P. R., Hamilton, S., Tran, P. V., & Tollefson, G. D. (1995). A clinical update in olanzapine treatment in schizophrenia and in elderly Alzheimer's disease patients [Abstract]. *Psychopharmacology Bulletin, 31.*

Schneider, L. S., Pollock, V. E., & Lyness, S. A. (1990). A metaanalysis of controlled trials of neuroleptic treatment in dementia. *Journal of the American Geriatrics Society, 38,* 553–563.

Schneider, L. S., Tariot, P. N., Lyketsos, C. G., Dagerman, K. S., Davis, K. L., Davis, S., et al. (2001). National Institute of Mental Health clinical antipsychotic trial of intervention effectiveness (CATIE)—Alzheimer Disease trial methodology. *American Journal of Geriatric Psychiatry, 9,* 346–360.

Shankle, W. R., Nielson, K. A., & Cotman, C. W. (1995). Low-dose propranolol reduces aggression and agitation resembling that associated with orbitofrontal dysfunction in elderly demented patients. *Alzheimer Disease and Associated Disorders, 9,* 233–237.

Street, J., Clark, W. S., Gannon, K. S., Cummings, J. L., Bymaster, F. P.,Tamura, R. N., et al. (2000). Olanzapine treatment of psychotic and behavioral symptoms in patients with Alzheimer's disease in nursing care facilities: A double blind, randomized, placebo-controlled trial. *Archives of General Psychiatry, 57*(10), 968–976.

Sultzer, D. L., Gray, K. F., Gunay, I., Berisford, M. A., & Mahler, M. E. (1997). A double-blind comparison of trazodone and haloperidol for treatment of agitation in patients with dementia. *American Journal of Geriatric Psychiatry, 5,* 60–69.

Tariot, P. N. (1999). Treatment of agitation in dementia. *Journal of Clinical Psychiatry, 60*(Suppl. 8), 11–20.

Tariot, P. N., & Blazina, L. (1993). The psychopathology of dementia. In J. Morris (Ed.), *Handbook of dementing illnesses* (pp. 461–475). New York: Marcel Dekker.

Tariot, P. N., Erb, R., Leibovici, A., Podgorski, C. A., Cox, C., Asnis, J., et al. (1994). Carbamazepine treatment of agitation in nursing home patients with dementia: A preliminary study. *Journal of the American Geriatrics Society, 42,* 1160–1166.

Tariot, P. N., Erb, R., Podgorski, C. A., Cox, C., Patel, S., Jakimovich, L., et al. (1998). Efficacy and tolerability of carbamazepine for agitation and aggression in dementia. *American Journal of Psychiatry, 155,* 54–61.

Tariot, P. N., Frederiksen, K., Erb, R., Leibovici, A., Podgorski, C. A., Asnis, J., et al. (1995). Lack of carbamazepine toxicity in frail nursing home patients: A controlled study. *Journal of the American Geriatrics Society, 43,* 1026–1029.

Tariot, P. N., Mack, J. L., Patterson, M. B., Edland, S. D., Weiner, M. F., Fillenbaum, G., et al. (1995). The Behavior Rating Scale for Dementia of the Consortium to Establish a Registry for Alzheimer's Disease. *American Journal of Psychiatry, 152,* 1349–1357.

Tariot, P. N., Salzman, C., Yeunc, P. P., Pultz, J., Rak, I. W. (2000). Long term use of the antipsychotic "seroquil" (Quetiapine) in elderly patients with psychotic disorders. *Clinical Therapeutics, 22*(9), 1069–1084.

Tariot, P. N., Schneider, L. S., & Katz, I. R. (1995). Anticonvulsant and other nonneuroleptic treatment of agitation in dementia. *Journal of Geriatric Psychiatry and Neurology, 8*(Suppl. 1), S28–S39.

Tariot, P. N., Schneider, L. S., Katz, I. R., Mintzer, J. E., & Street, J. (2002). Quetiapine in nursing home residents with Alzheimer's dementia and psychosis [Poster abstract]. *American Journal of Geriatric Psychiatry, 10,* 93.

Tariot, P. N., Schneider, L. S., Mintzer, J. E., Cutler, A., Cunningham, M., Thomas, J., et al. (2001). Safety and tolerability of divalproex sodium for the treatment of signs and symptoms of mania in elderly patients with dementia: Results of a double-blind, placebo-controlled trial. *Current Therapeutic Research Clinical and Experimental, 62,* 51–67.

Tariot, P. N., Solomon, P. R., Morris, J. C., Kershaw, P., Lilienfeld, S., Ding, C., et al. (2000). A 5-month, randomized placebo-controlled trial of galantamine in AD. *Neurology, 54,* 2269–2276.

Teri, L., Logsdon, R. G., Peskind, E., Raskind, M., Weiner, M. F., Trachtenberg, R. E., et al. (2000). Treatment of agitation in AD: A randomized placebo-controlled clinical trial. *Neurology, 55,* 1271–1278.

CHAPTER 13

Psychological and Nonpharmacological Aspects of Agitation and Behavioral Disorders in Dementia: Assessment, Intervention, and Challenges to Providing Care

Cameron J. Camp and Elizabeth H. Nasser

Behavioral disturbances among persons with dementia are consistently reported to be among the most stressful aspects of providing care to these individuals. Research has shown that between 50% and 90% of persons with moderate to severe symptoms of dementia may display clinically significant behavioral problems at some point during the course of their illness (Davis, Buckwalter, & Burgio, 1997; Swearer, Drachman, O'Donell, & Mitchell, 1990; Zimmer, Watson, & Treat, 1984). Behavioral disturbances among persons with dementia include agitation, verbally disruptive behavior, physically aggressive irritability, wandering, and mood lability (Burgio, 1996; Camp, Cohen-Mansfield, & Capezuti, 2002; Cohen-Mansfield, 2001; Drevets & Rubin, 1989), as well as apathy (Mega, Cummings, Fiorello, & Gornbein, 1996). Of these, apathy, physical aggression, agitation, and verbal disruption have been found to be the most common behavior problems (Holm et al., 1999; Mega et al., 1996). However, apathy may be less likely to be targeted for pharmacological intervention because its expression does not result in as much stress or strain on caregivers as other behavioral disturbances.

Preparation of this manuscript was partially supported through grant R21 MH57851 from the National Institute of Mental Health and grants R01 AG17908 and R03 AG19016 from the National Institute on Aging.

There are, however, nonpharmacological interventions available for behavioral disturbances commonly seen in persons with dementia. A number of reviews of such interventions and their theoretical bases have been written recently (e.g., Allen-Burge, Sevens, & Burgio, 1999; Arkin, 2001; Beck, 1998; Burgio & Stevens, 1999; Camp et al., 2002; Cohen-Mansfield, 2000a, 2000b, 2001; Kitwood, 1997; Koltai & Branch, 1999; Richards, Lambert, & Beck, 2000; Sloane et al., 1997; Woods, 1996a, 1996b; Woods & Bird, 1998; Zeisel & Raia, 2000). We do not attempt to reiterate everything that has already been covered on this topic. Rather, we first review some of the risk factors associated with problematic behaviors related to dementia, along with how these are assessed. We then describe factors that influence both the generation of problematic behaviors and the ability to implement interventions for them, for example, the influences of setting and culture. Next, we describe and illustrate an algorithm for determining underlying causes of behavioral symptoms, which in turn can lead to selection/development of nonpharmacological interventions for individual patients. Finally, we discuss challenges to providing nonpharmacological interventions to persons with dementia. These include issues of therapeutic nihilism, who will implement nonpharmacological interventions in real world settings, and difficulties in using clinical trial approaches for developing and documenting the effects of such interventions. It is suggested that nonpharmacological intervention be embedded in training models that bridge the gap between the development of an intervention from an applied research perspective and its effective implementation in real world contexts.

RISK FACTORS

Comorbidity

The risk for developing dementia is age related and increases substantially after the age of 75 years. Persons in this age range commonly suffer from a number of chronic conditions, which can exacerbate the behavioral symptoms associated with dementia. The treatment of choice for the behavioral symptoms of dementia has long been the use of psychotropic medications (L. S. Schneider, 1993). However, many patients do not respond favorably to such treatment (L. S. Schneider, Pollock, & Lyness, 1990). For example, Cariaga, Burgio, Flynn, and Martin (1991) found that medication is not effective in decreasing disruptive vocalizations without heavily sedating the patient, thus restricting the general behavioral repertoire of the persons with dementia. Further complicating the use of psychopharmacology with older adults is the fact that many are already taking multiple medications to manage other physical illnesses, making drug-drug interaction effects more likely in this population.

Stage of Impairment

Behavioral problems in persons with dementia are generally seen to increase as a function of increased cognitive impairment (Lyketsos et al., 1999; Reisberg, Franssen, Sclan, Kluger, & Ferris, 1989). However, there are large individual differences in manifestation of problematic behaviors, and relationships between specific problematic behaviors in persons with dementia and stages of dementia are not always progressive or linear. For example, wandering is curtailed when problems with mobility increase, as is often the case with advanced stages of dementia. Harwood, Barker, Ownby, and Duara (2000) found statistically significant correlations between overall level of behavioral pathology in persons with dementia of the Alzheimer's type (DAT) and level of cognitive impairment, but correlations were approximately 0.25 (about 5% of variance) in problematic behaviors accounted for by level of cognitive impairment. In addition, two measures of aggressiveness in their sample did not significantly relate to level of cognitive impairment.

Harwood et al. (2000) noted that manifestation of problematic behaviors in persons with dementia might be more strongly related to ability to manage activities of daily living (executive function) than other aspects of cognition, a sentiment that also was reached by Weiner et al. (1998). Perhaps the most appropriate summation of the current literature in this area is that there are contradictory findings concerning stage of dementia and manifestation of problematic behaviors, and individual differences seem to account for most of the variability in such behaviors.

Personality Characteristics

A few studies have examined linkages between premorbid personality traits and problematic behaviors in persons with dementia. Kolanowski, Strand, and Whall (1997) found a highly significant correlation between premorbid neuroticism and aggression in persons with dementia. Magai, Cohen, Culver, Gomberg, and Makatestsm (1997) found evidence that premorbid personality characteristics linked to emotionality show stability of expression across mid- to late-stage dementia. For example, premorbid attachment style predicted current degree of positive affect expressed by nursing home residents with dementia. Premorbid levels of hostility were associated with residents' levels of anger, contempt, and disgust. Their findings also suggested that high levels of premorbid hostility might put nursing home residents at risk for developing depression.

This linkage between hostility and depression in persons with dementia is echoed in Menon et al.'s (2001) finding that nursing home residents with dementia who manifested physical or verbal aggression had a higher incidence of depression than residents without such behaviors, though this relationship has not universally been supported in the literature (see Harwood et al., for a review of this topic). However, the relationship between personality characteristics and manifestation of problematic behaviors in persons with dementia has not been extensively researched to date.

ASSESSMENT TOOLS

To maximize the treatment of the behavioral and psychiatric symptoms in dementia, it is important to understand the causes of the underlying behavior. However, there is significant variability in the behavioral symptomatology of persons with dementia. There is also variability in the causes of behavior problems, even among individuals displaying similar symptomatology. Nevertheless, treatment providers are often focused on implementing treatments that have worked with some patients, without recognizing that not all treatments are effective with all types of individuals (Maslow, 1996). Using more comprehensive, though easily administered, assessment tools should enable providers to arrive at a more individualized understanding of patient behavior problems and choose interventions accordingly. In the following section, several thorough and easy-to-use tools to assess both agitation and behavior problems are described.

Agitation

Agitation affects between 70% and 90% of persons with dementia and significantly impacts the quality of life for people with dementia and their caregivers (Teri, Larson, & Reifler, 1988). Agitation may be considered "an unpleasant state of excitement experienced by the patient with DAT"

(Hurley et al., 1999, p. 118). Verbal and physical aggression, which are aspects of agitation, have been found to occur at least once a week in many nursing home residents (Cohen-Mansfield, 1988). Agitation is also one of the most commonly cited reasons for treatment with neuroleptics, yet attempts to understand the behavioral aspects of agitation are rare (Cohen-Mansfield & Billig, 1986). This may relate in part to an incomplete assessment of agitated behavior. For instance, using a visual analogue scale (i.e., 0 to 100) as a measure of agitation provides information as to the frequency or intensity of the behavior but does little to illuminate the complexities of agitation and the individual differences in agitated behavior.

Other measures exist that allow a more thorough assessment of aspects of agitation among persons with dementia. The Cohen-Mansfield Agitation Inventory (CMAI; Cohen-Mansfield, 1986) is a nurses' rating questionnaire consisting of 29 agitated behaviors such as cursing, screaming, pacing, and repetitive questioning, which are rated on a seven-point scale of frequency. The CMAI was developed for use with nursing home residents, but it has also demonstrated utility with adult day care participants (Koss et al., 1997). These behaviors can be broken down to four dimensions: aggressive behavior, physically nonaggressive behavior, verbally agitated behavior, and hiding/hoarding behavior (Cohen-Mansfield, Marx, & Rosenthal, 1989). The dimensional nature of the CMAI allows for the development of targeted interventions to address specific behavioral symptoms (Taft, Matthiesen, Farran, McCann, & Knafl, 1997). Further, the CMAI has proved useful in assessing agitation among persons who lack language (Weiner et al., 1998).

The Scale for the Observation of Agitation in Persons with DAT (SOAPD; Hurley et al., 1999) is a seven-item scale measuring total body movements from one place, up/down movements, repetitive body motions in place, outward motions, high-pitched or loud noise, repetitive vocalization, and negative words. Items are scored for both duration and intensity of the agitated behavior and can be useful as a means of categorizing and counting behaviors.

A similar measure, the Agitated Behavior in Dementia Scale (ABID; Logsdon et al., 1999) was designed to assess dementia-related problem behaviors in community-residing patients with DAT. This measure is composed of 16 items, scored from 0 to 3 based on the frequency of the behavior, which evaluate behaviors identified as the most problematic in individuals with mild to moderate dementia. These include verbal aggression toward others, inappropriate screaming, restlessness, and auditory and visual hallucinations. The ABID also includes a measure of caregiver reaction to particular agitated behaviors.

Finally, the Rating Scale for Aggressive Behavior in the Elderly (RAGE; Patel & Hope, 1992) is a 21-item, four-point Likert measure designed for unit staff to assess aggressive behavior in psychogeriatric inpatients. Nineteen items assess specific aspects of aggressive behavior divided into three categories: verbally aggressive behavior, physically aggressive behavior, and antisocial behavior. In addition, one item assesses whether the patient was restrained because of the aggressive behavior, and a final item measures overall aggressiveness. The RAGE has been used as an outcome measure in an intervention for inpatients with dementia and dysfunctional behaviors (Holm et al., 1999).

Behavioral Disorders

Other measures of behavior disorders assess a wider spectrum of behaviors than just agitation. The Consortium to Establish a Registry for Alzheimer's Disease Behavioral Rating Scale for Dementia (BRSD; Tariot et al., 1995) was designed to assess community-dwelling persons with mild to moderate Alzheimer's disease. Eight factors comprise the original version: depressive features, psychotic features, defective self-regulation, irritability/agitation, vegetative features, apathy, aggression, and affective lability. A second version is comprised of six factors: depressive symptoms, psychotic symptoms, inertia, vegetative symptoms, irritability/agitation, and behavioral dysregulation (Patterson & Mack, 1996).

Weiner et al. (1998) compared the CMAI and the BRSD in a community sample of persons with DAT. They concluded that while both measures were sensitive to the presence of agitation in persons with DAT, the CMAI might be more useful for assessing persons who lack language. The BRSD appeared more sensitive to apathy and depression, as might be expected from a more broadly focused instrument.

The Hierarchical Dementia Scale (HDS; Cole & Dastoor, 1980, 1987) is a standardized assessment of mental functions in people with dementia. The HDS was developed on the premise that functional decline in dementia follows Piaget's developmental stages in reverse (cf. Auer, Sclan, Yaffee, & Reisberg, 1994; Reisberg, 1986). Unlike many measures, the HDS is a measure of both strengths and weaknesses in persons with dementia. The HDS is composed of 20 subscales including perception, attention and memory, language, and orientation. Because the HDS focuses on both strengths and weaknesses, interventions can be designed to maximize an individual's strengths while compensating for weaknesses. Tailored interventions based on results from the HDS were used to achieve significant reductions in wandering behavior in one case study (Paterson, Hamilton, & Grant, 2000).

The Revised Memory and Behavior Problems Checklist (RMBPC; Teri et al., 1992) is a brief (24-item) self-report measure of the frequency of problematic behaviors in persons with dementia and the reactions of caregivers to these behaviors. The RMBPC is designed to be completed by the caregiver of the person with dementia. The RMBPC is composed of three factors (depression, disruption, and memory-related problems), which enables a more sensitive assessment of behavior problems and allows for interventions to be specifically targeted to address those areas particularly problematic for patients and especially upsetting to their caregivers.

Camp, Koss, and Judge (1999) reviewed cognitive assessment instruments for late-stage dementia and concluded by describing an assessment that was based on the use of Montessori-based activities for dementia (a topic to be covered in more detail later). This instrument, the Myers-Menorah Park/Montessori-based Assessment System (MMP/MAS), is designed to assess both strengths and weaknesses of persons with more advanced dementia. Consisting of several individualized activities for dementia, results from the MMP/MAS may be more readily translated into plans of care than results from assessments that are designed to assess change in overall cognitive or behavioral functioning (see also Plautz & Camp, 2001). Development of instruments designed not only to assess problematic behaviors and/or deficits in persons with dementia but also to aid in providing specific guidelines for developing individualized interventions would appear to be a growing, and highly valuable, trend in this area.

NONPHARMACOLOGICAL TREATMENTS

Focus on Unmet Needs

In some cases, behavior problems may be a manifestation of unmet needs of the person with dementia (Cohen-Mansfield, 2001; Crose, 2000; Richards et al., 2000). Many individuals, particularly in advanced stages of dementia, are unable to convey basic needs such as hunger, thirst, or need for toileting, much less the need for companionship or affection. Further, for some individuals, a need for independence or autonomy may be expressed as aggressive or agitated behavior. Finally, individuals who exhibit problem behaviors may be suffering from either a lack or an excess of environmental stimulation. Because the person with dementia may not be able to communicate his or her needs in traditional ways, caregivers must attempt to determine whether a need is not being met. Subsequently, caregivers must exercise patience and persistence in an often-frustrating, trial and error attempt to determine the root of the individual's behavior problem.

If an individual is expressing a less tangible need than hunger or thirst, determining the cause of the behavior problem becomes even more challenging. Fortunately, some interventions do exist to address some of the free-floating needs experienced by persons with dementia. The rise in popularity in the general population of holistic approaches to wellness and well-being can be adapted for demented elderly populations. One group intervention that combined breathing exercises, music, aromatherapy, the use of textured materials, and physical movement achieved significant reductions in agitation in nursing home residents (Lantz, Buchalter, & McBee, 1997). This intervention led to increased feelings of efficacy among staff members. Many individuals with dementia may suffer from a lack of physical contact, which may relate to their dysfunctional behavior. The use of brief (five-minute) gentle hand massage, combined with verbalization, has been found to decrease agitation, anxiety, and episodes of dysfunctional behavior such as aggression and verbal outbursts among persons with dementia (Kim & Buschmann, 1999).

Restraint Reduction

Despite the frequency with which restraints are used to manage dementia-related behavior problems such as aggression, agitation, and wandering, there is no scientific evidence supporting the effectiveness of restraints. In spite of this, one study found that mechanical restraints were used on 63% of patients with dementia in nursing homes at one time (Burton, German, Rovner, & Brant, 1992). In many cases, the use of restraints may hinder the implementation of other more effective means of managing problem behaviors because restraints do temporarily "resolve" the behavior problem. In addition, use of restraints such as side rails can increase the likelihood of injurious falls from a bed, entrapment injuries, and even death (Parker & Miles, 1997; Schwartz, Capezuti, & Grisso, 2001; Todd, Ruhl, & Gross, 1997).

Research has demonstrated that restraints can be removed without adverse consequences (Capezuti, 2000; Capezuti & Talerico, 1999; Capezuti, Strumpf, Evans, Grisson, & Maislin, 1998; Castle & Mor, 1998; Evans et al., 1997; Neufeld et al., 1999; Rader, Jones, & Miller, 1999; Si, Neufeld, & Dunbar, 1999; Strumpf, Patterson, Wagner, & Evans, 1998). Ejaz and Rose (1997) outlined three steps that were used to achieve restraint reduction in seven skilled nursing facilities. First, staff participated in an educational program that focused on education on the hazards of using restraints, dispelling myths about restraints and other methods of handling problematic behaviors including wandering and agitation. Next, multidisciplinary committees were formed composed of nurses, nursing assistants, physical therapists, social workers, and a director of education. A member of each committee was assigned as a case manager for each restrained resident, fostering individual motivation to reduce restraints. Finally, restraint reduction was implemented. Each resident who was restrained was assessed by the multidisciplinary team to reevaluate the initial causes and ongoing need for restraints. More challenging cases became the focus of the multidisciplinary team, and interventions to reduce and remove restraints were introduced on an individual basis.

The effectiveness of this program was contingent on finding alternatives to restraints. For some residents who were agitated, the use of rocking chairs and recliners proved to be an effective soothing technique, especially the use of gliding rockers to reduce risk of falling forward from the chair. To prevent wandering, some residents used chair, bed, and wrist alarms to signal staff when a resident was moving. For residents who were fall risks at night, soft floor mats were placed near their beds to lessen the impact of falls that might occur. This program resulted in the reduction of percentages of residents restrained across all facilities. The most dramatic results were from a facility that reduced restraints from a high of 39% of residents restrained to only 3% at the conclusion of the program.

Camp et al. (2002) also discuss the use of environmental interventions to reduce physical restraints for persons with dementia while promoting higher levels of functioning. Examples of such interventions include reduced bed height, concave mattresses or rolled blankets under mattress

edges, full body pillows, and so on. They emphasize the need for an individualized care philosophy, where alternative interventions for restraint
reduction are tailored to individual residents' needs. This involves not
only interventions as described earlier, but also an active, rehabilitation-
focused approach to caring for persons with dementia in general (see also
Camp & Mattern, 1999). For example, Camp et al. discuss the need to emphasize learning systems that are relatively preserved in persons with dementia on which to base training in the use of assistive devices. Thus, one
way to address issues of restraint reduction is to examine the underlying
cause of residents' agitation, identify unmet needs that might be motivat-
ing agitated behaviors, and then design interventions to address these
unmet needs.

Communication Problems

Communicating with persons with dementia is often challenging as expressive and receptive communication skills decline over the course of
dementing illnesses. Interventions in this area focus on caregiver training
and/or enhancing the abilities of persons with dementia. Several programs
to enhance caregivers' communication skills with persons with dementia
have been developed (e.g., Bourgeois, 1992a, 1992b, 1997; Clark, 1997;
Orange & Colton-Hudson, 1998; Orange, Ryan, Meredith, & MacLean,
1995; Richter, Roberto, & Bottenberg, 1995; Ripich, 1994; Ripich, Kercher,
Wykle, Sloan, & Ziol, 1998; Ripich & Wykle, 1996; Ripich, Wykle, & Niles,
1995; Tomoeda & Bayles, 1990). Most involve educating caregivers about
changes in communication abilities that accompany dementia. As part of this
education process, caregivers are shown how previous communication styles
must be adapted and new ways of communication must be developed to communicate more effectively with the individual with dementia. For instance,
when communicating verbally with the patient, caregivers should focus on
speaking slowly, annunciating, using simple language, and reducing the
amount of information conveyed (Harvis, 1990). Orange and Colton-Hudson
discuss strategies such as using specific names of persons or places rather
than ambiguous pronouns, stating the topic of conversation and signaling
changes in the topic of conversation, avoiding assumptions that the person
with dementia can follow aspects of the conversation that must be inferred,
and so on.

Ripich (1994) discussed the FOCUSED program, an intervention stressing that communication with persons with dementia must use these strategies:

- Face to face (face the person directly and maintain eye contact).

- Orientation (orient the person by repeating key words).

- Continuity (continue a topic of conversation as long as possible).

- Unsticking (suggest a word the person is looking for if he/she gets stuck or uses a word incorrectly).

- Structure (provide only two options at a time).

- Exchange (keep up a normal exchange of ideas during conversation).

- Direct (keep sentences short and direct).

These interventions attempt to train caregivers to help compensate for communication deficits seen in persons with dementia. Zeisel and Raia (2000) emphasized the importance of nonverbal communication and stated: "Much of what is communicated to people with dementia is not done with words. Feelings of safety, personal value, and purpose are communicated with a look, a tone, or a hug" (p. 339).

Other interventions involve the use of external aids that can enhance the communication capabilities of persons with dementia. The use of memory books and related aids (Bourgeois, 1992a, 1992b) is an example of this type of intervention. Camp (1999b) discusses aspects of printed materials that can enhance the ability of persons with dementia to perceive and use information contained in such materials. Some of the points he emphasized include:

- Use large print (e.g., 100-point type size for signage on walls).

- Use a sans serif font (e.g., Arial or Helvetica).

- Use high contrast between background and printed letters and so on.

It is possible for persons with dementia to read printed material and to use information so transmitted far into the course of dementia. For example, Bologna and Camp (1997) found that persons with dementia could read and understand printed material even when they evidenced the lack of ability to recognize their own reflections in a mirror (a condition usually associated with advanced dementia). One of the first things to consider when designing an intervention for a person with dementia is "Can this person read?" Too often, the answer is "We don't know." This is especially true for tests of printed materials that are configured for the persons with dementia (e.g., single words or very short phrases using the parameters for printing that were just described). This represents wasted opportunity for development of effective interventions (e.g., Camp, 1999a, 1999b).

Overcoming Language Barriers

A particularly challenging situation faces caregivers when persons with dementia speak a language that is different from that of the caregivers. For example, Runi, Doyle, and Redman (1999) note that persons with dementia of a non-English-speaking background (NESB) are at substantial risk for having unmet needs. They note that if English was acquired as a second language, it is often lost or impaired to a greater degree than their first language. Understimulation in terms of not taking part in activities or communicating regularly with staff is a typical concern in caring for NESB persons with dementia. Runi et al. described a case study in which a person with dementia had resorted to speaking Italian, her first language, and was exhibiting aggressive verbalizations and/or repetitive verbalizations not directed toward visible persons. Music was used as an intervention, in which both English-language and Italian-language music were played. They found that disruptive vocalizations were reduced when Italian-language music was played to a substantially greater degree than when English-language music was played.

Camp and his colleagues (Antenucci, Camp, Sterns, Sterns, & Sterns, 2001; Burant & Camp, 1996; Camp, Burant, & Graham, 1996; Mattern & Camp, 1998) have developed an intervention called *The InterpreCare System*[TM] that uses phonetics to enable caregivers to read English printing aloud and then be understood by speakers of Russian, Japanese, or Spanish. They have developed similar techniques for allowing NESB persons to speak English phrases while reading aloud in their native alphabets. This system now includes a substantial vocabulary of caregiving phrases that came from requests of both staff and NESB long-term care residents. It has now been used to reduce problematic behaviors (Burant & Camp,

1996) and to extend the availability of rehabilitation therapies to NESB persons with dementia.

Activities Programming

One of the most effective means of managing behavior problems, at least for short periods of time, is the implementation of activities that keep elders interested and engaged. Too often, persons with dementia are allowed to play a passive role during activities that may increase boredom and restlessness that may exacerbate behavior problems. This may result in part from the selection of inappropriate individual or group activities, which are either too challenging or not challenging enough to provide sufficient stimulation to the person with dementia. For instance, a typical scenario in a nursing home involves a nursing assistant or other staff member reading the newspaper to a large group of residents. Although a few residents may be able to attend to this activity, many more are likely to sleep or leave the room. Fortunately, options for activities programming do exist that increase the likelihood that persons with dementia will remain involved and decrease the likelihood that they will exhibit behavior problems. Zeisel and Raia (2000) noted that for persons with dementia, "Structured therapeutic activities are the motor that drives the entire treatment model. . . . Therapeutic activities should not be considered valuable merely because they fill time. Activities are therapeutic because they quickly change negative emotions and promote feelings of purpose and accomplishment" (pp. 338–339; see also Plautz & Camp, 2001, for an extensive discussion of the role of activities as a rehabilitation tool in providing care for persons with dementia).

Many long-term care facilities may be limited in the types of activities they can implement because of cost or staffing issues. However, by making small modifications to regular programming, it is possible to keep residents interested and may decrease the incidence of behavior problems. For example, when reading the newspaper, if attempts are made to make the material more accessible, attentiveness should increase. Many persons with dementia may not be interested in reading about the president of the United States visiting Europe. However, many individuals may have emigrated from other countries and may be able to discuss their experiences in their homelands or perhaps their favorite ethnic food. Perhaps some residents have traveled abroad and could answer questions about these experiences.

By personalizing the activity, particularly about past experiences, the individual with dementia is more likely to become and remain involved.

Camp et al. (2002) describe a host of activities serving as interventions for persons with dementia. Similarly, Orsulic-Jeras, Schneider, Camp, Nicholson, and Helbig (2001) describe a number of both individualized and group activities for persons with dementia that emphasize use of remaining skills such as motor learning, reading, and access to semantic memory. Most importantly, these activities have been implemented as part of the regular job routines of recreational therapists in a long-term care setting. A key element of this latter review is that such activities are based on the use of the Montessori method, developed by Maria Montessori as a means of teaching cognitive, social, and functional skills to children.

Montessori-Based Activities

The Montessori method has proved an effective means of developing activities for persons with dementia in both long-term care (Orsulic-Jeras, Judge, & Camp, 2000; Orsulic-Jeras, Schneider, & Camp, 2000) and adult day care settings (Judge, Camp, & Orsulic-Jeras, 2000). Montessori-based activities, such as sorting pictures into categories, can be implemented as both individual and intergenerational (with preschool children) and as group activities. Persons who have participated in Montessori-based group and intergenerational activities have demonstrated greater amounts of constructive engagement, defined as both direct verbal and nonverbal involvement in activities, than when participating in regular programming (Judge et al., 2000; Orsulic-Jeras, Judge, et al., 2000).

For example, Memory Bingo (Camp, 1999a, 1999b) is a Montessori-based group activity for persons with dementia. Participants receive four playing cards with answers that correspond to questions and/or phrases contained in calling cards that are read aloud. Participants alternate reading the questions or phrases and then look to see if they have the answer to each question or phrase on one of their cards. If so, they turn the card over. Once all participants have turned over all four cards, the game is finished. (See Camp, 1999a, 1999b, for more detailed descriptions of the game and its effects on behavioral indexes in persons with dementia.)

The critical importance of activities programming in fostering good quality of life is seen in Hellen's (1998, 2001) description of the "old" and "new" culture of dementia care. Aspects of the old culture involved ideas such as: Activities are just for entertainment, one size fits all—any activity will do, activity therapists are evaluated by the size of their group activities, don't repeat activities, and so on. Aspects of the new culture are represented by ideas such as: Activities offer therapeutic opportunities for overall wellness, activities should reflect personal strengths and life stories, smaller groups can foster friendships and participation more readily than large groups, repetitive activities can foster better participation and a sense of connectedness, and so on. Montessori's initial work involved attempts to reduce problematic behavior in young, slum-dwelling children by engaging them in meaningful activities. Her intervention was to educate children and offer them a chance to have meaningful roles in society. A similar approach can be used as a means of reducing problematic behaviors in persons with dementia by offering more meaningful activities and social roles for these persons.

THE INFLUENCE OF SETTING

Home Settings

Although behavior problems among persons with dementia are traditionally associated with long-term care settings, such problems exist among persons with dementia residing in the community (Teri, Borson, Kiyak, & Yamagishi, 1989). Care to persons with dementia residing at home is typically provided by family caregivers, home health aids, or some combination of the two.

Managing behavior problems at home can be challenging to family members for a variety of reasons, one of which is that home environments are not typically designed to maximize the functioning of a person with dementia. For instance, a room crowded with furniture or other clutter may increase confusion and agitation in a person with dementia (Skolaski-Pelliteri, 1985). Gwyther (1994) notes that persons with Alzheimer's disease can become suspicious of caregivers. "Accusations of theft or infidelity often result from feelings of loss of control, fear of abandonment, or confusion over lost or misplaced items" (p. 111). She notes that treating challenging behaviors involves changing the approaches and reactions of family members, as well as focusing on the routines, environment, and activities of persons with dementia. Books for caregivers such as *The 36-Hour Day* (Mace & Rabins, 1999) are widely read and include advice on handling problematic behaviors associated with dementia, such as using the six R's (Restrict—try to get the person with dementia to stop, especially if it might be harmful; Reassess—ask what might be causing the problem; Reconsider—think about how the situation looks from the point of view of the person with dementia; Rechannel—look for a way to let the behavior be manifested in a safer, more constructive way; Reassure—let the person know that he/she is safe and cared for; Review—think about the experience, what might have precipitated it, and how to handle it in the future. When nothing seems to work, the caregiver is encouraged to remember that negative attitudes and behaviors are part of the illness rather than a personal attack, to take the path of least difficulty, and to accept whatever compromise seems to work. A more formalized program of training caregivers to develop problem-solving skills in caring for persons with dementia has been described by Cotter, Stevens, Vance, and Burgio (2000).

The negative physical and emotional consequences of providing care to a family member with dementia have been well documented (for a review, see Schulz, O'Brien, Bookwala, & Fleissner, 1995). The consequence of behavior problems among community-dwelling residents tends to be strained family relationships and caregiver burden (Coen, Swanwick, O'Boyle, & Coakley, 1997; Deimling & Bass, 1986; Pearson, Teri, Wagner, Truax, & Logsdon, 1993). Family relationships may be strained both with the person with dementia and between family members attempting to care for the person with dementia. This may be particularly problematic when adult children attempt to share the responsibility of providing care to their elderly parents.

Providing care at home is also difficult because of the often unrelenting nature of providing care. Even if the person with dementia is able to become involved in an activity, the caregiver must usually be involved in the activity as well. Videotapes have been used to give caregivers respite by providing a meaningful independent activity for persons with dementia (Lund, Hill, Caserta, & Wright, 1995). This Video Respite© involves videotapes of actors and actresses simulating a visit with the person with dementia by asking questions, singing songs, telling stories, and asking the persons with dementia to do simple body movements and sing along. Preliminary results of this intervention suggest that 84% of persons with Alzheimer's disease are able to sit through the entire 33-minute video. By keeping a person with dementia occupied for 30 minutes, these videos should decrease behavior problems and give the caregiver at least a brief break from the demands of caregiving.

A benefit of providing care in the home setting is that the environment is usually familiar to the person with dementia, and routines have been developed that provide structure and support. On the other hand, this may also make accommodations to declining physical or cognitive capabilities difficult to accomplish. Decisions to prevent a person with dementia from driving, to use a home health worker, and so on can generate tensions between family caregivers and persons with dementia. Still, home settings are highly preferred to institutional settings for delivering care to persons with dementia. Use of home health workers and/or adult day health care services are seen as necessary compromises that enable persons with dementia to stay in home settings as long as possible.

Home health workers' training generally focuses on provision of physical care, such as bathing, dressing, and so on. Time spent not providing such care often involves serving the function of a sitter, with home health workers conversing with clients, watching TV, and so on. We have recently begun a training program to enable home health workers to provide Montessori-based activities to persons with dementia in home settings. Our preliminary results show that home health workers can effectively provide such activities and that doing so is seen as a more enjoyable use of time by both workers and clients. Training for home health workers needs to be expanded so that these individuals can become more effective providers of interventions for persons with dementia in home settings.

Adult Day Health Care Centers

The onset of dementia does not diminish an individual's need for autonomy and, in many cases, may increase this need. For some individuals, behavior problems may reflect a frustration with lack of independence. This may be particularly problematic for persons who reside at home and presumably have some independence there but attend adult day care centers for parts or all of the day. Access to enclosed outdoor areas has resulted in decreased agitation among participants of an adult day care center (Namazi & Johnson, 1992). The day care setting used in this study was designed so that residents could walk through interior walking paths that allowed access to an outdoor terrace and a secured park area. When clients were allowed access to the outdoors, decreases in verbal abuse, screaming, repetitive requests, walking, wandering, and agitation were seen. The quality of activities programming in adult day care centers can also reduce the incidence or severity of behavior problems by decreasing boredom (Acello, 1997).

While problematic behaviors associated with dementia in adult day health care clients are similar to those seen in home settings, this setting generates additional areas of concern. Wandering from a center is a key stressor for staff and administrators, especially when large numbers of clients attend a center. Another major concern involves clients insisting on leaving for home after lunch. At Menorah Park, we've used memory wallets (Bourgeois, 1992b) containing information about times of departure for home, pictures of automobiles and family members standing next to clients outside the center, and other cues to help orient clients and ease their anxieties. When large numbers of clients leave at one time, as on a bus, this can also create problems. Clients not riding on a bus may want to get on, or clients may attempt to board the wrong bus. Again, providing a fixed routine, extensive external cuing, and appropriate signage may reduce some problems associated with this situation.

Assisted Living

Assisted living is a residential setting that provides limited assistance with activities of daily living, such as meal preparation and activities planning, while still promoting independence in residents. Namazi and Chafetz (2001) review the various definitions of assisted living, noting that the concept of assisted living is far from uniform. It can range from a small board and care home to a corporate-owned facility that closely resembles a nursing home. Assisted living typically provides an intermediate level of care between home care and nursing home placement. As such, persons with dementia residing in assisted living facilities are typically higher functioning than those residing in nursing homes, but younger, less cognitively impaired, and less likely to need physical assistance than those in home settings (Kopetz et al., 2000). Some assisted living facilities specifically develop specialized dementia units (see Chafetz, 2001).

Behavior problems in persons with dementia have traditionally been studied among nursing home populations. However, dementia patients in assisted living facilities do exhibit behavior problems similar to those seen in long-term care residents. Behaviors such as aggression, wandering, falling, and depressive symptoms were highly correlated with time from admission to discharge to a nursing home (Kopetz et al., 2000). Assisted living facilities tend to have a lower tolerance for behavior problems than nursing homes. Less regulation of assisted living facilities concerning minimal training for staff and/or minimal levels of staffing produce the result that problematic behaviors in residents can place severe levels of stress on a setting that is not well equipped to handle such behaviors. However, because assisted living is usually less expensive than nursing home or providing paid care at home, families often want to extend the time spent in assisted living as long as possible. Thus, there is a fiscal motivation to determine a means to manage behavior problems so that the move to a nursing home can be delayed as long as possible.

The causes of behavior problems among residents of assisted living facilities are similar to those of residents of nursing homes. For instance, anxiety and depression have been associated with wandering among nursing home residents who may be attempting to relieve symptoms of anxiety and depression (Keily, Morris, & Algase, 2001). In addition, cognitive impairment and the physical ability to wander increase the likelihood that wandering will occur (Keily et al., 2001). These same characteristics may contribute to wandering behavior among residents of assisted living, who are under significantly less supervision than residents of nursing homes. Problems with finding their rooms can also impact wandering behavior, especially in large facilities where one floor or wing closely resembles another. Insufficient amounts of stimulation in terms of activities may increase boredom, which may in turn lead to wandering behavior among cognitively impaired residents of assisted living facilities. In addition, some problem behavior exhibited by elderly residents may be a means to control their environment and/or increase social attention (Baltes & Reisenzein, 1986).

Long-Term Care

One of the barriers to providing nonpharmacological interventions in long-term care is the significant variability in functioning and problem behaviors among residents of long-term care settings. Behavioral interventions are often initially focused on creating structure for persons who are no longer able to provide structure for themselves (Mintzer et al., 1993). However, this structure must often be provided through the implementation of *individualized* activities designed to decrease frustration and increase a sense of security in the individual (Holm et al., 1999). For example, while the use of classical music has been found to lead to decreases in agitation, selecting musical work preferred by the person with dementia (as noted by family members) resulted in more significant reductions in agitation than using traditional classical music (Gerdner, 2000). For many patients, decreases in agitation and aggressive behavior can also be achieved through either reducing levels of visual and auditory stimulation or altering the content of sensory stimulation. For example, bright light therapy has been found to lead to temporary decreases in agitation among nursing home residents who experience "sundowning" (Lovell, Ancoli-Israel, & Gevirtz, 1995). Similarly, the use of audiocassettes to play music the person with dementia used to like, books on tape, and so on may lead to reductions in behavior problems (Cohen-Mansfield, 2000a). However, other individuals may require more complex interventions to effectively address their particular behavior problem or level of agitation.

Some individuals in long-term care and other settings display behavior problems only at specific times or in specific settings. For instance, agitation and aggressive behaviors often occur when caregivers attempt to assist persons with activities of daily living such as bathing and dressing. One intervention designed to reduce agitation during bathing used natural environments such as the sounds of birds chirping combined with bright pictures for the patient to focus on during bathing. Although significant results on a group level were not found, individual successes using this method were noted (Whall et al., 1997). Rader and Barrick (2000) described a comprehensive approach to discovering underlying causes of problematic behaviors at bath time and offer a host of interventions for specific causes (e.g., if the person feels pain on movement, count with the person before moving; pad the shower chair to increase comfort; turn the heat on in the bathroom, and give the room time to warm up before giving a bath).

One of the most common and disturbing behavioral disorders is disruptive vocalizations (Cariaga et al., 1991). Disruptive vocalizations are distressing because they tend to upset the caregiver as well as other individuals near the individual. Disruptive verbalizations may involve both verbal (e.g., yelling, talking loudly) and nonverbal (e.g., moaning and sighing) behaviors. Individuals in advanced stages of dementia are more likely to exhibit more nonverbal disruptive verbalizations (Cohen-Mansfield & Werner, 1997). The purposes of disruptive verbalizations are heterogeneous as well, ranging from attempts to communicate basic needs (e.g., hunger, toileting) to attention seeking to self-stimulation. The frequency of disruptive verbalizations also varies, with nonpurposeful verbalizations tending to be more constant and need-based verbalizations tending to dissipate once the individual's need has been met (Cohen-Mansfield & Werner, 1997). Cohen-Mansfield (2000a) describes seven potential causes for verbal agitation, along with specific management approaches for each cause.

A key component of any intervention in long-term care settings is the nurse assistant (NA). It is the NA who will deliver the vast majority of personal care in long-term care settings and the NA who must deliver interventions over long periods. Burgio and Stevens (1999) described a model program in which NAs were trained to use behavioral interventions to address inappropriate behaviors of long-term care residents with dementia. They used a performance management system designed to encourage maintenance of behavior management techniques presented to NAs during training. This approach was referred to as the formal staff management (FSM) system. The components of FSM included:

- Clear definition of goals and tasks.
- Self-monitoring and supervisory monitoring of job skill performance (i.e., use of behavior management techniques).
- Verbal and written performance feedback.
- Rewards and corrective feedback tied to performance.

Their initial results as to NAs' maintenance of trained skills were encouraging, and similar approaches need to be developed, implemented, and assessed to determine how best to allow NAs to implement other interventions for dementia. N. M. Schneider, Diggs, Orsulic, and Camp (1999), for example, described a pilot program in which NAs were trained to implement Montessori-based activities in a long-term care setting.

MULTICULTURAL ISSUES

A manual for developing Montessori-based activities for persons with dementia has been developed (Camp, 1999b). In the course of having the manual translated into Japanese, the translator brought up a problem. One of the activities involved a tub of rice, in which were hidden objects (i.e., buried treasure). Participants were to use a slotted spoon to pick up one of the buried objects and to sift the rice by gently shaking the spoon until only the object was left in the spoon. The translator stated that older Japanese might take offense at treating rice in such a cavalier manner because each grain of rice would be held as important and almost sacred by these elderly adults. As a result, the materials used in the activity had to be changed. This illustrates how differences between cultural beliefs can create unanticipated problems for delivering care to persons with dementia.

Help-seeking and help-accepting in caregivers can be heavily influenced by culture. For example, Valle (1998) describes situations involving "cultural paralysis," in which help is neither sought nor accepted by caregivers of persons with dementia in large part because of cultural expectations. For example, Hispanic female caregivers may see their role of caring for an elderly relative with dementia as part of their *deber* (sense of obligation) to the relative.

Fried and Mehrotra (1998) noted that while Asian Americans were generally unwilling to use adult day health care services, African Americans often are more likely to use such services than older Whites—and to use them more frequently. As in the case of in-home services, this is in part due to African Americans' using Medicaid funding to pay for day care services. Fried and Mehrotra also stated that minorities are significantly underrepresented in nursing home settings. Asian/Pacific Islanders were said to generally cite language and cultural issues as critical factors in this outcome. African Americans identified cost and discrimination practices, while American Indians cited social and cultural factors as most important. Hispanics cited discrimination, cost, and isolation caused by language and cultural differences.

Cultural differences between persons with dementia and their caregivers can inhibit effective delivery of care, create behavioral disturbances stemming from such differences, or prevent persons with dementia from having unmet needs addressed. This is especially true in institutional settings. Crose (2000) notes: "The older women and minorities who currently live in nursing homes grew up in a time of unquestioned White male rule and have experienced discrimination throughout most of their lives. Many arrived in this country as immigrants or were born to immigrant parents for whom English was a second or third language" (p. 374).

──────────────── Case Study ────────────────

Mrs. C, a long-term care resident on a heavy physical care unit, had advanced dementia and spoke only Russian. Most staff on the unit were African American women from the inner city of an urban area. Staff complained that the resident was throwing orange juice at them when they would try to remove her food tray after meals. A psychologist spoke to the staff about what might precipitate such behavior and discussed the idea that the resident might be wishing to demonstrate some control over when her tray would or would not be removed. A printed card was then placed on the dining room wall, on which was written a phoneticized version of the Russian phrase "Are you finished?" Thus, when staff read aloud the phrase, printed in English, the resident could understand that nurse assistants were asking if she was finished. If the resident answered "Nyet," staff would leave and come back later to ask again. If the resident answered "Dah," the tray was removed without incident.

───

Crose (2000) notes that job satisfaction for NAs in long-term care settings (and the same is probably true for caregiving staff in adult day health care, assisted living, and home health care) centers around relationships with clients/residents. There is a strong tendency for these caregivers to project personal meaning into clients'/residents' actions and to interpret problematic behaviors as personal affronts. This may be especially problematic when language and/or cultural differences exist between caregivers and persons with dementia.

AN ALGORITHM FOR DETERMINING THE UNDERLYING CAUSE(S) OF BEHAVIORAL PROBLEMS

Whenever a problematic behavior occurs and an intervention is requested, it is critical that the first question be "Why is this person behaving in this way?" The answer cannot be "Because he/she has dementia." That is an extreme example of circular reasoning. ("And how do we know that he/she has dementia?" Because he/she is behaving in this way.) It is also not conducive to discovering an appropriate intervention.

Williams and colleagues (Williams, Wood, Moorleghen, & Chittuluru, 1995) developed a decision model to assist in the management of disruptive behavior problems among individuals with dementia residing in long-term care settings (see Figure 13.1). This model highlights four decision modules to assist clinicians (and caregivers) in the identification of causes of an individual's behavior problem. Before entering into the decision modules, it must first be determined whether the behavior has a somatic cause. At this point, an assessment should be made to determine if sensory deficits may be a factor in the problematic behavior (e.g., Is the person's hearing aid working or should the battery be replaced? Has his or her vision worsened?). Infections (e.g., UTIs), poor hydration, pain (e.g., Do poorly fitting dentures result in problematic behaviors at meals?), and so on also should be ruled out before proceeding to the first module and attempting to create interventions for functional causes. Of course, communication problems associated with dementia and/or cultural differences/use of a foreign language can exacerbate problems of somatic origins and make their detection and treatment more challenging.

If the behavior has a functional cause, the first module comes into play. It must then be decided if the individual is experiencing an appropriate amount of stimulation; that is, are they being over- or understimulated? Here, activities such as Montessori-based programming take on the role of an intervention for problematic behaviors. In our research, we have often seen persons with dementia exhibit behaviors such as repetitive vocalizations outside of Montessori-based activities programming but who exhibit no such behaviors during these activities. Rather than decry the lack of generalization of the effects of the intervention outside the context of providing activities, we recommend finding more opportunities for such activities to be made available throughout the course of the day.

Of course, problematic behaviors produced by overstimulation are generally approached by reducing the level of stimulation impinging on the person with dementia. Long-term care units can often be extremely noisy places, with call bells and alarms ringing throughout the day. Playing music can be a cause of overstimulation if it is too loud, especially if the music being played fits the tastes of staff as opposed to residents. Music played during meals should be subtle and subdued. Trying to have a meal and a conversation in an atmosphere that is too noisy is an uncomfortable experience, whether dining out in a restaurant or having lunch on a long-term care unit.

The second module involves determining who "owns" the problem—the person with dementia or the caregiver. Translating the original model to a

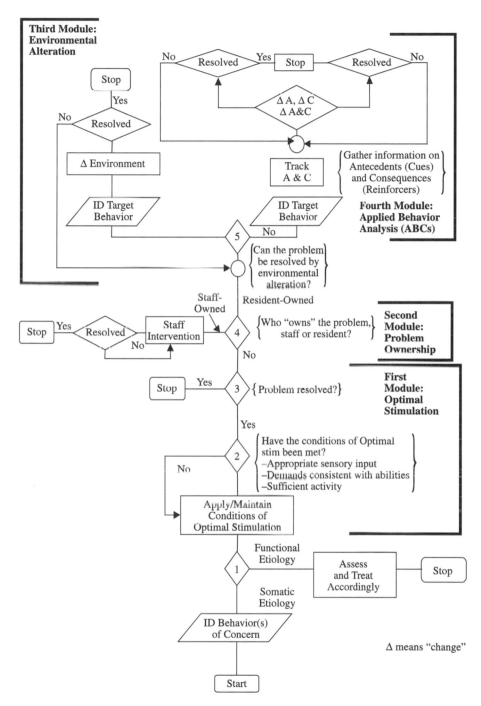

Figure 13.1   The disruptive behavior decision model. Printed with permission of the publisher.

home setting, consider the following situation. A woman was serving as caregiver for her spouse in their home. The wife reported that her husband would get frustrated when grandchildren came to visit because he could not remember their names. It was suggested that the grandchildren wear name tags during visits so that their grandfather could simply read their names and, therefore, circumvent his memory loss. His wife responded, "But that would be cheating!" In this case, intervention with the caregiver to reduce unrealistic expectations or assumptions was required. In long-term care, residents who have taken baths all of their lives may appear resistant to taking showers, or residents who were used to showers may exhibit "problematic behaviors" when told to take a bath. Developing some flexibility on the part of staff so that the means of cleaning residents fits residents' past experiences may be the best intervention in these circumstances.

If the behavior has a functional etiology and is owned by the person with dementia, the next module involves environmental alteration. Consider the case of holocaust survivors who develop dementia and are placed in long-term care. Taking these persons into a sterile, institutional shower can create catastrophic reactions. This is an example of how an environmental alteration is called for to alleviate "problematic behavior."

Lawton (2001) emphasized that environments for persons with dementia should address four general classes of needs: decreasing disturbing behavior, increasing social behavior, increasing activity, and increasing positive affect while decreasing negative affect. Note that most of his emphasis was on using environmental configurations to have positive impact on the quality of life for persons with dementia, not simply reducing problematic behaviors.

Cohen and Diaz Moore (1999) are exploring environmental correlates of cultural and ethnic experiences in assisted living settings. Day, Carreon, and Stump (2000) give an excellent overview of environmental alterations for persons with dementia, as does Brawley (2001). Calkins (2001) provides an integrated model of place, examining the effects of different dimensions of settings (organizational, social, individual, physical) and levels of settings (microsystem, e.g., rules, staff ratios; mesosystem, e.g., institutional values as to safety versus privacy; macrosystem, e.g., cultural values) that can serve as a useful heuristic for understanding how environment influences behaviors in dementia care settings.

Finally, if the behavior has not decreased or stopped after altering the environment, clinicians should engage in applied behavior analysis to attempt to control the problem. Antecedents and consequences of behaviors are identified and changed on an individual basis to attempt to control a problem. Consider a case in which several women with dementia in a long-term care setting began to refuse to take showers because they did not want to be seen naked by men. The "men" referred to in this case involved a group of female NAs who had decided to get their hair cut fashionably short. In this case, the antecedent was the length of the NAs' hair. The intervention, involving a change of the antecedent, consisted of the unit acquiring a set of cheap, long-haired wigs that could be donned by nurse assistants before taking female residents to the shower and taken off afterwards.

As to altering consequences, persons with dementia sometimes are inadvertently rewarded with attention (albeit negative attention) when they engage in problematic behaviors. By removing attention following an incident of problem behavior, the negative behavior is often extinguished. Camp and Foss (1997) described a case in which an adult day health care client was engaging in repetitive questioning behavior more than 800 times per day on a consistent basis; that is, "When is my husband going to pick me up?" It was next determined that the client already knew the answer to the question and that staff generally provided reassurance that he was indeed going to come for her that day in addition to saying "6:30" when answering the question. At that point, staff began providing reassurance that her husband was coming to pick her up when the woman was *not* asking the question, especially if the woman was engaged in a desirable behavior such as social interactions with other clients, taking part in a group activity, and so on. When she asked her question, staff would politely say, "When do you think?" The woman would respond "6:30" and staff would reply "That's right; now I have to help someone else," and leave to work with another client. By changing consequences, staff were able to significantly reduce the woman's problematic behavior and increase her ability to benefit from the center's activities.

Williams and colleagues (1995) reported a positive response from nursing staff who used this model in long-term care settings. It is a model that should work well across caregiving settings. The critical feature of the model, as is the case with designing any intervention for persons with dementia, is the assumption that behavior is not random. Persons with dementia are *persons* with dementia, and their behavior reflects genuinely human attempts to cope and make sense out of what is happening to and around them. Under the same circumstances, the readers of this work would (and will) behave similarly. We all, therefore, have a personal stake in the development of better nonpharmacological interventions for persons with dementia.

CHALLENGES TO PROVIDING NONPHARMACOLOGICAL TREATMENTS

Many challenges face the development and implementation of nonpharmacological interventions for persons with dementia. Camp (2001) described the first and, perhaps, most formidable, such problem—*therapeutic nihilism.* This refers to the belief that interventions for persons with dementia are doomed to failure because these individuals have a progressive illness and, it is assumed, cannot learn new information or new behaviors. If caregivers or facility administrators believe that palliative care is all that can or should be afforded persons with dementia, implementation of interventions is never attempted. Overcoming therapeutic nihilism first involves challenging this belief, usually by a demonstration that a person with dementia can do something (learn something new, change behavior, respond to external cues, etc.) that was considered impossible. Fortunately for interventionists, expectations of individuals who adhere to therapeutic nihilism are so low that it is relatively easy to enable persons with dementia to do the impossible. But, of course, this is only the first step. The next question raised is "You may be able to produce this change in behavior, but can I (or my staff) get the same results?" This leads to our next challenge.

Who delivers the intervention? Nonpharmacological interventions are generally designed by psychologists, nurse researchers, rehabilitation professionals, or recreational therapists. Territorial disputes among disciplines as to who is best qualified to deliver and assess the impact of such interventions can severely constrict the access of persons with dementia to such treatments. The need for developing an interdisciplinary approach to dementia care has been voiced (Lichtenberg, 1994, 1998), and we reiterate this position.

In addition, to the extent that nonpharmacological interventions are implemented in institutional settings, the ability to create and sustain positive outcomes will be placed in the hands of persons who receive both minimum amounts of training and minimum wages. A case in point is that of NAs in long-term care settings. In the state of Ohio, more training is required to become certified as a dog groomer than to become certified as a NA. This is not atypical. In an industry where staff turnover among NAs at facilities can range from 50% to 100% on a yearly basis, designing effective interventions may require that the infrastructure to support their implementation and maintenance be substantially improved. If this is not done, no matter how useful a nonpharmacological intervention may be, it will not be available for residents with dementia on a consistent basis. Beck (2001) reviews current recommendations for improving training of NAs, including developing better employee screening instruments to select persons for this job who have the best profile of personal characteristics to deliver care to persons with dementia. Attempts to better train nurse assistants in programs such as those using behavioral management techniques have demonstrated potential (Burgio & Stevens, 1999), but the energies of social and behavioral scientists must be spent to help create a work force that is stable, or our interventions will not have lasting impact over meaningful time frames.

Individualizing Treatment

To be successful, nonpharmacological interventions often must be highly individualized in nature. For example, finding an activity that will engage a resident whose occupation was plumbing (or contract law or playing in a symphony) can require the creation of a relatively unique set of materials. Enabling caregivers to develop such individualized treatment regimens is a challenge.

Undue Reliance on Clinical Trials Models

Another general barrier to knowledge is the mind-set that a clinical trials model is the only (or even the best) means of obtaining information as to the optimal form of treatment for dementia. A clinical trials approach uses highly selective inclusion and exclusion criteria, randomized selection and assignment to treatments, double-blinding for data collection, and standardized application of treatment and control procedures by well-trained staff. The model generally assumes that a single underlying cause produces a discrete symptom or small set of symptoms. The focus of a clinical trials model is to demonstrate the efficacy of treatment for that cause. The logic is that, before a treatment can be (or should be) tested for generalization, it must first demonstrate statistically significant effects.

Clinical trials in dementia research generally focus on development of drugs that can be administered early in the course of a disease process. Early diagnosis and treatment are the hallmarks of this type of research. Persons with dementia, especially those living in institutional settings and/or those in advanced stages of dementia, often are too frail or have too many comorbidities to be considered for clinical trials. Even when a "pure" sample of persons with a specific disorder such as Alzheimer's disease can be screened and tested, problematic behaviors can vary greatly within the sample.

As mentioned earlier, the desired nonpharmacological outcomes for persons with dementia are often highly individualized. "Success" treating a Hungarian immigrant assisted living resident with Pick's disease can be idiosyncratic. Ten long-term care residents demonstrating repetitive vocalizations on a unit may require at least five different interventions to alleviate or at least reduce the problematic behavior. This appears odd and inappropriate to researchers (and grant reviewers) who are used to conceptualizing variation in treatment as giving 5 versus 10 milligrams of a chemical compound.

Moreover, when chemical agents that have shown efficacy in clinical trials are implemented in real world settings such as long-term care, it is often difficult to demonstrate their effectiveness (i.e., ability to produce clinically meaningful results in real-world settings, for example, Camp, Lee, & Philips, 2000; Gifford et al., 1999). Camp (2001) describes the formidable challenges seen in attempts to translate efficacious treatments into effective treatments in the context of interventions for persons with dementia and provides a set of criteria that must be met for interventions to be considered truly effective.

Does this mean that nonpharmacological treatments for persons with dementia cannot or should not be manualized? That is a debate that is currently raging, and its conclusion is not known. Though manuals may be necessary for teaching methods and techniques, additional training may be needed to understand when, for whom, and how to alter parameters based on individuals' needs. However, alternative models focusing on demonstrating effectiveness of nonpharmacological treatment on a large scale must become available and accepted both as legitimate and of similar stature to clinical trials. This is a formidable but worthwhile task. Until it is accomplished, nonpharmacologic interventions for persons with dementia will be developed piecemeal and implemented sporadically, resulting in substantially lower quality of care than is actually obtainable.

Providing Bridging and Infrastructure Support for Interventions

A final, and perhaps most critical, challenge to designing effective nonpharmacological interventions is the need to provide bridging and infrastructure support for such interventions. Administrators charged with overseeing the delivery of services to persons with dementia (and in the case of many facilities, doing so at a profit) focus on three specific areas: reimbursement, marketing, and compliance with regulatory agency directives/inspections. It is simply not sufficient for an intervention to be developed, shown to be efficacious (i.e., it will produce a positive effect) and effective (i.e., it will produce a positive effect in real world settings). The intervention will not be implemented unless it can be explicitly shown to interface with one or more of these three areas of interest to administrators.

-------------------------------- Case Study --------------------------------

At the Myers Research Institute, we are currently engaged in a number of projects designed to address this issue. For example, we have been examining the use of a cognitive intervention for persons with dementia called spaced-retrieval (SR). SR involved giving persons with dementia (and other cognitive impairments) practice successfully recalling information over increasing time intervals. We have been working with speech-language pathologists to develop models for implementation of SR as a billable procedure. Working with rehabilitation staff, we now can provide detailed information about how to:

- Describe SR to medical directors or attending physicians to encourage their initial referrals of clients with dementia.
- Triage to determine which persons with dementia to select as initial clients when starting to deliver SR in facilities where it was never implemented before.
- Screen potential clients to document that they show potential for responding well to this treatment modality.

- Build a case load by increasing the number of persons with dementia being treated.

- Classify SR in clinical notes (e.g., it is a "modality" and not a "therapy" per se, listed under the "A" section in S.O.A.P. notes for speech-language pathologists).

- Do self-checks as a quality control procedure to insure that SR is being implemented appropriately.

- Document progress toward therapeutic goals.

- Determine which ICD-9 codes to use when requesting reimbursement.

- Describe SR to representatives of reimbursing agencies so that requests for payment based on use of SR won't be summarily dismissed because "persons with dementia cannot learn new things."

- Develop train-the-trainer programs to disseminate the intervention.

- Develop quality assurance protocols to ensure that the integrity of treatment does not dissipate across time, trainers, or implementation sites.

This approach, which includes provision of case studies with full documentation, enables therapists to implement SR quickly and appropriately. We also document changes in total number of clients seen and number of clients seen with dementia, along with levels of reimbursement received, before and after implementation of SR training within facilities. This lets us document improvements in the "bottom line" as a result of the implementation of this intervention, which is critical for obtaining administrative support for the implementation of this intervention.

We would not go to this trouble if there were not compelling evidence that SR can be an effective intervention for persons with dementia. Fortunately, such evidence exists (Brush & Camp, 1998a, 1998b, 1998c, 1999; Camp, Bird, & Cherry, 2000; Camp, Foss, Stevens, & O'Hanlon, 1996; Cherry, Simmons, & Camp, 1999). The key issue with SR, as is the case with any nonpharmacological intervention, is how to ensure that it will be applied where and when it is most needed. An intervention cannot have a positive impact on the quality of life of persons with dementia if it remains on journal pages and does not appear in the real world. Altruism alone is not a sufficient motivator to accomplish this end. In our applied research setting, we have a guiding motto: "It is not enough to be right; you must also help people." Tying an intervention to a key interest area of administrators is a way to improve quality of life for persons with dementia. Many times, it is the only way.

REFERENCES

Acello, B. (1997, March). Managing difficult behavior. *Journal of Nursing Assistants,* 24–26.

Allen-Burge, R., Stevens, A. B., & Burgio, L. D. (1999). Effective behavioral interventions for decreasing dementia-related challenging behaviors in nursing homes. *International Journal of Geriatric Psychiatry, 14,* 213–232.

Antenucci, V. M., Camp, C. J., Sterns, H., Sterns, R., & Sterns, A. (2001). Overcoming linguistic and cultural barriers: Lessons from long-term care settings. In K. H. Namazi & P. K. Chafetz (Eds.), *Assisted living: Current issues in facility management and resident care* (pp. 91–104). Westport, CT: Auburn House.

Arkin, S. M. (2001). Alzheimer rehabilitation by students: Interventions and outcomes. *Neuropsychological Rehabilitation, 11*(3/4), 273–317.

Auer, S. R., Sclan, S. G., Yaffee, R. A., & Reisberg, B. (1994). The neglected half of Alzheimer's disease: Cognitive and functional concomitants of severe dementia. *Journal of the American Geriatrics Society, 42,* 1266–1272.

Baltes, M. M., & Reisenzein, R. (1986). The social world in long-term care institutions: Psychosocial control toward dependence. In M. M. Baltes & P. B. Baltes (Eds.), *The psychology of control and aging* (pp. 315–343). Hillsdale, NJ: Erlbaum.

Beck, C. K. (1998). Psychosocial and behavioral interventions for Alzheimer's disease patients and their families. *American Journal of Geriatric Psychiatry, 6,* S41–S48.

Beck, C. K. (2001). Identification and assessment of effective services and interventions: The nursing home perspective. *Aging and Mental Health, 5*(Suppl. 1), S99–S111.

Bologna, S. M., & Camp, C. J. (1997). Covert versus overt self-recognition in late stage Alzheimer's disease. *Journal of the International Neuropsychological Society, 3,* 195–198.

Bourgeois, M. S. (1992a). *Conversing with memory-impaired individuals: Using memory aids.* Gaylord, MI: Northern Speech Services.

Bourgeois, M. S. (1992b). Evaluating memory wallets in conversations with persons with dementia. *Journal of Speech and Hearing Research, 35,* 1344–1357.

Bourgeois, M. S. (1997). Families caring for elders at home: Caregiver training. In B. B. Shadden & M. A. Toner (Eds.), *Aging and communication: For clinicians by clinicians* (pp. 227–249). Austin, TX: ProEd.

Brawley, E. C. (2001). Environmental design for Alzheimer's disease: A quality of life issue. *Aging and Mental Health, 5*(Suppl. 1), S79–S83.

Brush, J. A., & Camp, C. J. (1998a). *A therapy technique for improving memory: Spaced retrieval.* Beachwood, OH: Menorah Park Center for Senior Living.

Brush, J. A., & Camp, C. J. (1998b). Using spaced retrieval as an intervention during speech-language therapy. *Clinical Gerontologist, 19,* 51–64.

Brush, J. A., & Camp, C. J. (1998c). Using spaced retrieval to treat dysphagia in a long-term care resident with dementia. *Clinical Gerontologist, 19*(2), 96–99.

Brush, J. A., & Camp, C. J. (1999). Effective interventions for persons with dementia: Using spaced retrieval and Montessori techniques. *Neurophysiology and Neurogenic Speech and Language Disorders, 9*(4), 27–32.

Burant, C. J., & Camp, C. J. (1996). Language boards: Enabling direct care staff to speak foreign languages. *Clinical Gerontologist, 16*(4), 83–85.

Burgio, L. (1996). Interventions for the behavioral complications of Alzheimer's disease: Behavioral approaches. *International Psychogeriatrics, 8,* 45–52.

Burgio, L. D., & Stevens, A. B. (1999). Behavioral interventions and motivational systems in the nursing home. In R. Schulz, G. Maddox, & M. P. Lawton (Eds.), *Annual review of gerontology and geriatrics* (Vol. 18, pp. 284–320). New York: Springer.

Burton, L. C., German, S. P., Rovner, B. W., & Brant, L. J. (1992). Physical restrain use and cognitive decline among nursing home residents. *Journal of the American Geriatrics Society, 4,* 811–816.

Calkins, M. P. (2001). The physical and social environment of the person with Alzheimer's disease. *Aging and Mental Health, 5*(Suppl. 1), S74–S78.

Camp, C. J. (1999a). Memory interventions for normal and pathological older adults. In R. Schulz, M. P. Lawton, & G. Maddox (Eds.), *Annual review of gerontology and geriatrics* (Vol. 18, pp. 155–189). New York: Springer.

Camp, C. J. (Ed.). (1999b). *Montessori-based activities for persons with dementia* (Vol. 1). Beachwood, OH: Menorah Park Center for Senior Living.

Camp, C. J. (2001). From efficacy to effectiveness to diffusion: Making the transitions in dementia intervention research. *Neuropsychological Rehabilitation, 11,* 495–517.

Camp, C. J., Bird, M. J., & Cherry, K. E. (2000). Retrieval strategies as a rehabilitation aid for cognitive loss in pathological aging. In R. D. Hill, L. Bäckman, & A. S. Neely (Eds.), *Cognitive rehabilitation in old age* (pp. 224–248). New York: Oxford University Press.

Camp, C. J., Burant, C. J., & Graham, G. C. (1996). The InterpreCare System™: Overcoming language barriers in long-term care. *Gerontologist, 36,* 821–823.

Camp, C. J., Cohen-Mansfield, J., & Capezuti, E. A. (2002). Use of nonpharmacological interventions among nursing home residents with dementia. *Psychiatric Services, 53,* 1397–1401.

Camp, C. J., & Foss, J. W. (1997). Designing ecologically valid memory interventions for persons with dementia. In D. G. Payne & F. G. Conrad (Eds.), *Intersections in basic and applied memory research* (pp. 311–325). Mahwah, NJ: Erlbaum.

Camp, C. J., Foss, J. W., Stevens, A. B., & O'Hanlon, A. M. (1996). Improving prospective memory task performance in Alzheimer's disease. In M. A. Brandimonte, G. O. Einstein, & M. A. McDaniel (Eds.), *Prospective memory: Theory and applications* (pp. 351–367). Mahwah, NJ: Erlbaum.

Camp, C. J., Koss, E., & Judge, K. S. (1999). Cognitive assessment in late stage dementia. In P. A. Lichtenberg (Ed.), *Handbook of assessment in clinical gerontology* (pp. 442–467). New York: Wiley.

Camp, C. J., Lee, M. M., & Phillips, C. D. (2000, November). *Effects of donepezil on affect, engagement, cognition, and activities of daily living in residents of a dementia unit.* Poster presented at the annual meeting of the Gerontological Society of America, Washington, DC.

Camp, C. J., & Mattern, J. M. (1999). Innovations in managing Alzheimer's disease. In D. E. Biegel & A. Blum (Eds.), *Innovations in practice and service delivery across the lifespan* (pp. 276–294). New York: Oxford University Press.

Capezuti, E. (2000). Preventing falls and injuries while reducing siderail use. *Annals of Long-Term Care, 8*(6), 57–63.

Capezuti, E., Strumpf, N. E., Evans, L. K., Grisson, J. A., & Maislin, G. (1998). The relationship between physical restraint removal and falls and injuries among nursing home residents. *Journals of Gerontology: Series A, Biological Sciences and Medical Sciences, 53A,* M47–M53.

Capezuti, E., & Talerico, K. A. (1999). Review article: Physical restraint removal, falls and injuries. *Research and Practice in Alzheimer's Disease, 2,* 338–355.

Cariaga, J., Burgio, L., Flynn, W., & Martin, D. (1991). A controlled study of disruptive vocalizations among geriatric residents in nursing homes. *Journal of the American Geriatrics Society, 39,* 501–507.

Castle, N. G., & Mor, V. (1998). Physical restraints in nursing homes: A review of the literature since the nursing home Reform Act of 1987. *Medical Care Research and Review, 55,* 139–170.

Chafetz, P. K. (2001). Developing dementia care units in assisted living facilities. In K. H. Namazi & P. K. Chafetz (Eds.), *Assisted living: Current issues in facility management and resident care* (pp. 105–126). Westport, CT: Auburn House.

Cherry, K. E., Simmons, S. S., & Camp, C. J. (1999). Spaced-retrieval enhances memory in older adults with probable Alzheimer's disease. *Journal of Clinical Geropsychology, 5,* 159–175.

Clark, L. W. (1997). Communication intervention for family caregivers and professional health providers. In B. B. Shadden & M. A. Toner (Eds.), *Aging and communication: For clinicians by clinicians* (pp. 251–274). Austin, TX: ProEd.

Coen, R. F., Swanwick, G. R., O'Boyle, C. A., & Coakley, D. (1997). Behavior disturbance and other predictors of caregiver burden in Alzheimer's disease. *International Journal of Geriatric Psychiatry, 12,* 331–336.

Cohen, U., & Diaz Moore, K. (1999). Integrating cultural heritage into assisted living environments. In B. Schwartz & R. Brent (Eds.), *Aging, autonomy, and architecture: Advances in assisted living.* Baltimore: The Johns Hopkins University Press.

Cohen-Mansfield, J. (1986). Agitated behaviors in the elderly. II: Preliminary results in the cognitively deteriorated. *Journal of the American Geriatrics Society, 34,* 722–727.

Cohen-Mansfield, J. (1988). Agitated behavior and cognitive functioning in nursing home residents: Preliminary results. *Clinical Gerontologist, 7*(3/4), 11–22.

Cohen-Mansfield, J. (2000a). Nonpharmacological management of behavioral problems in persons with dementia. *Alzheimer's Care Quarterly, 1*(4), 22–34.

Cohen-Mansfield, J. (2000b). Theoretical frameworks for behavioral problems in dementia. *Alzheimer's Care Quarterly, 1*(4), 8–21.

Cohen-Mansfield, J. (2001). Nonpharmacologic interventions for inappropriate behaviors in dementia: A review, summary, and critique. *American Journal of Geriatric Psychiatry, 9,* 361–381.

Cohen-Mansfield, J., & Billig, N. (1986). Agitated behaviors in the elderly. I: A conceptual review. *Journal of the American Geriatrics Society, 34,* 711–721.

Cohen-Mansfield, J., Marx, M. S., & Rosenthal, A. S. (1989). A description of agitation in a nursing home. *Journals of Gerontology: Series A, Biological Sciences and Medical Sciences, 44,* M77–M84.

Cohen-Mansfield, J., & Werner, P. (1997). Typology of disruptive vocalization in older persons suffering from dementia. *International Journal of Geriatric Psychiatry, 12,* 1079–1091.

Cole, M. G., & Dastoor, D. P. (1980). Development of a dementia rating scale: Preliminary communication. *Journal of Clinical Experimental Gerontology, 2,* 46–63.

Cole, M. G., & Dastoor, D. P. (1987). A new hierarchic approach to the measurement of dementia. *Psychosomatics, 28,* 298–304.

Cotter, E. M., Stevens, A. B., Vance, D. E., & Burgio, L. D. (2000). Caregiver skills training in problem solving. *Alzheimer's Care Quarterly, 1*(4), 50–61.

Crose, R. (2000). The impact of culture and gender on mental health. In V. Molinari (Ed.), *Professional psychology in long-term care* (pp. 373–400). New York: Hatherleigh Press.

Davis, L. L., Buckwalter, K., & Burgio, L. D. (1997). Measuring problem behaviors in dementia: Developing a methodological agenda. *Advances in Nursing Science, 20,* 40–55.

Day, K., Carreon, D., & Stump, C. (2000). The therapeutic design of environments for people with dementia: A review of empirical research. *Gerontologist, 40*(4), 397–415.

Deimling, G. T., & Bass, D. M. (1986). Symptoms of mental impairment among elderly adults and their effects on family caregivers. *Journal of Gerontology, 41,* 778–784.

Drevets, W. C., & Rubin, E. H. (1989). Psychotic symptoms and the longitudinal course of senile dementia of the Alzheimer type. *Biological Psychiatry, 25,* 39–48.

Ejaz, F. K., & Rose, M. S. (1997). A stepwise approach to reducing physical restraints in nursing homes. *Nursing Home Medicine, 5,* 62–68.

Evans, L. K., Strumpf, N. E., Allen-Taylor, S. L., Capezuti, E., Maislin, G., & Jocobsen, B. (1997). A clinical trial to reduce restraints in nursing homes. *Journal of the American Geriatric Society, 45,* 675–681.

Fried, S. B., & Mehrotra, C. M. (1998). *Aging and diversity: An active learning experience.* Washington, DC: Taylor & Francis.

Gerdner, L. A. (2000). Effects of individualized versus classical "Relaxation" music on the frequency of agitation in elderly persons with Alzheimer's disease and related disorders. *International Psychogeriatrics, 12,* 49–65.

Gifford, D. R., Lapane, K. L., Gambassi, B., Landi, F., Mor, V., Bernabei, R., et al. (1999). Tacrine use in nursing homes: Implications for prescribing new cholinesterase inhibitors. *Neurology, 50,* 238–244.

Gwyther, L. (1994). Managing challenging behaviors at home. *Alzheimer Disease and Associated Disorders, 8*(Suppl. 3), 110–112.

Harvis, K. A. (1990). Care plan approach to dementia. *Geriatric Nursing, 2,* 76–80.

Harwood, D. G., Barker, W. W., Ownby, R. L., & Duara, R. (2000). Relationship of behavioral and psychological symptoms to cognitive impairment and functional status in Alzheimer's disease. *International Journal of Geriatric Psychiatry, 15,* 393–400.

Hellen, C. R. (1998). *Alzheimer's disease: Activity focused care.* Boston: Butterworth-Heinemann.

Hellen, C. R. (2001). Activities: The "old" and "new" culture. *Alzheimer's Disease Quarterly, 2*(3), 57–58.

Holm, A., Michel, M., Stern, G. A., Hung, T., Klein, T., Flaherty, L., et al. (1999). The outcomes of an inpatient treatment program for geriatric patients with dementia and dysfunctional behaviors. *Gerontologist, 39,* 668–676.

Hurley, A., Volicer, L., Camberg, L., Ashley, J., Woods, P., Odenheimer, G., et al. (1999). Measurement of observed agitation in patients with dementia of the Alzheimer type. *Journal of Mental Health and Aging, 5,* 117–133.

Judge, K. S., Camp, C. J., & Orsulic-Jeras, S. (2000). Use of Montessori-based activities for clients with dementia in adult day care: Effects on engagement. *American Journal of Alzheimer's Disease, 15,* 42–46.

Keily, D. K., Morris, J. N., & Algase, D. L. (2001). Resident characteristics associated with wandering in nursing homes. *International Journal of Geriatric Psychiatry, 15,* 1013–1020.

Kim, E. J., & Buschmann, M. T. (1999). The effect of expressive physical touch on patients with dementia. *International Journal of Nursing Studies, 36,* 325–243.

Kitwood, T. (1997). *Dementia reconsidered: The person comes first.* Buckingham, England: Open University Press.

Kolanowski, A. M., Strand, G., & Whall, A. (1997). A pilot study of the relation of premorbid characteristics to behavior in dementia. *Journal of Gerontological Nursing, 23*(2), 21–30.

Koltai, D., & Branch, L. G. (1999). Cognitive and affective interventions to maximize abilities and adjustments in dementia. *Annals of Psychiatry: Basic and Clinical Neurosciences, 7,* 241–255.

Kopetz, S., Steele, C. D., Brandt, J., Baker, A., Kronberg, M., Galik, E., et al. (2000). Characteristics and outcomes of dementia residents in an assisted living facility. *International Journal or Geriatric Psychiatry, 15,* 586–593.

Koss, E., Weiner, M., Ernesto, C., Cohen-Mansfield, J., Ferris, S. H., Grundman, M., et al. (1997). Assessing patterns of agitation in Alzheimer's disease patients with the Cohen-Mansfield Agitation Inventory. *Alzheimer Disease and Associated Disorders, 11,* S45–S50.

Lantz, M. S., Buchalter, E. N., & McBee, L. (1997). The Wellness Group: A novel intervention for coping with disruptive behavior in elderly nursing home residents. *Gerontologist, 37,* 551–556.

Lawton, M. P. (2001). The physical environment of the person with Alzheimer's disease. *Aging and Mental Health, 5*(Suppl. 1), S56–S64.

Lichtenberg, P. A. (1994). *A guide to psychological practice in long-term care.* Binghamton, NY: Haworth Press.

Lichtenberg, P. A. (1998). *Mental health practice in geriatric health care settings.* New York: Haworth Press.

Logsdon, R. G., Teri, L., Weiner, M. F., Gibbons, L. E., Raskind, M., Peskind, E., et al. (1999). Assessment of agitation in Alzheimer's disease: The Agitated Behavior in Dementia Scale. *Journal of the American Geriatrics Society, 47*(11), 1354–1358.

Lovell, B. B., Ancoli-Israel, S., & Gevirtz, R. (1995). Effect of bright light treatment on agitated behavior in institutionalized elderly subjects. *Psychiatry Research, 57,* 7–12.

Lund, D. A., Hill, R. D., Caserta, M .S., & Wright, S. D. (1995). Video respite: An innovative resource for family, professional caregivers, and persons with dementia. *Gerontologist, 35,* 683–687.

Lyketsos, C. G., Steele, C., Galik, E., Rosenblatt, A., Steinberg, M., Warren, A., et al. (1999). Physical aggression in dementia patients and its relationship to depression. *American Journal of Psychiatry, 156,* 66–71.

Mace, N. L., & Rabins, P. V. (1999). *The 36-hour day* (3rd ed.). Baltimore: Johns Hopkins University Press.

Magai, C., Cohen, C. I., Culver, C., Gomberg, D., & Makatestsm, C. (1997). Relation between premorbid personality and patterns of emotional expression in mid- to late-stage dementia. *International Journal of Geriatric Psychiatry, 12,* 1092–1099.

Maslow, K. (1996). Relationship between patient characteristics and the effectiveness of nonpharmacologic approaches to prevent or treat behavioral symptoms. *International Psychogeriatrics, 8*(Suppl. 1), 73–76.

Mattern, J. M., & Camp, C. J. (1998). Increasing the use of foreign language phrases by direct care staff in a nursing home. *Clinical Gerontologist, 19*(3), 84–86.

Mega, M. S., Cummings, J. L., Fiorello, T., & Gornbein, J. (1996). The spectrum of behavioral changes in Alzheimer's disease. *Neurology, 46,* 130–135.

Menon, A. S., Gruber-Baldini, A. L., Hebel, J. R., Kaup, B., Loreck, D., Zimmerman, S. I., et al. (2001). Relationship between aggressive behaviors and depression among nursing home residents with dementia. *International Journal of Geriatric Psychiatry, 16,* 139–146.

Mintzer, J., Lewis, L., Pennypacker, L., Simpson, W., Bachman, D., Wohlreich, G., et al. (1993). Behavioral intensive care unit (BICU): A new concept in the management of acute agitated behavior in the elderly demented patients. *Gerontologist, 33,* 801–806.

Namazi, K. H., & Chafetz, P. K. (2001). Introduction: The concept, the terminology, and the occupants. In K. H. Namazi & P. K. Chafetz (Eds.), *Assisted living: Current issues in facility management and resident care* (pp. 1–11). Westport, CT: Auburn House.

Namazi, K. H., & Johnson, B. D. (1992). Pertinent autonomy for residents with dementias: Modification of the physical environment to enhance independence.

American Journal of Alzheimer's Disease and Related Disorders and Research,
7(1), 16–21.

Neufeld, R. R., Libow, L. S., Foley, W. J., Dunbar, J. M., Cohen, C., & Breuer, B.
(1999). Restraint reduction reduces serious injuries among nursing home residents. *Journal of the American Geriatric Society, 47,* 1202.

Orange, J. B., & Colton-Hudson, A. (1998). Enhancing communication in dementia of the Alzheimer's type. *Topics in Geriatric Rehabilitation, 14*(2), 56–75.

Orange, J. B., Ryan, E. B., Meredith, S. D., & MacLean, M. J. (1995). Application of the communication enhancement model for long-term care residents
with dementia. *Topics in Language Disorders, 15,* 20–35.

Orsulic-Jeras, S., Judge, K. S., & Camp, C. J. (2000). Montessori-based activities
for long-term care residents with advanced dementia: Effects on engagement
and affect. *Gerontologist, 40,* 107–111.

Orsulic-Jeras, S., Schneider, N. M., & Camp, C. J. (2000). Montessori-based activities for long-term care residents with dementia: Outcomes and implications
for geriatric rehabilitation. *Topics in Geriatric Rehabilitation, 16,* 78–91.

Orsulic-Jeras, S., Schneider, N. M., Camp, C. J., Nicholson, P., & Helbig, M.
(2001). Montessori-based dementia activities in long-term care: Training and
implementation. *Activities, Adaptation, and Aging, 25,* 107–120.

Parker, K., & Miles, S. H. (1997). Deaths caused by bedrails. *Journal of the
American Geriatric Society, 45,* 797–802.

Patel, V., & Hope, R. (1992). A rating scale for aggressive behavior in the
elderly: The RAGE. *Psychological Medicine, 22,* 211–221.

Paterson, J., Hamilton, M. M., & Grant, H. (2000). The effectiveness of the
Hierarchic Dementia Scale in tailoring interventions to reduce problem behav-
iors in people with Alzheimer's disease. *Australian Occupational Therapy
Journal, 47,* 134–140.

Patterson, M. B., & Mack, J. L. (1996). *Manual for the administration of the
CERAD Behavioral Rating Scale for Dementia.* Cleveland, OH: Western Reserve University.

Pearson, J. L., Teri, L., Wagner, A., Truax, P., & Logsdon, R. G. (1993). The relationship of problem behaviors in dementia patients to the depression and
burden of caregiving spouses. *American Journal of Alzheimer's Disease and
Related Disorders and Research, 8,* 15–22.

Plautz, R. E., & Camp, C. J. (2001). Activities as agents for intervention and rehabilitation in long-term care. In B. R. Bonder & M. B. Wagner (Eds.), *Functional performance in older adults* (2nd ed., pp. 405–425). Philadelphia: Davis.

Rader, J., & Barrick, A. L. (2000). Ways that work: Bathing without a battle.
Alzheimer's Care Quarterly, 1(4), 35–49.

Rader, J., Jones, D., & Miller, L. L. (1999). Individualized wheelchair seating: Reducing restraints and improving comfort and function. *Topics in Geriatric Rehabilitation, 15,* 34–47.

Reisberg, B. (1986). Dementia: A systematic approach to identifying reversible cues. *Geriatrics, 4,* 30–46.

Reisberg, B., Franssen, E., Sclan, S. G., Kluger, A., & Ferris, S. H. (1989). Stage specific incidence of potentially remediable behavioral symptoms in aging and Alzheimer's disease. *Bulletin of Clinical Neuroscience, 54,* 95–112.

Richards, K., Lambert, C., & Beck, C. (2000). Deriving interventions for challenging behaviors from the need-driven, dementia-compromised behavior model. *Alzheimer's Care Quarterly, 1*(4), 62–72.

Richter, J. M., Roberto, K. A., & Bottenberg, D. J. (1995). Communicating with persons with Alzheimer's disease: Experiences of family and formal caregivers. *Archives of Psychiatric Nursing, 9,* 279–285.

Ripich, D. N. (1994). Functional communication with AD patients: A caregiver training program. *Alzheimer's Disease and Associated Disorders, 8,* 95–109.

Ripich, D. N., Kercher, K., Wykle, M., Sloan, D., & Ziol, E. (1998). Effects of communication training on African American and white caregivers of persons with Alzheimer's disease. *Journal of Aging and Ethnicity, 1*(3), 163–178.

Ripich, D. N., & Wykle, M. (1996). *Alzheimer's disease communication training manual: The FOCUSED program for caregivers.* San Antonio, TX: Psychological Corporation.

Ripich, D. N., Wykle, M., & Niles, S. (1996). Alzheimer's disease caregivers: The FOCUSED program. *Geriatric Nursing, 16,* 15–19.

Runi, S., Doyle, C., & Redman, J. (1999). An empirical test of language-relevant interventions for dementia. *International Psychogeriatrics, 11,* 301–311.

Schneider, L. S. (1993). Efficacy of treatment for geropsychiatric patients with severe mental illness. *Psychopharmacology Bulletin, 29,* 510–524.

Schneider, L. S., Pollock, V. E., & Lyness, S. A. (1990). A meta-analysis of controlled trials of neuroleptics treatment in dementia. *Journal of the American Geriatrics Society, 38,* 553–563.

Schneider, N. M., Diggs, S., Orsulic, S., & Camp, C. J. (1999, March). NAs teaching Montessori activities. *Journal of Nursing Assistants,* 13–15.

Schulz, R., O'Brien, A. T., Bookwala, J., & Fleissner, K. (1995). Psychiatric and physical morbidity effects of dementia caregiving: Prevalence, correlates and causes. *Gerontologist, 35,* 771–791.

Schwartz, A., Capezuti, E., & Grisso, J. A. (2001). Falls as risk factors for fractures. In R. Marcus, D. Feldman, & J. Kelsey (Eds.), *Osteoporosis* (2nd ed., pp. 795–803). San Diego, CA: Academic Press.

Si, M., Neufeld, R. R., & Dunbar, J. (1999). Removal of bedrails on a short-term nursing home rehabilitation unit. *Gerontologist, 39,* 611–614.

Skolaski-Pelliteri, T. (1985). Environmental intervention for the demented person. *Physical and Occupational in Geriatrics, 3,* 55–59.

Sloane, P. D., Davidson, S., Buckwalter, K., Lindsey, B. A., Ayers, S., Lenker, V., et al. (1997). Management of the patient with disruptive vocalization. *Gerontologist, 37,* 675–682.

Strumpf, N. E., Patterson, L. E., Wagner, J., & Evans, L. K. (1998). *Restraint free care: Individualized approaches for frail elders.* New York: Springer.

Swearer, J. M., Drachman, D. A., O'Donell, B. F., & Mitchell, A. L. (1990). Troublesome and disruptive behaviors in dementia: Relationship to diagnosis and disease severity. *Journal of the American Geriatrics Society, 36,* 784–790.

Taft, L. B., Matthiesen, V., Farran, C. J., McCann, J. J., & Knafl, K. A. (1997). Supporting strengths and responding to agitation in dementia care: An exploratory study. *American Journal of Alzheimer's Disease, 12,* 198–207.

Tariot, P. N., Mack, J. L., Patterson, M. B., Edland, S. D., Weiner, M. F., Fillenbaum, G., et al. (1995). The Behavior Rating Scale for Dementia of the Consortium to Establish a Registry for Alzheimer's Disease. *American Journal of Psychiatry, 152,* 1349–1357.

Teri, L., Borson, S., Kiyak, H. A., & Yamagishi, M. (1989). Behavioral disturbance, cognitive dysfunction, and functional skill: Prevalence and relationship in Alzheimer's disease. *Journal of the American Geriatrics Society, 37,* 109–116.

Teri, L., Larson, E. B., & Reifler, B. V. (1988). Behavioral disturbances in dementia of the Alzheimer's type. *Journal of the American Geriatrics Society, 36,* 1–6.

Teri, L., Truax, P., Logsdon, R., Uomoto, J., Zarit, S., & Vitaliano, P. P. (1992). Assessment of behavioral problems in dementia: The revised memory and behavior problem checklist. *Psychology and Aging, 7,* 622–631.

Todd, J. F., Ruhl, C. E., & Gross, T. P. (1997). Injury and death associated with hospital bed side-rails: Reports to the, U.S. Food and Drug Administration from 1985–1995. *American Journal of Public Health, 87,* 1675–1677.

Tomoeda, C. K., & Bayles, K. A. (1990). The efficacy of speech-language pathology intervention: Dementia. *Seminars in Speech and Language, 11,* 311–319.

Valle, R. (1998). *Caregiving across cultures: Working with dementing illness and ethnically diverse populations.* Washington, DC: Taylor & Francis.

Weiner, M. F., Koss, E., Patterson, M., Jin, S., Teri, L., Thomas, R., et al. (1998). A comparison of the Cohen-Mansfield agitation inventory with the CERAD behavioral rating scale for dementia in community-dwelling persons with Alzheimer's disease. *Journal of Psychiatric Research, 32,* 347–351.

Whall, A. L., Black, M. E., Groh, C. J., Yankoou, D. J., Kupferschmid, B. J., & Foster, N. L. (1997). The effect of natural environments upon agitation and aggression in late stage dementia patients. *American Journal of Alzheimer's Disease, 12,* 216–220.

Williams, D. P., Wood, E. C., Moorleghen, F., & Chittuluru, C. C. (1995). A decision model for guiding the management of disruptive behaviors in demented residents of institutionalized settings. *American Journal of Alzheimer's Disease, 10,* 22–29.

Woods, R. T. (1996a). Cognitive approaches to the management of dementia. In R. G. Morris (Ed.), *The cognitive neuropsychology of Alzheimer-type dementia* (pp. 310–326). Oxford, England: Oxford University Press.

Woods, R. T. (1996b). Psychological "therapies" in dementia. In R. T. Woods (Ed.), *Handbook of the clinical psychology of aging* (pp. 575–600). Chichester, England: Wiley.

Woods, R. T., & Bird, M. (1998). Nonpharmacological approaches to treatment. In G. Wilcox, R. Bucks, & K. Rockwood (Eds.), *Diagnosis and management of dementia: A manual for memory disorder teams.* Oxford, England: Oxford University Press.

Zeisel, J., & Raia, P. (2000). Nonpharmacological treatment for Alzheimer's disease: A mind-brain approach. *American Journal of Alzheimer's Disease and Other Dementias, 15,* 331–340.

Zimmer, J. G., Watson, N., & Treat, A. (1984). Behavioral problems among patients in skilled nursing facilities. *American Journal of Public Health, 74,* 1118–11121.

CHAPTER 14

Integrated Case Studies

Peter A. Lichtenberg, Daniel L. Murman, and Alan M. Mellow

──────── **Case Study I: Neurological Perspectives** ────────

Mrs. Regal is a 67-year-old woman who was initially treated by a geriatric psychiatrist three years ago for major depression complicated by generalized anxiety. Her depression improved with treatment, but she continued to have persistent anxiety symptoms. However, she did not return to see her psychiatrist. Mrs. Regal was functionally independent until she was hospitalized for a routine hysterectomy because of uterine bleeding caused by large fibroids. The second postoperative day, Mrs. Regal developed visual hallucinations (i.e., seeing a man in her room) and paranoid delusions (i.e., thought the nurses were plotting to kill her). The patient was given haloperidol orally for these symptoms in addition to the prochlorperazine that she was receiving for nausea. Within an hour of receiving haloperidol, she became very lethargic and immobile. She continued to have difficulty standing, dressing, and feeding herself for several days. After 10 days, she was discharged from the hospital improved, but not back to her cognitive or functional baseline.

In the past year since her hospitalization, she has had evidence of cognitive impairments. These often manifest as short-term memory loss but also include more difficulty in solving problems (e.g., learning to use a new microwave) and more visual-spatial difficulties (e.g., while driving, having trouble judging the distance and speed of oncoming traffic). She has had occasional visual hallucinations (e.g., seeing a small cat running under the coffee table). Mrs. Regal's cognitive symptoms fluctuate frequently. Often, she becomes very disoriented and confused in the late afternoon or may remain confused for several days before returning to a much more lucid state. Over the past year, Mrs. Regal's family has noticed that she is "slowing down," manifested as walking more slowly and having an "old man" posture and less expression in her face.

Mrs. Regal was referred for a neurological examination and was accompanied by her husband and two daughters, resulting in the following findings:

- *History:* Details of the events and symptoms were provided. Mrs. Regal was otherwise very healthy and taking no medications except for sertraline (100 mg/day), an estrogen patch (0.625 mg/day), and a calcium supplement. There was no history of stroke, closed head injury, alcohol or substance abuse, prior psychiatric illnesses (except for depression and anxiety over the past three years), and no family history of dementia.

- *Exam:* Bedside mental status evaluation demonstrated impaired attention, poor short-term memory, constructional apraxia, and impaired executive cognitive function as measured by Trails A and B tests. Mrs. Regal's neurological examination showed evidence of bradykinesia (decreased facial expression, decreased amplitude of fine finger movements, and decreased spontaneous movements of her extremities), mild postural tremor (without a resting tremor component), mild rigidity in her arms with passive limb movements, and an abnormal gait (stooped posture and absent arm swing).

- *Ancillary testing:* Laboratory tests were normal. Brain MRI showed mild generalized atrophy and a few scattered, punctuate high signal lesions in the periventricular white matter on T2 and FLARE weighted images.

Mrs. Regal's history, examination, and laboratory tests are consistent with a diagnosis of probable dementia with Lewy bodies (DLB). She has evidence of dementia, cognitive fluctuations, parkinsonism, and visual hallucinations that are not exclusively caused by medications or medical illnesses. Her extreme sensitivity to neuroleptic medications and pattern of cognitive deficits would be consistent with this diagnosis. By determining a specific dementia diagnosis in this patient, the neurologist is better able to understand, predict, and treat this patient's symptoms. A diagnosis of DLB would predict an increased risk of delirium, psychosis, falls, faster progression of symptoms, and sensitivity to neuroleptic medications. There is evidence that patients with DLB have improvement in cognitive and behavioral symptoms when treated with cholinesterase inhibitors.

After this evaluation, the diagnosis was discussed with the patient and family. We began discussing issues related to prognosis, the value of advance directives, and driving. I asked the patient to stop driving until formal neuropsychological testing could be completed, and we discussed the possibility of an "on road" driving evaluation. I suggested a trial of a cholinesterase inhibitor in hopes of improving cognitive symptoms, decreasing cognitive fluctuations, stabilizing functional abilities, and helping control her psychiatric symptoms. Because she was still having prominent symptoms of anxiety, I suggested she be reevaluated by her geriatric psychiatrist. Mrs. Regal was not having functional impairments from her parkinsonism, so I did not suggest any treatment for these symptoms.

After six months, the patient had had a good response to the cholinesterase inhibitor. Her cognition was slightly improved and psychiatric symptoms were under control. Mrs. Regal was able to do some cooking and all of her activities of daily living but was not driving. One year after her initial evaluation, her symptoms suddenly changed. Now, she was hallucinating throughout the day, frequently seeing a family sitting in her living room (i.e., a family that she did not know), including a man who would follow her around the house. She was very upset by this imaginary family and their behavior. She became convinced that her husband was having an affair with the imaginary mother of the family and thought that her daughters were giving all of her money to this family. She called 911 on two occasions to get this family out of her house. These symptoms prompted an evaluation by me. A laboratory evaluation did not identify any evidence of an infectious or metabolic cause of these symptoms, and she had not changed any of her medications. Neurologic examination did not reveal any evidence of a new structural lesion. Because of the disruptive nature of her psychotic symptoms, I prescribed a low dose of an atypical neuroleptic medication. These symptoms subsided substantially over the next six weeks without significantly worsening of her parkinsonism.

——————— **Case Study I: Psychological Perspectives** ———————

It is not coincidental that Mrs. Regal's first symptom was depression. Late-life depression has been linked, at least as a risk factor and perhaps as a prodrome, to dementia syndromes. It becomes important, then, when assessing and treating a patient for depression to assess cognition. The risks of dementia conversion in the three- to five-year window increase dramatically if there is even mild cognitive impairment at the time of the depression. Serial testing after the depression ceases can be useful as well.

The onset of new psychosis, such as exhibited by Mrs. Regal, is terribly difficult for family caregivers. Indeed, the fluctuations of both her cognitive and psychiatric symptoms typically leave caregivers feeling overwhelmed and frustrated. It is critically important to begin the educational and support process for caregivers during the time of the neurological work-up and treatment planning. The family can also be taught some strategies to help reduce Mrs. Regal's feelings of anxiety and depression.

Cognitive assessment should be linked to Mrs. Regal's remaining strengths as well as her deficits. What areas of strength can be used in functional and leisure activities? How structured do Mrs. Regal's days need to be and with what types of activities? Adaptation to disability is an important part of treating dementia, and this is usually most successful when the strengths of the patient are used in planning for care with the family.

—————— **Case Study II: Psychological Perspectives** ——————

Mr. Shell, an 85-year-old retired store manager, was evaluated by me at the request of his attorney to help determine his capabilities as to being his own guardian. Three years before my evaluation, Mr. Shell was visited by his daughter from out of state and was found to be in grave trouble. He was living in absolute filth, had turned off the heat during the winter, and was not attending to his own health care needs. The daughter took Mr. Shell to a psychiatrist, who concluded that Mr. Shell had mild Alzheimer's disease (AD) and needed a guardian. Mr. Shell's daughter was appointed by the court as his guardian, and he moved out of state with her. As a result of his self-neglect, he suffered from frozen feet and toe removals.

Mr. Shell had no other major medical problems and took only an aspirin a day to prevent heart disease. One year after he moved out of state, Mr. Shell became ill with pneumonia. After recovering in the hospital, he was discharged to a medical rehabilitation facility. While in the rehabilitation facility, Mr. Shell was evaluated by his attending physician, who administered the Mini-Mental State Exam (MMSE). Mr. Shell scored 28 on the MMSE and was pronounced by the physician as capable of being his own guardian.

After his discharge to medical rehabilitation, Mr. Shell convinced his daughter to take him to his home state for a chance to have guardianship rescinded. Mr. Shell's daughter agreed that Mr. Shell's cognition was somewhat improved but not to the extent that he should be his own guardian.

Mr. Shell came for a capacity evaluation. He stated that he had no cognitive problems and denied having any past problems living alone. He did not see any appreciable risks to his returning to living alone and denied any current or previous problems. Mr. Shell, a college graduate, was evaluated as follows:

- *Test scores interpreted:* Normative data used for persons of similar age and education.
- *Awareness interview:* Minimal awareness of any cognitive changes.
- *Wide-range achievement test reading:* ss = 14 (high average).
- *Multilingual aphasia exam:* Auditory comprehension 17 (WNL).
- *Mattis Dementia Rating Scale:* 122 (moderately impaired).
- *Hooper Visual Organizational Test:* 21.5 (WNL).
- *Trailmaking tests A & B:* 148″; 300″ (both severely impaired).
- *Boston Naming Test:* 15/15 (WNL).
- *Logical Memory I subtest:* 10 (moderately impaired).
- *Logical Memory II subtest:* 4 (moderate to severely impaired).
- *Rey Auditory Verbal learning test:* All scores moderately impaired.
- *Controlled Oral Word Test:* 26 (low average).
- *Animal naming:* 8 (moderately impaired).
- *Geriatric Depression Scale:* 6 (no depression).

Interpretation of the test results indicated that Mr. Shell exhibited above average premorbid intellectual functioning as seen in his reading scores. In comparison, his performance on tests of memory and certain tests of mental flexibility are in the moderate to severely impaired range. These represent a clear decline in cognitive function, deficits in at least two domains, and a decline that interferes with his ability to care for himself. Mr. Shell, it was concluded, met the criteria for a diagnosis of dementia. He also demonstrated a lack of awareness of deficit and thus did not see the need to use any compensatory strategies. It was recommended that guardianship be continued.

This case has several interesting elements to discuss. During his first evaluation when a dementia diagnosis was established, no psychometric testing was conducted. This is of concern. Lack of nutrition and impact of his significant medical illness (frozen toes) may well have been contributing to excess cognitive dysfunction beyond the effects of an early dementia. Without psychometric testing, however, serial evaluations lack a reliable standard for comparison. Use of the MMSE as evidence of cognitive recovery is a flawed strategy. The MMSE is a screening tool—not a comprehensive evaluation. It is well documented that the MMSE has a rate of false negatives (incorrectly finding no cognitive deficits) in more than one-third of patients. The use of neuropsychological tests that are more domain specific in their assessments and have higher specificity properties demonstrates that the MMSE was not sensitive enough to Mr. Shell's cognitive problems. Finally, the use of psychometric testing, along with clinical interview, and awareness of deficit testing can be of value in helping determine capacity and in guiding attorneys or courts in the competency arena.

─────────────── **Case Study II: Neurological Perspectives** ───────────────

Information in this case suggests that further neurologic evaluation would be warranted to better define the cause or causes of this patient's dementia and to determine whether additional treatment is needed. Specifically, the presence of significantly impaired executive cognitive functioning as measured by the Trailmaking A and B tests at a time when language and visual spatial skills are relatively intact would be somewhat atypical for an uncomplicated case of AD. However, AD complicated by cerebrovascular disease or other conditions that affect frontal or frontal-subcortical pathways could easily display this pattern of neuropsychological deficits. Similarly, the disease course has been marked by fluctuations and recent improvements that would be unexplained by uncomplicated AD alone.

To further evaluate this patient, it would be important to determine from history if there have been clinical strokes, alcohol abuse, closed head injuries, visual hallucinations, or frequent cognitive fluctuations. The neurologic exam would determine whether there are signs of stroke, gait disorder, or parkinsonism. Medical records should be reviewed to determine whether laboratory tests have been performed recently to rule out comorbid medical conditions (e.g., TSH, B12, serum chemistries) and whether brain imaging studies have been performed. Brain imaging studies should be reviewed or performed to evaluate for evidence of cerebrovascular disease or hydrocephalus. Depending on the results of this evaluation, the patient may need further treatment to control stroke risk factors (e.g., hypertension, diabetes, smoking, hyperlipidemia) or may need coumadin instead of aspirin if he has chronic, atrial fibrillation. If a diagnosis of AD or mixed AD and vascular dementia is reached, it would be appropriate to consider use of a cholinesterase inhibitor in this patient to improve or stabilize cognitive, behavioral, and functional impairments.

Case Study III: Psychiatric Perspectives

Mrs. Walker is a 76-year-old married woman who was referred by her internist for evaluation of depression and withdrawal.

Mrs. Walker was in her usual state of health, an active retiree (retired schoolteacher), until about three years before this evaluation when she developed some short-term memory difficulties. Over the ensuing year, this memory difficulty slowly progressed, and she found she was burning food on the stove and getting lost driving when she ventured beyond her neighborhood. She remained active, however (volunteering at her local church four days a week), and in good spirits. She was initially seen by her internist, who, after performing a physical examination and obtaining routine laboratory studies, found no immediate cause for this memory loss and referred her for neurologic evaluation. The consulting neurologist diagnosed early-stage AD and prescribed donepezil, 10 mg/day. Her Folstein MMSE score at that time was 26. An MRI scan was essentially normal, with only a question of minimal cortical atrophy.

Over the next year, Mrs. Walker did well, although her deficits did slowly progress. She remained active but gave up driving except for very short trips to her local grocery store. Her husband drove her to her volunteer job, which she had reduced to twice weekly. He also took over cooking for them. She depended more and more on lists to remember activities, names, and places. She and her husband joined a support group sponsored by the local chapter of the Alzheimer's Association. At her one-year neurologic follow-up, her MMSE was 24.

Over the following eight months, Mrs. Walker suffered several stressors. Her best friend of many years died, her husband was diagnosed with prostate cancer, and her eldest daughter was divorced. She became more forgetful and was unable to continue with her volunteer work. She confused the names of her grandchildren and even her children. At times, she appeared to be lost in her own house. She became tearful and withdrawn and ate only sporadically, losing 10 pounds over three months. Her personal hygiene deteriorated, and she often refused to bathe. Her husband took her to her internist, who found no abnormalities on physical exam other than the weight loss and, after obtaining normal laboratory studies, referred her for geropsychiatric evaluation.

Mrs. Walker's medical history was significant for hypertension, hypothyroidism, osteoarthritis, and osteoporosis. Her recent thyroid function tests performed by her internist were normal. Her medications included donepezil, Vitamin E, levothyroxine, lisinopril, and alendronate. She had a period of "the blues" for three weeks after the birth of her second child, which resolved without treatment. There is no other significant psychiatric history. She has never smoked; she drank socially when younger, but not at all in recent years. Mrs. Walker's mother died of "senility" at age 71. Mrs. Walker was the third of five siblings and grew up in a small town. She completed a master's degree in education and taught elementary school until her retirement at age 62. She has been married for 52 years to her husband, a retired businessman; they have three children and seven grandchildren.

On examination, Mrs. Walker appeared somewhat disheveled, had poor eye contact, little spontaneous speech, and appeared depressed, although she brightened when mention was made of her grandchildren. She could provide little detail as to the events of the prior several months, turning to her husband for help. She knew she had "memory problems" and said she wasn't "worth a damn" any more. She acknowledged "maybe it's time for me to go," but denied any suicidal intent. There was no evidence of delusions or hallucinations. Her MMSE score was 13.

After reviewing her internist's medical workup, a diagnosis of major depressive disorder complicating AD was made. It was felt that in addition to her psychiatric symptoms and worsened functional status, her mood syndrome was likely contributing, at least in part, to the recent dramatic decline in her cognitive function.

A trial of antidepressant therapy was begun with sertaline, beginning at 25 mg/day. With a dose increase to 50 mg/day, the patient developed diarrhea in the first 10 days of therapy and had no improvement in her depressive symptoms. Sertraline was discontinued, and a trial of venlafaxine was initiated, beginning with a dose of 37.5 mg/day, increasing to 75 mg b.i.d. She tolerated the medication and maintained good blood pressure control but showed little clinical response in the first three weeks of treatment. The dose was incrementally increased to 150 mg b.i.d., and within two weeks of achieving that dosage, her mood and appetite began to improve, and she began to attend to her personal hygiene. In addition, she was less confused and more accurate in remembering names of relatives. Over the next month, she continued to improve, regained the weight she had lost, and although she did not return to volunteer work, she did begin attending her neighborhood senior center several days a week. At a subsequent follow-up visit about six weeks after her initial improvement, she appeared in good spirits, denied any suicidal ideation, although she remained vague on any details of her life. Her MMSE score at that time was 20.

Over the next year, Mrs. Walker's course was fairly stable; she continued to show slowly progressive but minimal decline in her cognitive function. She then had a fairly abrupt decline, with development over the course of a week of confusion, agitation, and some physical aggressiveness toward her husband, who was now more frail physically and less able to care for her. She expressed a belief that her husband was having an affair and called the police several times complaining that he was plotting to kill her. Her daughter took her to her internist, who found, on urinalysis, a urinary tract infection. She was treated with antibiotic therapy, started on risperidone, 0.5 mg qhs, and re-referred urgently to the geropsychiatrist. When seen the same week, she appeared distracted, agitated, and initially refused to have her husband present during the visit. She eventually agreed but said he "couldn't be trusted." She was poorly cooperative with cognitive testing but scored 18 on a MMSE. Over the next two weeks, her behavior improved, she no longer suspected her husband, and she returned to her baseline. After one month, risperidone was discontinued. A visiting nurse was hired to assist with her care, and her children visited daily.

─────────── **Case Study III: Psychological Perspectives** ───────────

This case, which began as a seemingly straightforward case of progressive dementia, demonstrates the influence of multiple comorbidities (depression and delirium) that are integral to dementia care. As Mrs. Walker experienced significant loss (her best friend) and stress (her husband's illness and daughter's divorce), she became depressed. It is interesting to note that along with Mrs. Walker's overt vegetative symptoms of depression (e.g., not eating, losing weight, not bathing), she was also reporting mood problems as indicated in her statement "I'm not worth a damn." In addition to the antidepressant medication, there was some implicit behavioral treatment as well. Mrs. Walker began socializing more at the senior center and was likely engaging again in more day-to-day pleasant events than she had been before depression treatment. This, in addition to a focus on increasing her functional activity, would be psychological complements to the medication treatment. In addition, perhaps her husband was beginning to experience increased caregiver burden and/or depression himself. Teaching caregivers to increase pleasant events with their care recipients can also help the caregiver's depression. The onset of delirium, by virtue of a urinary tract infection, reflects the dramatic impact delirium can have on persons with dementia. Mrs. Walker became acutely psychotic, agitated, and aggressive. The attending psychiatrist did not simply accept these symptoms as inevitable outcomes of dementia, but evaluated Mrs. Walker for possible contributors to this dramatic decline in social functioning. Delirium is one of the most common comorbidities in dementia care but continues to be one of the most underrecognized.

Author Index

Subject Index

Activities of daily living (ADL), 9, 30, 31, 119
Activities programming, 371–373
Activity limitation framework, 314–318
ADDTC (Alzheimer's Disease Diagnostic and Treatment Center, California), 174, 175, 181, 184
Adult day health care centers, 375–376
Affect/mood. *See also* Depression in dementia:
  frontotemporal dementia, 132–134
  Lewy body dementia, 121–122, 278–279
  mixed dementia, 185–187
  Parkinson's disease, 66
Ageism, 280
Agelessdesign.com, 40
Aggression. *See also* Behavioral disturbances (nonpsychotic) in dementia:
  in Alzheimer's disease (AD), and long-term care placement, 36
  summary of general principles, 338
Agitated Behavior in Dementia Scale (ABID), 363–364
Agitation. *See also* Behavioral disturbances (nonpsychotic) in dementia:
  assessment tools, 362–364
  as paradigm of psychopathology, 337
  summary of general principles, 338
  sundowning and, 378
Alcoholic/toxic/metabolic dementia:
  diagnosis, 210–211
  epidemiology, 199–200
  genetic influences, 201–202
  pathophysiology, 203–204
  treatment, 217
Alzheimer's Association, 33–34
Alzheimer's disease (AD), 1–21, 25–41
  assessment, 13, 27–32, 34–35
    Alzheimer's Disease Assessment Scale, 13
    behavioral, 32
    cognitive, 27–30
    functional, 30, 31
    multicultural issues, 34–35
    psychiatric, 30–32
  biomarkers, 18
  caregiver role, 33–34 (*see also* Caregivers)

depression, 276–278 (*see also* Depression in dementia)
diagnosis, 9–12
  differential (VAD and PD), 71, 160
  issues in, 16–17
epidemiology, 2–4, 229
genetics, 3, 4–7
historical aspects, 1–2
molecular basis of, 3
multicultural issues in assessing/managing, 34–35
new directions, 17–21
vs. non-Alzheimer's disease dementia, 176–177 (*see also* Mixed dementia)
Parkinson's disease *vs.* (contrasting features of subcortical dementia of), 71
pathophysiology, 7–9
risk factors, 3, 17, 26
support groups, 37–38
treatment, 13–17, 35–41
  behavioral management techniques/therapies, 36–39, 41
  environmental strategies/modifications, 39–40
  issues in, 16–17
  medications, 13–15
  nonpharmacological approaches, 35–36
Alzheimer's Disease Assessment Scale, 13
Alzheimer's Disease Cooperative Study-Activities of Daily Living (ADCS-ADL), 31
Amitryptyline, 286–287
Amnesia, posttraumatic, 219
Amyloid cascade hypothesis of AD, 8, 13, 18
Amyloid precursor protein (APP) processing, 4, 5, 18
Animal assisted therapy, 41
Anticholinergic medications, 63
Anticonvulsants, 347–349
Antidepressants, 61, 70, 285–287, 346–347
Antipsychotics, 243–254, 340–345
  atypical, 246–247, 341–345
    clozapine, 60, 73, 246, 247, 253, 341
    olanzapine (Zyprexa), 60, 61, 73, 246, 249–250, 253, 342–343

atypical antipsychotics, 246–247
vs. benzodiazepines, 245–246
choice of conventional *vs.* atypical
antipsychotic, 252–253
conventional antipsychotics, 243–245
dose-finding studies, 251–252
optimal duration, 252
setting/location, 243
side effects, 246
trials, 229–233
Psychosis in Parkinson's disease (PD), 72–73
Psychotherapy, 37
Psychotropics, 339. *See also* Pharmacological
treatment
Public health aspects of vascular dementia,
164–165

Quetiapine (Seroquel), 73, 246, 251, 253,
343–344

Racial variation, 17, 34–35, 153, 289–290, 380
RAGE (Rating Scale for Aggressive Behavior
in the Elderly), 364
Restraint reduction, 366–368
Reversible dementia, 270
Revised Memory and Behavior Problems
Checklist (RMBPC), 365
Rey Auditory Verbal Learning Test, 69
Risk factors:
aging, 3, 26
for Alzheimer's disease (AD), 3, 17, 26
for behavior disorders, 360–362
comorbidity, 360–361
for depression, 277–278, 310–314
education, 277
environmental, 3
genetic, 3
premorbid personality traits (behavioral
disturbances), 361–362
race, 17
stage of impairment, 361
Risperidone, 60–61, 73, 246, 247–248, 249,
251, 341–342
Rivastigmine (Exelon), 164, 350

Scans. *See* Neuroimaging/MRI
Self-report measures: Geriatric Depression
Scale (GDS), 324–325
Semantic aphasia, 125
Semantic dementia, 99
Semantic memory, 101
Senile plaques (SP), 66
Seroquel (quetiapine), 73, 246, 251, 253,
343–344
Serotonergic deficits, 106–107
Serotonin reuptake inhibitors, 61, 70,
134–135, 286, 287, 346
Sertraline, 64, 286, 287
Settings:
adult day health care centers, 375–376
assisted living (residential), 376–377

behavior and influence of, 373–379
depression and, 285
home, 141, 373–375
institutional/long-term care, 141, 377–379
Shunting, ventricular, 217–218
Sleep disruption/disorder, 55, 72
SOAPD (Scale for the Observation of
Agitation in Persons with Dementia of
Alzheimer's Type), 363
Somatostatin, 69
Spaced-retrieval (SR) training, 389–390
Spastic paraparesis, 10
SSRIs. *See* Serotonin reuptake inhibitors
Stage of impairment (risk factor for behavioral
problems), 361
Statins, 14
STEP method (evaluation of cognitive/
psychiatric/neurological frontal
subcortical symptoms), 163
Stroke(s):
and dementia, 173–174
strategic, 155
survivors, 149 (*see also* Vascular dementia)
Stroop Test, 69, 102
Subcortical dementia, 64
Suicidal ideation, 283
Sundowning, 378
Support groups, AD, 37–38
Syphilis/infectious dementia, 197–199,
202–203, 207–210, 215–217

Tauopathies, 91, 93–94, 106
Thalamic dementia, 157–158
Therapeutic kitchen, 39
Thioridazine, 244, 246
Thiothixene, 244
Thyroid, 210–211
Tonically active neurons (TANs), 67
Topiramate, 349
Toxic/metabolic dementia:
diagnosis, 210–211
epidemiology, 199–200
pathophysiology, 203–204
treatment, 217
Trail Making tests, 102, 210
Transgenic mouse models, 19, 106
Traumatic brain injury (TBI), 179, 221
Traumatic dementia:
diagnosis, 214
epidemiology, 200–201
pathophysiology, 206
treatment, 218–219
Trazodone, 61, 64, 346
Treatment:
basic principles:
psychiatric perspective, xv
neurological perspective, xi–xiv
psychological perspective, xi
dementias/conditions:
alcoholic/toxic/metabolic dementia, 217
Alzheimer's disease, 13–17, 35–41